Handbook of Play Therapy
Volume Two: Advances and Innovations

WILEY SERIES ON PERSONALITY PROCESSES

IRVING B. WEINER, *Editor*
University of South Florida

Handbook of Play Therapy, Volume Two: Advances and Innovations *edited by Kevin J. O'Connor and Charles E. Schaefer*

Handbook of Group Psychotherapy: An Empirical and Clinical Synthesis *edited by Addie Fuhriman and Gary M. Burlingame*

Psychology and the Streets: Mental Health Practice with Homeless Persons *by Thomas L. Kuhlman*

The Working Alliance: Theory, Research, and Practice *edited by Adam Horvath and Leslie S. Greenberg*

Handbook of Developmental Family Psychology and Psychopathology *by Luciano L'Abate*

A Theory of Personality Development *by Luciana L'Abate*

Anxiety and Related Disorders: A Handbook *by Benjamin B. Wolman, Editor, George Stricker, Co-Editor*

Social Origins of Mental Ability *by Gary Collier*

Symptoms of Schizophrenia *edited by Charles G. Costello*

The Rorschach: A Comprehensive System. Volume I: Basic Foundations (Third Edition) *by John E. Exner, Jr.*

Symptoms of Depression *edited by Charles G. Costello*

Handbook of Clinical Research and Practice with Adolescents *edited by Patrick H. Tolan and Bertram J. Cohler*

Internalizing Disorders in Children and Adolescents *edited by William M. Reynolds*

Assessment of Family Violence: A Clinical and Legal Sourcebook *edited by Robert T. Ammerman and Michel Hersen*

Handbook of Clinical Child Psychology (Second Edition) *edited by C. Eugene Walker and Michael C. Roberts*

Handbook of Clinical Behavior Therapy (Second Edition) *edited by Samuel M. Turner, Karen S. Calhoun, and Henry E. Adams*

Psychological Disturbance in Adolescence (Second Edition) *by Irving B. Weiner*

Prevention of Child Maltreatment: Development and Ecological Perspectives *edited by Diane J. Willis, E. Wayne Holden, and Mindy Rosenberg*

Interventions for Children of Divorce: Custody, Access, and Psychotherapy *by William F. Hodges*

The Play Therapy Primer: An Integration of Theories and Techniques *by Kevin J. O'Connor*

Adult Psychopathology and Diagnosis (Second Edition) *edited by Michel Hersen and Samuel L. Turner*

The Rorschach: A Comprehensive System. Volume II: Interpretation (Second Edition) *by John E. Exner, Jr.*

Play Diagnosis and Assessment *edited by Charles E. Schaefer, Karen Gitlin, and Alice Sandgrund*

Acquaintance Rape: The Hidden Crime *edited by Andrea Parrot and Laurie Bechhofer*

The Psychological Examination of the Child *by Theodore H. Blau*

Depressive Disorders: Facts, Theories, and Treatment Methods *by Benjamin B. Wolman, Editor, and George Stricker, Co-Editor*

Social Support: An Interactional View *edited by Barbara R. Sarason, Irwin G. Sarason, and Gregory R. Pierce*

Toward a New Personology: An Evolutionary Model *by Theodore Millon*

Treatment of Family Violence: A Sourcebook *edited by Robert T. Ammerman and Michel Hersen*

Handbook of Comparative Treatments for Adult Disorders *edited by Alan S. Bellack and Michel Hersen*

Managing Attention Disorders in Children: A Guide for Practitioners *by Sam Goldstein and Michael Goldstein*

Understanding and Treating Depressed Adolescents and Their Families *by Gerald D. Oster and Janice E. Caro*

The Psychosocial Worlds of the Adolescent: Public and Private *by Vivian Center Seltzer*

Handbook of Parent Training: Parents as Co-Therapists for Children's Behavior Problems *edited by Charles E. Schaefer and James M. Briesmeister*

From Ritual to Repertoire: A Cognitive-Developmental Approach with Behavior-Disordered Children *by Arnold Miller and Eileen Eller-Miller*

Handbook of Play Therapy
Volume Two: Advances and Innovations

Edited by

KEVIN J. O'CONNOR
California School of Professional Psychology
Fresno, California

and

CHARLES E. SCHAEFER
Fairleigh Dickinson University
Hackensack, New Jersey

A WILEY-INTERSCIENCE PUBLICATION
JOHN WILEY & SONS, INC.
New York • Chichester • Brisbane • Toronto • Singapore

Library of Congress Cataloging-in-Publication Data:
(Revised for vol. two)

Handbook of play therapy.
  (Wiley series on personality processes, 0195-4008)
  "A Wiley-Interscience publication."
  Includes bibliographies and indexes.
    Content: v. two. Advances and innovations.
    1. Play therapy. I. Schaefer, Charles E.
II. O'Connor, Kevin J. III. Series.
RJ505.P6H36 1983   618.92'891   82-21818
ISBN 0-471-90462-5
ISBN 0-471-58463-0 (v. two)

Printed in the United States of America

10 9 8 7 6 5 4 3 2 1

With our thanks to the children, families, students, and fellow professionals who have contributed to our understanding of the value of play and to the growth of the field of play therapy.

Contributors

SUE AMMEN, Ph.D.
California School of Professional
  Psychology
Fresno, CA

GISELA DE DOMENICO, Ph.D.
Dynamic Play Therapy Training Center
Oakland, CA

DIANE E. FREY, Ph.D.
Wright State University
Dayton, OH

DEBRA HALDEMAN, Ph.D.
Independent Practice
State College, PA

MARY HAMMOND-NEWMAN, M.A.,
  L.P.C.
The Heart Center
Salem, OR

STEVEN HARVEY, Ph.D.
Independent Practice
Colorado Springs, CO

JOOP HELLENDOORN, Ph.D.
University of Leiden
Leiden, The Netherlands

SUSAN M. KNELL, Ph.D.
Child Guidance Center of Greater
  Cleveland
Cleveland, OH

TERRENCE J. KOLLER, Ph.D.
Independent Practice
Chicago, IL

TERRY KOTTMAN, Ph.D.
University of Northern Iowa
Cedar Falls, IA

SANDRA LINDAMAN, M.A.
The Theraplay Institute
Chicago, IL

JAMSHID A. MARVASTI, M.D.
Sexual Trauma Center
Manchester, CT

VIOLET OAKLANDER, Ph.D.
Violet Oaklander Institute
Santa Barbara, CA

KEVIN J. O'CONNOR, Ph.D.
California School of Professional
  Psychology
Fresno, CA

KAREN BELINGER PETERLIN, C.S.W.
Brooklyn Center for Short-Term
  Psychotherapy
New York, NY

CHARLES E. SCHAEFER, Ph.D.
Fairleigh Dickinson University
Hackensack, NJ

MARGARETA SJOLUND, Ph.D.
Erica Institute of Child Psychology
Wilton, CT

RICHARD E. SLOVES, Ph.D.
State University of New York
Brooklyn, NY

SCOTT J. VAN DE PUTTE, Ph.D.
Visalia Youth Services
Visalia, CA

RISË VAN FLEET, Ph.D.
Family Developmental Services
Harrisburg, PA

Series Preface

This series of books is addressed to behavioral scientists interested in the nature of human personality. Its scope should prove pertinent to personality theorists and researchers, as well as to clinicians concerned with applying an understanding of personality processes to the amelioration of emotional difficulties in living. To this end, the series provides a scholarly integration of theoretical formulations, empirical data, and practical recommendations.

Six major aspects of studying and learning about human personality can be designated: personality theory, personality structure and dynamics, personality development, personality assessment, personality change, and personality adjustment. In exploring these aspects of personality, the books in the series discuss a number of distinct but related subject areas: the nature and implications of various theories of personality; personality characteristics that account for consistencies and variations in human behavior; the emergence of personality processes in children and adolescents; the use of interviewing and testing procedures to evaluate individual differences in personality; efforts to modify personality styles through psychotherapy, counseling, behavior therapy, and other methods of influence; and patterns of abnormal personality functioning that impair individual competence.

IRVING B. WEINER

University of South Florida
Tampa, Florida

Preface

The *Handbook of Play Therapy, Volume One,* published in 1983, has been considered the primary reference source for practitioners, teachers, and students involved in conducting and studying play therapy. The *Handbook of Play Therapy, Volume Two: Advances and Innovations* considerably expands on the first volume by presenting the theoretical, technical, and methodological advances coming out of this steadily growing field.

In order to match the standard created by *Volume One,* we did two things. We have, once again, invited leading authorities on the various aspects of play therapy to write original chapters presenting the developments that have occurred in the field since 1983. And, we have included material that is interdisciplinary in approach, eclectic in theory, and comprehensive in scope.

Volume Two begins with a discussion of recent developments and additions to some of the theoretical models underlying the practice of play therapy.

Psychiatrists, psychologists, social workers, nurses, and counselors at all levels of training and experience will find this *Handbook of Play Therapy, Volume Two: Advances and Innovations,* informative, thought provoking, and clinically useful.

KEVIN J. O'CONNOR
CHARLES E. SCHAEFER

Contents

Handbook of Play Therapy
Volume Two: Advances and Innovations

Theoretical Approaches to the Practice of Play Therapy

CHAPTER 1

Adlerian Play Therapy

TERRY KOTTMAN

INTRODUCTION

Adlerian play therapy is an approach to working with troubled children that is based on the integration of the concepts and strategies of the Individual Psychology of Alfred Adler with the methods of play therapy (Kottman, 1987; Kottman, 1993; Kottman & Johnson, 1993; Kottman & Stiles, 1990; Kottman & Warlick, 1989; Kottman & Warlick, 1990).

Adlerian Theory

Alfred Adler (1870–1937) developed a psychological theory based on the idea that people are proactive, creative, and unique (Ansbacher & Ansbacher, 1956; Dinkmeyer, Dinkmeyer, & Sperry, 1987). According to the tenets of Adlerian psychology, when individuals are born, they have a predisposition to develop social interest: a sense of connectedness to other people (Ansbacher & Ansbacher, 1956). As an individual grows and matures, he or she begins to form a life-style based on the individual's subjective interpretation of how he or she can belong and gain significance in relationships with other people (Adler, 1930; Ansbacher & Ansbacher, 1956). An individual's life-style is a compilation of his or her subjective convictions about self, others, and the world and his or her cognitions, actions, and emotions based on those convictions. As the life-style develops, the individual retains the capacity to examine his or her life and to make conscious choices about thoughts, feelings, and behaviors (Dinkmeyer, Dinkmeyer, & Sperry, 1987). Although their motivation may be out of their awareness, individuals' behavior is always purposive and self-consistent—every action moving them closer to a goal (Dinkmeyer, Dinkmeyer, & Sperry, 1987; Manaster & Corsini, 1982). Because there is usually a discrepancy between how individuals view themselves and how they view what they *should* be, they are constantly striving to overcome feelings of inferiority and inadequacy (Manaster & Corsini, 1982). These feelings of inferiority frequently combine with mistaken beliefs in individuals' life-styles to cause discouragement and maladjustment (Ansbacher & Ansbacher, 1956; Manaster & Corsini, 1982).

In attempting to conceptualize clients' life-styles and to help them better understand themselves and make changes in their lives, Adlerian therapists must always consider the social context in which clients live. In this process of understanding, Adlerian therapists take a holistic view of clients' lives, examining every possible aspect to try to "see with the eyes of another, to hear with the ears of another, to feel with the heart of another" (Ansbacher & Ansbacher, 1956, p. 135).

Each of the following sections will include an explanation of an essential concept in Individual Psychology and a description of how that idea applies to the practice of Adlerian play therapy.

Social Interest

"This term [social interest] refers to the individual's awareness of belonging in the human community and the extent of his or her sense of being a fellow human being. Social interest is a capacity inherent in all human beings which must be developed and trained, analogous in this way, to the capacity for language and speech" (Griffith & Powers, 1984, p. 7). Adlerians believe that social interest is one of the most important factors in human personality development. Although children have the innate potential for learning social interest, they must have someone in their lives to teach them how to connect with others. They must learn to relate to others, first through attachment to a primary caretaker and later through their relationships with siblings and peers. Adlerian counselors can use their clients' degree of social interest to measure their mental health and their potential for growth and positive change (Ansbacher & Ansbacher, 1956).

In Adlerian play therapy, the play therapist looks at social interest as a therapy goal with the children, as a component of parent consultation, and as a measure of progress. Since many of the children who come to play therapy have an underdeveloped sense of connectedness to others, one of the primary goals of Adlerian play therapy is to increase clients' social interest. As the Adlerian play therapist begins to build relationships with clients, he or she will cultivate the attachment to others that is the necessary first step in learning social interest. The play therapist will use empathy, genuineness, and warmth to let children know that they are important and cared for. After this initial contact is secure, the Adlerian play therapist may begin to expand clients' social interest by introducing siblings or other children into the sessions. In this way, the therapist helps children generalize their connectedness with this important adult in their lives to other people. Initially, when a new child begins to invade their sessions, many children experience a sense of abandonment, betrayal, or jealousy. The play therapist lets the clients know that they are just as important as ever and concomitantly encourages them to interact with the newcomer and to build a relationship with this sibling or peer. As time passes, clients start to experience a stronger sense of social interest.

While the play therapist teaches social interest directly to children, it is also important to help parents learn to encourage social interest at home. The play therapist must never become a substitute parent, so the parents need to understand how to build attachment with their children and how to teach children to broaden that allegiance to include siblings, friends, relatives, neighbors, teachers, and other important people in their children's lives.

As the play therapy progresses, the Adlerian therapist can use the expression of social interest as a measure of children's progress. Initially, children in play therapy frequently evidence little connectedness to others. Their play may be characterized by insular, egocentric themes, and they may show little interest in building a relationship with the play therapist or with siblings, peers, or other adults. As the therapy progresses, the Adlerian play therapist looks for ways in which clients express an enhanced interest in others and an increased willingness to cooperate and work on interpersonal relationships. The higher the level of social interest, the closer clients are to being ready for termination. With a client who does not evidence enhanced social interest over time, the play therapist may want to consider a different form of therapy or a referral.

Life-Style

"The Style of Living refers to (1) the person's characteristic way of operating in the social field, and (2) the basic convictions concerning self, others, and the world which form the person's schema of biased apperceptions" (Griffith & Powers, 1984, p. 13). According to Adlerian theory, children form their own unique, individual life-styles before the age of 6. They base their life-styles on conclusions that they make about how they can belong and gain significance, first in their families and then in the rest of the world. Children subjectively observe the interactions and atmosphere in their families and decide which of their behaviors gain approval, attention, power, and the other elements of belonging. Although children are excellent observers, they are frequently mistaken in their interpretation of the events and interactions they observe (Dinkmeyer, Pew, & Dinkmeyer, 1979). Based on their biased apperceptions (Powers & Griffith, 1987), they may come to faulty conclusions ("basic mistakes"), which they overgeneralize and include in their ideas and attitudes about self, others, and the world.

These basic mistakes are usually predicated on "only if" thinking (Dinkmeyer, Pew, & Dinkmeyer, 1979). Thus, children may tell themselves, "Only if I am pleasing others will they love me and I will belong" or "Only if I am in control of all of the aspects of my life will I be safe and protected." Because children think that these mistaken beliefs are true, they may engage in a kind of "private logic" (Manaster & Corsini, 1982), which they use as the foundation of all their beliefs about themselves and their interactions with others. They will spend a great deal of time and energy proving and reproving what they already believe about themselves.

One of the primary functions of the Adlerian play therapist is to use the process of play to begin to understand clients' life-styles, mistaken beliefs, and private logic. As the play therapist gains an understanding of all of the elements of clients' life-styles, he or she will formulate a plan for helping them gain insight into how they see themselves, others, and the world. The play therapist will also attempt to communicate to clients his or her understanding of how their thoughts, feelings, and behaviors grow out of their life-styles and how they can begin to alter the way they see themselves and the ways they interact with others. Although a client's life-style itself very seldom changes radically (Powers & Griffith, 1987), clients can change their attitudes, their mistaken beliefs, and how they act upon them. They can change their "only if" thinking and begin to learn how to more fully accept themselves. As children experiment in the playroom with the idea that they can belong in new and more constructive ways, they begin to exhibit changed attitudes and behaviors. In the final phase of Adlerian play therapy, the play therapist encourages clients to practice those altered attitudes and interactional patterns outside the playroom so that they can experience external validation of their new ways of gaining significance.

Goals of Behavior

"In Individual Psychology all behavior (thought, feeling, and action) is understood as purposive, that is, as movement in line with the individual's Life-Style goals (whether or not the purpose of the movement is consciously understood by the individual)" (Griffith & Powers, 1984, p. 2). Adlerians believe that all behavior is based on individuals' creative choices about how they can move toward their goals (Dinkmeyer, Pew, & Dinkmeyer, 1979). They may or may not be conscious of the direction in which they are moving or the motivation for their behavior. Regardless of whether their purposes are in or out of their awareness, this movement toward life goals is the essence of personality. In the process of their development, individuals choose the goals of their behavior (Dinkmeyer, Pew, & Dinkmeyer, 1979). According to Individual Psychology, when individuals' behaviors are incomprehensible to others, it is because the observers do not yet understand the purpose of their behavior. Once the purpose becomes clear to the observers, they will also comprehend the behavior because there is a unity and a pattern within the behavior related to that purpose (Dinkmeyer, Dinkmeyer, & Sperry, 1987). One of the primary intervention strategies in Adlerian counseling is to help clients become aware of their goals and to bring their decision-making processes into their conscious awareness. As clients understand the purposes of their behavior, they have the freedom to shift their goals or to alter their methods of striving and their behaviors.

Within the Adlerian framework, children's problem behavior falls into four primary goals: attention, power, revenge, and the display of inadequacy (Dinkmeyer & McKay, 1976; Dreikurs & Soltz, 1964; Pepper, 1980). Children who strive for attention believe that they are only significant when they are being noticed or served. Children whose goal is power believe that they are only safe and significant when they are in control—of themselves and/or of others. Children who are attempting to gain revenge believe that they have a need to protect themselves from hurt and that the only way to accomplish that is to hurt others. Children who display inadequacy believe that they are incapable, so they refuse to engage with others or to make attempts at accomplishments.

In order to discover these goals, the counselor examines the behavior, the feelings of those who encounter the child, and the child's reactions to correction. Based on an analysis of these patterns, the counselor can usually make an educated guess about the child's goal. The next step in the process is to share that guess with the child in a tentative way, to help the child gain insight into the goal, and to give him or her the opportunity to reevaluate both the goal and the behaviors used to strive toward the goal. If the child agrees with the tentative hypothesis and wants to begin to make changes, the counselor will design a program to help the child begin to execute these changes.

In play therapy, the Adlerian play therapist uses play, the interaction in the playroom, observations of the child with parents and teachers, and reports of the child, parents, and teachers to discover individual goals. The play therapist then uses both the toys and conversations to convey tentative hypotheses to the child. If the child agrees and expresses interest in realigning goals and learning new, constructive ways of interacting, the play therapist uses the play media, role-playing, and other play-therapy techniques to help the child. Sometimes the child may deny the goal interpretations. This may mean that the play therapist is mistaken, or it may mean that the child is not ready to change. Sometimes the child may agree with the goal interpretation but not show any interest in changing. This is usually due to the fact that the behavior is working for the child; for instance, if the child's goal is power, he or she may have total control of what happens in the family or at school. This is not appropriate because, from a developmental perspective, it is not healthy for a child to have complete power, authority, or responsibility. When the child has total control, the child has very little motivation for change. Until the system (the home, school, or both) changes, the child will be extremely resistant to change. With this type of child, the Adlerian play therapist must shift the therapeutic focus by changing the system to ensure that the behavior no longer works for the child. With the example of the power-motivated child, the play therapist would work to empower parents and teachers so that the child does not have total control of situations in the family and in school. The play therapist would also teach the parents to encourage the child to get his or her needs for significance and belonging met in ways that do not relate to power and control. When this happens, the child begins to feel a need for realigning goals and learning new behaviors.

Feelings of Inferiority

"Inferiority feelings are those universal human feelings of incompleteness, smallness, weakness, ignorance, and dependency first experienced by the infant and small child.

Inferiority feelings continue to be experienced to greater or less degree in adult life . . ." (Griffith & Powers, 1984, p. 19). According to Adlerian theory, all individuals have feelings of inferiority. These usually consist of some type of "less than" feeling or some lingering belief that if others really knew all of their weaknesses and faults, the others would not continue to care about them. The difference between well-adjusted individuals and discouraged individuals is the way in which they act upon those feelings. Well-adjusted individuals acknowledge these self-doubts but do not let them interfere with personal functioning. They may even use the feelings of inferiority as motivation for growth and self-improvement (Griffith & Powers, 1984). Discouraged individuals most often follow one of two paths: they either overcompensate for their feelings of inferiority by developing a superiority complex, or they become so disheartened that they give up. Those who develop superiority complexes, in their process of denying their inferiority feelings, convince themselves that they can do no wrong—that they are all-seeing and all-powerful. This arrogant attitude tends to distance other people, which effectively keeps those people from getting close enough to notice or recognize these discouraged individuals' vulnerable areas. Those who become so discouraged that they give up are so convinced that they cannot succeed that they simply do not try. They allow themselves to become immobilized by their feelings of inferiority. This immobilization may be confined to one area in their lives, or it may be generalized to all aspects of their lives.

In Adlerian play therapy, the therapist must remember that children are usually in the process of discovering and developing feelings of inferiority. The play therapist uses the toys and the relationship in the playroom to (a) help children explore these areas of vulnerability, (b) check out the objective reality of certain beliefs and attitudes, and (c) encourage children to accept their own assets and liabilities in a realistic manner. One important idea for the Adlerian play therapist to remember is that, because all individuals have feelings of inferiority, the play therapist's primary job is not to eliminate those feelings but to help children to accept the feelings and to use them in constructive ways, rather than to be overwhelmed by them.

Discouragement/Maladjustment

"The loss of courage, or discouragement, is understood by Individual Psychology to be the basis of mistaken and dysfunctional behavior" (Griffith & Powers, 1984, p. 57). Adlerians define *maladjustment* as a form of discouragement. Those individuals who are unable to cope with the developmental tasks of life are those who are having difficulty finding useful ways of belonging and being significant. They may be feeling overpowered by their feelings of inferiority; they may have so many negative mistaken beliefs that they cannot function adequately; they may have limited social interest (Dinkmeyer, Pew, & Dinkmeyer, 1979; Manaster & Corsini, 1982). Whatever the reason, individuals in need of therapy are struggling, due to lack of the strength, courage, and skills, to overcome the problems in living that they encounter.

Children who come to play therapy manifest these same symptoms of discouragement. They may have experienced abuse, neglect, abandonment, rejection, or other type of trauma. Sometimes they are pampered and spoiled. Sometimes they have too little power or too much power. Some children come from chaotic environments in which there is little structure and security. Many of the children who come to play therapy have parents who are separated or divorced or have parents who abuse drugs or alcohol. The Adlerian play therapist must remember that these children are not bad, regardless of what they or their parents or teachers believe and regardless of their behaviors. A key element in Adlerian play therapy is to counterbalance clients' feelings of helplessness and hopelessness with hope and encouragement.

Social Embeddedness

In Adlerian Psychology human being is seen as inherently social being, and human problems are therefore regarded as social problems requiring the cooperation of others for their solution. The individual cannot be considered or understood apart from the social context in which he or she plays a part. (Griffith & Powers, 1984, p. 3)

Because of this sense of social embeddedness, Adlerian counselors always look at their clients' difficulties systemically. Whenever possible, Adlerian counselors like to see the entire family. When this is not possible, they still examine clients' situations using information about the present family and social context and from the family of origin and the developmental social context.

Based on this concept of social embeddedness, the Adlerian play therapist does not simply work with the child in play therapy. He or she incorporates parent consultations and family sessions into the process of play therapy. The Adlerian play therapist uses these parent consultation sessions and works with the family to gather information necessary for a thorough understanding of the client. These sessions can also be the forum for the play therapist to offer corrective suggestions and to teach parenting skills, communication skills, and other strategies designed to help the family learn new ways of interacting. The play therapist may also visit the child's school and/or consult with the child's teacher and the school counselor. This affords the play therapist the opportunity to begin to restructure the child's school social context so that the child attains academic success and builds relationships with peers and authority figures.

The concept of *social embeddedness* is also a motivating factor in the Adlerian play therapist's introducing a second or third child into the play sessions before the client terminates. The inclusion of peers and/or siblings in play sessions helps to consolidate the client's evolving constructive attitudes and behaviors.

Further Information

An exhaustive explanation of Adlerian theory is beyond the scope of this chapter. The author has attempted to describe the basic principles and attitudes underlying therapy, but a complete understanding of the theory will require further study. Readers who are interested in learning more about Individual Psychology should explore the Adlerian works listed in the references.

Research

The development of Adlerian play therapy is a relatively recent application of Individual Psychology (Kottman & Stiles, 1990; Kottman & Warlick, 1989; Kottman & Warlick, 1990). In the author's dissertation (Kottman, 1987), she conducted an ethnographic study of a training program designed to teach counselors how to use Adlerian play therapy. The subjects of this study reported increased use of many Adlerian techniques and attitudes in their play-therapy sessions. The author is presently conducting an outcome study designed to examine the pre- and posttherapy behaviors of children participating in Adlerian play therapy, but this study is not yet complete.

There is substantial research indicating that using other systems of intervention with children and families from an Adlerian perspective is highly successful (Dinkmeyer & Dinkmeyer, 1983; Kern, Matheny, & Patterson, 1978). Most of this research centered around school counseling and parent education. Children experiencing problems with classroom behavior, school achievement, self-concept, and interpersonal relationships showed consistent improvements after Adlerian-based interventions (Kern, Matheny, & Patterson, 1978; Ritchie & Burnett, 1985).

PROCEDURE

Therapist Qualifications/Characteristics

The foremost qualification of the Adlerian play therapist is a belief in the basic philosophical constructs of Individual Psychology. The Adlerian play therapist shares the following beliefs about children: (a) children are unique and creative; (b) children have a natural tendency to connect with other people; (c) all children have a basic need to belong—if they cannot find a way to belong in a positive, constructive way, they will find a way to belong in a negative, destructive way; (d) children can make conscious decisions about themselves, others, and the world; (e) children's behavior always has a purpose, even though that purpose may be out of their awareness; (f) all children have some feelings of inferiority; and (g) children who are experiencing problems are discouraged but not mentally ill.

Because Adlerian play therapists believe that children belong in a social context, they do not usually work with children in isolation. They want to include all of the people in their clients' environments as part of the intervention strategy. This may include parents, siblings, grandparents, friends, teachers, neighbors, and a host of other people who come into contact with their clients. Adlerian play therapists are flexible and willing to visit homes, schools, neighborhoods, and other locations in order to gain a better understanding of their clients and to help the people in these locations learn new ways of interacting with the clients.

In order to practice Adlerian play therapy, therapists must have a thorough understanding of the principles, attitudes, and intervention techniques of Individual Psychology. They must also have training and experience working with children in play therapy. They should have at least a master's degree in counseling, psychology, social work, or some equivalent field. These therapists should also have supervision in Adlerian applications in a play-therapy setting. Professionals who practice Adlerian play therapy may work as school counselors, in agencies, or in private practice. Adlerian play therapy is an appropriate treatment strategy in all of these settings.

The role of the therapist in Adlerian play therapy is that of an equal partner with the child. The therapist and the child share the power in the session. Sometimes the counselor takes the lead by setting up different play scenarios, making suggestions, telling therapeutic metaphors, role-playing, setting limits, teaching new behaviors, and/or consulting with parents. Sometimes the child takes the lead and the counselor follows by reflecting feelings, restating content, and tracking behavior. Because of this sharing of control, Adlerian play therapists must also be comfortable with their own power. Many of the children who come to play therapy have issues of power and control. Play therapists who have not learned to deal constructively with their own feelings of inferiority and their need to belong frequently engage in power struggles with these children.

Since Adlerian play therapists take a very active role, they must be willing to be spontaneous and playful with the client. They must also be willing to trust their own intuition because many times they will decide whether to direct or to let the child direct based on their intuitive sense of what the child needs at that particular moment of the relationship.

Client Characteristics

Adlerian play therapy seems to work best with children whose goal is either attention or power. The following is a list of behaviors frequently manifested by children whose goal is attention. These behaviors are amenable to treatment using an Adlerian orientation:

1. Needs constant attention from teacher or parent.
2. Needs instant gratification of desires.
3. Excessive requests to visit the bathroom in school.
4. Seeks constant approval from peers or adults.
5. Acts as class clown.

With children whose goal is attention, adults who come into contact with them usually feel slightly annoyed by their behavior (Dreikurs & Soltz, 1964). When they receive negative feedback or correction, these children will stop the annoying behavior for the time being but will eventually return to the behavior or a similar behavior designed to draw attention to them. Not very many children who are striving for attention are referred for play therapy in community agencies or private practices because their behavior is not problematic enough to cause major problems. However, quite a few school counselors work with children who manifest this type of problem, and Adlerian play therapy is appropriate for this population (Kottman & Johnson, 1993).

The majority of the children referred for Adlerian play therapy are children who seek power, either actively or passively. Children who actively seek power exhibit the following types of behavior:

1. Refuse to finish assignments in school or chores at home.
2. Are unwilling to abide by limits or rules.
3. Argue or otherwise get into power struggles with authority figures.
4. Are extremely defensive when accused of misbehavior.
5. Have temper tantrums.
6. Repeatedly wet or soil themselves.
7. Contradict others.
8. Frequently fight with or bully peers.

Children who passively seek power exhibit the following types of behavior:

1. Are stubborn.
2. Forget repeatedly, but not due to organic problems.
3. Excessively day dream.
4. Neglect to finish assignments in school or chores at home.

5. Resist change; adjust poorly to new situations.
6. Are selectively mute.
7. Withdraw from contact with others.

When adults encounter children motivated by power and control, the adults usually feel angry and frustrated (Dreikurs & Soltz, 1964). In reaction to correction, these children will escalate their behavior, trying to prove to the adults that they have little power to control them. Because adults feel powerless in dealing with children motivated by power, they frequently bring them to play therapy so that the play therapist will "fix" them. Due to the play therapist's egalitarian role in the sessions, Adlerian play therapy works extremely well with these clients. Confronted by an adult who does not try to control them, power-oriented children have no need to prove that they cannot be controlled. By sharing the power in the session with these children, the Adlerian play therapist engages their interest and their willingness to change.

There are not as many children whose goal is revenge referred to Adlerian play therapy as there are children whose goal is attention or power. Most children who are motivated by revenge seem to have been abused—sexually, physically, or emotionally—and seek to protect and avenge themselves (Pepper, 1980). However, it is important to note that not all abused children seek revenge as the goal of their behaviors. These children will manifest the following types of presenting problems:

1. Manifesting malicious behavior.
2. Hurting others, especially smaller, less powerful children.
3. Vandalizing.
4. Being cruel to animals.
5. Threatening revenge.
6. Teasing or picking on others.

When these children interact with adults, the adults usually feel threatened or hurt by them in some way (Dreikurs & Soltz, 1964). Some adults seek to repay these children for any hurts they have inflicted. Upon being corrected, revenge-oriented children usually become more vicious and escalate their attempts to get even. While these children do benefit from Adlerian play therapy, the play therapist must have a great deal of patience and a willingness to not take their attempts to hurt him or her personally.

Unfortunately, children who are trying to prove their own inadequacy frequently do not get referred to play therapy because adults have already given up on them. These children will not try, constantly give up, and seem severely depressed and withdrawn. When adults encounter these children, the adults usually feel hopeless and helpless (Dreikurs & Soltz, 1964). These children are so needy that those trying to work with them may feel overwhelmed and unable to cope. Because encouragement is a major focus of Adlerian play therapy, this intervention strategy works well with these children, but the progress is extremely slow and energy-consuming.

Adlerian play therapists can also work successfully with children who are experiencing or have experienced traumatic or stressful life events such as the following:

1. Parents separating or getting divorced.
2. Recent move to a new home or school.

3. The death of a family member, close friend, or a pet.
4. Recent birth of sibling.
5. Some type of abuse.

Indications and Contraindications

The clients most amenable to treatment with Adlerian play therapy are those with relatively well-developed verbal reasoning skills. Because life-style investigation and tentative hypotheses processing require a certain level of abstract reasoning ability and verbal skills, very young children and children with limited intellectual capacity are unsuited to this intervention. Adlerian play therapy seems to have limited success with children under the age of 4 and with children whose IQs are below 80.

This strategy also seems to work better with children who have a strong grasp of reality. Because of the emphasis on letting go of private logic and on increasing social interest, Adlerian play therapy is not particularly effective with children who are diagnosed as having schizophrenia, bipolar disorder, or organic brain syndromes.

The best results in Adlerian play therapy come about with children whose parents, siblings, and teachers are willing to participate in the treatment and are open to making systemic changes. These children make the most rapid and sustained growth through this process. Children whose parents are not willing to participate as active members of the therapy process do not have as significant or long-lasting positive results.

Logistics

Settings and materials for Adlerian play therapy can vary. Many Adlerian play therapists see children in a standard playroom or office. Other Adlerians conduct play therapy in other settings such as schools (Kottman & Johnson, 1993) or in children's homes. Adlerians usually use a wide variety of play materials similar to those used in client-centered play therapy (Landreth, 1991). The most essential elements of the toy complement are:

1. Family toys and puppets
2. A dollhouse
3. Kitchen items
4. Several dolls
5. Weapons, such as a dart gun, plastic knives
6. Toy soldiers
7. Stand-up punching bag
8. Handcuffs and rope
9. Mask, hats, and other disguises
10. Telephone
11. Alligator, rat, snake(s), and other "scary" creatures
12. Play dough
13. Crayons, markers, paper
14. Paints and fingerpaints

Clients can use the family toys and puppets, dollhouse, and kitchen items to describe and gain insight into what happens at home and with family members. They can also express a need for being nurtured or a desire to nurture others with these toys and with the dolls. They can use the weapons, toy soldiers, and stand-up punching bag to express anger and aggression and to explore control and revenge issues. They can also use the handcuffs and rope to examine issues about power and revenge. Children frequently use the masks, hats, other disguises, and the telephone to pretend to be someone different or to explore ideas they are not yet ready to own. They can also use the telephone to have conversations with the therapist and with important other people in their lives. The alligator, rat, snake(s), and other scary creatures can symbolically represent clients' fears and alternative ways of handling threats to their psychological and/or physical safety. They can use the play dough, crayons, markers, paper, paints, and finger paints to express and explore emotions, thoughts, and relationships.

This list is certainly not exhaustive. The Adlerian play therapist can alter the setting or materials in response to needs of the child or practical considerations. The setting and materials are not as important as the consistency of the time and place and the egalitarian attitude of the play therapist.

The frequency of sessions in Adlerian play therapy is also variable, depending on the needs of the child and family. Most Adlerian play therapists see their clients once a week. The author usually divides sessions into two parts, with 30 to 40 minutes for the child and 15 to 20 minutes for the parent(s). Some parent(s) and some children need more time than this, so the author may have two separate 50-minute sessions: one for the parent(s) and one for the child. Other Adlerian play therapists who work with children in schools or other settings may arrange their time with clients differently. School counselors, for instance, cannot necessarily meet with parents on a weekly basis. They may suggest that the parents of the children they see in play therapy come to a parenting class, or they may discuss issues on the telephone with them once every 2 weeks or so (Kottman & Johnson, 1993).

The average duration of treatment in Adlerian play therapy is 6 to 9 months. This, too, is variable, however, depending on the type of presenting problem(s) and the willingness of the child and other family members to change their attitudes and patterns of behavior. The author has had successful interventions that lasted as short a period of time as 3 or 4 sessions and has other play-therapy relationships that lasted (intermittently) for 3 to 4 years.

Treatment Stages and Specific Strategies

Adlerian play therapy is a four-phase process (Kottman & Warlick, 1989; Kottman & Warlick, 1990). The first phase is building an equal relationship between the therapist and the child. The second phase is exploring the child's life-style, goals of behavior, and mistaken beliefs. In the third phase, the therapist begins to help the child gain insight into his or her life-style, goals of behavior, and mistaken beliefs. The fourth phase is the reorientation/reeducation phase. In this final phase, the therapist helps the child to learn new ways of viewing self, others, and the world and to acquire more constructive ways of gaining significance and interacting with others. While they are sequential, these phases are not discrete. The therapist continues to build the relationship throughout the therapy process. The play therapist does not have to wait until he or she understands every aspect of the child's life-style before beginning to help the child gain insight into it. When the child decides that he or she is ready to change a behavior or a mistaken belief, the therapist can use some of the techniques from the reorientation/reeducation phase, even if the child does not have total insight into all of the aspects of the life-style. Even though the phases may overlap somewhat, it is necessary for the therapy relationship to progress through all four phases. The play therapist should not attempt to help the child gain insight or learn new interactional skills before they have built a relationship and explored the child's life-style together.

Building an Egalitarian Relationship

Before meeting the child, the author always has an initial session lasting at least 50 minutes with the child's parent(s). During this session, the play therapist has three primary goals: (a) beginning to build a therapeutic partnership with the parent(s); (b) explaining the process of play therapy to the parent(s); and (c) beginning to gather information about the child's life-style. The first aspect, building a relationship with the parents, is the most important element of this initial contact. One of the key aspects of this interaction is for the play therapist to communicate to the parent(s) that he or she has heard and understood parental concerns and issues. The play therapist also needs to communicate to the parent(s) the essential nature of parental involvement in Adlerian play therapy. This involvement will definitely entail parent consultations and parent education. It may also involve marital counseling, working on personal issues, and other commitments to change on the part of the parent(s).

In addition to providing an explanation of play therapy during the session, the play therapist may want to ask the parent(s) to read *A Child's First Book about Play Therapy* (Nemiroff & Annunziata, 1990) to or with the child. This book will help both parent(s) and the child gain a clearer understanding of the process of play therapy.

In order to gather information about the child's life-style from the parent(s), the Adlerian play therapist will ask a series of questions designed to elucidate how the child gains a sense of belonging in the family (Dinkmeyer, 1977). This will include information about the family constellation (Pepper, 1979), family atmosphere (Dewey, 1978), traumatic events, functioning at home and school, and family relationships. The author prefers to avoid simply asking the parent(s) questions and filling out an assessment instrument. She tries to weave these basic queries about the child and how the child fits into the family into the flow of the conversation with the parent(s). For this reason, this process of information-gathering may stretch out over several meetings with the parent(s). However, after that first initial session with the parent(s), it is time to proceed with the process by conducting the first play session with the child. No matter how important the perspective of the parent(s) is, the Adlerian play therapist must always remember that the first obligation is to the child and the child's perceptions.

During the first meeting with the child, the Adlerian play therapist will attempt to normalize the counseling process and the presenting problem to him or her. Some time during the course of the session, the play therapist will describe the process of play therapy, including logistical concerns such as how often the sessions will occur, how long they will last, and what will usually happen. At this point, the play therapist will also discuss with the child confidentiality, the limits of confidentiality, and parent consultations. The author usually says something like, "I will not tell your parent(s) anything that we do or say in the playroom, unless I think you might be going to do something to hurt yourself or another or if I think someone is doing something to hurt you. I will talk to your parent(s) about things that I think the family can do differently and about better ways to get along with one another." It is also important to ask the child what he or she understands about the presenting problem and/or what it is that the parent(s) told him or her about coming to play therapy. Quite often, parents feel so overwhelmed by the presenting problem that they explain play therapy in a negative light ("You are so bad that I am going to have to take you to the doctor to be fixed" or some variation on the theme). The Adlerian play therapist will want to reframe any negative interpretations of the presenting problem and the play-therapy process and suggest to the child that this is a place to have fun and to learn more about him- or herself and others.

Throughout the play therapy relationship, the Adlerian play therapist will use the following strategies to build the equal relationship with the child:

1. Tracking behavior.
2. Restating content.
3. Reflecting feelings.
4. Encouraging.
5. Giving explanations and answering questions.
6. Interacting actively with the child.
7. Cleaning the playroom together.
8. Setting limits.

TRACKING BEHAVIOR. Tracking behavior is an intervention technique that transverses many theoretical approaches. When play therapists *track*, they reflect what the child is doing back to the child. An example of tracking would be, "You're picking that up" or "You're painting something." The purpose of tracking is to communicate to the child that what the child is doing in the playroom is important and that his or her behavior is the center of attention and respect. When Adlerian play therapists use tracking, they usually try to avoid labeling objects in the playroom in order to encourage the child to be creative and to avoid imposing their own reality on the child. This way, if the child picks up something that looks like a plastic cabbage to the therapist, that object can still be a giant's head to the child. The author has noticed over the course of many sessions that usually when the therapist labels an object as something that does not fit into the child's schema, the child will correct the therapist. Adlerian play therapists use tracking more at the beginning of the relationship than they do later in the therapeutic process. This is due to the fact that, initially, they want to create an intense kind of contact with the child. Later in the relationship, after they have established contact and rapport with the child, they usually decrease the amount of tracking they use.

RESTATING CONTENT. Adlerian play therapists use restating content for the same purpose as tracking behavior—to let the child know that what he or she says is important. In restating content, play therapists simply say back to the child what the child has said. It is important not to parrot directly what the client said, but to distill the content and, at the same time, to use vocabulary that is comprehensible to the child. Again, Adlerian play therapists use restating content more at the beginning of the relationship as a way to build a sense of connectedness.

REFLECTING FEELINGS. Reflecting feelings is an important strategy for building a relationship between Adlerian play therapists and the child. When play therapists reflect the child's feelings, they must be careful to reflect both surface feelings and underlying feelings. When Jimmy comes into the playroom and starts ferociously hitting the punching bag with a scowl on his face, for example, the reflection of a surface feeling would sound something like, "You seem really angry." By looking for patterns and relying on their knowledge of the child's life situation and psychological issues, Adlerian play therapists could also add a reflection of an underlying issue: "I'm guessing maybe you feel hurt by something someone did, and you're taking it out on the punching bag." With this reflection, therapists can draw the client into a more in-depth exploration of feelings.

When Adlerian play therapists reflect feelings, they try to avoid using the phrase ". . . makes you feel . . ." because this phrase implies that children are not responsible for their feelings. This phrase allows children to avoid owning feelings and allows them to shift the blame for their emotions onto some other person or event. Since Adlerians believe that people must take responsibility for their thoughts, feelings, and behavior, they attempt to refrain from using language that allows people to eschew responsibility for all of the aspects of their lives.

ENCOURAGING.   Adlerian play therapists use encouraging to help children recognize and acknowledge their own strengths and assets (Dinkmeyer, Pew, & Dinkmeyer, 1979). Applying an encouraging strategy means that the play therapist (a) emphasizes the deed, not the doer; (b) emphasizes the satisfaction and joy of effort; (c) focuses on the positive part of what was done; (d) is positive in comments made, avoiding the words *don't* and *can't*; (e) focuses on the child's feelings and not the adult's feelings; and (f) never makes acceptance conditional by building up the child one minute and deflating the child the next minute (Baruth & Eckstein, 1978). When play therapists want to be encouraging to children, they can:

1. Point out improvements and progress. ("You couldn't do that last week, but this week you did it all by yourself.")

2. Concentrate on effort, rather than finished product. ("You're really trying hard to get that just the way you want it to be.")

3. Avoid doing things for them that they can do for themselves. ("You want me to do that for you, but I bet you can figure it out for yourself.")

4. Model the courage to be imperfect. ("I'm sorry. I picked up the green marker, and you asked me for the red one. Oh well, sometimes I make mistakes like that.")

5. Point out personal assets and his or her feelings about them. ("You really know how to fix things that are broken. You look very proud of yourself.")

Encouraging remarks can come in many different forms, but the most important element for Adlerian play therapists to remember is that they must be sincere in their belief in the child and the child's abilities. Counselors must feel trust, confidence, and acceptance and convey those emotions verbally and nonverbally. If the therapist is feeling distrustful or insincere, the child will almost certainly recognize this and discount any encouraging comments.

GIVING EXPLANATIONS AND ANSWERING QUESTIONS.   One aspect of developing an equal relationship with the child involves honest and forthright communication. When children ask questions or want to have something explained, it is important for Adlerian play therapists to answer them as simply and completely as possible. Understanding children's goals is an essential element in Adlerian counseling. In order to explore children's goals, whenever they ask questions, whether they concern playroom procedures, the therapist's relationship with other children, factual information, or anything else, the therapist tries to understand their purpose in asking that particular question. The play therapist makes a guess about their purpose and then answers the question. When the child is frantically trying to finish an art project and he asks, "What time is it?", for example, the play therapist might make the guess, "You're kind of afraid you might run out of time. It's about 10 minutes until it is time for us to leave." The therapist observes a child's reactions to these goal disclosures in order to learn more about the child and his or her purposes. If guesses about the purposes are incorrect, the child will almost always correct the therapist. A willingness or reluctance to rectify a misconception and the corrected answer will give the therapist more information about the child's interactional patterns and self-images.

INTERACTING ACTIVELY WITH THE CHILD.   In Adlerian play therapy, the counselor frequently plays with the child. This can be at either the child's or the play therapist's instigation. It can be role-playing, puppetry, or simply playful interaction. The purpose in doing this is to build an equal partnership with the child and to use the child's own form of language in order to better understand the child and to communicate that understanding to the child.

CLEANING THE PLAYROOM TOGETHER.   One way Adlerian play therapists create a sense of shared responsibility in the playroom is to pick up the toys and materials at the end of the session together with the child. If this activity seems appropriate for the child, 10 minutes before the end of the session, the play therapist says, "In 5 minutes, it will be time for us to clean up the playroom together." When the 5 minutes have passed, the play therapist says, "What do you want to pick up and what do you want me to pick up?" This way the child controls the cleaning-up process, but it is a joint effort.

With some children, this is not an effective method of building the relationship. The author does not use this technique with children who are overresponsible or "pleasers." She also does not use this method with children who are motivated by revenge or who have such a strong need for control that this activity would become an opportunity for a power struggle. However, with most children, this is a productive way to activating a team connection between the play therapist and child clients.

SETTING LIMITS.   Adlerian play therapists set limits on the same types of behavior as many other play therapists (Axline, 1969; Landreth, 1991). They limit harm to self and others, damage to the property, and leaving the playroom before the end of the session. Adlerian limit-setting is a variation on client-centered limit-setting (Axline, 1969). Adlerian play therapists limit in a four-step process:

1. Set the limit in a nonjudgmental manner. ("It's against the playroom rules to hit the mirror with the hammer.")

2. Reflect the feeling or purpose involved in the infraction. ("I can see that you are angry, and you'd like to show me that I can't tell you what to do.")

3. Engage the child in generating acceptable alternative behaviors. ("I bet you can think of something that you can hit with the hammer that is not against the playroom rules.")

4. If the child chooses not to engage in finding an alternative acceptable behavior or does not abide by the agreement set up in this negotiating process, engage the child in generating logical consequences (Dreikurs & Soltz, 1964; Gilbert, 1986) for the next transgression.

This method engages children in the limit-setting process. Because they are involved in setting the limits and consequences for the playroom, they learn that they can control their behavior. This inclusion also enhances their sense of personal responsibility and teaches them problem-solving skills they can use in other relationships.

Exploration of Child's Life-Style

The second phase of Adlerian play therapy involves the investigation of the child's life-style, which may involve the following strategies:

1. Examining goals/purposes of behavior.
2. Exploring family atmosphere.
3. Exploring family constellation.
4. Soliciting early recollections.
5. Formulating life-style hypotheses.

The Adlerian play therapist uses observation, questioning strategies, and art to discover the child's beliefs about self, others, and the world and how his or her behavior evolves from those apperceptions.

EXAMINING GOALS/PURPOSES OF BEHAVIOR.   During this phase of the play therapy, counselors observe the child's behavior in the playroom and in other settings, monitor their own reactions, and notice the child's response when limited. The play therapist will also question parents and teachers about behavior patterns, their reactions to the child's behavior, and the child's response to correction and discipline. All of these factors will help the play therapist decide what the primary goal of the child's behavior is.

Once play therapists have clarified children's goals, they will tailor their interactions with them in accordance with those goals. With children whose goals are attention, counselors will try to avoid giving them attention when they ask for it and give them attention when they least expect it. This strategy is designed to teach these children that they are valuable and important whether or not they are the center of attention. With children whose goals are power, counselors will try to avoid power struggles and to let them control as many age-appropriate decisions as possible. The play therapist will want to eventually share equal power in the playroom with these children. With children whose goals are revenge, counselors must carefully avoid hurting them in any way or taking their hurtful behavior personally. With children whose goals are proving themselves inadequate, counselors will focus on encouragement and self-affirming activities.

EXPLORING FAMILY ATMOSPHERE.   Family atmosphere is the characteristic attitude of family members toward one another and the typical patterns of interaction in the family (Dewey, 1978). Most times, the family atmosphere grows from the relationship of the parents and their attitudes toward discipline and their children. Family atmospheres can be rejective, authoritarian, inconsistent, hopeless, suppressive, overprotective, pitying, high-standard, materialistic, competitive, disparaging, inharmonious, or democratic (Dewey, 1978). These patterns affect the way children view themselves, others, and the world. They have a major impact on family members' life-styles and on their characteristic way of interacting with the world.

In play therapy, the Adlerian counselor watches how the child plays in the dollhouse, with the doll family, with the kitchen items, and in the sandbox to see how the child perceives the family atmosphere. This will also show the play therapist how the child feels about and reacts to the family atmosphere. Alternate methods of exploring the family atmosphere are to ask the child and/or the parent(s) about the parent(s)' relationship, their methods of discipline, and their feelings about their children. Some Adlerian play therapists also ask the child to use drawing or art to illustrate how the family gets along. All of these techniques will give the play therapist a basis for understanding the impact of the family atmosphere on the child.

EXPLORING FAMILY CONSTELLATION.   One of Adler's primary contributions to the field of psychology was the concept that one's position in the birth order affects self-image and behavior (Ansbacher & Ansbacher, 1956; Pepper, 1979). Adlerians believe that each person fits into a psychological position in the family constellation. This psychological position is more impactful than any actual, chronological placement within the birth order. Each psychological position has certain characteristic behaviors and attitudes and distinctive assets and liabilities. Most oldest children, for instance, are responsible and like to tell others what to do. They may be overachievers and overly invested in pleasing others, especially adults. If Lee were a psychologically oldest child, he might come to play sessions and want to play teacher. He would be a bossy teacher who ordered his students around and insisted that they always get 100% on all their papers.

In the play session, Adlerians will observe children's interactions and behavior patterns. They will probably ask the children and/or their parents about birth-order position. They may also ask the children to use family drawings to illustrate the relationships within the family. Play therapists gather this data in order to help them more fully understand their clients. Knowing children's psychological positions in their family constellations can help Adlerian play therapists build upon their clients' strengths and remediate their weaknesses. With Lee, the play therapist might say, "It's important for this teacher that all the children do what he wants and always get 100% on assignments. I choose not to get 100% on my assignment though. I want to play and have a good time, and I can still get a good grade." In this scenario, the play therapist is attempting to make a guess about Lee's purposes and to "spit in his soup." This is an Adlerian technique in which the therapist gently points out the absurdity in the client's private logic and mistaken beliefs and suggests alternative possibilities.

SOLICITING EARLY RECOLLECTIONS.   Early recollections are incidents from a person's life that he or she chooses to remember (Borden, 1982; Dewey, 1978). Adlerians believe that these specific memories represent the essence of the client's life-style. In gathering early recollections, the therapist usually asks the client to recount six to eight early memories, including a setting, cast of characters, interactions, and any associated feelings. In order to interpret early recollections, the therapist looks for a central theme in each memory and an overall pattern that permeates all of the recollections. The therapist examines these patterns to gain an understanding of the client's level of social interest, mistaken beliefs, self-ideal, and goals of behavior. As the therapy progresses, the therapist can base interpretations on the patterns found in early recollections and how they relate to thoughts, feelings, and behaviors present in the client's current relationship with the therapist and in interactions with others.

This technique is a very quick method for gaining an understanding of a child's life-style. It may also be used to help a child gain insight into his or her basic convictions and private logic. The author does not use this strategy with all of her play-therapy clients. She has found that soliciting early recollections works better with children who are 7 or older. If the play therapist decides to use this intervention strategy, he or she asks children to describe or draw a scene that "happened one time when you were little. Pretend it is on a movie screen or video. Tell me exactly where it was, who was there, what happened, and how you felt." The play therapist then writes down exactly what the child says. Since the interpretation depends on serial memories, this activity works best in play therapy if it is extended over several sessions, with the child recounting two or three memories per session.

FORMULATING LIFE-STYLE HYPOTHESES.   As Adlerian play therapists find patterns in the goals of behavior, family atmosphere, family constellation, and early recollections, they will begin to formulate life-style hypotheses. This conceptualization of the client can take the form of completing the following statements:

1. I am . . .
2. Others are . . .
3. The world is . . .
4. Therefore, it makes sense for me to . . .

For Juan, a 7-year-old boy whose mother abandoned when he was 4, his life-style might be summed up by the following statements:

1. I am not worth loving and taking care of.
2. Others are not going to be there for me.
3. The world is a place filled with pain.
4. Therefore, it makes sense for me to protect myself from the pain by not trusting others and not taking a risk that they will reject and hurt me.

As they develop these hypotheses, Adlerian play therapists begin to design strategies for sharing these ideas with their clients. They cannot simply sit down and directly make these interpretations. Most children do not have the abstract verbal reasoning skills to understand such interpretations and would probably resist them even if they did. Play therapists gradually share ideas with children about their life-styles. They do this gently, with humor and respect. As they begin to share their understanding with children, they shift into the third phase of the play-therapy process, helping children gain insight into their life-styles.

Helping the Child Gain Insight into Life-Style

One of the main goals of Adlerian play therapy is to help the child recognize and understand his or her life-style. The play therapist uses the following strategies to assist the child to understand himself or herself better:

1. Making interpretations.
2. Using metaphors.
3. Connecting the playroom to the real world.

With these techniques, using the toys and play media in the playroom to communicate with the child, the Adlerian play therapist reveals goals of behavior, mistaken beliefs, private logic, assets and liabilities of psychological position, and influences of family atmosphere. These therapeutic intervention methods can also help a child gain a more complete comprehension about his or her self-ideal, ways of gaining significance and belonging, and relationships with adults and peers.

MAKING INTERPRETATIONS.   Adlerian play therapists interpret verbalizations and behaviors to help children learn more about themselves and how they interact with others. Everything that happens in the playroom and in any other arena of their clients' lives is available to them to use in their attempts to reveal children's life-styles to them. This may include play sequences; conversations with children; discussions with parents, siblings, and teachers; drawings, paintings, and other art work; early recollections; observations of behavior in the waiting room; or any other revealing components of children's lives. Play therapists take these bits and pieces of information, analyze the patterns in them, and share their inferences about children and their lives with them. Sometimes Adlerian play therapists may make these interpretations directly to their clients. Other times they may use the dolls, puppets, and various toys to communicate the interpretations, or they may use storytelling or some other metaphoric technique to help children gain insight about themselves.

Whenever they use direct methods of sharing inferences, Adlerians always try to phrase their interpretations in the form of tentative hypotheses or guesses (Dinkmeyer, Dinkmeyer, & Sperry, 1987). By keeping their interpretations tentative, they convey respect to clients and communicate their belief that clients should always have the final word on what fits for them at that time. This also allows clients to have control over whether or not they are ready to accept the insight or information that the counselor wishes to share. Phrasing interpretations in tentative terms avoids potential power struggles between counselors and clients about the accuracy of the interpretation.

In play therapy, tentative hypotheses frequently involve guesses about the goals of children's behavior. Goal disclosure usually follows a four-step sequence:

1. Point out the behavior in a nonjudgmental way. ("I notice that sometimes you stand very close to me when I am talking to your sister.")

2. Make a tentative hypothesis about the purpose of the behavior. ("I have a guess that you stand close to me when I am talking to Sally because you want me to pay attention to you instead of her.")

3. Wait and observe the child. One important component of incorporating tentative hypotheses in play therapy is that children must have the freedom to choose not to answer or confirm the guess. Watch for some type of recognition reflex (Dreikurs & Soltz, 1964). Although children may not acknowledge or agree with the guess, they will almost always have some type of recognition reflex, that is, some nonverbal sign that they sense the significance and/or accuracy of the interpretation. Sometimes they will say "No!" but their smile or other nonverbal cues will give the counselor an indication that the hypothesis was important to them. Sometimes they will simply stop an activity or move somewhere else in the room. This could indicate that the hypothesis had an impact on them but that they could not or chose not to confirm it directly.

4. Acknowledge the recognition reflex. Many times, children's recognition of the significance of the hypothesis is out of their awareness. While Adlerian play therapists never demand a response, they always try to point out any kind of reactions their clients have to their guesses. ("When I said that you wanted attention, you kind of smiled and looked at me. I bet you even like the attention you are getting right now.")

USING METAPHORS.   Another method of sharing inferences about life-style with children in Adlerian play therapy is the use of metaphors. The predominant method for doing this is to simply use the metaphor inherent in children's communication (Brooks, 1985). All play is a form of metaphoric communication. Every act of fantasy and every story children tell in their interaction with the play therapist is a metaphor for their own beliefs about themselves, others, and the world and how they act on those beliefs and for situations they are experiencing in their lives. When James, for instance, tells his play therapist a story about how the walls in the dollhouse are cracking and breaking down and how they need to use the glue to make sure the house does not come apart, he may be telling her about the breakup of his mother and father's marriage and his desire to avoid that tragedy. Or when Sue has the wolf puppet attack the crying puppy and none of the other animals will help the puppy, she may be telling her play therapist that she believes that no one will help or protect her.

The author has found that the most productive way to use children's metaphors in play therapy is for the play therapist to communicate through them instead of directly interpreting them. By taking children's metaphors and using their characters, settings, and situations, the therapist can effectively co-opt children's own language and best method of communication. With James, for instance, the play therapist might reflect how sad and scared the house feels when its walls are cracking and breaking. The therapist might ask James what the house would say if it could talk. With Sue, the play therapist might reflect the puppy's feelings and ask the puppy how it can get help from others or how it can protect itself. In this way, the play therapist can help children begin to look at their situations and perceptions a bit differently. Metaphors can also help children consider alternative convictions and goals and learn new more adaptive behaviors.

Another method for using metaphor to help children gain insight in Adlerian play therapy is mutual storytelling (Gardner, 1971; Kottman & Stiles, 1990; Stiles & Kottman, 1990). In mutual storytelling, the play therapist asks the child to tell a story with a beginning, a middle, and an end. Using the same characters, setting, and beginning, the play therapist retells the story with a more appropriate and constructive ending. The play therapist may want to construct the middle of the story so that it has some parallels to the child's situation and may want to use some of the characters to explore the child's feelings and perceptions. The new ending gives the therapist a chance to show the child alternative ways of viewing experiences and of solving problems.

CONNECTING THE PLAYROOM TO THE REAL WORLD.   While helping children gain insight into their life-styles, the therapist must be sure that the children's insights generalize from the relationship with the play therapist in the playroom to the rest of the world. Clients will not automatically bring what they learn in therapy sessions into their interactions with others. In order to help this process, the Adlerian play therapist provides ways for children to make the connection between the playroom and the real world. One way of doing this is to simply point out the parallels in attitudes, feelings, and behaviors that children manifest in the playroom and those that others report observing or experiencing. When Sarah, for example, tries to use a tantrum to make the play therapist comply with her wishes, the therapist could say, "I bet that sometimes you try to use this same kind of yelling and screaming to get your mom to do what you want her to do." When Andre tries to work a math problem on the chalkboard in the playroom, the play therapist could guess, "You look pretty proud of yourself for trying that. I'm guessing that you might be kind of proud of yourself if you tried that at school sometime." By verbalizing the relationship between behavior and attitudes manifested in the playroom and those present in the rest of the world, the play therapist helps children to begin to make the transference of the skills and perceptions learned in the play therapy relationship.

Reorientation/Reeducation

In the reorientation/reeducation stage, the play therapist tries to continue the play therapy process to help the child consolidate insight and altered perceptions gained in the first three stages, learn specific skills and new behaviors, and prepare for termination. During this stage, there may be a slight shift in the role of the play therapist. With many children, the play therapist becomes a teacher, providing new experiences, information, and skills designed to help clients learn to interact more appropriately with others. In this stage, the Adlerian play therapist uses the following techniques:

1. Helping the child generate alternative behaviors and attitudes for outside the playroom.
2. Teaching new behaviors and skills for outside the playroom.
3. Practicing new behaviors, skills, and attitudes for outside the playroom.
4. Encouraging.

HELPING THE CHILD GENERATE ALTERNATIVE BEHAVIORS AND ATTITUDES FOR OUTSIDE THE PLAYROOM.   As children gain insight into their own life-styles and learn new ways of looking at themselves, others, and the world, they are more open to trying out new ways of interacting with others. During this stage of therapy, children who have had difficulty coping with life's problems frequently generate their own positive ideas of how to get along with others. They sometimes come into the playroom recounting situations in which they would have formerly struggled and are now handling with ease. This is cause for celebration and encouragement, with the play therapist pointing out how they have changed and how much they have learned.

Children may come into the playroom and ask the play therapist for suggestions of how to get along with others or how to responsibly solve a problem. Or they may encounter a problem with the play therapist, with a parent or sibling, or with a friend who has joined their play therapy sessions. When children experience a situation that they are unsure of how to handle, the play therapist should respond with some type of comment that indicates he or she believes that they will be able to generate a solution to the problem. This first step communicates the play therapist's confidence in clients' newly acquired ability to handle difficult situations. The second step in this process is to ask them to brainstorm possible solutions (either behavioral or attitudinal adjustments) to the problem. This opens the avenue to a standard problem-solving strategy in which the play therapist helps clients to generate alternative behaviors and attitudes to be used to cope with problems. This is a joint process in which the play therapist and clients collaborate on generating ideas, explore the advantages and disadvantages of each idea, decide on the most likely solution, and devise a plan for execution. This process can take place on a literal, conversational level or on a metaphoric, play level.

TEACHING NEW BEHAVIORS AND SKILLS FOR OUTSIDE THE PLAYROOM.   Sometimes children will not have the skills needed for solving certain problems within their behavioral repertoire. When this is the case, the Adlerian play therapist will use teaching techniques to help children learn these skills. All children have certain skill areas that are specific weaknesses for them. There are many children who do not have the social skills to be able to make friends; other children have never learned how to get attention in a positive way; other children do not know how to negotiate for what they need. These are examples of the types of skills that the Adlerian play therapist may choose to teach children. In order to assess the skill areas needed, the play therapist watches clients interact with others and listens to the types of alternative behaviors they generate in the brainstorming process. There will be some skills that children obviously do not have or do not know how to apply. These are the skills that the play therapist will teach.

Like the generation of alternative behaviors, this teaching can take place on either a literal or metaphoric level. With some children, direct teaching methods work better. With Jill and Sam, siblings whose parents argue constantly, the play therapist might want to use didactic, conversational methods to teach negotiation skills. When a situation came up in the playroom in which they would usually fight over a toy, the play therapist could have them take turns asking for what they wanted, teaching them a step-by-step plan for working out conflicts peacefully. With Karen, a little girl who usually hits others when she is angry, the play therapist might decide to use a more metaphoric teaching approach by using the puppets. The play therapist could initiate a play sequence in which his or her puppet continually hit another puppet. A third puppet could come up and use I-messages and empathic responses to reflect both of the original puppets' feelings and thoughts. The first puppet could then comment that maybe this "talking stuff" might be a better way of handling feelings than just going around and being mad and hitting all the time.

The play therapist must design the teaching of new skills and behaviors for each individual child, based on what he or she knows about the child and how the child learns and interacts with others. Teaching strategies can change based on the child's reactions to initial skill lessons. If metaphoric strategies do not work, the play therapist may want to switch to more didactic techniques and vice versa.

PRACTICING NEW SKILLS, ATTITUDES, AND BEHAVIORS FOR OUTSIDE THE PLAYROOM.   After the child has generated alternative behaviors or has learned new skills and attitudes, the play therapist must provide an opportunity for him or her to practice those new skills, attitudes, and behaviors. First, the child should probably practice these learnings one-on-one in the safe relationship with the therapist. Next, the child would practice with another child, sibling, or parent in the safety of the playroom. Then the child would try out the new methods of interacting with coached siblings, parents, or teachers outside the playroom— at home or school. The final step of transferring these new relationship skills would be for the child to practice them as homework assignments with friends, siblings, parents, or teachers, without these other people having any kind of forewarning. While it is not always necessary to provide all of these levels of practice for every new skill the child learns, it is essential that the play therapist remember that he or she cannot expect the child to act on newly acquired knowledge without some kind of practical preparation.

ENCOURAGEMENT.   During the reorientation process, the child will need a great deal of encouragement. As the child's attitudes toward self, others, and the world change and he or she learns new ways of gaining significance and interacting with others, self-confidence and self-respect will grow. One of the primary roles of the play therapist at this point is to serve as a cheerleader, pointing out effort, progress, and pride in accomplishment.

Consulting with Parents and Teachers

Simultaneously with the ongoing process of play therapy with children, Adlerian play therapists consult with parents and teachers. The purpose of the consultation is to help parents and teachers change their own patterns of interaction so that the changes brought about by the play therapy will have a chance to flourish. In consulting with parents and teachers, Adlerian play therapists teach skills and work on personal issues.

In the skills area, they teach parents and teachers to recognize the four goals of behavior and how to constructively use that information in their interactions with children. They make suggestions for ways that parents and teachers can be encouraging to children. Adlerian play therapists give parents and teachers instruction in using I-messages and empathic responses in order to improve communication in families and in classrooms. They also teach them how to set up logical consequences in order to make discipline more effective and democratic.

Adlerian play therapists may also challenge parents and teachers to begin to look at any personal issues that might be keeping them from effectively using appropriate, positive interactional skills. Sometimes parents or teachers have their own control issues that prevent them from sharing power appropriately with children. Sometimes parents or teachers have family-of-origin issues that keep them from making empathic responses or from using democratic discipline strategies. Play therapists should restrict working on these issues to the context of the adults' parenting or teaching. If these issues are more pervasive or if the consultation threatens to turn into personal counseling on a deep level, the play therapist may decide to refer the consultee to a personal counselor for further work on these issues.

CONCLUSION

Adlerian play therapy is a four-stage process that combines the concepts and attitudes of Individual Psychology with the strategies and techniques of play therapy. This method of working with troubled children and their families can be highly effective in helping clients learn more about themselves and their relationships with others. It can also be helpful in teaching clients new ways of viewing themselves, others, and the world and in teaching them the skills that they need to act upon these altered perceptions and attitudes.

REFERENCES

Adler, A. (1930). *The science of living*. London: Allen & Unwin.

Ansbacher, H., & Ansbacher, R. (Eds.). (1956). *The Individual Psychology of Alfred Adler*. New York: Basic Books.

Axline, V. (1969). *Play therapy* (rev. ed.). New York: Ballantine.

Baruth, L., & Eckstein, D. (1978). *The ABC's of classroom discipline*. Dubuque, IA: Kendall/Hunt.

Borden, B. (1982). Early recollections as a diagnostic technique with primary age children. *Individual Psychology, 38*, 207–212.

Brooks, R. (1985). The beginning sessions of child therapy: Of messages and metaphors. *Psychotherapy, 22*, 761–769.

Dewey, E. (1978). *Basic applications of Adlerian psychology for self-understanding and human relations*. Coral Springs, FL: CMTI Press.

Dinkmeyer, D. (1977). Concise counseling assessment: The children's life style guide. *Elementary School Guidance and Counseling, 12,* 117–124.

Dinkmeyer, D., & Dinkmeyer, D. (1983). Adlerian approaches. In H.T. Prout & D. Brown (Eds.), *Counseling and psychotherapy with children and adolescents: Theory and practice for school and clinic settings* (pp. 289–327). Tampa, FL: Mariner.

Dinkmeyer, D., Dinkmeyer, D., & Sperry, L. (1987). *Adlerian counseling and psychotherapy* (2nd ed.). Muncie, IN: Accelerated Development.

Dinkmeyer, D., & McKay, G. (1976). *Systematic training for effective parenting (STEP)*. Circle Pines, MN: American Guidance Service.

Dinkmeyer, D., Pew, W., & Dinkmeyer, D. (1978). *Adlerian counseling and psychotherapy* (1st ed.). Monterey, CA: Brooks/Coles.

Dreikurs, R., & Soltz, V. (1964). *Children: The challenge.* New York: Hawthorn/Dutton.

Gardner, R. (1971). *Therapeutic communication with children: The mutual storytelling technique.* New York: Jason Aronson.

Gilbert, J. (1986). Logical consequences: A new classification. *Individual Psychology, 42,* 243–254.

Griffith, J., & Powers, R. (1984). *An Adlerian lexicon.* Chicago: The Americas Institute of Adlerian Studies.

Kern, R., Matheny, K., & Patterson, D. (1978). *A case for Adlerian counseling: Theory, techniques, and research evidence.* Chicago: Alfred Adler Institute.

Kottman, T. (1987). *An ethnographic study of an Adlerian play therapy training program.* Unpublished doctoral dissertation, University of North Texas, Denton, TX.

Kottman, T. (1993). Billy, the teddy bear boy. In L. Golden & M. Norwood (Eds.), *Case studies in child counseling* (pp. 75–88). New York: Macmillan.

Kottman, T., & Johnson, V. (1993). Adlerian play therapy: A tool for school counselors. *Elementary School Counseling and Guidance Journal, 28,* 42–51.

Kottman, T., & Stiles, K. (1990). The mutual storytelling technique: An Adlerian application in child therapy. *Journal of Individual Psychology, 46,* 148–156.

Kottman, T., & Warlick, J. (1989). Adlerian play therapy: Practical applications. *Journal of Individual Psychology, 45,* 433–446.

Kottman, T., & Warlick, J. (1990). Adlerian play therapy. *Journal of Humanistic Education and Development, 28,* 125–132.

Landreth, G. (1991). *Play therapy: The art of the relationship.* Muncie, IN: Accelerated Development.

Manaster, G., & Corsini, R. (1982). *Individual psychology: Theory and practice.* Itasca, IL: F.E. Peacock.

Nemiroff, M., & Annunziata, J. (1990). *A child's first book about play therapy.* Washington, DC: American Psychological Association.

Pepper, F. (1979). The characteristics of the family constellation. *Individual Psychology, 16,* 11–16.

Pepper, F. (1980). Why children misbehave. *Individual Psychology, 17,* 19–37.

Powers, R., & Griffith, J. (1987). *Understanding life-style: The psycho-clarity process.* Chicago: The Americas Institute of Adlerian Studies.

Ritchie, M., & Burnett, P. (1985). Evaluating the effectiveness of an Adlerian-based self-enhancement program for children. *Journal of Individual Psychology, 41,* 263–271.

Stiles, K., & Kottman, T. (1990). Mutual storytelling: An alternative intervention for depressed children. *The School Counselor, 37,* 337–342.

CHAPTER 2

Time-Limited Play Therapy

RICHARD E. SLOVES AND KAREN BELINGER PETERLIN

INTRODUCTION

The growth and popularity of brief psychotherapy is not surprising, given a variety of social, institutional, and economic forces pushing therapists to serve a growing number of constituents with declining resources. The acceptance by therapists of more limited, circumscribed goals is the result of several concurrent factors. Along with significant advances in the classification of emotional disorders, and the development of an array of varied treatments and approaches, came a growing awareness that prolonged treatment might have an iatrogenic effect on children. When the community mental health movement made psychotherapy available to populations that were previously underserved, treatment protocols became more pragmatic and progressive, less utopian in their goals, and much less likely to be guided by a single dogma. As the result of an increased individualization of treatment, the traditional private-practice model of psychotherapy was reexamined, and this led to a more tolerant use of less orthodox approaches and the development of new theoretical and technical treatment modalities (Bonstedt, 1965). Three independent, albeit concurrent, therapeutic strategies blossomed during this period: Laboratory-based behaviorism was adapted to clinical use (Bandura, 1969; Lazarus, 1976); ego psychology provided a theoretical rationale that sanctioned increased therapist activity (Blanck & Blanck, 1974); and structural and strategic family therapy forced greater attention to be paid to the external, interpersonal world of children (Papp, 1980; Minuchin, 1974)

However, psychotherapy became a victim of its own success when increased need and limited resources created unacceptably long waiting lists, and this, in turn, led to an unacceptably high drop-out rate. Even when treatment is provided without delay, the rate of premature termination from long-term therapy reaches staggering proportions. Because statistically, the average stay in therapy is only eight sessions, Garfield and Affleck (1959) coined the phrase "the myth of long-term therapy." When clinics subject families to long, protracted, and unnecessarily comprehensive intake procedures, it is not all that surprising that families drop out of the process in frustration. Valuable time expended on detailed assessments that are never put to good use, along with costly broken appointments and premature terminations, leave both clinicians and their constituents wondering, is there not a better way? One interpretation of the high patient-drop-out rate is that consumers of mental health services expect treatment to be provided in a timely fashion and to be of brief duration and that they terminate only when faced with the prospect of interminable therapy. In other words, families act as though they want brief psychotherapy and demonstrate their displeasure by firing the therapist and leaving treatment. A different subset of clients leave psychotherapy after a few sessions because they have gotten all the treatment they feel is needed. While some clinicians might regard such experiences as treatment failures, there is growing evidence that brief contacts can produce changes as meaningful as those produced by long-term treatment (Welter, 1982).

The problem of how to meet high demand with limited resources and maintain client interest in the treatment process is especially acute in mental health clinics located in urban centers where the working class, working poor, and poor are served. This population, almost exclusively dependent on emergency room services for medical and psychiatric needs, are treated on a first come, first served basis, and they, more often than not, are treated by a different health-care provider each time they come for service. While the public health delivery system requires families to arrive early and stay late, outpatient child and adolescent psychiatric clinics require them to play by an entirely different set of rules—they are expected to arrive and depart at specified times, and, further, they are informed that their problem(s) require continuous and prolonged treatment to be provided by one clinician over a relatively extended period of time.

This state of affairs led some in the mental health movement to feel that long-term psychotherapy is an expensive, time-consuming, and highly restrictive modality quite out of synch with the modern family's immediate psychological, social, and economic needs. Brief play therapy with children grew out of pragmatic need for an efficient and cost-effective method of treatment as demand increased for clinical services. Shortened treatment has an advantage of saving time for a family by avoiding prolonged absences from school and work, costly commutes, and the general inconvenience engendered by an endless series of clinic appointments. For clinicians, brief treatment represents a significant reduction in the number of clients awaiting treatment, along with a lower dropout rate between the time of the initial intake and the eventual onset of treatment (Sloves, 1988). In fact, a more recent study revealed that the dropout rate for patients in time-limited psychotherapy was one-half the dropout rate for brief and long-term psychotherapy (Sledge, Moras, Hartley, & Levine, 1990). Episodic, intermittent, or what Budman Stoen (1983) call discontinuous brief psychotherapy can reduce the attrition rate rampant in long-term therapy and decrease the likelihood that a family will become overly dependent on the therapist because it predisposes families to use psychotherapy in the future should the need arise. In fact, brief psychotherapy has a paradoxical benefit in that it significantly reduces children's use of medical services, especially acute primary care visits (Cummings, 1977; Finney, Riley, and Cataldo, 1991).

The dramatic expansion in the use of brief psychotherapy in the treatment of adults is well documented with a broad variety of patient populations, with a multiplicity of psychiatric disorders, and employing a formidable array of innovative methods (Sifneos, 1979; Davanloo, 1980; Malan, 1976). The same cannot be said for the use of brief individual psychotherapy with children. In this regard, there exists a veritable therapeutic black hole. When Mandel (1981) published an exhaustively researched, annotated bibliography on brief psychotherapy from 1920 to 1980 inclusive, only 7% of the 1,552 citation make direct reference to children, and only seven of these articles deal specifically with time-limited treatment. Dulcan (1984) found the situation fundamentally unchanged when she surveyed the short-term therapies available for children and families. The benign neglect that characterizes brief individual therapy may be due, in part, to the long shadow cast by structural and strategic family therapy over more traditional formats of treatment. However, there are many clinical circumstances when family therapy is either contraindicated or is best used as a collateral intervention.

Time-Limited Play Therapy with Children

At the onset, it is important to note that time-limited psychotherapy is not an elongated form of crisis intervention, not a supportive anxiety-suppressing intervention, and not an abbreviated, truncated form of long-term psychotherapy (de la Torre, 1978). This said, time-limited therapy has much in common with crisis intervention/emergency psychotherapy, as well as with its distant relation long-term psychodynamic therapy. Both crisis intervention and emergency psychotherapy demand rapid assessment and reasonably high levels of activity and directness on the part of the therapist, as does time-limited treatment. The point of departure is that while all formats of emergency psychotherapy seek the rescue of an embattled and exhausted ego from attack and the return of it to a precrisis level of stability, the primary focus of time-limited psychotherapy is on the structural deficits that made the ego vulnerable to attack in the first place. The goal is to enable children to develop more effective techniques for coping with a core psychodynamic conflict. Whereas crisis intervention uses emotional support and environmental manipulation to restore homeostasis, time-limited play therapy, like long-term treatment, is more heavily dependent on the uncovering of the core conflict. However, it differs from the more traditional treatments in the way it attempts to accelerate the development of the working alliance, to avoid at all costs the development of a negative transference, and to intensify the interpretative process (Marmor, 1980).

The technique of time-limited play therapy is predicated on the assumption that many children have experience that put a strain on their development but do not require extensive psychotherapeutic intervention or major structural change to resume forward momentum. Experiences such as these are typically stimulated by focal stressors that have the potential to derail the developmental process. They are what Chethik (1989) calls "reactive disturbances," and, as distinguished from more pathological reactions to environmental stress, they are triggered by events that arouse in the child fears of loss (death), separation (divorce), dependency (illness and/or hospitalization), helplessness (parental job loss), or social isolation (relocation). At these moments, children usually feel frustrated, victimized or frightened by external circumstances as they strive to maintain existing defenses and attempt to emulate the autonomous functioning of their elders. More often than not, children's presenting symptomatology is the result of a preservative, defensive reaction undertaken by an ego that momentarily fears a loss of autonomy. Time-limited therapy is most effective with this kind of child who is temporarily blocked or inhibited in the individuation process. As in all forms of developmental psychotherapy, the primary goal of time-limited play therapy is to return children to a healthy developmental pathway. The time-limited therapist helps children to safely negotiate a difficult developmental transition before they withdraw. As a means of fostering children's's progressive momentum through key transitional points in development, time-limited play therapy avoids overtreatment that can interfere with the child's natural resilience or foster excessive dependence on the therapist that would weaken the child's attachment to significant others in the natural environment. This intense, yet brief, therapeutic contact conveys to both child and family the message that they are regarded as competent to handle life's problems (Vernberg, Koocher, & Routh, 1992).

Time-limited therapy offers the latency child an opportunity to gain new skills and insight into the current developmental problems that are causing the discomfort. The focus is on strengthening those defenses that help children deal effectively with strong emotions,

emotions that may hamper cognitive, social, and affective growth. The goal of this treatment is to have children gain a more objective view of themselves and a greater appreciation of their role in bringing about the difficulties at hand, and acquire more adaptive ways of handling life's conflicts. While treatment does not focus primarily on behavioral excesses, the reduction of exaggerated behavioral responses is one positive side effect of treatment. Furthermore, the treatment is oriented in the present with adaptation, development, and differentiation emphasized. Time-limited play therapy takes, as one of its goals, the child's greater acceptance of a role as an individuated person, and this means that treatment must help the child to overcome pathological attachments to parents or other significant adults.

Clinical experience suggests that the therapist's power to effect change, as well as the family's receptivity to change, is at its peak during the first 8 to 10 months of contact. Time-limited therapy attempts to take advantage of this force by giving it shape and structure. Among the various formats of brief psychotherapy, only time-limited therapy fixes the total number of sessions with a specific date for termination set before treatment begins. Once this is established, time becomes the dominant fixture in treatment because it significantly alters the manner in which therapist and child relate to one another and how the central work of therapy is conducted. The mere imposition of a time limit does not necessarily mean that therapy will be brief. However, when the total number of sessions is reduce to 12 or less, time takes on a singular power to reawaken in children earlier psychological conflicts related to separation and loss. In practical terms, a therapy of this length is said to possess an urgency and intensity that is absent when time is unlimited. To paraphrase Parkinson's Law, if psychotherapy expands or contracts to fill the amount of time available to it, then the central work of treatment accelerates when time is restricted (Applebaum, 1975).

The adult model of brief treatment advocated by James Maan is an individual psychotherapy, 12 sessions in length, wherein the termination date is predetermined at the onset of treatment (Mann, 1973). Intrigued by Mann's work, several child psychotherapists took up the challenge of how to adapt the paradigm to work with latency-aged children who have a less than optimal sense of time (Lester, 1968; Mackay, 1967; Proskauer, 1969, 1971; Peterlin & Sloves, 1985; Sloves & Peterlin, 1986).

Although Mann does not provide direct guidance about how to adjust the time-limited model to work with children, the model is deemed acceptable for this population because it focuses on the "here and now" crisis of separation-individuation rather than on the resolution of an Oedipal conflict. Further, it directly addresses strong emotions in a supportive and nonconfrontational manner, as it encourages a warm and empathetic relationship nurtured within the positive transference. The aim of therapy is to free children from inappropriately held dependent relationships and to help them be less afraid to separate from sustaining figures of authority. Coincidentally, these aims happen to be at the core of many developmental conflicts experienced by children who, between the ages of 6 and 12, are in the process of shedding their dependent, fearful selves by looking for less ambivalently held representations than their parents. During latency, children struggle daily to defend and repulse assaults on their self-esteem, autonomy, and emotional separateness. Treatment makes an explicit alliance with the child's potential for mastery, and this, it is hoped, becomes a catalyst for the resolution of their neurotic conflict. Time-limited treatment is organized in such a way as to compliment and reinforce independence and self-directness, while it provides a blanket of security against any perceived loss of self-control. The format of treatment appeals to the child's wish for meaningful change as well as the acquisition of new and purposeful modes of action.

Time-limited play psychotherapy (TLPT) is a dynamically oriented, close-ended, individual psychotherapy with a duration of no more than 12 sessions and with a termination date irrevocably fixed at the onset of treatment. TLPT has several unique characteristics that distinguish it from the traditional long-term therapies:

1. This treatment demands the selection of a single dynamic focus or central theme that underlies the child's difficulties, the resolution of which is the principal aim of therapy.

2. Therapy is theme driven. The central theme, which represents a reenactment of the separation-individuation process and is related to the child's feelings of separation and loss, becomes the sole focus of treatment. The theme represents, at any one moment, the child's cognitive, psychodynamic, and interpersonal struggle to gain mastery over the environment.

3. The brevity of treatment dictates an unusually high level of therapist activity that serves to nurture and sustain a positive transference throughout the entire length of treatment.

4. Structured play therapy is used exclusively to support and empower the child so that regression, dependency, and a sense of helplessness are avoided.

5. Time, embodied in a written therapeutic contract, is used in a unique way to maintain therapeutic momentum and to help the child appreciate time's passage.

TLPT is a highly structured, aggressively managed, interactive treatment modality. Because the therapist is an active, coequal participant in the play and not a participant observer or neutral commentator, an energized working relationship develops between child and therapist but always with an eye on limiting the expression of primary processes and restricting flight from phase-appropriate responsibilities. TLPT uses play as the primary medium through which the therapist communicates an empathic understanding of the child's distress. Treatment is not predicated on an analysis of resistance or a negative transference. On the contrary, children are selected because they offer minimal resistance to a therapeutic and working alliance and because they are easily dissuaded from any activity that might elicit a negative transference.

Time

Time is an influential strategic variable that imposes upon the therapeutic relationship a series of expectations, pressures, and constraints that are consciously manipulated in the interest of structural change. The termination date casts time into a metaphor that comes to stand for several concurrent issues: the conflicted past, the symptomatic present, and optimistic future. More importantly, time represents the child's progression from a passive, dependent infant to an autonomous, fully individuated adult. Strategically, the experience of time's passage, and the fear of loss and separation it evokes, is a powerful engine that drives the treatment.

In order to understand the importance of time in TLPT, one has to go back to the child's earliest sense of time. Because of the infant's fusion with the mother, the newborn feels omnipotent. All things, could, would, and should be possible, and time does not exist because it is without end. However, the infant, faced with external demands and frustrations, begins to experience the precursor of finite time. Separation, loss, and their accompanying emotions take on new importance as the infant learns to wait for need fulfillment. In this regard, the child's realization of time is a watershed event that defines one as an individual and forever marks the child as distinct, separate, and alone. This feeling of infinite time lies on or persists in the unconscious mind of children, adolescents, and adults.

Ego and cognitive psychologists from Freud to Mahler have addressed the development of the child's sense of time. Piaget (1927) speculated about the relationship between the development of a child's sense of time and their awareness of rhythmic internal bodily functions. The perception of present needs and sensations and the expectation that gratification will be afforded within an endurable period ushers in the infant's first experience of time. Initially egocentric, the infant's awareness gradually expands to incorporate changes external to the self. This event marks the infant's ability to differentiate between an internalized self and object representations. It should be noted that positive feelings of expectancy, engendered by optimal frustration and fulfillments, lead to a normal ego development and sense of time. Only with object constancy (Spitz, 1965) and a fused self-image (Hartocollis, 1974) can the sense of past, present, and future be consolidated.

In Piagetian terms, it is only when children enter the stage of concrete operations (ages 7 to 8) that an appreciation for conventional time's passage and measurement is said to exist. However, it is only with adolescence that the sense of past, present, and future time becomes constant and fixed. With this in mind, it is reasonable to ask whether a normal 6- to 12-year-old, with good enough parenting, is capable of responding to time-limited therapy and whether latency-aged children with inadequate mothering can respond. It is known that parentally deprived or impoverished children have a more limited ability to conceptualize time than their peers who have not been so deprived. Yet, Proskauer (1969), who coupled object relations and cognitive developmental theories of child development, suggests that while deprived children may never find the unlimited parental provider for whom they yearn, they do need to learn that limited givers are available and trustworthy, otherwise the outside world offers nothing but disappointment. For TLPT to serve as a metaphor for life, children are told when to expect the disappointment of termination so that they will have less basis in reality to fear betrayal by sudden abandonment.

Because children conceptualize the passage of time in a state of flux, it might be expected that they will regard any therapeutic relationship as an experience that will continue forever. Children's perception of psychotherapy as rooted in infinite time is enhanced by the benign and noncompetitive nature of the therapeutic alliance and positive transference and is reinforced by a seemingly endless number of contacts with the therapist. The longer the therapist remains nondirective and therapeutically neutral, the greater the expectation that children will view each treatment session as disconnected in both time and purpose from one another. When children do not know exactly how long they will be in treatment, a sense of timelessness pervades the therapeutic relationship. In a context of timelessness, an adaptive resolution of the separation-individuation theme cannot take place. Time-limited psychotherapy with children arouses a sharply focused awareness of the finite quality of all relationships, in which the loss, separation, and inevitability of sadness is an ever-present problem to be confronted. For each time the future is acknowledged, termination is consciously evoked and separation-individuation issues are unconsciously aroused. Resolution of these issues in TLPT has a corollary utility to that of the analysis of the transference neurosis in psychoanalytic psychotherapy. Drisko (1978) points out that, of the two partners in individual therapy, at least one, the therapist, has a developed sense of time. He went on to suggest that an established time limit influences the therapist to establish goals, mobilizes the family toward more adaptive functioning, and engenders a spirit of cooperation between the family and therapist.

TLPT, with its preset termination date, protects children so they feel less threatened by feelings of engulfment by the therapist; perhaps it is for this reason that children appear so willing to take risks and engage in the essential work of treatment. Time, limited from the onset, provides an inherent structure that permits children to engage in treatment with more intensity than they would in long-term open-ended psychotherapy. Treatment addresses finite, limited time as it interfaces with one's grasp on reality and as it effects one's adaptive behavior. Time makes the response to that reality less conflicted and less guilt and anger laden. The imposition of adult time emphasizes the recurrent struggle for separation and individuation against the regressive force of infantile time. The struggle against reality represents a core conflict that is more basic to children than any phase-specific conflict or any current life problem. Because the conflict between merger and separateness is such a fundamental one, treatment takes this existential issue as its major focus.

PROCEDURE

Format of Treatment

TLPT with children is organized into four stages. The first stage is the assessment stage, which takes no more than two sessions to complete. It provides the therapist with an opportunity to (a) evaluate the family's appropriateness for treatment, (b) abstract a central theme from the history, and (c) draft a therapeutic contract that is signed by each member of the family. Treatment begins without delay the following week.

The 12 weekly, individual, play-therapy sessions progress through the second, third, and fourth stages, which are overlapping and progressive: the opening, working through, and termination stages of treatment. The individual play sessions are supplemented by two family meetings: the first is scheduled midway through the treatment (session 6), and the second follows immediately after the child's last individual session (session 12). Six months after termination, an individual session and a family follow-up session are arranged.

Therapist Selection, Training, and Supervision

The process of selecting the best match of therapist, patient, and type of therapy is a key issue and, therefore, one deserving of some thought. Literature underscores the importance of selecting the best therapy: whether group treatment might address a particular patient's issues best or whether an individual would be able to tolerate the demands of analysis. Colden (1978) goes further and delineates what aspects of a therapist's style or technique best suit the time-limited treatment model. Flegenheimer (1982), Mann (1973), and Budman and Gurman (1992) expand on the criteria. Mann (1973, p. 82) observed time-limited psychotherapy as an emotional and intellectually demanding modality of treatment; short treatment does not mean easy treatment.

Activity of the therapist is an important characteristic in any clinician who engages in the briefer treatments. While the basic neutrality of the therapist must be maintained, it is clear that, because of the directive, intense nature of the treatment, more of the therapist is revealed than what would be normal in the longer term models. In the classically oriented long-term treatments, the therapist's personality increasingly becomes less and less important with the patient projecting onto the clinician whatever issues or needs might be on the therapeutic table at the time. With TLPT, therapists must engage the patient immediately and positively and are also required to display the utmost confidence, not only in the model but in themselves as clinicians. Therapists must feel comfortable in manipulating the transference, that is, in convincing the patient that, without question, help is at hand.

Addedly, in TLPT, the therapist must be a skillfull assessor of dynamics so that the ideal transference can be effected quickly and accurately. A flair for the dramatic is an asset to the therapist so that the transference can be communicated with credibility.

On the other hand, the therapist who is engaged in the time-limited models must see life as having more substance, more importance than psychotherapy. Further, TLPT clinicians must feel comfortable with the fact that treatment will continue and, in fact, must continue once the formal sessions have ended. They must subscribe to the fact that treatment happens outside of the "hour" and must reject the concept of *cure*, rather, perceiving treatment as iterative. TLPT therapists emphasize strengths rather than weakness and look for supports rather than concentrating on presenting problems, on curing pathology. They must be skilled in dynamic formulations and in making critical and sensitive interpretations during the treatment itself. For those individuals who choose to work in a time-limited manner with children, creativity, spontaneity, and flexibility are all essential. One must be able to go with the flow, to use what the child brings in to the session, and to shape it in such a way as to bring about a further realization of the central theme without drawing out a negative transference. Humor is a major asset.

It would be wrong to view TLPT as simply an abridged form of long-term psychotherapy and then conclude that it requires little in the way of specialized training to gain mastery. However, the primary obstacle standing in the way of those who want to learn the technique of TLPT is that many of the conceptual and technical skills that are so effective in long-term psychodynamic therapy are either not readily transferable or actually run counter to TLPT's guiding goals and objectives. Clinicians trained in long-term therapy need a brief, albeit concentrated, period of retraining to adjust to TLPT's requirements. This is necessary because the principles of evenly suspended attention, therapeutic neutrality, low therapist activity, a nondirective reflective therapeutic stance, as well as the air of timelessness that permeates long-term psychotherapy, encumber rather than facilitate the practice of TLPT. The therapists may need to recognize, acknowledge, and work through their misconceptions or outright prejudices about short-term treatment, which include seeing brief therapy as superficial or as a form of second-best treatment to be used only when a family does not have the time, money, or inclination for a long-term commitment. Furthermore, at first glance, the directive, active stance assumed by the TLPT therapist can be misunderstood as manipulative, whereas the structured and theme-directed play may be regarded as a technique that fails to pay due respect to children's autonomy and independence. And lastly, these therapists must be comfortable and able to tolerate frequent losses, separations, and feelings of sadness. They must be able to endure these same intense feelings in their patients and must be willing to relive their own personal issues of loss over and over again. Because, in this model, one begins treatment and ends it in rapid succession, the therapists must be willing to prove themselves repeatedly. Facing issues such as, will this patient like me, will I be able to help, will I be able to facilitate change in this patient, do I understand the dynamics correctly, can I formulate a theme that is personal enough yet central enough to help to this end, time-limited therapists do well to have a strong support system of their own to endure the demands of this demanding and draining form of treatment. At this point, it should be self evident that psychotherapists who are overly introspective, passive, and contemplative or who have difficulty either beginning or finishing things on time would do well to avoid TLPT.

When to begin training in TLPT is a problem that is not easily resolved. One can take the view that it is by far easier for a therapeutic novice to learn a technique than it is for an experienced psychotherapist precisely because the former has less to unlearn. On the other hand, the danger for the inexperienced therapist is that in his or her enthusiastic rush for a magical, quick fix, they may under estimate the complexities and uncertainties inherent in the majority of diagnostic and treatment situations. Teaching short-term therapy to advanced psychology, social work, and psychiatric students who are at least midway through their training program has its advantages; but because TLPT distills, condenses, and concentrates in 12 sessions all that occurs in a year of long-term therapy, supervisory safeguards need to be established so that the trainee is not overwhelmed. It is for this reason, that trainees should be provided with more than hour-for-hour supervision for their first two or three cases. On a more positive note, the compressed nature of TLPT offers the novice a chance to observe and experience in a relatively controlled context and in a relatively short period of time changes in resistance, shifts in defenses, and a whole range of transferential and countertransferential phenomena that would take years to experience if they were treating a child in long-term therapy.

Client Selection and Pretreatment Process

Assessment

The therapist's first task is to determine whether a child is suitable for TLPT. The selection process is a calculated exercise in prediction, and most treatment failures are traceable to the assessment phase when the therapist miscalculated the good-enough fit between child and modality. One factor working against the therapist is time. The therapist must conduct the assessment quickly so that the family's motivation for treatment is intensified rather than diluted by the process.

Assessment is a relatively circumscribed undertaking that is completed in no more than two extended diagnostic interviews. Keep in mind that the detailed assessment of psychopathology is not the primary goal and may not be particularly helpful in the development of a central theme. The usual assessment protocol is to first interview the family as a whole. Only after learning the etiology of the presenting problem, obtaining a developmental history, and having an opportunity to directly observe the interaction of the various family members are the parents asked to leave the room and the child interviewed. Because of the vigorous structured nature of TLPT and the unique pressures it brings to bear on children, the interview is significantly more intense and probing than if a child were being evaluated for long-term treatment. Prior to the second diagnostic interview, the parents complete an Achenbach Behavioral Checklist (1981) and the child's teacher is asked to fill out a Connors' Teacher Rating Scale (1972). At the beginning of the second meeting, the rating scales are scored and reviewed, the family's history is examined in greater detail, and a second interview with the child is completed. Once the family has agreed to TLPT, the central theme is presented and the therapeutic contract is signed by all in attendance. Treatment begins promptly the following week.

The selection criteria for TLPT are more liberal and inclusionary than they are conservative and exclusionary. Basically, the child needs to have experienced at least one sustained, meaningful relationship with an adult and must be willing to form a rapid, positive therapeutic alliance with the therapist in spite of the therapist's challenging and occasionally confrontational response. But in the end, it is the child's developmental competence, or how well the child has navigated safely through lift's worst disturbance periods, that qualifies him or her for TLPT.

Inclusionary-Exclusionary Guidelines

In the assessment stage, one evaluates the relative ease or difficulty with which children have entered and mastered successive development stages without arrest. Many children, burdened with extensive conflicts that go back many years, are able to marshal sufficient defenses to make a reasonable adaptation. However, it may take only a single potent psychosocial stressor or a series of stressors in close proximity to one another to destabilize the defensive system. As noted by Wolberg (1980), stress can reopen "closed traumatic chapters" along developmental fault lines from the past. Here, it is important to emphasize that patient selection is not solely dependent on the severity of the psychopathology but on the stability of the child's defenses, ego strengths, and premorbid personality.

Lester (1968) looks for evenness along cognitive, affective, and social lines of development, and, if these are found to be within relatively normal limits, children are considered for treatment. In this view, the ideal child for TLPT would exhibit symptoms that are neither too fixed and rigidly held as part of the personality structure nor represent a significant deviation from normal developmental pathways. Chronicity, alone, is not a negative prognostic sign. But if a symptom is stable over time, it is important to know whether it has become a functionally autonomous part of the personality or an ongoing reaction to an external stressor. Primitive, rigid, or brittle defenses, such as massive denial, can render TLPT useless because the child's character structure will not permit a rapid resolution of the core conflict.

The quality of the defensive system is directly related to the child's capacity for basic trust. Perception of adults as benign is critical to the time-limited process because the early termination needs to be experienced as a positive growth experience and not as an act of rejection. The relative presence or absence of basic trust provides an important clue as to the quality of the child's experiences with primary caretakers. A child with shifting and unstable maternal objects in early life usually shows a characterological proclivity for regression such as rage, dependency, or passivity that cannot be reversed in TLPT. In this vein, a child with a history of multiple losses through death or separation, frequent changes in domicile caused by homelessness, or placement in foster care or a history of moderate to severe emotional/physical neglect cannot adequately tolerate the anxiety of separation and loss engendered by TLPT. Children such as these do not fully engage with the therapist because they perceive the early termination as yet another abandonment (Turecki, 1982). Children in reasonably stable foster-care placements, especially kinship foster care, are responsive to TLPT when a positive unequivocal relationship exists between child and guardian.

In time-limited psychotherapy, psychiatric nosology does not dominate the assessment process, but the diagnostic criteria set forth in the *Diagnostic and Statistical Manual of Mental Disorders*, (DSM-III-R) (APA, 1987) can augment the evaluation. Children with an Axis I diagnosis of "Conduct Disorder, Solitary Aggressive" are appropriate so long as their behavior is driven by neurotic rather than characterological acting-out. Therefore, a history of persistent destructiveness or of an impulse disorder as well as the presence of masochistic or self-destructive behavior needs to be ruled out. Likewise, children with an oppositional defiant disorder are poorly suited for TLPT because they struggle for control when they need to collaborate with the therapist. Acute phobias, with or without psycho-physiological reactions (somatization disorder), are treatable with one caveat: parents need to experience the phobia as a highly noxious and disruptive irritant and cannot be so invested in the benefits of the symptom that they collude with the child. The vast majority of multiple phobias with a duration of more than 3 months have proven resistant to brief treatment. Children with a diagnosis of posttraumatic stress disorder are suitable for TLPT so long as the symptom is of recent onset. However, TLPT is of questionable value for children who have witnessed a violent physical assault on a family member. It should come as no surprise that the entire category of adjustment disorders lends itself to time-limited treatment because the diagnosis rests on a presumption of an underlying adaptive, nonneurotic character structure and adaptive, conflict-free spheres of functioning.

All children with precharacter disorders, developmental retardation, or complex neu-rotic structures are excluded, as are children with severe symptoms including recent, potentially lethal suicide attempts, withdrawal and isolation from social relationships, and extremely aggressive children such as those with attempted homicides (Rosenthal & Levine, 1970). In families where the identified child, sibling, or parent suffers from a potentially life-threatening or terminal medical illness, TLPT is inappropriate. However, the time-limited approach has proved beneficial to children who have recently lost a parent to a chronic terminal medical condition (Christ, Siegal, Mesagno, & Langosch, 1991).

THE DIAGNOSTIC PLAY INTERVIEW: IN SEARCH OF THE ALLIANCE.   The therapist attempts to harness the energies released by a family in crisis and, thereby, illuminate and define a central theme. It is this experience of energy released and movement directed that is at the heart of the assessment process.

Assuming that neither the child nor family are grossly dysfunctional, it is most likely that the child will be brought to the clinic in the midst of a maturational crisis such as divorce, parental separation, or death of a parent or sibling. The therapist needs to know whether or not the child is capable of developing an immediate and positive relationship with the therapist. In this view, the therapeutic alliance is born out of the therapist's effort to help children clearly define those obstacles in the environment that impede adaptation. The most important trait, quality, or characteristic that the child can possess is whether or not there is a willingness and ability to make room for the therapist as both engage in diagnostic play.

It is the therapist's job to actively probe the child's capacity and willingness to engage in the therapeutic process as measured against several developmental forces that impede or hamper the alliance. The latency-aged child is baically pleasure oriented, avoiding unpleasant affects, the toleration of which is vital if treatment is to proceed smoothly. The latency-aged child prefers to live in the present, tends to act rather then remember, and externalizes the source of any problems instead of assuming responsibility for the conse-quences of his or her actions. With this in mind, the therapist makes a direct and unequivocal appeal to that part of the child that takes a profound interest in the concrete, physical world; derives immense satisfaction in learning how things work; and is capable of verbalizing inner thoughts and feelings. Because children can intuitively sense thoughts, feelings, and memories that are just beyond their expressive range, they can understand the inductive quality of the therapist's psychological interpretations when these inferences are backed up with the concrete examples in play. One of the most valued measures in the assessment is how long it takes the child to realize that the therapist is speaking in children's "language" through the modality of play. A child's willingness to discuss painful feelings with a relative stranger implies a belief that adults are potentially trustworthy and can serve a purpose beyond the satisfaction of immediate needs or impulses.

Because TLPT places a premium on active participation, as well as direct and vigorous interaction between therapist and child, diagnostic play therapy is used during the interview to gauge the child's ability to handle the therapeutic directedness that is to follow. The purpose of diagnostic play is to challenge the neurotic defenses. The therapist constructs a play scenario that closely resembles an event, incident, or conflict described by the family as problematic. As the therapist acts and speaks to the child through the play materials, much as a ventriloquist speaks through a dummy, clarifications, confrontations, and frustrations may mobilize resistance. Resistance, in and of itself, is not a negative result; but, should resistance become overt and conscious, such as with a child's outright refusal to respond, the use of massive denial, or regressive defenses (crying or passivity), then another therapeutic approach is best sought. When it is working well, diagnostic play liberates affect-laden unconscious material that throws a bright light on the core dynamic conflict.

Diagnostic play therapy is used to assess whether a child has the basic competence to engage in imaginative play and to join with the therapist in an alliance for change. The child who makes little room for the therapist in play or forces the therapist to assume the role of a helpless spectator is incapable of the kind of intimacy that is so necessary for time-limited treatment to succeed. Children who avoid all realistic, imaginative play materials and favor board games that force the contestants into highly stereotyped roles either do not know how to play, not an unusual occurrence in this age of electronic video games, or are so rigidly defended that it would take weeks before they could engage in the real work of treatment.

If the child's ability to become engaged in a meaningful and collaborative relationship with the therapist is a key variable in predicting a positive result, then the child who remains sullen, avoidant, negativistic, or oppositional throughout the two diagnostic interviews and cannot be engaged in any productive work is unsuitable. Obviously, distrustful, schizoid, and severely depressed children are unable to meet this criteria because their pathology prevents them from engaging quickly with the therapist.

The child's appreciation of time's passage is another critical element that needs assessment. An awareness of time helps children to understand the brevity of treatment, and it sustains them through the inevitable periods of frustration that are to follow. While the child's sense of time is evaluated indirectly by assessing such conflict-free ego functions as delay, anticipation, and intention, there are more direct means available to obtain this information. Integrated into the mental status exam are questions about the child's age, date of birth, and the current month, season, and day of the week, as well as the ages of any siblings. The child is asked to estimate how much time will be needed to accomplish certain tasks or the amount of time that has transpired between two important life events. Time projections, such as asking children how old they will be when they can drive a car or get married, are equally useful. Another technique is to ask them to pretend that their family has moved to a new neighborhood and then estimate how long it would take for them to make three new friends.

The Parental Alliance

The parental alliance is based on the level of parental motivation, flexibility, stability, and capacity to tolerate change. The child's environment must be sufficiently supportive so that treatment is not undermined by powerful unidentified pathological forces in the home. Significant parental pathology, severe and chronic marital discord, and/or significant environmental changes, such as impending divorce and family dissolution, contraindicate brief therapy. The therapist wants to know what the parent(s) like best about their child. Some parents begin with a laundry list of grievances or a litany of complaints, but it is the relative ease with which the interviewer can reframe anger as concern that provides the true test of the parental-child bond. Parents, who despite the therapist's best effort, cannot stay focused exclusively on the child's needs to the exclusion of their own narcissistic concerns are unable to work with the therapist in laying out realistic treatment goals. While some parents initially try to disassociate themselves from their child's distress, this may be a defense against feelings of hurt, rejection, and failure. It is the extent to which they resist the therapist's effort to join with them as adults that indicates the degree to which they are capable of supporting the child. Parents who do not want to become involved in the treatment process, who insist that "He needs to talk with someone" or "This has nothing to do with me or my spouse," are not suitable.

TLPT is an ill-considered therapeutic strategy when a child is preoccupied with an acute, life-threatening, or terminal illness of a family member or with the dissolution or a threat of dissolution of the family as a consequence of parental divorce or separation, imminent loss of domicile, or unemployment. A family that plans to relocate within the next 4 months is rarely enrolled in TLPT because of the proximity between the fixed termination date and the actual loss to come. Most, if not all, of these cautions apply equally to the therapist. It would be improper to engage in TLPT when illness on the part of the therapist means cancellations of sessions or when the therapist plans to relocate in the midst of treatment. For reasons that should now be obvious, the termination date of TLPT is never scheduled to fall on or near any regular or planned separation in the life of the child, family, or therapist; for example, therapy is never scheduled to end on a date that falls within 3 weeks of a school or family vacation because to do so would only contaminate the experience of separation from the therapist. The failure to pay attention to the timing of the termination date only encourages the child to fantasize that therapy will continue after the vacation or when school starts up again.

Critical to the success of TLPT is the child's understanding that both the therapist and the parent(s) are in agreement as to the rationale, purpose, goals, and course of treatment. Besides the fact that it is simply good practice to involve a child's parent(s) in each step of treatment, assisting them to become an integral part of therapy significantly reduces the likelihood that they will feel threatened by or become resentful of the therapist's role. Parents can be threatened by their child's initial idealization of the therapist ("I wish my daddy talked to me like you do") or by the knowledge that the child speaks of private and intimate thoughts and feelings to a stranger and not to them. While some narcissistic injury can be anticipated and handled through scheduled and impromptu parent conferences, those parents who have personal needs that supersede those of their children often require a concurrent therapy of their own by a different therapist. Furthermore, the parent who experiences the treatment as destabilizing the existing parent-child or marital system may obstruct or directly sabotage the treatment.

The parental alliance reduces the opportunity for children to act out in the treatment or to collude with the parents against the therapist, a problem that often occurs during the termination phase. To help parents and children understand both the anticipated and usual resistances, they are told:

> Children respond to short-term therapy in predictable ways. For the first few sessions, your child's problems will be less pronounced, and they will enjoy coming to see me. You may feel that treatment is no longer needed. Let me assure you that this is not the case. Later, as treatment continues and your child and I continue to talk about their painful feelings, the symptoms may well reappear, and again you may consider stopping treatment. Your uncertainty may be reinforced by your child's not wanting to come, complaining of stomach aches, or an urgent school assignment.

The evaluation ends with an assessment of ease with which the mechanics of treatment, including fee, resolution of scheduling conflicts, and transportation to the clinic, are arranged.

Formulation and Use of the Central Theme

The search for a central theme or core conflict is predicated on the belief that if the therapist can translate and condense the child's presenting complaint and psychodynamic conflict into a single overriding theme and can express it in such a way that he or she can take ownership of it, the child will work with the therapist toward its resolution. It is anticipated that the resolution of the theme will bring about growth in areas other than those specifically addressed by the theme; this is based on the assumption that psychological growth will continue after treatment has ended. This stems from the fact that, in treatment, the child has been empowered to confront the future with renewed confidence. Changes brought on by therapy are reinforced by others' positive response to their newly acquired behavior and more engaging affect.

Children in TLPT, encouraged by the tangible, realizable goal in therapy, seem more willing to take risks, trust more quickly, and more productively use the limited time that is theirs. One can not underestimate the enormous therapeutic benefit to be derived from the act of advising children that their pain is not as overwhelming as they feared and that they can resolve it successfully in a relatively short period of time. This is especially true for children who, before coming to therapy, encountered a host of unsuccessful helper/ adults such as parents, guidance counselors, principals, teachers, grandparents, clergy, neighbors, or pediatricians. It is enormously chathartic for children to hear from an authority figure that not only does their problem have a name but that it can be described in such a way as to be understood. With this accomplished, children's sense of entrapment, helplessness, and shame dissipates as self-esteem is enhanced. By lending support to children, by saying in effect, "Here is what is wrong and this is what we are going to do about it," the therapist frees within the child the capability of change.

The central theme is a clear and direct statement to children that explains how the presenting symptomatology and its attendant psychological discomfort are related to an unresolved core conflict. The central theme should not be confused with an ad hoc clinical case formulation because it must be sufficiently broad in order to explain the child's difficulties yet specific enough to permit a clear and circumscribed focus to be communicated to the child. When presented to a child in the form of a life story or allegory, the theme becomes a statement of therapeutic intent and purpose. The central theme serves several distinct purposes at different points in the treatment. During the assessment phase, the theme is a summary statement that connects all that is known about the problem, its historical antecedents, and etiology. Once treatment begins, the theme is used to guide the therapeutic relationship toward its objectives. It maintains the therapeutic focus, wards off distractions, and reduces the possible intrusion of irrelevant side issues into the therapy. The theme is a form of therapeutic blinders that are worn by both therapist and child.

The presenting symptomatology and dynamic conflict originating from the parts are joined together in the central theme. In other words, the theme reveals the child's hidden painful feelings of loss that persist in the present. The goal of treatment is to allow children to understand the cause of these painful feelings, the discovery of which adds to and intensifies their sense of self-control and well-being. The theme is the most important way in which the therapist conveys understanding of children's fear of dependency and their need for an array of effective psychological tools that increase the prospect of greater competence in the future. There exists in the child a need to resolve the conflict between the wish to remain connected to one's parents and the necessity of learning how to tolerate separation and loss without undue damage to the self. Because a failure to tolerate separateness is at the core of many children's behavioral and psychological problems, the iterative process of separation-individuation becomes the basis for conceptualizing a therapeutic focus. An emphasis on separation-individuation is consistent with a life-stage developmental framework wherein recurrent systematic developmental changes occur throughout life. In this view, the process of separation-individuation begun in infancy is never fully resolved and remains a powerful, yet dormant, force until reactivated by a psychosocial stressor. Children present with problems that are the direct result of external threats to newly acquired defenses, due to environmental stress, actual or psychological loss of the idealized parental object (disillusionment), and loss of narcissistic supplies through parental illness, death, or divorce. To traverse these developmental milestones may be difficult, challenging, or crisis-laden (Budman & Stone, 1983). TLPT with children emphasizes adaptation and the strengthening of existing defenses and, as a consequence, sets its sights on the future rather than on the past. If the overall thrust of the child's life is toward separation, differentiation, growth, and autonomy, then effective treatment must capitalize on these powerful developmental forces despite the fact that they may be temporarily inhibited or diverted by external constraints not under the child's direct control.

In long-term treatment, children are expected, even encouraged, to have periods of regression, and, for this reason, no time limit is placed on the working-through phase. In contrast, everything about TLPT is calculated to restrict dependency and regression in order to guard against this possibility. The central issue is always phrased and dramatized play in derivative terms that are nonthreatening, that enhance ego functioning, and that bypass the child's defensive system. Primary, primitive, or infantile affects are never directly addressed out of concern that they might exert a regressive pull on the child's defensive system. However, defensive feelings that represent the past and present are incorporated into the central theme. Therefore, one speaks of a child's feelings of disappointment, worry, or uncertainty, but never of feelings of rage, fearfulness, or abandonment. In psychoanalytic parlance, the development of a transference neurosis is actively thwarted, and this is accomplished by the therapist consistently stressing adaptation over passivity.

When a central theme is psychologically on the mark, it jump-starts the therapeutic alliance and quickly accelerates the formation of a positive transference. Children judge very quickly that the therapist is on their side. Viewed in this light, the theme sets the tone for the entire treatment because it is one of the most effective means available by which the therapist can convey an appreciation of the child's pain. The theme adds to the child's understanding of treatment beyond the vague assertion that "you will feel better if you can talk with someone about your problems." Furthermore, the theme provides a feeling of familiarity and provides a forward motion from one session to the next. In TLPT, the theme is not reserved for the exclusive use of the therapist but is, instead, shared directly with the child.

Terry is an 8-year-old boy of average intelligence who has lived for the past 5 years with his maternal grandmother, Ms. R., in kinship foster care. Six months prior to the referral for TLPT, Terry was diagnosed with an attention deficit hyperactivity disorder, and he had an excellent response to psychostimulants. At the time of referral, his grandmother cited a host of problems that suggested an oppositional defiant disorder. Over the past year, Terry had demonstrated his increasing lack of "respect" for the grandmother's authority. The event that precipitated the referral occurred 2 weeks ago after Terry was given permission to play with a peer in the apartment hallway after school. On his own accord, Terry left the building and walked two blocks to a classmate's home, where he spent the next 3 hours before returning home to his distraught and angry guardian.

We found several points of information relevant in our search for a central theme. Terry was placed with the grandmother as a consequence of neglect on the part of the biological mother. Ms. R. revealed that on more than one occasion, Terry was left alone by his mother for several hours at a time, which was discovered when he went door to door in search of food. Here, we thought, is the source of his pseudoindependence. He was only oppositional and defiant when in his grandmother's custody. His school reported, and his grandmother confirmed, that Terry was rarely if ever antagonistic, rebellious, or belligerent in the classroom. With these facts in mind, Terry was offered the following theme.

"I can see that you are a smart boy who has learned how to take care of himself. When you were a little kid and even though you loved your mommy a whole lot, you had to act real grown-up because you were never sure grown-ups would be around to take care of you. Now you live with grandma, who wants to take care of you. But, you want to show grandma that you don't need her all the time. You said that you know grandma loves you and won't leave you alone, but inside you still worry about this. Maybe you are getting ready for the day when grandma will leave you like mommy did.

You and I, together, are going to meet in this room for the next 12 weeks. We are going to work together for 12 times to find a way for you to get grandma to treat you like a strong, smart 8-year-old boy but without making her angry at you and without you being worried she is going to leave you or being angry at her because she doesn't realize you are so smart and able to do a lot of things for yourself. You can be a big boy and still let grown-ups take care of you."

The example of Terry illustrates how the central theme is the outgrowth of a process that begins when the therapist selects one representative core conflict from the myriad present. The therapist examines the history for recurrent events that are symbolically connected to one another, those which have caused the child enduring pain. For as children move through latency and become increasingly enmeshed in the complex social order of childhood, they experience an ever-increasing number of situations that can cause pain.

They may feel unaccepted, separate, or unusually distinct from others, become sensitive to real or imagined signs of rejection by peers, or feel victimized or unfairly treated by others. The fact that the theme is not all inclusive, that alternative interpretations or formulations may "fit the facts," is of minimal concern. As a form of discontinuous psychotherapy, TLPT does not have to be overly comprehensive in scope.

Three basic complementary elements are included in the theme for the treatment to have any meaning to the child. First, the child is offered a statement that condenses the developmental conflict currently being experienced. In a sense, the therapist exposes a painfully hidden part of the child. Next, the therapist conveys how the child's problematic behaviors represent an erstwhile attempt to resolve or alleviate the source of the pain. Here, the therapist reframes the symptom(s) that have aroused the displeasure, disapproval, or disappointment of significant others as an understandable occurence; that the presenting problem is a maladaptive solution to a real problem plaguing the child. Finally, the history of the problem is reviewed to illustrate both the ineffectiveness of the applied solution and the need to find a more appropriate, less conflictual means to achieve adaptation. The central theme embodies the future in that it supports the child in seeking new behaviors and higher more flexible levels of defense while creating a sense of optimism. It is a way to demonstrate to children what it is they want, how efforts in the past failed to achieve their anticipated results, and how they can achieve these goals in the present.

After the therapist has located in the history and present symptomatology the core conflict responsible for the child's distress, the dynamic formulation is translated into an affectively meaningful story that the child can readily understand. The therapist dramatizes the theme with the appropriate play materials as she encourages the child to customize and/or modify the story and, thereby, make it even more relevant to the child's experience. Once treatment has begun, the very idea of the theme acts to support children when they "forget" or lose sight of the purpose of therapy. It is something they can refer back to whenever they become confused, and it helps them to tolerate the constraints imposed on them by the therapist. So that children do not feel controlled or dominated by their therapist, they need to understand how each session serves their enlightened self-interest. The theme increases the likelihood of enlisting the child's observing ego in the battle against the infantile and irrational self. In practice, the therapist presents the theme in the form of a "family story" that summarizes the therapist's recognition of the child's distress.

Crystal is a 10-year-old who was brought to the clinic because of multiple hospitalizations for pain in her leg that prevented her from walking. The repeated hospitalizations did not find anything medically significant, despite numerous Xrays, CAT scans, MRIs, and specialty consultations. After a period of hospitalization and inpatient rehabilitation therapy, Crystal's ability to walk would return and she would be discharged. Before her referral to psychiatry, she was hospitalized four times in the prior 20 months.

Crystal's mother works at a department store as a secretary, and her father was killed in a suspected drug war when Crystal was 2 years old. There are two other daughters by this father, one a year younger and one a year older than Crystal. The older one is in a class for very bright children and is at the head of her class. She also excels in violin, jazz ballet, and debate. The youngest daughter is exceptionally pretty, has participated in junior beauty pageants, and has won several trophies. She is also "Ms. Personality" and has legions of friends. Crystal is an attractive child and is a B student in regular class. She has friends, relates well to adults as well as peers, and is in the Girl Scouts. She "hates" music and dancing and "those stupid beauty shows." Mother is very busy taking the older child to music and dance lessons and the younger to beauty competitions, often traveling out of state to do so.

While in the hospital, Crystal was the star of the ward, making quick progress and achieving ambulatory skills at a faster rate than anyone. She was doted upon by the family, and her classmates, all of whom came to visit, brought flowers and milk shakes and showered her with attention. Crystal was diagnosed with a conversion disorder.

The central theme was stated as such: "You are a very special person and are able to have many, many people sit up and take notice of just how special you are. That is your gift; you can get your mother, who is very, very busy, to have time for you; you can get your classmates to take time to visit you; and you can get your sisters to pay attention to you; and you can do this without having to be a star in class or a beauty queen. That is an amazing talent. However, you have figured out how to do this when you are not feeling so well, and we know that sometimes you feel OK. So together, let's use some time, 12 meeting times, to figure out ways together to have you be special when you are feeling strong and your leg doesn't hurt you. You can be your own star all the time and not just when you are in the hospital."

Once treatment begins, the therapist enhances the continuous aspects of the therapeutic process and the psychodynamic conflict through a repeated explication of the central theme as it is enacted within each session. The theme, repeated over the course of 12 sessions and woven into the very fabric of the structured play, significantly reduces the experience of randomness that characterizes much of long-term play treatment. Each succeeding session is the logical and thematic extension of the session that preceded it. The theme is restated at the beginning of each session as the contract is being signed. Theme derivations are abstracted from the child's verbal and nonverbal play during the sessions, and this occurs with such regularity that the child soon internalizes the process. Movement within treatment is measured by the child's response or lack thereof to each statement of the theme. Some children use the theme as a starting point by integrating it into their play; others, threatened by the eventual loss of the therapist, sarcastically invoke the theme or mimic the therapist. At the end of each session, the therapist takes the time to summarize the child's work, to review how the theme made itself known in the play, and to note how a particular variation on the theme will require further exploration. Before the child leaves, the therapist ties up any loose ends, extending a single common thread through any disparate elements, and draws the child's attention ahead to the next session. This review enables the child to bridge the potentially timeless gap between the present and the future because it implies that the work of treatment will continue in the interval between sessions. When the goals and procedure of therapy are clearly explained to children, they invariably come to the sessions with a plan of how to best use the time in the service of the central theme.

The Therapeutic Contract

TLPT begins both with the presentation of the central theme to the child in front of the parents and with the development of a written therapeutic contract (Peterlin & Sloves, 1985). The contract appeals to the latency child's need for discernable rules and regulations, as well as to the desire for concrete evidence of accomplishments. The process of contract making represents a fusion of the central theme, the working alliance, and the beginning of the positive transference. It is the latency child's variable sense of time that is of greatest concern for the time-limited therapist (Proskauer, 1969). Given the fact that children do not possess a fully developed sense of time, consideration must be given to how this relative deficit can be addressed throughout the process of therapy. Clarification and concretization of the passage of time are helpful in mitigating the sense of loss, disappointment, and rejection that occurs at the end of treatment.

In order to maintain the goal-directed nature of TLPT, several techniques are required to assist the child in coming to grips with the dynamic issues related to time (loss, separation, and individuation). The therapist educates the child as to the importance of remaining attuned to the central theme that prompted the treatment. Contracts make the central theme concrete. The therapist, together with the child, draws up a contract at the end of the assessment stage. This contract includes the central theme, or focus, of the treatment: "I will figure out ways to be important in my school and to have lots of friends without having to take money to buy stuff for them"; or, "I will figure out ways to be important in my school and to have lots of friends and have my dad pay attention to me without having to beat up kids to do it." The contract contains the child's name, a statement of the central theme in age-appropriate language, the total number of sessions, and the exact date of termination (see Figure 2.1).

Because cognitive and dynamic factors collude in permitting the child to deny or distort the reality of loss engendered by the termination, it is particularly useful to supplement the contract with graphic or pictorial materials that emphasize the passage of time. One example would be to give the child a photocopied calendar that has each session date highlighted in a distinctive color and numbered in decreasing order from 12 to 1. Obviously, the therapist must take into consideration the chronological as well as the cognitive age of the child when choosing an appropriate mnemonic device. An intellectually accelerated 10-year-old might consider such a reminder patronizing, whereas an equally intelligent younger child might be quite eager to use the materials to demonstrate his or her knowledge of time. The child receives a copy of the contract; the family receives another; and the therapist holds several copies in reserve, in the case the child destroys the original, which often happens during the termination stage. The contract is not the only symbol of time that is the subject of the child's conscious and/or unconscious anger. One of the authors has had so many clocks dropped or thrown out the window that they are routinely secreted away before each session. One child who entered the playroom and found the clock missing from the therapist's desk remarked, "No clock! No clock! Now we have to go forever." At the beginning of each treatment session, the central theme is reviewed, and the child marks off the date as attended. The therapist counts off the remaining sessions and might say, "This is our first session; after today we have 11 left." At the end of the session, the therapist reminds the child: "I'll see you next Monday at the same time for our second session." This serves several purposes. Reviewing the central theme at the beginning of each session grounds both child and therapist and orients them to the work at hand. Marking off the dates and reminding the child of how many sessions there are until the end helps the child understand life in a more realistic way.

While this procedure may seem somewhat obsessive in nature, its importance cannot be overemphasized because, as the termination date grows closer, children deny the impending reality or attempt to renegotiate termination. Even when meticulous and clear

MY THERAPY CONTRACT

Central Theme:

Therapy Begins:

Therapy Ends:

Number of Visits:

We promise to make a very special effort to keep all of our appointments, and to call when we are going to be late or when we can't come.

| 1 | 2 | 3 | 4 | 5 | 6 | 7 | 8 | 9 | 10 | 11 | 12 |

_____
Child

_____
Parent(s)

_____
Therapist

Figure 2.1. An example of a therapy contract.

records are maintained, children frequently assert that the therapist has miscounted. The therapist substitutes, externally, what is lacking in the internal structural development of a particular child. In those children where the passage of time is poorly developed, the therapist, who does experience time's passage, lends this awareness and its ensuing anxieties to the child.

The Treatment Process

Structured Play

TLPT demands considerable modification of technique and a thoughtful examination of many assumptions that govern more traditional, open-ended formats of play therapy. The modality necessitates a highly efficient, focused, and organized approach so that a child's level of interest and motivation for change are held consistently high throughout the 12 sessions.

Several major characteristics of latency shape the structure and technique of TLPT. The child's predilection for primary process expression, or, as described by Piaget, preoperational and concrete operational cognitive development (Ginsberg & Opper, 1969), requires a structured format that limits regression and dependency (Kramer & Byerly, 1978). Children need to maintain and guard newly acquired defenses. This raises the question of how treatment can emphasize adaptation and learning and, at the same time, allow the therapist to challenge self-defeating and maladaptive defensive strategies. The idealization of action by children and their inability to be inactive in therapy demand an active, play-oriented treatment.

In important ways, structured play is quite distinct from the prevailing orthodoxy of Axlinian/Rogerian play therapy. Rather than assume a posture of therapeutic abstinence or neutrality, the therapist's role is both directive and facilitative, with therapy geared toward helping children to develop age-appropriate psychological (internal) and behavioral-social (interpersonal) competencies. Structured play is an outgrowth of the psychodynamic play interview techniques of Conn (1989) and Erikson (1950) and the cognitive-behavioral approach explicated by Meichenbaum (1974). Because each session begins with a preplanned scenario, the therapist spends as much time and energy focused on the future as reflecting on past. This orientation is based on the premise that therapeutic play is not free. The therapist develops a plan for each session, designs specific play scenarios, selects the appropriate play materials, introduces the major players, and gets each session rolling with an opening narrative; all the while trying to make the play resemble the child's inner as well as external life circumstances. While respect is given to the child's ability to solve problems, the child is not allowed to do it in his or her own time, especially when the therapist is in the position to convey to the child the collective knowledge of children who, in similar circumstances, have struggled to confront similar problems. Rather than let children hunt and search out the implicit rules that govern treatment, the therapist gives them a helping hand. Therefore, the dynamic formulation, the length of therapy, and the basic mechanics of the process are spelled out to them ahead of time. They learn that psychotherapy is not play, and the play area is the work area.

Play-in-progress is a term that describes the process by which guided fantasy, mutual storytelling, cognitive restructuring, and symbolic work are integrated into the therapy. The therapist sets the stage, arranging the play materials into a scene shortly *before* the child enters the room. The play is not always a literal representation of the child's life circumstances, and it can take on a highly symbolic portrayal of the child's inner world (Sloves & Peterlin, 1993).

The trick is to drive the play as close as possible to preconscious awareness without triggering maladaptive defenses. At times, the play is a barely disguised representation of the child's inner thoughts, feelings, and object relationships. Materials are used to illustrate in as direct a way as possible the conflict-free spheres of ego and cognitive functioning, such as memory, delay, intention, and cause-and-effect reasoning. Therapists are explicit in their efforts to identify and strengthen the observing ego and to use any type of image, metaphor, and allegory to help children decenter and strengthen their capacity for self-observation and regulation; for example, the therapist might move the narrative in the direction that best illustrates how a child can experience simultaneously positive and negative thoughts and feelings about one person. Illustrated with drawings and acted out with puppets or dolls, children gain a greater understanding of their driving forces. Pictographs are used extensively to provide children with graphic representations of their internal emotional states and cognitive processes—dynamics that are intuitively sensed by children but lie just beyond their linguistic and conceptual powers. The therapist, as ally, does everything to hurry the therapy along without frightening a child into passivity, active resistance, or flight. As therapist and child take turns acting out the central theme, the play offers an opportunity for objectification and a reshuffling of perspective that will hopefully lead to a greater acceptance of responsibility by the child.

Structured play pushes the central theme to the forefront of each session so that a different theme or conflicting subtheme does not emerge for each session. In a sense, this prevents each session from becoming a series of endless new beginnings. Therapist and child do not begin each session with a tabula rasa because the therapist plans the opening gambit in such a manner as to keep issues raised in the previous session alive in the present. The selected story line contains the overriding theme as well as the specific details that emerged during the previous session, and, in this regard, the therapist is the repository of the therapeutic memory. It is the therapist who remembers what was repressed or denied, connects the child's play directly to his or her extratherapeutic experiences, and gives voice to the child's intuitive, experiential self. With the kind of thematic continuity provided by structured play, it is a relatively easy task for the child and therapist to pick up from where they left off at the last session. Instead of a plethora of daily, transient, situational events dictating the pace and direction of work, the shared conscious and observing ego of child and therapist takes charge and directs the process. Children do not usually look ahead with great precision; but, with the help of the central theme, the therapy becomes an algorithm for growth and development and helps them accept adult time, or reality. When, at the close of each session, the play is summarized and reworked into the core conflict, the child's attention is drawn naturally to the next session and toward the inevitable separation that will bring enhanced self-esteem and psychological competence.

While limited time may seem to constrain what can or cannot be accomplished within the therapy, it exerts a paradoxical and liberating effect on the therapist. High therapist activity is one of the hallmarks of TLPT, and structured play is its logical outgrowth. An active therapist, in collaboration with the child, can orchestrate the tempo and rhythm for each session and for the treatment as a whole. Once the therapist's role is conceptualized as participatory, the therapist is free to engage in one of the major tasks of treatment, that is, to act as the child's theme detector. This is shown in the following example: A child in the course of treatment raised the issue of sibling rivalry when the central theme had to do with helping her come to grips with her anger toward her recently divorced parents. Because the therapist was unable to directly link her feelings toward her sister with the central theme, she was told:

"That is a very important problem, but we don't have enough time for that. Maybe you can talk to your mother about it or figure it out by yourself. We have another big worry to solve—how to tell your Mom and Dad what you are feeling but without you getting into trouble. We have to find a way so they can really understand you. It has to be a solution where they won't get mad at you, won't punish you, and won't go away so you won't see them ever again. If we can do all that, I am sure that you will be able to figure out what to do about your baby sister messing up your stuff."

The play material for each session must be carefully selected by the therapist beforehand. In fact, the whole session is organized and planned before the child comes into the office. Several factors are taken into consideration: the phase of treatment the child is in, what happened in the preceding session, and where the therapist wishes to go in this session. Therefore, specific play materials are used and others are avoided. Puppets, dolls, dollhouses and furniture, action figures, toy animals and vehicles, wooden building blocks, and water-soluble drawing materials are the primary tools of treatment and are chosen for their ability to recreate, in reasonably concrete, literal ways, the core conflict. At the same time, any play activity that is too cumbersome, takes too much time to set up, offers the child sanctuary from the therapeutic focus, or is so complicated that it takes too long for the theme to be played out is avoided. Board games are never used, no matter how therapeutic their intent. They are totally dominated by and dependent on fixed, invariant rules and, thus, serve to limit spontaneity, constrain fantasy, and force the players into a competitive relationship. Materials resistant to psychological regression are acceptable. This means finger paints, play dough, water play, and other primitive materials are banished from the playroom because they only lead to transferential difficulties, which include issues of control and repression, rather than encouraging freedom of expression.

At the end of the second and last assessment session and at the end of each treatment session, the child is asked to bring to the next session dolls, action figures, or toy vehicles that they think will help dramatize the central theme. This makes efficient use of time and, under the right circumstances, can accelerate the treatment because, unlike toys in the therapist's playroom, the child's toys have been already cathected and, therefore, have an important and unique history. In other words, each toy is imbued with distinctive aspects of the child's past and present experiences. They are replete with a rich psychosocial subtext. Children and their possessions share a wealth of experiences that are easily revealed to the therapist with little resistance. More importantly, these personalized toys enhance generalization from treatment session to natural environment because children can take the play home with them. Once children catch on to the routine of structured play, they often produce from their pockets or knapsack useful and, at times, wonderful illustrative materials. The therapist can often modify the session play to incorporate whatever the child has offered by chance or design. This speeds up the treatment momentum because one can begin almost immediately to play out the central dynamic issues.

Children are never forced or coerced to conform to a prescribed script, but the play materials and restrictions placed on their use in the playroom are perforce limiting. In fact, if there is a part of TLPT that requires quick reflexes and improvisational skill, it is manifested on those occasions when a scenario fails to spark the child's imagination. The child is quite free to play out any resistance and any defenses, but the therapist channels the means of expression. Because the child and therapist play as equals, each has as much right as the other to question and to comment upon the play character's thoughts, feelings, and motives. Watching the therapist play, the child becomes at once an interested observer and an active participant in the process of problem clarification and conflict resolution. This improvisational switching of roles helps the child to think about his or her thinking (Hartner, 1977) or to be a bystander to their own thoughts and feelings (Meichenbaum,

1974). With both child and therapist at play, the therapeutic alliance and positive transference are enhanced, making it easier for both to endure conflict. The therapist is now free to shift at will from commentator to observer and then to participant. Engaged in either parallel or communal play, the therapist is free to ask the child, "What am I supposed to be doing here? How is this story (action) helping you? What is the point of all this?"

Stages of Treatment

Children in TLPT move through three more or less distinct stages in much the same manner as Mann's adult patients (Mann, 1973). In the opening stage, the therapist nourishes the therapeutic alliance, offering children an empathic umbrella from the interpersonal and intrapsychic storm that surrounds them. At this stage, the transference is not interpreted because doing so might interfere with the child's wish to cast the therapist in the role of the all-comprehending special friend. During the working-through stage, the therapist, who serves as a stand-in for ambivalently held objects, interprets the transference in light of the child's past and present relationships with significant others. It is in the termination stage that the therapist helps the child choose between the ambivalent past and the imperfect future, between magical wishes for restitution and tangible, albeit flawed, sources of gratification in the present and future. During termination, the relationship between the therapist and the child is the primary source for all transference interpretations.

In order to keep the child focused on both time's passage and the central work of treatment, each session begins the same way. First the child checks off the current session date on the therapeutic contract. Then, the therapist verbalizes the passage of time: "Today is session number three, we now have nine sessions to go." The formalities end with the therapist reading the central theme from the contract. The session ends on a similar note: "Today we finished session three, and next week is session four. That means we have nine sessions to go."

OPENING STAGE.   The opening stage of therapy actually begins when the central theme is presented in the diagnostic stage and continues, unabated, through the third and fourth sessions. The primary goal at this stage is to nurture the therapeutic alliance, which is something that most children can understand and to which they can relate: the desire for independence, the novelty of feeling empowered, the triumph of defending one's own self. The therapist makes a direct appeal to that part of the child that craves security without dependency and support without regression.

In this stage of treatment, the child, like an infant, reexperiences the golden glow of infancy and feels a sense of omnipotence that is rooted in the archaic feeling of infinite time. The central theme makes the conflict between infinite time (desire) and finite time (reality) concrete to the child, and this serves to underscore the therapist's role as an ally in the process of individuation. The therapist unconditionally accepts the child's wish for a wordless perfect bond, and, along with his or her empathic support, they begin to explore the core conflict. The therapist bridges the gap between infant time (symbiosis) and adult time (identity). Children know, through the therapist's statement of the theme and the structured play, that they are supported. At the same time, the therapist's reflective and problem-solving orientation, dramatized in the structured play, communicates to children the belief that they are capable of understanding themselves in new and potentially liberating ways.

While the opening stage of TLPT revives archaic fantasies of symbiotic merger, it also provides a structure that keeps the child developmentally in phase. This structure, provided by the central theme, the therapeutic contract, and structured play, empowers the child and gives a sense of hope that the goals of therapy can be attained. At this point, the central theme reinforces the child's belief that a magical friendship exists, and this strengthens the therapeutic alliance. Later, both the alliance and the strong positive transference will support the child as the therapist slowly challenges the wish to prolong the fantasy of an infinite childhood.

In this opening stage, an overwhelming number of children discard their presenting symptoms and behave as though the therapeutic alliance, alone, was sufficient to obviate the need for the very defensive system that gave rise to it. Perhaps children expect the therapist to replace, permanently, the past and present ambivalently held objects. In any case, the result is diminished intrapsychic conflict. Symptomatic relief is further hastened as the therapist dramatizes, in play, the central conflict. The calm, purposeful manner in which the core conflict is explored tends to desensitize children to whatever powerful and frightening affects caused them to avoid problem solving and mastery in the past. Symptom reduction during the opening stage is attributed to the therapist's empathic exploration of the central issue, the process of abreaction, the promotion of positive feelings about the self, and the supportive nature of the therapeutic alliance.

The therapeutic alliance is realized through the following application of technique: the play materials are manipulated in order to avoid all issues related to authority and control. At the same time, the therapist assumes the role of a benign and nonpunitive figure who has the power to understand all that the child experiences. The goal, here, is to recapture the first fusion between the mother and child when the mother and, therefore, the child were omnipotent. This reenacted symbiosis enables the child to feel a renewed sense of power. The therapist reinforces the positive thrust by lending his or her ego to that of the child. "Together, we will figure out a way to get the bad dreams and tummy aches to go away, and, together, we will find a way to get your Mommy to spend more time with you." This rather straightforward technique is marvelously enabling to children, for it inspires confidence and increases the level of energy available to tackle tasks that were, heretofore, their undoing. The therapist is empathic but never in a way that might be misconstrued as seductive and certainly never in a manner that could undermine the child's sense of connectedness with the primary caretakers. The alliance never assumes an "us against them" mentality, and, for this reason, the therapist never takes credit for any of the child's accomplishments.

With the alliance well established, the therapist begins to challenge the illusion of perpetual symbiosis that was so carefully nurtured. As the date for each session is checked off on the contract, the child begins to realize that loss (ending) looms in the not so distant future. Along with this realization comes an awareness that neither participant is able to control time's passage. Gradually and painfully, children come to the awareness that the therapist cannot make all wishes possible: the therapist, once the embodiment of power, perfection, the holder of all entitlements, is going to disappointment them the way others have done in the past.

CASE ILLUSTRATION FOR OPENING STAGE

Within the span of the first 15 minutes of the fourth session, Terry made several related comments. First he noted, "You don't have a lot of good toys; you should get some more." This was followed in quick order by the multiple requests: "Do you have something to eat?" "Can I take one of these (a mechanical pencil)? You have a lot of them," and "Can I take this fan home with me? I broke the one at home, and my mom said I have to pay her back."

Therapist: Today you have asked me for many things. You seem very hungry today.

Terry: Yeah. My mother said I'm going to eat her out of everything in the refrig.

Therapist: You want something from me, too, but you keep asking for things that I can't give to you. What do you really want that you are not getting at home?

Terry: I don't know.

Therapist: It says here in your therapy contract that you want to get grown-ups to help you without them treating you like a little kid.

Terry: (Smiles) That's not going to fill my stomach right now!

Therapist: You're absolutely right, but it can fill up another part of you that's a little empty.

Terry: (Silent for a while and fiddles with the blocks on the table). Yeah, well, OK, I mean, I know how little kids get stuff by climbing up into their Mom's lap and stuff like that, but I can't figure out how I can, exactly . . .

Therapist: You mean get love?

Terry: (Looks a bit embarrassed) Well, yeah, I guess so. (Silence) So, how *do* you do it?

Therapist: That is exactly what we have to figure out together. That is the work that you and I will be doing for the next 8 weeks, to get love and attention in a way that makes sense for 8-year-old boys like you.

If children are allowed to perceive the therapist as a restitutive object (all good) and are permitted to cast the therapeutic relationship into the framework of the symbiotic past, they will ignore the need to solve the conflict that constitutes the core of their present difficulties. The desire, to have the therapist restore the symbiotic state, is enacted in the transference and represents the child's first resistance to change; and it is this resistance to accepting the finiteness of time that signals the beginning of the working-through stage. It is at this juncture that reality confronts fantasy. It is here that children have an opportunity to renegotiate past issues of separation and individuation, to reassess their assets and liabilities, and to emerge better equipped to confront the future.

WORKING-THROUGH STAGE. In the second stage of treatment, children begin to confront the reality that time is indeed passing, that therapy is not limitless, and that the therapist is not omnipotent and is incapable of stopping time. Children come face-to-face with the fact that not all goals in life are attainable. Like an infant during the separation and individuation stage of development, disillusionment sets in. Reality pushes out fantasy and brings with it real time, time that is limited and finite. Ceaseless and immediate gratifications are not to be had. With time, with reality, the child confronts mortality and one's ultimate death, facing personal imperfections as well as those of others. During this phase, the child experiences the ambivalence that ensues when one is confronted with the limits of time, with reality. This second stage is critical because it is here that the child reexperiences the pains and anxieties of separation. The therapist's role is to help the child struggle with this painful reality, to bridge the gap between child (infinite) time and adult (limited) time and to work through the resulting anxieties in a more adaptive manner than in infancy.

Because the termination date, representing separation and loss, holds such a commanding and prominent position in each session, children gradually begin to deny the inevitable loss of the therapist by distancing themselves from the therapeutic work, or they try to bargain for more time. At this stage, it is the therapist's responsibility to interpret all forms of resistance as fear of growing up. As children begin to assert themselves vis-à-vis the therapist, a reworking of earlier attachments that constitute higher levels of adaptation and separateness takes place.

The therapeutic contract and calendar, relatively unimportant and often ignored during the opening phase, begin to take on meaning that is both metaphoric and tangible. Time begins to intrude into the therapeutic alliance and attack the positive transference. Children, who only a few weeks before, gazed at treatment across the wide expanse of time, start to contemplate separation: separation not only from this newly developed relationship, but from the remnants of the infantile past that was dramatized in the structured play scenarios. Further irritation is provided by the session number, which is mentioned at the beginning and end of each appointment. This becomes a particular source of annoyance to children and a target of their disdain or ridicule. Both ambivalence and discouragement are expressed in the play and in the transference, and it is at this point that there is a momentary loss in therapeutic momentum as children pause to reassess the therapeutic alliance. The pervasive sense of energy, therapeutic movement, and cooperation that characterized the opening stage is now mitigated. Children appear more reserved as the idolization of the therapist begins to diminish.

With the ever-present reminder that time is passing and separation (termination) looms on the horizon, children begin to resist the treatment in myriad ways. They might begin to question the therapist's choice and arrangement of play materials, criticize their performance ("You're not doing it right"), or demand that the therapist "play." Often they express an aversion to the "work" of therapy. When this happens, the therapist confirms the importance of having fun, while stressing the need to work on the core conflict. In addition to the choice of play materials, children frequently challenge the central theme or call into question the number of sessions remaining in treatment. Some will claim that they had not attended the previous week's session, that another child checked off the date on the contract, or that they have coming to them more sessions than are listed.

Throughout this phase, as children experience the passage of time with ever-greater intensity, the therapeutic alliance becomes increasingly ambivalent. Whereas in the opening phase the therapist represented a restitutive object, the therapeutic relationship now becomes a transitional one between the past and the future. Fears as well as positive expectations evolve from this new relationship. Children become torn between feelings of disappointment (sadness) and anger (oppositional and defiant behaviors). As the child moves from anger over the loss of the idealized object to fear of separateness, the therapist reinforces those phase-appropriate structural and affective states that will maintain a positive transference while challenging the child to adopt functional and purposeful psychological tools to deal with these feelings.

It is at this point in treatment that the techniques of confrontation and interpretation are employed to cut through resistance. Confrontation may arouse anger in the child and its expression provides opportunities rich for interpretation of feelings about how their parents and other significant adults have disappointed them in the past. However, Wolberg (1980) offers a stern word of warning: Whenever confrontation is used too early in therapy, it might cause the child to perceive the therapist as unsympathetic or malicious and, thereby, endanger the positive transference.

The emergence of a negative transference is the most damaging event to sabotage

TLPT, so, whenever it emerges, decisive action on the part of the therapist is required. The therapist is vigilant to any shift in the therapeutic alliance in order to avoid becoming embroiled in an unproductive struggle for control. Given the importance of collaboration within the context of the positive transference, the therapist needs to determine whether opposition is a reenactment of the central issue (transference), an avoidance of the core conflict (defense), or a valid criticism of the play's irrelevance (self-assertiveness). Disagreements over power will almost always lead to the child's perception of the therapist as either impotent or inadequate. The therapist does not engage the child in a struggle for control because to do so might convey the wrong idea: that the child has sufficient emotional clout to dominate the therapist. At the same time, as the therapist demonstrates in play how the conflict replicates those with other significant figures of authority in the natural environment, he or she needs to derail, defuse, and reframe the negative affect without becoming embroiled in it.

The therapist joins with or reframes all expressions of frustration and anger that have the capacity to overwhelm or damage the therapeutic alliance. This process helps the child to bind unneutralized aggressive affects and to facilitate the development of age-appropriate defenses. The goal is to strengthen all of the autonomous ego functions of delay, anticipation, reflection, and cognition. The therapist appeals directly to the child in understanding how time, embodied in the fixed termination date, is a metaphor for what has been lost (both real and imagined) and for what can be attained. Of course, the therapist has as an ally, the child's normal developmental press for autonomy. This force carries the child and therapist forward in time and allows them to view the therapy as a means of achieving individuation. The child's gradual internalization of the therapist's adaptive ego functioning holds forth the promise of a finite, yet still hoped for, relationship in the future. Children may fight time's passage through the defiance of limits (resistance) but they also demonstrate their desire for independence through a gradual acceptance of finite time.

TERMINATION STAGE.   The termination stage is an intensification of all that precedes it and emerges somewhere around the ninth session. A sense of loss is so palpable that it permeates every aspect of the treatment, and it is here that the alliance is most endangered. The therapist begins each session with the understanding that some unforeseen event might cause the bond between the child and therapist to break, thus ending treatment. Despite this risk, the therapist has but one path to follow: the aggressive management of the termination. It is a most difficult process because it arouses a tremendous amount of resistance in the child, the parents, and even the therapist. An active and appropriate management of the termination permits the child to internalize the therapist as a positive replacement or substitute for the earlier ambivalent objects, thereby making separation a genuine maturational event. Separation, as a universal experience, as played out within this context of a successful termination, becomes yet another successful adaptation by the child's developing ego.

The termination stage is undermined when either therapist or child act on their conscious or unconscious desire to prolong the relationship. If the termination phase is difficult for children, it is equally problematic for the parents. Initially pleased by a dramatic reduction in the presenting symptomatology during the opening stage and satisfied with the child's progress during the working-through stage, parents are frequently alarmed by symptom's return. "He was acting like a completely different child, listening to us and all, but now he's even more stubborn than before." Parents may lose confidence in the treatment, the therapist, or, more importantly, their own competence should the therapist fail to remind them that it is a normal feature of the treatment.

When the therapist is ambivalent about termination, this too will undermine TLPT and cause the patient to avoid the basic issue of separation and individuation that termination symbolizes. The therapist might question the accuracy of the original diagnosis, the severity of the underlying psychopathology, or ruminate on a host of systemic and psychodynamic variables that were overlooked during the earlier stages of treatment. The unconscious purpose of such doubt is to prolong the treatment and, thereby, ward off the impending emotions associated with separation. A therapist dominated by these dynamics cannot maintain a clear thematic focus and will be distracted by irrelevant details or will be preoccupied by extraneous subthemes. In any event, self-doubt and loss of focus inevitably lead the therapist to convey a false sense of time to the child. The therapist who postpones the termination date ostensibly to pacify the child's and/or parents' anxieties merely colludes with the longing for infinite time. Behavior such as this ends up not only validating the low self-esteem of the child but places the therapist in a position of power over the family.

It is in this final stage of treatment that the child is asked to make an explicit, existential choice. The child can leave treatment in a way that replicates earlier unsatisfactory separations, but this only preserves and perpetuates the conflicted past. On the other hand, the child can leave treatment in a rehabilitative manner, but this means that he or she must relinquish all prospects that the lost relationship will ever return. Children are quite naturally frustrated by this predicament, and it is the source of much of their acting out in termination. The therapist counters this resistance by remaining empathic. However, emotional support at this point is not enough. The therapist expresses an appreciation of the idea that while it is perfectly acceptable to feel dissatisfaction or disillusionment with one's caretakers, the child has available a wide variety of friends, siblings, teachers, neighbors, and relatives who might be available to pick up the slack. Further, the therapist underlines the child's own unique store of inner resources and strengths. As mastery and self-esteem are enhanced, the ability to tolerate separateness is simultaneously strengthened. The termination date is held inviolate except for all but the most extreme of circumstances, such as the onset of a serious illness or the death of a parent, relative, family, or close friend. For the therapist to concede to a request for a few more sessions is tantamount to saying, "You really can't make it on your own, and you are too weak or helpless to leave therapy." To act in accordance with this wish is to reinforce the most maladaptive need to remain dependent on the permanent fusion with a significant other and stay rooted in infinite time. It is the therapist's responsibility to dramatize the conflict between the infantile past and the imperfect future in such a way as to make the future more appealing than the past. No matter how children make known their fears and anxieties, the therapist expresses confidence in them and models an age-appropriate problem-solving orientation.

Of all the responses to termination, anger is the most difficult to manage because of the danger of a premature termination. In this last stage of treatment, all resistances are interpreted in conjunction with the child's difficulties in separation from the therapist and from treatment. The therapist tells both child and family that they will know how to deal with the symptom should it reappear. If the therapist is ambivalent about termination, the treatment is in danger of being undermined, for it causes the therapist to avoid the basic issue of separation and individuation that termination symbolizes. This gives the child a false sense of time, and it implies that treatment is limitless and that life, itself, has no limits. Should the therapist pull back from the brink of separation, the child's disillusionment with the therapist's omnipotence cannot occur, and the entire treatment process is derailed and rendered ineffective. Because separation is such a universal experience, it is critical that not only the central issue be related to it, but that the actual termination of treatment be seen within its context. Interpretation of transference is key but only within the framework of the central issue and as it is played out by the child's behavior in termination. When the child is encouraged to internalize the therapist as a positive replacement of an earlier, more ambivalently cathected object, the level and intensity of anger is substantially reduced.

It will come as no surprise that the child in TLPT responds to termination in a manner that resembles the five stages of death and dying described by Kubler-Ross (1969). Some children deny the impending termination date when they announce, "I didn't know we had to stop." Should the therapist counter by invoking the therapeutic contract, anger and disappointment are the natural consequence: "You're really stupid! You can't even count! We have two more times together." When the therapist stands firm and expresses confidence in the child's ability to survive the separation, the child may bargain for more time: "But if we keep going, I could find better things to talk about, not like now." Toward the very end, many children seem sad as they struggle to accept the impending reality of loss. During the final session, it is not at all unusual for children to acknowledge, for the first time, that the therapist is a person and exists outside of the treatment hour. One 9-year-old said, "Don't be sad. Here is a picture of me from school." While another child remarked, "Here, me and my dad got these Lincoln logs at the flea market so you and your other kids can play with them." A final comment is in order. Although the final session is dynamically significant and special, it is not an opportunity for the therapist to relax. The therapist expects the child to continue with the work of therapy throughout the final session. It is only in the final minutes of the session that the therapist takes the time to congratulate the child for all his or her accomplishments, to express confidence in their ability to manage, adaptively, events in the future, and to wish the child a warm and fond farewell.

CONCLUSION

Time-limited play therapy with children represents a significant departure from the traditional norm of Axlinian play therapy, yet it is a modality that is distinct from crisis intervention and from other forms of emergency psychotherapy. It is a dynamically oriented, theme-driven, close-ended, individual psychotherapy with a usual duration of 12 sessions, with the termination date irrevocably fixed before the onset of therapy.

TLTP is a highly structured, aggressively managed, and interactive treatment modality. The modality necessitates a highly efficient, focused, and organized approach so that children's level of interest and motivation for change is held at a consistently high level throughout the 12 sessions. The therapist is neither a participant observer nor a neutral commentator but an active participant in the play. An energized relationship between child and therapist is nurtured but always with an eye to limiting all regressive phenomena and to setting limits on the child's flight from phase-appropriate responsibilities. Unlike psychoanalytically oriented, long-term therapy, successful TLPT is not predicated on the emergence or analysis of a negative transference. On the contrary, children are selected for TLPT precisely because they offer minimal resistance in joining with the therapist in a working alliance and because they are easily dissuaded from any activity that might elicit a negative transference.

The authors do not believe that TLPT is appropriate for every child; nor have they meant to imply, either overtly or covertly, that TLPT is superior to the more traditional forms of treatment. It is an alternative method of treatment, no more, no less. In the end, it is the responsibility of each clinician to know the relative costs and benefits of any given modality in their therapeutic repertoire so that it will not be applied in an inappropriate or unreasonable manner. In this view, it is more important to know when *not* to use TLPT. Parents and guardians in search of psychotherapeutic help for their child have good reason to expect that the therapist will conduct a comprehensive evaluation and that the proposed course of treatment was selected because it represents the best prospect for relief. It serves neither the interests of the child nor the psychotherapeutic profession when a regimen of treatment is applied in an arbitrary or ad hoc basis that fails to take into consideration the best fit of the presenting psychopathology, the child, the therapist, and the technique.

REFERENCES

Achenbach, T. M. (1981). *The child behavior profile.* Burlington, VT: University of Vermont.

American Psychiatric Association. (1987). *Diagnostic and statistical manual of mental disorders* (3rd ed., rev.). Washington, DC: Author.

Applebaum, S. A. (1975). Parkinson's law in psychotherapy. *International Journal of Psychoanalytic Psychotherapy, 4,* 426–436.

Bandura, A. (1969). *Principles of behavior.* New York: Holt, Rinehart and Winston.

Blanck, G., & Blanck, R. (1974). *Ego psychology: theory & practice.* New York: Columbia University Press.

Bonstedt, T. (1965). Psychotherapy in a public psychiatric clinic: An attempt at "adjustment." *Psychiatric Quarterly, 39,* 1–15.

Budman, S. H., & Gurman, A. S. (1992). A time-sensitive model of brief-therapy: The I-D-E approach. In S. H. Budman, M. F. Hoyt, & S. Friedman (Eds.), *The first session in brief therapy.* New York: Guilford Press.

Budman, S. H., & Stone, J. (1983). Advances in brief psychotherapy: A review of recent literature. *Hospital and Community Psychiatry, 34,* 939–946.

Chethik, M. (1989). *Techniques of child therapy.* New York: Guilford Press.

Christ, G. H., Siegel, K., Mesagno, F. P., & Langosch, D. (1991). A preventative program for bereaved children: Problems of implementation. *Journal of Orthopsychiatry, 61,* 168–178.

Colden, C. (1978). Implications of the interviewer's technique and selection criteria. In H. Davanloo (Ed.), *Basic principles and techniques in short-term dynamic psychotherapy.* New York: SP Medical and Scientific Books.

Conn, J. H. (1989). Play interview technique: Its history, theory and practice—A fifty year retrospective account. *Child Psychiatry and Human Development, 20,* 3–13.

Connors, C. (1972). Pharmacotherapy of psychopathology in children. In H. Quay & J. Werry (Eds.), *Psychopathological disorders of children.* New York: Wiley.

Cummings, N. A. (1977). Prolonged (ideal) versus short-term (realistic) psychotherapy. *Professional Psychology, 8,* 491–501.

Davanloo, H. (Ed.). (1980). *Short-term dynamic psychotherapy.* New York: Jason Aronson.

de la Torre, J. (1978). Brief encounters: General and technical considerations. *Psychiatry, 41,* 184–193.

Drisko, J. W. (1978). Time-limited therapy with children. *Smith College Studies in Social Work, 48,* 107–131.

Dulcan, M. K. (1984). Brief psychotherapy with children and their families: The state of the art. *Journal of the American Academy of Child Psychiatry, 23,* 544–551.

Erikson, E. (1950). *Childhood and society.* New York: Norton.

Finney, J. W., Riley, A. W., & Cataldo, M. F. (1991). Psychology in primary health care: Effects of brief targeted therapy in children's medical care utilization. *Journal of Pediatric Psychology, 16,* 447–461.

Flegenheimer, W. V. (1982). *Techniques of brief psychotherapy.* New York: Jason Aronson.

Garfield, S. L., & Affleck, D. C. (1959). An appraisal of duration of stay in out-patient psychotherapy. *Journal of Nervous and Mental Disease, 129,* 492–498.

Ginsberg, H., & Opper, S. (1969). *Piaget's theory of intellectual development: An introduction.* Englewood Cliffs, NJ: Prentice-Hall.

Hartner, S. (1977). A cognitive-developmental approach to children's expression of conflicting feelings and a technique to facilitate such expression in play therapy. *Journal of Consulting and Clinical Psychology, 45,* 417–432.

Hartocollis, P. (1974). Origins of time. *Psychoanalytic Quarterly, 43,* 243–261.

Kramer, S., & Byerly, L. J. (1978). Technique of psychoanalysis of the latency child. In J. Glenn (Ed.), *Child analysis and theory* (pp. 205–236). New York: Jason Aronson.

Kubler-Ross, E. (1969). *On death and dying.* New York: Macmillan.

Lazarus, A. A. (1976). *Multimodal behavior therapy.* New York: Springer.

Lester, E. P. (1968). Brief psychotherapies in child psychiatry. *Canadian Association Journal, 13,* 301–309.

Mackay, J. (1967). The use of brief psychotherapy with children. *Canadian Association Journal, 12,* 269–279.

Malan, D. H. (1976). *The frontier of brief psychotherapy.* New York: Plenum Press.

Mandel, H. P. (1981). *Short-term psychotherapy and brief treatment techniques: An annotated bibliography 1920–1980.* New York: Plenum Press.

Mann, J. (1973). *Time-limited psychotherapy.* Cambridge, MA: Harvard University Press.

Marmor, J. (1980). Crisis intervention and short-term psychotherapy. In H. Davanloo (Ed.), *Short-term dynamic psychotherapy* (pp. 237–244). New York: Jason Aronson.

Meichenbaum, D. (1974). *Cognitive-behavior modification.* New York: Plenum Press.

Minuchin, S. (1974). *Families and family therapy.* Cambridge, MA: Harvard University Press.

Papp, P. (1980). The Greek chorus and other techniques of family therapy. *Family Process, 19,* 45–57.

Peterlin, K., & Sloves, R. (1985). Time-limited psychotherapy with children: Central theme and time as major tools. *Journal of the American Academy of Child Psychiatry, 24,* 788–792.

Piaget, J. (1927). *The child's conception of time.* New York: Basic Books.

Proskauer, S. (1969). Some technical issues in time-limited psychotherapy with children. *Journal of the American Academy of Child Psychiatry, 8*(1), 154–169.

Proskauer, S. (1971). Focused time-limited psychotherapy with children. *Journal of the American Academy of Child Psychiatry, 10,* 619–639.

Rosenthal, A. J., & Levine, S. V. (1970). Brief psychotherapy with children: A preliminary report. *American Journal of Psychiatry, 127,* 646–651.

Sifneos, P. E. (1979). *Short-term dynamic psychotherapy.* New York: Plenum Press.

Sledge, W. H., Moras, K., Hartley, D., & Levine, M. (1990). Effect of time-limited psychotherapy on patient dropout rates. *American Journal of Psychiatry, 147,* 1341–1347.

Sloves, R. (1988). *The impact of therapeutic contracts on patient attendance and treatment outcome.* Unpublished manuscript, The State University of New York, Health Science Center of Brooklyn, New York.

Sloves, R., & Peterlin, K. (1986). The process of time-limited psychotherapy with latency-aged children. *The Journal of the American Academy of Child Psychiatry, 25*, 847–851.

Sloves, R., & Peterlin, K. (1993). Where in the world is my father: A time-limited treatment of video game addiction. In C. Schaefer & T. Kottman (Eds.), *Play therapy in action: A casebook for practitioners* (pp. 301–346). New York: Jason Aronson.

Spitz, R. A. (1965). *The first year of life.* New York: International Universities Press.

Turecki, S. (1982). Elective brief psychotherapy with children. *American Journal of Psychotherapy, 37*, 479–488.

Vernberg, E. M., Koocher, G. P., & Routh, D. K. (1992). The future of psychotherapy with children: Developmental psychotherapy. *Psychotherapy, 29*, 72–80.

Welter, J. S. (1982). One to three session therapy with children. *Family Process, 21*, 281–289.

Wolberg, L. R. (1980). *Handbook of short-term psychotherapy.* New York: Thieme-Stratton.

CHAPTER 3

Ecosystemic Play Therapy

KEVIN J. O'CONNOR

INTRODUCTION

Ecosystemic Play Therapy is a hybrid model that derives from an integration of biological science concepts, multiple models of child psychotherapy, and developmental theory. Unlike most theories of play therapy, Ecosystemic Play Therapy does not focus solely on the functioning of the child client, but rather on optimizing the functioning of that child in the context of his or her ecosystem, or world. Conceptualizing and practicing Ecosystemic Play Therapy does not require one to be eclectic in the sense of maintaining familiarity with many different models and techniques of play therapy. For, although Ecosystemic Play Therapy does draw from multiple models, once these are integrated, they become a freestanding model that is different from the sum of its parts. In order to best understand Ecosystemic Play Therapy theory and practice, it is best to begin with an understanding of its component parts.

The Ecosystemic Model

First, one must understand the implications of the term *ecosystemic* and accept that this is not only a viable but also a valuable base for the conceptualization of any therapeutic intervention. *Ecosystem* is defined as "a complex of community and environment forming a functional whole in nature" (Webster's, 1967). Most often, people associate the term with biology and the study of all of the factors that impinge on any given organism. In psychology, the term is often used to describe a series of nested systems in which an individual is embedded. The concept of nested systems, however, is not sufficiently complex to reflect the nature of any individual's real ecosystem. Similarly, the chart shown in Figure 3.1 does not do the concept justice but will serve as a starting point for this discussion. The reader should note that neither this chart nor any element within it is meant to be all inclusive or even necessarily stable over time.

The very nature of an ecosystemic model is such that it is readily inclusive of additional points of view and evolves as time passes.

As it is used here, the ecosystemic model has, as its basic unit, the individual. Yet, even at this level, one sees that the individual is a system that consists of the interaction of the mind and body. Depending on one's philosophy, personal beliefs, and theoretical orientation, one might include other elements in the description of the individual as a system. These other elements might include the soul, id, ego, superego, anima, animus, and so forth. At a minimum, however, it is important for the play therapist to recognize that children's bodies affect their thoughts and feelings and vice versa. A simple example is the high frequency of anxiety symptoms in children with severe asthma. Often these feelings are as much a result of their ingestion of large amounts of the asthma medications

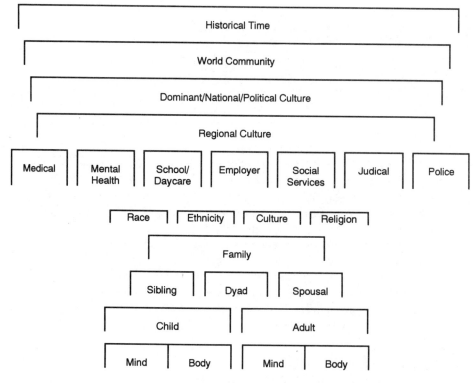

Figure 3.1. Ecosystemic model.

that act as major stimulants as they are the result of any psychological aspects of the disease.

In the chart, the interaction of one adult and one child immediately brings several other systems into play. The pair form a dyad with interactions unique to the two individuals involved. The pair, with or without other individuals, also forms a family. The very nature of families brings at least two roles, if not actual systems, into play: those of siblings and spouses. This is to say that even if one is discussing a single parent/single child family, one must understand that, within the dyad, it is acceptable for these two to interact as parent and child but it is not acceptable for them to interact as either siblings or as spouses. The regression of the adult to the level of sibling or peer is seen as preventing the adult from providing for the best interests of the child. Similarly, spousal interactions with children invoke levels of emotional and potentially sexual intimacy viewed as harmful. These roles, as reflections of actual systems, exist even when the systems themselves do not exist. At this point, the value of ecosystemic thinking becomes more obvious as it forces the play therapist to recognize environmental complexity at all times.

As one moves up the chart, the roles or systems of sibling/parent-child/spouse are subsumed under the broader heading of family. At this level, many other roles and relationships must be considered. The concept of *family* has no simple definition in this day and age. There are nuclear, blended, multigenerational, adoptive, and step families. There are families where the child is biologically related to one or even both parents but was carried in utero by a nonfamily member. There are families headed by gay and lesbian couples. There are even families that consist of several adults agreeing to share the responsibility of childrearing. Needless to say, such seemingly endless variability makes it imperative that the play therapist attempt to identify the child's view of family in order to develop suitable treatment goals and implement appropriate interventions.

As one moves beyond the "simple" concept of family, one is immediately struck by the number of other systems in which families or individual family members are, or may be, involved. The adult(s) may be involved in an employment system with all of its pressures and rewards. The child(ren) may be involved with peers and with school or daycare. Suddenly, the number of people involved and the complexity of their interactions increases dramatically. Initially, one could imagine making a global evaluation of the interaction between an adult and a child. These two are either good together or they are not. As one takes a more ecosystemic perspective, one sees that the dyadic interaction may be severely affected by the adult's bad day at work or the child's bad day at school or, worse still, the coincidence of the two.

Moving still further up the chart, one encounters the many systems established by modern American society. These include the medical, legal, educational, law enforcement, social service, and, of course, mental health systems, to mention only the most obvious. While most of these systems have some equivalent in virtually every society and cultural group, the exact makeup of each may vary dramatically. The medical system in Ann Arbor, Michigan, is represented by a mega-hospital run by the University of Michigan. The site resembles a small city or even an industrial complex. The medical system in some California Native American villages is represented by a shaman. Even when one works hard not to value one system over another, it is difficult for the average play therapist to keep the impact of such substantial differences in mind as he or she treats a variety of child clients.

For the sake of relative simplicity, more abstract systems, such as race, religion, culture, and ethnicity, were not introduced until relatively high up on the chart. This was done to reflect the nature of these systems rather than to overlook or deny the possibility that these systems will have a dramatic impact at the individual or familial level. In fact, intrafamilial differences with respect to membership in any of these systems may prove to be a significant stressor.

Race is difficult to define as it is not as much of a biological reality as one tends to think. While there is general recognition of three racial groups (Black, Caucasian, and Asian), the variability within those groups is significant. Each race resembles a continuum more than a distinct group and may contain members easily confused with members of another race. As global mobility increases the mixing of the races, it makes the orthogonal categorization of individuals even less meaningful.

The remaining three systems at this level are often highly interrelated and have an impact on the nature and interaction of many, if not most, of the other systems mentioned so far. Religion may have an impact on the medical practices in which a family will engage, such as the use of birth control or transfusions. Additionally, religion may affect the type of school in which a child is enrolled. Culture plays a significant role in everything from one's style of dress, to one's diet, to the degree one will access other systems in times of need. Lastly, ethnicity allows for substantial variations within broader cultural and racial groups, thus increasing the complexity of the ecosystemic model.

The next higher order system in the model is one reflected by the individual's national or political context. Often this system is the equivalent of a dominant culture. In the United States, this system is usually thought of as being represented by middle-class, white, Anglo-Saxon Protestants. Usually, the dominant culture represents the majority of the people in a given country or region. In many places, this is not the case. California is an example of a region where the nondominant groups are rapidly exceeding the traditional dominant group in numbers. South Africa is another example of a place where a statistical minority has established the political context for the majority.

Each geopolitical region or country is part of the world community. In this day and age of rapid electronic communication, the earth seems to be an ever-shrinking community. Places that once seemed impossibly distant are now brought directly into one's living room. This results in greater exposure to a greater number of systems than has been experienced by any previous generation. And, it is a phenomenon that shows no signs of slowing. Children in the future are likely to know as much about what happens around the globe as they will know about what happens in their own neighborhood.

The last system to be considered here is that of historical time. By recognizing this system, the Ecosystemic Play Therapist simply recognizes that any system is not static and that each may change dramatically with the passage of time. The previously mentioned exposure to world events, for example, has some significant benefits in terms of helping to break down stereotypes; however, it also tends to produce a level of overload that causes many people to minimize catastrophic world events. Interestingly, the very perception of whether a world event is catastrophic or even important now depends largely on media coverage. An earthquake in China may kill thousands but is not likely to get much media coverage in the United States and, in turn, it is not likely to trigger significant relief efforts in the United States. An earthquake in Italy may have a much lower death toll; but it is likely to have much greater news coverage and elicit much more of a response from other Western countries.

The mental health system is one on which the passage of time has had a profound impact. Just over a century ago, children were still considered to be the disposable property of their parents with no real moral rights and certainly no legal rights of their own (Mead & Westgate, 1992). Even the idea that children can think and are not mere victims of instincts and impulses is relatively new. Time has dramatically changed the view of mental illness. More and more diagnoses are found to have biological bases and that, in turn, tends to reduce the social stigma their sufferers must face (Weiner, 1993). The various conceptualizations and even names for the phenomenon of excessive motor behavior in children have undergone such a revolution that it has become hard to keep up with current trends. Twenty years ago, the phenomenon of sexual abuse, when recognized at all, was thought to be a relatively low-frequency problem (Summit, 1985). Now it is widely recognized and considered to have reached virtually epidemic proportions. Given such a dramatic shift in the conceptualization of the problem, it becomes very difficult to ascertain whether the base rate of the problem has changed. Certainly, such a dramatic transition has had an impact on the number and types of treatment now available to children who have been sexually victimized (Summit, 1985).

It is also important to recognize the impact of the passage of time on the systems further down the chart. Each and every system is not static, and, no matter how much each may attempt to maintain a status quo, change is inevitable. This includes change at the familial and individual levels as well. At the familial level, one needs to consider the normal phases of family development. Families begin when two or more people make a decision to become a couple, a parent-child dyad, or a family. This group may grow to include more people over time or change membership through such events as death, divorce, or adoption. At some point, the original family will disappear as the founding members die off and the remaining members form new family groupings. At the individual level, one must consider the impact of development over the course of the life span. Lastly, the development of the individual interacts with the development of the family to produce many changes, some predictable, some not, over time.

One issue that bears consideration in a discussion of systems is the relative value placed on each of the systems when viewed from the perspective of any one system. This valuing or evaluating seems to be a somewhat inevitable result of the very interaction of these same systems. The fact that some people value medicine to the point that they think a parent should be forced to care for his or her child in a certain way in spite of the parent's religious beliefs that place God over the desires of humankind is an example of such relative valuing. At present, there seems to be a growing consensus that it is important for everyone to preserve and work to value differences on many levels. While this is not particularly threatening when it comes to preserving the cuisines of the world, it tends to be quite threatening when it comes to differential patterns of child rearing. The whole field of child-abuse research and treatment is just beginning to come to grips with this problem (O'Connor et al., 1993).

Several styles of reconciling individual differences are evidenced as people from one cultural group move into lands dominated by another cultural group. In some areas, the new group may work to preserve differences; the children may be taught the language of their culture of origin. In other areas, the new group may attempt to acculturate, that is, to reach a compromise between their own and the surrounding cultures (Padilla, 1980). Such is the case for a Southeast Asian family in the United States that continues to practice traditional medicine but limits certain practices to adults for fear of violating American child abuse laws. Lastly, the new group may assimilate (Gordon, 1964), or become like the surrounding culture as, for example, they adopt the region's style of dress. Generally, the individuals who fare the best in these situations seem to be those who find a balance between self-serving (survival) instincts and their individual attachment or group affiliation needs.

This balancing occurs naturally in every system. It must be reached at the individual level when the child must weigh attachment to his or her caretakers against independence. It happens at the dyadic level when the parent and child must find a balance that ensures that each gets their critical needs met. It happens at the level of the family when the family struggles to exist against those forces that push it to become a mere collection of individuals and against those competing systems that would subsume one or more members. Every parent who has chosen to not to attend a critical work/business function in order to go home to be with his or her child knows the reality of this struggle. It happens at the cultural level as was described above. And, it happens between individuals and society at large. Society suffers when one of its members fails to be adequately socialized, as in the case of sociopaths, but it also suffers when its members have been so completely socialized that no variability and, therefore, no creativity exists.

In summary, it is imperative that the play therapist be able to view the child and his or her behavior as existing within a very complex set of interacting systems. The play therapist must further recognize that these systems are not static but very fluid and that none is inherently more valuable or better or worse than any other. The play therapist will use this ecosystemic view to conceptualize the difficulties the child is experiencing, to anticipate the support and interference each system will generate as the child begins to change with treatment, and to facilitate the generalization and maintenance of those changes over time. At the same time, the play therapist should be committed to preserving and valuing differences whenever and wherever possible. Having discussed the ecosystemic model and some of its philosophical and social implications, it is time to examine the impact of this model on the theory and practice of Ecosystemic Play Therapy.

Ecosystemic Play Therapy Theory

Before proceeding with a discussion of the details of Ecosystemic Play Therapy theory and practice, it is important to clarify those aspects that are structural and, therefore, less variable as opposed to those aspects that are fill and open to substantial interpretation by each practitioner. Structural elements define a theory. Structural elements are stable, internally consistent, and form the basis for the comparison of one theory to another. In Ecosystemic Play Therapy, there has been a deliberate attempt to keep the structural elements to a minimum in order to ensure that the model is as flexible and adaptable as possible. This is consistent with an ecosystemic world view in which all things are always open to change even if that change is simply the result of evolution over time.

The concept of fill in a theory, as it is used here, is probably unique. Most theorists strive to develop theories that consist solely of structural elements, that is, universal rules or truths. To accomplish this, they rely on a logical-positivist philosophy in which all things are seen as understandable and explainable relative to an absolute truth (Bevan, 1991). This philosophy proposes that, to every question, there is a single, correct answer that needs only to be discovered. It is possible to integrate this positivistic view with the ecosystemic model by saying that one can understand and explain all things if one can only come to grasp the principles underlying the interaction of each and every system. While possible, such a task seems unending as the number, type, and interaction of systems in existence are constantly changing. Alternatively, a phenomenological philosophy reconciles with the ecosystemic model much more easily.

Within phenomenology, absolute truth does not exist; rather, one's understanding of events is always an interactive process between the individual and the environment, or systems, by which he or she is surrounded (Giorgi, 1985). It is within this philosophy that most of Ecosystemic Play Therapy has been developed. This, in turn, has led to two observations. One is that even the structural elements of Ecosystemic Play Therapy must be considered relative and open to change as the understanding of the world changes. The other is that there is real value in each Ecosystemic Play Therapist filling the basic structure provided with details suited to his or her own experience as well as to the experiences of his or her clients. Because Ecosystemic Play Therapy will be used by individuals who are embedded in a multitude of systems to guide their work with individuals embedded in yet other systems, no single set of beliefs or techniques could be developed that would address all the possible permutations. Similarly, the adoption of such a unitary theory would work against the goal of preserving diversity that the model itself supports.

Aside from accepting the underlying philosophy, the practitioner must meet two criteria to be consistent with Ecosystemic Play Therapy theory. One is that Ecosystemic Play Therapists must be committed to maintaining an ecosystemic world view in all aspects of their work from case conceptualization to treatment implementation. The other is that Ecosystemic Play Therapists must develop or adopt a personal theory, a theoretical fill, for each of the structural elements to be described later in this discussion. This theory must be internally consistent and must be able to be readily communicated to others. This personal theory allows for two things: consistency and clarity, that seem central to the practice of effective psychotherapy.

While the structural elements of Ecosystemic Play Therapy allow for a certain amount of consistency in the thinking and practice of Ecosystemic Play Therapists, those elements do not assure that each therapist will work consistently over time. It is the development or adoption of a personally relevant theory within the structural elements that allows a play therapist to do consistent work with any client over a period of time. If the theory is experienced as internally consistent by the therapist, then he or she will become invested in it and strive to make it work. This personal theory actually helps foster empathy because it gives therapists a basis for comparing and contrasting their experiences with those of their clients. This personal theory also fosters the therapist's behaving consistently over time so that the client is able to understand and implement the therapist's approach to problem solving.

Additionally, the adoption of a personal theory ensures that the therapist will be effective at communicating his or her understanding of the client's experience to the client. This is consistent with the research that suggests that one of the elements clients experience as most helpful in therapy is a shift in their perception of their life situation (Frank, 1973). The direction or the nature of the shift seems less important than the coherency of the shift, that is, clients come to therapy because their view of the world and, therefore, their response to it has become stuck. The therapist is able to provide an alternative view consistent with a model different from the one that the client is using. So long as the client can integrate even a part of this alternative view, he or she will be able to break set and experience the freedom to engage in alternative behaviors. This is comparable to the psychoanalytic view that insight makes behavioral change possible by reducing the client's use of defense mechanisms and allowing the client to resolve more appropriately his or her underlying conflicts (O'Connor, 1991).

What are the implications of this discussion for those who wish to become Ecosystemic Play Therapists? Those who wish to become Ecosystemic Play Therapists are advised to begin by developing or selecting theories or theoretical elements that seem to best fit their own experience. This will allow them to become invested in their theory and to use it consistently. This is critical, for virtually every aspect of Ecosystemic Play Therapy depends on the therapist being able to first develop and then to convey to the client a clear understanding of the client's functioning and transactions with his or her world. At first, the Ecosystemic Play Therapist will be most effective at applying his or her selected theory to clients who are relatively similar to him or her. Over time, the Ecosystemic Play Therapist will become more adept at theorizing about personality and will be able to modify the model to suit a variety of clients who are very different from the therapist.

Ecosystemic Play Therapy theory and practice are most readily described if the structural elements and the fill are presented simultaneously. One strategy for proceeding with a discussion of Ecosystemic Play Therapy would be to present several alternative fills of each of the structural elements. The risk this poses for the reader is that it will be difficult to discern and fully appreciate the internal consistency of each example. An alternative strategy for presenting the discussion is to present a single example of how the structural elements might be filled. While this strategy makes it much easier for the reader to see the internal consistency of the fill, it risks that no aspect of the example will ring true to the reader's experience. This may lead the reader to dismiss the entire theory rather than to attempt filling the basic structure in a way he or she would find useful. The importance of demonstrating internal consistency seems to outweigh the risk of the reader dismissing the theory altogether, so only one example of fill is presented in the remainder of this chapter. To further ensure the internal consistency of the material presented, the author will present the structural elements with the fill he has found to best match his experience and that of this clients. The presentation of this example is not meant to establish it as any better or worse than other possible fills, but only to address the issues just raised.

The structural elements that form the basis of Ecosystemic Play Therapy are derived from psychoanalytic play therapy (A. Freud, 1928; Klein, 1932), humanistic play therapy (Axline, 1947; Landreth, 1991), behaviorally oriented play therapy (Leland, 1983), Theraplay (Jernberg, 1979), and Reality Therapy (Glasser, 1975). These theories have been integrated with several models of child development using an ecosystemic world view. The developmental models that have been used are those of Piaget (1952, 1959, 1963), Anna Freud (1965), Sigmund Freud (1905/1957), Mahler (1967, 1972), Erikson (1950), and the Developmental Therapy model (Wood, Combs, Gunn, & Weller, 1986). Rather than reviewing each of these models separately, this section of this chapter will focus on their integration into the structure of Ecosystemic Play Therapy theory. For a brief review of each of these models and for a general description of children's functioning at different developmental levels, the reader is referred to *The Play Therapy Primer* (O'Connor, 1991). While these particular theories and theorists have had a significant impact on the model to be described herein, this list is not meant to be either exclusive or exhaustive. The work or influence of many other writers may be recognized in Ecosystemic Play Therapy. Certainly, as the theory evolves, the work of many more will come into play. The structural elements that evolved from this integration and that form the frame for the theory and practice of Ecosystemic Play Therapy include the concepts of *personality* and *psychopathology*, the notion of treatment goals or a definition of *cure*, a description of the role of play in the treatment, and the technique itself.

Personality Theory

The concept of *personality* seems to be an essential structural element in Ecosystemic Play Therapy theory. Personality theory allows the Ecosystemic Play Therapist to explain the interaction of the systems thought to be at work within an individual. As noted previously, what is somewhat different about Ecosystemic Play Therapy theory relative to certain other psychological theories is that the emphasis is not on the value or accuracy of a given theory of personality but rather on the therapist's developing and consistently using a theory, that is to say, neither the psychoanalytic theory, the object-relations theory, nor any other theory of personality is seen as inherently superior or closer to the truth about human functioning. However, the absence of a true theory of personality does not automatically imply that personality does not exist. Rather, the fact that different theories seem most useful both when used by different therapists and when applied to different clients speaks to the phenomenological nature of this concept labeled *personality*.

Most widely used personality theories seem to have several elements in common. Each postulates some type of elemental force motivating individual behavior; each takes into account developmental changes in individual functioning over the life span; and each explains pathological functioning in a manner consistent with the first two elements. All three of these elements are treated in the following discussion.

Since the ecosystemic world view readily incorporates biological concepts, it is *easy* to incorporate the idea that at least a portion of human behavior is biologically driven. Humans, like all other animal species, appear driven to survive individually and, consequently, to perpetuate the species. At its most basic level, this drive motivates humans to seek rewards and to maximize personal gratification in a relatively egocentric way.

Secondarily, this drive motivates humans to avoid punishment as a potential risk to survival. If the human infant's development and socialization proceed optimally, the drive is modified to the point that the individual will seek to maximize his or her own gratification while minimally interfering with other individuals seeking to do the same. The drive is then channeled into more social behavior, and the child becomes less egocentrically focused. When framed in this way the drive is not so different from the psychoanalytic concept of libido (S. Freud, 1933), from Maslow's hierarchy of needs (Maslow, 1987) or from the concept of self-actualization (Rogers, 1951, 1959, 1961).

It also seems likely that humans experience a secondary drive to affiliate very much the way their simian ancestors still form fairly stable social groups. It appears, however, that this drive may not be as strong as the survival instinct that pushes people toward self-gratification. As with other instincts, humans seem to have the capacity to completely override the affiliation instincts, as in the case of those who become hermits or social isolates. If one posits the existence of such a social drive, then there is a force beyond early interpersonal experience that pushes children toward social interactions. The existence of such a drive would help to explain how some children grow up desirous and capable of warm relationships in spite of severe early abuse or neglect.

As noted previously, even humans' basic drives are thought to be modified over the course of their lives; therefore, a viable theory of personality must have some way of accounting for such changes. There exist developmental models to account for virtually every aspect of human functioning. Psychoanalysis, for example, proposes a line of psychosexual development that is relatively independent of other developmental lines (S. Freud, 1957). If development proceeds normally, the child advances through the oral, anal, phallic, latency, and genital stages. However, the model does not readily account for the development of, say, children with mental retardation or even learning disabilities because the interaction of psychosexual development and cognitive development is not considered. In spite of this, it seems only logical that a child cannot progress beyond the oral stage if he or she is incapable of engaging in some degree of organized thinking. Similarly, the types of issues involved in the Oedipal conflict, whether one accepts these as real or not, require a level of cognitive understanding that a child has not achieved prior to the age of 3 or 4. Further, the resolution of the conflict requires concrete types of thinking not acquired until early school age. Therefore, the author posits that development in all social, emotional, and behavioral areas is cognitively driven; that is to say, children cannot progress in other areas beyond the limits imposed by their cognitive development. Accordingly, an individual's personality is a result of an interaction between his or her life experience and his or her developmental progress.

In spite of the emphasis placed on cognitive development, it is imperative that one continues to conceptualize development as an interactive process. The child's developmental progression produces certain environmental responses that either facilitate or inhibit further progression. Once the environment inhibits progress in one or more areas, the course of the child's subsequent development is altered, sometimes irrevocably. Because more human development occurs within the first 2 years of a child's life than occurs in the entire remainder of its life, it is not surprising that those early interactions the child has with the environment are herein viewed as crucial (Caplan, 1978; Caplan, 1980). The relevance of the child's interactions with his or her early environment, including all significant others, to the conceptualization of the child's personality functioning and psychopathology and to the development of an effective Ecosystemic Play Therapy treatment plan cannot be overstated.

Pathology

The concept of pathology as a way of describing individual, interactional, and systemic dysfunction is another structural element of Ecosystemic Play Therapy theory. As any personality theory is expanded to include a model of psychopathology, there is some risk that it will become pathology rather than functionally focused. To some extent, this has been the case with psychoanalysis where there tends to exist the view that the best a person can hope for is to be a well-analyzed neurotic. The existence of internal conflicts, defense mechanisms, and, to some extent, symptoms is assumed for all individuals. Alternatively, there is very little benefit to personality theories that deny the existence of any individual pathology, attributing these conditions solely to social forces or cultural definition. One model does not validate a state of optimal functioning, thereby becoming overly pessimistic; the other ignores the reality of individual behavior and the progress of biological science in identifying bases for some conditions previously thought to be purely psychological.

A model of personality that balances internal and external attributions of causality as well as allowing for the possibility of different mechanisms triggering the same or different dysfunctions seems most useful. First, it is imperative that the Ecosystemic Play Therapist recognize that some pathology has its origins in the individual. These conditions include those that are genetic, biologic, neurologic, cognitive, or even constitutional in nature. While these types of disorder are easily recognized in their extreme, such as with autism or manic-depressive illness, they are less fully understood in their more subtle variants. There is a tendency to accept, for example, that there is a biologic basis for psychopathy; and yet the social response to this disorder is still very harsh and punitive.

Second, some forms of psychopathology seem to have interactional origins; that is to say, neither of the people involved nor the environment in which they are embedded seem particularly pathologic, but their interaction produces pathology in one or more individuals. Certain cases of child abuse seem to fall in this category. Evaluated individually, both the child victim and the abuser may not manifest any particular psychopathological syndrome. The ecosystem in which the dyad exists may not appear dysfunctional. The abuser may not even be tempted to abuse any other children, and yet the interaction within this dyad has resulted in pathologic behavior. Obviously, other variants on the interactional basis of pathology are possible. Any one individual may bring his or her individual psychopatholgy to an interaction and, thereby, produce pathologic behavior on the part of another. The ever-burgeoning interest in the children and families of alcoholics attests to the impact one pathologic individual may have on all those around him or her (Hammond-Newman, Chapter 17, this volume).

Of interest is the fact that disorders may move from one causal category to another as understanding changes. Autism is probably one of the more recent examples of such a move. When the author was a graduate student, he was trained in a model that hypothesized that autism was the result of a healthy infant's exposure to a "refrigerator" mother — the mother's cold and distant style directly caused the autism — an interactional view of the disorder (Bettleheim, 1967). A few years later, the model shifted to one in which the cause of autism was biological, the result of a defect in the infant (Schwartz & Johnson, 1985). The explanation for the phenomenon of refrigerator mothers then became interactional. Mothers develop this more distant caretaking style as the result of interaction with an infant with autism.

Lastly are considered those disorders that seem to arise when a healthy individual is embedded in a pathologic or pathogenic system: some children begin to abuse substances secondary to gang involvement at school; some medically ill children cannot cope with the separation from family imposed by a well-meaning medical system; other children fail to develop adequate interpersonal relationships subsequent to placement in a virtually endless string of foster homes. In each of these cases, the children have the capacity to develop and function normally, and yet they are thwarted by the very systems on which they depend.

Irrespective of its origins, psycholpathology is not viewed simply as a deviant response on the part of the individual but as that person's best attempt at coping with his or her internal or external circumstance. The child with autism who bites is not biting simply to be difficult but somehow experiences biting as addressing his or her needs. Perhaps the biting is experienced as adaptive because it keeps others away; perhaps it is stimulating. In any case, the phenomenology of the behavior is that it has more positive than negative associations, or it would not continue. The child who learns to provoke abuse is also exhibiting the same "best attempt" at adapting to an abusive situation. In this case, the ability to provoke abuse may facilitate splitting and the preservation of the fantasy of having a good parent, or it may foster an illusion of control. Whatever the motive, the experience of provoking the abuse is somehow worth the pain experienced. In either case, once the child develops these pathologic ways of responding, he or she is likely to use them over and over again, even if they are only intermittently successful. Children become stuck with their behavior; they cannot change because they are unable to view their world or experience differently, and, therefore, they cannot engage in alternative problem solving. Once stuck, the child becomes a candidate for play therapy.

Goal/Cure

The concept of a *therapeutic goal* or the criteria for assessing cure is another structural element in Ecosystemic Play Therapy. Given the proceeding descriptions of *personality* and *pathology,* one can readily derive an overarching goal statement that applies to children brought to play therapy. Namely, the ultimate goals of play therapy are to facilitate the child's resumption of normal development and to maximize the child's ability to get his or her needs met while interfering as little as possible with the gratification of others' needs.

To accomplish this goal, the Ecosystemic Play Therapist must first understand the origins of the child's psycholpathology. Next, the Ecosystemic Play Therapist must help the child to break set, to become "unstuck," that is, the Ecosystemic Play Therapist helps the child to reconceptualize his or her experience. The Ecosystemic Play Therapist does this in one of two ways. One way is to provide the child with alternative experiences. The very aggressive child who has experienced only abusive interactions with adults is engaged in a relationship with the play therapist that does not become abusive no matter what the child does. This experience breaks the child's expectations and provides him or her with additional information about the nature of the world. This new information allows the child to think about how he or she might want to behave when abuse is not an overriding concern. Alternatively, the play therapist may help the child break set by directly altering the child's cognitive understanding of his or her life experience by using verbal interventions. The most common verbal interventions of this type are interpretation and education. With interpretation, the play therapist reorganizes the information that the child provides. With education, the play therapist provides the child with new information that is useful in developing an alternative world view.

While much of play therapy tends to emphasize the role of alternative experience, it seems reasonable to place the relative emphasis on either alternative experience or verbal and cognitive work with children in a manner consistent with their developmental level. Children depend on experience for their primary learning only during the very early years of their lives. By early childhood, they acquire at least as much information through language as through experience. By young adulthood, children learn dramatically more from language than they do from experience. In fact, a marker of adequate formal operations development is the ability to engage in "as if" thinking (Piaget & Inhelder, 1969). Specifically, children must be able to cognitively manipulate an event they have only heard about never experienced. Given the developmental emphasis on cognition and language, it seems only appropriate for the Ecosystemic Play Therapist to strive to match the level of cognitive and verbal work the child is expected to do in session to the child's developmental level.

Beyond the developmental suitability of language-based interventions for most children, the use of language in therapy has two other distinct advantages. One is that language greatly speeds the child's acquisition of new information. It is much easier to teach children appropriate social behavior by teaching them some basic rules than it is to walk them through numerous variations on social behavior until they come to discover the rule themselves. The other advantage is that language greatly facilitates the generalization of learning. One of the problems play therapists often experience is the failure of their clients to generalize the improvement they make in session to life beyond the confines of the playroom. Some children are quite explicit in stating the fact that they see no connection between what happens in the playroom and their "real" lives. By consistently using language, the Ecosystemic Play Therapist can directly connect the child's in-session experience to his or her life experience. Similarly, the child can be encouraged to use solutions generated in session to problems experienced out of session. As previously stated, the play therapist should not rely solely on either corrective experience or cognitive-verbal work to accomplish the goals of therapy but should seek a balance between the two that matches the developmental level of the child.

Given all of the preceding, what is the role of play in Ecosystemic Play Therapy? Without question, play has a role as another of the structural elements of this theory. As noted in the *Handbook of Play Therapy* (Schaefer & O'Connor, 1983), play serves four broad functions in the daily lives of children. First, it serves biological functions in that it provides a medium through which children can learn basic skills, be kinesthetically stimulated, and relax. Second, it serves various intrapersonal functions, including the gratification of "functionlust" (Slobin, 1964) and the ability to work toward mastery of situations and conflicts. Third, play serves interpersonal functions, including serving as a medium for practicing separation/individuation and for acquiring social skills. Lastly, play serves a sociocultural function by allowing children to imitate desired adult roles.

In the context of Ecosystemic Play Therapy, play promotes healthy development through each of these four basic functions. As stressed in *Theraplay* (Jernberg, 1979), children learn best when in a state of optimal arousal. It is the role of the child's caretaker to help the child maintain a level of arousal that maximizes learning and, consequently, maximizes developmental progress. In this context, learning is a very inclusive concept denoting everything the child comes to understand about his or her ecosystem, including all aspects of interpersonal relationships. The play therapist as an extension of the child's caretaker then assumes the role of moderator of the child's arousal level. Play serves as a natural medium in which to fulfill this role. Because play is so positively loaded, it serves to reinforce the development of a relationship between the child and the play therapist. Children are usually minimally motivated to come for psychological treatment, but they are usually motivated to come and play. Lastly, play, with its enormous symbolic potential, serves as an excellent tool for linking corrective experience, interpretation, and cognitive understanding or insight. At first, the child may need to have direct experience in order to understand. Later, the child may be able to act out an issue and even its resolution through play and may not need to experience direct gratification. Still later, the child may be able to talk about the issue and be gratified without engaging in any direct action. Play serves as the link between these steps.

Summarizing, Ecosystemic Play Therapy theory includes three different structural elements. One is a *theory of personality* functioning that needs to be adapted by each play therapy practitioner to be internally consistent with his or her phenomenological experience of the world. This allows the Ecosystemic Play Therapist to operate in a way that is consistent and logical. Unfortunately, it also means that not all Ecosystemic Play Therapists will be optimally suited for work with all clients and that each must strive to recognize the constraints that their views of personality and ecosystemic interactions place upon their work. Ecosystemic Play Therapy theory also includes a *concept of psychopathology* that allows for the origins of the difficulties the child is experiencing to lie within the child, in the child's interactions with specific other persons, and/or in the child's exposure to a pathogenic environment. Lastly, consistent with this multifocal view of psychopathology and the emphasis on development within the theory of personality, Ecosystemic Play Therapy theory frames the *cure* sought through the use of play therapy as the resumption of the child's normal development while maximizing the child's ability to get his or her needs met without interfering with others doing the same. The theory creates a frame for the role of play in the treatment process. The further implications of this theory for the practice of Ecosystemic Play Therapy will be discussed in the remaining sections.

TECHNIQUE

Therapist Qualifications/Characteristics

In any discussion of the qualifications of play therapists, it is important to remember that the field of play therapy is one that crosses many disciplines. Play therapists may be nurses, social workers, counselors, psychologists, psychiatrists, and graduate students in any of these fields. In addition, there are therapists in many related fields such as Art Therapy who also use play in their work. For purposes of this discussion, it is assumed that the practitioner is already well trained and qualified with respect to his or her chosen mental health field or specialty.

Education and Clinical Experience

It is suggested that a play therapist have a minimum of a master's degree in a mental health field. Furthermore, the individual should have a minimum of 150 clock hours of instruction in play therapy. The play therapist should obtain a minimum of 2,000 hours of supervised clinical experience in work related to his or her master's degree. At least 500 hours of supervised experience specifically in play therapy is recommended. Finally, any play therapy practitioner should regularly obtain additional training or continuing education units in order to stay current with the developments in the field. These guidelines are taken from the Association for Play Therapy criteria for status as a Registered Play Therapist (1993).

Personal Characteristics

Over the years, much has been written about the characteristics that make someone a good therapist (Rogers, 1942, 1951) and some about what makes for a good play therapist (Axline, 1947; Jernberg, 1979; O'Connor, 1991). While there seems to be some agreement among these descriptions, there also seems to be a great deal of reluctance to tie good therapy too closely to the personality of the practitioner. Perhaps mental health professionals are afraid that in so doing they will return to the days when psychotherapy was considered more of an art than a science and, therefore, somehow less valid. Perhaps mental health educators fear that their role will be minimized. Or perhaps those in the field are simply reluctant to entrust something so important as any one individual's mental health to something as unknown as the personality style of another individual. Whatever the reason, it seems past time for play therapy professionals to begin some serious research on this issue. In the meantime, they must abide by some combination of ethical standards, logic, and some old-fashioned intuition.

The role of the play therapist, especially in an ecosystemic model, logically leads one to believe that some people would be better suited to it than others. After all, every play therapist is a system unto him- or herself and represents a point of convergent influence for all of the systems in which he or she is embedded. In spite of this inevitable variability, it is still worth addressing the issue of beneficial characteristics. First, the play therapist should be able to place the needs of the child client ahead of his or her own needs at all times. Second, the play therapist must be able to recognize and maintain the kinds of personal and systemic boundaries needed to be an effective therapist and occasional advocate for children. Lastly, the therapist must be willing to preserve diversity wherever and whenever possible in spite of his or her own beliefs about what may be optimal in any given area of human behavior (American Psychological Association, 1991).

With respect to being able to place the client's needs first at all times, it seems imperative that the play therapist have the capacity for genuine adult gratifications in his or her personal life. Such gratifications make it much less likely that the therapist will seek to obtain primary gratification from either a client or the therapy process. Anecdotal evidence suggests that therapists are much more prone to making errors ranging from simple case-management mistakes to major violations of various ethical codes when they are under stress in their personal lives. This is not to imply that play therapists need to be happy and satisfied at all times or else cease or suspend their practice. Such a standard is not only unrealistic but fails to recognize the very human nature of even the most well-trained play therapist. Rather, the implication is that play therapists need to be ever vigilant as to where they are getting their basic needs met and to the balance of need gratification occurring in the play session. In addition to obtaining gratification outside of the session, the play therapist who is empathic is also likely to be much more successful at recognizing the child's basic needs than one who is not.

The ability to recognize and maintain boundaries is a skill that seems teachable, especially to individuals who are relatively healthy and secure in themselves. One aspect of maintaining good boundaries is a thorough understanding of the nature of Ecosystemic

Play Therapy and the role of the Ecosystemic Play Therapist. Each of these has been discussed in the section on Ecosystemic Play Therapy theory. The play therapist who understands the limits of play therapy is less likely to try to usurp the role of the child's teacher or physician than the therapist who believes play therapy can potentially cure everything that ails the child. Similarly, the play therapist who understands the limits of the role is less likely to become embroiled in a battle with the child's parent(s) to see who can be the best caretaker.

With respect to working to preserve diversity, it seems imperative that the therapist have adequate self-knowledge and self-acceptance. Play therapists who are either unaware or not accepting of the components of their own identities are much more likely to react negatively to differences between themselves and their clients than are more secure therapists. Again, this is not meant to imply that all play therapists must be open and accepting with respect to all clients. First and foremost, the therapist is obliged to consider the welfare of society at large. If the client's differences present a danger to another individual or group of individuals, then that difference should not be preserved but rather addressed as a treatment issue. Such is the case when one is working with an egosyntonic pedophile. These individuals see nothing wrong with their behavior. They even have a lobbying group in Washington that works to legalize sexual contacts between adults and children. The reality of present knowledge in psychology, however, suggests that, while the pedophile may be comfortable with his behavior, the children with whom he or she has contact are not. The children in such contacts are harmed; they are victims. Clearly, this type of diversity cannot be supported. Alternatively, play therapists may need to recognize that there are some beliefs, practices, or behaviors that they personally cannot support, and they must limit their practice accordingly.

How does one address the issue of preservation of diversity in the face of one's own beliefs about what is optimal in any given area of human behavior? The standard reference for an answer to this question is *Counseling the Culturally Different* (Sue, 1981). Some specific suggestions are described here. First, one should inform clients of such specific views prior to the onset of therapy. If the therapist believes that all clients must have a set of religious beliefs in order to function optimally, then clients should know this at the outset in order to make an informed decision about entering therapy. Second, therapists should be prepared to refer out the client whose beliefs are so different from their own that they are unable to help the client maintain them. This assumes that the client was informed about potential problems beforehand and chose to stay or that the differences were not uncovered until after therapy had begun. Lastly, in areas where the differences are not critical to the client's functioning, the therapist may help the client to explore the pros and cons of his or her beliefs or behaviors. A therapist who maintains particularly feminist views may, for example, find it very difficult to support a young woman from a traditional Japanese family who wants to learn how to suppress her own needs in favor of those of her family and new husband. In such a case, the therapist might begin by pointing out to the client that there exist in the world different views about what is optimal female behavior. Some examples from different cultural groups might then be discussed. Lastly, the therapist would help the client to explore the pros and cons of the different female roles as they apply to the client's life situation.

There are some additional play therapist abilities and characteristics that facilitate the conduct of effective Ecosystemic Play Therapy. Play therapists should be able to inspire confidence as a result of their faith in the therapy process, in their own skills, and in their ability to protect both themselves and their clients should the clients begin to act out. It is also useful for play therapists to have a substantial tolerance for ambiguity and for severe regression. Both of these occur more often than not in work with children. Regression in particular is a problem in play therapy because children are by definition so much closer to the beginnings of their developmental progression. A 4-year-old who regresses by 1 year has lost a quarter of his or her developmental gains, whereas an adult who regresses 1 year has lost virtually nothing. And, in all of this, therapists will find the ability to be flexible extremely useful. After all, it is quite rare that either a single play session or, much less, the entire course of a child's play therapy treatment goes as planned.

Client Characteristics

Every treatment modality and every theory and technique of psychotherapy or play therapy has their limitations with respect to one population and/or their strengths with respect to another. This continues to be true with respect to Ecosystemic Play Therapy as practiced by any one play therapist. However, consistent with the ecosystemic model, these limitations are due to the limits of the specific therapist and the systems in which he or she is embedded rather than on the limits of the model itself. By its very definition, Ecosystemic Play Therapy is inclusive rather than exclusive and should, therefore, be adaptable to all client populations. No matter how flexible the theory, however, there are limits to the flexibility of both individuals and systems. The best play therapist working in the best facility will not be able to be equally responsive to the needs of every client. The key to making the best match between the services to be provided and the client's needs is the conduct of a thorough, ecosystemically oriented intake and treatment planning procedure.

Logistics

Setting

Because the population of children who may potentially be treated with Ecosystemic Play Therapy is so diverse, it seems most pragmatic to have a playroom that is easily adapted to suit a wide range of needs. In order to accomplish this, the room should be as simple and clutter free as possible. A room that is approximately 10 feet by 10 feet, or slightly larger, will work well. It is advantageous to have one side carpeted and one side covered with linoleum tile. This will provide the play therapist with environmental cues he or she can give the child to signal when an activity is a quiet one and when it is a messy or active one. The other key element is the safety of the room. Any glass, including windows, should be either unbreakable or safety glass. All electrical outlets should have childproof caps. And any furniture or equipment in the room should be as close to indestructible as possible. This safety helps to ensure that neither the play therapist nor the child will be injured during the session, and it allows the play therapist to focus on the therapy process rather than on the setting.

Materials

Consistent with several elements of Ecosystemic Play Therapy theory, the primary material made available to the child is the play therapist. As noted, play and specifically play with toys does have a function in and of itself and may be therapeutic with only a minimum of input from the play therapist. However, in most cases, the child plays outside of session;

what makes play therapy different from play or childcare is the presence of the therapist. The therapist is an integral part of the treatment because it is through the interaction with the therapist that the child comes to an alternative understanding of his or her experience and then practices the behavior changes made possible by that shift in thinking. If the toys are allowed to become the focus of the session, the work of play therapy may never get done, and the child may fail to progress.

The number and type of materials available will be limited in session to those items that directly address the child's predetermined goals. Ecosystemic Play Therapy places on the play therapist the responsibility for maintaining the child in an optimal state of arousal. To do this, the therapist needs to have maximum control over the environment, both the physical space and the materials. For this reason, neither toys nor other play materials are freely available to child clients. The therapist preselects a few toys and makes only these available. The toys are selected according to the following general guidelines: (a) Select one toy that is suited to the child's present developmental functioning, (b) select one toy that is suited to a child functioning slightly below the client's current developmental level; (c) select one toy that is suited to a child functioning slightly above the client's current level; and (d) select one or two toys for their ability to symbolize the conflicts the child is experiencing or for their ability to pull for content related to the treatment goals.

Besides the toys and play materials, there are several pieces of equipment that are often useful in the conduct of play therapy. A small table and some chairs make the completion of art projects and table games more comfortable. A sandbox, preferably one with a removable cover, appeals to a wide variety of children and can be used for many different types of activities that range from the sensory motor exploration of the sand to the construction of elaborate miniature worlds accompanied by complex stories. Lastly, a large solid dollhouse or its equivalent may be widely used. A good alternative to a dollhouse is a collection of sturdy cardboard or wood boxes that are open on one side. Each of these can be used to represent a room in the house, and the child can put the house together as suits him or her.

Frequency and Duration of Treatment

One of the drawbacks of Ecosystemic Play Therapy is that it requires a somewhat longer intake to allow the play therapist to gather sufficient information about the child's ecosystem. Typically, the intake can be accomplished in one or two sessions. It is easiest if the first session is with the parent(s) (or parent equivalents) alone because that allows the play therapist to begin to formulate the context in which the child's problems are occurring. One should be aware that this arrangement will make some children, especially those who are over the age of 9 or 10, uncomfortable because they may feel that the therapist has taken the side of the parent(s) against them. The second session focuses on obtaining information from the child and the development of treatment goals with the child and his or her parent(s). The treatment itself begins in the third session.

Because children enter Ecosystemic Play Therapy for very different reasons, both the frequency and duration of their treatment may be extremely variable. Some children who were developing normally and who have access to stable and supportive systems but who have become symptomatic in response to a focal trauma or crisis may respond in as little as one session. Children whose symptoms arise out of attachment-related problems or those children who have difficulty with object constancy may need to have two or more sessions scheduled per week. On the other hand, most children do not seem to make good use of sessions more than two weeks apart. Children whose ecosystem is chaotic or unable to change to meet the child's needs may benefit from long-term, supportive psycho-therapy. What is most important is that both the frequency and the duration of the treatment be tailored to the child's developmental level and to the specific treatment goals.

Specific Strategies

Therapist Behaviors in Session

All of the play therapist's in-session behavior should be geared to achieving the ultimate goals of play therapy, which are, as previously stated, to facilitate the child's resumption of normal development and to maximize the child's ability to get his or her needs met while interfering as little as possible with the gratification of others' needs. To accomplish these goals, the play therapist must help the child to break set, to become "unstuck." The therapist uses two specific strategies: providing the child with alternative or corrective experiences and using verbal interventions.

There are two broad categories of corrective experiences that the Ecosystemic Play Therapist can provide. One category includes symbolic play experiences; the other includes direct interaction with the therapist. The provision of corrective, symbolic play experiences underlies the majority of play therapy. The therapist provides the child with the setting and materials that, in turn, allow the child to create a reality different from the one that he or she has experienced. The abused child is provided with miniature human figures that he or she uses to recreate elements of the abusive situation. In the play, the child may exact revenge upon the abuser or call for help or be rescued at the last minute. While none of these positive outcomes happened in reality, the fact that they can occur in fantasy helps the child to master the situation, to regain a sense of control, and to practice behaviors that might prevent the problem from recurring. The play therapist may facilitate these experiences by providing the child with toys that elicit relevant symbolic material in an environment that is as supportive as possible.

Corrective experiences that are the result of direct interaction between the therapist and the child are also common to most forms of play therapy, but there is substantial difference in emphasis on these experiences as one moves from one model to another. Psychoanalytic play therapy minimizes the role of reality-based child/analyst interaction (A. Freud, 1928). Humanistic therapy stresses the importance of the play therapist being warm and support-ive but severely limits the amount of direct involvement the therapist should have in the child's play (Axline, 1947). Theraplay (Jernberg, 1979), on the other hand, views the child's direct, real interactions with the therapist to be the primary curative force in play therapy.

Theraplay emphasizes the importance of the child's early interactions with a caretaker in healthy development and interpersonal functioning. The role of the caretaker is to maintain the child's arousal at an optimal level so that development can proceed and so that the child will learn as much about his or her environment as possible. Learning, in this context, includes the acquisition of intra- and interpersonal knowledge. In this context, it is important for the child to have the experience of interacting with an adult who is fully in control (on whom the child is dependent) and who can use that control to recognize and meet the child's needs. When there have been problems in the child/caretaker dyad that have prevented the child from having such experiences, it becomes the therapist's task to provide them.

The play therapist creates these experiences by following two rules and engaging in one of four types of behavior to regulate the child's level of arousal (Jernberg, 1979). The first rule is that the therapist remains in control at all times. The second is that the therapist works to remain in contact with the child, preferably by maintaining eye contact. The four categories of behavior are structuring, challenging, intruding, and nurturing. Structuring behaviors are those that are designed to reduce the child's arousal level by limiting the amount of stimulation the child is receiving. Any active limit setting, the preselection of the materials or the arranging of the environment, are structuring in nature. Challenging behaviors are used to increase the child's arousal level. These are behaviors the therapist uses to push or encourage the child to function at the upper limits of his or her developmental capacities. Encouraging a child to jump higher, to sing the rest of a song, or even betting a child that he or she cannot complete a specific task are all challenging behaviors. Intruding behaviors are also geared to increasing a child's level of arousal. Intrusions prevent the child from withdrawing and maintain an active interaction with the therapist. Finally, nurturing behaviors are used both to reduce the child's level of arousal and to maintain it once optimal. Physical soothing, verbal reinforcement, and positive attention are all examples of nurturing. When implementing these types of interaction, Theraplay therapists are much more active and directive than therapists would be in other play therapy modalities. These interactions provide children with new information about the nature of human interaction and help them to become unstuck.

While corrective experiences are very useful in the treatment of children, they should not be the sole vehicle for producing change and achieving the therapeutic goals. The therapist also needs to use language to help the child come to a developmentally suitable cognitive understanding of his or her experience. The use of language has two primary benefits in play therapy. One is that is fosters children's processing of events they have not or cannot experience. The child who has a severely alcoholic mother may not be able to engage in corrective symbolic play because he or she has no awareness of what nonalcoholic mothers are like. Language can be used to help the child imagine what such a mother might do or say. Similarly, language may help a child develop a response plan for an anticipated traumatic event without that event having to actually occur. The other benefit of language use is that is greatly facilitates generalization. The play therapist can use language to help the child solve problems outside of the playroom and to specifically generalize in-session learning to out-of-session experience.

While there are many types of verbal statements made by play therapists in the course of a play therapy session, interpretation is the primary verbal tool used to accomplish the work of the session. Interpretations are most effective in facilitating movement towards the therapeutic goals when they are offered in a systematic and logical way in language the child understands. One way to make the interpretive process more systematic is to deliver them sequentially using a hierarchical model. One such model (O'Connor, 1991) proposes a hierarchy that moves through five levels: from Reflections at its lowest, least intrusive point to Genetic interpretations at its highest. Reflections are statements made by the play therapist that add a feeling or motive to an action or statement just completed by the child. The child hits the therapist and the therapist reflects, "You are very angry at me for . . ." or "You think if you can hit me hard enough you can get me to do what you want." Present pattern interpretations are simple statements noting the repetitive or predictable nature of the child's behavior. The therapist points out repetitions in actual behavior or in the symbolic content of the behavior within or across sessions. Simple dynamic interpretations require the therapist to make an explicit connection between previously made reflections and pattern interpretations. The therapist has reflected the child's anger on several occasions. The therapist has also identified a pattern of aggressiveness in the sessions. The therapist now makes the simple dynamic interpretation that the child seems to have no other way to communicate anger beyond being aggressive. Generalized dynamic interpretations allow the therapist to make an explicit connection between the child's in-session behavior and his or her out-of-session behavior or experience. Through the first three interpretive levels, the therapist uses only material that has been directly observed in the session or reported by the child. At the level of generalized dynamic interpretation, the therapist begins to connect the learning the child is accomplishing to events and experiences in the child's current life. It is still best if the therapist is working from information the child has provided, but this level of interpretation also allows the therapist to introduce information gleaned from the child's parents, teachers, or other reporters. Finally, Genetic interpretations are used to connect the child's present experience to those events in his or her history from which these experiences are derived. At this level, the therapist connects the child's present anxiety about facing anger with his her early abuse experiences at the hands of a chronically enraged father. For a more complete discussion of each of these steps in the interpretive process, the reader is referred to *The Play Therapy Primer* (O'Connor, 1991).

What is most important in the conduct of optimally effective Ecosystemic Play Therapy is not the specific use of either corrective experiences or verbal interventions but the matching of the balance of the two to the child's developmental functioning across the therapy process. At birth and through the first few years of their developmental progress, children learn primarily through experience. Piaget's (1952, 1967) labeling this phase *the sensory-motor phase* is a reflection of that reality. As the child acquires language, the balance of learning begins to shift until by late school age children are expected to learn more through language than experience. While every child will continue to have a preferred learning mode, the environmental valuing of language is quite extreme. An Ecosystemic Play Therapy treatment plan needs to take into account where on the experiential versus language learning curves the child in currently functioning and design sessions accordingly.

One other potential therapist role, namely that of advocate, needs to be discussed here as it is an implicit part of Ecosystemic Play Therapy. Psychoanalytic play therapists may be able to isolate themselves from interaction with their clients' worlds because the theory supports such isolation. Ecosystemic Play Therapists cannot isolate themselves because the model stresses the contextual nature of all problems experienced by children. While Ecosystemic Play Therapists cannot isolate themselves, they do not automatically need to become advocates for the child in every situation. In fact, a pervasive advocacy role would be both countertherapeutic and out of line with the ecosystemic model.

Before assuming any advocacy role, Ecosystemic Play Therapists need to assess whether another person (or other persons) operating in the problem system might better take on the advocacy role. Generally, a physician is a much better advocate for the needs of a medically ill child in the medical system than is a play therapist. This is not to say that the play therapist may not have valuable input, but only to recognize that, in many cases, a "native" to the system is in a much better position to be an advocate than is an outsider, although the reverse is sometimes true. Potentially, the most valuable task Ecosystemic Play Therapists can do for their clients is to take on the task of assessing the relevant systems, helping to identity resources within those systems, and facilitating the child's access to those resources. This moves Ecosystemic Play Therapists beyond the traditional role of individual therapists and into more of a case manager role. This shift seems well suited to the needs of child clients who are entirely dependent on individual adults and various systems to meet all of their needs.

Treatment Stages

The stages of Ecosystemic Play Therapy do not vary significantly from those seen in any other play therapy modality. The stage model that seems particularly well suited is that proposed in the *Theraplay* (Jernberg, 1979) literature that lists six phases: Introduction, Exploration, Tentative Acceptance, Negative Reaction, Growing and Trusting, and Termination.

Introduction

During this phase, the child becomes familiar with the playroom, the materials, the play therapist, and the essentials of the play therapy process. This child is literally introduced to the play therapist, and some basic expectations for the interaction are established.

Exploration

During this phase, the child begins to interact with the play materials and the play therapist and to gently test the limits of the process. Children in this phase are more active in their interactions with the environment. They have yet to make any significant judgments about the therapist or the process of play therapy, but they are taking it all in. Often during this phase, children are learning how to play.

Tentative Acceptance

Once acquainted with the concept of play therapy, most children have an initial positive reaction especially if the treatment is not specifically problem focused. In this Tentative Acceptance phase, the child is basically saying, "Well, I haven't found anything I really dislike just yet, but I'm still on guard." During this phase, children temporarily yield to the therapist's control.

Negative Reaction

The Negative Reaction phase is the only phase of this process that is substantially different from the those proposed by other models. This model anticipates that there will be a point in the treatment when the child will react against the therapy, the therapist, or both. It is likely that the Negative Reaction phase in Theraplay is more obvious because of the level of control the therapist assumes during the sessions. Due to the fact that Ecosystemic Play Therapists will also be assuming a great deal of control, it is likely that children in Ecosystemic Play Therapy will also go through a Negative Reaction phase. The existence of this reaction is not viewed as problematic but as a natural part of the child's response to change. Children who come to treatment are used to controlling their worlds through either positive or pathologic means. They take control because they fear that when others are in control their own needs will not get met. When these children encounter the controlling but benevolent Ecosystemic Play Therapist, they struggle to maintain the behaviors they are used to, and the struggle may become quite pronounced.

Growing and Trusting

Once the child learns that the therapist will only use his or her control for the child's welfare, then the struggle of the Negative Reaction phase comes to an end and the child enters the Growing and Trusting phase. During this phase, the real work of the therapy is done. The child has corrective experiences and, through these, comes to an alternative understanding of his or her experience and is able subsequently to engage in new behaviors.

Termination

After the changes of the Growing and Trusting phase are accomplished and have both generalized to new situations and stabilized over time, the child is ready for termination. During this phase, many of the problems that brought the child to therapy may be reactivated and need to be addressed once more. Unless the regression during this phase is massive, the Termination may proceed as planned.

CONCLUSION

In this chapter, the author has attempted to present the essential, structural elements of a new theory of play therapy. The theory and practice of Ecosystemic Play Therapy are characterized by an adherence to an ecosystemic world view. This world view requires that one conceptualize each individual's experience as unique and as the result of the impact and interaction of all of the systems in which the person is embedded. This belief in the uniqueness of human experience is derived from phenomenologic philosophy. As a result of this focus, Ecosystemic Play Therapy also emphasizes that each play therapist must develop a theoretical frame that he or she experiences as internally consistent. Such personal theoretical models actually make the therapist more responsive to clients because they provide a secure base from which the therapist can compare and contrast his or her own experience with that of the client. In this way, therapists are able to make use of the majority of their life experience and to maintain boundaries that ensure that the client's needs will take precedence over the therapist's needs throughout the course of the therapy. As therapists struggle to develop their personal theory, they are encouraged to "try on" a variety of established theoretical frames and to assess them for complete or partial fit. To this end, the author has attempted to describe the theory from which he works. Hopefully, it will serve to help others to identify their own beliefs and to become maximally effective in their role as Ecosystemic Play Therapists so that they can facilitate a client's resumption of normal development while increasing this child's ability to get his or her needs met while minimally interfering with others getting their needs met.

REFERENCES

American Psychological Association. (1991). *Guidelines for providers of psychological services to ethnic, linguistic and culturally diverse populations.* Washington, DC: Author.

Axline, V. (1947). *Play therapy.* Boston: Houghton Mifflin.

Bevan, W. (1991). Contemporary psychology: A tour inside the onion. *American Psychologist, 46,* (5), 475-483.

Caplan, F. (1978). *The first twelve months of life.* New York: Bantam.

Caplan, F., & Caplan, T. (1980). *The second twelve months of life.* New York: Bantam.

Erickson, E. (1950). *Childhood and society.* New York: Norton

Frank, J. (1973). *Persuasion and healing.* Baltimore: John Hopkins University Press.

Freud, A. (1928). *Introduction to the technique of child analysis* (L. P. Clark, Trans.). New York: Nervous and Mental Disease Publishing.

Freud, S. (1933). *Collected papers.* London: Hogarth Press.

Freud, A. (1965). *Normality and pathology in childhood.* New York: International Universities Press.

Freud, S. (1957). *Three essays on the theory of sexuality.* The standard edition (Vol. 16). London: Hogarth Press. (Original work published 1905).

Giorgi, A. (1985). *Phenomenology and psychological research.* Pittsburgh, PA: Duquesne University Press.

Glasser, W. (1975). *Reality therapy.* New York: Harper & Row.

Gordon, M. (1964). *Assimilation in American life: The role of race, religion and national origins.* New York: Oxford Press.

Hammond-Newman, M. (1994). Play therapy for children of alcoholics and addicts. In K. J. O'Connor & C. E. Schaefer (Eds.), *Handbook of play therapy, Volume Two.* New York: Wiley.

Jernberg, A. (1979). *Theraplay.* San Francisco: Jossey-Bass.

Klein, M. (1932). *The psycho-analysis of children.* London: Hogarth Press.

Landreth, G. (1991). *Play therapy: The art of the relationship.* Muncie, IN: Accelerated Development.

Leland, H. (1983). Play therapy for mentally retarded and developmentally disabled children. In C. Schaefer and K. O'Connor (Eds.) *Handbook of Play Therapy.* New York: Wiley.

Mahler, M. (1967). On human symbiosis and the vicissitudes of individuation. *Journal of the American Psychoanalytic Association, 25,* 740-763.

Mahler, M. (1972). On the first three subphases of the separation-individuation process. *International Journal of Psycho-Analysis, 53,* 333-338.

Maslow, A. (1987). *Motivation and personality* (3rd ed.). New York: Harper & Row.

Mead, J. & Westgate, D. (1992). *Investigating child abuse.* Canyon Lake, CA: For Kids Sake.

O'Connor, K. (1991). *The play therapy primer.* New York: Wiley.

O'Connor, K., Ammen, S., Schmidt, M., Anderson, S., Bantugan, C., Mouanoutoua, V. L., O'Sullivan, D., Brown, L., Davis-Russell, E., & Shibuya, P. (1993). *The development of the parenting self-efficacy scale to assess at-risk parenting in ethnically diverse families: A preliminary report.* Unpublished manuscript.

Padilla, A. (1980). *Acculturation: Theory, models and some new findings.* Boulder, CO: Westview Press.

Piaget, J. (1952). *The origins of intelligence in children.* New York: International Universities Press.

Piaget, J. (1959). *The language and thought of the child.* London: Routledge & Kegan Paul.

Piaget, J. (1963). *The psychology of intelligence.* Patterson, NJ: Littlefield-Adams.

Piaget, J. (1967). *Sex psychological studies.* New York: Vintage.

Piaget, J., & Inhelder, B. (1969). *The psychology of the child.* New York: Basic Books.

Rogers, C. (1942). *Counseling and psychotherapy.* Boston: Houghton Mifflin.

Rogers, C. (1951). *Client-centered therapy.* Boston: Houghton Mifflin.

Rogers, C. (1959). A theory of therapy, personality and interpersonal relationships as developed in the client-centered framework. In S. Koch (Ed.), *Psychology: A study of science* (Vol. 3). New York: McGraw-Hill.

Rogers, C. (1961). *On becoming a person.* Boston: Houghton Mifflin.

Schaefer, C., & O'Connor, K. (1983). *Handbook of play therapy.* New York: Wiley.

Schwartz, S., & Johnson, J. (1985). *Psychopathology of childhood.* New York: Pergamon Press.

Slobin, D. (1964). The fruits of the first season: A discussion of the role of play in childhood. *Journal of Humanistic Psychology,* 4, 59-79.

Sue, D. (1981). *Counseling the culturally different.* New York: Wiley.

Summit, R. (1985). Causes, consequences, treatment and prevention of sexual assault against children. In J. Meier (Ed.) *Assault Against Children* (pp. 47-97). San Diego, CA: College Hill.

Webster's seventh new collegiate dictionary. (1967). Springfield, MA: Merriam.

Weiner, B. (1993). On sin versus sickness: A theory of perceived responsibility and social motivation. *American Psychologist, 48* (9) 957-965.

Wood, M., Combs, C., Gunn, A., & Weller, D. (1986). *Developmental therapy in the classroom* (2nd. ed.). Austin, TX: Pro-Ed.

CHAPTER 4

Dynamic Play Therapy: Expressive Play Intervention with Families

STEVEN HARVEY

INTRODUCTION

Definitions

Dynamic Play Therapy is a style of family intervention that integrates movement, dramatic play, art, and video expression within therapy sessions. The goal of these activities is to help a family bring more creativity into their day-to-day interactions. A central premise of this intervention style is that creativity is a naturally occurring ability that greatly influences the quality, form, and meaning of interpersonal interaction, especially among family members. Both the process and the content of family interactions are seen as being created in an ongoing, effortless fashion by family members. This is especially seen in their process of ongoing, nonverbal communication. However, much of this creative process is unconscious. In Dynamic Play Therapy, family interactive patterns, themes, and metaphors are identified through expressive play activities. Families are then coached to create new family metaphors, as well as to change ongoing, day-to-day conflict-related behavior.

When families engage in interactive play, their patterns of communication influence their expressions and are easily recognized. The spontaneous play themes and dramatic imagery that emerge during these activities give indications of a family's unconscious feeling tone. Nonverbal/play expression and dramatic imagery reflect the emotional experience of a family, as was illustrated during an observation of a family of three: The father described how his father had physically abused him for many years, which has led to his low self-esteem. This father, in turn, had assaulted his wife and tended to be too demanding of his 2 ½-year-old son. The son had difficulty eating and had lost a considerable amount of weight. When this family began to play together in a large room with several stuffed animals and pillows, the father quickly approached the boy while his wife watched from several feet away. The boy responded by first laughing and then retreating from the approach by withdrawing behind a pillow. The father followed the boy and tried to grab him, but the son withdrew even further. The father then attempted to get the boy's attention by wrapping a large, stuffed snake around his own neck, as if he were being strangled, and shouting for his son to save him. The quality of this strong approach, coupled with the son's withdrawal, resembled the family's behavior during an observed mealtime. During the observation, the father began using forceful gestures and a loud voice encouraging his son to eat faster. The boy responded by running away from the father and around the table while the mother sat quietly. The father's feelings from his history of physical abuse and neglect by his own father were reflected in the dramatic imagery of the snake strangling him while he begged his son for help and influenced his enaction during the meal. This enactment provided a metaphor for the family feeling tone, as well as indications of the pattern of relationships.

The use of expressive activities from the creative arts therapies proves very helpful in providing concrete examples of interactive problems. Ineffective power relationships, continuing conflict, and attachment difficulties emerge within common, everyday games (such as Follow the Leader) through, for example, ineffective interactive movement, facial expressions, or dramatic role enactments. In therapy, interactive problems or themes that are identified in one expressive play modality are then extended into other modalities to help concretely lead family members in the sometimes difficult process of metaphor making. An example of this process includes having family members engage in a scribble argument on a single piece of paper following enacted disagreements generated in a more dramatic activity such as pretend argument in which participants use shouting facial expressions and gestures while not making any noise. This activity may then be videotaped and labeled as the family argument. A homework assignment might then be given for family members to watch their family movie and then to alter their role behavior, add lines, and develop additional scenes. Such activities are seen as ways to provide family members with concrete steps in experiencing the creative process of making metaphors, images, and play symbols that have relevance to their ongoing, interactive, day-to-day problems and their developing solutions.

With the development of the emergent ability to express difficulties, to identify them, and to make metaphors that have relevance, families are given the opportunity and encouragement to develop conscious choice making within their therapeutic activity. It is this development of an atmosphere in which individual choice making can occur while interacting with significant others that is thought to provide one of the active ingredients of change in Dynamic Play Therapy. This process of choice making is also seen as emergent because family members can engage in active negotiation as they develop varying choices with a family expression. An example might be for a parent-child power struggle to be expressed within a slow- or fast-motion race within a family context, with each participant given the option of choosing how fast is fast and how slow is slow. The creative negotiation introduces a family's opportunity to experience change firsthand while creating new expressions within their metaphor. Homework assignments are given to help families connect in-office interactive scenes to home behavior as a way to extend their creative experience from office sessions into day-to-day behavior and as a way to bring new home behavior to the office to engage in the outlined creative process.

In Dynamic Play Therapy, families are guided to extend initial interactive activities such as Follow the Leader, group and individual drawings, and dramatic play enactments using their unique movement, dramatic, and artistic expressive styles. These extensions are developed as first the therapist and later the therapist and family members notice certain patterns, breaks, and cues in their ongoing expressive process. These elements are then integrated to form a dynamic metaphor or series of metaphors. The therapist then helps the family draw parallels between its subjective experience of the problems in the home and the process and style that their creative expressions take. Through the constant use of shifting expressive modalities and discussions of family life and the incorporation of play breaks, deviations, and emotional states encountered during expressive activities, families are assisted in developing their creative potential to transform more simple, everyday games into activities that can have metaphorical significance.

Once this step of active metaphor making can be accomplished, family members are then coached into making in-office solutions that can be transferred to home. This process of generalization of change within the office to a more creative home life is accomplished by use of small, practical, overt steps, as well as being accomplished more indirectly as families begin to experience different states of intrinsic motivation and enjoyment of the process of more creative play and negotiations together.

Usually towards the end of the therapeutic sessions, families develop a central dynamic play metaphor that has been built through previous sessions and homework assignments. This dynamic scene usually contains movement and dramatic play enactment that come from previous expressive patterns, drama themes, and play images. This metaphor is constructed to contain elements of the family's core problem as well as the seeds for a more basic creative solution. The enactment of this scene usually offers the family members their most basic creative challenge for change. The solutions generated during this *core scene* are usually quite cathartic and offer insight into future change strategies of emotional expression and intimacy.

One recent example of such a core metaphorical scene occurred with a 4-year-old child who repeatedly played dead during family play sessions while his mother and stepfather were passive. After several sessions, the parents were guided over to the boy's passive and motionless body as he again played dead. When the young boy began to make small, peripheral movements with his fingers, both his stepfather and his mother were encouraged to make complementary "finger dances" with him. Within a brief time, the boy's movement spread throughout his body, and he was able to joyously embrace both his parents. The finger dances served as a creative link between the boy and his caretakers, who had been quite alienated prior to treatment. Following this core scene, the family was able to discuss the boy's extreme fears and his feelings of abandonment following quite traumatic abuse at the hands of another family member and to discuss the parents' feelings of joy at being able to experience emotional reconnection with their son. Before treatment, this boy had been showing the strong posttraumatic symptoms of nightmares, fears, and overtly sexual behavior, which had introduced conflict into the family home for an extended period of time. Clearly, this finger activity highlighted the boy's choice to again reconnect with his parents in a positive way and the parents' choice to approach the boy with understanding and sensitivity. The resulting positive feelings between parents and child proved to be a significant family experience and offered both motivation and insight into how to accomplish this scene more often in the home.

Theoretical Background

This author (Harvey, 1989, 1990, 1991, in press) and others have described ways of using expressive activities within the context of family therapy. Landgarten (1987) presented the use of expressive drawing activities and their use in family therapy. Bell (1984) presented a model of how a family's interaction can be seen and worked with using directed- and nondirected-movement activities; she described how such dynamics as inclusion and exclusion are readily seen in such simple movement activities as milling or the enactment of everyday family interactive scenes. Meekums (1991) described how the interactions between mothers and young children who are at risk for abuse can be observed and transformed using simple games such as rocking with blankets. Meekums described how observations of children's access to their mothers' bodies, amount of shaping or molding behavior between pairs, and rhythmic synchrony are helpful in distinguishing successful from unsuccessful interactions. Lequit and van der Wrel (1989) also reported using nondirective, creative, dramatic enactment to identify and intervene with roles and communication patterns within families. In these case studies, families were provided with play materials, costumes, and discussions as the therapist helped families construct and understand their family dramatic productions to express and change their major family themes of concern.

Dance therapists have noted the importance of interactive movement elements in reflecting the emotional context and meaning of relationships. Dulicai (1977) reported that elements such as molding (how the shape of bodies fit into each other in a sculptural manner), how individual members negotiate actual physical touch, and the quality of movement when entering intimate reach space (approximately 6 to 12 inches from each body) are related to the qualities of interaction. Loman and Brandt (1992) reported that qualities of physical tension/flow rhythms can be identified and matched even prenatally in successful mother-neonate relationships. This concept of *rhythm matchings* of postural shifts, gestural movement, and vocal expressions is further defined and outlined by Stern (1977, 1985, 1990) in the concept of *affective attunement*. Patterns of expressive rhythm shared between family members are worked out between parents and children during the first years of a child's life. Such expressive patterns underlie the ability of parents and children to effectively express emotional content and intimacy among themselves. In successful family relationships, a process of nonverbal negotiation develops that seems to be absent among dysfunctional families. Parents and children who are intimate can improvise more freely. In their negotiations, initial mismatches serve as cues in a flow of communication adjustments until emotional expressive matches are achieved. This use of matching and rhythm sharing is effortless and quite motivating in healthy situations. However, in more difficult and conflictual families, when such clashings of rhythm occur, the mismatching of expressive rhythm halts and interrupts the communication process.

Several psychologists studying the development of social-emotional attachment relationships between parents and children (Ainsworth, Blehar, Waters, & Hall, 1978; Maine, Kaplan, & Cassidy, 1985; Maine & Solomon, 1990) have identified children's strategies of using approach and holding behavior in their interactions with their parents as reflective of emotional security within parent/child dyad. Children who are able to approach parents easily and in a comfortable manner when they are distressed show secure attachments, whereas children who have difficulty and tend to show avoidance, resistance, or disorganization in use of such approach behavior show problems and more insecure attachment. Stern (1985, 1990), Crittenden (1988), Bertherton, Ridgeway, and Cassidy (1990), and Solomon and George (1991) report that such strategies of approach behavior and/or affective attunement become reflected in narrative play and storytelling as children reach preschool age and older.

CASE ILLUSTRATION

In a recent longitudinal case study, Harvey and Kelly (1993) observed interactive movement elements between a young boy and his birth mother and between the same boy and his foster adoptive parents at 18 months and 36 months of age. The same boy was seen at 44 months in conjoint family therapy with his foster adoptive parents. This child had been removed from the birth mother's home at approximately 12 months of age because of extensive physical abuse. Visits between the boy and his birth mother were continued, however, until 38 months. Observational categories included number of rhythm matchings or affective attunements that occurred over a 45-minute segment of free play during each observation session. Amount of time spent in face-to-face interaction was recorded, as well as the amount of time spent within reach space. A category was included that reflected the number of breaks in interaction introduced by either the parents or the child in this situation. A break consisted of an interactive strategy that effectively stopped an attunement or matching from occurring. Breaks functioned as a way to limit the amount of attunement or rhythm sharing allowed into the relationship. Observations of reunion behavior that followed a brief separation of the parents from the interaction were also included. Observations of these reunion behaviors included an estimate of approach, comfort-seeking behavior, resistance, and amount of avoidance present.

Interestingly, the patterns of interaction remained constant between 18 months and 36 months. During both these observations, the young boy showed a decidedly avoidant yet passive-compliant attachment interactive style with his birth mother. Avoidance was shown by little or no approach behavior and by distance taking upon reunion. Also, the young boy's only engagement with the birth mother's ideas was passive in nature. A secure style was observed between the foster adoptive parents and this boy. The secure style was shown with spontaneous, clear approach behavior, in combination with active exploratory behavior when security was achieved. Similar patterns of use of interaction breaks and overall use of close or far space were noted during both observation sessions. At 18 months and 36 months, this young boy and his foster adoptive parents showed a high use of attuned, nonverbal expressions; high use of face-to-face in interactions; and high proportion of time spent within 6 inches and within 3 feet. Also, this boy introduced relatively few active breaks within interactive play with the foster/adoptive parents. However, this young boy's interactions were virtually the opposite with his birth mother on both occasions. These observations reflected little use of attunement and face-to-face communications, and little use of close intimate space. This boy showed a high reliance on breaks to influence the interaction. These breaks were accomplished as the young boy distanced himself or turned his back when his birth mother attempted to initiate contact or a shared activity.

Shortly after the observation session conducted at 36 months, the birth mother's rights were terminated, and the boy was adopted by his foster family. He was seen at this point in a relatively nondirected Dynamic Play Therapy session to address a recurrence of nightmares and aggressive symptoms following a final goodbye visit with the birth mother. During these sessions, this young boy identified his birth mother as a large bear who had spiders on her stomach and who was threatening to break down a "safe house," that he and his foster/adoptive parents had built, in order to steal younger figures, identified as stuffed animals. During these stories, the boy continually identified his foster/adoptive parents in a positive light as animal figures who would protect and save the younger figures. Clearly, the patterns of nonverbal behavior previously mentioned—ratio of attunements, breaks, use of close space, approach behavior, and avoidance—appeared to have been incorporated into these dramatic metaphors, themes, and images. Interestingly, the young boy and his adoptive parents maintained the interactive style within the dynamic play as well. During these play sessions, the boy was able to continue to attune to his parents' expressions and to use clear approach behavior as he completed enactments of being saved from the large, scary, other-mama bear with spiders in her stomach.

Attachment and Process Creativity in Family Therapy

In describing his approach to family therapy, Byng-Hall (1991) utilized Bowlby's concept of the *secure base* in organizing his strategies for intervention. The concept of mother or parent caregiver being a secure base from which a young child is able to explore is basic to the attachment model (Bowlby, 1982). Using this idea, secure children show an appropriate balance between approach/security-seeking behavior toward their parents and distancing/exploration. As more threat is experienced, secure children tend to rely on approach behavior. When children feel secure, they are then able to engage in more exploration. In applying this concept of family therapy, Byng-Hall developed an overriding goal: to assist a family as a whole in developing an adequate amount of security by which its family members can develop more appropriate exploration behaviors. To accomplish this, the therapist offers interventions to establish security and stability and then coaches the parents to gradually develop the role of a secure base between them. Children's behaviors are then guided into developing more age-appropriate exploration within the secure container of the family.

The concepts of the *security/exploration balance* and the *family as secure base* are central in guiding the development of the expressions and metaphors in Dynamic Play Therapy. Throughout all the expressive activities, one goal is to help balance distancing behavior and exploration strategies with approach/security seeking. Many movement activities are set up in which the parent(s) build a house that children can leave and come back to during their exploratory play. If children tend not to return, a large stretch rope is introduced into the enactment to encourage the leaving and the return. Often, these games turn into long, highly motivated and engaging tugs-of-war whereby parents and children actively negotiate distance and closeness. The ropes themselves are given metaphorical significance, such as being called the "saving rope," "rescue rope," "love rope," or even "angry rope," depending on the relevance of the game being enacted. On the other hand, children who have difficulty initiating exploratory behavior are often given the opportunity to make their own drawings as an initial step towards exploration with their expression. In dramatic enactments, parents are usually cast in protective, caretaking roles, whereas children are in roles that require them to both leave and return. The dramatic strategies and deviations away from these roles are used to develop the dramatic next steps in metaphor making.

Creativity is also a major ingredient in the Dynamic Play Therapy process. Throughout family expressive interventions, it is assumed that individuals and families have a greater or lesser amount of creativity available to them. *Creativity* in this context refers to the ability to sense conflicts and tension or a gap, to generate hypotheses and solutions to fill this gap, and to communicate those solutions (Torrence, 1974). In this sense, the *tension* represents the problem or conflict in the family's interactive process, and *creativity* represents the attempts at generating creative behaviors and metaphors to solve the problem. This process often involves making connections and combinations among elements that were previously unrelated and quite often incidental and peripheral to the initial problem. *Intervention* is the attempt to redefine the initial images and felt tension.

Getzels and Czikszentmihalyi (1976) present a concept of *problem finding/problem solving* as the force that drives this creative process of reframing and reconnection. In developing this idea, these two authors used research in which they found that the most creative artists improvise with their materials in artistic expression until a problem emerges, rather than attempt to solve a problem preset from the beginning. When this problem does emerge from the expressive process, the solution usually is quite simple. This process is in contrast to some of the more linear problem-solving strategies of defining the problem first, before attempting a solution process, which is typical in some other family intervention strategies. Interestingly enough, Getzels and Czikszentmihalyi found, when examining the journals and dreams of and when talking to the artists who use the problem-finding/problem-solving process in their creativity expression, that their ultimate solutions involved elements of their personal lives of which they were unaware prior to the beginning of the creative expression and that would end up being integrated into the final solutions.

Taken together, these ideas suggest the model of creative expression in which a family can first experience subjective tension in the form of emotional and behavioral conflict. In this model, the process of therapy becomes one in which this family is then introduced to various forms of expression that concretely engage their creative process whereby they improvise with the elements of that problem until the conflict becomes more concretely defined. At this point, creative solutions involving recombinations and new connections of personal elements become integrated into a new creative solution. As Torrence (1974) pointed out, it is highly important for these solutions to be communicated clearly and to be shared with the therapist as well as with family members.

When these parallel concepts of attachment and creativity are united in treatment, the resulting metaphors are designed to help families literally recreate their system of attachment, to creatively balance security and exploration among family members. Using the various expressive processes of movement, drama, art, and video, families are guided into a situation in which they can experientially learn the improvisational tools needed to explore, find, and solve problems, creating new solutions around these attachment-related themes; to develop metaphors; and to communicate them. Families are engaged in this experiential process through the use of simple, organized, expressive games. Such games first depend on therapist observation and coaching and later include family input. These solutions and new metaphors are constructed from a family's unique interactive movement, dramatic images, stories, expressive art process, and play themes. These elements serve as the basic building blocks in the therapeutic creative process.

Movement aspects include elements of body shaping, rhythm matching/clashing, development and use of body boundaries as expressed in movement, and approach and distancing behavior between parents and children. The dramatic elements include role enactment and influence, shaping of dramatic episodes into conflict identification, and resolution. The artistic elements include properties such as expressive choice, metaphor making, and graphic imagery. Observation of self and family enactments in videotapes is also used. Stories and play themes become combined into an integrated metaphor that can be related to family life. As family members can engage their creativity in successfully developing these metaphors, they can begin to infuse this creativity into their day-to-day interactions in more playful and imaginative ways.

CASE ILLUSTRATION

An example of this attachment/creative process occurred when a therapist and family were able to use movement, dramatic, and story elements to resolve the dilemma of a young boy's fear of his parents' death and the family's resulting helplessness as experienced within this conflict. This family was seen only briefly as part of ongoing research on the development of the creative process throughout the life of a family. This boy and his parents were seen each year for a videotaped series of creative, nondirective, and directive play episodes. Shortly following the boy's fourth birthday, he and his parents were asked to play Follow-the-Leader. During this enactment, the boy quickly identified himself as the leader while his parents followed in a playful manner; there was a large amount of playfulness and good feeling generated. The boy and his parents shared similar levels, and their playful body behavior showed a good deal of matching. There was an adequate balance of distancing and approach behavior throughout the game, as well. The parents were able to suspend their parental role briefly to allow their young son to influence their movement in creative process to great enjoyment.

However, when it came time for the mother to lead, the boy refused to follow. During her leadership turn, as well as the father's, the boy introduced several breaks of conflicting body shaping and rhythm mismatching and of distancing behavior. At one point, when the mother and father began crawling in a playful game, the boy stood up and left. When the parents stood up, he then began crawling, distancing himself from them both times. As his parents' activity quickened, the boy became quite still. Finally, as the parents noticed this, they stopped moving and assumed very stable postures for a period of 3 to 5 minutes while their son continued to move away from them quickly. Some amount of conflict was introduced to the family during this enactment. At one point, the boy briefly lost sight of his mother and asked where she was as she was crawling under one of the pillows. At another point, he demanded that the father not enter the game. Though none of these episodes added up to a major break by itself, these elements led to difficulty for the family, and they began to experience some tension. At this point, the mother and father were quite still and stable in their seated position, asking the boy to follow them while he was running from side to side in the room at some distance from them. As this style was quite different from family play from previous years, the therapist stopped and asked if anything had occurred recently. Mother and father reported that the young boy had witnessed the death of his babysitter's cat. They began to wonder if this experience had bothered the boy.

The next intervention consisted of asking the family to tell a story about a family of bears; during that time, the boy identified one of the large, stuffed dogs as being a "dead mama." Using the conflicting nonverbal behavior from Follow the Leader and the play imagery of the dead mother, the play therapist had the family change the story using the theme of the dead mother and the smaller animals as puppies who might be sad. The boy then reintroduced the movement style of clashing rhythms and distancing behavior by jumping away from his parents. For the next intervention, the therapist incorporated this jumping behavior by having the puppies begin to jump in a similar rhythm and direction as the boy, saying the puppies were jumping because they had some feeling. The boy and the therapist then developed a jumping game in which the puppies began jumping all over the room looking for their mother. As the boy became excited and engaged in this image, the therapist asked him to teach his mother and father the jumping puppy game, and asked what feeling he might have. He then said he and the puppies were happy.

After a brief period of "puppy jumping" in which the parents began to match the boy's jumping rhythm, the therapist then asked the parents to swing/jump the boy between them with the therapist saying the family was using the swinging because boy was so happy that he might again be able to find his parents. This intervention included a shift from dramatic play to movement enactment, extending the boy's play theme to direct interaction with his parents. The boy then stated that he wanted to be thrown up into the air between his parents in direct face-to-face contact with both mother and father in an excited manner. During this activity, the therapist began telling a story about a boy, how the boy had parents who were with him and how these parents would not leave him during this game.

As the jumping game wound down, the therapist asked the boy what the puppies needed to do then to find their mother, and the boy replied, "Make a house." At this suggestion the mother, father, and son made a house for themselves and the stuffed animals, and the boy calmed down in his mother's lap. The therapist then introduced a story about how a young boy saw a dead cat and how the cat made the boy feel afraid that he might lose his mother and father; the therapist asked each family member to continue the story and to enact any appropriate feelings. Throughout the story, the boy was able to make contact with his mother and father in a physical way by crawling into their laps in a secure manner, and the parents were able to assure him they were not going away.

Because the session was in the late afternoon, the therapist asked the parents and the boy to integrate the activities of that evening's dinner into their stories, with both parents making assurances not only that they were not going to die, but also that they would make a special "alive" family meal for their son. The family was asked to draw a special picture that they were to put up over their kitchen table during the "alive" meal. This family was seen again approximately 1 week later, and the parents reported that their boy had been very affectionate and happy throughout the week and showed no problems; in fact, he had had dreams of flying in the therapy office and was very excited about returning. A subsequent Follow the Leader game was completed in an extremely creative manner whereby each family member's leadership turn and movement ideas seemed to stimulate some new idea and movement in the other family members. The game transformed through many variations and was accomplished without break for the entire hour.

In this example, the family showed various movement clashes, including rhythm and shape mismatching and some distancing and avoidance in the initial game. As they were playing this game, both mother and father were unaware of the impact the death of the babysitter's pet 1 week earlier had had on their son. By calling attention to the contrasting movement style, a tension point was identified. The boy then introduced his disturbing dramatic image of the dead mother. At this point, the therapist helped the family to creatively extend their expressive activity. The emotional problem within the family began to take shape. The therapeutic activity shifted to helping the family improvise with story and movement elements to find some resolution that included a swinging/happy game and a story whereby the parents and the boy could generate movement/dramatic metaphors to regenerate security. This metaphor was then extended into an art piece and was integrated into an everyday activity of having dinner. The significance of this meal was highlighted both in the picture and in the definition of it as being an "alive meal." This case proved to be a successful resolution of a problem of which a family was unaware at the beginning of the session: that of their boy's reaction to the dead cat and his fear of their death. Their creative process was coached, using the integration of movement, storytelling, and art through an improvisation to achieve a new attachment metaphor.

PROCEDURE AND TECHNIQUE

Therapist Qualification and Characteristics

Ideally, the Dynamic Play therapist should have educational background in family systems theory, in attachment, and in one of the major expressive arts therapies. Training in dance, drama, art, or play therapy usually prepares the clinician for the process aspects involved in using expressive activities. Central to the education of the creative/expressive arts therapist is the idea that psychological aspects of meaning are revealed in the process of expression used by clients. Training includes how to incorporate these process elements into the activity such that psychological meaning is made relevant and workable. While various theories may identify and organize these expressive elements in different ways, the focus on viewing the creative expressive processes as the primary therapeutic material is important. This training is essential in Dynamic Play Therapy.

Further, this author has found that some additional experience and training, particularly in dance/movement therapy is especially relevant. For more traditionally trained therapists, movement is usually the least understood and used of the modalities. Often, therapists who have not been trained or who have no experience in dance therapy or movement expression have little understanding of how elements of meaning reflect themselves in interactive movement. Because of this lack of appreciation, such therapists tend to avoid using movement or simply do not allow movement in sessions. Another mistake often made is that movement expressions are thought to represent only some literal version of a verbal concept rather than to express underlying interactive dynamics so important to accessing attachment and core affective expression.

As in many fields of family therapy, the more clinical experience the Dynamic Play therapist has in working with children and families the better. Perhaps the most helpful suggestion for a therapist who wishes to be a successful Dynamic Play therapist is to have experience watching normal, healthy families engage in expressive interactive experiences. While this can be done at almost any playground or park, it is important to also observe these family interactions in a playroom. These observations prove invaluable in grasping how the process of expressive improvisation at play comes naturally for healthy families. In normal situations, various expressive problems present themselves, and successful families orient themselves improvisationally to better identify and solve the situations in a creative, playful, and flexible manner. Humor, catharsis, security, and support, as well as individual choice making and expressive exploration, are present.

Experience watching healthy families create expressive improvisations to solve problems is invaluable in recognizing how families with more difficult situations become stuck and trapped by their own expressive process. Families, for example, whose children have experienced sexual abuse, who have major attachment difficulties, or who are in developmental crisis can find even simple activities such as drawing together, playing tag, or storytelling truly painful and frustrating. Also, when a therapist can become familiar with what the normal play/expressive process looks and feels like, he or she knows what to encourage when families enter therapy who are stuck in conflict situations. Often, the most difficult thing is not only identifying how a problematic family reaches a conflict, but also generating enough motivation, playfulness, and imaginative ability to encourage personal creativity to meet such challenges. To do this, the therapist needs to have experience to encourage small, creative movements when they are seen.

Clearly, creativity is one of the strongest personal characteristics demanded of an effective Dynamic Play therapist. A Dynamic Play therapist should be able to tolerate the frustration of leaving some expression processes open from premature closure. Often, the Dynamic Play therapist is called on to model the expressive-creative process in difficult situations so as to set up and reframe problematic situations as more playful experiments in which the answer is not known or readily seen. In such situations, the therapist must guide the next creative solution. This demands that the therapist trust his or her own creative ability to see the problem and its solution as it is happening rather than expecting to see it before it happens.

Parallel to this personal creative ability is the therapist's ability to have security and trust in his or her own human and professional abilities to engage in interactions in which strong intimacy and affect are being expressed, negotiated, and defended against, even if only in a playful manner. Without such trust and security, the therapist may be tempted to stop, redirect, or offer boundaries that are so rigid that families are unable to truly explore creative options.

A final personal characteristic is the therapist's ability to negotiate between principles of form and energy. In this context, *form* is the ability to offer boundaries, definition, and focus to expressive activities, whereas *energy* refers to more freely generated expression. For any intervention to work, clearly the therapist must balance these two elements. When too much form is added to an intervention through the use of rules, boundaries, and expectations, not enough improvisational spirit or intrinsic motivation are present to generate the expression needed for creative change. On the other hand, if too much energy is present through too may expressive ideas, interventions can become random, scattered, and unfocused. Therefore, the Dynamic Play therapist must have the ability to read interactions and add more or less form or energy to an expression in a moment-to-moment fashion as the situation demands.

Client Characteristics

Dynamic Play Therapy is a highly flexible form of therapy and can be applied in almost any clinical setting. Because of the reliance on creative, imaginative, and movement-expressive elements, this method is particularly useful in engaging young, preschool children. Families with infants whose parents show potential difficulties in the attachment process may also receive much assistance in developing social/emotional relationships with infants. Often, young mothers or fathers who have had difficult histories themselves are quite fearful of engaging in emotional relationships with their infants and show this in rigid body behavior. While it is true that some more appropriate holding behavior can be modeled, it is very useful in helping such parents spontaneously, intrinsically develop more molding and shaping behavior in direct response to their infant's weight shifting, eye contact, and emerging exploratory movement and motor behaviors.

When using Dynamic Play Therapy approaches with older children, adolescents, or adults wishing and/or needing to work on family-of-origin issues, the expressive activities need to be more dramatically focused to engage them. Rather than engaging in a Follow-the-Leader process, for example, adolescents and young adults may be asked to sculpt their families into scenes, adding "go" and "stop" aspects; that is, on "go," other family members can move freely. The balance between uncontrollability during the "go" phase of this dynamic sculpturing and the meaning of the sculptured scene often yields quite interesting movement and emotionally laden information that can be discussed and integrated into further movement and dramatic scenes.

With appropriate accommodations and adaptations, Dynamic Play Therapy can be adapted to fit adults in individual, couple, or group therapy who wish to address, for example, their family-of-origin conflicts or their current abilities as parents. By using the same improvisational expressive process that integrates movement, story, drama, art, and video, quite powerful dynamic metaphors can be generated for such clients. An example of this process involves an initial game that two parents can play to address difficulties they may be having in parenting their children. The children can be defined as different props, and the parents are given the initial task of moving the props from one side of the room to the other in a cooperative fashion. A further limit can be imposed that requires the parents to place the props (metaphors for children) between them without using their hands so they both must work with each other with mutual leaning to carry their "children" across the room. This initial game can be made more dramatic by creating an obstacle course through the placement of other props that represent the various conflicts this couple may be having, for example, disagreements on discipline and bedtime. The resulting process of a movement/dramatic enactment can provide important information on how this couple's interactive process may be contributing to the problem. These props can be identified as how their creative, improvisational abilities are blocked or stopped or lack coordination.

This concept of stimulating personal creativity to create new dynamic metaphors that address past family core-relational issues can be extended to work with individual adults.

CASE ILLUSTRATION

A recent one-to-one session with a 28-year-old woman whom this therapist had seen several times before in group treatment provided a good example of this process for adults. In this session, the woman developed a quite moving, rich, and complex metaphor in which she was able to express, understand, and creatively engage her feelings about the tragic death of her younger brother. This brother had died suddenly as a result of a freak accident several years earlier. In previous uses of dynamic family sculpting, this woman would find herself in a physical confrontation with the character she identified as her brother. The confrontation usually consisted of her standing in front of the identified actor holding his hands, pushing him away quite strongly with her eyes closed. As this was extended over several sessions, she was able to open her eyes gradually and to relax somewhat in order to stand in front of this figure. Though she was unable to verbally identify or make sense of this position, she able to say that it "felt right."

Some 5 years later, this woman sought out an individual session when she began to have strong migraine-type headaches after she was very assertive with a boss when he reminded her of her brother. In this session, the young woman was encouraged to begin to move with large dance scarves as if they were the headache. After several minutes of different styles of moving, she left the scarves in the center of the room, distanced herself, and assumed a sitting posture that seemed very sad. Using these movement and emotional cues, both patient and therapist recognized the sad feeling. The therapist suggested the woman change the dance to develop a leaving movement to distance herself from the scarves. After a short time of moving, the young woman described the death of a younger brother some 12 years earlier that had left her with the feeling that she had always had to attend to others' needs or they might die as well if she "left" them behind. She then designed a dance ritual in which she was able to use two scarves as the spirits of herself and her brother. In this dance, she was clearly able to say goodbye to the scarf identified as the brother, leaving it on the other side of the room, and to begin to move with her own spirit.

This scene was quite cathartic and moving, and, within the short time of 45 minutes, her dynamic play activity had transformed, creatively expressing the past tragedy of the death in her family. The cues of the scene, feeling sad and distancing movement, became integrated into a final goodbye dance. In this way, the initial interactive scenes of the confrontation with the brother figure were symbolically transformed whereby the leaving dance from the scarves could be metaphorically associated with leaving the headache, saying goodbye, setting a boundary, and finding herself all in one activity. Even though this was accomplished in a one-to-one session, the symbolic material clearly was related to past attachment and loss issues within the family.

Dynamic Play Therapy is particularly powerful with preschool and elementary school children who are unable to use other forms of verbal therapy and even play therapy to generate helpful metaphors. Through the use of the interactive expressive elements of movement, art, and dramatic play, even this aged client can be assisted in developing metaphors that they can understand. Very often, therapists using other forms of treatment are tempted to ask such children to leave family therapy sessions in order to accomplish the real work of therapy or verbal interaction, leaving these children unable to grasp the meaning of therapy in any tangible or experiential way. In Dynamic Play Therapy, such children are usually able to generate extremely motivating and enjoyable play quite naturally with the large pillows, stuffed animals, gymnastic balls, and scarves. By observing such play using Dynamic Play Therapy, the therapist can then observe how such children's movement is organized in relation to their parents and can identify elements with which to begin to form metaphors; for example, as some children play in the room, they may be unable to approach or get close to and include their parents in their natural play. Using this movement cue, the therapist could easily construct a beginning metaphor of having the parents form a house with the pillows while the children might be "outside." The other props, such as scarves and balls, might be identified as "feeling letters" that can be sent back and forth between these two spots in the room. In videotaping this scene, the children and parents might be able to then add lines to their videotaped moving figures to change this scene into a movie or cartoon that could then be related to typical family interactions.

Some families or even individual family members seem unable to use the expressive process to form meaningful metaphors for themselves. This is usually apparent when such families are offered initial activities such as playing Follow-the-Leader or developing a family mural together. During these expressive activities, their resistance to these interventions is seen in confusion or overt refusal to show any preference in using movement, art, or video. For such families, more typical behavioral and/or verbal interventions may be more appropriate. Even within some ongoing family sessions, a family member occasionally becomes too disoriented to use even a very guided and structured expressive activity in relation to other family members. At this point, one strategy would be to exclude this family member, temporarily, from the expressive aspects of the treatment.

CASE ILLUSTRATION

In one such case involving a mother and an 8-year-old daughter, the mother became highly distracted and confused as she and her young daughter were asked to chase away a monster. During a following session, this woman's verbal statements made it clear that she had experience of incest, which she was unwilling and unable to deal with in a play way. While this woman was seen in more individually oriented verbal treatment, her daughter was helped to continue to develop her story through dynamic play. During some 2 months of treatment, this young girl was able to extend her movement/drama story to include how she, as a tiger, was able to be hurt by, fight with, and ultimately chase away a menacing figure and later crawl to a heart hospital to seek nurturance and treatment. This metaphor was developed to address this young girl's experience with sexual molestation. With this successful development, the girl was then asked to draw pictures of the relevant scenes of her tiger story. Her mother was then included. Both mother and daughter wrote the different scenes of the story under these pictures and made a book. This book was then used to extend the therapy activity into the home where the mother and daughter would continue to both read and tell the story of the successful tiger before the girl's bedtime. This technique was quite successful in addressing the posttraumatic nightmares, night terrors, and bedwetting that the girl had demonstrated for quite some time. The mother was able to use this specific activity as generated by her daughter quite easily, whereas she had been unable to participate in the more process-oriented, movement-based development of the tiger story.

Logistics

Therapy Setting and the Playroom

Up until this point, Dynamic Play Therapy has primarily been used in family sessions involving younger children or an outpatient basis. As in some of the previous illustrations, this author has also used this format with groups of adults working on core family issues using dynamic family sculpting, drawings of families of origin, and more psychodramatic movement techniques to generate initial material. Current projects, however, include some attempt to incorporate Dynamic Play Therapy in residential treatment centers for children with attachment difficulties. The clear advantage in this situation is that children could be helped to make very concrete connections between their expressive behavior and their ongoing behavior in the treatment home. An interesting project currently underway is to provide multifamily experiences using Dynamic Play Therapy whereby different family units are seen together and separately. The goal of this group is to address couple, parenting, and family issues with the development of new family metaphors. One valuable use of multifamily groups is that people from other families can begin to play, enact, or move roles for families addressing particularly difficult situations. The main practical goal of these sessions is to have each family generate their own videotaped movie that addresses their particular family issue. Using the Dynamic Play Therapy creative process, such a movie would be the end result of expressions that have been extended using shifting modalities and incorporation of each family's unique expressive characteristics.

Play Props

The play material and props used in Dynamic Play Therapy are there to both stimulate and organize interactive movement and dramatic play in families. At the beginning of a session, the props are spread out in a relatively organized fashion throughout a large, open space. These play props are flexible enough either to design structured play tasks or to stimulate, organize, and help reflect meaning from nondirected free play situations. These props include pillows and stuffed animals of various sizes and shapes, ropes, scarves, canopies, parachutes, gym balls, large sheets of paper along with various markers, and a video camera. The pillows are made out of blocks of foam covered with brightly colored soft material. Five to ten large square or rectangular pillows are useful, as are several small pillows, approximately 12 inches square, and several large heart-shaped pillows, approximately 4 feet in diameter and approximately 6 inches deep. The pillows can be used to help define areas and to build rooms, houses, walls, or various lands. In more structured situations, families are often asked to build their own house. These pillows can be used to define "Angryland," "Madland," "Happyland," and so on. The heart pillows are especially good for defining "Mom/Dadland" or for using in rocking, swinging, and soothing activities. In free play, young children find these pillows quite stimulating to crawl over, around, or through. During such free play, the therapist can label such activities as "climbing through Madland" or "finding one's room." Or he or she can place them in the play to develop boundaries between people.

It is important to have several stuffed animals of varying sizes in at least two family groupings so that projective play can be used to develop separate groupings if necessary. To accomplish this, there is a bear family and a dog family. These animals are life-size; adult bears being approximately 5 to 6 feet tall and large in diameter. Smaller bears are approximately the size of preschoolers or toddlers. Several normal-sized animals are also included. The dog family consists of a large wolf and a mother dog with puppies designed so they can nurse from the mother. Another figure that can simulate more threatening characters include a large, 5-foot-long snake. The varying sizes of animals have proven useful not only in stimulating projective play, but also in generating movement interaction with such props. The movement interaction between the child and the prop proves important in helping to develop dynamic metaphors. Often, when children first begin, strong attachment-related feelings or aggression can be expressed to the larger animals. Even very young children are able to identify adult and young figures in their play because of the clear size differences, and dramatic metaphors are readily developed.

Other play props that are useful for encouraging interaction also prove quite helpful. These include stretch ropes in which family members can engage in tugs-of-war and stretch fights. Often these ropes can be labeled to help with expressive feelings, such as a stretch rope being called "rescue rope" that a mother or father might use to try to rescue a young child from a more threatening large bear or snake in play enactment. Large, multicolored scarves and canopies are also helpful. The scarves can be useful to costume and identify character as well as to show feelings as they are thrown into the air or placed on the ground. The large, colored canopies can be used to identify beginnings and ends of scenes as family members move them up and down. This enables children, while underneath the canopies, to do expressive movement that has a definite beginning and end.

Large, gymnastic balls are helpful in establishing other kinds of physical exchange between family members. Parachutes are used in the construction of houses, as well as in defining different kinds of feeling areas. Large pieces of paper in combination with markers, pastels, and colored pencils are helpful so that family members can move freely from movement activity to drawing. Often, these drawings can be used to define or make action maps of interactions that just take place or, conversely, to define and preplan future interactive activity. Finally, a video camera with a monitor available in the room is very helpful so that movement and drama enactments can be videotaped and viewed directly. Sometimes, videos can be made consciously by the therapist and/or family saying, "Now, we'll make a movie." Families are given different themes, such as being in their rooms or enacting having breakfast together. More metaphorical play can also be videotaped, such as having children and parents have fights under piles of pillows called "a volcano" or encouraging family members to imagine themselves waking into a dream. Either such videos can be seen directly afterward to plan the next scene and identify feelings and relationships or the videos can be taken home to be viewed as family homework. Homework can include the addition of new scenes, characters, or lines, the development of dances or artwork, as well as finding the allegorical significance of such a movie in their day-to-day lives.

Frequency of Therapy and Duration of Treatment

Dynamic Play Therapy has been used very flexibly to achieve different goals, one example being family evaluation. This author has been asked to perform assessments for adoptions in attempst to match children and parents with similar expressive styles. During these assessments, children can be seen separately or with the foster family, while the adoptive parents are seen at another time. Observations of style and preference of movement and interactive characteristics are obtained. Such evaluations are conducted over a period of three or four weekly sessions. More short-term treatment issues include helping adoptive parents understand issues of attachment. This may be accomplished by setting up a particular scenario involving a parent's house and observing children and their play with new parents. Such scenes are videotaped, often with the therapist discussing the meaning of play behaviors and interactive distancing, avoidance, and approach to help new parents get an idea of how children's play and interactive style might reflect deeply seated fears and needs. Such sessions usually occur on a weekly basis as well.

However, most Dynamic Play Therapy sessions are carried out on a relatively long-term basis over 6 months to 2 years, including various family subgroupings and individuals. The process of these longer term therapies includes some form of initial assessment followed by therapist-structured games that then lead into more family- and child-generated expressive movement and free play situations that are coached to address more core family issues. The family is ready for termination when they are able to set their own goals and develop their own dynamic metaphors about day-to-day issues and need only slight coaching and reflection from the therapist.

Attendees at Sessions

As previously stated, the general goal of Dynamic Play Therapy is for an entire family to develop an expressive metaphor that addresses family issues in a way that infuses daily life with creativity and helps with developing attachment and appropriate transitions. Within this general goal, different family members or groups may be asked to attend at different times. Ideally, the entire family is asked to participate in the first series of sessions, which include history taking and initial drawings, movement, and dramatic activities. The entire family, of course, is asked to attend a series of termination sessions. Likewise, it is important that all family members actively participate in core expressive activities. However, within this, different family members are asked to attend individually or in various groupings.

With young children, clearly the most obvious dyad is the mother and child because time is needed to develop a positive interactive relationship between this pair. As this couple is able to develop important interactions or drawings, these scenes are either videotaped or the drawings taken home with some homework assignment that involves other family members. As work with this dyad continues to improve, other members of the family are included as necessary. However, if therapy does not progress and/or the other family members request it, larger groupings may be drawn into the treatment.

Additionally, some children may be seen for some time alone to develop their own expression and metaphors with the understanding that parents will be shown or involved in the interaction as important activities develop. Although some confidentiality is important, the therapist coaches the child in ways that the child can show the parent the important expressions through making movies or drawings and in ways to later involve his or her parents in some interactive way. Likewise, parents may be asked to participate in separate sessions in which family problems are discussed in a verbal way. Parents are then asked to develop ways to involve their children in some activities to better help meet their goals. Such splitting up of therapy can either be by whole, concurrent sessions or within the session itself. Often, when using a cotherapist, parents and children are asked to go into different rooms to address various issues that arise from expressive activities, with the goal of returning to generate some solution. Another variation that has been successfully used with children of divorce is to have one parent involved with the child one week and the other parent the next week. In the most successful of these cases, both parents may be asked to attend together with the child on important holidays to develop ritual or symbolic activity that expresses love and respect for the new family situation.

One example of the strategy just mentioned occurred when a young boy would not produce any activity with his mother and stepfather present. It was later found out that this boy was afraid of the personal threats from his abusive father who had threatened to kill the mother if the boy told of the threats. In this situation, when the mother and stepfather were asked to leave, the boy was able to generate several dramatic themes, such as falling dead, needing a doctor, and needing safety. The mother and stepfather were then reintroduced into the therapy using these themes, and they were asked to take protective roles within such metaphors.

Another example occurred in a session when a mother and father became angry when their 9-year-old adopted daughter had run away. While one cotherapist worked with the young girl, who described her feelings and developed a play-story about her leaving, the other therapist discussed the feelings and solutions with the parents. Ultimately, the parents were asked to think of a play activity in which they could welcome their daughter back into the home when she and parents were reunited. Play negotiations were given the added significance of trying to work out the actual family behavior that led to the daughter leaving.

A final example involving the strategy of having both divorced parents attending a session included a 7-year-old girl who had difficulties with visitation. During a series of individual sessions, she was able to make a visitation map in which she drew herself going from one home to another and having to go through various emotional stages, such as the Angry Forest and Fearful Pond. This girl then developed enactments based on this map. Both parents were then asked to attend a single session in which the girl showed her picture and her enactments concerning her feelings. Both parents were then involved and coached to help understand the daughter's feelings and difficulties with visitation. This session was used for more verbal discussion with each parent separately in later sessions.

Specific Strategies

Dynamic Play Therapy sessions typically begin with the therapist discussing the past week's feelings and behavioral episodes with family members. After each member responds for him- or herself, each is asked how he or she thinks the mother, father, brother, or sister would answer the same question. Answers are then compared and discrepancies noted. Younger children are engaged in this by being asked to make brief scribble drawings or facial expressions about how they feel and how they would like to feel at the end of the session. Here, the therapist may reflect their movement behavior back to them. Later, parents are coached into doing the same. An example might be, "Jimmy, you look really angry right now. Can you show me how angry you are in your face?"; both therapist and boy come to an agreement of just how angry the facial expression should be. The boy then uses the same facial expression to answer the questions, "How angry does your mother think you are?" and "How would you like to feel at the end of the session?" When pictures are used, they can be put up in the therapy room and used for comparison at the end of the session.

Using the material, the therapist then helps a family decide on an initial structure or starting place for their drawing, movement, or dramatic activity. During this activity, the therapist uses the roles of participant and observer. It is sometimes very helpful for the therapist to model creative behavior and to generate simple interactions such as rolling balls back and forth or using the parachute to develop a game of feelings. Sometimes the therapist can also be cast in various roles such as an approaching monster or a ghost throughout the drama. However, it is important for the therapist to guide the activity in different directions or to stop and make reflective comments or coaching to help guide the interactive activity in a more metaphorically relevant activity. An occasion for guidance might be when a child begins to build a house with his parents and then refuses to do so and distances himself. The therapist at this point notes the deviation or play break and then asks the boy to build his own house, pointing out how the story has changed. The therapist comments by saying "Your game tells me that . . . " and then reflects on how the actual interactive behavior has changed the initial starting place. Feeling questions may also be used at this point: "I notice you have your own house. How does it feel to be in your own house?" If the child refuses to answer, the therapist may use the child's body movement as an answer, for example saying, "Oh, I see, you're wiggling your foot. This story must really be about wiggling-feet feelings."

Throughout the session, it is quite likely that the therapist will shift from movement, drama, or art in an effort to help build the actual metaphor. Sometimes, art pieces are reintegrated back into the movement and drama as props or as maps or suggestions for the next activity. When the therapist notices that parents and children are becoming somewhat irritated with each other in a movement activity, a shift of expressive modalities can be used: The family might be asked to stop their activity and draw their argument out on a scribble board, with each member given a marker. After the scribbles are completed, the family can be asked to identify characters or animals within the scribbles and to draw them. Using the drawn characters, the family can then be encouraged to continue the original movement activity. An example of a prop piece being used in a dramatic enactment could occur when a child introduces fear into play action; the child is then stopped and encouraged to draw a monster, ghost, or other large, threatening figure. This drawing might then be reintroduced into the drama to be used as a prop piece.

With the approach of the end of the session, the therapist then asks the family to clean up the playroom, putting away pillows, prop pieces, and art materials that have been used. Often, this is very difficult for younger children. One technique is to ask them the number of props they will put away; for example, "Jimmy, will you put away six things or seven things?" Then the family is coached to improvise songs about how the child puts the things away. Often, with young children, the sessions are ended with some kind of rocking or calming activity. During this time, the therapist introduces a story that reflects the connections between the activities completed, emphasizing all the feeling aspects, especially those involving attachment, and the positive interactions that occurred. For older children and adults, this summary might include a connection between the therapy activities and particular metaphors or real-life issues. Such stories or summaries are often taped and given to the family as homework assignments to develop their own versions of stories for endings and transitions.

Treatment Stages

Introduction and Orientation

During initial meetings, an interview is conducted with parents and children explaining general kinds of activities. The children are shown the playroom and are asked what ideas they might have for developing dramas or movement activity with the various props. Parents are similarly asked what kinds of things they could imagine themselves and the children doing together. In this interview, information is gathered about the presenting behavioral problems, perception of family difficulties, parenting and discipline style, and about ongoing family rituals involving mealtime and bedtime. A family developmental history of parents' meeting and marriage and the birth of their children is also gathered. A developmental history of each child and information concerning any major separations or traumatic events are also gathered. Even within this general, verbal interview, questions are asked like "What kinds of stories do you imagine your family telling or playing out that might reflect this problem?"

For the remainder of the first session and the next, the family is asked to complete initial observation and evaluation activities, as the therapist watches. These activities are listed more extensively elsewhere (Harvey, 1990, 1991). Examples of such activities include the family playing Follow the Leader, with everyone getting a chance to be the leader; going from one part of the room to the other, while tied together with stretch ropes, over obstacle courses and pillows; and completing dramatic play activity such as enacting a story about a family of bears or dogs. Observations of free movement and dramatic play are then conducted with the whole family together, children alone, and parents alone. Episodes of parents returning to the playroom are also scheduled. Comparison of such play states and reunion sequences between parents and children are really quite revealing. Art activities include having the family make murals together, draw their families separately doing things together, individually and as a whole, and drawing pictures of themselves as their favorite animals.

The goal of these activities is for the therapist to gain some understanding of how the interactive dynamics of the family complete expressive play together. These activities have also proven very helpful in introducing the family to expressive play through therapist-defined structures. Often, families are quite able to see how their problematic, day-to-day dynamics affect their play together. It is also important for children to have some concrete idea of their experience of the problem as well. This may be later stated by the therapist, "I notice you always wanted to lead your parents and they wouldn't follow you. Maybe the game you really wanted to play was Tell Them What to Do or Play Chase." The general purpose of this initial observation is to gain some understanding of how the family process influences the style and content of their expressive play. The questions are which nonverbal elements are present and interfere with family functioning, how expressive roles influence behavior, of how well and easily the family and its individual members generate metaphors, and which salient and repeatable themes appear present. Once these questions have been answered, it is important for the therapist to then reflect back these observations in concrete-activity terms to the family and children.

In the next stage of therapy, following the initial observation sessions, the therapist offers the family specific structures that relate to both the presenting problem and the problematic interaction dynamics identified. These structures are called *initial games* and are central to Dynamic Play Therapy. These games are a starting place for the family's beginning improvisation and are expected to generate a wide variety of responses from families. In many cases, these games are expected not to work but rather fall apart quite easily. It is the interactive strategy used by the family in breaking up that is identified and incorporated into later games. Such strategies are called deviations or play breaks. These initial games can be generated to fit the initial situation or can be chosen from several generic games that have been discussed in earlier works (Harvey, 1990, 1991). Generally, initial games involve all family members in an organized, interactive format. The games can be as simple as rolling a ball back and forth or as complicated as having an entire family transform the playroom into a series of rooms, or one room for each member to control who comes in and out or having the family complete a family mural of a particularly important family member who is absent from the situation for some reason.

As was stated, it is expected that these interactive structures will break down through a series of physical, dramatic, and social/emotional state changes. Physical cues or deviations include body twistings; odd facial expressions; inability to coordinate simple, physical interactions such as rolling a ball back and forth; difficulty matching rhythms or shaping behavior; introduction of slight bumps and small injuries during enactments; excessive, repeated use of distancing or close behavior; and any unexpected break, change, or deviation from the interactive rules. Dramatic elements to be noted include observations of influence and control; development of beginning, middle, and end of the episode; repeated and incongruous dramatic themes and imagery; and an overt use of metaphorical activity in coordinating interactions. Cues involving emotional state changes include changes in emotional states that have no obvious cause or lead to no clear catharsis, such as inappropriate or odd laughing, or silliness, or sudden change to anger or sadness during the enactments.

As these deviations are noticed, the Dynamic Play therapist attempts to incorporate these deviations into the structure of the game. The deviations are thought to be generated from core family problems relating to deeper attachment- and loss-related issues. As such deviations become more integrated into the story, the initial games change to represent second- and third-level scenes. As the family and therapist are able to accomplish this transformation successfully, such deviations can be seen in any free play or activity that the family engage in.

One case involved a mother and an 8-year-old girl who was very fearful and withdrawn. The initial game presented was that the girl be able to tell a monster to go away. The therapist used a dance scarf as a monster that slowly approached. The girl became quite frightened, and the therapist stopped the activity and asked the girl and her mother to use pillows to make a safe land into which the monster could not come. Using the movement cues of fright, the mother and girl were able to develop the safe land, including a protective wall. As the game proceeded, the girl changed the image of the monster to hot lava, which was on the floor. She and the mother were then encouraged to make different safe places throughout the room. The rest of the session included the girl and her mother enthusiastically jumping from safe island to safe island over the monster changed to lava, which had once been fearful.

In another example, a 10-year-old girl and her mother were asked to play a game of wall ball, by hitting a ball in turn against a wall. It was noticed that the mother's hits varied from light to medium, while the girl continued to hit the ball as hard as she could in a very competitive manner. The girl and mother were then asked to see if they could begin to match each other as the game progressed, such that when the mother hit the ball lightly, the girl was to hit it lightly, and when the girl hit the ball hard, the mother was to hit it hard. The game progressed into quite a competitive match between mother and daughter. At this point, both mother and daughter agreed that this was very much like the intensity of their conflict. When asked for a specific example, the mother cited their frequent angry confrontations concerning the girl's failure to pick up her clothes. The homework assignment then consisted of both mother and daughter having a clothes fight, in which they would throw the girl's dirty clothes as hard as they could against the wall for 5 minutes at least once a day. The next week, both mother and daughter reported that the clothes fights and the continuing game of wall ball were quite intense yet enjoyable, and the girl began to add some lightness in her play, as well.

Negative Reactions

The whole structure of Dynamic Play Therapy is designed to identify and incorporate negative reactions and difficult family dynamics within small episodes (deviations) of play behavior and interactive elements. Because of this structure, through constantly incorporating deviations and seeming play failures within a new play context, the amount and style of negative reaction is somewhat contained by the therapy itself. However, occasionally, some of the enactments produce intense feelings. The technique then is to separate family members and to discuss the activities with an eye toward gaining some understanding and reframing the more difficult behaviors. Even using these techniques, however, some children who exhibit strong posttraumatic stress difficulties need more containment than outpatient treatment provides. At that point, more traditional behavioral techniques are employed in the home as well as in possible out-of-home placement or hospitalization.

Termination

Ideally, treatment continues until the family is able both to identify their own day-to-day problems and to use their dynamic play expressions to address these problems in a motivated and useful manner and until the core dynamic play metaphor is formed. Treatment is then usually reduced to a twice-a-month or once-a-month meeting over a period of approximately 3 months. At this time, the family's art and video expressions are reviewed. Family members are asked about their most memorable and favorite metaphors. These metaphors and games can be enacted or drawn again, and discussions as to how these metaphors relate to their changes in family life usually can occur. As the families leave treatment, they are given the art materials and videos that were made throughout the session to help them review their treatment and progress. Because the Dynamic Play Therapy sessions usually have involved direct, strong affect or expressions of this feeling, it is also important to include a goodbye-saying ritual. Exchanging presents is usually quite helpful (Imber-Black, Roberts, & Whiting, 1988). Presents can be art pieces that can be exchanged between the therapist and family members.

CASE MATERIAL

A description of a family's expressive process as they developed their core dynamic metaphor within approximately 3 months of treatment will be presented as an illustration of the use of the emergent expressive process as presented throughout this chapter. The following single session is an example of a working-through process using creativity to help redesign a family's attachment. This case illustration was presented briefly in one of the author's previous works (Harvey, 1991). However, this particular session was not described in full.

CASE ILLUSTRATION

The Brandon family consisted of a mother and father in their mid-30s with two birth children, a boy aged 8, and a girl aged 6. At the time of this session, the family was in the process of adopting a 4-year-old boy who had been extensively physically abused and neglected in his first 2 years and had already experienced two failed adoptions prior to his placement. Prior to this session, the family had been in Dynamic Play Therapy for approximately 4 months, and therapy activities had included development of swinging games, of placing all children into a "love sandwich" (pillows), and of using stretch ropes in such a way that children attempting to pull away from their parents would subsequently be pulled back into large piles of pillows. The family had defined these ropes as "love ropes." Additional activities included several sessions in which they had made a house only to knock it over and reform larger lands where the children could both sleep or could alternatively identify various feeling lands.

Prior to this session, after the birth children had identified several ambivalent feelings concerning the adoption of the 4-year-old, they were asked to draw a family of their favorite cartoon characters involved in some feeling interaction. Both children chose to draw turtles in a larger turtle family who were angry. The parents had helped their adoptive son use mark making to identify several feeling states as well during the week.

The session began by using the pillows to set up different feeling lands throughout the room, lands such as Angry and Calm and another the parents spontaneously identified as Rough Play to match the physical activities the children were engaging in during the initial setup. As this play progressed, all family members were going through each of the feeling lands quite easily and adding a great deal more expression with each transition. Gradually, this activity calmed down after about 10 minutes, and the older children were asked to tell their turtle stories.

At this point, the young girl elaborated on her story, stating that she had had two parents who had been killed by a little boy. She had now become lost and needed to be adopted by a turtle family. Both parents and therapist then helped guide the little girl to identify what she wanted from her new, adoptive "turtle parents" and what she missed from her old parents. The girl identified such things as being tucked into bed, being read stories, and being loved. The new turtle family consisted of the mother and father turtle, an older boy turtle (who identified himself as a teenage turtle), and the younger adoptive turtle, who was a full-fledged turtle family member in this story, all voted that they would like to include the new girl in their turtle family, and each took turns presenting their favorite imaginary things about the family. The girl sat in her turtle mother's lap, teaching her how her old mother would hold her. The girl was asked if she wished to join the family and she answered that she did, and the turtle family readily accepted her. Clearly, the girl was using this story to metaphorically help her with the transition of family relationships following the adoption.

The family then came up with the idea of giving some kind of party to celebrate their new arrival. The therapist made a suggestion that this party include physical activity. The mother and father quickly organized swinging the children into a pile of "turtle love pillows." Just as the activity was to shift to calm pantomime eating of a pretend cake, the older boy became slightly hurt during his swinging turn. However, the mother, the father, and the other family members ignored this boy in their preparations for eating their pretend cake. The therapist's intervention was to point out that there was a hurt turtle who might need attention. The activity then changed to placing the older, hurt turtle on a pillow and attempting to give him surgery by touching him. However, the touch was initially quite rough and the therapist continued to say, "Does this help? Is the healing for real?" Again, as the family was about to eat its pretend cake, the boy said that the touch had not helped.

The parents then laid the boy in the large heart pillows to begin to rock him. At this point, the younger girl became "hurt" as well, as she slightly fell over while getting up. The younger boy, too, became hurt, and the parents decided that all three turtle children needed to be placed on the heart pillows in order to receive a large "heart hug." This solution did not quite work either because each of the children continued to exaggerate their "hurtness." The parents then said that this was exactly the feeling they had at home as their attention had been divided with the arrival of the new adoptive son. The therapist then encouraged the three children and the parents to all exaggerate and develop dances and mime gestures to show exactly how hurt they were, and a hurt contest was established in which the most hurt turtle, including the parents, would get a prize. The family continued to escalate their behavior quite enthusiastically, with their mood notably changing to a very playful and happy one. As this escalation died down, the family was given the task of cleaning up and finding an end. The therapist helped negotiate with the three children in developing a combination of their various ideas with the result being that all the family would hold hands with the older boy teaching them "turtle kicks" as a family signature. After this, the family left quite invigorated and satisfied. This scene was often mentioned in termination sessions as being something that even the youngest child remembered. The therapy ended with an "adoption room" scene in which all family members were asked questions by the "adoption judge" (therapist) about whether they wanted to adopt each other; if so, they needed to make promises to each other to remember each other's uniqueness. During that final scene, the metaphor of the turtle family was often used in describing their feelings towards each other.

In this scene, the initial metaphor was introduced clearly enough by the young daughter with her request to be adopted into the new turtle family, her old parents having been killed by a little boy. This idea clearly introduced the idea of transition, the emotional changes felt with the addition of the 4-year-old adoptive brother, and the need for both the 6- and 8-year-old to adapt to their new roles while continuing to establish feelings of security. Throughout the process of the scene, however, it became very clear that no simple cathartic play end could be achieved because each child and parent ultimately found themselves faced with the creative and unsettling challenge of needing to flexibly adapt their expression to others. While the parents kept trying to find the final acceptance in this scene through celebration cakes, love hearts, helping hospitals, and so on, each of the children continued to become hurt, each demanding different kinds of shifting attention. The final creative solution to this metaphoric and interactive problem, interestingly enough, became the paradox of the "hurt contest," with each family member trying, through escalated expression, to show the other how much more hurt they were. Given this framing, their activity could become quite fun and creative, offering them a more emotionally satisfying final expression. In this way, using a process in which the interactive deviations in play were being constantly incorporated into the play metaphor, the process as well as the content of a metaphor became realized in a more fully expressive way. As the family experienced this, they creatively adapted to end this scene, and they were able to create an actual experience of togetherness rather than just relying on the content of the image of the "new turtle family." They changed their unsettledness to fun rather than relying on their initial beginning metaphor. This strong experience proved to be very important for them, with even the 4-year-old remembering it some months later during termination. It should be pointed out that the discovery of the ending metaphor emerged from the activity itself and was not planned. The therapist merely incorporated the family deviations into a new scene that the family transformed until they reached a satisfactory play answer.

CONCLUSION

Dynamic Play Therapy is an intervention style that integrates the expressive modalities of movement, drama, art, and video within the family context. The goal of these interventions is to both infuse a family's day-to-day life with more creativity and help them create metaphors for addressing deeper issues of attachment, loss, and reattachment through periods of transition, change, and experiences of trauma. This strategy of developing and creating attachment and security is developed both in a general way within the family by establishing the family itself as a secure base and in a more specific way in parent-child relationships.

This is accomplished using the concrete elements of nonverbal and dramatic expressive behaviors as they present themselves in clashes of expressive rhythm and dramatic conflict that produce mismatching within simple game formats. Such elements are identified concretely, and families are encouraged to use their creativity to express, negotiate, and generate new solutions in active metaphor making that incorporates these disparate elements. This interactive process can be seen in the simple process of a mother and child rolling a ball back and forth, or it can be seen in more complicated dramatic imagery and repeated themes that fail to achieve solution or catharsis. As the families are encouraged to extend their expressions, they are helped to identify these patterns and the accompanying feelings of tension, to find metaphorical solutions through switching of media, and to extend these expressions to everyday home life. Finally, through creative negotiation, more basic problems are uncovered and solutions are generated in final metaphors so that the family members can concretely experience their creation of new solutions.

The driving, healing force behind this process appears to be especially present in healthy families who engage in creative problem creation and problem solving continually throughout their day-to-day life. This can be seen on the nonverbal level in their gesture-by-gesture flow as it creates small problems and solutions, as well as in more dramatic play and enactments in which solutions are created, intrinsically generating enjoyment and pleasure. One mother of two wonderful preschool aged boys recently told this author that her basic experience of parenting was discovering that it was "never too late" to recognize and respond to her children's needs throughout the day or even on a weekly basis. After observing her behavior after the birth of her boys, this mother's greatest fear was that having once studied developmental psychology, she was introducing major trauma into her children's lives. However, she discovered over 6 years of parenting that both she and her husband had developed natural rhythms to respond to their children, and her children, for their parts, continued to generate movement and dramatic situations in their interactive behavior that called for their parents to engage with them in finding solutions. Such solutions always brought enjoyment. This enjoyment, therefore, insured the continuation of very healthy, creative, and flexible interactions. In successful cases using Dynamic Play

Therapy with families who have experienced major conflicts such as prior abuse and neglect, this process of introducing expressive improvisation to engage in problem finding/problem solving is used in small, concrete ways. As this process becomes more successful, the families are guided to use this process to develop their problems and solutions in more metaphorical ways.

As families are able to develop more creative problem-finding/problem-solving methods, the elements and themes of their conflict can be brought together so that these expressions can also be part of their solutions. This combinatorial ability that creativity includes is one of its most powerful avenues of change. Throughout this chapter, several examples have been presented in which images and initial interactions were used to identify continuing conflict that later became incorporated within a core dynamic metaphor and served as a springboard for developing new behavior. The Headache Scarves, the Jumping Puppies, and the story of the Adopted Turtles provided their families not only with effective labels for identifying and describing their difficulties, but also furnished them with new ways to exchange feelings. Each of these examples produced strong experiential meaning for even the youngest family members as years later they discussed their times in therapy.

REFERENCES

Ainsworth, M. D. S., Blehar, M. C., Waters, E., & Hall, S. (1978). *Patterns of attachment: A psychological study of the strange situation.* Hillsdale, NJ: Lawrence Erlbaum.

Bell, J. (1984). Family therapy in motion: Observing, assessing and changing the family dance. In P. L. Bernstein (Ed.), *Theoretical approaches in dance/movement therapy* (Vol. 2). IA: Kendall/Hunt.

Bertherton, I., Ridgeway, D., & Cassidy, J. (1990). Assessing internal working models of the attachment relationship: An attachment story completion task for three-year-olds. In M. Greenberg, D. Ciccetti, and E. Cummins (Eds.), *Attachment in the pre-school years: Theory, research, and intervention.* Chicago, IL: University of Chicago Press.

Bowlby, J. (1982). *Attachment and loss: Vol. I. Attachment.* London: Hogarth Press.

Byng-Hall, J. (1991). The treatment of attachment theory to understanding and treatment in family therapy. In C. M. Parks, J., Stevenson-Hinde, and P. Marris (Eds.), *Attachment across the life cycle.* London: Tavistock-Rutledge.

Crittenden, P. M. (1988). Relationships at risk. In J. Belskey and T. Nezworski (Eds.), *Clinical implications of attachment.* Hillsdale, NJ: Lawrence Erlbaum.

Dulicai, D. (1977). Movement therapy with families. *The Arts in Psychotherapy, 4,* 77–80.

Getzels, J. W., & Csikszentmihalyi, M. (1976). *The creative vision: A longitudinal study of problem-finding in art.* New York: Wiley.

Harvey, S. A. (1989). *Dance of intimacy: Expressive arts therapy approaches to intimate relationships within the family context.* Paper presented at the 10th Nordic Conference of Expressive Arts Therapies, Copenhagen, Denmark.

Harvey, S. A. (1990). Dynamic play therapy: An integrated expressive arts approach to the family therapy of young children. *The Arts in Psychotherapy, 17*(3), 239–246.

Harvey, S. A. (1991). Creating a family: An integrated expressive approach to adoption. *The Arts in Psychotherapy, 18* (3), 213–222.

Harvey, S. A. (1992). Strategies in the interactive observation of families. *Proceedings of the 27th Annual Conference of the American Dance Therapy Association,* (pp. 55–58), Columbia, MD.,

Harvey, S. A. (in press). The development of attachment: Long-term family intervention with the adoption of a sexually abused child. In F. Levy, *Dance/Movement Therapy: A healing art* (Vol. 2). Reston, VA: The American Alliance for Health, Physical Education, Recreation, and Dance.

Harvey, S., & Kelly, E. C. (1993). The influence of the quality of early interaction in a three-year-old's play narratives: A longitudinal case study. *The Arts in Psychotherapy, 20*(4), pp. 387–395.

Imber-Black, E., Roberts, T., & Whiting, R. (1988). *Rituals in families and family therapy.* New York: Norton.

Landgarten, H. B. (1987). *Family art psychotherapy: A clinical guide and casebook.* New York: Brunner Mazel.

Lequit, G., & van der Wrel, D. (1989). A family plays itself better. In J. Houben, H. Smitskaun, & J. te Velde (Eds.), *The creative process.* Amsterdam, The Netherlands: Phaedon.

Loman, S., & Brandt, R. (Eds.). (1992). *The mind-body connection.* Keene, NH: Antioch University Press.

Maine, M. & Solomon, J. (1990). Infants as disorganized/disoriented during the Ainsworth strange situation. In M. T. Greenberg, D. Cicchetti, & E. M. Cummings (Eds.), *Attachment in the preschool years.* Chicago, IL: University of Chicago Press.

Maine, M., Kaplan, N., & Cassidy, J. (1985). Security in infancy, childhood, and adulthood: A move to the level of representation. In I. Bertherton & E. Waters (Eds.), Growing points of attachment theory and research. *Monograph of the Society for Research in Child Development, 50* (1–2, Serial No. 209), 66–104.

Meekums, B. (1991). Dance movement therapy with mothers and young children at risk of abuse. *The Arts in Psychotherapy, 18*, 223–230.

Solomon, J., & George, C. (1991). *Working models of attachment of children classified as controlling at age six: Disorganization at the level of representation.* Paper presented at the biennial meeting of the Society for the Research of Child Development, Seattle, WA.

Stern, D. N. (1977). *The first relationship: Mother and infant.* Cambridge, MA: Harvard University Press.

Stern, D. N. (1985). *The interpersonal world of the infant.* New York: Basic Books.

Stern, D. N. (1990). *The diary of a baby.* New York: Basic Books.

Torrence, E. P. (1974). *Torrence test of creative thinking.* Lexington, MA: Ginn.

CHAPTER 5

Cognitive-Behavioral Play Therapy

SUSAN M. KNELL

INTRODUCTION

Despite the high incidence of behavior problems in preschool-age children, few of these children exhibit difficulties indicative of serious psychopathology (Campbell, 1990). When treatment is warranted, interventions should be developmentally appropriate and, when possible, empirically sound. Often, therapies for young children have been adapted from those used with older children and adults, with little consideration for the developmental level of the child being treated. One treatment specifically designed for young children is Cognitive-Behvioral Play Therapy (CBPT), which integrates cognitive, behavioral, and play therapies (Knell, 1993a, Knell, & Moore, 1990). Although developed for preschool-age children, CBPT can be used with individuals from a wide spectrum of ages and presenting problems.

THEORY

Cognitive-Behavioral Play Therapy is based on behavioral and cognitive theories of emotional development and psychopathology and on the interventions derived from these theories. These theoretical roots are each considered here, particularly in regard to their influence on CBPT.

Behavior Therapy

Behavior Therapy includes three models: Classical Conditioning, Operant Conditioning, and Social Learning Theory. Classical Conditioning, along with its emphasis on a systematic approach to research, is used to explain certain behaviors, (e.g., fear) and is the basis for some behavior therapy techniques, such as systematic desensitization. In contrast, the emphasis in Operant Conditioning is on responses, with the basic premise that behavior is a function of its consequences; behaviors with rewarding consequences are strengthened, whereas those with negative or aversive consequences are weakened or extinguished. Techniques based on Operant Conditioning are numerous and include positive reinforcement and token economies. The most recent model, Social Learning Theory, considers more than a stimulus-response paradigm, with its emphasis on learning through observation and cognitive control (Bandura, 1977).

Behavior therapies for children were developed, in part, as an effort to help children and parents translate knowledge gained in therapy to the natural environment. Behavioral approaches to child management are often taught directly to parents or significant adults (e.g., teachers). However, behavior therapies can also be implemented directly with a child. In either case, the therapist attempts to discover factors that reinforce and maintain the child's problematic behaviors so that these behaviors can be altered. Social Learning Theory considers an additional component with its emphasis on observational learning and more cognitive aspects of behavior. The broadening of behavior therapies past the stimulus-response paradigm provided the impetus for the development of cognitive therapy.

Cognitive Therapy

Although ground was broken with the introduction of Social Learning Theory, acceptance of the role of cognitive factors in behavior therapy has been slow. With the introduction in the mid-1960s of self-control strategies to modify behavior, there has been more emphasis on internal factors, such as thought processes, and their impact on behavior and pathology. Although the cognitive movement has been challenged by some behaviorists, others argue that cognitive theories bridge the gap between behavior change and thought.

Cognitive therapy is a structured, focused approach that helps an individual make changes in thinking and perceptions and, ultimately, in behavior. Two pioneers in the area, Beck (e.g., 1963, 1964, 1972, 1976) and Ellis (e.g., 1958, 1962, 1971), developed Cognitive Therapy and Rational Emotive Therapy, respectively. Although cognitive therapies were designed for therapeutic work with adults, they have been recently adapted for use with children and adolescents. Downward extensions of cognitive treatments for adults to work with children have begun to address younger populations of children and adolescents, with some interventions adapted from adult interventions. However, these adaptations for use with children have not been subjected to the same empirical study as have adult interventions. In addition to the need for empirical support, more focus needs to be placed on developmental issues so that cognitive interventions can be used most appropriately. The need for more emphasis on normal development and developmental psychopathology has been evident in much of the child therapy literature to date (Masten & Braswell, 1991).

Cognitive-Behavioral Therapy

Recently, cognitive-behavioral therapies for children have begun to address children from a developmental perspective; for example, interventions specifically geared to depressed children (Emery, Bedrosian, & Garber, 1983) and to impulsive children (Kendall & Braswell, 1985) have shown promising effects. Cognitive-behavioral therapy (CBT) offers a potentially powerful method for children to learn to change their own behavior and to become active participants in treatment.

The significance of a child's involvement in treatment may be understood from a number of perspectives. Developmentally, children need to demonstrate a sense of mastery and control over their environment. Such mastery can be seen as children exhibit increasing levels of management of their own behavior. Ollendick and Cerney (1981) described the increasing interest in teaching children to regulate their own behavior. Teaching the child self-control might be more efficient (Lovitt & Curtis, 1969) and more durable (Drabman, Spitalnik, & O'Leary, 1973) than parent-administered programs; and it also might permit significant adults to engage in more positive activities with the child. Finally, in parent-implemented programs in which the child is not involved directly in treatment, the adult might become a discriminative cue for the child to emit the appropriate behavior or to suppress and inappropriate one. Thus, children might only behave in certain ways when these cues are present (Kazdin, 1975). Integrating cognitive and behavioral interventions can provide the missing link to promoting the child's active involvement in a focused, goal-directed treatment.

Cognitive Behavioral Play Therapy

Cognitive-Behavioral Play Therapy incorporates cognitive and behavioral interventions within a play therapy paradigm. Play activities, as well as verbal and nonverbal communication, are used. Although behavioral and cognitive interventions are a critical component, CBPT is more than the use of specific techniques. CBPT provides a theoretical framework that is based on cognitive-behavioral principles and integrates those principles in a developmentally sensitive way.

CBPT places a strong emphasis on the child's involvement in treatment and on a framework for the child's involvement by addressing issues of control, mastery, and responsibility for one's own behavior change. By incorporating the cognitive components, the child can become an active participant in change; for example, by helping children identify and modify potentially maladaptive beliefs, a sense of personal understanding and empowerment can be experienced. Integrating cognitive and behavioral interventions offers effects of the combined properties of all approaches, which might not be available otherwise.

PRINCIPLES OF COGNITIVE THERAPY

The literature on cognitive-behavioral interventions with very young children is still quite limited, largely due to the belief by many that such work cannot be done. The first published case integrating cognitive-behavioral intervention in play therapy of a preschooler was reported by Knell and Moore (1990), with other cases reported since that time (Knell, 1993a). Despite arguments that cognitive-behavioral interventions are inappropriate for use with preschoolers (Campbell, 1990), Knell (1993a) contends that, with minor modifications, the principles of cognitive therapy apply to young children.

Ten principles of cognitive therapy were delineated by Beck and Emery (1985), who contended that the strategies and techniques used in cognitive therapy with adults are based on principles of psychotherapy. In order to create a more developmentally appropriate CBT for young children, the 10 principles must be reconsidered and then labeled as those that do apply to young children, those that apply with modification, and those that do not apply. (The principle numbers are those assigned by Beck and Emery.)

Principles That Do Apply to Children

Principle 1: Cognitive therapy is based on the cognitive model of emotional disorders.

The cognitive model of emotional disorders is based on the interplay among cognition, emotions, behavior, and physiology. Behavior is mediated through verbal processes, with disturbed behavior considered to be an expression of irrational thinking. Therapy is focused on cognitive change, which is comprised in part of altering irrational, maladaptive, or illogical thinking. A wide range of techniques has been developed to modify cognitions.

The cognitive model of emotional disorder is applicable to children. The interplay among cognition, emotions, behavior, and physiology is as important for children and adolescents as it is for adults. However, the role of cognition must be carefully considered for children. The thinking of a preoperational-stage or a concrete-operational-stage child can be illogical or irrational, with little verbal mediation of behavior. Young children can be impulsive, with behavior and activity often preceding thought and reflection. Thus, even when young children are functioning optimally, they are not capable of thinking in the same way as an adult can. Cognitive therapy does not try to make children think like adults; rather, it focuses on helping the child behave most adaptively. Therefore, interventions for young children focus on the absence of adaptive thoughts (cognitive deficits), as well as on cognitive errors (distortions).

Principle 2: Cognitive therapy is brief and time-limited.

Cognitive therapy is brief and time-limited, typically lasting less than 6 months. Brief therapy encourages the individual to be self-sufficient and discourages dependency on the therapist. Because therapy is brief, it is task-oriented and focused on problem solving. Beck and Emery (1985) proposed several strategies for keeping treatment brief: making interventions simple, specific, and concrete; keeping sessions task-related; and focusing on manageable problems.

Brief and time-limited treatments are also appropriate for children. In fact, a task-oriented, problem-solving focus is indicated for many of the more common childhood difficulties. Because problems in the preschool and early school years are rarely indicative of serious psychopathology, they can often be dealt with in a brief, time-limited manner.

Principle 3: A sound therapeutic relationship is a necessary condition for effective cognitive therapy.

Cognitive therapy relies on the establishment of a warm, therapeutic relationship based on trust and acceptance. As in all forms of psychotherapy, the development of a positive, accepting therapeutic relationship is the best predictor of good treatment outcome (Brady et al., 1980; Rogers, Gendlin, Kiesler, & Truax, 1967).

CBPT is no exception. If a child is to view therapy as a safe, accepting place where communicating about oneself is permissible, the therapist will need to be seen as trustworthy and nonjudgmental.

Principle 6: Cognitive therapy is structured and directive.

Cognitive therapy provides a structured, directive format, both for individual therapy sessions and for therapy as a whole. The degree of structure is determined by individual needs but often involves setting an agenda for each session and focusing on specific targets.

For children, specific targets and agendas may be set for each session. In addition, children might need open-ended therapy time in which they can bring spontaneous material that can be incorporated into the more directive, structured interventions.

An example of using structured, directive interventions as well as more open-ended time is highlighted in the treatment of a 5-year-old encopretic child.

Terry demonstrated, through a toy bear, a fear of falling into and being flushed down the toilet. Through play with the bear, the therapist helped him identify the fear and become more comfortable with the toilet. During treatment, the bear and Terry both received stars for using the toilet (Terry's toilet use was reported by his parents, and reinforced via stars at home). The therapist introduced issues related to feelings about soiled pants through the bear. Despite an "agenda" for sessions developed by the therapist, there was time for the child's spontaneous play, which was incorporated into the treatment (Knell & Moore, 1990).

Principle 7: Cognitive therapy is problem-oriented.

Initially, cognitive therapy is focused on problem solving of current concerns. With adults, focusing on current concerns can provide more accurate data and can allow the therapist and patient to work together to resolve specific problems. Later, a focus on past and future information might be helpful. The individual and therapist work together to identify and correct maladaptive thoughts and behaviors that might be maintaining a problem or impeding its solution. With adults, Beck and Emery (1985) recommend conceptualizing the problem, choosing a strategy and technique to implement the strategy, and assessing the effectiveness of the technique.

With children, it is equally important to be problem-oriented. When children present with discrete problems (e.g., toileting or eating problems), treatment approaches should be focused on the presenting problem, without losing sight of a more global picture of the child's situation.

In problem-oriented treatment, particular life experiences or stressors (e.g., sexual abuse, parental divorce) need to be considered. Treatment should not be based solely on symptom alleviation; for example, sexually abused children often present with well-defined symptoms (e.g., enuresis, sleep disturbances) but often also struggle with issues related to trust and control. Children who are maltreated by a known and trusted adult may experience significant feelings of betrayal and confusion. The therapist must be sensitive to these issues without losing sight of the presenting problems.

Principle 8: Cognitive therapy is based on an educational model.

One premise of cognitive therapy is that symptoms develop because the individual has learned inappropriate ways of dealing with life situations. In helping the individual change coping styles, the therapist functions as a teacher who imparts positive coping skills and alternative behaviors. One aspect of this is teaching the individual to learn from experiences so that coping skills can be applied on an ongoing basis. Beck and Emery (1985) refer to this as "learning to learn" (p. 186).

The educational model is particularly relevant with children in teaching them how to replace maladaptive behaviors with more adaptive ones, as well as in teaching them specific alternative ways of coping. Because the young child cannot generate alternatives and test them out, the therapist will need to provide, often through example, an alternate coping method. Teaching new skills in play therapy is often accomplished via modeling with puppets and other toys. The following illustrates the use of the educational model in helping a fearful 5-year-old child learn to remain calm in anxiety-provoking situations:

Jim exhibited a fear of closed spaces, after he was accidently locked in a bathroom by his younger sister. He screamed intensely and froze in place when a door was closed behind him. He also refused to enter elevators and was beginning to become anxious when in a car. A systematic desensitization paradigm was utilized. A hierarchy was developed which consisted of graduated steps from a larger to a smaller room with the therapist in attendance, to a small room without the therapist.

Graduated stages of a door being closed were added until the child was comfortable being in the room, with the door closed, without the therapist. Jim was taught relaxing play as a behavior mutually exclusive with anxiety. Additionally, hew was taught to make simple, positive self-statements, such as "I can stay in this room," "I feel good playing in here," "I feel good, I am brave." The therapist provided positive feedback (e.g., "That was great," "Good job") after successful completion of increasingly difficult items. Jim gradually learned to tolerate graduated stages in the hierarchy, and to generalize his calmness to closed spaces in his natural environmeht (Knell, 1993a).

Principles That Apply to Children, with Modification

Principle 4: Therapy is a collaborative effort between therapist and patient.

Cognitive therapy utilizes a team approach to solve an individual's problems: the patient supplies information; the therapist provides structure and expertise in problem solving; and the patient and therapist work together to develop strategies and plans to help the patient deal with difficulties. Collaboration is approached by avoiding hidden agendas, designing treatment plans and homework together, and maintaining a "collaborative environment" (Beck & Emery, 1985).

Although young children do not have the capacity to be truly collaborative in their treatment, this does not suggest that the therapist should be authoritative. The therapist must find a balance between imposing structure on the child and not interfering with the child's wishes and spontaneous behavior. With young children, this may involve creative efforts to follow the child's lead, as well as to convey certain information. This balance helps define how the child and therapist will collaborate.

An example of collaboration with a young child is highlighted in the case of a 4-year-8-month-old boy who had been sexually abused by his baby-sitter:

Richard resisted any attempts by the therapist to introduce information regarding abuse. When material was presented via puppets, books, or conversation, he either changed the subject or regressed to speech about "poopoo" or "kaka." However, he did tolerate the introduction of such materials if he did not need to interact with them directly. For example, the therapist read a book about abuse to a puppet and interacted with the puppet in conversation about past experiences of maltreatment. As the therapist read to the puppet, Richard listened and interacted with the puppet about the material in the book (Ruma, 1993).

In this example, the collaboration exists in part through the therapist's flexibility and the child's stated, and implicit, communication about how treatment should proceed.

Some of the collaboration occurs between the parent and therapist, rather than directly between the child and therapist. Because parents and caregivers control the child's environment, their cooperation and collaboration are essential. Collaboration with parents does not replace a collaborative relationship with a child, although it may be supplemental to it. Parent-therapist collaboration can provide invaluable information that is incorporated into the CBPT sessions with the child.

Principle 9: The theory and techniques of cognitive therapy rely on the inductive method.

In cognitive therapy, adult patients are taught a scientific approach to their problems. Beliefs are viewed as hypotheses, which can be revised based on new data. "Experiments" are conducted by the patient to test hypotheses. Similarly, the therapist inductively processes information about the patient. The therapist generates, tests, and revises hypotheses according to therapy-generated data. The choice of therapeutic techniques is also driven by the inductive method; various techniques are tested, until a suitable one is found.

The inductive method is beyond the cognitive capabilities of most children and, therefore, cannot be used effectively. However, from the therapist's perspective, the inductive method is still important. Hypotheses about the child and treatment techniques are tested and case conceptualization and treatment plans are adapted and changed accordingly.

Principle 5: Cognitive therapy uses primarily the Socratic method.

The cognitive therapist uses the question as a lead and avoids direct suggestions and explanations. Questions are often used to help the individual alter maladaptive thinking; for example, the therapist might ask "What is the evidence? What do you have to gain or lose? What can you learn from this?" Such questions eventually become incorporated into the patient's repertoire in order to counter irrational thoughts and to develop a more rational, adaptive thinking style.

Direct questions are usually not effective with children, although the use of open-ended questions, if phrased in statement format, can be helpful for young children; for example, a child may be more likely to respond to "I wonder what you think about that than to the more directive question "What do you think about that?" Such phrasing of a question in the form of a statement could be considered to be Socratic in nature, albeit quite different from what one traditionally considers to be the Socratic method.

The use of this type of Socratic statement is highlighted dramatically in the case of an elective mute 6-year-old child.

Chris spoke freely with her parents and other children but would not speak to other adults. In therapy sessions, she presented with a smile and interacted nonverbally, but would not speak with the therapist. Her efforts to communicate usually consisted of facial expressions and drawing pictures. The therapist did not want to pressure her to talk, but also did not want to remain silent. Therefore, efforts were made to provide a dialogue with the child, although Chris did not answer. For example, when a topic would arise (e.g., through a drawing), the therapist would say, "I wonder what you think about that," rather than asking a more direct question such as "What do you think about that?" At one session, it was clear that Chris was going somewhere after therapy, and the therapist "wondered" about where that might be. Chris responded, "Ho Ho"; although it was near Christmas, the therapist appeared not to understand, commenting, "Ho Ho . . . I wonder where you are going." Finally, Chris responded with, "Santa Claus," the first two-word utterance that she spoke in treatment (Knell, 1993a, 1993b).

A Principle That Does Not Apply to Children

Principle 10: Homework is a central feature of cognitive therapy.

One important aspect of cognitive therapy is the use of new, more adaptive behaviors by patients in their everyday functioning outside of therapy. Patients are given homework assignments in the form of between-session tasks that are geared to reinforce and supplement the work that is taking place in the therapy session.

Although homework assignments have been used with older children, they are rarely used with young children. When homework is given, it is more often completed by the parent(s) or by the child with significant contribution from the parents. As a rule, however, homework is not an integral aspect of CBPT.

PROPERTIES OF COGNITIVE-BEHAVIORAL PLAY THERAPY

The potential efficacy of CBPT may be related to six specific properties:

1. *CBPT involves the child in treatment via play.* As an active participant in therapy, issues of resistance and noncompliance can be addressed. Additionally, the therapist can deal with the child's issues directly, rather than via a parent or significant adult.

2. *CBPT focuses on the child's thoughts, feelings, fantasies, and environment.* In this way, it is possible to focus on a combination of situation-specific factors (e.g., soiling) as well as the child's feelings about the problem (e.g., anger, sadness). CBPT is focused neither on feelings nor on thoughts exclusively, nor is it focused only on situations or environmental circumstances.

3. *CBPT provides a strategy for developing more adaptive thoughts and behaviors.* Through CBPT, the child is taught new, more adaptive strategies for coping with situations. An example is the cognitive strategy of replacing maladaptive thoughts with positive self-statements. Learning more positive adaptive coping skills is highlighted in all cases employing CBPT, and is frequently taught through modeling positive self-statements by toys and puppets. In clinical use, the puppets present situations that are similar to the child's situation and then model adaptive coping strategies, as well as appropriate verbal expression of feelings.

4. *CBPT is structured, directive, and goal-oriented.* Treatment is structured rather than open-ended. The therapist works with the child and family to set goals and helps the child work towards these goals. Movement toward the goals is an important part of CBPT.

5. *CBPT incorporates empirically demonstrated techniques.* Drawing heavily from the behavioral and cognitive traditions of utilizing empirically based intervention, CBPT employs, when possible, empirically demonstrated interventions. One of the most commonly used, well-documented, and perhaps most powerful techniques used is modeling (Bandura, 1977). Modeling is the basis of much of CBPT because of the need to demonstrate concretely, nonverbally, and specifically for young children.

6. *CBPT allows for an empirical examination of treatment.* The importance of using techniques that can be evaluated cannot be overstated. The ultimate question in psychotherapy outcome research is "**What** treatment, by **whom**, is the most effective for **this** individual with **that** specific problem, under **which** set of circumstances?" (Paul, 1967). CBPT offers the opportunity to study the specific effects of well-defined interventions for well-delineated problems. CBPT can be set up in a way that maximizes empirical study of therapy outcome.

CBPT VERSUS TRADITIONAL PLAY THERAPIES

Similarities

CBPT shares some similarities with traditional play interventions, while proposing other assumptions that run counter to the basic philosophy of traditional play therapies. A discussion of similarities and differences between CBPT and traditional therapies, delineated by Knell (1993a), is considered in the following sections and summarized in Table 5.1.

TABLE 5.1. Comparison of CBPT and Traditional Play Therapies

Similarities	Differences		
	Psychoanalytic	Nondirective Axlinian	CBPT
Therapeutic Relationship	**Direction and Goals**		
Establish contact with child	Direction does not come from therapist	Direction is not accepted because it imposes on child; does not accept child as he/she is	Therapeutic goals are established; direction toward goals is basis of intervention
Engage child in treatment			
Engender child's trust			
Play as Communication	**Play Materials and Activities**		
Play is treatment modality as well as means to communicate	Therapist is "participant observer" not playmate	Play materials, activities, direction of play *always* selected by child	Both child and therapist select materials and activities
Therapy as a Safe Place	Therapist does not suggest any materials or activities		
Provide child with sense of security and safety	**Play as Education**		
	Play is not used to educate; education is not the goal of therapy	Education is not appropriate because it is a form of direction	Play is used to teach skills and alternative behaviors
	Interpretations/Connections		
	Interpretation as ultimate tool	Not made by the therapist unless child introduces them first, therapist communicates unconditional acceptance, *not* interpretation of symbolic play.	Introduced by therapist, therapist brings conflict into verbal expression for child
	Praise		
	Not considered appropriate	Praise should not be used by therapist; praise communicates acceptance of child.	Praise is crucial component, communicates appropriate behaviors and reinforces child

Therapeutic Relationship

A positive therapeutic relationship is critical in psychotherapy and is considered to be predictive of good treatment outcome (Brady et al., 1980; Rogers, et al., 1967). This is just as true in play therapy as it is in any other form of therapy because the therapist attempts to establish a positive therapeutic contact with the child via play. Psychoanalytic play therapy, particularly as practiced by Anna Freud (1928, 1946) and her followers, emphasized play as the means of establishing the therapeutic relationship. Axline (1947), influenced primarily by the Rogerian school, felt that the therapist should develop a warm, friendly relationship with the child in which good rapport is established as soon as possible. Similarly, the therapeutic relationship is of utmost importance in CBPT. The therapist must make contact with the child, engage the child, and engender the child's trust if treatment is to be effective.

Play as Communication

In play therapy, play is not only the treatment modality but also the method of communication between therapist and child. Observing the child's play offers an understanding of the child's thoughts, feelings, and view of the world. Children bring their conflicts and fantasies into treatment; the less able they are to verbalize the conflicts and fantasies, the more they reveal through play. The implications of children's play are endless: Play is the window through which adults see how children view themselves and others, how they interact with the therapist, how they approach problems, and how they understand the world around them.

Therapy as a Safe Place

Play therapy should provide the child with a sense of security and safety. It is important for the child to know that therapy is a safe place to deal with problems. Criticisms and uncertainties are part of the real world; they should be in the therapy setting only in that the child brings them there and can deal with them in a comfortable, nonthreatening way.

Differences

There are a number of differences between CBPT and traditional play therapies. The contrast is made between CBPT and nondirective (Axlinian) and psychoanalytic approaches, respectively, since they have received the most attention in the literature and in clinical settings.

Direction and Goals

In traditional play therapy, direction from the therapist is not accepted. In Axlinian therapy, specifically, direction came only from the child; Axline felt that direction imposed on the child by the therapist did not accept the child as he or she was. In CBPT, therapeutic goals are established and movement toward those goals is an integral part of treatment. Whereas goals and direction are counter to the basic philosophy of Axlinian play therapy, they form the basis of CBPT. The cognitive-behavioral therapist's selection of a direction may be based on the child's lead or on knowledge of the child's situation gleaned from an outside source. In CBPT, it is acceptable for the therapist to introduce themes based on parent or teacher report of the child's behavior in situations outside the therapy setting; for example, the cognitive-behavioral play therapist may provide direction by purposefully and systematically employing a puppet that behaves in certain ways or verbalizes issues that the child reportedly is exhibiting.

Play Materials and Activities

In Axlinian play therapy, the child always selects the play material, activities, and direction of play. Similarly, in psychoanalytic play therapy, the therapist is a "participant observer," not a playmate (Esman, 1983). The therapist is expected to maintain a position as a neutral observer in order to understand the child's behavior. Thus, the psychoanalytic therapist does not suggest the use of any particular play material because he or she must maintain a position as a neutral and permissive observer not director. In CBPT, both the child and therapist play a role in the choice of play materials and activities. From the child's spontaneous use of particular toys and activities, the cognitive-behavioral therapist gleans information that is then used by the therapist to structure play sessions geared specifically for the child.

Play as Education

In psychoanalytically oriented play therapy, play is not used to educate a child. Esman (1983) noted that play in nontherapeutic contexts can be used for instructional purposes. However, play in psychoanalytic therapy is used to resolve conflicts. Although educational benefits may be derived secondarily from therapeutic processes, education is not the goal of therapy. Nondirective play therapy also did not view education as an appropriate part of play therapy. Clearly, CBPT is not used solely to educate the child. However, utilizing play to teach skills or alternative behaviors is one aspect of CBPT. Educating the child often takes place in CBPT as a model, such as a puppet, behaves in such a way that teaches the child.

Interpretations/Connections

Axline considered interpretations or connections important but contended that they should not be made until the child introduced them. The relationship between therapist and child was used to provide a corrective emotional experience for the child. The therapist demonstrated unconditional acceptance, rather than interpretation of symbolic play. In contrast, in psychoanalytic play therapy, the ultimate tool is interpretation. Melanie Klein (1932) felt that play was a substitute for verbalization and that the therapist's role was to interpret the child's play. Anna Freud (1928, 1946) placed less emphasis on play as the equivalent of the child's verbalizations; instead, she stressed play as the means by which the therapeutic relationship was built. Anna Freud allowed the child to "work through" resistances before offering interpretations. Although the Freudian and Kleinian schools differ in this regard, there is still an emphasis on interpretation. In this respect, CBPT is actually more similar to psychoanalytically oriented treatment in which the therapist brings the conflict into verbal expressions **for** the child.

Praise

In psychoanalytic therapy, praise is not considered appropriate. Axline (1947) contended that praise was not acceptable. She felt that praise communicated that the therapist did not accept the child as he or she was but rather wanted the child to be a certain way. In contrast, praise is a critical component of CBPT, as it helps children feel good about themselves and incorporate positive perceptions in their self-appraisal. Praise also communicates to the child which behaviors are appropriate and which ones are not.

Summary of Similarities and Differences

CBPT is similar to other play therapies in its reliance on a positive therapeutic relationship that is based on rapport and trust, in the use of play activities as a means of communication between therapist and child, and in its message that therapy is a safe place. It differs from other play therapies with respect to establishment of goals, selection of play materials and activities, use of therapy to educate, and the use of praise and interpretations.

PRACTICE

Methods

The wide range of techniques and strategies that may be used in CBPT are considered later in this chapter. First to be considered are the methods through which specific interventions are typically delivered: modeling, role-playing, and behavioral contingencies (Braswell & Kendall, 1988).

Modeling

Most cognitive-behavioral interventions with children include some form of modeling. Although modeling is important in work with children of all ages, with young children with whom verbal therapy cannot be used extensively, modeling is particularly important. Extensive research shows that modeling is an effective way to acquire and strengthen behaviors, as well as to weaken them (Bandura, 1977). In many situations, learning through modeling can be more efficient and effective than learning through shaping and direct reinforcement. In CBPT, modeling is used to demonstrate adaptive coping methods to the child. Although CBPT is not primarily verbal, the model may verbalize problem-solving skills as a particular behavior is demonstrated. In this way, the model may talk in a manner that is compatible with positive problem solving. Talking out loud provides a number of cues (e.g., auditory, visual), as well as a concrete example of the behavior.

When used in therapy, modeling exposes the child to someone (often a stuffed animal or other toy) who demonstrates the behavior that the therapist wants the child to learn. It can be particularly useful if the child can relate positively to the model. Modeling can also be presented in a variety of other forms, such as films, books, and dolls. Because of the nature of the young child's limited cognitive and verbal abilities, modeling is an important component of play therapy.

Role-Playing

Through role-playing in therapy sessions, the child practices skills with the therapist and receives ongoing feedback regarding progress. Role-playing between child and therapist is usually more effective with school-age, rather than preschool-age, children. However, it is possible to deliver role-playing through a modeling technique so that the models are actually role-playing and the child is observing and learning from watching the models practicing particular skills; for example, a shy child may observe a shy puppet, one that is reluctant to be with others, as it "practices" interacting with other children. The child would listen as the puppet practices and receives feedback from the therapist.

Behavioral Contingencies

Behavioral contingencies are often a significant component of CBPT. With young children, this typically involves reinforcing or rewarding the child for acquiring new skills. For example, the therapist may label the child's behavior and praise the child for attempts to develop new skills. The child may also be taught and encouraged to use positive coping self-statements. The therapist can use specific behavioral contingencies in the session, and also can encourage and assist the parents in setting up contingencies in the home and other environments.

Behavioral Techniques

There is a wide array of behavioral techniques that may be used in CBPT. Some of the most common techniques are described in the following sections and summarized in Table 5.2.

Systematic Desensitization

Systematic desensitization is the process of reducing anxiety or fear by replacing a maladaptive response with an adaptive one (Wolpe, 1958, 1982). This is accomplished by breaking the association between a particular stimulus and the anxiety or fear response that it usually elicits: the stimulus is presented, but the anxiety is prevented from occurring.

With adults, systematic desensitization is usually accomplished through teaching muscle relaxation, which is incompatible with anxiety (Jacobson, 1938). For children, if muscle relaxation is not used, other alternatives that are enjoyable and counter anxiety can be taught. A viable alternative for very young children is the use of play activities that are not anxiety provoking.

Contingency Management

Contingency management is a general term describing techniques that modify a behavior by controlling its consequences. These management programs can be set up for the child for behaviors in the natural environment or for behaviors within the play therapy session. Several techniques based on contingency management can be used within the play therapy setting. Positive reinforcement, shaping, extinction, differential reinforcement of other behavior, and time-out are all commonly used forms of contingency management.

POSITIVE REINFORCEMENT.   Positive reinforcement often involves social reinforcers (e.g., praise) or material reinforcers (e.g., stickers). It is often used in combination with other procedures and may be direct (e.g., praise for playing appropriately) or more subtle (e.g., encouraging the child to explore certain topics rather than others). If a particular problem is the focus of treatment, the therapist might use praise as the child exhibits mastery over the problem. Positive reinforcement is a powerful technique, and, therefore, it is important for the therapist to exercise good clinical judgment in its use.

SHAPING.   In some instances, a child is missing certain skills necessary to behave in a particular way. The therapist can reinforce the child through shaping successive approximations to a desired response; positive reinforcement is given for a behavior that is not the desired response but is close to it. As therapy continues, the child is rewarded for behavior that is closer and closer to the desired response. Eventually the child reaches the desired behavior.

STIMULUS FADING.   If a child has some of the requisite skills for a behavior but only exhibits the behavior in certain circumstances or with certain people, stimulus fading may be used. In such situations, the therapist can become a discriminative stimulus for behaving. The child learns to use some of these positive skills in a setting with the therapist and then transfers the skills to other settings.

TABLE 5.2.   Examples of Behavioral Techniques in Cognitive-Behavioral Play Therapy

Behavioral technique modeled via puppet	Vignette
Shaping/Positive reinforcement	Child is afraid to go to school. Therapist helps puppet go near the school building, visit the school, and gradually stay in the classroom (shaping). Puppet receives encouragement and positive feedback (reinforcement) from therapist as it makes closer and closer attempts to be in school.
Shaping socially appropriate expression of feelings	Child makes doll hit father whenever he comes to visit. Therapist knows the child is angry with father because he visits infrequently. Therapist has doll turn hitting into verbal expression, "I am mad at you, Daddy, because you don't visit."
Extinction/Differential reinforcement of other behavior (DRO)	Child makes puppet slap another puppet. Therapist knows nursery school teacher is concerned that child deals with anger by hitting other children. The puppet's slapping is ignored (extinction). When appropriate behavior is shown (e.g., shaking hands), puppet is praised (differential reinforcement of other).
Systematic desensitization	Sexually abused child depicts abuse through drawings or play, beginning with least threatening material and gradually dealing with most threatening issues.
Contingency management	Child earns stars for sleeping in own bed.
Self-monitoring	Child monitors feelings by marking "happy," "sad," or "neutral" face chart.
Time-out	Child removed from therapist's attention for 1 minute for breaking "No throwing toys" rule in therapy.

EXTINCTION AND DIFFERENTIAL REINFORCEMENT OF OTHER BEHAVIOR.   Behaviors can be extinguished by withholding reinforcement. Extinction itself does not teach new behaviors, so it is frequently used in conjunction with a reinforcement program. In this way, a child can be reinforced for learning a new behavior at the same time that another behavior is being extinguished. This if often done through differential reinforcement of other behavior (DRO); that is, behaviors that are different from or incompatible with the maladaptive behavior are reinforced. The main idea is that the unacceptable behavior cannot occur if a competing, more desirable behavior is taking place (e.g., reinforcing a child for appropriately playing with a toy while extinguishing the child's efforts to break toys.)

TIME-OUT.   When a child has maladaptive behaviors, it is important to look at the environment to see what is reinforcing and, therefore, maintaining the behaviors. Frequently, it is attention from a significant adult that maintains a child's maladaptive behavior. Removing that focus on negative behaviors can promote more adaptive behaviors.

Sometimes children need to be removed from whatever is reinforcing their behavior. This may literally mean removing the child from the immediate environment. One technique for this is time-out, which is more frequently used in the natural environment, such as school or home, but may be used within the play therapy session as well. Although, technically, *time-out* means time away from reinforcement, it has come to mean removing children from what they perceive as a desirable environment to a less attractive one.

Time-out may be used in play therapy when a child does not follow a preestablished rule, such as "No breaking toys in the therapy session." In that situation, there may be a time-out from therapy: the child is removed from the situation for a brief period. This might involve moving the child to a part of the therapy room where there are no toys. During the time-out period, the child would not have access to the reinforcing aspects of therapy (e.g., the therapist's positive attention).

Time-out is considered effective because it keeps the child from whatever is reinforcing the maladaptive behaviors. The duration of the time-out interval is considered less important than the fact that the child is not being reinforced for maladaptive behavior. The disadvantage of time-out in therapy is that it might remove the child from interaction with the therapist, and, thus, it should be used sparingly and for maladaptive behaviors that cannot be dealt with in other ways. It is important that the child understands what *is* acceptable, and that positive reinforcement is forthcoming for such adaptive, appropriate behaviors. When time-out is used, it should be needed less frequently over the course of therapy as the child learns more appropriate responses.

Self-Monitoring

In self-monitoring, clients observe and record information about certain aspects of their behavior. Monitoring activities and moods can serve several useful purposes. First, it may be the only means of obtaining information from the natural environment. Second, it allows the individual to record subjective reactions to specific events. Third, it serves as a baseline for later comparisons and can be used throughout therapy. Fourth, hypotheses can be tested using self-monitoring because it may provide more accurate data than could be recalled otherwise. Finally, it may serve as a beginning point for discussion in therapy (DeRubeis & Beck, 1988) by providing structured information about the client's experiences.

Self-monitoring can be used accurately by children as young as 4 or 5 years old (Fixsen, Phillips, & Wolf, 1972; Risley & Hart, 1968) and is especially useful if the child is asked to monitor activities or events, rather than mood. Young children usually need parental help with this task, because they cannot be expected to complete it by themselves. If it is explained carefully and simply, however, the child can be expected to understand the task and complete it with supervision.

Although monitoring of mood is difficult, it can be done, especially if simple, concrete scales are used. Older children can understand simple scales, with zero representing *the worst you ever felt in your whole life* and 10 standing for *the best you ever felt in your whole life* (Emery et. al., 1983). Preschoolers are more inclined to have all-or-nothing thinking about feelings and to lack understanding of the complexities of mood. Scales used with young children may need to be very concrete (e.g., three faces representing *mad, happy,* and *sad*). Alternative scales for monitoring mood with young children include those anchored with faces (Garber, 1982) and simple feelings words (Barden, Zelko, Duncan, & Masters, 1980). It is often helpful to devise scales that progress in a *worst* to *best* order, such as faces that gradually progress from *sad* to *happy*. Scales should not include more than three or four options. Parents can monitor the accuracy of these perceptions by helping the child to clarify his or her feelings (e.g., "How did you feel when you hurt yourself? You were crying. Which picture looks like how you felt?").

Activity Scheduling

With activity scheduling, specific tasks are planned and then implemented by the client. Scheduling specific activities may increase the probability that the individual will participate in activities. Scheduled activities for children and adolescents might reduce time spent in passive or ruminative activities. This can be particularly useful for depressed, withdrawn, or very anxious children. These children may avoid activities because they do not expect to enjoy them or because they perceive themselves as a failure when they try. When pressure is removed and the child is encouraged only to *attempt* the activity, many realize that they can have fun, despite expectations that they will not. Even if they do not enjoy the activity, they can still be reinforced for their efforts.

When activity scheduling is used with young children, it is best done with parent and child working together. Although parent involvement is critical, it is equally important that the child have an active sense of control in activities planned. Providing the child with choices and control can be useful, particularly for the preschooler who is struggling with issues of autonomy and control (e.g., eating, toileting).

Systematic planning should provide the child with as much sense of control as possible. Providing "no-choice choices" can help young children feel that they have some input in their lives. An example of giving a no-choice choice is the parent asking the child "Do you want to play with dolls outside or with the board games in the basement?" This clearly communicates that the child has no choice but to play; yet still maintains control over the choice of the toy and the place.

In order for this to be effective, the parent must provide a limited range of *acceptable* and *real* options. The question, "Do you want to play with the toys outside or to go to the amusement park?" is a false choice if going to an amusement park is not a real option. It is also important that the child maintain control in making the choice. If the choice is given to the child but is clearly made by the parent, anything gained by offering a choice may be lost.

It is important that the child feel a sense of competence at the assigned tasks and that significant adults provide contingent reinforcement for activities well done. Reinforcement should not always be based on the final product; it should also involve positive feedback for the child's efforts and perseverance. Such positive reinforcement can improve the child's mood as well. To ensure success experiences, tasks can be broken down into small steps, thus reducing the difficulty of the activity and providing reinforcement for successive approximations to the completed activity.

Summary of Behavioral Techniques

In summary, behavioral techniques can be used for clients of all ages. Many of these techniques can be adapted for children as young as 4 or 5 years old. With some of the techniques (e.g., self-monitoring), young children often need an adult's assistance to accomplish the task. With other techniques, such as activity scheduling, parent involvement may take different forms but should include the parent's participation in helping he child play and carry out a particular activity. Parental encouragement and positive feedback are also useful. Additionally, tasks usually need to be relatively simple and concrete and not verbally complex. As the child gets older, more difficult tasks and verbally oriented tasks may be presented.

Cognitive Techniques

Whereas the behavioral methods used in CBPT usually involve an alteration in activity, cognitive methods deal with changes in thinking. This is an important distinction because cognitive theories suggest that changes in affect *and* behavior occur as a result of changes in thinking. In cognitive therapy with children, the therapist helps the child to identify, modify, and/or build cognitions. Table 5.3 provides commonly used cognitive techniques and examples.

Recording Dysfunctional Thoughts

Cognitive therapists frequently ask individuals to monitor and record their thoughts (e.g., in written or oral form). Although older children can be encouraged to record their thoughts, this is difficult if not impossible to do with very young children. Many times, this may be accomplished indirectly by having a parent monitor the child's activities and statements. Although this is the parent's perception of the child's statements, it is possible to obtain a recording of dysfunctional statements made by the child, rather than the child's self-recording of thoughts. The astute parent will listen and watch for such comments not only in direct communication with the child, but via the child's play. Although overheard and repeated by the parent as opposed to being directly reported by the child, these comments can be invaluable in providing clues to the youngster's perceptions.

An interesting example is offered by a 5-year-old girl, Karen, whose father was diagnosed with obsessive-compulsive disorder. The father engaged in repetitive checking rituals in which he spent hours checking to make sure that certain activities had been performed (e.g., turning off the light).

Karen's mother overheard her say, "I must be a witch." When her mother asked why, Karen replied, "Because I make Daddy do all those crazy things" (referring to his checking compulsions).

This example provided the therapist with an important clue to the child's perception

TABLE 5.3.   Examples of Cognitive Techniques in Cognitive-Behavioral Play Therapy

Cognitive technique modeled via puppet	Vignette
Cognitive Change Strategies (identifying and correcting beliefs)	Child states that doll's private parts were hurt. Therapist responds by stating that although they had been hurt in the past, they were alright now.
Positive coping self-statements	Child is destroying clay model of perpetrator and says to therapist, "Don't rip me up." Therapist models positive statement by saying "We won't rip you up. You are a special and good person." Child is encouraged to learn to use positive self-statements.
	Child afraid of being in closed room learns to make self-statements, "I am OK, I can stay here."
Bibliotherapy	Therapist reads stories to child depicting children in similar circumstances and how they deal with them (e.g., divorce, sexual abuse).

that she was responsible for her father's difficulties. It also highlights the magical thinking of young children.

Cognitive Change Strategies

With adults, hypothesis testing is used to change faulty cognitions. Thoughts, beliefs, assumptions, and expectations are treated as hypotheses to be tested scientifically. Problem areas are identified and experiments designed to test these thoughts. This examination typically involves a three-pronged approach: Look at the evidence, explore the alternatives, and examine the consequences.

These strategies are difficult to use with children. Their cognitive abilities are more limited than those of the adolescent and adult; therefore, the hypothesis testing inherent in this approach is problematic. Children may have difficulty exploring situations, providing alternative explanations, and understanding consequences. Because children have the capacity to misinterpret and distort reality, their inferences may be consistent with *their* perceptions of reality, although they are not necessarily accurate.

An example of how children make inaccurate, although personally consistent perceptions is provided by the typical response to the breakup of their parents' marriage. Parental divorce is often viewed by children as their fault, or at least due in part to some behavior on their part. The child makes assumptions such as "Daddy is leaving because I am a bad kid" or "If my behavior were better, Mommy wouldn't have left." If encouraged to provide an alternative explanation (such as "Daddy is leaving because he and Mommy fight all the time"), the child may remain stuck with the previous, more personal explanation.

Therefore, helping children to change cognitions means that the child will need assistance from adults in generating alternative explanations, testing them, and altering beliefs (Emery et al., 1983). To challenge one's beliefs, it is necessary to distance oneself from the beliefs, something that is very difficult for young children to do. Additionally, the child needs an "accumulated history of events" in order to understand the ramifications of certain situations (Kendall, 1991). Learning occurs, in part, from experience, and the very young child still has limited experiences on which to build. At this age, thought and reality are not always separate. Although still difficult, play does provide the means for the therapist to help the child bridge the gap between beliefs and reality and to build experiences that may help the child.

Play also allows the child to reenact problem situations and to potentially gain mastery over events and circumstances. The therapist can assist in this mastery by providing the experiments in the play situations and by assisting the child to look at the evidence, to explore the alternatives, and to examine the consequences. For example, the therapist may structure some of the play with the child to reflect alternative scenarios so the child experiences different reactions and consequences for the same situation.

Changing cognitions through play therapy may be highlighted by the case of a five-year-old boy, Mark, whose mother was able to provide information through her recording of his play and conversations at home. Additionally, the therapist's observations were used to form hypotheses about the meaning of his play.

In spontaneous play, Mark would repeatedly have the daddy doll steal the puppets and return them to mommy. Mark acted this scenario out via puppets. The therapist could use this play to help understand Mark's sense of confusion, frustration, and fear with the family situation. Mark's labeling of the dad as "Super dad" also provided information about the child's perceptions that his father had certain "magical powers." The therapist could use Mark's play to help him see that he was indeed safe at home with his mother and would not be hurt by his father. Given Mark's interest in the puppets, the therapist used them to reenact alternative scenes for Mark. Scenes were enacted that verbalized the puppet's confusion and fears about his dad, ways that he could feel better about himself, as well as the fact that he could be safe (Knell, 1993a).

Coping Self-Statements

The way an individual interprets events, not the events per se, affects the person's ability to cope. When one believes negative self-thoughts, maladaptive physiological reactions may follow. These negative experiences may then prompt continued negative self-statements, which may lead to poor decisions. This feedback loop is illustrated by the school-age child who predicts he will do poorly on a test, supported by his negative self-statements (e.g., "I did not study, I will fail, I do not understand this"), which may lead to physiological reactions, such as upset stomach or sweaty palms.

Individuals of all ages can be helped to develop adaptive coping self-statements (e.g., Meichenbaum, 1985). However, treatment strategies must be modified based on the age and the cognitive level of the individual; teaching coping self-statements must be modified when working with young children. Children in the preoperational stage of cognitive development may benefit most from learning simple statements about themselves. Often in the form of self-affirmation, these modified self-statements can be used with children as young as 2 1/2 to 3 years old. At that age, the self-statements are very simple, both linguistically and conceptually (e.g., "I can sit"; "Good sitting"). Such self-statements contain a component of self-reward (e.g., The message: "I am doing a good job"). This can be thought of as "the little engine that could" approach, reflecting Walter Piper's (1950) story in which the engine gets up the hill while repeatedly saying "I think I can, I think I can."

Positive self-statements can be modeled by the parent for the child. For example, the young child loves hearing praise for accomplishments, such as "good girl" or clapping one's hands. Even more helpful is specific verbal labeling of what the child has done well (e.g., "Good boy, you did the whole puzzle"). Turning praise into self-statements does not always happen spontaneously; parents must learn to prompt positive self-affirmative comments from their children. In addition, children's positive self-comments are often short-lived and situation specific, and, thus, it is important both to teach generalization as well as to ensure that parents reinforce the positive message for the child. For some parents, this concept is a difficult one, as they *expect* good behavior from their child and do not feel that such behavior needs to be praised. It is important for parents to understand that children will not internalize positive feelings unless taught the value of their actions. One way children learn the positive value of what they do is through specific labeling with positive feedback.

Bibliotherapy

Although not technically a cognitive intervention, bibliotherapy is used increasingly as an adjunct to therapy. Many self-help books for adults are based on cognitive theory (e.g., Burns, 1980) and provide an arena where individuals can question their irrational beliefs and consider alternative options.

The use of bibliotherapy with children may have a somewhat different focus. Rather than specifically teaching concepts and suggesting ways for using these in one's life, children's books provide more of a storytelling approach. Although children's literature has always had messages and morals, only recently has there been a proliferation of stories about children who have experienced particular stressors or traumas (e.g., divorce, death, moving). Such stories may model a child's reaction to a particular situation with the hope that the listener will learn something.

When published materials are not available or not appropriate, they may be created specifically for a child. The following is an example of the use of a therapist-created book in short term intervention with a 2-year-5-month-old child.

Billy and his family had experienced numerous fires in abandoned homes in their neighborhood. Immediately prior to being seen in a mental health setting, the garage of the home next door had burned. To insure his safety, he had been carried from his bed in the middle of the night. Billy's language was limited and the family was having great difficulty helping him understand that everything was going to be all right. He became upset when he heard any kind of siren, or saw a fire truck, and could not fall asleep at night.

The therapist wrote a brief story about a child who experienced similar fires near his home. The story ended with the boy learning that he and his family could be safe. In the story, the child felt safe when he went to bed at night, could talk about his feelings, and tell his family about his fears. The child drew pictures to go with the story. The story was read to the child over the course of several sessions, and the parents read it to him nightly before he went to bed. At the point of termination, Billy was sleeping without difficulty and was not exhibiting any other difficulties (Knell, 1993a).

Summary of Cognitive Techniques

Cognitive methods in therapy help individuals make changes in their cognitions. Young children can be taught to modify thoughts, beliefs, and assumptions. However, they will need help in considering alternative explanations and approaches. Cognitive techniques can be incorporated into play in order to help the child gain mastery over life events. Coping self-statements are also effective and can be modeled for the child by therapist, parent, or others. Finally, the use of bibliotherapy is ideal with young children who often enjoy having stories read to them.

Behavioral and Cognitive Techniques in Practice

Some authors have questioned the applicability and appropriateness of using CBT with preschool-age children (e.g., Campbell, 1990). Frequently cited are developmental issues that might preclude the young child from understanding and benefiting from such interventions, because cognitive-behavioral approaches often rely on fairly sophisticated cognitive abilities (e.g., abstract thinking, hypothesis testing). Further, the use of "collaborative empiricism" as described by Beck, Rush, Shaw, and Emery (1979) is difficult for very young children.

At first glance, one might assume that preschoolers and young school-age children lack the cognitive skills to engage in cognitive interventions, in the same way as they are currently used with older children and adults. However, there is evidence that cognitive theorists, such as Piaget, underestimated the abilities of young children. Recent theorists (e.g., Gelman & Baillargeon, 1983) contend that young children should be viewed on the basis of what they *can* do, rather than what they *cannot* do. Further, there is ample data to suggest that preschoolers' ability to understand complex problems may be enhanced by specific techniques, such as providing concrete examples and using less-open-ended questions. Part of this task is the creating and maintaining of a collaborative therapy environment. Rather than assuming preschoolers lack the cognitive abilities to engage in CBT, therapists must consider ways to make interventions more developmentally appropriate and, therefore, accessible to young children.

In order to make interventions available, there should be a match between the developmental level of the child and the level of complexity of the intervention chosen. Therapists must capitalize on the child's strengths and abilities rather than deferring to weaknesses. Obviously, experiential therapies incorporating play and deemphasizing complex cognitive and verbal capabilities are likely to be the most useful for young children. With careful planning, the egocentric functioning typical of young children can be decreased, and reasoning abilities can improve.

One important arena for therapeutic intervention is in encouraging and facilitating the child's language for describing experiences and emotions. Language development takes great strides during the preschool period. However, despite dramatic growth in general vocabulary during this period, the child's descriptive vocabulary for words depicting emotions is still limited. Many youngsters do not even have even the most rudimentary words to express their feelings (e.g., happy, mad, sad).

In addition to a feeling-word vocabulary, young children may benefit from efforts to help them match their behaviors with their feelings and learn to express certain maladaptive behaviors in more adaptive, language-based ways. A common example is the young child's expression of anger through aggression. One child is angry about the birth of a new sibling, so he tries to kick the baby carriage and, thus, hurt his new sister. Another child is mad about being left with a baby-sitter when her parents go out for the evening, so she tries to break a toy. Teaching these youngsters to understand that they are angry, why they are angry, what it means to be angry, and how to express it in words instead of behavior may be a beginning to helping them deal with their feelings. Children at this age benefit from a sense of control, and using language rather than aggressive behaviors might provide some of this sense of mastery and control.

In therapy, learning may take place for the child in a very experiential way. Children can practice different facial expressions, as modeled by the therapist, drawings, or puppets, and can learn to associate these expressions with appropriate words. The boy who was angry about the new baby sister can play with puppets and toys to understand his feelings and to practice adaptive behaviors. While acting out his anger by kicking the play carriage, a punching bag, or a puppet representation of his sister, the therapist can help the child label his feelings. Merely acting out aggression in therapy does not teach the child that there are alternatives. Labeling the aggression and learning other verbal and nonverbal ways to cope can offer the child some other, more adaptive way of dealing with frustration and anger.

RESEARCH

All therapy-outcome research is complex, although the very nature of play therapy makes it particularly difficult to subject to empirical study. Although some early studies were concerned with nondirective play therapies (e.g., Cox, 1953; Dorfman, 1958), very little systematic research has taken place with other types of play therapy, particularly with regard to process and outcome issues. In a review of play therapy research, Phillips (1985) contended that the integration of cognitive-behavioral techniques into play interventions offered a promising direction because the specificity of treatment goals and methods of study might account for a positive outcome. However, CBPT has yet to be subjected to systematic empirical study.

PROCEDURE

Therapist Qualifications and Characteristics

It is assumed that the therapist is professionally trained, having received clinical course work and supervised experience through a graduate degree in an appropriate discipline (e.g., psychology, social work, psychiatry). Individuals trained to work with adults or older children/adolescents will need specific background in a play therapy approach, as well as experience working with very young children. Additionally, therapists should be well versed in cognitive-behavior theory and clinical application and should be comfortable adapting CBT for use with children. The training and supervised experience should be of high quality. Learning to become a cognitive-behavioral play therapist should include an understanding of the literature as well as experience through role-playing therapy sessions, observation of experienced therapists, and direct supervision of cases. Obtaining such training may be difficult because of the limited number of experienced play therapists utilizing cognitive-behavioral approaches. Until there are more cognitive-behavioral play therapists, clinicians-in-training will need to stay up-to-date with the growing literature in this field and utilize sources outside the specific educational/training setting for educational and supervisory purposes (e.g., national conventions).

Treatment Stages

Assessment

Most child therapists will consider the first few play therapy sessions as part of an intake or assessment period. The nature of this assessment may range from informal observation to formal interviews or testing. Information is usually gathered about the child's current functioning, the level of development, presenting problems, and a sense of the child's perspective of the problem. For young children, it is particularly important to gather assessment information from multiple sources, particularly if the child is in a number of settings other than home (e.g., day care). In order to develop a treatment plan with specific goals, the situation should be understood from the parents' perspective as well as the child's. The evaluation should always use normal child development as a basis from which to understand behavior. The child's thoughts, feelings, beliefs, and underlying assumptions are all important but are not always gathered directly from the child, because self-report is difficult for young children. The assessment of perceptions in young children is most frequently obtained through parents who may contribute to an understanding of the child's perceptions. More direct assessment of the child would be obtained via observation, interaction, interview, and play assessment.

PARENT-REPORT INVENTORIES.   If the parents are considered to be reliable informants, parent-report inventories can be used in assessing young children. These measures can be completed fairly easily and quickly, and, because these measures have norms, they may provide a background of normal development from which to view the child's individual development. Commonly used are The Child Behavior Checklist (CBCL) (Achenbach & Edelbrock, 1983) and The Minnesota Child Development Inventory (MCDI) (Ireton & Thwing, 1972). The CBCL, which can be used with children as young as 2 years old, measures social competence and behavior problems. The MCDI, for children from 1 to 6 years old, measures development on six separate scales. Both inventories are completed by parent or caretaker.

CLINICAL INTERVIEW.   Interviewing preschoolers is possible if one is aware of the cognitive-developmental characteristics of youngsters of that age and conducts the interview accordingly. According to Hughes and Baker (1990), the cardinal prerequisite of developmentally sensitive child interviewing is *flexibility*. Such flexibility is determined in part by the child's developmental level, the purpose of the interview, the relationship between child and interviewer, the setting, and the interpersonal styles of both child and interviewer.

Interviews are largely a combination of verbal questioning and play observation and assessment. Standard verbal-interview techniques will not be effective with young children, and interviewers must adjust their techniques according to the developmental level of the child. The child may need concrete referents, options, and structure in order to understand the interviewer and respond appropriately (Bierman, 1983).

PLAY ASSESSMENT MEASURES.   Despite the development of several play assessment measures (e.g., Lowenfeld, 1939, 1950), play assessments are typically informal and lack any methodological rigor. They may provide the therapist with a large quantity of information about the child, albeit not in a systematic fashion. There are no standardized play interviews that confirm a particular diagnosis or elicit specific symptoms. However, play interviews can be used to support parent report or can suggest a direction different from the problem as described by the parent. Commonly, they are used in as somewhat "projective" manner as a way for the clinician to observe and understand how the child views the world as conveyed through play.

COGNITIVE/DEVELOPMENTAL TESTS.   Individually administered psychological measures are sometimes used with young children. Tests of cognitive/intellectual development offer information about the child's cognitive abilities, and may provide some information regarding the child's capacity to benefit from more verbally oriented therapies. Although much of this information can also be gathered from observation over time, and from other sources, formal testing often provides a starting point that is critical in treatment planning.

The child's overall test-taking behaviors and response style can provide information that adds to specific tests results. Interpretations based on behavior in testing situations are subjective and open to much interclinician variability. However, when tests are given in a standardized way, the testing situation is relatively uniform, and, therefore, hypotheses about a child's test-taking behaviors are open to less subjectivity than if such interpretations were being made about a child in a free-play setting.

PROJECTIVE TESTS.   Projective tests are not typically used by cognitive-behaviorally oriented therapists, even though they may offer information about the child's conflicts, coping styles, style of organizing information, and view of he world. Certain projective tests may provide the very young child with structure that might be similar to the structure provided by dolls and puppets. With very young children, projective tests may provide concrete, pictorial representations to which the child can respond (for example, the Thematic Apperception Test (TAT) (Murray, 1943); the Children's Apperception Test

(CAT) (Bellak & Bellak, 1949); and Robert's Apperception Test for Children (RATC) (McArthur & Roberts, 1982).

Another commonly used projective technique is the sentence-completion task, which was designed to provide information about the individual's thoughts, perceptions, assumptions, and underlying beliefs. Although there are many versions of this task, none are standardized for use with children. The typical sentence-completion task allows the individual to complete sentence stems, such as "I get upset when . . ." or "My mother . . ." If able to, older children or adults usually write in their responses, whereas younger children respond orally. The traditional sentence-completion task is usually not used with children under the age of 5 or 6 years because of their difficulty in comprehending the expectations and, therefore, in responding in a coherent manner.

The Puppet Sentence-Completion Task (Knell, 1993a) was developed to make the traditional sentence-completion task more accessible for preschool-age children. It is modeled after the traditional sentence-completion tasks that are used with older children, adolescents, and adults. The task employs three puppets, two controlled by the therapist and one by the child. The task consists of two parts: In the first part, the sentence-completion activity is modeled for the child by the therapist's two puppets; in the second part, the child completes sentences. The second part begins only when it is clear that the child understands the task (see Table 5.4).

The Puppet Sentence-Completion Task is structured to facilitate the child's understanding of what is expected. It is developmentally suited to the preschooler for two reasons: First, the task itself is not begun until it is clear that the child understands the directions. The directions are conveyed via modeling with the puppets, and the child's responses to the first part of the task indicate to the therapist if the child understands what is expected. Second, the child has the opportunity to complete the stem through the puppet or without

TABLE 5.4.   Puppet Sentence-Completion Task (Knell, 1993a)

Directions: The therapist should let the child choose a puppet. After the child has chosen a puppet, the therapist chooses two puppets. If the child would like, the therapist can let the child pick the puppets for the therapist.

The following code is used in the directions:
Puppet A–Therapist's
Puppet B–Therapist's
Puppet C–Child's

Part One
Directions: Puppet A states the sentence stem. Puppet B quickly responds. The therapist then turns to Puppet C (held by the child) for a response. The therapist supplies answers for Puppet B and moves to Part Two as soon as it is clear that the child understands the task by providing a response for Puppet C.

Puppet A: My name is:
    [turn to Puppet B:] My name is
    [turn to Puppet C:] My name is
Puppet A: My favorite ice cream is:
    [Puppet B:] chocolate ice cream
    [Puppet C:]
Puppet A: I am:
    [Puppet B:] 4 years old.
    [Puppet C:]

Puppet A: My favorite toy is:
   [Puppet B:] my teddy bear
   [Puppet C:]
Puppet A: My favorite color is:
   [Puppet B:] blue
   [Puppet C:]

If the child does not understand the task, the therapist should go back through the statements and have Puppet B prompt the child to help Puppet C give a response. This continues until the task is clearly understood by the child. Part Two should not be begun until it is clear that the child understands the task. If the child does not seem to understand what is expected in Part One, Part Two will probably not be understood.

Note: Some children catch on quite quickly and do not seem to like the repetition necessary in Part One. For these children, it is permissible to go directly to Part Two. Although it is preferable to write down the child's responses immediately, because the therapist has a puppet on each hand, it may be necessary to record responses immediately following the administration of Part One.

Part Two
Directions: In Part Two, Puppet A states the sentence stem. The sentence is stated directly to Puppet C. The response made by the child (Puppet C) should be written in the blank immediately. Some children will give two responses, one for the puppet and one for themselves. Both responses should be noted.

1. My favorite food is _____ .
2. I love to _____ .
3. Outside, I play with _____ .
4. Mommy is _____ .
5. Daddy is _____ .
6. My favorite TV show is _____ .
7. (If applicable) My brother's name is _____ .
8. (If applicable) My sister's name is _____ .
9. I like to pretend to be _____ .
10. If I were bigger, I would _____ .
11. At night when I sleep, I _____ .
12. I am afraid of _____ .
13. I hate _____ .
14. The best secret is _____ .
15. The worst secret is _____ .
16. Mommy is nice when _____ .
17. Daddy is nice when _____ .
18. Daddy is mean when _____ .
19. Mommy is mean when _____ .
20. I am happiest when _____ .
21. I am saddest when _____ .
22. I get scared when _____ .
23. My biggest problem is _____ .
24. The worst thing about me is _____ .
25. With my hands, I like to touch _____ .
26. With my hands, I don't like to touch _____ .
27. Someone I don't like to touch me is _____ .
28. Someone I like to touch me is _____ .
29. My body is _____ .
30. I don't like to be touched on my _____ .
31. A secret I am not supposed to tell is _____ .
32. I am the maddest when _____ .
33. I am the happiest when _____ .
34. I like to pretend to be _____ .

the puppet as a prompt. For some children, the use of the puppet provides a tool that makes the task easier because they do not need to directly tell the therapist how they feel. For others, modeling with the puppet explains the task to them; thereafter, they are comfortable responding freely to the task without the puppets. In either case, the task is introduced with puppets, which are familiar to and enjoyed by most children.

Any sentence stems can be used with the Puppet Sentence-Completion Task. This is helpful because particular sentence stems may elicit information about certain areas. Stems such as "The worst secret is . . ." or "When I am in bed, I think about . . ." may provide structure for the sexually abused child to convey information that would be difficult to reveal in an interview. Stems such as "When my mommy and daddy stopped living together . . ." may be useful with children experiencing the divorce of their parents. Ideally, a set of common stems might be used with all children, with special stems, unique to specific life situations or presenting problems, added (e.g., children of divorced parents, children who have been sexually abused). Preliminary use of this instrument suggests that it can be understood by children as young as 3 years of age.

THERAPIST-CREATED MEASURES.   Various authors have written about the use of drawings to depict feelings in assessment and treatment of young children (e.g., Bierman, 1983; Harter, 1977, 1983; Hughes & Baker, 1990). By providing concrete referents, such as pictures depicting people with various facial expressions, children may be able to provide information about their own feelings. A preschooler may not respond to questions such as "How do you feel about your new sister?" However, if the child is offered pictures with faces showing simple emotional expressions (e.g., sad, happy, mad) he or she may be able to point to the picture that describes his or her feelings. Another option is for the therapist to show pictures of a family with a new baby to which the child can respond by telling what the child in the picture is feeling. Numerous variations exist and are limited only by the creativity of the therapist and child together.

Since young children have difficulty understanding the existence of contradictory feelings, their all-or-nothing thinking offers a very limited view of their own emotions. Harter (1977) used drawings depicting conflicting views (e.g., smart/dumb: happy/sad; good/bad) to show that sometimes an individual can feel two seemingly conflicting feelings. The use of pictures to help describe feelings seems to be particularly useful for the child with limited verbal abilities.

Introduction/Orientation to Therapy

PREPARATION OF THE CHILD FOR CBPT.   What the parents tell the child about treatment is important, although preparation for CBPT is similar to preparation for other types of play therapy. The parents should be encouraged to be straightforward with the child. It is often helpful for parents to explain to the child that they are concerned about the child's problem. The problem should be described to the child in a simple, concrete, nonjudgmental manner. Further, the parents should indicate that they are all going to talk to someone who "helps kids by taking and playing with them." It is important not to lie (e.g., "We are going shopping"), threaten (e.g., "You need to behave or the doctor won't talk to you"), or bribe ("If you talk to the doctor, I will buy you a treat") the child (Dodds, 1985).

Bibliotherapy is one useful source for preparing a child for treatment. A picture book recently published by The American Psychological Association, *A Child's First Book about Play Therapy* (Nemiroff & Annunziata, 1990), provides an introduction to play therapy for 4-to-7-year-old children. This and other related books can be used by the parent(s) to help the child begin to understand the experience of play therapy. Therapists might also consider its use in therapy sessions.

INVOLVING SIGNIFICANT ADULTS IN TREATMENT.   Children are referred to therapy because their behavior is of concern to an adult, often the parent. Therefore, the inclusion of the significant adult(s) in the child's treatment is an important consideration. Parents are usually involved from the beginning, when the therapist meets with them to gather assessment data. After the parents are interviewed and the initial evaluation of the child is completed, it is usually best to meet with the parents to present the evaluation findings and to agree on a treatment plan. The treatment plan may primarily involve individual CBPT with the child, work with the parent(s), or a combination of CBPT and parent work. Decisions are made based on the therapist's assessment regarding whether or not the parents will need help in modifying their interaction with the child or if the child will need assistance in implementing a treatment program outside of therapy.

When the primary work is with the child, it is still important to meet with the parents regularly. During these parent sessions, the therapist will obtain information about the child, continue to monitor the parents' interaction with the child, and work on areas of concern. The therapist may also provide, as needed, support for the parents as well as information on issues related to child development. Although the nature of the work with parents will vary, parents are usually seen regularly when their child is in CBPT.

Middle Stages

As treatment progresses into the middle stages, therapy is focused on assisting the child in learning adaptive responses to deal with individual situations, problems, or stressors. As gains are noted, the therapist will also need to focus on two key concerns: First is helping the child generalize what is learned in therapy so that it may be applied in other settings. Second is helping the child avoid relapses after therapy is terminated.

GENERALIZATION ACROSS SETTINGS.   One obvious goal of treatment is for the child to maintain the adaptive behaviors learned in therapy in the natural environment after treatment has terminated. Despite successful outcome in many studies of cognitive-behavioral therapy with children, an overall lack of generalization of treatment effects and a lack of maintenance of gains is often noted (Braswell & Kendall, 1988). For children, the maintenance of newly acquired skills may depend in part on the attitudes and behaviors of significant adults in the child's life. Additionally, therapy should be designed to promote and facilitate generalization, rather than assuming that it will occur naturally.

In order for generalization to occur, specific training might be required. There is no reason to expect that children will generalize from one setting to another or from reactions from one caretaker to those of another. The therapist needs to build in mechanisms for this. As noted previously, generalization may be enhanced by interventions that address it directly and resemble real-life situations as much as possible; significant individuals in the child's natural environment should be involved in treatment and should be a source of reinforcement of the child's adaptive behavior; procedures that promote self-control of behavior should be utilized; and interventions should continue past the initial acquisition of the skill to ensure that adequate learning has taken place.

RELAPSE PREVENTION.   Setbacks are part of learning. Both child and parent must be prepared for setbacks and not be discouraged by them. Part of the original treatment must be geared towards the possibility of setbacks. This may involve preparing the parent and the child for what to expect, but also for what to do when certain things happen. In so doing, the therapist and the family identify high-risk situations as those that might present a threat to the child's sense of control and ability to manage situations. Marlatt and Gordon (1985) describe "inoculating" individuals against failure, so that, when there are road blocks, the individual does not panic. Although some of this inoculation will occur in CBPT, much work will take place between parent and child outside of therapy.

Termination

Preparation for termination is usually a gradual process during which, over several sessions, the therapist and child talk about the end of therapy. Children and parents (and therapists, too) often approach termination with mixed feelings. It is often helpful to remind the child of the number of sessions remaining until the final appointment. With younger children, the therapist might need to provide a concrete reference to the number (e.g., a piece of paper with marks for the number of appointments remaining). Termination may mean intermittent appointments until the therapy is eventually ended. These appointments may be scheduled over a period of time with a particular end event in mind (e.g., beginning of school year, remarriage of a parent). Thus, for example, a child who appears to be ready to terminate in March but who has concerns about the new school year may be seen sporadically through the spring and summer so that the final appointment can take place *after* the child begins school. By spacing the final appointments several weeks apart, the therapist communicates a message that the child can manage without the therapist. This can also be conveyed by positive reinforcement from the therapist for how well the child has been doing between appointments.

It may be difficult for the young child to think about therapy as finished. Many children are upset by the thought of never seeing the therapist again. For this reason, it is important that the children not believe that bad behavior will insure that they will return to the therapist. Some reassurance may be felt by children if they are told that it is all right to send a card to the therapist. Alternatively, they may appreciate knowing that the parent will call periodically to let the therapist know how the child is doing. It is important in CBPT to have an open-door policy. For children, knowing that one can return to treatment can be very important, regardless of whether or not they ever need to return.

Materials

Play materials used in CBPT are similar to those found in any type of play therapy. These include, but are not limited to, crayons and paper, blocks, dolls, dollhouse, and puppets. Axline (1947) provided a list of toys that is still cited as a guideline for materials in a play therapy office, despite the numbers of new toys created since that list was published. In general, the more directive techniques found in CBPT require planning and forethought regarding the choice of materials. However, it is probably more important that options are available than that the therapy room is stocked with an infinite range of toys and play materials (e.g., the therapist and encopretic child mentioned previously used a plastic storage container to represent the toilet used with the toy bear). It may be possible to buy materials to fit every possible therapeutic situation, but it may be neither necessary nor desirable. By encouraging flexibility, the child is encouraged to be creative, and the therapist need not buy specific toys for each child.

SUMMARY AND DISCUSSION

The application of cognitive-behavioral interventions with very young children is still in its early stages, largely due to disbelief by many that such work can be done. CBPT incorporates behavioral and cognitive interventions into a play therapy paradigm and integrates these in a developmentally sensitive way. It places a strong emphasis on the child's involvement and active participation in treatment. The principles of cognitive therapy apply to children with minor modifications. Thus, CBPT is based on the cognitive model of emotional disorders. It is brief, time-limited, structured, directive, and problem-oriented. It depends on a sound therapeutic relationship in which one role of therapy is educational. CBPT is a collaborative process, although the nature of collaboration between child and therapist is different from that between adult and therapist. Both the inductive method and Socratic method are important, but they play a different role in CBPT.

CBPT is similar to other play therapies in its reliance on a positive therapeutic relationship, with rapport and trust considered critical elements in engaging the child in treatment. Similarly, play activities as a means of communication between therapist and child are universal to play therapies. Finally, in all play therapies, efforts are made to communicate the message that therapy is a safe place.

Differences among various play therapies include: the establishment of treatment goals, therapist selection of play materials and activities, use of therapy as educational in CBPT as contrasted with more child-directed, noneducationally oriented traditional therapies. CBPT builds on the child's strengths by using praise and reinforcement appropriately and by providing connections or interpretations where appropriate. In contrast, more traditional therapies attempt to avoid the use of praise, and, in nondirective therapies, interpretations must come first from the child.

Initial efforts to make CBPT developmentally appropriate have suggested that cognitive-behavioral approaches can be adapted for very young children. This chapter has reviewed the theory and practice of CBPT and used case examples to highlight the application of CBPT. Further clinical work and empirical study will be important in continuing to refine this therapeutic approach.

REFERENCES

Achenbach, T. M., & Edelbrock, C. (1983). *Manual for the Child Behavior Checklist and Revised Child Behavior Profile.* Burlington, VT: University of Vermont, Department of Psychiatry.

Axline, V. (1947). *Play therapy.* Boston: Houghton-Mifflin.

Bandura, A. (1977). *Social learning theory.* Englewood Cliffs, NJ: Prentice-Hall.

Barden, R. C., Zelko, F. A., Duncan, S. W., & Masters, J. C. (1980). Children's consensual knowledge about the experiential determinants of emotion. *Journal of Personality and Social Psychology, 39,* 968–976.

Beck, A. T. (1963). Thinking and depression. *Archives of General Psychiatry, 9,* 324–333.

Beck, A. T. (1964). Thinking and depression: 2. Theory and therapy. *Archives of general psychiatry, 10,* 561–571.

Beck, A. T. (1972). *Depression: Causes and treatment.* Philadelphia: University of Pennsylvania Press.

Beck, A. T. (1976). *Cognitive therapy and the emotional disorders.* New York: International Universities Press.

Beck, A. T., & Emery, G. (1985). *Anxiety disorders and phobias: A cognitive perspective.* New York: Basic Books.

Beck, A. T., Rush, A. J., Shaw, B. F., & Emery, G. (1979). *Cognitive therapy of depression.* New York: Guilford Press.

Bellak, L., & Bellak, S. S. (1949). *Children's Apperception Test (CAT).* New York: CPS.

Bierman, K. L. (1983). Cognitive development and clinical interviews with children. In B. B. Lahey & A. Kazdin (Eds.), *Advances in clinical child psychology* (Vol. 6, pp. 217–250). New York: Plenum Press.

Brady, J. P., Davison, G. C., Dewald, P. A., Egan, G., Fadmina, J., Frank, J. D., Gill, M. M., Hoffman, I., Kempler, W., Lazarus, A. A., Raimy, V., Rotter, J. B., & Strupp, H. H. (1980). Some views on effective principles of psychotherapy. *Cognitive Therapy and Research, 4,* 269–306.

Braswell, L., & Kendall, P. C. (1988). Cognitive-behavioral methods with children. In K. S. Dobson (Ed.), *Handbook of cognitive behavior therapy* (pp. 167–213). New York: Guilford Press.

Burns, D. (1980). *Feeling good.* New York: New American Library.

Campbell, S. (1990). *Behavior problems in preschool children.* New York: Guilford Press.

Cox, F. N. (1953). Sociometric status and individual adjustment before and after play therapy. *Journal of Abnormal and Social Psychology, 48,* 354–356.

DeRubeis, R. J., & Beck, A. T. (1988). Cognitive therapy. In K. S. Dobson (Ed.), *Handbook of cognitive behavior therapy* (pp. 273–306). New York: Guilford Press.

Dodds, J.B. (1985). *A child psychotherapy primer.* New York: Human Sciences Press.

Dorfman, E. (1958). Personality outcomes of client-centered child therapy. *Psychological Monographs, 72,* (whole No. 456), 1–22.

Drabman, R., Spitalnik, R., & O'Leary, K. D. (1973). Teaching self-control to disruptive children. *Journal of Abnormal Psychology, 82,* 110–116.

Ellis, A. (1958). Rational psychotherapy. *Journal of General Psychology, 59,* 35–49.

Ellis, A. (1962). *Reason and emotion in psychotherapy.* New York: Lyle Stuart.

Ellis, A. (1971). *Growth through reason: Verbatim cases in rational-emotive therapy and cognitive-behavior therapy.* New York: Lyle Stuart.

Emery, G., Bedrosian, R., & Garber, J. (1983). Cognitive therapy with depressed children and adolescents. In D. P. Cantwell & G. A. Carlson (Eds.), *Affective disorders in childhood and adolescence — An update* (pp. 445–471). New York: Spectrum.

Esman, A. H. (1983). Psychoanalytic play therapy. In C. E. Schaefer and K. J. O'Connor (Eds.), *Handbook of play therapy* (pp. 11–20). New York: Wiley.

Fixsen, D. L., Phillips, E. L., & Wolf, M. M. (1972). Achievement place: The reliability of self-reporting and peer-reporting and their effects on behavior. *Journal of Applied Behavior Analysis, 5,* 19–30.

Freud, A. (1928). *Introduction to the technique of child analysis.* New York: Nervous and Mental Disease Publishing.

Freud, A. (1946). *The psychoanalytic treatment of children.* London: Imago.

Garber, J. (1982). The children's events schedule. Unpublished manuscript, University of Minnesota.

Gelman, R., & Baillargeon, R. (1983). A review of some Piagetian concepts. In J. H. Flavell & E. M. Markman (Eds.), P. Mussen (Series Ed.), *Handbook of child psychology: Vol. 3. Cognitive development* (pp. 167–230). New York: Wiley.

Harter, S. (1977). A cognitive-developmental approach to children's expression of conflicting feelings and a technique to facilitate such expression in play therapy. *Journal of Consulting and Clinical Psychology, 45,* 417–432.

Harter, S. (1983). Cognitive-developmental considerations in the conduct of play therapy. In C. Schaefer & K. J. O'Connor (Eds.), *Handbook of play therapy* (pp. 95–127). New York: Wiley.

Hughes, J. N., & Baker, D. B. (1990). *The Clinical Child Interview.* New York: Guilford Press.

Ireton, H., & Thwing, E. (1972). *Minnesota Child Development Inventory.* Minneapolis: Authors.

Jacobson, E. (1938). *Progressive relaxation.* Chicago: University of Chicago Press.

Kazdin, A. E. (1975). *Behavior modification in applied settings.* Homewood, IL: Dorsey.

Kendall, P. C. (1991). *Child and adolescent therapy.* New York: Guilford Press.

Kendall, P. C., & Braswell, L. (1985). *Cognitive-behavioral therapy for impulsive children.* New York: Guilford Press.

Klein, M. (1932). The psycho-analysis of children. London: Hogarth Press.

Knell, S. M. (1993a). *Cognitive-behavioral play therapy.* Northvale, NJ: Jason Aronson.

Knell, S. M. (1993b). To show and not tell: Cognitive-behavioral play therapy. In T. Kottman & C. Schaefer (Eds.), *Play therapy in action: A casebook for practitioners* (pp. 169–208). Northvale, NJ: Jason Aronson.

Knell, S. M., & Moore, D. J. (1990). Cognitive-behavioral play therapy in the treatment of encopresis. *Journal of Clinical Child Psychology, 19,* 55–60.

Lovitt, T. C., & Curtis, K. A. (1969). Academic response rate as a function of teacher- and self-imposed contingencies. *Journal of Applied Behavior Analysis, 2,* 49–53.

Lowenfeld, M. (1939). The world pictures of children. *British Journal of Medical Psychology, 18,* 65–101.

Lowenfeld, M. (1950). The nature and the use of the Lowenfeld World Technique in work with children and adults. *Journal of Psychology, 30,* 325–331.

Marlatt, G. A., & Gordon, J. R. (1985). *Relapse prevention: Maintenance strategies in the treatment of addictive behaviors.* New York: Guilford Press.

Masten, A. S., & Braswell, L. (1991). Developmental psychopathology: An integrative framework. In P. R. Martin (Ed.), *Handbook of behavior therapy and psychological science* (pp. 35–56). New York: Pergamon Press.

McArthur, D. S. & Roberts, G. E. (1982). *Roberts Apperception Test for Children Manual.* Los Angeles, CA: Western Psychological Services.

Meichenbaum, D. (1985). *Stress inoculation training.* New York: Pergamon Press.

Murray, H. A. (1943). *Thematic Apperception Test Manual.* Cambridge, MA.: Harvard University Press.

Nemiroff, M.A., & Annunziata, J. (1990). *A child's first book about play therapy.* Washington, DC: American Psychological Association.

Ollendick, T. H., & Cerney, J. A. (1981). *Clinical behavior therapy with children.* New York: Plenum Press.

Paul, G. L. (1967). Outcome research in psychotherapy. *Journal of Consulting Psychology 31,* 109–118.

Phillips, R. D. (1985). Whistling in the dark? A review of play therapy research. *Psychotherapy, 22,* 752–760.

Piper, W. (1950). *The little engine that could.* New York: Platt & Munk.

Risley, T. R., & Hart, B. (1968). Developing correspondence between the non-verbal and verbal behavior of school children. *Journal of Applied Behavior Analysis, 1,* 267–281.

Rogers, C. R., Gendlin, G. T., Kiesler, D. V., & Truax, C. B. (1967). *The therapeutic relationship and its impact: A study of psychotherapy with schizophrenics.* Madison, WI: University of Wisconsin Press.

Ruma, C. (1993). Cognitive-behavioral play therapy with sexually abused children. In S.M. Knell (Ed.), *Cognitive-behavioral play therapy* (pp. 199–230). Northvale, NJ: Jason Aronson.

Wolpe, J. (1958). *Psychotherapy by reciprocal inhibition.* Stanford, CA: Stanford University Press.

Wolpe, J. (1982). *The practice of behavior therapy* (3rd ed.). Oxford: Pergamon Press.

CHAPTER 6

Gestalt Play Therapy

VIOLET OAKLANDER

INTRODUCTION

Gestalt therapy is a humanistic, process-oriented mode of therapy that is concerned with the healthy functioning of the total organism—senses, body, emotions, and intellect. A number of theoretical principles from the body of Gestalt therapy theory directly relate to and influence work with children. These include the kind of relationship developed between client and therapist; the concept of organismic self-regulation; contact-boundary disturbances as manifested by children; how the sense of self is perceived from this framework; and the role of awareness, experience, and resistance.

BASIC CONCEPTS

The I/Thou Relationship

The *I/Thou relationship* is a particular type of relationship derived from the philosophical writings of Martin Buber (1958). Several principles are involved in this kind of relationship. For one, the therapist brings herself or himself fully to the session, willing to be affected by the client. There is no artificial wall set up between therapist and client. Of this relationship, Buber (1966) stated:

> I-Thou can be spoken only with the whole being. Concentration and fusion into the whole being can never take place through my agency, nor can it ever take place without me. I become through my relation to the Thou; as I become I, I say Thou. All real living is meeting. (p. 48)

Further, the therapist has a responsibility to meet the child, however he or she presents the self, with respect and honor. The therapist is genuine and congruent, never manipulative. At the same time, the therapist must respect her or his own limits and boundaries and not lose herself or himself to the client. The therapist, too, holds the attitude that supports the full, healthy potential of the child.

Organismic Self-Regulation

Gestalt therapy emphasizes the process of *organismic self-regulation*. Fritz Perls (1973), one of the founders of Gestalt therapy, wrote:

> All life and all behavior are governed by the process which scientists call homeostasis, and which the layman calls adaptation. The homeostatic process is the process by which the organism maintains its equilibrium and therefore its health under varying conditions. Homeo-

stasis is thus the process by which the organism satisfies its needs. Since its needs are many, and each need upsets the equilibrium, the homeostatic process goes on all the time. (p. 4)

Children react to family dysfunction, trauma, crises, and loss in fairly common developmental ways. They tend to blame themselves and take responsibility for whatever happens. They fear rejection, abandonment, and not having their basic needs met. So, in their everlasting quest for health and their thrust for growth and life, they will do anything to get their needs met. Often, due to lack of emotional and intellectual maturity, they will develop inappropriate ways of being in the world—ways that they assume will serve to make life better and that they hope will meet their needs. One child may become quiet and withdrawn—behaviors that are often positively reinforced—as a result of some undue stress in the family. As the child grows, withdrawn and quiet behavior becomes his or her process, or way, of being in the world. Another child may repress much anger, having learned that anger is an unacceptable emotion in his or her family. The organism, in its crusade for balance and equilibrium, appears to cause the child to express this anger in harmful, devious ways.

Contact-Boundary Disturbances

The child, in his or her quest for survival, will inhibit, block, repress, and restrict various aspects of the organism: the senses, the body, the emotions, the intellect. These restrictions become contact-boundary disturbances and cause interruptions of the natural, healthy process of organismic self-regulation.

When the child inhibits the organism, adversarial behaviors and symptoms develop. Some children will retroflect (i.e., pull in) the energy that appears to need to be thrust outward. In essence, they will, instead, do to themselves what they might like to do to others. They will have headaches, stomachaches, tear their hair out, gouge themselves. Other children will deflect their feelings, turning away from the true feelings of grief or anger. They will have tantrums, punch and hit others, and generally engage in acting-out behaviors.

Some children will avoid their painful emotions by spacing out, daydreaming, fantasizing. Others become hyperactive. These and other behaviors are called *contact-boundary disturbances* (sometimes called *resistances* in Gestalt therapy literature) because they affect the child's healthy contact with the self and the environment.

According to Korb, Gorrell, and Van de Reit (1989):

Contact takes place at the boundary between the organism and the environment or between the organism and other parts of itself. The process of assimilation or rejection of owning or disowning, of identification with or alienation from takes place at the boundary. It is in this process that we define ourselves in relation to our environment. We become clear as to what is "me" or "not me." As we grow, we constantly change our boundary to include new learnings and experiences. (p. 55)

When children restrict and inhibit aspects of the organism, particularly emotions, the sense of self is diminished. The major developmental task of children, from birth through adolescence, is to separate and develop their own boundaries and self-support. However, children basically have very little self-support. They lack the ability to deal with the environment on their own. It is terrifying for a child to imagine that he or she might be disapproved of, and perhaps rejected and abandoned, and not get basic needs met. Yet the struggle for separation is essential.

When children are thwarted in this endeavor, they attempt to find a semblance of self in any way they can. Sometimes deflection such as hitting or outbursts of anger gives them a feeling of self and energy. However, the feeling quickly dissipates. A child never says, "What I am doing isn't working, isn't meeting my needs. Maybe I can try something better." Instead, the child will continue, and even accelerate, the inappropriate behavior.

Sense of Self

Other contact-boundary disturbances are confluence, projection, and introjection. *Confluent behavior* is common among children who have difficulty establishing their own boundaries. Confluence has to do with merging: the antithesis of separateness. The infant feels as one with the mother, and the struggle to separate and individuate becomes a life-long process. When the child has been injured, traumatized, abandoned, or rejected, the struggle for separateness is fraught with anxiety for the child. The self is so fragile that the child needs enormous assurance that he or she exists. Being good, pleasing others, literally hanging onto someone, are typical aspects of confluent behavior among children and deceptively provide some sense of self. Children who behave in that manner need continual feedback and reinforcement from others.

Projection is a classic way that children have of denying their own personal experience. Many children will lie and deny because they have little ego strength to take responsibility for their own actions. They will blame others for bad things that have happened. They will project many of their own feelings onto others because it is too difficult and dangerous to own these feelings. For some children, saying "My father is always angry at me" is less difficult to proclaim than "I am very angry at my father." Projection is a way of protecting one's fragile self and often results in the loss of one's own perceptual abilities.

Introjects play an important part in the growth and development of children. *Introjects* are basically messages about the self and how to be in the world that children absorb and incorporate into themselves. A child lacks the maturity to reflect and discriminate about whether or not something is true and whether or not it appropriately applies to him. The child believes everything he or she hears about the self. Many of these messages are faulty and in direct conflict with the healthy developmental needs of the child. The child might hear, in overt or covert ways, that he or she is stupid, bad, lazy, inconsiderate, and so forth. These introjects, in combination with the child's basic egocentricity (taking responsibility for whatever happens), play havoc with the sense of self, self-esteem, and self-concept. Messages about the self and about how one ought to be in the world become deeply ingrained and can follow the child into adulthood.

Process Therapy

Gestalt therapy is considered to be a process therapy; attention is paid to the *what* and *how* of behavior rather than the *why*. An awareness of one's process can lead to change. When the therapist can help the client become more aware of what he or she is doing and how he or she is doing it within the context of dissatisfaction, the client then has the choice to make changes.

Polster and Polster (1973) wrote:

The awarenesses which concern us in Gestalt Therapy are also those which help restore the unity of the individual's total and integrated function. Before he can alter his behavior in any way the individual must first encompass the sensations and feelings which go along with it. Recovery of the acceptability of awareness—no matter what it may reveal—is a crucial step on the road to the development of new behavior. (p. 210)

Awareness and Experience

Awareness encompasses many aspects of life and of the individual. Along with becoming aware of one's process, awareness of sensations, feelings, wants, needs, thought processes, and actions strengthens one's sense of self and self-determination.

As the child finds himself through the therapy experience, he becomes more aware of who he is, what he feels, what he needs, what he wants, what he does and how he does it. He then finds he has choices to make and often will experiment with them. He will drop the unproductive behaviors that bring him into therapy. "I don't have to steal any more to get attention," said one boy. "I just ask for it now." (Oaklander, 1982, p. 71-72)

Experience is the key to awareness, especially in work with children. Remembering what it is like to eat an orange pales in comparison with the actual eating of an orange. Providing varied experiences for children is an essential component of the therapeutic process and will be discussed in the Procedure and Technique section.

Resistance

Resistance in the Gestalt therapy context plays an important part in therapy. It is not seen as a client's unwillingness to participate cooperatively in the therapy process, but as a loss of contact on the part of the client. Children reveal many behavioral manifestations, as previously discussed, in their efforts to cope and survive in their lives. These manifestations are seen as resistances because they sidestep the real issues and emotions. Resistance implies a closing down, a cutting off of aspects of the organism, be it the senses, the body, the emotions, or the intellect. This inhibition impairs the sense of self and results in faulty contact with the environment.

The manifestation of resistances is the main focus of therapeutic work. Resistances help the therapist make assessments regarding the kinds of therapeutic experiences the child needs; for example, if a child displays resistance by desensitizing the self, presenting her- or himself as rigid and mechanical, the therapist may need to include in a treatment plan a variety of activities, experiments, and experiences that will gradually free the functioning of the child's self.

Resistance takes many forms with children. It is to be expected because it is their only way of protecting themselves. In fact, a confluent child will need experiences that will call forth some resistance. As the child begins to trust the therapist, he or she will allow him or herself tentatively to open and to risk. Resistance is met over and over during the course of therapy. The child will open for a bit and then close up, retreating into his or her shell much as a turtle might. Each time the child comes up against a fearful place, he or she will resist. This kind of resistance must be honored.

Every time we come to this place of resistance we are making progress, for within the wall of resistance there is a door that opens into new areas of growth. This place is fearful to the child and is akin to what Fritz Perls called the impasse. When we come to an impasse we are witnessing a person's process of giving up old strategies and feelings as though there were no support. When we recognize the impasse (resistance place) for what it is, we can anticipate that the child is on the verge of a new way of being, a new discovery. So each time resistance appears we can know that we are encountering not a rigid boundary, but a place that has just beyond it a stretching, a growing edge. (Oaklander, 1982, p. 71)

When the therapist respects the child's resistance and as the child develops more and more self-support, the child is more amenable to going a little farther in his or her therapeutic journey.

PROCEDURE AND TECHNIQUE

There is a specific process to this form of therapy with children that is directly related to the theoretical assumptions made in Gestalt therapy. This process consists of the following components:

- Developing the relationship
- Evaluating and establishing contact
- Strengthening the child's sense of self and self-support
- Encouraging emotional expression
- Helping the child learn to nurture the self
- Focusing on the child's process—particularly aspects of his or her way of being in the world that may be inappropriate
- Finalizing the therapy

Relationship

Essential to any good therapy is the *relationship* between the therapist and the client. In work with children, the relationship takes on very great proportions, for it is the foundation of the therapeutic process. Moreover, the relationship itself can be curative.

CASE ILLUSTRATION

Jeannie, age 8, was left in a foster home for almost a year after her birth. Her birth-mother was unsure if she wanted this baby, and was plagued by ambivalence about giving the child up. She took her back when the year was up. Then, when Jeannie was almost 2, the mother finally gave her up for adoption. Jeannie's trust level was severely impaired. She was withdrawn and distant even from her adoptive parents, and they brought her into therapy fearing that she had schizoid tendencies.

The therapist focused treatment on the relationship. Honoring Jeannie's mistrustfulness, the therapist was gentle and cautious in her interactions as she offered activities that the child might enjoy, such as coloring together in an attractive coloring book. Within a few weeks, Jeannie appeared to feel safe enough to chat with the therapist and then to tentatively experiment with more expressive activities. Her adoptive parents were guided toward a mild, sensitive, though loving approach toward Jeannie, rather than the over-whelming stance they had previously employed. Gradually Jeannie become more and more responsive.

Contact

Contact involves a connection with the environment as well as the self. When the child is fully engaged in reading a book, he or she is contactful with that book. The child's mind is not wandering—his or her concentration and energy are completely directed toward the book. The therapist comes into such contact with the client in order to facilitate the I/Thou relationship. The therapist is not only in contact with the client, but with him- or herself—having awareness of his or her own body sensations, emotions, and thought processes. The therapist brings his or her senses into the present situation, cognizant of what he or she sees, hears, touches, smells, tastes. In other words, the therapist is fully present. The child, however, may have difficulty staying in contact.

Children who are anxious, worried, and disturbed—children who are blocking feelings—cannot sustain contact but must avoid awareness of self as well as of aspects of the environment in order to protect themselves. They will engage in one or more of the contact-boundary disturbances described previously. When children avoid contact, the self is diminished. They block full expression of aspects of the self. Full use of their senses is restrained, the body is restricted, the emotions are repressed, and the mind is not available for its fullest potential. Some children find it so painful to sustain contact that they will find any means to avoid it. The focus of therapy at that point, then, is to help the child maintain contact—to bring the self fully to the session.

CASE ILLUSTRATION

Jason had many good reasons in his life to avoid contact. He presented himself as extremely hyperactive (medication had been tried to no avail). In the therapist's office, he ran around and around the room, picking up one object after another and throwing it down. The therapist attempted, in a gentle, accepting way, to engage Jason. She followed after him, commenting about each object he discarded. He appeared not to hear. At each subsequent session, it appeared that Jason stopped a few seconds longer before running on to the next thing. By the fourth session, he actually responded to the therapist's puppet with a puppet of his own. Gradually, Jason was able to interact with the therapist and engage in self-enhancing activities and emotional expression. His hyperactivity diminished not only in the therapy sessions, but in his outside life as well.

Staying with the client, without judgment, appears to promote contactful interaction. Starting with anything that may interest the child can be helpful, even if it appears to have little therapeutic value. Contact is a prerequisite for deeper therapy.

Resistance is closely related to contact. A highly resistant child is not contactful. Others, who appear to be in contact for part of the time, will abruptly close down. They become resistant during the course of the therapy, evidenced often by a sudden depletion of energy. This is an indication that behind the resistance is material that the child is not ready to confront. This kind of resistance must be respected because the child is evidencing a lack of self-support—ego strength—to deal with such material. As the self is strengthened, the child becomes more amenable to deeper work.

Strengthening the Self

Children need *support within the self* in order to express blocked emotions. Children who have experienced trauma, be it molestation, abuse, the death of a loved one, or the divorce of their parents, block their emotions relating to the trauma and have little experience in knowing how to express them. Because children are basically egocentric and take everything personally as part of their normal developmental process, they take responsibility and blame themselves for whatever trauma occurs. Children, too, take in many negative introjects—faulty beliefs about themselves—because they do not have the cognitive ability to discriminate between the accurate and the inaccurate. These negative messages cause fragmentation, inhibit healthy growth and integration, and are the roots of a self-deprecating attitude and low self-esteem.

Helping the child develop a *strong sense of self* gives him or her a sense of well-being and a positive feeling of self, as well as the inner strength to express those buried emotions. Giving the child experiences that will stimulate and intensify the use of the senses is an important step toward empowering the self. Most children who are troubled will desensitize themselves as a way of armoring and protecting. Experiences with seeing, hearing, touching, tasting, and smelling—modalities that are actually the functions of contact—focus new awareness on one's senses. Activities are designed depending on the age of the child. Jason spent one entire session looking through a kaleidoscope and contactfully directing the therapist to see what he could see.

The Senses

The following are some brief examples of experiments with the senses for enhanced sensation:

Touching: finger painting; putting objects in a bag and guessing what they are; describing the feel of various textures; using wet clay; moving the child's hands through sand

Seeing: looking at various pictures that have much detail; doing simple sketches of flowers and fruit

Listening: painting while listening to music; matching sounds with percussion instruments; using a toy xylophone, hitting various tones to see which are higher or lower, louder or softer

Tasting: tasting segments of an orange and comparing that taste with the therapist's segments; talking about favorite (and not so favorite) tastes; tasting something sweet and something sour

Smelling: provide experiences with the smell of flowers, fruit, grass, and so forth; place distinctive aromas in opaque containers—perfume, mustard, banana, apple slice, onion, and others—and ask the child to identify the smell (Oaklander, 1988)

The Body

Consistent with Gestalt therapy's attention to all aspects of the child's organism, attention is paid to the child's use of the body. Troubled children restrict and disconnect themselves from their bodies, particularly children who have been molested and abused. The therapist can provide numerous experiences to help children heighten awareness of their bodies.

Pantomime games, for example, are useful for this kind of awareness—children learn to exaggerate the movements of various parts of the body in order to get the message across. Also useful would be participation in a therapeutic body movement group. In the safe boundary of the therapy setting, children can experience various self-enhancing activities. Giving children opportunities to make choices, feel mastery, and to exert some power and control can strengthen the sense of self.

CASE ILLUSTRATION

Ten-year-old Julie had suffered years of sexual molestation and physical abuse before disclosure. She walked woodenly, hunched her shoulders, and had little awareness of her body sensations. Although she progressed well in therapy, her body posture remained the same. Some body movement and body awareness activities helped, but the most improvement occurred after she was referred to a therapeutic body movement group.

Julie, who had never had any control over her life, and, in fact, was rendered utterly powerless, after several weeks in therapy, began to take control of the sessions. She invented games with a soft ball; she directed various play activities such as school, doctor, and restaurant, advising the therapist of her role and dialogue in the games. The therapist energetically submitted to Julie's directions, much to Julie's obvious delight. Though this was a play situation, Julie appeared to revel in her power and her control within the limits of the play. This was a new and valuable experience for her.

Defining the Self

Helping the child strengthen the self can be a cognitive experience at times. To define the self is to make statements regarding the likes, dislikes, wants, and needs of the self. Expressing thoughts, opinions, and ideas further defines the self. Learning to discriminate—drawing a distinction between the self and the environment—is another extension of determining the boundaries of the self: "This is who I am—this is who I'm not."

Emotional Expression

Aggressive Energy

To take action requires aggressive energy. To meet needs, whether it be eating food or expressing an emotion, involves movement. Joel Latner (1986) stated:

> Both gestalt formation and destruction are the working out of structural processes intrinsic to existence. In the process of living, we must create and destroy. These processes are aggressive ones. They do not happen by themselves. They require our active participation. (p. 25)

Gestalt destruction, in this context, refers to the closure made when a need is met. That particular need has been met, has taken another form, and a new need comes forth to be dealt with.

Aggressive energy is more than a sense of power within; it involves action. Disturbed children are confused by this kind of energy. They either push it down (retroflect) and present themselves as fearful, timid, or withdrawn; or they express the energy beyond their own boundaries (deflect) through hitting, punching, power struggles, and generally acting aggressive. Helping children to feel this energy from a solid place within themselves and to be comfortable with it is a prerequisite for the *expression of suppressed emotions*. Experiences with this kind of internal force are encapsulated in a play setting involving contactful interaction with the therapist.

CASE ILLUSTRATIONS

Julie, heretofore extremely restricted and timid, was encouraged to exhibit aggressive energy in puppet play. Although many children manifest aggression with puppets, it is usually done in a reactive rather than in a contactful way. The therapist attacked Julie's alligator puppet with a shark puppet, the shark advising the alligator, with great emphasis, "Do not bite me with your big mouth." Julie tentatively had the alligator bite the therapist's shark puppet, which "died," making loud, dying sounds. This scenario was replayed many times until Julie's puppet was biting the therapist's puppet with vigor and Julie was obviously enjoying the repeated agonizing death of the therapist's puppet. Further experiences with this kind of energy were employed through smashing clay, encounter foam-bat fights with the therapist, and other energetic games. Becoming comfortable with expressing her inner power helped Julie talk about her years of abuse and move toward the expression of her deep feelings of rage and grief.

Eight-year-old Ivan had witnessed violence in his home until his mother fled, taking him with her and leaving behind everything with which he was familiar. In his new environment, Ivan was disruptive in the classroom, bullied other children, and fought both physically and verbally with his mother. At about the midpoint in Ivan's therapy, the therapist introduced various activities involving the use of aggressive energy. Ivan enjoyed playing games of attack with the therapist using He-Man figures, shooting at a target with a rubber dart gun, and other similar games. Only then was he able to sort out and articulate his feelings about his trauma and losses. His behavior at school and at home dramatically improved.

It would appear that the child, particularly as he or she reaches latency and adolescence, will avoid dealing with the deeper feelings that are kept hidden and that interfere with healthy growth. The child has little support to deal with the intensity and weight of these feelings, and often the child suppresses the feelings to such an extent that he or she has little awareness of them.

Interventions of the therapist, through activities and experiences, based on assessment of blocked and lost aspects of the self, would appear to lead the child toward expression.

Expressing Feelings

To help children express emotions that they have kept hidden, as well as to experience and strengthen lost and stagnant parts of themselves, many creative, expressive, projective techniques are used in the therapeutic process. These techniques involve drawing, painting, and collage making and the use of pottery clay, fantasy and imagery, storytelling, puppetry, the sand tray, creative dramatics, music, metaphors, body movement, sensory awareness, and photography. Many of these mediums lend themselves to powerful projections that can evoke strong feelings.

As indicated previously, self-support is a prerequisite to emotional expression. Further, some children need to first approach expression in a cognitive manner. Talking about various feelings, making lists of their feelings, playing games that involve articulating feelings, experimenting with feelings through music, drawing happy and sad feelings, and so forth, help some children become familiar and comfortable with the *idea* of feelings. This, together with self-support activities, helps them toward authentic expression.

One way that expressive, projective techniques are used is to help the child express feelings metaphorically and then, perhaps, to own the projection. A 13-year-old girl named Susan drew a picture of a rabbit that was alone and lost in the forest. She and the therapist developed a story about this rabbit that found ways to survive in spite of its isolated state. The rabbit, though, was very sad to have lost its mother and father and sometimes sat under a tree and cried and cried. When asked by the therapist if she ever felt like that rabbit, Susan began to cry and talk about her own mother, who had abandoned her.

In another case, 10-year-old Jeffrey made a sand scene with pairs of animals fighting each other. He took the part of each animal, expressing much anger. When asked, "Do you ever feel angry like that lion?" Jeffrey began to express his own anger at his father's death.

The projective techniques can also assist the child in direct expression of emotions. The therapist asked Julie, the abused and molested child referred to earlier, to make a figure of her molester out of clay. Both the therapist and Julie began to yell loudly at the figure, and Julie subsequently smashed the clay figure with a rubber mallet.

The brother of 11-year-old John had died. John made a clay form of his brother. The therapist suggested that John talk to his brother. Tears came down his face as he told his brother how much he missed him and then, on his own, said good-bye to his brother as he picked up the clay figure and kissed it.

Not only do these devices provide concrete objects that the child finds easier to address, but also, the very act of creating them helps the child open to deeper places within the self. The child can express him- or herself through creative media in ways that would be difficult for a child to merely articulate.

Nine-year-old Gina made a graveyard scene in the sand tray and said the divorce of her parents was like a death. Eleven-year-old Michael arranged army men and army vehicles in the sand and said that the divorce of his parents was like a war. In both cases, the creations led to expression of deep emotions and, subsequently, to feelings of relief and calm.

Self-Nurturing

Self-nurturing involves helping children learn to accept the parts of themselves that they hate and to work toward feelings of integration and self-worth. Further, it teaches them skills for treating themselves well. This latter concept is revolutionary for most children because they have learned that it is selfish and bad to treat oneself well. They look, then, to others to do this job and feel disappointed when it does not happen. Adolescents feel guilty when they do nice things for themselves, which debilitates rather than strengthens.

> Even a young child, particularly the disturbed child, has a very well-developed critical self. . . . He develops powerful negative introjects and often does a better job of criticizing himself than his parents do. This judgmental stance, often well hidden from others, is detrimental to healthful growth. The child may say to himself, "I should be a better boy," but the enactment of this wish is beyond his power and comprehension. The will to "be better" enhances his despair. Self-acceptance of all of one's parts, even the most hateful, is a vital component of unimpaired, sound development. (Oaklander, 1982, p. 74)

The first part of the self-nurturing process involves digging out those hateful parts of self, which are usually negative introjects, messages about the self absorbed in early years. Children tend to identify themselves totally with those hateful parts (even though they actually cause fragmentation). Realizing that this is only one aspect of themselves is usually a new concept. Once a part is identified, the child may be asked to draw it, to make it out of clay, or to find a puppet to represent that part. The part is fully described, even exaggerated, in this manner. A dialogue ensues between the part and the child, usually evoking critical, angry statements toward the part by the child. In this manner, the child expresses the aggression outwardly, rather than inwardly, toward the self, providing self-support for the next step, which involves finding a nurturing element within the self. Projective techniques may be used, such as a fairy godmother puppet, to accept and nurture the hateful part. Realizing that the part is actually a belief from a much younger age often helps the child to develop a nurturing stance.

CASE ILLUSTRATIONS

Stephen, age 10, expressed much anger and disgust at a drawing of the clumsy part of himself, which he claimed could not do anything right and fell down and bumped into things all the time. He was then directed to choose a fairy godmother puppet from among the many puppets available who would speak to the clumsy part. He did so, and she said, in Stephen's own words, "You're not afraid to try things and I like that!" Stephen turned to the therapist with wonderment, and shouted, "That's right! I try things!" Integration was achieved at that very moment. The therapist directed Stephen to imagine that fairy godmother sitting on his shoulder each time he fell, telling him that she liked him and was glad he tried. Stephen reported in subsequent sessions that he really was not as clumsy as he originally thought.

Joanne, age 7, believed she was stupid because she had trouble learning to read. Her fairy godmother puppet said, through her own projection, "You're not so dumb—you're pretty good in math."

Julie admitted that deep down she felt she was a very bad person and deserved her abuse. She made a figure of a 4-year-old Julie out of clay, the age that she first remembered abuse. It was not difficult for her to see that this concrete little figure could not have deserved such treatment, and Julie was able to talk to her little-girl self in a nurturing way. Julie was directed by the therapist to designate one of her stuffed animals at home to be her 4-year-old self and to hug it and tell it she loved it every night. Julie followed these instructions with delight and appeared to be strengthened by this exercise.

Children have been asked to make lists of nice things they can do for themselves; this is not an easy task for some. They are then directed to do one each day, within a set time limit, keeping a record of what they do. Children have reported feelings of joy and power through these experiments. Beginning to take responsibility for one's choices in life can begin with choosing to be kind and actively loving to the self.

Focusing on the Child's Inappropriate Process

Usually, the child is brought into therapy because of symptoms and behaviors that cause concern and that interfere with healthful life and growth. These symptoms and behaviors appear to be the only way that the child, and his or her organism, know how to cope and survive in his stressful world. Generally, when the child has been in therapy and has moved through the therapeutic process, these behaviors basically drop away, and the child evidences a much more healthful mode of living and interacting.

After several months of therapy, most children have a stronger sense of self and develop appropriate behaviors: Jeannie gradually grew to trust others and to develop a strong sense of self. She began to express her emotions clearly and finally transformed herself from a meek, timid child into one who could comfortably stand up for herself. Jason, who had presented himself as severely hyperactive, no longer needed to move incessantly in order to avoid contact. He now had good contact skills, and was calm and present in most situations. Ivan no longer was disruptive at school, no longer bullied other children or was abusive to his mother.

However, with some children, hoped-for change does not take place and some of the inappropriate behaviors are retained even after much therapeutic work. It is at this time that the behaviors or symptoms are focused upon.

The Gestalt therapist's purpose in focusing on those inappropriate behaviors in this stage of the child's therapy is to provide the child with the opportunity to *fully experience the self within his or her process.* The therapist and the child can then devise experiments that will allow the child to experience himself or herself in a new light.

Gestalt therapy is considered to be process-oriented therapy, centering on the *what* and *how* of behavior. It is through the awareness and experience of behavior that change begins to take place. Change within this context is actually paradoxical in nature. Arnold Beiser (1970) stated: "Change occurs when one becomes what he is, not when he tries to become what he is not" (p. 77) Korb, Gorrell, and Van de Riet (1989) stated:

> The important change processes are not connected with trying to change. . . . Interventions, appropriately timed and directed, may lead the client to an experience and an understanding of the forces and resistances within the client's experience. The intervention, thus, may delineate more specifically what is being experienced and also may expose when the problem emerged and how the problem is maintained. Change happens through present-centered, spontaneous concentration on any figural aspect of the client's experience. (p. 70)

Thus, devising activities and experiments to help direct the child's awareness toward his or her behavior is the key to this work. Prerequisite, however, is the child's new feeling of self-worth and self-support, as well as skills for aptly expressing feelings, particularly anger.

CASE ILLUSTRATIONS

Jenny, age 12, was very shy. She lived in a large, chaotic family and somehow had been lost in this atmosphere. The therapist worked with the family and individually with the child, and, though it seemed that much good work had been done, Jenny remained painfully shy when she was with other children. A therapeutic group would have been helpful to allow Jenny to practice her new-found skills, but one was not available. The therapist devised an experiment whereby Jenny would attempt to approach a group of children on the playground at school and to pay full attention to the feelings in her body and the thoughts in her head. At the next session, Jenny drew a picture of these feelings, using many different colors, and listed her thoughts: "They don't like me; I'm not good enough." Jenny was able to recognize these thoughts as old messages about herself.

The therapist suggested a further experiment that involved Jenny actually asking other children if she could join in their game, just to see what would happen. Jenny was intrigued by the idea of an experiment and felt that she could handle any rejection because it was what she usually expected anyway. And so, with the support of the therapist, and with the idea that this was merely an experiment, Jenny agreed to do it. She approached a group playing jump rope, timidly asked if she could play (as she reported to the therapist), and was accepted into the game without fanfare. With further similar experiments, Jenny gradually forgot about her shyness.

Barbara, 17 years old, who had originally come into therapy for her persistent lying, admitted to the therapist that she continued to lie sometimes, even when she truly did not want to. She and the therapist had never actually focused on this behavior, since it was seen as a symptom of deeper problems. Barbara was encouraged to discover the first time she had lied, and her memory brought forth a nursery school experience where she felt that, unless she fabricated a story, she would not be accepted by the other children. Barbara spoke in a nurturing way to her 4-year-old self, advising her that she, 17-year-old Barbara, liked and accepted her even if she had nothing exciting and wonderful to talk about. It took some practice and work, but soon Barbara was able to actually catch herself in the act of lying and to realize that this was an old pattern no longer needed. An important aspect of this procedure was the acceptance and understanding of her lying self.

Ten-year-old Stuart come into therapy for a variety of maladaptive behaviors, including stealing. Although there was much improvement, he continued to occasionally steal. The therapist asked him to pay particular attention to how he felt and to what was happening around him the next time he had the urge to steal. Stuart was able to become aware that he stole because he was angry at his parents. Through this awareness, the therapist was able to help Stuart learn more acceptable ways of dealing with his angry feelings.

Termination Procedures

Closure is not just a mere ending but a vital component of the Gestalt therapy process. In a sense, therapy has been the foreground, the figure in the client's life, and the completion of this Gestalt allows the child to move on to a new place. As needs are met, new masteries achieved, and new discoveries made, there is a period of homeostasis and satisfaction. This is closure, and, from this place, the child can grow and develop in healthy ways.

The concept of *termination*, or closure, is a misconception because there is no actual ending to therapy, particularly in work with children. Children are limited in working through situations therapeutically only as far as their developmental levels will take them. Closure is made at that particular stage. If a 3-year-old girl has been traumatized in some way, she may work through her anxieties and feelings over that trauma, but only to the extent of her 3-year-old cognitive and emotional abilities. At various levels of her life, issues may present themselves related to that early trauma, causing inappropriate behaviors or symptoms to emerge, calling for further therapy geared to her current development.

Children reach plateaus that indicate a stopping place. The ideal indicator occurs when the child is doing well in life outside the therapy setting and appears, in therapy sessions, to lack the energy that was previously evident. Unfortunately, therapy often must end when the child has not yet reached this plateau. Sometimes the child is doing well at home and at school, and much good work continues to take place in sessions. Parents, anxious to stop for financial reasons, time constraints, or insurance company limitations, will remove the child from therapy.

No matter what the reason for the ending of therapy, a special session must be scheduled, and particular attention must be paid to this time of conclusion. Ideally, three or four sessions prior to the last one, the child will be advised that the ending of the therapy time is close at hand. At the last session, a particular ritual may take place, depending on the child's age. Some of the ways to give the last session special emphasis are for the child and the therapist to choose a favorite game, medium, or activity; to make good-bye cards for each other; or to review drawings and photographs of sand scenes that were made over the course of therapy. Honoring mixed feelings related to the completion of therapy relieves the child's confusion regarding the splits within her. Jeannie, for example, enjoyed drawing pictures of her happy feelings as well as her sad feelings regarding the conclusion of her therapy.

CONCLUSION

The varied theoretical concepts and principles of Gestalt therapy fit well in working with children. The therapist respects the uniqueness and individual process of each child, while at the same time, providing activities and experiences to help the child renew and strengthen those aspects of the self that have been suppressed, restricted, and, perhaps, lost. The therapist never intrudes or pushes, but gently creates a safe environment in which the child can engage in a fuller experience of himself or herself. The sessions take on the phenomenon of a dance: sometimes the therapist leads and sometimes the child leads. In this way, the child sets off on his or her own rightful, healthy path of growth.

REFERENCES

Beiser, A. (1970). The paradoxical theory of change. In J. Fagan and I. L. Shepherd (Eds.), *Gestalt therapy now* (pp. 77–80). New York: Harper.

Buber, M. (1958). *I and thou.* New York: Scribner.

Buber, M. (1966). *The way of response.* New York: Schocken.

Korb, M., Gorrell, J., & Van de Reit, V. (1989). *Gestalt therapy: Practice and theory.* New York: Pergamon Press.

Latner, J. (1986). *The Gestalt therapy book.* New York: Center for Gestalt Development.

Oaklander, V. (1982). The relationship of Gestalt therapy to children. *Gestalt Journal, 1,* 64.

Oaklander, V. (1988). *Windows to our children.* New York: The Gestalt Journal Press.

Perls, F. (1973). *The Gestalt approach and eye witness to therapy.* Palo Alto, CA: Science and Behavior Books.

Polster, E., & Polster, M. (1973). *Gestalt therapy integrated.* New York: Brunner/Mazel.

Developmental Adaptations of Play Therapy

CHAPTER 7

Adolescent Theraplay

TERRENCE J. KOLLER

INTRODUCTION

Adolescence can be a difficult time not only for the child, but for the clinician whose job it is to evaluate the child and to create a treatment plan when things go wrong. The literature describes the normative upheaval and turmoil of adolescence (Freud, 1958), the identity struggle (Erikson, 1950), the depression (Loeber, 1982), the importance of the peer group (Offer & Boxer, 1991), and the myriad biological changes that occur during adolescence. Not only do changes occur in a rapid and sometimes frightening way, but according to Giovacchini (1985), adolescents "have a propensity for creating problems within the treatment setting because of their reticence about becoming engaged or their inclination to express themselves through action rather than words and feelings" (p. 447). Add to this the fact that adolescence recapitulates many of the developmental steps attempted during infancy (Jones, 1922), including a second period of individuation (Blos, 1962), and it is no surprise that Anna Freud's description of this period as "an interruption of peaceful growth" (Freud, 1958, p. 275) is indeed almost an understatement.

Some theorists, on the other hand, disagree with the notion that adolescence is a period of recapitulation of earlier developmental steps. Kaplan (1984) viewed the separation and individuation of adolescence as quite different from that of infancy. He described adolescence as a time when the infantile period is revised from narcissism to a more general moral attitude towards others. According to Kaplan, separation-individuation occurs only once, and it is during the first 3 years of life (p. 94). Offer, Ostrov, and Howard (1981) disagreed that adolescence is a time of turmoil. They reported that, in their research population, the norm was one of confident maturation and comfortable relationships with others. Their work, however, was limited primarily to middle class and upper-middle class, white, intact families.

Striving for Autonomy versus Attachment

Rather than being a single time period or episode in life, adolescence is a time of stages unto itself. Many authors describe early, middle, and late periods of adolescence (Blos, 1962; Mishne, 1986). Thus, although the older adolescent may be making appropriate strides toward independence, the younger one may engage in pseudoindependent behavior only—behavior that can be extremely dangerous. At a time when parents can feel the most hurt by the rejection they experience from their adolescent, that adolescent is relying heavily on external rather than intrafamilial supports to bolster his or her self-esteem (Holmes & Wagner, 1992, p. 314). At age 13, for example, high-risk adolescents given social support showed improvement in cognitive functioning (Seifer,

The author dedicates this chapter to the memory of Dr. Ann Jernberg who generously assisted in its preparation.

Sameroff, Baldwin, & Baldwin, 1992). In their study of 935 adolescents, Raja, McGee, and Stanton (1992) found that those whose perceived greater attachment to their parents and peers had the highest scores on measures of self-perceived strengths. Adolescents who perceived a lower attachment to parents scored significantly lower on measures of well-being. When it came to adolescents' mental health, attachment to peers did not compensate for their low attachment to parents. Adolescents who move away from parents to peers, as part of a too-early striving for autonomy, are susceptible to peer group pressure, especially in the area of antisocial activity (Steinberg & Silverberg, 1986).

Adolescent attachment to parents, thus, is very important to wholesome adolescent development. Those teenagers who are securely attached report significantly higher self-esteem than those who are insecurely attached (Armsden & Greenberg, 1987). This is consistent with Klaus and Kennell's (1976) conviction that, at any age, one benefits from attachment to another: "a call for help after even forty years may bring a mother to her child and evoke attachment behaviors equal in strength to those in the first year" (p. 2).

During times of stress, it is physical contact from a caregiver that can be the most effective means of comfort. Thus, it is the adolescent's psychotherapist, another significant caretaker, who must also provide a period of support and acceptance (Bemporad, 1988). The psychotherapist must allow for autonomous development while encouraging intimacy.

Attachment Failure

Typically, literature about the normal development of the adolescent was written at a time when family values were very different. Earlier writers had not experienced the current divorce rate (Glick, 1984), the increase of substance abuse (Dryfoos, 1990), the rising numbers of teen pregnancies (United States Congress, OTA, 1991), or the frequent family necessity that both parents work. The stresses of urban life, furthermore, make normal development a difficult task for the adolescent. Kelleher, Taylor, and Rickert (1992) found that children and adolescents in rural environments have rates of mental disorders equal to those in metropolitan areas.

Environmental stress alone does not account for all the problems adolescents encounter, however. Some adolescents are particularly rejecting of adult efforts to meet their developmental goals. This can be seen as a problem relating back to the child's inability to form a satisfying attachment to a primary caretaker (Jernberg, 1989; Jernberg and Koller, 1984). Jernberg (1989) pointed out that this is especially common among adoptees, foster placements, and children who, in other ways, have lost their parents. A parent does not have to be physically absent for the child to experience parental loss. Experiences such as substance abuse and mental illness in the family (Kazdin, 1992) as well as physical and sexual abuse (Kazdin, 1987) can have a profound impact on the child's ability to form an attachment and, thereby, be able to proceed with normal development.

Adolescent developmental and psychiatric disorders may also make him or her resist adult contact. These are the children suffering from autism, obsessive-compulsive disorder, oppositional defiance, learning disabilities, attention-deficit disorder, and phobias.

Consequences of the Failure to Attach

Every clinician who specializes in working with adolescents has experienced a child who has lost one or both parents through some form of neglect (even benign neglect, by state definition of *child abuse*). On the other hand, what clinician has not seen adolescents, even in the middle classes, who spend most of their time out of the home, wandering around from one friend's house to another, while their parents pursue successful careers. These children may inconsistently attend school with barely passing grades, only occasionally redeeming themselves through hasty efforts to complete last-minute work. Their experimentation with personal appearance seems to last too long, and they look bizarre and disheveled. These adolescents take inadequate care of their health and maintain a poor dietary regimen. They undertake experimentation with sexuality without the much-needed base upon which to build those experiences. Anxiety and depression increase, and, with it, so do their unsuccessful attempts to cope. Like any individual in crisis, those adolescents become tunnel-visioned, repeating over and over the same behavior that created the problem in the first place. They remain isolated from healthy adult contact and become vulnerable to the quick, unhealthy fixes offered by those who exploit. Only rarely do they look to appropriate adult caretakers for guidance and nurturing. Indeed, they become hypersensitive to anything that may seem like criticism. Sometimes, because of its antisocial quality, this behavior does, in fact, call out criticism from adults, thus further alienating the child and concealing more basic needs for nurturance, soothing, structure, and appropriate stimulation.

Challenges for the Psychotherapist

The psychotherapist approaches young children who have needs for attachment, nurturance, or tension reduction with relative comfort. If these children have difficulty communicating verbally, the therapist can temporarily replicate, nonverbally, the early parent-child relationship. Like a parent, the therapist can take charge and interact in ways that are joyful, physical, and good for the child. The psychotherapist knows what will ultimately help the child and can use this knowledge to remain persistent and optimistic, even in the face of the child's protests.

Whereas a variety of techniques exist for the treatment of young children, adolescents are frequently given a modified version of the talking therapies developed primarily for the highly motivated adult. Adolescents, however, rarely meet the criteria required of adult candidates for psychotherapy.

Adolescents love to talk to their friends but are uncomfortable talking to adults. Many resist the suggestion that they seek mental health help. They see this type of help as indicating that they are crazy or that someone sees their behavior as bad and something needing to be controlled. Even more difficult for adolescents is the fear that their friends will know that they are in therapy.

When parents tell adolescents that they need to talk to someone about their acting out, adolescents react with opposition and anger. They do not want to be remade into something that adults want them to be. Thus, therapists of adolescents generally see the parents first in order to help them deal with their adolescent's protest and to devise a plan to get the child to treatment. The adolescent is often not given the choice about attending psychotherapy sessions as is the case with pediatric and dental appointments. However, unlike the dentist or pediatrician who has a treatment plan that can readily be carried out with a completely passive adolescent, the traditional psychotherapist counts on the patient's cooperation and verbalizations. Psychotherapists attempt to gain some trust by assuring the adolescent that what is said will be kept in confidence. However, the adolescent cannot ignore the warning that this confidence will be broken if he or she becomes a danger to self or others. To avoid colluding with the adolescent, many therapists also explain to their adolescent patients that confidence will also be broken if the adolescent misses appointments (Mishne, 1986, p. 35).

Inpatient Hospitalization

It is not surprising, given the fears and distress that adolescents call out in others, that they account for a substantial share of inpatient hospitalizations (Frank, Salkever, & Sharfstein, 1991). An inpatient setting can give a psychotherapist a sense of security akin to the power a parent experiences with a much younger child. Additionally, the psychotherapist can confront the hospitalized adolescent knowing that help is available to handle threats and misbehaviors. The inpatient milieu allows the adult to take charge without worrying that adolescent patients will exploit their independence, thus placing the caretaker in a helpless position. In a sense, hospitalization allows the adolescent to regress to tantrum-like behavior while experiencing support and protection.

The inpatient setting also provides a greater opportunity for the psychotherapist and adolescent to experience intimacy. The greater frequency of adult-child contact and the greater ease of confronting difficult issues allow the adolescent to experience the very closeness to others that had been missing in the family.

Another Approach

Theraplay, as will be described later, does not require the adolescent to be verbal, to be motivated, or to be hospitalized for the psychotherapist to gain control of most forms of acting-out. Theraplay does not require the adolescent to reveal deep-seated secrets (although appropriate confidentiality is assured if secrets are told). If parents are ambivalent or ineffective, Theraplay therapists are certainly not. Rather than play to parental regression to helplessness, the Theraplay therapist appeals to the regressive needs that are hidden behind an adolescent's smoke screen of misbehavior. While respecting teenagers' needs to withhold thoughts about their developing identities, the Theraplay therapist engages the adolescent at a more primitive, playful level directed to his or her more basic needs. Nonetheless, to the outside observer, Theraplay looks intrusive.

Those who teach classes or run workshops designed to train mental health professionals in the use of more active, intrusive forms of psychotherapy have certainly experienced firsthand the tremendous resistance that many of these students demonstrate. Any attempt at psychotherapist intrusion is viewed as having the potential to harm the patient. This protest sometimes comes from the students' theoretical (client-centered, self-psychological, etc.) belief system. Yet Kohut (1977) wrote:

> The analyst's muted response is not adopted in consequence of the specific need of his analysand, is not adopted in consequence of his deep comprehension of the genetic core of the analysand's disturbed personality; it is adopted in obedience to the tenet that contamination of the transference has to be avoided. The analyst's mutedness and reserve would therefore be experienced as unempathic . . . . (p. 258)

Other students resist activity, however, not because of theory but because of their personal background. Many psychotherapists enter the field of psychotherapy hoping to engage in a passive career. Unlike physicians and parents who must tolerate some pain in those under their care, these psychotherapists find patient protest uncomfortable and, thus, view as inappropriate any therapeutic behavior that results in discomfort.

Some psychotherapists may have experienced a difficult adolescence themselves, and, thus, may understate the problems and dangers inherent in adolescent suffering. Having physically survived this period, some adults may take a laissez-faire attitude, thereby failing to consider the harmful, long-term, emotional consequences of some forms of adolescent rebellion.

Many psychotherapists began their lives as good children (Miller, 1981). They took care of others and tried to stay out of trouble. These therapists may then feel discomfort around another's defiant, oppositional behavior and may overreact or overcontrol those behaviors.

Development of Theraplay

Much of the theory and practice of Theraplay came from the work of Austin DesLauriers (1962), whose focus was primarily on autistic and schizophrenic children. Compared to the prevalent theories of his time, DesLauries's focus on the here and now and on intrusive and physical aspects of play was radical. Ann Jernberg and colleagues (Jernberg, 1979, 1989; Jernberg, Hurst, & Lyman, 1969), at the Theraplay Institute in Chicago, applied these principles to children with less severe forms of pathology. She retained Des Lauriers's

> ... vigor; intrusiveness; body and eye contact; focus on intimacy between child and therapist (particularly with regard to individuation; that is, helping the child to see himself as unique, different, and separate from others); emphasis on the here and now; and ignoring the bizarre, the past, and fantasy. (Jernberg, 1979, p. 2)

Theraplay differs from DesLauriers's work in the degree to which the therapist initiates, structures, and takes charge of the session. The Theraplay therapist is far more intrusive and, thus, is more likely to encounter resistance in the form of temper tantrums. Although it may seem natural to apply this technique to a very young child—indeed, Theraplay's first clients were several thousand preschool (Head Start) children—it is the purpose of this chapter to outline its application to adolescents.

Theraplay can best be understood by looking at the parent-infant interaction. Studies of this interaction look at the adult's behavior, the child's behavior, and the impact that each has on the other. The simple act of making a funny face at a baby sets into motion a reciprocal series of behaviors in which each player in the drama significantly influences the other (Lewis & Lee-Painter, 1974). This interaction helps both participants understand how each feels about the other, eventually generalizing into a view of the world as a "fun, caring, and loving place" (Jernberg, 1979, p. 5). It allows both to experience the comfort of intimacy and to develop self-confidence.

To say that this interaction stops at infancy goes against adult experience. The need for intimacy and validation continues throughout the life span. People often find partners who best continue this very interaction into adulthood. If abusive parental interchanges were part of one's childhood, similar partner choices may result later on. Theraplay assumes a number of significant ingredients that go into a healthy parent-child relationship and applies these in the treatment setting.

PROCEDURE AND TECHNIQUE

The Therapist

Selection of Therapists

The first Theraplay therapists were selected not for their academic achievements but for their native ability to provide a healthy, optimistic, playful relationship with another human being. Rather than being asked for a curriculum vitae, potential Theraplay therapists were asked to assemble in a large room, free of the usual playroom props except for gym mats and large floor pillows for sitting. These Theraplay therapist candidates were then divided into two groups and paired off. Individuals in one group were asked to play the role of *unhappy child*. Individuals in the other group were given one instruction: "You are therapists. Help this child feel better about himself or herself." Participants were then asked to switch roles so that the *child* became the *therapist*.

The following approaches were observed by the Theraplay staff: Some *therapists* approached the *unhappy child* tentatively and stopped a comfortable distance away from him or her. These *therapists* would say "hello" and search their pockets for some object to offer the *child*. Other individuals immediately began sympathizing with the *child's* pain and waiting for a response. If the *child* did not respond, those *therapists* sat back and remained silent until instructed to "Switch roles." Some individuals took a more daring approach. They directly approached the child and gently stroked the child's back or hair. Ultimately, these *therapists* withdrew if the *child* protested.

When the described *therapists* were asked about their behavior, they explained the importance of "respecting the *child's* need for distance." They warned about the potential disorganizing, sexual, and abusive effects of pushing a child to interact if the child protests. Many said it would be cruel to intrude when the child wanted to be left alone. When asked how long they might wait for the child to respond, most said, "As long as it took; months, even years if necessary." Some defined an arbitrary time before they would demand more responsiveness from the child: "If I didn't get a response in 6 weeks, I might insist that the child look at me." These therapists were often well-trained, kind, and theoretically correct, but they were not selected for further Theraplay training.

A small number of individuals distinguished themselves during these group interviews. These potentially successful Theraplay therapists did not hesitate to enter the *child's* space. They insisted on eye contact and were not afraid to touch the *child*. They were playful, upbeat, and confident. They persevered in doing things that a normal child truly enjoys, such as playing patty cake, even if the *unhappy child* tried to say "no." They insisted that the *child* interact personally with them while yet remaining empathic to the *child's* feeling. They understood how painful this insistence could be for the *child* and experienced some pain themselves. These were the individuals selected for the Theraplay training.

Adults were also interviewed about their experience role-playing the *unhappy child*. They were asked what it felt like to be in the role of a child interacting with their particular partner's style. The *unhappy child* paired with a cautious, nonintrusive *therapist* sometimes reported that, although it initially felt good to be left alone, he or she began to feel uncomfortable, lonely, misunderstood, unlovable, and pessimistic about any prospect for change. The *child* with the more intrusive *therapist* often reported the opposite experience. "At first I wanted her to go away from me. I was embarrassed that she wanted to do these babyish games with me. When I could see that she wouldn't go away, I began to give in.

I was surprised to find that I actually liked playing like this. I got the feeling that my therapist also had fun and liked me." Another common response was, "I wanted to throw a temper tantrum, but, as I became more upset, my therapist took even more charge. When I realized what was happening, I felt safe and much more secure."

Participants were asked an important question about their experience when role-playing the *child*. They were asked to recall what they remembered doing during the *session*. The *children* whose *therapists* were nonintrusive talked about experiences going on inside their heads. They reported, "I said to myself, I'm just going to remain quiet. If I close my eyes, I don't have to think about that other person." The *children* with more active *therapists* often described, in some detail, the games played and the physical characteristics of the *therapists*. "I would try to close my eyes, but my therapist took my hands and played patty-cake anyway. I remember that she had the warmest eyes."

Professional Requirements for Training

All types of individuals have been trained at the Theraplay Institute in Chicago, including psychologists; psychiatrists; social workers; teachers; occupation, speech, and physical therapists; pediatricians; and child care workers. The film *Here I Am* (Jernberg, Hurst, & Lyman, 1969), produced by the Theraplay Institute, even outlines the training of lay persons to provide Theraplay to Head Start children. Thus, individuals at all levels of education can be trained in Theraplay if they have a good understanding of their motivation, a healthy ability to relate flexibly and joyfully, and a willingness to undergo and learn from appropriate training experiences. Some parents of disturbed children have become outstanding Theraplay therapists as observed during their participation in family Theraplay sessions.

Personal Characteristics for Acceptance to Candidacy

Theraplay therapists are courageous but not reckless. They know the difference between sympathy and true empathy. Like a good parent, they know when a child needs more contact and when to allow the child some personal space. They are energetic and willing to take responsibility for the session. They are not discouraged by the child's resistant "Go away." They constantly analyze their own motivation but do not become paralyzed by self-analysis. Most of all, they have confidence in the healing value of good parent-child relating. These individuals are playful and optimistic. They know when humor works and when the child's pain requires more serious attention.

Individuals who make poor Theraplay therapists prefer to remain distant and intellectual in their therapeutic efforts. They work toward establishing a talking relationship. They place a great deal of responsibility for what happens in the sessions on the children themselves. Although this is not a negative in itself, some of these individuals are too quick to give up if their patient does not respond on a verbal level. Some describe the child as resistive. Others play the kinds of games that children could play with any other interested adult. Theraplay therapists always ask themselves whether a particular activity is something the child could do alone. If so, they must try to do something different. Furthermore, trainees learn always to ask themselves the question: "Whose need is being met by this response or by this activity?" Some individuals are uncomfortable with this degree of activity, however, and support their stance by quoting warnings in psychological literature about how too much activity on the part of the therapist overstimulates the patient and ruins the therapeutic relationship. Depressed adults do not make good Theraplay therapists.

The Patient

Selection for Treatment: Traditional Models

Much has been written about selection criteria for patients being considered for psycho-therapy. Contemporary theorists have become increasingly interested in developing spe-cific treatments for select populations. As psychotherapy has developed to become more short term, patient characteristics become even more important. Typically, an appropriate patient is seen as one who can quickly engage with the therapist (Malan, 1976), one who has a good history of interpersonal relationships with at least one significant person (Sifneos, 1972), and is motivated, psychologically minded, and intelligent (Davanloo, 1978). The patient should not engage in promiscuous sexual relationships (Davanloo, 1978), substance abuse or self-destructive acting-out (Malan, 1976), and must not have a life that "centers exclusively around the need for and incapacity to tolerate object rela-tions" (Mann, 1973, p. 74). It would be difficult to find a theorist whose technique is especially suited to a nonverbal patient. Although it certainly makes sense to be very specific in selecting a patient for a briefer psychotherapy, these characteristics are also valued in the selection of long-term patients.

A review of the selection criteria can be very discouraging for the psychotherapist who works with adolescents. The adolescent, because of his or her acting-out behavior, fre-quently comes to treatment at the insistence of another. The adolescent may not trust adults and is still in the process of developing meaningful relationships. If motivated for treat-ment, the adolescent may have a different agenda from that of the person who referred him or her. The psychotherapist, if unable to keep perspective, may fall into a trap of siding with either the parent's or the adolescent's agenda. Indeed, neither the adolescent or the caretaker may be aware of the underlying need that resulted in the referral for treatment. This brings the therapist back to the position where he or she must decide what is best for the patient.

Obstacles to the Treatment of Adolescents

With encouragement, many psychotherapists can be trained to apply active, playful, and intrusive methods to a 4-year-old child. Many more find these methods almost impossible, however, when faced with a resistant adolescent.

Many psychotherapists have become defeated by the conduct-disordered adolescent's unwillingness to show respect or submission. Sherwood (1990) noted "The delinquent's sense of entitlement, unstable self-esteem, egocentric cognitive focus, and grandiosity serve as profound resistances to treatment and, for that matter, generally lie behind events that bring such patients to treatment" (p. 38). Anyone who has worked with an adolescent knows that, at that age, even the nondelinquent feels that he or she does not have to take the time to learn and earn the privileges of adulthood. The word *fair* again enters their vocabulary, and they constantly compare their own rights to what they perceive to be their friend's rights.

The book *Theraplay* (Jernberg, 1979) outlines just some of the reasons why adolescents pose a more difficult challenge than do younger children:

1. *Physical Size.* Because the adolescent is so much larger, the therapist cannot rely on physical measures alone to control activities.

2. *Sexual Development.* Because the adolescent is sexually aware, many Theraplay activities more typically geared to younger children are not appropriate for the adolescent.

3. *Intellectual Development.* Adolescents are more self-conscious and certainly less naive than younger children. This must be considered when approaching this age group in a more regressive way.

Other issues may also prevent the adolescent from engaging in more physically playful and intrusive activities. These include:

1. Striving for independence.
2. Wishing to perceive adults as peers.
3. Perfected "conning" or manipulation skills.
4. Mistrust of adults.
5. Propensity toward narcissistic injury.
6. Inflated grandiosity.

Contraindications to the Use of Theraplay

The intake interview gives the therapist the opportunity to eliminate, as Theraplay candidates, those children for whom Theraplay is contraindicated. This decision is a critical one because the exclusion of a child who is, in fact, an appropriate Theraplay candidate may mean that he or she may be subjected instead to a slower moving, less appropriate form of treatment. On the other hand, an inappropriate selection for Theraplay may mean that other more specific problems do not get addressed.

Traumatized children, as a rule, should not be treated with Theraplay. These children, by virtue of their upsetting experience, need to talk to someone in order to come to understand what happened to them, to express feelings aroused by trauma, to gain reassurance, to feel that what happened is not necessarily going to happen again, and to know that what happened is not their fault and that they will not be punished for it. Although these children can benefit from a number of Theraplay dimensions (i.e., nurture, attachment, empathy), these are needs that are specifically trauma-related. The goal is to restore the child to his or her previous level of homeostasis. Although these children need to feel safe and to be encouraged to express themselves through whatever means they can, Beverly James (1989) stated that Theraplay can provide the mistrusting abused child the experience of "safe touch" and joyful body confirmation.

Theraplay is also contraindicated for the "fragile child" (Jernberg, 1979, p. 28). Such a child reacts in a distraught way when approached in even the most gentle manner, true sometimes of children with vestibular damage (Rieff, 1991). It should be noted, however, that, although many children initially protest the therapist's initiative, few are truly fragile to the point where the therapist must wait for the child to take the initiative.

Since the abused child needs crisis intervention, Theraplay was heretofore thought to be contraindicated, and symbolic play with toys and dolls was the more traditional way these children were encouraged to communicate their distress. The nurturing elements of Theraplay for purposes of enhancing the child's self-esteem were, however, considered appropriate.

Some therapists maintain that Theraplay is appropriate for children whose abuse has already been dealt with through traditional talking therapy methods and whose abuse was an event in the distant past. Family Theraplay is frequently used to help reunite families by training more appropriate behavior. It is also used to begin the attachment process in stepfamilies, foster families, and potentially adoptive families (Jernberg, 1989, 1990).

All this having been said, the skill and training of the Theraplay therapist is still the best aid in the identification of children who are appropriate or inappropriate for Theraplay treatment. It is rare, however, that all elements of Theraplay are excluded from the treatment of any child.

The Treatment Room

The Theraplay room must be constructed so that the principles of Theraplay can be carried out in an easy and fluid manner. Since the focus of treatment is the relationship between the adolescent and the therapist, the room must be free of the usual playroom props. It should not contain sand tables, puppets, paper and pencils (for projective drawings), dollhouses, board games, or the kinds of toys used in representative play by more traditional play therapists.

The playroom itself should appear simple but appealing. Mats should cover the floors, and there should be a number of large floor pillows on which to sit. It should also contain a large mirror, a cork board on which to hang drawings, a scale, and, if possible, a sink with water. The Theraplay room should be constructed so that the therapist can be completely spontaneous and comfortable and, thus, should be soundproof and easy to clean. If the budget allows, the Theraplay room should contain a large one-way viewing mirror and videotaping equipment. By simply adding a folding table and chairs, the room can double as an evaluation room for the Marschak Interaction Method to be described later.

Materials

Theraplay does use props, but these props are stored in closed cabinets and taken out only by the therapist after he or she has developed an individualized treatment plan and decided which props are appropriate for that plan. These items should be easily accessible. The flow of the session should never be interrupted either because the therapist cannot find a prop or because he or she runs out of ideas.

The following list is a good beginning complement for a Theraplay playroom:

Towels for tug of war and for drying

Blank pieces of paper, both large and small, and markers for tracing the whole body or body parts (e.g., hands)

Chalk

Bubble-blowing solution

Food (including pretzels, M&M's, juice, donuts, etc.)

Body lotion

Baby powder

Small adhesive bandages

Necklaces, hats, and clothing for dressing up

Quick drying nail polish for manicures

Combs and manicure tools

Crepe paper

Yardstick and/or tape measure

Squirt guns and large plastic trash bags

Theraplay Dimensions

Theraplay activities are designed to call out patient behaviors, attitudes, and reactions that have been culled from the literature and through clinical practice. Each Theraplay session consists of activities that ensure that all essential Theraplay dimensions be included. Some children may require more of a particular dimension, but it is unlikely that any dimension would be dropped entirely from a session.

The following dimensions best define the elements of Theraplay:

1. *Structure.* The activities in this dimension are designed to allow the therapist to set limits, to inform the child about his or her body boundaries, and to provide an appropriate, orderly, understandable environment for the child. Structuring takes place through the therapist consistently adhering to the definitions of time and space (e.g., the duration of the session, the duration of any one activity, the space in which the activity takes place beyond which the child may not roam).

2. *Challenge.* These activities allow the therapist to stimulate the child's development, to set appropriate expectations, and to enhance the child's achievement. They encourage the child to stretch and reach just a little beyond his or her present level of functioning.

3. *Intrusion.* Intrusive activities discourage the child from retreating into his or her own world, from keeping others at bay, from indulging in too pervasive a fantasy life, and from withdrawing.

4. *Nurturing.* It is assumed that everyone, at any age, has the need to be nurtured: to be cared for, to be consoled or comforted, and to be nourished. However, some children's needs are so intense that the failure to attain nurturing interferes seriously with day-to-day functioning.

5. *Playfulness.* Although not truly a discreet dimension, this fifth category is so important that it has been given a separate listing. This dimension can cut across all tasks. The therapist must be lighthearted and joyful and must communicate to the child a sense of pleasure in the interaction. This attitude is particularly important for children whose lives are grim, intense, and worrisome.

There is, of course, considerable overlap between dimensions. A single activity may contain elements that are both challenging and intrusive. A water pistol duel, for example, can be built into the Theraplay session during the hot summer months. Arm and head holes are cut out of large plastic trash bags, and adolescent and therapist wear them like raincoats. The two stand back to back and take five paces away from each other (or however many the room size allows). The therapist counts the paces, and, on the final one, each turns and tries to be the one to squirt the other first. The *structure* of this task is a function of the therapist taking charge and counting. If one participant fails to conform to the structure, there is a consequence (e.g., the other person is allowed three free squirts). The *challenge* of this task is that each must use good aim to squirt the other.

Structure Activities

Body Boundary Measurement: The therapist asks the adolescent to take off his or her shoes and socks and lie on the mat. The therapist places one sock by the adolescent's head and another by his or her feet. The adolescent then stands up and observes the distance between socks. The therapist asks him or her to again lie down, but this time with arms outstretched so the adolescent's *hands* span the distance between the socks. Most are amazed to see that arm space is approximately equal to height.

Quiet Movement: The adolescent stands at one end of the room and the therapist at the other. The therapist turns his or her back to the adolescent. The adolescent is then instructed to quietly walk toward the therapist who, at any time, can spin around quickly and try to catch the adolescent in the act of moving. If caught, the adolescent must return to the point of origin. If not caught, the adolescent can proceed on toward the therapist. The stated goal is to sneak up and tap the therapist on the shoulder. The adolescent is given three tries to do this before the two reverse roles.

Statue Making: The therapist instructs the patient to become a statue that accurately represents the adolescent's current interest (e.g., playing soccer). This statue must be so accurate that the therapist can guess the activity.

Structured tasks are best for adolescents who come from households where rules are rarely or inconsistently enforced. Parents from these households fold under the pressure to be fair, and they idealize the notion of family democracy. These parents frequently fear that they cannot enforce a structure, or they view their adolescent's protest as an indication that they (the parents) are wrong in their decisions or that their child does not like them.

Although most of the Theraplay is structured and has the therapist in charge, this dimension should not be emphasized with adolescents who are already too rule-bound either externally (e.g., by their parents) or internally (e.g., by their own guilt, high self-expectations, etc.). These are the adolescents who complain about others breaking rules and often find it difficult to socialize with peers who engage in normal experimentation.

Challenge Activities

Adolescents love the challenging aspects of Theraplay and, since these types of activities are relatively easy to develop, so do therapists. Challenging tasks include the following:

Tug-of-war

Wrestling

Arm wrestling

Thumb wrestling

Leg wrestling

Basketball: One person uses his or her hands to form a basketball rim and the other tries to shoot a crumpled piece of paper into the rim.

Watermelon seed spitting contest

Hockey games: Straws are used to blow air at dried beans or a table tennis ball.

Pillow balancing: Pillows are placed, in increasing numbers, on the adolescent's head. He or she is asked to walk a certain distance in the room. The game ends when the pillows fall off the adolescent's head. The game is repeated three times to see if the adolescent can improve his or her performance. A variation of this is a round or two timed with a stopwatch for speed.

Weighing: Standing on a scale, leaning against the therapist, the adolescent is challenged to increase or decrease his or her weight.

Challenging tasks are clearly not appropriate for children whose world is already too demanding of them. These children are overscheduled and have become competitive and tense. They are academically competent but have difficulty relating to parents and sometimes even to peers.

Adolescents who are unmotivated and directionless, on the other hand, benefit tremendously from these activities. These are the adolescents who spend their time hanging around with their friends and arguing with teachers who want them to perform. They are generally lacking a passion for anything. They are nonathletic, have no hobbies, and appear disinterested in school in spite of good intellectual ability. Their parents make token efforts to encourage them to complete their work but lack follow-up. By the time these children reach adolescence, their parents find it extremely difficult to challenge them. Many adolescents take advantage of this freedom.

The metaphorical value of challenge (and of all Theraplay dimensions) is powerful. The adolescent learns to enjoy the feeling of competition in a supportive atmosphere. He or she can apply the experience to others outside the Theraplay session.

Intrusion Activities

Any activity that moves the therapist into the adolescent's space is intrusive. The very act of a therapist's sitting closer to a teenager decreases the ease with which that teenager can screen the therapist from awareness. Intrusive activities include the following:

Dressing up: The therapist tries hats on the adolescent.

Tracing: The therapist traces the adolescent's hands, feet, and so on, on paper.

Measuring: The therapist uses a yardstick or tape measure (as appropriate) to measure the adolescent's height, arm length, neck size, and so on.

These activities are necessary for adolescents who are withdrawn and isolated. These are the children who spend home time in their rooms and away time wandering around. Intrusive activities are also indicated for adolescents with obsessive-compulsive defenses. The surprise inherent in the intrusion makes it difficult for the obsessive-compulsive adolescent to maintain his or her intellectual distance. Because activities are designed to be pleasurable, the withdrawn or obsessive adolescent gradually comes to experience satisfaction in relating in a new way. These tasks are not appropriate, however, for the adolescent who comes from an intrusive environment. These individuals need the respect, distance, and protection that they do not receive from snooping, prying, manipulative others. Some adolescents have intrusive parents. Their parents use them to meet their own (the parents') needs or are so paranoid that they constantly burst into the adolescent's space to see what he or she is doing. These parents do not know their children well enough to trust them.

Nurturing Activities

By definition, tasks that overtly nurture are those typically geared toward a younger population. Although they might not seem age-appropriate, nurturing activities are appropriate for individuals of any age up to and including marriage. Nurturing activities promote attachment, communicate understanding, and reduce stress. They take over where cognition breaks down. They work quickly.

Because adolescents are moving toward independence and adulthood, they begin to become self-conscious about being nurtured. The underlying need for nurturance, however, is especially problematic for those who covertly must crave it. They evidence this need by displaying behavior that conceals a bad self-image, an inability to relax, and/or the development of stress-related illnesses.

Nurturing activities include the following activities the therapist does for the child:

Grooming: Hair combing, manicuring, applying lotion to dry hands, and so on

First-aid task: Looking at cuts and scrapes, and applying adhesive bandages and lotion to bruises or dry skin when appropriate

Making dress-up items that are put on the adolescent such as crepe paper bow ties, hats, necklaces, bracelets, and so on

Singing: The therapist sings to the adolescent

It is rare to find an adolescent for whom nurturing is inappropriate. Although nurturing tasks may not be of primary focus for some adolescents, these activities are always appropriate for helping the adolescent relax after a more active and lively Theraplay activity.

Playfulness Activities

It cannot be stressed enough that all Theraplay activities should be done in the spirit of play. The Theraplay therapist should have a good sense of humor and communicate confidence and comfort. This playfulness should be communicated not only in the therapist's selection of tasks but also in the therapist's voice, stance, and gestures.

The Therapist and Theraplay Dimensions

Reviewing each of the preceding dimensions and imagining what it might feel like to do these activities with an adolescent, some readers may feel uncomfortable with one or more of the dimensions. They may overidentify, as have parents, with the adolescent's discomfort and, thus, avoid giving the very experience the adolescent needs.

1. An adult who experienced an overly controlling parent may find it difficult to provide *structure* to an adolescent. Having no experience with appropriate order, this therapist may too easily become tempted to collude with the adolescent's chaos.

2. Therapists who were successful students, and many obviously were, may have been overly organized and may not be in touch with how difficult demands and overregimentation are for some adolescents. These therapists find it difficult to apply *challenge* in a way that adolescents can understand.

3. If therapists themselves were allowed no privacy as children, they may not feel comfortable *intruding* upon someone who is withdrawn, especially when that individual's protests sound like those once belonging to the therapist.

4. An adult who has not experienced the pleasure of a *nurturing* relationship and who has coped with this deficit through distance may find it difficult to nurture someone who, like him- or herself, is also distancing.

5. Finally, many therapists approach their patients in a way that confuses intensity with respect. Adolescents who already fear that adults think they are disturbed are further distressed by a therapist who takes a serious stance. The adolescent then feels that the therapist, like the parents, is disapproving, angry, and unempathic. *Playful* therapists

communicate that they know that the adolescent is experiencing pain, that there is hope, and that this relationship can be different. They can, thereby, help the adolescent fill the gaps necessary for movement on to the next stage of development.

As evidenced in the foregoing, Theraplay therapists must be aware of their own motivations. Personal therapy, supervision, and ongoing self-analysis are necessary to ensure that it is the adolescent's, and not the therapist's, needs that are being met through the Theraplay process.

Treatment Phases

The duration of Theraplay treatment is not open-ended. Treatment plans are well thought-out and activities are designed to adhere to these plans. Theraplay activities are tailor-made to each particular patient's personality, pathology, goals, and so on. Consequently, therapists can generally anticipate a predictable sequence of events. Therapists should alert parents and teachers about unsettling, but temporary, potential future behavior. Indeed, the Theraplay therapist treating adolescents should warn the parents to contact other adult caretakers about the potential for negative behavior as adolescents may generalize from their attempts at resisting treatment.

The most frequent adolescent maneuver is to claim that he or she is being physically abused. This complaint will be applied not only to the Theraplay sessions but to the parents' new-found ability to set limits. One adolescent, for example, called the state child abuse hotline to complain that her father would not allow her to leave her desk until she finished her homework. She also complained to her high school principal, to her guidance counselor (whom she had met for the first time), and to the father of a friend. All but the hotline had been warned of this potential behavior.

Although one cannot expect that each child will adhere to the following schedule, the stages generally characterize the course of adolescent Theraplay.

1. The Introductory Phase

The Introductory Phase begins with session one. The therapist's first greeting of the adolescent is engaging. He or she escorts the adolescent to the Theraplay room and communicates the rules of Theraplay, not by lecture but by the therapist's behavior. The rules are:

1. The therapist is in charge of the sessions.
2. The sessions are fun (often not because of but in spite of the adolescent's intentions).
3. The sessions are active. They are not verbal, not focused on the past, and not fantasy or insight oriented.
4. The sessions are well structured in terms of regular duration, scheduling, use of space in the room, and so on.
5. The sessions are free from physical hurts. All activities are conducted in a safe way. Violence is never permitted.

2. The Exploration Phase

This phase also begins with session one. Therapist and adolescent both learn the ways in which they are alike and how they are different (with respect to strength, hand size, height, eye color, etc.). The therapist makes these comparisons with humor, thus taking the adolescent off guard. Many Theraplay therapists begin each session with some form of therapist-patient exploration so that, week after week, each can discover something different about the other.

3. The Negative-Reaction Phase

In young children, this phase usually *follows* the Tentative-Acceptance Phase. Adolescents, however, when confronted with their painful ambivalence about closeness, become negative very quickly. Adolescents try to back away from the therapist; then they realize that the therapist is not doing the expected. Finding that his or her intellectual, verbal defenses do not work, the adolescent's only escape is to become difficult. Theraplay therapists must be secure in their own self-concept so as not to be sidetracked by the adolescent's barrage of complaints.

4. The Tentative-Acceptance Phase

At times, the adolescent may drop his or her defenses and momentarily laugh or cooperate with an activity. These are the times when he or she could not resist the playfulness inherent in Theraplay. Although verbalizing that the therapist's behavior is ridiculous, the adolescent sometimes inadvertently participates in the games. While not sold on the idea of enjoying the pleasure a relationship can bring, he or she is becoming curious.

5. The Growing-and-Trusting Phase

Adolescent and therapist eventually interact with one another in a warm, pleasurable way. Each feels he or she knows the other well. The therapist enjoys the sessions and begins to feel that they are all play and no work. This signals that the time has come to prepare the adolescent for termination.

6. The Termination Phase

The stage for termination is set in the therapist's pointing out the adolescent's strengths. Next the adolescent is told that Theraplay will be over in a few more sessions. The final session is scheduled as a termination party.

Although there is some debate as to whether transference can occur in such a brief therapy, many psychodynamically oriented brief therapists stress the importance of transference in their treatment (Bloom, 1992, p. 27). Theraplay therapists report that their patients form a close attachment to them and that patients react to Theraplay termination in ways similar to the adult patient's reaction to long-term therapy termination. Thus, for example, parents and adolescents must be prepared for a regression to previous behavior. Adolescents who had academic problems prior to Theraplay may stop doing homework. Withdrawn, depressed adolescents may retreat to their rooms. Defiant adolescents may temporarily pick fights. Well-prepared parents can take over where the therapist left off. Initially, this is reassuring to the adolescent. However, the adolescent's newfound pleasure in relating to others in a better way will soon take over to help him or her feel confident about the future.

A final warning about termination: Termination is a difficult time for both the patient and the therapist. The patient may want to cancel the last session, claiming that there is nothing left to do, that all problems are resolved. The therapist should not allow this retreat from the pain of separation. The therapist must be emotionally involved during this last phase of treatment and seek consultation if he or she experiences too much anxiety or depression. The therapist must demonstrate the courage to complete the treatment process as planned.

Variation of Treatment: Family Theraplay

Used with adolescents, Theraplay is a powerful tool. One variation, Family Theraplay (Jernberg & Jernberg, 1993), makes this an even more effective technique. Parents of adolescents need to communicate, sometimes through reproach, that they are capable of protecting and caring for their child (Shafer, 1960). Parents sometimes overunderstand their child's pain to the point of allowing unacceptable behavior (Weisberger, 1975). To ensure that they can offer more to their adolescent, parents must truly understand their own upbringing.

Sherwood (1990) described a treatment approach that significantly confronted the narcissistic resistance in conduct-disordered adolescents. Sherwood's approach works to help adolescents surrender their "infantile omnipotence" (p. 382) that has continued into adolescence making these children unwilling to submit to the demands of their parents. The goal is to help these children surrender this omnipotence in the interest of identification with the therapist. This is accomplished through "benevolent humiliation," which is "the humiliation of being treated like a child" (p. 382). This treatment allows adolescents to see that they are not their parents' equals and that they are not as smart, wise, experienced, successful, or even, in some cases, as physically strong. Only then can adolescents come to idealize their parents and to begin to take the steps necessary to attain the power of adulthood. Only then can they look up to their therapists for help in attaining status.

Family Theraplay helps parents regain status over their children. It also helps parents directly meet the adolescent's other needs. Rather than focusing only on the child, Family Theraplay helps parents regain control. Because it gives something to both adolescent and parent, it is especially effective. When the going gets rough, parents can be supported by therapists who serve as models and educators for handling difficult situations. Family Theraplay uses more resources than other therapies but is usually briefer, more powerful, and, thus, more worthy of the investment.

Family Theraplay is divided into the following seven segments (Jernberg, 1983):

1. *Intake Session.* Unless there is a crisis calling for immediate intervention (e.g., hospitalization), the parents are seen without the adolescent for the first session. This is a traditional intake session wherein the worker collects a thorough history of the child and family and a description of the problem. Family dynamics and developmental progress are explored. A substance abuse history is taken. If the clinician deems the family to be appropriate for Theraplay, the process described in the following segments continues. If it is not so deemed, they are referred to appropriate services (e.g., a substance abuse program).

2. *The Marschak Interaction Method* (MIM) (Jernberg, 1988; Jernberg, Allert, Koller, & Booth, 1983; Jernberg & Booth, 1991; Jernberg, Booth, Koller, & Allert, 1982; Jernberg, Wickersham, & Thomas, 1985; Koller, 1980, 1991; Marschak, 1960, 1967, 1980; Marschak & Call, 1966; Ritterfeld & Franke, 1993; Scholom & Koller, 1980). By selecting tasks that call out certain behaviors from adolescent and parent, the therapist is able to test out hypotheses about the family relationship. The MIM allows the clinician to

become an observer in the live interchanges that help and harm the adolescent. The MIM allows the therapist to decide which Theraplay dimensions to stress in the treatment. Only one parent at a time interacts on the MIM with the adolescent.

3. *MIM #2.* A second MIM session is scheduled if the adolescent comes from a two-parent family. This second MIM session could be scheduled on the same day as the first one; however, for reasons of boredom, practice effects, and so on, a one-week hiatus between the two sessions is preferable.

4. *MIM and Intake Feedback Session.* Parents meet with the therapist for one feedback session. If the MIM session was videotaped, select parts of the tape are shown to demonstrate parent and adolescent strengths and weaknesses. Weaknesses are demonstrated constructively in order not to further damage the already vulnerable parents. If, for example, a parent looks to the adolescent for direction about how to perform a task and that task breaks down into a power struggle, this can be pointed out to the parent but only if such an observation is followed by an example, within the interaction, of when the parent was in charge and the task, therefore, ran without incident.

The feedback session is very important. Parents must understand the philosophy of Theraplay and the resistance that they or their adolescent may put up to sabotage successful treatment. In order to help those parents who are prone to sabotage the treatment, the process of confrontation begins here. The therapist must prepare these parents for the anxiety they will feel when their child attempts to resist the therapist's efforts. Parents are asked whether they are ready to engage in such a struggle or whether they prefer to continue living with the present problem. With support and modeling, this confrontation continues throughout the Theraplay treatment. Parents are always consciously reminded that they have the option to continue their current situation or to do something different. A clear hierarchy is set up in the course of Theraplay. The therapists are at the top of this hierarchy and, in a playful, ego-enhancing way, communicate confidence and authority. Parents are next in line, and they are taught to imitate the therapist's behavior. The parents, like the adolescent, also must respect a line of authority. Adolescents remain at the bottom of the ladder. Their needs and pain are recognized, but the adults use their own judgment and they are the ones who call the shots. The feedback session ends with a contract to engage in a certain number of sessions, usually eight. A reevaluation may be made after session six.

5. *Theraplay: Adolescent and Parent Apart.* Parents sit behind a one-way viewing mirror (or at the far end of the Theraplay room possibly behind a video screen and videotape equipment). An Interpreting therapist sits beside or between the parents while the adolescent concurrently interacts with the therapist in the center of the Theraplay room. The parents must be trained to stay disengaged from the adolescent. If a mirror is used, the adolescent is told that he or she is being observed, and, in fact, some of the activities may be directed toward the one-way viewing mirror (e.g., showing off to the parents a handmade hat). The Interpreting therapist teaches the parents the principles of Theraplay and helps them to see what their child needs. Parents are encouraged to ask questions. The Interpreting Therapist answers these questions directly and additionally demonstrates how the parents' own history relates to the adolescent's development. Child sessions are physically active, and, therefore, Theraplay is scheduled for only 30 minutes.

6. *Theraplay: Parent and Adolescent Together.* During the first four (individual) sessions that follow the feedback session, the Interpreting therapist teaches the parents about Theraplay and about their child's underlying needs. They are prepared for their

eventual entry into the Theraplay sessions. The next four sessions are divided into two halves. The first 15 minutes run as described. The final 15 minutes are structured so that the parents enter the room and join the adolescent and his or her therapist in their Theraplay activities. The Theraplay therapist gradually helps the parents take over the treatment of their child, while at the same time providing the parents with support. It is not unusual for the parents to be given nurturing or structuring Theraplay activities so that they (the parents) can experience these firsthand.

It is deemed that Theraplay can be successfully terminated after these eight sessions, parents and adolescent are prepared for termination. The therapist points out individual strengths and the strength of the parent-child relationship. The final session becomes a termination party that may include photographs and party food.

If more Theraplay is needed or if the therapist determines that another form of treatment is appropriate, he or she discusses this with the parent in the first half of the Theraplay session six and presents this observation to the adolescent when the parents join child and therapist for the last 15 minutes of session six.

7. *Follow-up Sessions.* After termination, the therapist sets up a predetermined checkup schedule. This could be on a monthly or quarterly basis, continuing until an annual schedule seems appropriate.

Family Theraplay is an excellent training ground for new therapists. Potential Theraplay therapists can join forces with a senior therapist in the Theraplay room and learn by doing. Additionally, this second set of hands can be very helpful when working with more difficult adolescents.

CASE MATERIAL

Although there is, of course, no such thing as a typical adolescent Theraplay case, the following characterizes a good many of the kinds of adolescent referrals made to Theraplay therapists.

CASE ILLUSTRATION

John is a 15-year-old boy referred for poor school performance. John does not know his biological father. When he was 4 years old, his mother married his stepfather. In spite of numerous moves, he was an average student throughout grammar and middle school. His teachers, nonetheless, claimed that he was working below his ability. Although he says he has "lots of friends" at school, his parents have never seen one and worry that he is isolated. He is not involved in extracurricular activities, and, when his parents enroll him in an activity, he drops out saying "I'm bored."

When left to his own devices, John is quiet, almost nonexistent in the home. The moment a demand is made (e.g., "Turn off your radio and do your homework"), however, he becomes oppositional and hostile, sometimes even violent. His parents fold under his pressure to "get off my back" and remain silent until the next report card.

When John's parents are asked what they have tried to do to motivate John, the mother answers, "We ask him to study. We cajole him. We say we will buy him new basketball shoes if he could get just one C. We threaten to take his stereo away. We explain the importance of an education. We've said these things hundreds of times, but nothing works. We get excited when he goes for a new activity, but he bursts our bubble when, after one session, he returns complaining about the coach, the teacher, or the camp counselor. His teachers worry about him, but they're afraid to confront him because of his temper. They feel he has a lot of anger stored up inside that he needs 'to get out.' I think he has low self-esteem. His stepfather thinks he needs more discipline. Our nextdoor neighbor thinks he should attend one of those motivational seminars. One counselor we consulted told us to back off, that we were pressuring him too much and that he had to learn by suffering the consequences. Well, we backed off, and now he has failed everything." His mother continues, "He's still not doing his homework, and he's even more difficult to live with. When he was younger, we tried to punish him by taking his toys away. At one point, he had nothing left and never once asked for them back. We're worried he will never get a job or be able to live independently."

John and his parents were scheduled for an MIM, and his parents were scheduled for a feedback session. Some of what they said during the intake session became graphically clear during their performance of the MIM.

Both parents introduced each task by asking John a question. After his mother read the MIM instruction card, "Parents teach the child something he doesn't know," for example, she said to John, "What should I teach you? What don't you know?" John shrugged his shoulders, and, after a moment of silence, his mother asked, "Would you like to know what ISBN stands for in the front of books?" John's predictable answer was "No." His mother continued to propose other ideas, but John rejected each one. She asked, "How about if I teach you the Latin word for *hand*? Do you want me to teach you how to count to 10 in Spanish? Can I teach you how to sew a button on your clothes?" Eventually John became restless and annoyed. He picked up the next MIM card and handed it to his mother to read. She read the next instruction: "Comb each other's hair." John did not like this idea and handed her the next card. They repeated this interchange for two more cards until John's mother finally decided to stick with the task on the card in front of her. A power struggle ensued, but the mother managed to complete the task: "Try dress-up hats on each other." After concluding the task, she looked at the camera and, in a frustrated tone, said, "This is what we have all the time at home."

Although John's stepfather had been described as more strict than his mother during the intake session, he, too, asked many questions. After reading "Teach child something he doesn't know," he said, "What should I teach you?" John answered, "I don't know." His stepfather repeated "C'mon, what should I teach you?" This time John said angrily "How should I know what I don't know." The stepfather responded angrily, "Look! We have to do this. I need some cooperation here! You think you know everything, but you don't! Now tell me something you don't know." John responded, "How to drive." The stepfather then proceeded to give an imaginary demonstration about how to start a car, put it in gear, and so on. This task was characteristic of the entire MIM and ended with the stepfather reporting that he did not feel that the examiner got a good picture of John. He said that this MIM went smoothly, compared to life at home, that one would get the idea that John was not a problem.

The Interpreting therapist pointed out two main themes to John's parents during the feedback session. He helped John's parents to see John's need for both structure and challenge. The therapist also pointed out that John and his parents might feel better if they were more playful.

The MIM and feedback sessions were administered by the Interpreting Therapist. The videotape was reviewed by both the Interpreting Therapist and John's Theraplay therapist. Accordingly, the two clinicians planned the following activities for session one:

1. Introductions and tour of the Theraplay room
2. Body-part check
3. Pillow pushing
4. Cool down with paper fans and wet towels
5. Weight measurement and weight manipulation on a scale
6. Thumb wrestling
7. Water pistol duel
8. M&M feeding (hand to mouth)
9. Height/arm span measurement
10. Newspaper-hat making (not appropriate with children who are slow-moving or compulsive)

During this first Theraplay session, the Interpreting therapist planned to point out to the parents the fast-moving, playful, and well-structured nature of the Theraplay sessions. In future sessions, the Interpreting therapist would point how Theraplay therapists are always in charge, how they do not waiver from a playful attitude. The parents will be encouraged to ask questions but will be shown how the Theraplay therapist, even by tone of voice, avoids the answering of inappropriate, unnecessary, or self-defeating questions.

Session one: John and therapist alone

John and his parents arrived for the first session and sat in the waiting room. John sat at one end of the room and sullenly read a magazine. His parents sat together at the other end and talked to each other in a cheerful but nervous manner.

The Interpreting and Theraplay therapists entered the waiting room. The Interpreting therapist introduced the Theraplay therapist to John's family. John's therapist took over from there. He (John's therapist) walked up to John, shook his hand, and cheerfully said, "Follow me; I'll show you our room." On the way to the Theraplay room, he showed John the observation room with its one-way viewing mirror and told him that his parents and their therapist would be watching the session from there.

The two then entered the stark Theraplay room, and John's therapist humorously said, "I'll give you a tour. This is a scientifically designed room. Notice the walls: four of them, not three, not two. Also please check out the ceiling, high enough so we can stand up. And, on the floor, mats to prevent all injury. Have a seat." John looked bewildered as his therapist handed him a pillow on which to sit. The following is their interchange as they do the first task: Body-part check.

THERAPLAY THERAPIST: John, before we begin, I have to be sure that your parents gaveyou everything you were supposed to bring to the session so that we can do what we need to do.

JOHN: They didn't tell me to bring anything.

THERAPLAY THERAPIST: I hate when this happens. Oh well, let's see anyway. Let's see your hands. (Therapist takes John's hands.)

JOHN: What are you doing?"

THERAPLAY THERAPIST: Yes, you have all the fingers we need. Five on this hand and five more. Wait—one, two, three, four, right, five on this one.

JOHN: Stop! What are you doing? This is weird. You are weird!"

THERAPLAY THERAPIST: Before you call *me* weird, let me see how many feet you have. (The therapist takes John's shoes off.) Yep, two feet. Wow, and two good arms, and . . . Oh no! Stop! Wait! No! Have you lost your mind? What's the point of this?

THERAPLAY THERAPIST: I'm glad you asked that question. You must have all these parts in order to do the next activity. (John's therapist picks up a large pillow, holds it chest high, and pushes against John.) On the count of three, I want you to try to push me back a step, and I'll do the same. One, two, three, push! (Therapist pushes against John, who has no choice but to push back to maintain his balance. Three rounds are attempted, but, after the second round, John sits on the floor. His therapist sits in front of him and does round three from a sitting position.) That's great. Good arm strength. I'll write that down after the session. (Claps hands.)

JOHN: Wait, Wait! Hold on! You've lost it, man.

THERAPLAY THERAPIST: Whew, that was hard work. (John's therapist fans John with a pillow.) Someday you'll be able to beat me at that game. Let me feel your arm muscles.

JOHN: (John unsuccessfully attempts to withdraw his arm from his therapist's grasp.)

THERAPLAY THERAPIST: (John's therapist takes a wet towel and pats John's arms with it.) There, that should cool you off. (Continues to fan John.)

JOHN: I'm not hot.

John has already begun to resist the therapist's efforts. This resistance is mostly verbal, but John also backed away physically. His therapist was not deterred, and John attempted to resort to his old defenses of sitting passively while the adult tried to engage him. However, the intrusiveness of the Theraplay approach made this difficult so that John had to actively deal with his newfound friend.

The first session ended with John joining his parents in the hallway. He shook his head and walked in front of them. They, however, smiled in approval of what they had just witnessed. Later, the Interpreting therapist told John's therapist that the parents had not seen John move so much in years. They also liked that he expressed some emotions, even though it was negative. In their experience, his opposition would have caused them to back away and avoid his anger.

Session two: John and therapist alone

John knew what to expect during his second Theraplay session. He clicked his tongue and sighed with disapproval when his therapist entered the waiting room. In spite of this, he energetically stood up from his seat and followed his therapist to the Theraplay room. The session began.

THERAPLAY THERAPIST: Hi, John. Checkout time. Last week I forgot to see if you brought all your knuckles. I won those thumb wrestling matches so easily that I later worried that you might be missing some knuckles. (John's therapist takes John's hand and starts counting his knuckles.) Let's see. One, two, three, . . ., fourteen. Well, that looks right to me. Let's see the other hand. (John holds his hand out to his therapist.) One, two, three, . . ., fourteen. That one's good, too. Let's try that thumb wrestling game again.

JOHN: Here we go again. (John rolls his eyes.) (John is curious about this knuckle-counting activity and watches closely as his therapist counts). Let's not.

THERAPLAY THERAPIST: This time I'm going to make it more difficult. I'm going to put baby lotion on each of our thumbs and see who wins. (After lotioning both thumbs, the contest began.)

JOHN: Gross. (Taken by surprise at how difficult it was to catch a slippery thumb, John laughed for two rounds before catching himself and becoming serious.)

John verbally protested each Theraplay activity during this second session but never refused to participate. Unlike his usual defense, John could not withdraw into day dreams or other forms of self-stimulation. He had to deal with his therapist who was not discouraged by John's negativity.

Session four: John and therapist alone

By session four, John was more engaged. At times, he retreated from an activity, but, rather than express hostility toward the therapist, he looked sad. His therapist recognized John's sadness and switched to more nurturing activities, as in the following example:

THERAPLAY THERAPIST: (John and his therapist are engaged in a game of tug-of-war) That's right. Pull, John. Harder. I don't know if I can hold on much longer. You did it! You pulled me over the line.

JOHN: (John is doing what he should, even trying to conceal a smile. However, when the game is over, John looks sad.)

THERAPLAY THERAPIST: (Noting John's sadness, his therapist moved a nurturing activity, scheduled for later, into the treatment at this point. John, of course, does not know the order of the activities or what will come next, so this transition is very smooth.) Here, John, put your head on this pillow while I fan you. I brought some oranges for us to eat.(John's therapist feeds him orange slices, hand to mouth.)

JOHN: (John relaxes, sighs.) "What kind of orange is this?"

When the feeding was finished, John looked more relaxed and engaged. His therapist returned to the normal schedule and ended the session by making a crepe paper bow tie for John. Later, when John left the session, he spontaneously took this tie off and attached it to his stepfather. Both stepfather and John laughed as the family left the office.

Session five: John and parents together

John's parents were brought into the last 15 minutes of sessions five through eight. During the first half of the session, John and his therapist played as usual. Both were aware that his parents would enter the room during session five. John and his therapist planned a way to invite his parents into the room.

THERAPLAY THERAPIST: John, get up on the scale. We'll weigh you, and then you pull my arms and see how heavy you can make yourself. We'll see how many pounds you can increase your weight. Then we'll call your parents into the room. They can try this using each other, and we'll see how well they can do.

JOHN: (John stands on the scale and easily increases his weight to the maximum possible on this particular scale.)

JOHN: Okay, c'mon in! Come over to the scale. (Forgetting that his parents watched him plan this activity, John explained to them what they were to do.)

PARENTS: John's mother strains to increase her weight.)

JOHN: (John laughs joyfully.)

PARENTS: That's harder than it looks. (John's stepfather tries to pull her, but she cannot hold on.)

THERAPLAY THERAPIST: Okay, everybody sit down.Another contest. I'm going to put this donut on my finger and pass it around. I'll ask each of you to take a bite. Be careful. The one who takes the bite that makes the donut fall off my finger loses the game.

PARENTS: (John's parents are good sports and cooperate with the game.)

THERAPLAY THERAPIST: (With small amount of donut left . . .) You guys are good. I quit!

JOHN: No, you have to take your turn.

THERAPLAY THERAPIST: Okay, that was the deal. (The therapist takes the last bite, and the remaining bit of donut falls to the floor.)

(JOHN: Cheers rise from John.)

PARENTS: (And from his parents.)

At times, John becomes quiet during the sessions. His parents, alerted to this by the Interpreting therapist, easily follow John's therapist's lead to rub lotion on his hands and arms. They also feed him orange juice through a sports water bottle. This always perks John up, and activities can resume at a higher pitch. His parents are beginning to understand John's need for nurturance and how important it is to meet this need if they expect him to take initiative and show ambition. They realize that they have to refuel him after he engages in a challenge and that this need for refueling is not a defect in John but simply something he missed from an earlier age. His parents also get a taste of what it feels like to be nurtured during Theraplay. They then realize that they themselves have more sources for nurturance (each other, for example) than does John.

John's need for nurturance and his ability to accept it made his Theraplay progress quickly. His parents stopped pressuring him about his school work during the initial Theraplay sessions but, with the Interpreting therapist's help, began to raise expectations. John fought them, but, by refueling him before, during, and after homework, the parents were able to encourage him to complete his work.

The therapists recommended four additional Theraplay sessions beyond the original eight. They did this to help the parents deal with John as they increased their demands on him. Whenever he complained, they sympathized, gave him a shoulder rub or a piece of fruit, and he returned to his work until he again depleted his own resources.

John's parents were obviously highly motivated. They were willing to put their own needs on hold and make John the center of attention. They stopped trying to control him by verbal "remote control." They also stopped complaining about what he *should* be able to do if he *tried*.

John is a bright teenager. The fact that he did any homework increased his grades well into the passing range. He became less phobic about school and more relaxed in the classroom. His parents reported that he was now showing a good sense of humor and that this attracted other children to him.

The termination session

The final session was planned as a termination party. The therapists hung crepe paper from the ceiling and placed balloons around the room. They brought cookies, party hats, noise makers, and punch to the session. They hung up a large piece of paper with the following written on it:

JOHN

Height	# of Fingers
Weight	# of Knuckles
Arm Span	# of Feet
Eye Color	# of Ears
	# of Noses
Hand Outline	Foot Outline

Face Profile Outline

John and his therapist began this session alone. His therapist talked about John's progress (e.g., "You're really so much quicker now. I can hardly ever beat you in thumb wrestling anymore.") After some time together, the two called his parents to join the party. John's therapists then filled out his form by measuring him and tracing his hands, feet, and face profile. They shared stories about prior Theraplay sessions while eating party food and making hats for each other.

John's formal Theraplay sessions were terminated after this party. A follow-up, check-up session was arranged for 3 months later. His parents were given follow-up questionnaires to complete and goodbyes were exchanged.

CONCLUSION

Theraplay gives adolescents some of what they want and some of what they need. They may not want to talk to adults, but they cannot resist laughing. They may want to be "junior adults," but they need time to develop, learn, and experience life. Parents must not allow children's grandiosity and impulsiveness to take over. The child may want immediate gratification, but parents must realize that this leads to disaster.

Sometimes parents, like teenagers, need help to see that it takes time to grow up, and that their child's good language development or adult-like size does not substitute for life experience. Adolescents who accuse their parents of not trusting them may be guilty of manipulation, even though parents, of course, should not completely trust their children. As the child grows older, parents use their own judgment to decide how far out of the nest a child can go. Some parents' apprehensions notwithstanding, setting limits will not stifle ambition or creativity. Structure allows children to invest more time on creative ventures rather than to engage in a "costly legal battle" with parents over a curfew.

Theraplay helps adolescents become young children again for awhile. It gives parents the opportunity to regroup and to fill the gaps—necessary before adolescents can pass to the next level of trust. This process does not have to be serious, overly intellectual, or performed in a vacuum—yet it would be misleading to imply that it is easy.

Theraplay helps parents and adolescents make decisions about their future. If parents decide to retain the status quo, they will do so with full knowledge of the consequences. If they want to bring about change, they can do that with the help of a therapist who recognizes both the strength and wisdom of parents and the adolescent's desire for empathic parenting.

REFERENCES

Armsden, G. C., & Greenberg, M. T. (1987). The inventory of parent and peer attachment: Individual differences and their relationship to psychological well being in adolescence. *Journal of Youth and Adolescence, 16*, 427–453.

Bemporad, J. R. (1988). Psychodynamic treatment of depressed adolescents. *Journal of Clinical Psychiatry, 49*, 26–31.

Blos, P. (1962). *On adolescence.* New York: Free Press.

Bloom, B. L. (1992). *Planned short-term psychotherapy: A clinical handbook.* Boston: Allyn and Bacon.

Davanloo, H. (1978). *Basic principles and techniques in short term dynamic psychotherapy.* New York: SP Medical & Scientific Books.

DesLauriers, A. (1962). *The experience of reality in childhood schizophrenia.* New York: International Universities Press.

Dryfoos, J. G. (1990). *Adolescents at risk: Prevalence and prevention.* New York: Oxford University Press.

Erikson, E. H. (1950). *Childhood and society*. New York: Norton.

Frank, R., Salkever, D. S., & Sharfstein, S. S. (1991, Summer). Growth in expenditure for mental health services under private insurance, 1986–1989. *Health Affairs*, 116–123.

Freud, A. (1958). Adolescence. In *Psychoanalytic Study of the Child* (Vol. 13, pp. 255–278). New York: International Universities Press.

Giovachinni, P. (1985). Introduction: Countertransference responses to adolescents. In S. Feinstein, M. Sugar, A. Esman, J. Cooney, A. Schwartzberg, & A. Sorosky (Eds.), *Adolescent psychiatry: Development and clinical studies* (Vol. 12, pp. 447–480). Chicago: University of Chicago Press.

Glick, P. C. (1984). Marriage, divorce and living arrangements: Prospective change. *Journal of Family Issues, 5*, 7–26.

Holmes, W. D., & Wagner, K. D. (1992). Psychotherapy treatments for depression in children and adolescents. *Journal of Psychotherapy Practice and Research, 1*, 313–323.

James, B. (1989). *Treating traumatized children*. Lexington, MA: Lexington Books.

Jernberg, A. (1979). *Theraplay*. San Francisco: Jossey-Bass.

Jernberg, A. (1983). Therapeutic use of sensory-motor play. In C. E. Schaefer & K. J. O'Connor (Eds.), *Handbook of play therapy* (pp. 128–147). New York: Wiley.

Jernberg, A. (1988). Untesuchung und therapie der pranatalen mutter-kind-beziehung. *Praxis kinderpsychologie und kinderpsychiatrie, 37*, 161–167.

Jernberg, A. (1989). Training parents of failure-to-attach children. In C. E. Schaefer & J. Briesmeister (Eds.), *Handbook of parent training: Parents as co-therapists for children* (pp. 392–413). New York: Wiley.

Jernberg, A. (1990). Attachment enhancing for adopted children. In P. V. Grebe (Ed.), *Adoption resources for mental health professionals* (pp. 271–279). New Brunswick: Transaction Publishers.

Jernberg, A., Allert, A., Koller, T., & Booth, P. (1983). *Reciprocity in parent-infant relationships*. Chicago: The Theraplay Institute.

Jernberg, A., & Booth, P. (1991). *Clinical research and teaching uses of the Marschak Interaction Method: Observing and evaluating controlled interactions between parents and children*. Chicago: The Theraplay Institute.

Jernberg, A., Booth, P., Koller, T., & Allert, A. (1982). *Manual of the administration and the clinical interpretation of the Marschak Interaction Method: Preschool and school age*. Chicago: The Theraplay Institute.

Jernberg, A., Hurst, T., & Lyman, C. (1969). *Here I am* [Film]. Chicago: The Theraplay Institute.

Jernberg, A., & Jernberg, E. (1993). Family Theraplay for the family tyrant. In T. Kottman & C. E. Schaefer (Eds.), *Play therapy in action: A casebook for practitioners*. New York: Jason Aronson.

Jernberg, A., & Koller, T., (1984, August). *Attachment failure in older adopted children*. Paper presented at the Biannual Training Conference of the North American Council of Adoptable Children, Chicago, IL.

Jernberg, A., Wickersham, M., & Thomas, E. (1985). *Mothers' behaviors and attitudes toward their unborn infants*. Chicago: The Theraplay Institute.

Jones, E. (1922). Some problems of adolescence. *British Journal of Psychiatry, 13*, 41–47.

Kaplan, L. J. (1984). *Adolescence: The farewell to childhood*. New York: Simon and Schuster.

Kazdin, A. E. (1987). *Conduct disorder in childhood and adolescence*. Newbury Park, CA: Sage Publications.

Kazdin, A. E. (1992). Child and adolescent dysfunction. *Clinical Psychology Review, 12*, 795–817.

Kelleher, K. J., Taylor, J. L., & Rickert, V. I. (1992). Mental health services for rural children and adolescents. *Clinical Psychology Review, 12*, 841–852.

Klaus, M. J., & Kennell, J. H. (1976). *Maternal-infant bonding*. St. Louis, MO: Mosby.

Kohut, H. (1977). *The Restoration of the self.* New York: International Universities Press.

Koller, T. (1980). *The relationship of infant temperament to mother-infant and father-infant interaction.* Unpublished doctoral dissertation, Illinois Institute of Technology, Chicago, IL.

Koller, T. (1991, March). *Evaluating interactions in foster/adoptive families.* Workshop presented at the Annual Family and Schools Conference sponsored by the Institute for Juvenile Research, Chicago, IL.

Lewis, H., & Lee-Painter, S. (1974). An interactional approach to the mother-infant dyad. In M. Lewis & L. A. Rosenblum (Eds.), *The effect of the infant on its caretaker* (pp. 21–48). New York: Wiley.

Loeber, R. (1982). The stability of antisocial and delinquent childhood behavior. *Child Development, 53,* 1431–1446.

Malan, D. H. (1976). *The frontier of brief psychotherapy.* New York: Plenum Press.

Mann, J. (1973). *Time-limited psychotherapy.* Cambridge, MA: Harvard University Press.

Marschak, M. (1960). A method for evaluating child-parent interaction under controlled conditions. *Journal of Genetic Psychology, 97,* 3–22.

Marschak, M. (1967). Imitation and participation in normal and disturbed young boys in interaction with their parents. *Journal of Clinical Psychology, 23*(4), 421–427.

Marschak, M. (1980). *Parent-child interaction and youth rebellion.* New York: Gardner Press.

Marschak, M., & Call, J. (1966). Observing the disturbed child and his parents: Class demonstration of medical students. *Journal of the American Academy of Child Psychiatry, 5,* 686–692.

Miller, A. (1981). *Prisoners of childhood: The drama of the gifted child and the search for the true self.* New York: Basic Books.

Mishne, J. M. (1986). *Clinical work with adolescents.* New York: Free Press.

Offer, D., & Boxer, A. M. (1991). Normal adolescent development: Empirical research findings. In M. Lewis (Ed.), *Child and adolescent psychiatry: A comprehensive textbook* (pp. 266–278). Baltimore, MD: Williams & Wilkins.

Offer, D., Ostrov, E., & Howard, K. (1981). *The adolescent: A psychological self-portrait.* New York: Basic Books.

Raja, S. N., McGee, R., & Stanton, W. R. (1992). Perceived attachments to parents and peers and psychological well-being in adolescence. *Journal of Youth and Adolescence, 21*(4), 471–485.

Rieff, M. L. (1991). Theraplay with developmentally disabled infants and toddlers. *The Theraplay Institute Newsletter,* 4–6.

Ritterfeld, U., & Franke, U. (1992). *Die heidelberger Marschak-Interaktionmethode (H-MIM): Zur diagnostischen beurteilung der dyadischen interaktion mit vorschulkindern.* Stuttgart, Germany: Fischer-Verlag.

Scholom, A., & Koller, T. (1980). *Relating infant temperament to mother- and father-infant interaction.* Paper presented at the Annual Meeting of the American Psychological Association (Division 12, Section 1), Montreal, Canada.

Seifer, R., Sameroff, A. J., Baldwin, C. P., & Baldwin, A. (1992). Child and family factors that ameliorate risk between 4 and 13 years of age. *Journal of the American Academy of Child and Adolescent Psychiatry, 31*(5), 893–903.

Shafer, R. (1960). The loving and beloved superego in Freud's structural theory. *Psychoanalytic Study of the Child, 15,* 163–190.

Sherwood, V. R. (1990). The first stage of treatment with the conduct-disordered adolescent: overcoming narcissistic resistance. *Psychotherapy, 27,* 380–387.

Sifneos, P. E. (1972). *Short-term psychotherapy and emotional crisis.* Cambridge, MA: Harvard University Press.

Steinberg, L., & Silverberg, S. B. (1986). The vicissitudes of autonomy in early adolescence. *Child Development, 57,* 841–851.

United States Congress, Office of Technology Assessment. (1991). *Adolescent Health* (OTA-H-468). Washington, DC: U.S. Government Printing Office.

Weisberger, E. (1975). *You and your child.* New York: Dutton.

CHAPTER 8

The Use of Play Therapy with Adults

DIANE E. FREY

INTRODUCTION

Mention the word *play* to adults, and it is much like mentioning the word *love*. Everybody knows about it, but no one can really define it. Mention the words *adult play therapy* to adults, and the response is much like the song title, "What's Love Got to Do with It?": What's play got to do with it?

Although everyone can relate to play, many adults think play therapy approaches have nothing relevant for them. Just how relevant play is for adults is aptly captured in this incident entitled, "Tooth Sayer."

> A child's tooth had been loose for weeks, but when it finally wriggled out, her parents still hadn't decided the Tooth Fairy's going rate. They debated back and forth. The quarter they'd received for their baby teeth was worth much less now and they could risk disappointment when their daughter looked under her pillow. The higher dollar bounty that some classmates were getting seemed higher and conveyed the wrong value. So, in the name of tradition, the parents settled on a quarter, which the mother, undetected, substituted for the tooth that night.
>
> "She came, she came!" the girl shouted the next morning, waving the coin; "The tooth fairy came! I saw her! She was dressed in pink with big purple lace wings."
>
> Her parents had forgotten: What the Tooth Fairy is all about is not money, but magic. (Tooth Sayer, 1991, p. 117)

Adults and Play

Such adults may have lost sight of their "child self," the childhood experience, and/or the benefits of play. They have lost the "magic" and perhaps do not realize the value play has for adults as well as for children.

There is a reciprocal relationship between play and learning. There is a *play-competence spiral* in which learning leads to more sophisticated play and play results in a mastery that leads to more learning, which leads to more play, and so forth. Children play so much that the major learning experiences of individuals can be said to be developed through play. The play-competence spiral helps children reach an adult level in the cognitive, affective, and behavioral domains.

While play contributes immensely to the child's physical development (behavioral domain), play's current and ongoing contribution to adults is mainly in the cognitive and affective domains. Play is an apprenticeship for adult life. The cognitive, affective, and behavioral learnings that a person develops through play in childhood are those that are useful in his or her culture. It is through play that individuals become integrated into society. Play opens thoughts and feelings. Through this process is developed a flexibility that enables society to change.

Those adults who did not play much in childhood, therefore, have had little apprentice-ship for adult life. They often lack the skills for dealing with rejection, cooperation, and competition that are gleaned from childhood play. It becomes evident, then, why they do not feel integrated into society.

According to Aldis (1975), most play is between the young. Typically, play begins in a fragmentary way in infancy, reaches its peak in childhood years, and tapers off in adolescence. Usually, when adults play, it is activity that is initiated by infants or children. There are, of course, many reasons why therapists need to guide adults back to the world of play.

Play enhances the physical, social, emotional, and intellectual growth across stages of human development. Play, stated Sutton-Smith (1975, p. 199), "potentiates novelty" and increases a person's ability to adapt to a changing world.

In elucidating about how he thought about a problem, Einstein stated that "play seems to be the essential feature in productive thought—before there is any connection with logical construction in work or other kinds of signs which can be communicated to others" (Koestler, 1964, p. 171). Thus, playing with ideas was essential before Einstein began to think more completely.

Play can be very vitalizing. Playing has neurophysiological effects on children and adults. During play, customary rules of conduct are suspended, thus allowing for the release of feelings and aggression, disapproval of authority figures, and resolution of conflicts. Thus, play transcends ordinary behavior, becoming a diversion from routine and societal demands.

Types of Play

Since play can be so valuable in therapy with adults, it is helpful to explore the many types of play and the major characteristics of play. A schema that most experts agree upon identifies four types of play: physical play, manipulative play, symbolic play, and games (Chance, 1979).

In the *physical* type of play, action is primary. Running, jumping, wrestling, tag, and king of the mountain are examples of play in which the major emphasis is in the sensorimotor domain. Adult play that is primarily physical includes such activities as football, golf, swimming, baseball, and cycling. In adult play therapy, any activities that are primarily action-oriented would fall in this category. An activity commonly referred to as "I like my neighbor who" is frequently used as an icebreaker in adult group therapy: In a group of eight adults, for example, seven chairs are placed in a circle. The person without a chair begins by saying something like, "I like my neighbor who has brown eyes." All who have brown eyes get up from their chairs and move to another chair. The person remaining standing then can state, "I like my neighbor who . . . " (e.g., enjoys movies, likes classical music, works second shift, . . .). Play continues until the therapist believes people have become well acquainted in the group. The emphasis on action and movement qualifies this play activity as primarily the physical type.

When individuals try to gain control or master the environment, they are engaging in *manipulative* play. Such play attempts to answer a question like, "What will someone do?" or "What will happen when I do this?" Playing with jigsaw puzzles can be an example of this type of play. Exploring broken pieces of a large object or taking apart objects can also be considered manipulative play. The use of puppetry in adult play therapy is often an example of manipulative play because the adult, through the puppet, often seeks to discover "What will happen if I do this?" By using puppets in family therapy, the play therapist frequently discovers how members of the family manipulate each other.

Symbolic play, a third type of play, involves fantasy play. Daydreaming is a type of symbolic play for adults. Symbolic play is characterized by a lack of rules or constraints. Sociodrama could be a type of symbolic play used with adults. The use of art therapy in play therapy with adults is also frequently symbolic.

When the play involves rules and conversions, it is called a *game*, the fourth category of play. Interactional board games used with adults in play therapy include such games as "The Ungame" (Zakich, 1975), "Social Security" (Barten, 1976), and "Reunion" (Zakich & Monroe, 1979). Card games, chess, and checkers can also be used with adults in play therapy.

These four categories of play provide a taxonomy for the enhanced understanding of play. It should be noted, however, that these categories are not usually exclusive and, in some ways, are arbitrary classifications.

Characteristics of Play

Experts in the field of play therapy agree that at least five characteristics are common to all types of play (Chance, 1979).

The first characteristic is that *play is fun*. When people play, they enjoy what they are doing. Play is most often something one *feels* more so than something one *does*. Those who enjoy play describe a mental state called *flow*. Most characteristic of this state of flow is a high degree of concentration to the extent that the participant is unaware of other events. A person does not think about doing something during flow, rather he or she is just doing it.

Secondly, *play is more a process than a product*. Play is enjoyed as an end in itself. When adults play in therapy, the end comes from the activity itself not the end product. Play is innerdirected; it has intrinsic motivation. While there may be intrinsic rewards of play, the external elements are not necessary for the maintenance of play. Whether it be an infant reaching for a mobile, a child playing with building blocks, an adolescent playing football, or an adult playing chess, there is a common element of the rewards of play coming from within. Extrinsic rewards can change what is ordinarily playful into something that is more like work.

It is possible to turn work into play. In work, the activity involved is usually a means to an end—a paycheck, praise, words of encouragement. In play, the activity is the end; the process more than the product is the emphasis. Work becomes play when the means and the end are both internally and externally rewarding. While this may be a rare occasion for adults, a play therapist may assist adults aiming toward this goal.

Another characteristic of play is that *play is nonliteral*. In play, the activity is processed more as a medium of expression than a literal interpretation. If taken literally, the game of "Monopoly" would be somewhat absurd! Several people compete to acquire plastic hotels and paper money. It is not the objects in and of themselves that are important, but more the fact that these objects facilitate the play. These objects only provide the experience for play. Similarly, the laugh that accompanies a teasing remark or the insult that is delivered with a wink are all methods of saying, "I'm playing." Play is obviously more than it seems on the surface.

A fourth characteristic is that *play provides a challenge*. If an activity is too difficult or too easy, it is not thought of as play. To qualify as play, the activity must be difficult enough to be interesting but not so difficult as to be frustrating. Play is most successful when the challenge matches the skill level of the individual as closely as possible. A grandmaster chess player would be bored if competing against a novice. What is difficult for one person, of course, can be easy for another. Hence, a skilled play therapist realizes that the same activity can be play for one adult client but not for another.

Lastly, *play exists in relaxed settings.* In play, a person has a type of diplomatic immunity from the usual expectations and conventions of life. As a person matures, the permission to play becomes more restricted. For adults, permission is often limited to certain places and times. Some places where adults have permission to play are at amusement parks, New Year's Eve parties, nightclubs, and the play therapist's office.

PROCEDURE AND TECHNIQUE

Therapist Qualifications

To be an effective play therapist, one has to feel comfortable with the arena of play and with its application to adults. Adult clients will sense any anxiety or hesitancy that the therapist may have regarding play. It is also extremely helpful if the therapist has enjoyed play as a child.

Winnicott (1971) stated that "psychotherapy is done in the overlap of the two play areas, that of patient and that of therapist. If the therapist cannot play, then he's not suitable for the work. If the patient can't play, then something needs to be done to enable the patient to become able to play, after which psychotherapy may begin" (p. 54).

Appropriate Adult Populations for Play Therapy

While play therapy is appropriate for almost all adult clients, there are some adult clients for whom play therapy is an especially effective treatment modality. These adult clients benefit considerably from play therapy approaches.

Adults who as children were subject to early parentification are excellent clients for play therapy. A child who had to parent his or her father or mother because the parent was physically or mentally ill or unable to cope with life stressors is an example of parentification. A child who had to parent younger siblings because one or both parents were unable or unwilling to parent them is also an example of parentification. The child's time was spent primarily in parenting, not playing, and as a result, the child often lost the playfulness of childhood.

Adult children of alcoholics (A.C.O.A.) and adult children of divorce (A.C.O.D.) are also clients who can benefit from the use of play therapy. As children, these clients often had serious issues to deal with and, as such, lost part or all of their childhoods.

Those adults who are emotionally constricted are also good candidates for adult play therapy. Adults who live primarily in the cognitive domain have lost touch with their affective side and their own playfulness.

Adults who prefer to function primarily by using left brain approaches are benefited by play therapy (McCaulley, 1990). On the Myers-Briggs Type Indicator, for example, those adults who are primarily sensors, judges, and thinkers (S.J.T.) are benefited by play therapy, which helps them to become more whole-brained in their approaches to life.

Adults whose jobs require extensive in-depth thought often forget to play. As such they frequently lose touch with the creative aspects of themselves.

Individuals who are highly stressed can be assisted by play therapy approaches. Play therapy helps them to engage in a catharsis for the stress and develops more effective methods of managing stress.

Workaholics are also good candidates for play therapy. For them, life has become work. With no play in their life, life can become boring and depressing for these adults.

Parents of the children play therapists see in therapy are also a very suitable population for play therapy. These parents often need to learn how to play with their children.

Adults who are developmentally handicapped are frequently excellent candidates for play therapy. While more traditional approaches might be too abstract for these clients, play therapy approaches provide an excellent modality for communicating with such adults.

Elderly clients are good clients for the use of play therapy also. Such clients might be threatened by traditional approaches to therapy but often will respond to art or music therapy approaches.

Play therapists who themselves are overworked and stressed can also benefit from becoming more playful and using these techniques. During the demands of building a successful career, play therapists can often lose sight of their playful side. If a play therapist cannot play, his or her client will find it difficult to play in therapy.

Psychological Dynamics Suitable for Play Therapy with Adults

In addition to these specific client types, clients who have certain psychological dynamics are also very suited to play therapy approaches. These clients include adults who are resistant to therapy. While such a client might resist disclosing information to a therapist or resist transferring information learned in therapy into everyday life, play therapy approaches help the therapist to engage the client in this manner. An adult who, for example, refuses to talk to a therapist will usually draw or play a board game.

Adults involved in denial also benefit from play therapy. Although they consciously deny alcoholism, for example, they will discuss the elements related to it through game play or drawing.

Adults who are psychologically unaware of the etiology, or cause, of their difficulties will often manifest this through play approaches; for example, an adult client who was unaware of being raised in a dysfunctional, alcoholic family displayed these characteristics through the play of the "Adult Children Game" (Miller, 1987).

Those adults who are verbally deficient in their ability to describe a problem are also good candidates for play therapy. Often such clients draw out their concerns even though they do not have the vocabulary to express them.

Clients who are inhibited can often benefit from play therapy; for example, clients who are inhibited about discussing sexual concerns in a relationship will often do so through the use of the board game "An Enchanted Evening" (An Enchanted, 1989).

Adult clients who are usually disclosing and cooperative but who reach a particular topic that is vulnerable for them also find play therapy helpful. Such a client is frequently doing well in therapy and then reaches a plateau due to a particularly sensitive concern. This concern can be surfaced more readily through play therapy.

Contraindications for the Use of Play Therapy with Adults

There are contraindications for the use of play therapy with adults. Adults for whom playfulness is threatening are adults for whom this modality is not advised. Often this type of adult has a history of damage in play or close relationships. Perhaps the adult felt seduced by playful intrusions, only to be betrayed. A relative may have, for instance, introduced incest as a "game."

Play can represent defensiveness for some clients. The play can be calculated or driven by the client as a defense mechanism. Play can serve to mask hostility of some clients and, as such is not facilitative. Clients can become playful to avoid dealing with hostility and anger. Some adult clients use play as a means to become seductive or disarming. As such, this retards the progression of therapy and contraindicates play therapy.

Adults can use play as a means to manipulate and control the therapy environment. Such adults use playful techniques to avoid dealing with issues; for example, an adult client might insist on always playing chess with the therapist, long after the value of chess playing as a therapeutic process has ceased. It is possible to start traditional therapy with such clients and gradually begin the use of play therapy when the client has a readiness for it. In general, however, great caution is needed when working with such clients in adult play therapy.

It is necessary for play therapists to monitor the impact of play therapy with adult clients in order to avoid the dangers of defensiveness, seduction, manipulation, and transference. Failure to identify these dynamics or going along with client pseudoplayfulness can result in collusion. Monitoring the degree to which play is client-initiated, therapist-initiated, or cojointly initiated is also important in the therapeutic process. The therapists's acute awareness of these interactional dynamics is extremely important for the successful use of play therapy with adults.

While such monitoring is necessary, it is also important for the play therapist to be spontaneous in play approaches with adults. Play therapists need to be playful themselves. It is also crucial for play therapists to trust their intuition while engaging in play therapy with adults.

Strategies

Uses of Play Therapy

Play therapy can have many uses with adults. It can be used:

• For diagnosis. One adult client had so successfully repressed the death of her young triplets that she neglected to inform the therapist of this life event while discussing her major depressive episode. The use of drawings assisted the therapist in discovering an anniversary syndrome cause of depression that more formalized testing did not reveal.

• To enhance the therapeutic relationship. When adult clients refuse to discuss relevant information with a therapist and chastise the therapist, the therapist could use, for example, "The Ungame" board game (Zakich, 1983) to enhance the relationship.

• To break through the defenses of clients. Adult clients who insist, for example, that they are not sexist often have revealed to them, through the play of "Gender Bender," (Gerber, 1988) that they are sexist.

• To help clients who find it difficult to verbalize their concerns. Often this is accomplished through drawings.

• To relieve tension and, thus, achieve some catharsis. Clay play and/or puppetry is often used for this purpose.

• To develop insight. Adults who play, for example, the "Adult Child Boardgame" can gain considerable information about dysfunction in their family of origin.

- For reality testing. Role-playing and/or sociodrama are often used in this regard.
- To enable the therapist to communicate with the adult client at several levels simultaneously. Play utilizes the auditory, visual, and kinesthetic modalities of learning, thus making the communication more powerful.
- To transcend communication barriers. Clients who find it difficult to discuss issues, for example, might act them out or draw them out in play.
- To cut through the distance and defenses of the client. The client may defend himself or herself in the traditional verbal interactions of therapy but frequently does not know how to or is unable to do this in play therapy. A father who insists he is not domineering or controlling often reveals such in the enactment of a puppetry play with his family in family therapy.
- To learn how to communicate in other modalities other than just auditory. An adult can draw a picture of how he or she feels, rather than just telling about it.
- To restructure the relationship in therapy by calling attention to interactive and relational concerns. This is often accomplished by role-playing.
- To help clients discover and integrate disowned or repudiated aspects of self. These aspects are often discovered, for example, through drawings, games, and fantasy.
- For discovering underdeveloped aspects of self. Often these aspects surface through play when they were unknown at the conscious level. One adult who viewed himself as quite independent discovered the dependent side of himself through the use of an interactional game.
- For the positive association with the affective domain. Feelings are not then seen as so ominous. Adults frequently develop profound insight when they develop a positive connection with the affective domain. Such adults can then develop the capacity for tenderness, affection, and humor, which had never been expressed before then. Such results often develop from the use of fantasy, game play, and artwork.

Some adults, however, have difficulty playing for a variety of reasons, but one of the most prevalent reasons is the fear of loss of control. In actuality, play is an excellent modality in which to learn healthy self-control without regression.

Adults who experience difficulties in their current life often had distortions in their play in childhood and adolescence. Such difficulties manifested in adult life include the tendency toward addiction; tendency to shyness and discomfort among others; reluctance to experiment with singing, dancing, drawing, or drama; awkwardness when around others who are playful; lack of knowledge about how to play with children; vague and generalized depression and/or restriction of their own play to competitive or structured activities.

Adults often lack role models of other adults in healthy playful situations. Bill Cosby's television family was a good model for playfulness and creative problem solving. Adult clients who are very inhibited in play are sometimes directed to view this television program or other programs where appropriate models exist.

Other techniques, according to Blatner (1988) that can help adults to become less inhibited in play include asking them to recall:

- A time in your childhood when pretend play occupied more time than other forms of play. When did this change? What factors influenced this change?
- Whether any adults played creatively and imaginatively with you. Who were they?
- People you knew who modeled playfulness.

- How long you were able to sing, color, or draw without inhibition.
- How many playmates you had. Were you isolated by reasons of geography or other restrictions?
- What play was like in your family.
- How often you laughed in your childhood. What was the rate of humor in your family of origin?

When adults recall such topics, it assists them in developing insight about their inhibitions and learning more about how to overcome these inhibitions towards play.

Play Therapy Techniques for Adults

When a readiness level for play exists in both the play therapist and the adult client, there are many different activities from which to choose.

One type of play therapy especially helpful for adult clients is the use of board games. Much can be learned from analyzing the play of adults in chess, for example. The play therapist can learn about how the client engages in problem solving, how he or she reacts to success or failure, and how the client engages in conflict management—there are adults clients who will argue extensively about the rules of chess; who try to manipulate the play therapist through chess play; who succumb to defeat long before the play is over and during the time they could still win; who blatantly or covertly cheat; who are relentless at reminding everyone around them that they won the game; who make a particular nonlegal chess move appear to be an accident when it was actually intended to assist the client in winning. Those are just a few examples of the many ways people reveal themselves during chess play.

There are other adult board games that can be beneficial in play therapy. One such game is the "Adult Children Game" (Miller, 1987). The main purpose of this game, designed specifically for adults in therapy, is to gain insight about feelings associated with childhood experiences. Players draw an image of how they perceive themselves as children. This image card is then placed by a column of discussion topics, such as childhood games, sharing, mother, father, abuse, secret places, secrets, affection shown, and losses. The first player places a token on a topic she or he wants to discuss. Each player then has a turn to discuss this topic. Players take turns choosing topics. If a player becomes stuck on a topic, he or she proceeds to the middle of the board and spins an arrow. The stuck player receives a hug from the player to whom the arrow points, and then the turn is ended. Processing occurs after the topics are shared; the inner child card (the picture of the perceived self from childhood) is passed in a clockwise direction to all other players. Each player shares what was learned about the card owner during the play. Each player receives feedback from all other players. This game provides ample opportunity for the exploration of the inner child, childhood experiences, and the development of insight. It can be played individually with a client or in a group.

"Getting to Know You . . . Better" (Getting, 1990) is another board game designed for play by two adults. The purpose of the game is to assist players in learning more about their preferences, life experiences, accomplishments, and goals. The game is intended for people who are friends, dating, or married. There are four card categories in the game: one in which one player guesses the answer of the other, one in which both players answer the card, one in which the player who drew the card answers the question, and one in which the focus is on the attitudes of the players. Examples of the cards include:

- "The only way to get rid of temptation is to yield to it." *Oscar Wilde*
- What indulgence is likely to make you feel the least guilty?

  A. Sleeping late

  B. Leaving work early

  C. Overeating

  D. Overspending

  E. Fudging on a tax return
- "Billie Holiday had a white gardenia; Texas has a yellow rose . . ." What flower represents you?
- "Think about the past only as its remembrances give you pleasure." *Jane Austen*
- Describe a childhood memory that makes you smile.
- "There are no winners in life, only survivors." *Unknown*
- What gets you through very difficult days?

Play continues with each person taking turns until one player rolls the exact number needed to land on the last space of the board. The winner then receives a prize that she or he chose at the beginning of the game. The prize is an activity, such as going to a play or concert, having dinner, or taking a hike, that the other player facilitates.

Another board game for adults is entitled "An Enchanted Evening" (An Enchanted, 1989). The goal of this board game, developed for adult players, is to increase self-disclosure and sharing about intimacy. The game is played by two players and has some cards that elicit verbal responses that are positive and supportive and other cards that suggest gentle touching. One card states, "If you saw your partner at a dinner party, what might first attract you?" Another card instructs, "The 'How Much Feeling Can You Put into a Kiss?' contest has just begun. You are a contestant. Give your partner the winning kiss." Much of the content of the game helps couples to express their wants and desires about human sexuality and intimacy. This game is an excellent one to assist couples in learning more about each other's desires on this topic. It facilitates discussion on a topic that some adults find difficult to discuss in more direct ways.

Other appropriate board games include "The Ungame" (Zakich, 1975), which is aimed at the ages of 5 to 105. This noncompetitive game explores attitudes, feelings, motives, and values. Two to six players can play this game, which comes with two decks of cards—one lighthearted and the other entitled "deep understanding." There are also a few blank cards on which adults or the therapist can write their questions. An additional set of cards relevant to adults can be obtained (these cards focus on enriching family communication), and another additional set of cards was developed by marriage counselors and psychologists. There are also "tell it like it is" spaces on the game board, which elicit the player to self-disclose or which ask the player a question.

"Reunion" (Zakich & Monroe, 1979) is another board game for two to six players, ages 8 years to adult. This noncompetitive game focuses on the topics of feelings, perceptions, empathetic understanding, and self-understanding. Visual imaging cards ask players to imagine what they would do if they won $90,000 in a sweepstakes. Picture cards of items in different categories ask players to imagine how the other player might answer. Players might also land on a recall space and be asked to remember certain childhood experiences. As in other noncompetitive games, there is no winner or loser. Play continues until the therapist and/or client decide to stop.

"Social Security" (Burten, 1976) is appropriate for ages 6 to 106. Six major theme areas are indicated in this game: ownership of problems, feelings exploration, problem solving, adaptation to change(s), conflict management, and values exploration. Players are also given the opportunity to fantasize and express whatever is on their mind by landing on spaces on the game board. Sample cards include: "What was the most recent change in your life?"; "What two ideas do you have that you think others also believe in?"; "For 30 seconds, name different things you would do or say if you were angry"; "Just using your eyes, show how you might look if you were shocked by someone's behavior"; "Who has a problem? Your plumber smashes his thumb and runs to get some ice. Meanwhile, you see the water pipe beginning to spray to the ceiling"; and "You need more time by yourself but find it difficult to arrange. Name three solutions to this problem."

Of course, these board games are just a representative sample of the many different board games available for adults. There are other adult board games for therapeutic use on the topics of, for example, gender bias, midlife crisis, and communication skills. The American Association for Retired Persons (AARP) is currently involved in the development of a board game called "Limbo," a game designed to assist retired adults in transitions in their lives. In addition, play therapists can design their own board games for specific purposes using blank board games or designing boards themselves.

Card games are another type of play therapy modality very suitable for adults. The Ungame card game—Families Version (Zakich, 1983) helps individuals to learn how to communicate more effectively in a family environment. The author states that the first time she and her family played the game, they learned more about each other in 20 minutes than they had in 12 years. This card game comes with two decks containing a total of 140 cards. The first deck is more lighthearted, whereas the second deck deals with feelings, values, and memories. Examples of these cards are: "What is likely to cause you to 'blow up?'"; "Who do you think is the most loving member of your family?"; and "You may ask a player one question or comment on any subject you choose." The game is noncompetitive and encourages active listening and self-disclosure about family issues.

Frequently, such games as "UNO" or "O'no 99" (both produced in 1973 by International Games, Inc.) can be used to establish rapport, build a relationship, relieve tension, and/or break through defenses. The fact that such card games are nonthreatening and so do not require advanced skills such as those needed for Bridge, for example, make the games an excellent medium through which to do therapy. These card games blend skill and luck in such a manner as to be ideal for therapeutic use. They do not rely totally on luck, nor are they so difficult as to require extensive concentration, thus taking the focus away from therapy. Other card games of similar structure would also be useful for adults.

The play therapist can, of course, obtain blank playing cards and design a game especially for a certain unique adult problem. Or a traditional deck of cards can be used and assigned a therapeutic purpose. When each card is assigned a feeling, for example, an average deck of cards can be used to help improve the nonverbal communication skills of adults. Players are dealt six cards each. The player decides which feeling card from his or her hand is going to be played. Then the player acts out the feeling in a nonverbal way (i.e., no words are permitted). Other players assess what feeling is being portrayed. If they possess that card, they place it face down in front of them. If there is a successful match between the feeling sent and the feeling received, all cards are discarded. If no match occurs, all players retrieve their cards and take penalty cards. The first player to discard all cards is the winner. This game's purpose is to improve communication by focusing on the nonverbal domain. The player learns how to give and receive accurate nonverbal messages.

"Self-Esteem Bingo" (Frey & Carlock, 1991) is a game designed for adults to foster increased awareness of the characteristics of those with high self-esteem and how to attain these qualities. Twenty-five techniques known to foster high self-esteem are placed on a bingo card. Players try to obtain bingo by finding individuals who engage in these self-esteem-enhancing activities. The game is a fun way of learning how to improve self-esteem.

Objects can also be used in play therapy with adults. A stuffed bust of Freud, called a Freud Toy (Myrstad, 1988), has been used by adults as a method of catharsis. Speaking to the stuffed object has a lower threat level than speaking directly to the play therapist.

Other therapeutic dolls are often used in cases of incestuous sexual abuse. By talking with such dolls, adult incest victims are often freed from the repression of other childhood memories. An opportunity for catharsis exists. As the adults cradle the doll, they are also able to lessen tension levels. Such dolls come to represent the adult's child self (The pain, 1991).

One adult client used a doll to make a three-dimensional replica of her therapist, accurate in every detail. She informed the therapist that she often spoke to the therapist doll between sessions when the therapist was not available to her. Such interaction allowed her to process issues on her own and enabled her to become more independent and self-sufficient. If she were angry at the therapist during the process of therapy, she often used the therapist doll to help her manage this anger. At times, she would talk with the doll as a type of therapy behavior rehearsal, which assisted her in talking directly to the therapist about a concern in the next session.

Music can also be used in play therapy with adults. To assist clients in dealing with stress, for example, often clients are acquainted with the song "Stress Yourself" sung to the tune of "Row, Row, Row Your Boat" (Tubesing & Tubesing, 1983).

Stress, stress, stress yourself
All throughout the day—

Verily, verily, verily, verily
Distress is on the way!

By introducing the topic of stress in a playful manner, the therapist often makes it easier for denying and resistant clients to be open to the topic. Using this technique makes the discussion of stress management less threatening, and it aids in tension relief.

The use of crayons, paints, or pastels by clients often facilitates therapeutic growth. Such use can be unstructured (the adult clients might draw "anger" on a piece of paper) or more structured (the adult clients are asked to draw a specific event or to respond to a specific stimulus, such as those in an anti-coloring book). The *Anti-Coloring Book* by Stricker & Kimmel (1978) provides ample opportunities to engage adults in expressive drawing. A pictorial stimulus value is placed on the page and then the client is asked to draw, for example, the "nicest dream you ever had." Another page asks the client to draw "the worst nightmare you ever had."

Of particular note for adults is the *Anti-Coloring Book of Masterpieces* (Stricker, 1982). Thirty-eight works of art with part of the original missing are presented to be completed by the colorer. Such art inspires the client to view the world from a different perspective; it increases creativity. Picasso stated that he wished he could draw as well as a child. Such drawings are intended to free the child in the adult client and to stimulate imagination, creativity, and fantasy.

Another expressive drawing technique that a play therapist might use with adults is the *Symbolic Profile* (Fry, 1976). The Jungian technique involves the use of symbolic drawings by the client to help the individual gain awareness and insight into different aspects of his or her life. The client is asked to utilize a symbol in each of six squares as a stimulus value to make and entitle a complete drawing. The symbolic representations are in the areas of ego, fantasy, family, self-determination, spirituality, and future potential. This technique is especially effective for adult clients who are resistant, denying, inhibited, verbally deficient, or psychologically unaware of what is concerning them. It is also helpful in aiding clients in breaking through defenses, verbalizing material, developing insight, and resolving unconscious material.

Games and interactive activities can also be facilitative for adults in play therapy. One such game often used as a warm-up technique in group therapy with adults involves the use of a Koosh ball or any other type of ball. A participant simultaneously says his or her name and throws the ball to another person. The recipient catches the ball, then states his or her name and throws the ball to another person. This continues in kind until everyone has had a chance to state his or her name when throwing the ball. The next phase involves each person stating the name of the person to whom they are throwing the ball as they throw it until everyone has had a turn. The next phase involves throwing the ball to another person while the thrower calls his or her name and then tells something about his- or herself to the recipient. The activity can progress to the next phase in which the person throwing the ball expresses his or her feelings after stating the recipient's name. The activity can be concluded by the thrower asking the recipient of the ball a question. Play continues until everyone has had a turn. This is a playful way of getting to know others.

To ensure awareness of others and to perceive others more accurately, clients can play a game called "Three Changes." (This is also a good introductory activity for adults in a group.) Two teams of equal number are formed. Team A faces Team B in parallel lines. Each person on Team A has a partner on Team B. Each person is given time to closely look at his or her partner. Then the members of Team B turn their backs to Team A while each person on Team A makes three changes in their appearance (such as changing rings on fingers, undoing a button, and so on). Team B then faces Team A again and tries to discern what changes were made in his or her partner. Play continues with the teams reversing roles several times. This activity is helpful in increasing a person's ability to accurately observe others.

Another interactive activity that can be used with adults is self-esteem fortune cookies (Frey & Carlock, 1991). Fortune cookies with a self-esteem quotation or message are given to each person in the group as individual therapy. The client is asked to open the cookie, read the self-esteem message, and then comment about how that message pertains to them. The individual can then eat the cookie. This approach represents a very nonthreatening method of discussing the topic of self-esteem and is often helpful as a first step with the type of adult client discussed earlier who has a repudiated, disowned, or unknown self.

Scavenger hunts can be playful ways for adults to learn coping skills. Clients could get sent on a scavenger hunt to find six different ways, for example, that people effectively manage their stress or enhance their self-esteem or cope with difficult people. The topics can be changed according to the needs of the adult client.

If the adult play therapist searches for appropriate games and activities, the number of such activities is quite large. It is helpful to keep a file folder of suitable games for specific adult clients in certain phases of therapy.

Humor can be used in play therapy with adults. Many adults will accept constructive criticism, confrontation, or other feedback through humor that they would not otherwise accept. This humor is sometimes spontaneous and sometimes planned. It can be valuable to keep a collection of cartoons and jokes that have relevance to reoccurring themes in adult therapy.

CASE ILLUSTRATION

Two jokes were told to an adult client who is an attorney. This client had a good sense of humor, and these comments were made after rapport had been established and the middle phase of therapy was in process. The client entered the therapy room complaining about how few people really understand how frustrating and difficult the practice of law can be. He was concerned about media images of lawyers. The therapist, in an attempt to communicate empathy, recounted a joke she had just heard: "How many lawyers does it take to screw in a light bulb?" Answer: "How many can you afford?" Also related to the client was the joke: "What form of contraception does an attorney use?" Answer: "His (her) personality." Laughter ensued, and both adults discussed how easy it is for many people to form stereotypes of others and, thus, not fully understand them. When the session ended, the client told the therapist a psychologist's joke. The humor on this issue, as was intended, enhanced the relationship and communicated empathy.

Caution needs to be used when using humor with clients, however. It is important that sarcasm not be used and that the client sees the humor as facilitative to the therapeutic process. Too much humor used in a session can lead individuals away from established therapeutic goals. Quite extensive literature exists on the use of humor in psychotherapy.

Drama and guided imagery can also be used with adults in play therapy. Dayton (1990) offered a guided imagery in which the client imagines having what he or she wants very much in life. The client is then asked to imagine participating in life as though this desire were a reality. After the client has fulfilled this desire in his or her mind, the client returns to consciousness in the room and processes the experience.

Dayton (1990) shared another activity, entitled "Taking Care of the Child Within." She described this as an activity she learned from Zekra Moreno, the doyenne of psychodrama. After the client has relaxed, he or she is asked to see an image of his or her child self. The client is asked to imagine that the child self needs something from the client, something that the client is able to give. The client actually stands up, puts the child self in his or her chair, and gives the child self whatever he or she is needing. The client nurtures the child self and lets the child know that he or she will be back to visit again. When the client is ready, he or she returns attention to the room and processes the experience. This is a very powerful way to reparent the inner child. The insights resulting from this method are easier to obtain than those from other, more traditional therapeutic approaches.

Another creative dramatic game effective with adults is focused on the topic of social interaction. The goal of this activity is to identify power and leadership that formal and informal organizations and families have. In corporate America, many adults do not succeed as well as they could because it is difficult for them to ascertain the difference between formal and informal power types. In this activity, a group of adults form a circle.

One person is asked to leave the room; the rest of the group chooses a leader. The job of the leader is to initiate movement such as clapping hands or head shaking. The role of the group is to follow the leader without making it obvious. No speech is used. The leader can change the activity at any time. The person who left is called back into the room to guess who is the leader.

Many of these dramatizations exist. This discussion is just a brief review of a few effective techniques. The play therapist working with adults can develop an extensive repertoire of techniques.

Role-playing can assist adults in problem solving, rehearsing behavior, developing empathy, and reenacting or reconstructing a situation. One such example of behavior rehearsal might involve the client rehearsing through role-playing how he or she is going to prosocially express anger to a sibling. The therapist becomes the sibling, and, after the role-playing is completed, the activity is processed. A client can develop empathy by playing the role of a significant other while the therapist plays the role of the client. Many opportunities exist in the therapeutic relationship for the use of role-playing. Simulation games for adults would also fall into this category.

While this review is a representation of various categories of play that can be used by play therapists with adults, often unstructured and spontaneous activities might occur that are especially unique to the therapeutic session. The more playful the therapist, the more these opportunities will be incorporated into play therapy with adults. One such activity occurred when a therapist met with a particularly hostile, resistant adult client who was reacting to a previous session during which therapeutic confrontation happened between the therapist and the client. The client insisted she did not want to talk to the therapist at all during the session. The session was October 31. The therapist was wearing jack-o-lantern pantyhose in an attempt to be in the holiday spirit with the child clients she was also seeing that day. The client, in an attempt to avoid eye contact and interaction, turned her eyes to the floor. Upon seeing the pantyhose, she immediately began to comment about how she wondered sometimes about whether the therapist was more child than adult or vice versa. She began to laugh and, after a few minutes of discussion about this topic, began to easily self-disclose about her current feelings and how they reflected her reaction to the prior therapy session. This "Halloween pantyhose" technique served as an ice-breaker, and its humor enabled the client to continue. It was a unique, specific event that was spontaneously used for facilitative purposes. Looking for such opportunities can be very rewarding for the play therapist and client.

Processing Guidelines

Regardless of the type of play therapy activity used with adults, it is recommended that each technique be processed using the following learning model, which includes six steps (Frey & Carlock, 1991):

Step 1, Introduction. The therapist discusses with the client the rationale for participating in the play therapy activity to insure that the client understands why the technique is being used and how it is to be done.

Step 2, Participation. The client responds to the direction given by the therapist. The therapist should allow clients to not respond if the technique evolves into one that is too threatening. On the other hand, it is valuable to encourage clients to risk.

Step 3, Publishing. The client shares reactions and observations about what has happened.

Step 4, Processing. Clients are asked to discuss patterns or dynamics that they noticed while engaging in the technique.

Step 5, Cognition. Clients are asked to think about principles, hypotheses, and generalizations that can be inferred from the technique.

Step 6, Application. Clients begin to recognize the relevance of their learning to everyday life.

By utilizing this process, the learnings from play therapy become more relevant for adults, and, as a result, adult clients are usually more motivated to engage in the next play therapy technique. The problematic dynamics of adult clients discussed earlier in this chapter seem to diminish. The play therapist is then able to move more readily to assist clients in meeting their therapeutic goals.

CASE STUDIES

A few brief case illustrations of the use of play therapy are helpful in discussing the effectiveness of this technique for adults.

CASE ILLUSTRATION 1

A 42-year-old mother of two rebellious teenage daughters sought therapy because the uncontrolled behavior of her daughters was threatening her current marriage, her second marriage; her first husband had died. This client was a good example of an individual who was in denial and who had early parentification issues herself. She was unable to use the connection between her parenting skills and the unruly behavior of these young adolescents. Since she lacked much of the childhood experience herself and since the children had lost their father due to death, the mother insisted that the children needed to be treated very gingerly and given a lot of freedom. The adolescents had little knowledge of boundaries, and household rules and chores were virtually nonexistent. The stepfather coming into this family had great difficulty adjusting. His response was to withdraw from the conflict. The play therapist in this case began by discussing directly what she had assessed to be the family dynamics. The mother's response was complete denial. The therapist then engaged the mother and daughters in "The Ungame" family card game. The mother and daughters also played several board games. After each technique, the process model discussed earlier was used. Gradually, the family began to become more aware of the family dynamics. Continued use of interactive games and role-playing with all members of the family helped everyone gain insight about the nature of the problem and what needed to be done for remediation.

CASE ILLUSTRATION 2

A 39-year-old man entered therapy upon the suggestion of his friend. He was an A.C.O.A. who was adopted at age 1 year by his aunt. He was quite verbally expressive about most aspects of his life except the actual concern—repressed anger. His case illustrates a person who repudiated aspects of self, namely the angry self. In play therapy, he utilized stuffed objects to vent his anger. He was unable to discuss or vent this anger to the therapist. Over time in therapy, he began to express his anger through his drawings. Eventually, he processed his anger directly with the therapist and learned effective anger-management techniques.

CASE ILLUSTRATION 3

A 32-year-old woman came to therapy because she felt generally unhappy with her life. She did not know what bothered her most but was unhappy with her life and her parenting. The client was a workaholic who was psychologically unaware of what bothered her. Play therapy helped her to uncover unconscious material. The use of expressive drawings helped to reveal that this client had been sexually abused as a child and had repressed this problem. Play therapy, in this case, helped to diagnose the problem and to provide insight to the client. The use of drawings continued to allow the client to express herself. Drama games also aided her in successfully dealing with this problem.

CONCLUSION

Perhaps what has been discussed about the value of play therapy for adults can best be summarized in this quotation by Marthaler (Frey, 1991).

> When a child is born he/she is loving, lovable, intelligent, creative, energetic, powerful, gentle, sociable, and cooperative. We never lose these qualities; because they are the essence of being human. Our bodies age, but the child within each of us remains the same. Each night the stars are shining, even though on some nights they cannot be seen because of the clouds. So it is with the child within us. What must be done, then, is for the clouds, which have accumulated along the way, to be cast off. And then the stars within us will shine with all their brilliance. (p. 58)

The process of play therapy is certainly a very effective way to help adults "shine with all their brilliance."

REFERENCES

Adult children games. (1987). Tuscon, AZ: Sobriety Publications.

Aldis, O. (1975). *Play fighting.* New York: Academic Press.

An Enchanted Evening. (1989). San Francisco, CA: Games Partnership Ltd.

Barten, R. (1976). Social Security. Anaheim, CA: The Ungame Company.

Blatner, A. (1988). Spontaneity. In *Foundations of Psychodrama.* New York: Springer.

Caplan, F., & Caplan, T. (1973). *The power of play.* New York: Anchor/Doubleday.

Chance, P. (Ed.). (1979). *Learning through play: A symposium.* New York: Johnson and Johnson Co./Gardner Press.

Dayton, T. (1990). *Drama games.* Deerfield Beach, FL: Health Communications.

Frey, D. (1991). *100 inspirational quotations for enhancing self-esteem.* Dayton, OH: Author.

Frey, D., & Carlock, J. (1991). *Practical techniques for enhancing self-esteem.* Muncie, IN: Accelerated Development.

Fry, R. (1976). *The symbolic profile.* Houston, TX: Gulf Publishing Co.

Gender bender. (1988). New York: LoKi Games Ltd.

Getting to Know You . . . Better. (1990). San Francisco, CA: Games Partnership Ltd.

Koestler, A. (1964). *The act of creation.* New York: Macmillan.

McCaulley, M. (1990). The Myers-Briggs Type Indicator in counseling. In E. Watkins & V.

Campbell (Eds.), *Applications of psychological testing in counseling practice.* Hillsdale, NJ.: Lawrence Erlbaum.

Miller, D. (1987). Adult children game. Tucson, AZ: Sobriety Publications.

Myrstad, B. (1988). *Freud Toy.* New York: Freud Toy Inc.

O'no 99. (1973). Joliet, IL: International Games, Inc.

Stricker, S. (1982). *The anti-coloring book of masterpieces.* New York: Holt, Rinehart and Winston.

Stricker, S., & Kimmel, E. (1978). *The anti-coloring book.* New York: Holt.

Sutton-Smith, B. (1975). The useless made useful: Play as variability training. *School Review, 83,* 197–215.

The pain of the last taboo. (1991, October 7). *Newsweek,* pp. 70–72.

Tooth Sayer. (1991, October), *Reader's Digest,* p. 117.

Tubesing, M., & Tubesing, D. (1983). *Structured exercises in stress management, Vol. 1.* Duluth, MN: Whole Person Press.

UNO. (1973). Joliet, IL: International Games, Inc.

Winnicott, D. W. (1971). *Playing and reality.* New York: Basic Books.

Zakich, R. (1975). The Ungame. Anaheim, CA: The Ungame Co.

Zakich, R. (1983). The Ungame, Families Version. Anaheim, CA: The Ungame Co.

Zakich, R., & Monroe, S. (1979). Reunion. Placentia, CA: The Ungame Co.

CHAPTER 9

Geriatric Theraplay

SANDRA LINDAMAN AND DEBRA HALDEMAN

INTRODUCTION

Can Theraplay, an attachment- and relationship-enhancing treatment, be meaningfully applied to troubled older adults? This chapter will describe the adaptation of Theraplay to aging individuals.

Historically, Theraplay has been used with selected adult clients. These tended to be clients who displayed inappropriate or flat affect, who had problems of relating, who were passive or obsessive, who suffered from bizarre thought processes, or who had overwhelming reality problems. Others were adults whose own childhoods were lacking in self-enhancing experiences, which resulted in a lack of personal autonomy and difficulty encouraging their children toward emotional growth. Theraplay has been used as the only treatment or as a preparation, follow-up, or adjunct to traditional psychotherapy. Jernberg (1979) noted that participation in the structuring, challenging, intrusive, nurturing, and playful activities of Theraplay discharged tensions in these clients, raised self-esteem, and focused attention. Some adult clients engaged in a Theraplay session recalled painful childhood relationships, experienced current sadness, or developed valuable insights. Parent group Theraplay sessions were tailored to improving parent-child relationships by helping the adults understand what their children were experiencing (Jernberg, 1979). Robbins (1987) described a group Theraplay program with Head Start parents who were found to be needy of being cared for and nurtured; the goal was to enhance the parents' capacity to accept and practice healthy self-nourishing behaviors.

Geriatric Theraplay grew out of the belief that in aging, as in any other phase of development, there is the need for and the potential for feelings of self-worth, competence, attractiveness, lovability, and satisfaction in responding to others. In the Theraplay approach, age is regarded as an asset rather than as a degenerative process.

> In what they like and don't like, in their joys and worries, in what hurts and doesn't, and in what they need in order to keep their days exciting, old people require others to respect them. Like all of us, as proof that they are touchable, old people need others to touch them. They need others to look at them as proof that they are attractive, and to speak to them as a demonstration that they themselves have something to say. Like all of us, old people need to feel that they are part of an ongoing, vested relationship—a relationship which is fun at some times, and caring and tender at others. Intimacy with another provides indisputable evidence that "I'm not terrible . . . People still look at me, and touch me. People seem to enjoy being with me. That, in itself, means I'm still lovable. And that means I'm still alive." (Jernberg, 1987, p. 1)

The authors wish to acknowledge the work of Carol Adamitis, Theraplay Therapist, in developing Geriatric Theraplay; the case studies of Marge, Sarah, and the Group Theraplay session are excerpted from her case reports. The authors also wish to thank Ann M. Jernberg, Ph.D., the creator of Theraplay and the Clinical Director of The Theraplay Institute since its inception in 1968, for her assistance in writing and critiquing this manuscript.

Because many older individuals do not receive the feedback that younger people do as a part of their daily lives, they have no chance to confirm their worthiness. Having been *decathected*—deinvested of energy and love—by uninterested others, they begin to decathect themselves. It is only as one begins to decathect oneself that the word *still* begins to enter one's vocabulary (H. Bolgar, personal communication, 1986). Except perhaps following a broken romance or a disfiguring illness, a young adult would rarely ask the question, "Am I still . . . ?" "Am I still beautiful? Am I still bright? Am I still the entertaining person I once was?" And certainly a young or middle-aged adult would never ask the question "Am I still alive?" Yet, as older adults hear the decathecting message, take note of the averted gaze, feel the exclusionary response on buses and at social functions, the "Am I still . . . ?" questions inevitably become increasingly persistent.

With a decreased feeling of self-worth and a growing hopeless expectation of others, the old person may begin to act in ways that become self-fulfilling prophecies. The feelings of low self-worth and hopelessness may lead to the kinds of behaviors guaranteed to keep friends and caretakers at a distance and oneself in a state of bitter solitude. Old people, like all people, are proud. They do not go where they are not wanted. They go to great efforts to save face. For old people in nursing homes or with their families, saving face may mean withdrawing or it may mean being cantankerous and difficult. In both cases, the message is the same: "Stay out of my life, keep away from my person." In both cases, it says, "I'll decide how I want to run my days, and you can't make me change my mind. I'll be mute and immobilized as one alternative, or curse and carry on as another."

In both cases, others must respect the *reason* for the message, while at the same time asking if the withdrawn or aggressive behavior is getting the person what he or she really needs." "Is Mrs. Grey's behavior—sitting stonily in her wheelchair neither hearing nor speaking hour after hour, day after day—really getting for her what she so badly needs: the warmth, tenderness, appreciation, and joyful engagement that will let her know she is *still* beautiful, *still* special, *still* bright and fun to be with? and yes, she is *still* alive?" And "Is Mr. Burton's hurling invectives—and sometimes his cane or a shoe—at any passerby getting him what he really needs? Is it getting him the respect that will affirm that he is *still* charming, *still* intelligent, *still* good looking? and, yes, that he is *still* alive?" Rather than invite love, the conviction that one is unlovable and the behavior consequent upon that conviction only serves to drive candidates for intimacy away. Theraplay's intention is to reverse this process. Theraplay aims to affirm lovability in the face of even the most determined effort to refute it.

> The Theraplay therapist makes the assumption that, among the needs underlying the tyranny there is the need for intimacy, for recognition, and for fun, as well as the need to value oneself and to value others. Recognizing those underlying needs, the Theraplay therapist offers experiences that are challenging, nurturing, and playfully intruding. The Theraplay therapist makes one further assumption: that, in spite of overt behavior, the patient is not emotionally fragile, can draw on his or her lifelong inner resources and does have the capacity for improvement. Thus the theraplay sessions are health- not pathology-oriented." (Jernberg, 1988, p. 77)

Geriatric Concerns

A review of the literature in geriatric mental health reveals that older people suffer from depression, anxiety disorders, isolation, grief, anger, sexual concerns, and somatic complaints (Knight, 1992).

Some therapy outcome studies show depression to be the predominate target complaint (Gatz, Popkin, Pine, & Vandenbos, 1985), whereas others find the prevalence rates for anxiety disorders to be greater than the rate of depression (Myers & Weissman, 1980). Depression often is evidenced by a significant drop in participation in pleasant life activities and by feelings of helplessness and hopelessness often being identified in the therapy session. Some elderly individuals view suicide as a romanticized alternative to boredom. The suicide rate is higher among the elderly, yet little has been written about it (La Rue, Dessonville, & Jarwick, 1985). Constant worrying, confusion, and disorientation, a sense of loss of control, and physical health changes may result in feelings of anxiety (Knight, 1992). Isolation as a function of a number of factors including loss of spouse, family, or friends, relocation of residency, and disability is not necessarily correlated to a lack of socialization opportunities (Knight, 1992). Personality traits themselves (disorders) may result in isolation. These then need to be considered in treatment. However, as Knight suggests, the viewpoints that isolation equals loneliness and that friendships are easily made and worthwhile are the viewpoints of younger people and not necessarily that of older adults. Many older people, in contrast, experience unresolved grief for the loss of spouse, child, health, work, and independence. It is this loss that may be associated with low self-esteem (Gatz, et al., 1985). A recent study in the state of Georgia of a group of individuals 100 or more years of age revealed that engagement in the present, optimism, and the ability to resolve losses characterized the group (20/20, 1993). Knight (1992) defined the anger experienced by some elderly clients as "irritation" because the elderly seem to experience this affect with less intensity than do younger people.

Knight (1992) noted that many professionals are misinformed about aging—they ascribe differences between older and younger people to the aging process (and to dementing illness) and, so, consider the differences to be unchangeable and insurmountable. Although there are a number of variables unique to the older adult (e.g., patterns of cognitive strengths and weaknesses, experience with different models of education, different personality dispositions, different use of words, and the different world view that comes from being of different times) that, therefore, require a specialized treatment, recent research suggests that this age group benefits from treatments similar to those utilized with other age groups (Knight, 1992). Gatz et al. (1985), in fact, suggested that clinical progress with the elderly may have been limited in the past due to the overemphasized notion that the elderly require entirely different treatment than younger clients do.

Geriatric Mental Health Intervention

A number of different models of mental health intervention are in use for the geriatric population. In the *loss-deficit model*, aging is portrayed as a deterioration of functioning and a regression to a second childhood. This model focuses on the loss of physical ability, grown children leaving home, and reduced income. Knight (1992) disputed the loss-deficit model for two reasons: (a) losses and illnesses are not specific to the aged, and (b) the loss-deficit model neglects optimizing functioning. It presents the deficit side without suggesting methods for improving life. The *maturity-based model* proposed by Knight (1992) addresses the potential for continued growth throughout the adult life span. Knight explained maturity as cognitive complexity, emotional complexity, androgyny, and expertise in areas of competency, including work, family, and interpersonal relationships. The *selective optimization with compensation model* views older adults as often not functioning at full capacity due to developmental and illness-imposed limitations. This model advocates that areas of competency could be optimized by practice and that loss or reduced ability could be replaced by compensating strengths (Baltes & Baltes, 1990). The *psychoeducational model* downplays the psychological aspect of treatment while focusing on prevention for those who are unidentified as having mental health problems (Gatz et al., 1985).

Other approaches for providing mental health services to the elderly include family and marital counseling, friendly visiting-home visits, use of volunteers and paraprofessionals, and pet therapy (Gatz et al., 1985).

Life review therapy (Butler & Lewis, 1982; Sherman, 1981) or reminiscing about past achievements enhances self-esteem. Life review therapy includes writing autobiographies, participating in reunions and pilgrimages, and looking at old photographs. Kaminsky (1984) suggested that reminiscence may be considered a culturally valuable form of play.

Ingersoll and Silverman (1978) sought to compare the effectiveness of an insight-oriented approach versus a behaviorally oriented approach for older adults. The insight-oriented approach, named "Then and There," used memory, journals, genograms, reminiscing, and loss and grief sharing to improve self-esteem and maintain self-identity. The behaviorally oriented approach, entitled "Here and Now," used relaxation training, relationship building, record keeping, and increasing activity level to improve self-esteem. Members of both groups improved self-esteem and decreased anxiety and somatic complaints on posttest measures.

Group therapy with the elderly may have certain advantages: efficiency (McGee & Lakin, 1977), increasing positive social effects (Gilbert, 1977), and normalizing and generalizing personal problems (Ingersoll & Silverman, 1978). Butler and Lewis (1982) utilized reminiscing in a group format. Birren (1982) reported group work as a means of improving insight, sense of personal identity, self-esteem, sense of control, and group cohesion.

Therapist Attitudes and Characteristics

Older adults are less likely than younger adults to receive mental health services (Myers & Weissman, 1980). Gatz et al. (1985) proposed client, therapist, and mental health system variables for this underserved status.

Many therapists have misconceptions of the aged that restrict their involvement with this age group. Lopez (1984) defined four biases that may impact interventions with older adults: (a) overpathologizing—the older person is seen as more impaired than a younger person; (b) minimizing—symptoms in the older adult are ignored ("it's just old age"); (c) equalizing—symptoms are considered equally appropriate across all age groups; and (d) misinterpreting—insensitivity to normal differences of aging.

Knight (1992) suggested that therapy with the older adult frequently "calls forth" countertransference issues. Unresolved issues abut the therapist's own mortality are raised and must be confronted. Work with older adults may force therapists to deal with problems with their own parents, their own fear that the patient may die during treatment, their own decline, and their own anticipated losses (Gatz et al., 1985; Butler & Lewis, 1982; Hiatt, 1971).

Other studies dealing with the therapist's role and style in working with the elderly suggested that the therapist typically is active and directive (Pfeiffer & Busse, 1973). Weinberg (1981) suggested that the therapist of an older adult may need to be more empathic, and Oberleder (1966) suggested that physical touch may be therapeutic.

THE THERAPLAY TECHNIQUE

Theraplay (Jernberg, 1979, 1989, 1993a, 1993b) is a method modeled after Des Lauriers's therapeutic approach for "waking up" autistic children (DesLauriers & Carlson, 1969). Theraplay has been used subsequently in a variety of settings, including homes (Jernberg, 1979), poverty preschools (Jernberg, 1976), nursing homes (Adamitis, 1982), and mental health and adult day-care centers (Booth, 1986). These settings serve individuals with low self-esteem, minimal trust in others, and little belief that life can be fun.

Features of Theraplay

Depending upon the needs of the client, the Theraplay therapist reenacts one or more of the primary features characterizing the ideal parent-child relationship: structuring, challenging, intruding, and nurturing (SCIN). As much as possible Theraplay therapists interact with the clients in the context of a playful, physical, empathic engagement.

1. **Structuring** activities state clearly articulated rules, set limits, and define body and other boundaries (e.g., "First I'll have a turn, then you will" or "When you're with me, I put your shoes on").

2. **Challenging** activities encourage the client to try, to risk, to stretch, and to move forward, without being frustrating (e.g., "Let's see how tightly you can squeeze my hand").

3. **Intruding** activities are exciting, stimulating, and surprising; their variety serves to engage the client and maintain his or her interest. Intruding activities are designed to "bring out" the withdrawn client (e.g., "There I blew on that nice, soft cheek").

4. **Nurturing** activities indulge, reassure, approve, and demonstrate caring. They make the world feel safe, warm, and secure (e.g., lotioning, powdering, stroking, and singing to).

Therapists working with older people must gauge carefully, for example, with whom to be more nurturing, with whom to be challenging. They must determine with whom to be more structuring, with whom to be more intruding. Having made those decisions, therapists working with older persons will next determine what kinds of Theraplay activities are appropriate and which activities promise to be optimally therapeutic. To quote Franke (1991), a Theraplay therapist working with an older client with nonorganic breathing difficulty and anxiety, "I have to find out what makes her attentive but doesn't make her tense" (p. 10). A challenge to a shoe-hurling match may be therapeutic for Mr. Burton but would be quite impossible for Mrs. Grey. By the same token, softly combing hair or lotioning arms would be appropriate for Mrs. Grey but would be contraindicated for Mr. Burton—at least at the outset. Although he so decries it, there is no question that, in the deepest recesses of his soul, Mr. Burton longs for nurturing. The innovative Theraplay therapist will find a way to supply it to him while still allowing him to save face. By the same token, Mrs. Grey's unspoken message, "I'm not communicating with no one, no how" surely belies a longing to be engaged. Ultimately, challenge will prove a helpful way to engage her. Again, the creative therapist will find a face-saving way to begin the challenge.

Theraplay therapy is not democratic (Jernberg, 1979). Decisions about and execution of the sessions lie with the therapist. The therapist does not wait to see what the client will do. It does no good for the client to have the therapist sit passively while the client hallucinates or withdraws deeper into himself or herself. Theraplay differs from client-centered therapy. Theraplay therapists operate with the assumption that they have the right, indeed the obligation, to intrude into the client's pathology (Jernberg, 1979).

Theraplay is a short-term therapy. Typically, individuals or families are seen for an initial series of 8 to 10 half-hour sessions, one week apart, followed by four follow-up sessions at quarterly intervals over the next year. Sessions involve direct Theraplay duplicating (regardless of age) the kind of playful behavior and activities that parents and infants or marital couples naturally engage in together.

Phases of Theraplay

Four phases occur during the course of treatment: The *honeymoon phase* is basically a time of "feeling each other out," enjoying the newness of the relationship and wondering what will come next. This phase is followed by the *negative phase*, which is characterized by oppositional behavior and attitudes and appears to be a function of warding off newfound feelings of trust and enjoyment. Next is a *growing and trusting phase* in which the client and therapist interact with warmth, pleasure, and spontaneity—and in which gains are consolidated. Finally, there is the *termination phase* at which clients are prepared to end their sessions with the therapist. They have come to enjoy, trust, and welcome new experiences and new relationships.

Theraplay with Older Clients

Theraplay with older individuals differs in some respects from Theraplay with children; yet, without being demeaning or infantilizing, in many ways, it is similar. Similarities arise from similarities in client behavior—concealing low self-esteem, for example. Thus, clients may become tyrannical in their effort to keep the world at bay. Often, it is this behavior that eventually turns off caregivers, thereby depriving the individual of the very care he or she so badly needs. Unlike other caregivers, Theraplay therapists demonstrate that nothing will turn them off; that no matter what it takes, they are prepared to hang on; and that tyranny is unnecessary and self-defeating. Theraplay therapists focus on the positive characteristics of the client—her soft hair, his strong fingers, his sparkling eyes, or her musical voice—and what a pleasure it is to get together for the session. Theraplay therapists do not discuss the gloomy, the bizarre, or the hopeless. "Actions speak louder than words" might be the therapist's motto.

In working with older adults, the Theraplay therapist must be alert to certain possible conditions: older people sometimes do not hear or see or feel as well as younger people; they may have trouble remembering; they may have difficulty changing position from sitting to standing or balancing comfortably when they stand. Theraplay therapists working with older people need to accommodate. The following guidelines have been found to be helpful in using Theraplay with geriatric clients:

1. *Slow the pace.* Be lively and inviting but take it easy to avoid feelings of confusion or of being overwhelmed. Move gradually and speak slowly. Do not offer too-abrupt surprises.

2. *Value spontaneous reminiscence.* When it occurs, listen intently and appreciate this vital form of self-expression.

3. *Conduct activities in a manner allowing face-saving.* Regardless of age, all clients should be treated with respect. Older adults, especially, require gracious treatment. Pay deliberate attention to their need for pride and dignity.

4. *Be alert to diminished sensitivity in sight, hearing, smell, taste, and touch.* Develop ways to enhance sensory experience. Face the client directly when addressing him or her.

5. *Give special consideration to feet and hands*—appreciate an older person's hands in and of themselves. This is more caring than is a comparison of the therapist's hands with the client's hands. Although the feet frequently are the part of the body that cause the most discomfort, they are often the part most neglected both by the older person and by those around him. (Adamitis, 1985)

Therapist Qualifications and Characteristics

Theraplay therapists working with adults should have developed prior competence doing Theraplay with children and should have access to ongoing evaluation or supervision if at all possible. Achieving competence in Theraplay involves participation in a program of training and supervision developed by The Theraplay Institute. Jernberg (1979) has described Theraplay therapists' personalities as confident, certain, appealing, delightful, responsive, empathic, cheerful, optimistic, spontaneous, flexible, and displaying leadership qualities. The behavior of Theraplay therapists as it relates to adults particularly should include using every opportunity to make physical contact with the client, focusing on the client in an intensive and exclusive manner, focusing on the client as he or she is, responding to cues given by the client, and using every opportunity to make the client feel unique and special. Jernberg (1979) noted that the new Theraplay therapist, given the rules that govern "appropriate adult conduct," may have more difficulty *giving* therapy than the client may have *receiving* it. Geriatric Theraplay therapists may at first find it difficult to work with adults because of

> the therapist's own uneasiness, identification, defensiveness, self-consciousness, and so on, all brought into focus by doing "silly," physical, infantile activities with another adult who has the potential to demean, ridicule, reject, or expose the therapist's weakness . . . in working with adults it is essential for the therapist both to know himself and to plan for all eventualities . . . therapists doing adult Theraplay are confident, flexible, undefensive, and comfortable with physical intimacy . . . they play their sessions carefully and tailor them particularly to the individual's specific needs. (Jernberg, 1979, p. 408)

Individual Theraplay Procedures

Theraplay therapists schedule 8 to 10 regular, weekly, half-hour, individual sessions on-site at the client's home, nursing home, or apartment complex. The sessions should be carefully scheduled and planned for. They should coincide with the client's time of heightened alertness and should find clients in the most active posture of which they are capable (sitting in bed rather than lying; sitting in a wheelchair rather than sitting in bed, etc.). Stimuli other than the two interacting individuals should be kept to a minimum (no television, radios, roommates, social room participants, etc.).

The purpose of the first session of diagnostic Theraplay is to assess whether a particular client is a good candidate for Theraplay. "Will this form of treatment," it asks, "be likely to produce significant change?" The answer to that question is based on questions such as "What is his or her capacity for intimacy?" and "How able—and how motivated—is he or she to forego old, self-defeating behaviors for new, self-enhancing ones?" In this and all sessions, the therapist may use lotions, powder, simple foods (e.g., yogurt, applesauce), a comb, a bowl with warm soapy water, and a terry towel. Other props are unnecessary.

Assuming an eight-session treatment schedule, advance notice of termination is given in the sixth session. In the seventh session, the client participates in planning the final session, which will be a "good-bye" party, including food and simple decorations.

At the party itself, client and therapist may exchange handprints and together compose a song to remember. The therapist might adorn the client with a paper crown or a flower for the hair, and then, embracing or holding hands, the therapist and client will sing their "special song," list all the memorable features of the client, and say a tender good-bye.

A plan should already have been made for another person in the client's world to take responsibility for maintaining with the client the warm, engaging contact made during Theraplay. This ensures that the client is not abandoned after experiencing regression with and connection to another person.

Individual Theraplay—Case Studies

The Development of Geriatric Theraplay

In an effort to widen the awareness of the uses of Theraplay for the aging adult, The Theraplay Institute invited Marge, a well-adjusted woman of 79 years, to participate in a series of videotaped Theraplay sessions. The following is therapist Carol Adamitis's description of these sessions.

MARGE

Marge reflected an optimistic view of her aging from the very start. While the therapist admired her soft hands during the process of "finding" her, Marge spontaneously offered the comment that what people commonly referred to as age spots were, in her case, "spots of experience." (Theraplay therapist Phyllis Booth referred to these spots as "cinnamon sprinkles" for an adult Theraplay client who was distressed about these signs of aging. The client later reported that this was one of her favorite memories of the sessions.) (Booth, 1986, personal communication)

Marge delighted in being "discovered." She seemed to respond most readily to touch and to challenge. She relished, as though it were new information, hearing personal details such as that she had "soft" eyes, naturally wavy hair, and "velvety" skin. Frequently, her response to sensory activity (e.g., singing, looking in the mirror, having her feet bathed) was to report long-forgotten memories. The following interaction illustrates her characteristic response to one of the many Theraplay activities:

THERAPIST: (Admiring Marge's hand) I love your nails.

MARGE: You do?

THERAPIST: Such a nice shape to your nails and fingers, too. I can tell you take real good care of your hands.

MARGE: I do! Even during the Depression, I never went without hand cream. (Marge pauses briefly as if thinking.)

Because Geriatric Theraplay was in a developmental stage, Marge was requested to give her therapist detailed feedback on her sessions. She said that *Dressing up in hats* and *Making soap bubbles with the therapist* were her favorite Theraplay activities. After termination, Marge and her therapist sat together and viewed Marge's Theraplay sessions on videotape; the following were among her verbal and nonverbal reactions:

1. Marge was quiet but intensely engrossed as she watched, in sharp contrast to her lively talking during the Theraplay sessions.

2. She frequently smiled or laughed as she relived the experience. At one point, she turned to her therapist and said, in anticipation, "Here comes the fun part."

3. She expressed a desire for her family to see the videotapes of her sessions.

4. Her interpretation of the experience was that she and her therapist (some 40 years younger) were communicating and enjoying each other.

5. She seemed particularly moved by the scenes that showed the therapist taking care of her feet. She called this activity "respect for an older person" because, she said, that was the part of her that was often neglected and frequently the part that hurt the most.

The sessions with Marge provided important clues about both the adaptation of Theraplay to the older adult and implications for further applications. It was felt that Theraplay would be a valuable group modality in a nursing home or adult day-care center. Members of such a group would be guided to enhance their self-esteem, stimulate reminiscence, and promote meaningful contact with others—all necessary ingredients for a sense of well being and adjustment at any age.

A short time after the work with Marge, an adult day-care center called on The Theraplay Institute for help in better engaging the group members with one another and in encouraging each client to more fully express his or her personality. In a Theraplay training videotape of this group, a day-care staff member commented on the group members' reactions to Theraplay: "People weren't staying away; they didn't seem bored. They seemed to be really excited about what was going on. Somebody like Dave who always says, 'I can't, I don't want to do none of that,' he seemed to be really enthusiastic about participating. He raised his hand and he laughed; he showed he was having fun. They really appreciated having the attention." (Booth, 1986). (Group Theraplay will be discussed in detail later in this chapter.)

It also was felt that Theraplay would be a useful method for increasing families' opportunities to appreciate an aging member. Families, too, could learn to provide esteem-building and trust-enhancing experiences. Jernberg (1988) described Theraplay with Mrs. K, a 92-year-old woman who was withdrawn, mute, and wheelchair-confined without organic basis. She lived in the house of her daughter and was cared for by round-the-clock staff. The staff and family members observed Mrs. K's eight weekly sessions during which her therapist, Russell Reisner, praised her physical attributes, challenged her to athletic matches (sliding a slippery lotioned hand out of the therapist's hand), nurtured her (fanning, a cool drink, a cool cloth to her hands or face), and calmed her (singing personalized songs). At the point of termination, Mrs. K's caregivers reported that she had become cooperative and responsive, following their moves with interested eyes and nodding in response to their questions. Her daughter stated, "After all this time, she is beginning to communicate with me . . . it is as though she is finally telling me she loves me" (p. 78).

Individual Theraplay in the Nursing Home

Adamitis also reported on Theraplay with Sarah, age 85, who resided in a nursing home and moved about in a wheel chair.

SARAH

Sarah was considered depressed by the nursing home staff and this was confirmed by her pretherapy testing. During the eight-week course of Theraplay, Sarah was introduced to delighting, intruding surprises, sensitive nurturing, organizing structure, and inviting challenge. It was evident early in treatment that Sarah delighted in being "found" (discovered). She took pleasure in references to personal details about herself. She loved the therapist's cheerfully observant commentary while her legs were decorated with soap crayons, while hats were being tried on her, or while her fingers were outlined with frosting. She savored the therapist's remarks as though she had never experienced such attentiveness before.

Frequently it happened that sensory activities (e.g., hiding perfume on her, singing, making a mustard-and-ketchup handprint) seemed to trigger a memory. At these times, the therapist listened, as sharing these memories was another way for Sarah to have an impact on her environment and a way to reorganize, to reintegrate, and, therefore, to resolve preoccupying thoughts, concerns, and conflicts.

Sarah resisted, too, of course. The following sequence was typical, showing that, in spite of persistent resistance, she enjoyed the activity.

SARAH: (Building a tower of hands with her therapist) What kind of trick is this? (Interest in her voice)

THERAPIST: The silliest kind, but you haven't seen anything yet. Now put your foot up here on my leg . . . (Therapist begins to take off her shoe.)

SARAH: Don't take my shoes off! (She curls up her toes.)

THERAPIST: You're curling up your toes inside there! My goodness, you're really strong! (Therapist continues to remove her shoe.) I've got a special place to put your feet.

SARAH: Why do you have to do all this to me? I feel like throwing up.

THERAPIST: (Therapist puts her feet down on a soft rug.) Oh, your feet are very warm today.

SARAH: You aren't going to monkey around with my toes, are you? (Expressing a wish)

THERAPIST: That's a good idea! This toe looks like it has a little sore. I'll bet your shoe rubs there. (Therapist continues to inspect her foot.)

SARAH: Yeah. (Looking attentively)

Sarah's initial reactions to Theraplay strongly resembled those reactions of children in the initial phase of Theraplay. Sessions 1 and 2 reflected a tentative acceptance, followed by negativism in session 3. A growing-and-trusting phase, as indicated by fewer instances of resistance and an increasing number of positive self-references, spanned sessions 4 through 6. During session 7, the reminder of termination was followed by a slight increase in resistance that continued through session 8. By these last sessions, however, the number of positive self-references was high and remained so thereafter.

Testing results, as measured by pre- and post-Theraplay administrations of the House-Tree-Person Test (Buck, 1964), consistently showed improved self-esteem. In addition, Sarah had become more aware of herself; for example, whereas her original female figure drawing showed no legs, her post-testing figure was complete with feet and legs (Figures 9.1 to 9.8).

Sarah's depression also seemed to have been lifted by the Theraplay experience. Although it might appear that just spending time with Sarah on a regular basis in itself could have reduced depression, that does not seem to be the case. In an independent study carried out at the same time as her Theraplay, Sarah indicated by questionnaire that she received and enjoyed considerable physical contact and attention from weekly visitors. Rather than just alleviating loneliness—a frequent component of geriatric depression—testing results and feedback suggested that Theraplay altered Sarah's sense of self in a positive way. Her more positive self-concept may have been responsible for her lessened depression.

Figure 9.1. Sarah's drawing of a house, pre-Theraplay.

Figure 9.2. Sarah's drawing of a house, post-Theraplay.

Figure 9.3. Sarah's drawing of a tree, pre-Theraplay.

Figure 9.4. Sarah's drawing of a tree, post-Theraplay.

Figure 9.5. Sarah's drawing of a man, pre-Theraplay.

Figure 9.6. Sarah's drawing of a man, post-Theraplay.

Figure 9.7. Sarah's drawing of a woman, pre-Theraplay.

Figure 9.8. Sarah's drawing of a woman, post-Theraplay.

Individual Theraplay in the Hospital

Ruth had been hospitalized on an orthopedic unit of a general hospital for treatment of the broken hip that she incurred when she fell off her kitchen step stool several weeks before her 85th birthday. Following her recovery, she was transferred to the psychiatric unit because of her subsequent self-mutilating behavior.

At the point of her psychiatric hospitalization, she not only was refusing to eat and to comply with medical recommendations but also was refusing to engage in activity of any kind. The nursing staff had tried cajoling her, reasoning with her, rewarding her, and ignoring her. Eventually, their kindness threatened to turn into abuse. Following one particularly punitively toned unit staff meeting, the Theraplay therapist was called in on a consultation. "Can anything be done to turn Ruth into a more reasonable human being?"

RUTH

At the first diagnostic session, the Theraplay therapist entered Ruth's room. Ruth was nowhere to be seen. The therapist, thinking she had misunderstood the room number, was about to leave when her attention was caught by a large bundle of crumpled sheets in one corner of the hospital bed. The therapist moved over to bundle of sheets and gently began to poke the nooks and crannies of the white fabric. Eventually a small hillock undulated.

THERAPIST: Well, look at that! There's something in there a-wiggling.

The response was silence. This was followed shortly by a quick, muffled clearing of a throat.

THERAPIST: And making little noises yet. (Moving in closer to the bundle and tentatively extending one finger) I wonder what will happen if I just gently touch this corner.

The "corner" recoils.

THERAPIST: Well! Can you beat that? It jumped. Whatever's in there, it jumped!

And so the game of cat and mouse continued. The therapist's journey around the sheet produced all manner of surprises.

THERAPIST: Well, lookee here—there's something that feels a whole lot like an ear . . . and look over here—I think I have myself a foot. (Wiggling intensifies) And this surely does resemble a nose.

At about this time, the bundle emitted a short but unmistakable giggle. Eventually the patient and therapist confronted each other directly.

THERAPIST: Whoever thought I'd find such a beauty all wrapped up inside there!

A small, obviously involuntary smile played on Ruth's lips. She seemed a promising candidate. The recommendation was made to proceed with eight weekly half-hour Theraplay sessions. The goal was to entice Ruth out of her reclusive stance.

Each of the sessions that followed began with the therapist "checking out" her client. Sometimes she checked her fingernails, sometimes the profile of her chin, sometimes the strength of her grip or the softness of her hair. The activities in any one session ranged from lively to calm. Since the plan for Ruth was to focus on experiences that would be intrusive, challenging, and nurturing, activities tended to concentrate on arm or thumb wrestling, delighting surprises, and feeding, lotioning, or foot bathing.

Each session ended with a hug and a familiar, very personal song. At first, Ruth resisted listening to the singing. Then she listened but refused to participate. Eventually she not only participated but sang rounds with her therapist. As the time for each of her weekly

Theraplay sessions drew nearer, the nursing staff reported that she appeared to look forward to the day and time of her appointment and to search for her therapist.

Ruth's increasing engagement, rising self-esteem, and participation in joyful, playful experiences led, by week four, to her becoming a more valued member of the unit community. The nursing staff began to report that they actually enjoyed caring for her and that Ruth herself was becoming helpful in engaging other withdrawn patients, first by offering to teach them needlework and, eventually, by engaging them in conversation. In spite of her initial, tyrannical efforts to save face and to keep others at arm's length, it was becoming increasingly apparent that she was falling in love with herself and with the world around her.

Group Theraplay Procedures

Caretakers or family members may observe or join in the Theraplay sessions. Thus, in that sense, the sessions are not always "individual." In time, the client may entice others to engage with him or her. Indeed, Theraplay is effective when conducted with a group as well as with individuals.

Group Theraplay is designed to enhance engagement through the use of activities that increase trust, self-esteem, and the capacity for pleasurable interaction with others. The therapist conducts the group in such a way that each participant is ensured stardom and the opportunity to share with one or more others.

Eight 45-minute sessions are scheduled at regular (usually weekly) intervals. Group coherence is important. Activities vary from quiet nurturing to challenging, from delightful surprising to structuring—all in a playful and upbeat atmosphere. The therapist opens the sessions by paying particular, personal attention to some positive, physical attribute(s) of each individual ("Helen, I can see you brought your lovely smile today; and Herbert, there is that friendly handshake of yours. Martha, I just love the way you grin with your eyebrows"). Next, this individual focus is expanded to include the whole group ("Sam, can you tell us some equally neat feature of Nancy, today?"). The joy of having been "discovered" by a group member may be concealed at first, but, sooner or later, there is no longer any hiding the joy this evokes. As the members show readiness to become more active, the therapist may organize a "hand tower" ("Let's pile our hands one on top of the other . . . higher. . . higher . . . higher . . . ") or divide the group into two teams, distributing marshmallows for a "snowball fight." As the therapist cheers the two teams on, the members of each team become ever more determined to achieve a victorious outcome. Even chronic depressives have been known to catch the spirit in their eagerness to win.

The therapist makes sure that highly charged, challenging activities like the snowball fight are followed with more nurturing, quieter ones, like feeding each other grapes or pear slices. And, having settled the group, the therapist may next organize group singing. The theme of the song is always personal (e.g., "the more we get to know Jan, the better we like Jan; the more we get to know Jan, the more we see that she's a gem. The more we get to like Hank, to like Hank, to like Hank, the more we get to like Hank, the more special he becomes"). At the session's closing, the therapist again moves from one individual to the next saying something like 'What I'm going to remember all week about Beth is . . . about Ray is . . . " and so on. Depending upon the members' comfort with group intimacy, the sessions may or may not end with a group hug.

It goes without saying that Group Theraplay therapists must be extremely sensitive to the thresholds and limitations of individual participants. Whereas one person may speak freely and join in readily, another may be considered to be making an effort if he or she only nods or grunts once in a while. Both individuals must be treated with equal respect by the therapist as well as by fellow group members.

In Group Theraplay, as in individual Theraplay, the final session is a goodbye party. Favorite activities are repeated at the goodbye party, and each member reiterates some of the outstanding qualities of each of the other members. Sometimes each member leaves the final session with a souvenir—perhaps a sheet of paper on which each participant has autographed a handprint.

Group Theraplay—Case Studies

Theraplay was introduced as an adjunct to an ongoing support group of five depressed women following hospitalization. This group was selected for Theraplay because the individual group members exhibited a high level of personal needs, and the group had previously resisted various interventions to promote interaction. For 8 weeks, Theraplay was used in the last part of their 90-minute therapy session. Initially, Theraplay was conducted for 30 minutes, but the necessity for a slower pace and the positive responses of the group and individuals were factors in increasing the time to a more optimal 45 minutes.

Each session had a definite beginning, which focused on actively making group members aware of each other's presence; a middle, which consisted of a flow of active activities and then quiet activities; and a closing, which ended the session without ending the relationships. Throughout the session, the therapist interspersed group activities (e.g., creating and passing around a handshake) with individual attention (e.g., taking the hand of one woman at a time and telling her what she, the therapist, liked best about the woman that day).

The sessions were preplanned yet flexible enough to accommodate to the mood of the group or to individual emergent needs. The therapist, while providing structure and clearly remaining in charge, also allowed the women a sense of control (e.g., following an activity, the group often had an opportunity to express pleasure by a show of thumbs up or thumbs down). Both verbally and nonverbally, group members indicated their enjoyment of such activities as trying on hats, singing, engaging in a "snowball fight" with marshmallows, group hugs, hand stacking with lotion, and cooling each other off with paper fans.

While anxious for an approach that would be more effective than the therapy that already had been conducted, the two initial group therapists (non-Theraplay therapists) and at least one of the individual therapists of these women were, nevertheless, skeptical. Their specific concerns were (a) that the activities would seem infantilizing to the women; (b) that the women would resist to the point of nonparticipation; and (c) that physical contact would be difficult for these women because of their low levels of trust and fears of intimacy.

Prior to beginning the Group Theraplay, these therapists participated in a one-day Theraplay workshop. They were introduced to the Theraplay approach and philosophy through lectures and videotapes. During the role-playing segment of the day, they portrayed the anticipated reactions of various women in the group as the Theraplay therapist conducted a variety of activities with this simulated group. The Theraplay therapist and the group therapists then contributed to the generation of ideas for other group activities designed to meet the specific needs of this particular group of women. In order to minimize disruptive changes and to maximize the benefits of group interaction, it was determined that the two group therapists would act as cotherapists to the Theraplay therapist when Theraplay was in progress.

Adamitis' (1986) transcription of session 6 of the eight-session series shows the format, content, and reactions that were typical of the entire program.

CASE ILLUSTRATION

When the Theraplay therapist entered the room, the women moved from their places around a large table to chairs in a circle.

THERAPIST: (Extending her hand to Sadie, with a smile) Give me your hand. (The therapist then had all the women join hands.) Now we've got a lady chain. (They smiled and several repeated "A lady chain!") Come on! (The therapist led them around the room.) We'll get a new view of the room today. (They continue walking about.) My, we make a long chain! (The women reenter the circle of chairs.) Now, I know we aren't back to your own chairs yet. That's so we can do something sort of tricky first. (The women watch with interest.) Take your hands and cross them in front of you like this. (The therapist shows them and everyone joins crisscrossed hands.) Now, we'll move back to where we were sitting. (The women move into position.) Let's see if we can all sit down at the same time without breaking hands. Ready, set, go! (Everyone sits together, shaking hands with the two people she is joined to.) Well, hello there! We have a new way of saying "Hello!" (The women smile and continue the handshake.) I told you when I first entered your group that I would be here for eight sessions. This is already number six! So we've got today and then two more times. After that, your group will continue with _____ and _____ (regular group leaders). At our last session together, we'll have a special goodbye party.

GRACE: A surprise party? (Her eyes lighting up)

THERAPIST: A goodbye party, Grace, but there'll be a lot of surprises in it! (The group laughs.) Next week, we'll plan the party together, but I'll still save some surprises for you, too.

SADIE: (Smiles) I'll bet she will surprise us.

THERAPIST: What we'll do now is to go around the circle telling the group about the view from your bedroom window when you were a child.

The women entered into the sharing rather quickly with brief accounts. Several of the women became animated at this time, embellishing their accounts with hand gestures as if drawing a picture for the group to see. Elizabeth could not recall a scene from her childhood but did remember something from her young adulthood in descriptive terms. Sadie had previously entered group conversations rather inappropriately and with little self-reference. In this instance, she began by recalling the view from the window of a character in a book she had once read but spontaneously returned to a sharing of her own childhood. Several times during this sharing, others would inquire with interest about further details from the speaker.

THERAPIST: (Looks around the group) Snow was predicted for today.

ELIZABETH: I know, I've got my boots on.

GRACE: Me, too.

THERAPIST: I think today is just right for a snowball fight! (Looks of surprise quickly turn to smiles and laughs.) OK, we'll need two teams. (Therapist arranges this.) Now we need a fort! (The women move into their teams while the therapist builds a fort with chairs and her coat.) And now for the snowballs.

LYDIA: (Turns to Fern) She brought snowballs?

Therapist produces two bags of marshmallows. Several women say "Marshmallows?!" and laugh. The therapist passes piles of marshmallows out to each one. Several women pop a marshmallow into their mouths immediately, with a giggle.

THERAPIST: Of course, it's fair to sample them before we begin. Get your pitching arm ready, ladies, and let the snowball fight begin!

The air is immediately filled with hurled marshmallows and gales of laughter. They begin seated in their chairs, but their energy and enthusiasm quickly have them up retrieving snowballs or trying to get into a better throwing position. The women were so engrossed in their enjoyment that there was little talking. Occasionally, however, such things were heard like "Here's one with a bite out of it" or "Hey, I have a curve to my throw" or (laughing so hard she could hardly speak) "Look at that, Grace is throwing at her own team!"

THERAPIST: I call a truce!

GROUP MEMBER: (A voice from somewhere calls out.) Not yet, not yet!

GRACE: (Leans back in her chair to rest at last.) Wasn't that the funniest thing!

FERN: You were funny, Grace; you were attacking your own team! (Both laugh.)

ELIZABETH: Who won?

As each woman begins to settle back in her chair again, the Theraplay therapist goes to each woman and fans her with a paper plate.

THERAPIST: (Fans Lydia) I'll fan you like a queen after that.

LYDIA: Me, a queen?

THERAPIST: You're just as special as a queen! (Lydia beams) then returns to her chair. Everyone come closer into the circle. (While they move in, the therapist puts a small, soft throw rug on the floor in the center of the circle.) Thinking about snowball fights makes me think of how good it feels to get warmed up afterward. (Kneels down beside Sadie.) I'll begin with you. (Takes her boots and shoes off.) I have a good place on this rug for your feet while I get them warmed up.

GRACE: (Begins to take her own boots off) Shoes off, too?

THERAPIST: I'll be around to you shortly, Grace. Today I get the fun of taking off your shoes! (Everyone laughs.) Therapist moves to Fern. OK, Fern, you're next. (Fern lifts up her foot in anticipation.) Off come your shoes, and hello toes! (Fern smiles. Therapist moves to Lydia, who sneezes as her shoes are being taken off.) Look at that! I took your shoes off and you sneezed! Bless you!!

The therapist continues around the circle, taking their shoes off and putting their feet on the rug. The women seem fascinated by the sight of everyone's bare feet on the rug.

THERAPIST: (Returns to Sadie and picks up her foot to massage it.) Your feet are nice and warm. (Sadie watches intently.) Therapist moves to Fern, who is wearing heavy socks instead of stockings.) I can't see your feet, but I sure can warm them up. Let's see. (Counting her toes from big to little) "1–2–3–4–5, yes—just the right number of toes in these socks.

FERN: Toes! (Smiles with delight.)

THERAPIST: (Picks up Fern's other foot and counts the toes from the little toe to the big one.) And 10–9–8–7–6. Hey, 6 and 5 are 11!

FERN: (Laughs.) Oh, you know I don't have 11 toes!

THERAPIST: (Recounts the toes with her fingers.) You're right! There are 10!! (Therapist moves to Elizabeth.) Now for your hardworking feet. (Picks up her foot and begins massaging it, watching her face for signs of expression.) I'll be careful not to get the tickles on the bottom though!

ELIZABETH: (Smiles.) I don't have tickles!

GRACE: Unless it's with a feather.

THERAPIST: (Moves to Grace and picks up her foot.) Now this one. (Points to her little toe.) Watch out for this one and be careful.

Grace points out the sore on her foot with concern; but, in the quick interchange that follows, she is clearly playing with the therapist's words and enjoying it.

THERAPIST: I'll be very careful.

GRACE: You'll handle it with care.

THERAPIST: (Winks at Grace.) I'll take good care of you.

The group seems to have been following this interchange and the other women laugh along with Grace.

LYDIA: (Comments as she watches therapist massage feet.) Smelly feet. (The group giggles.)

THERAPIST: (Moves to Lydia and picks up her feet.) Oh, these are toasty ones!

While the foot massaging continues, someone mentions that they never had a snowball fight that ended like this. Her comment seemed to spark further memories of snowdrifts, snow forts, and warming up cold toes and cold noses in the winter.

THERAPIST: (Returns to her chair in the circle.) You know, we can say hello to each other with our feet. (Models this by wiggling her toes in a "wave." As the hello continues, amid giggles, all feet busily tap a friendly hello to each one in reach.) I felt a tickle. Who did that? (More giggles by the group) Our feet are wonderful! They can do lots of things, you know. We can tap them like this. (They all join in.) We can make our toes wiggle. (The women look about at the wiggling toes.) This feels so good; we'll just leave our feet on the rug like this for a while. I've got another song for us today, and you can sing or not sing while we do the actions together. (Begins to sing.) She'll be coming round the mountain when she comes . . . (The women all begin to pick up the familiar tune.)

As the song continues, the therapist begins to change the words a bit to things like, "She'll be waving to her friends . . . bouncing up and down . . . tapping her toes." The women catch on quickly and add more actions of their own . . . nodding her head, winking at her neighbor, twiddling her thumbs, shaking hands with everyone, and even sticking out her tongue.

THERAPIST: That was terrific! All of you have such good ideas! (Looks around the group.) We've really been on the move today, so now, with partners, we'll try arranging each other's hair. I don't have any combs, but we can blow like this. (Turns to Lydia and gently blows her hair to illustrate.) Or, use your fingers for a comb.

The therapist pairs the women, and the blowing begins. In spite of some initial negative reactions of "Oh my, no" and "I don't think my hair is clean today." their faces showed enjoyment as the arranging progressed.

FERN: (Turns to the group.) Elizabeth's hair is so nice and soft. It blows real good.
ELIZABETH: My hair is thin.
THERAPIST: (Gives Elizabeth's hair a soft blow.) It sure wiggles good!
FERN: Mine's so tight it doesn't move.
THERAPIST: I'll tell you what, I think it takes more than one person to make yours wiggle, so we'll all help. (Laughter) Come on everyone. Gather around Fern, and let's make her hair dance. (Fern smiles as the other women gather around her and begin blowing her hair.)

The women return to their circle of chairs. The therapist puts shoes back on each one. When some ask if they should put their own on, the therapist responds, "I helped you out of your shoes, so I get to help you into them again, too."

THERAPIST: (Returns to her chair in the circle.) It's almost time to stop; but before we do, we're going to say good-bye in a special way today. Everyone stand up for this one. Now turn around like this (Turns half way around.) and back up so we all meet in the center. (Everyone backs into a tight circle.) There! We have a backward hug!! (Laughter) But this isn't nearly as much fun as a forward hug. (Turns around and spontaneously the women begin to hug each other.)

With each encounter, the therapist adds something like "What a nice warm hug," or "Mmm, you feel so good!" or "I'm so glad you came today!" When the hugging concludes, the therapist winks at the group. "I'll see you next week!"

It was evident from the start that the group dynamics quickly changed when the women moved from the more open-ended, cognitively oriented, problem-solving atmosphere of the support group to the more highly structured, active, intensely personal, yet playful Theraplay atmosphere. In contrast to their previous group behavior, they rarely resisted but rather seemed to absorb the Theraplay experiences. Their overall attendance improved, they participated and interacted, and their willingness to try new experiences increased.

Their response to challenge was frequently lively and creative. They verbally indicated a greater awareness of themselves as separate individuals and became more interested and aware of those around them.

A major impact of eight sessions of Theraplay with this group was a shift in affect. It was observed, for example, that several women became more attentive to their personal care. Further, individual members as well as the group repeatedly exhibited the capacity to "come alive" in this highly structured, nurturing atmosphere.

CONCLUSION

In summary, whether conducted individually or in groups, for young and for old, Theraplay is designed to enhance self-esteem, increase trust in others, and reinstate the philosophy that there can be pleasure in day-to-day experiences. Thus, Theraplay is an appropriate intervention for the elderly who often lack self-esteem, trust, and the pleasure of intimacy. Above all else, Theraplay answers a positive "Yes!" to the question "Am I still alive?"

REFERENCES

Adamitis, C. (1982, Spring). Theraplay with the elderly: A case study. *The Theraplay Institute Newsletter*, pp. 2–3.

Adamitis, C. (1985, Winter). Theraplay with an older adult. *The Theraplay Institute Newsletter*, pp. 2–4.

Adamitis, C. (1986). *The use of Theraplay with older adult women in a group setting.* Unpublished paper.

Baltes, P. B., & Baltes, M. M. (1990). Psychological perspectives on successful aging: The model of selective optimization with compensation. In P. B. Baltes & M. M. Baltes (Eds.), *Successful aging: A psychological model* (pp. 1–34). Cambridge, MA: Cambridge University Press.

Birren, J. E. (1982). *A review of the development of the self.* Paper presented at the annual meeting of the Gerontological Society of America, Boston, MA.

Booth, P. (1986). *Group Theraplay for the elderly: Part I. Group Theraplay in a day-care center for older adults. Part 2. Theraplay with an outpatient group.* [Videotape.] Chicago: The Theraplay Institute.

Buck, J. (1964). *House-Tree Person Projective Drawing Technique.* Los Angeles, CA: Western Psychological Services.

Butler, R. N., & Lewis, M. I. (1982). *Aging and mental health: Positive psychological approaches.* St. Louis, MO: C. V. Mosley.

DesLauriers, A., & Carlson, C. F. (1969). *Your child is asleep: early infantile autism.* Homewood, IL: Dorsey.

Franke, U. (1991). Theraplay mit Elisabeth Maier, 79 Jahre alt [Theraplay with Elizabeth Maier, 79 years old]. *Theraplay Journal, 4,* 9–11.

Gatz, M., Popkin, S., Pino, C., & Vandenbos, G. (1985). In J. E. Birren & K. W. Schaie (Eds.), *Handbook of the psychology of aging,* 2nd ed., (pp. 755–785). New York: Van Nostrand Reinhold.

Gilbert, J. G. (1977). Psychotherapy with the aged. *Psychotherapy: Theory, Research, and Practice, 14,* 394–402.

Hiatt, H. (1971). Dynamic psychotherapy with the aging patient. *American Journal of Psychotherapy, 25,* 591–600.

Ingersoll, B., & Silverman, A. (1978). Comparative group psychotherapy for the aged. *The Gerontologist, 18,* 201–206.

Jernberg, A. (1976). Theraplay technique. In C. Schaefer (Ed.), *The therapeutic use of child's play* (pp. 345–349). New York: Jason Aronson.

Jernberg, A. (1979). *Theraplay: A new treatment using structured play for problem children and their families.* San Francisco: Jossey-Bass.

Jernberg, A. (1987). *Theraplay for the elderly.* (Available from The Theraplay Institute, Chicago, IL)

Jernberg, A. (1988). Theraplay for the elderly tyrant. *Clinical Gerontologist, 8,* 76–79.

Jernberg, A. (1989). Training parents of failure-to-attach children. In C. E. Schaefer & J. M. Briesmeister (Eds.), *Handbook of parent training: Parents as co-therapists for children's behavior problems,* (pp. 392–413). New York: Wiley-Interscience Publication.

Jernberg, A. (1993). Attachment formation. In C. Schaefer (Ed.), *The therapeutic powers of play* (pp. 241–265). Northvale, NJ: Jason-Aronson.

Jernberg, A. (1993). Family Theraplay for the family tyrant. In T. Kottman & C. Schaefer (Eds.), *Play therapy in action: A casebook for practitioners* (pp. 45–96). Northvale, NJ: Jason-Aronson.

Kaminsky, M. (1984). The uses of reminiscence: A discussion of the formative literature. *Journal of Gerontological Social Work, 7,* 137–157.

Knight, B. (1992). *Older adults in psychotherapy: Case histories.* London: Sage Publications.

LaRue, A., Dessonville, C. & Jarwick, L. (1985). Aging and mental disorders. In J. Birren & W. Schaie (Eds.), *The psychology of aging, 2nd ed.,* (pp. 664–702). New York: Van Nostrand Reinhold.

Lopez, S. (1984). *In search of clinical judgment bias: Some conceptual guide posts.* Paper presented at the Western Psychological Association Annual Meeting, Los Angeles, CA.

McGee, J., & Lakin, M. (1977). Social perspectives on psychotherapy with the aged. *Psychotherapy: Theory, Research, and Practice, 14,* 333–342.

Myers, J. K., & Weissman, M. M. (1980). Psychiatric disorders and their treatment. *Medical Care, 18,* 117–123.

Oberleder, M. (1966). Psychotherapy with the aging: An art of the possible? *Psychotherapy: Theory, Research, and Practice, 3,* 139–142.

Pfeiffer, E., & Busse, W. E. (1973). Mental disorders in later life: Affective disorders, paranoid, neurotic, and situational reactions. In E. W. Busse & E. Pfeiffer (Eds.), *Mental illness in later life* (pp. 217–228). Washington, DC: American Psychiatric Association.

Robbins, J. (1987). Nurturing play with parents. *Nurturing Today: For Self and Family Growth, 2,* 6.

Sherman, E. (1981). *Counseling the aging: An integrative approach.* New York: Free Press.

20/20. (1993, July 9). [Television]. Capital Cities, ABC. "100 and Still Growing." Fred Peabody, Producer.

Weinberg, J. (1981). Comments: Need for healthcare providers: Implications for training. *Gerontology and Geriatric Education, 1,* 260–262.

PART 3

Play Therapy Techniques and Methods

CHAPTER 10

The Erica Method of Sand Play Diagnosis and Assessment

MARGARETA SJOLUND AND CHARLES E. SCHAEFER

INTRODUCTION

The Danish philosopher Soren Kirkegaard said in 1847 that the best way of getting to know children is by observing them play—and the best way of getting to know adolescents is by listening to what their wishes are. Obviously, the need for children to play in order to express experiences and emotions has been recognized for many years. However, it was not until the 1930s that play began to be used in a systematic way to understand childhood problems.

Child's play is often described as the territory between the real world and the child's inner world. In an attempt to reach this inner world of children, the Erica Method of Play Assessment was developed during the late 1940s at the Erica Foundation in Stockholm, Sweden. The Erica Method uses sand and toys in a standardized way to assess children's psychological functioning (Sjolund, 1981).

The Erica Method is named after the plant *Erica Telralix*. This plant is noted for its strength and hardiness as well as for its soft, pink, lovely flower. In like manner, the Erica Method combines the two elements of structured observation and clinical intuition. More specifically, the Erica Method combines the hardiness of a formal, reality-based observation with the softness and fragility of empathic contact with the child.

HISTORICAL ROOTS

Play therapy and play diagnosis have strong connections between them, and they often go hand in hand. It is difficult for clinicians to practice play therapy without making diagnostic observations and even harder to avoid starting a therapeutic process during the diagnostic phase. However, the purposes of diagnosis and therapy are different: The diagnostician is observing with the intent of developing a better understanding; the therapist's goal is to influence the child's psychopathological processes. In 1929, the English pediatrician and child psychologist Margaret Lowenfeld developed the Lowenfeld World Technique (Lowenfeld, 1960). At the Institute for Child Psychology in London, she collected miniature toys and objects and put them into a sandbox that the children called a "wonderbox." She then invited the children to use the small objects to build a world in the wonderbox and, thus, to construct a "microcosmos." In so doing, children had an opportunity to express and work through inner feelings and conflicts (Lowenfeld, 1979).

As her work became well known, Lowenfeld was visited by clinicians from all over the world who wanted to study and learn about play techniques. Charlotte Buhler, a child psychologist from Germany, visited the Institute in 1934 and subsequently developed the

World Test. This test uses standardized materials in order to study how children of different ages build their play world (Buhler, 1951a, 1951b). Buhler observed that children with psychological problems constructed worlds that were different from those of normal children; more specifically, the maladjusted children were more likely to produce worlds that were aggressive, empty, chaotic, or rigid.

Lucas Kamp, a child psychiatrist from Holland, further modified Lowenfeld's method in order to study the developmental aspects of child's play. Erik Erikson (1940, 1951) also employed the modified methods studying the differences in the way girls and boys used the materials.

Both Kamp and Erikson used the general idea of combining small toys with a sandtray in order to create a situation that allowed the child free creativity but that provided some boundaries for the observation and study of the play process. The collection of toys was guided by personal preferences and adapted to the study in question, and no attempts were made to standardize the technique.

The Swedish psychologist Hanna Bratt visited Lowenfeld in 1933 and later became one of the founders of the Erica Foundation in Stockholm (Danielson, 1986). Out of Bratt's work grew a modified version of the World Test, but it was used only for therapeutic purposes and, again, with a private collection of toys and no standardization.

The question facing the psychologists at the Institute was whether it was possible to go beyond traditional intelligence testing, and, through a technique of diagnosing children's natural play, find a method that could be taught and shared by others and that would give the clinician a tool for better understanding of childhood problems.

When the Swedish child psychiatrist Gosta Harding was introduced to the idea of letting children play in the sandtray, he became intrigued with the possibilities of actually developing a standardized procedure and using it as a diagnostic tool. Inspired by the work of Dr. Lowenfeld in London, Harding started to collect miniature toys. He found that the children responded well to the task of creating worlds in the sandtray and that, frequently, these worlds were very personal and often described the child's situation in a way much more meaningful than that described with words. Together with the child psychologist Allis Danielson (1986), Harding (1965) developed the method and gradually assembled an impressive collection of miniature toys, each toy having a particular symbolic meaning. In their daily clinical work with children at the Erica Foundation in Stockholm, Danielson and Harding came to realize the uniqueness and usefulness of the technique that was given the name *the Erica Method*.

Gradually, over many years, the method and the theories behind it evolved into an accepted and frequently used assessment tool. Today, it is used in schools, hospitals, and child guidance clinics throughout the Scandinavian countries.

PROCEDURE AND TECHNIQUE

Therapist Qualifications

The Erica Method is used primarily by psychiatrists, psychologists, and social workers in child guidance settings. However, the method is increasingly being used by school counselors as an effective way of communicating with children.

Even though child clinicians can easily understand the Erica Method and incorporate it into their daily work, they should have a thorough background in child development and some knowledge of projective methods. A year-long course is taught at the Erica Institute in Stockholm, Sweden, where theories of psychodynamic psychology and projective testing are interspersed with clinical experience. A similar training program is taught by The Erica Institute in Connecticut, and workshops are presented throughout the United States on a regular basis.

Client Characteristics

The Erica Method is most commonly used with children between the ages of 3 and 12, but the concept of combining toys and sand is really ageless. Both adolescents and adults, at times, welcome the opportunity to give gestalt to their life experiences without necessarily using words for communication.

The nonverbal aspects of the method make it possible to communicate with a population who, for developmental or other reasons, cannot respond to verbal tasks. The Erica Method is used very successfully in a number of schools for deaf children.

Children who have experienced trauma and abuse are also good candidates for the Erica Method because they might have difficulty discussing their experiences. The toys and the sandtray give them an opportunity to vent their feelings and reveal their background in a nonthreatening and safe manner.

Most children need very little encouragement to start building a world with the 360 different miniature toys that are provided, and they find the experience pleasurable and fun. A rare exception would be the hyperactive or impulse-disordered child who might have difficulty with the abundance of the material.

Throwing sand or destroying the toys is usually not productive to the therapeutic process, and limits should be set for such behavior. A child who will continuously challenge these limits is probably overwhelmed by the situation and not ready to function within the structure of the method.

The great majority of children adapt easily to the task of building a world and can use the materials in a very productive manner.

Logistics

When children enter the playroom, they are introduced to the toys, which are kept in an open cabinet with shelves divided into 12 compartments. It is a good rule to try to keep the observations as "clean" as possible by removing other kinds of toys or materials from the observation room. In order to make the toys easily accessible and to give the child a good overview of the contents of the cabinet, the toys are divided into 10 categories:

1. Soldiers, cowboys, and Indians
2. Other people
3. Wild animals
4. Farm animals
5. Traffic vehicles
6. War materials
7. Buildings
8. Fences
9. Houses and trees
10. Interior objects

The toys are arranged in the cabinet along a continuum from peaceful to aggressive on the vertical axes. They are arranged on the horizontal axes by whether they are moving, active, or static. A small piece of clay is also provided so the child can create whatever they might miss from among the collection of types. All of the different Erica toys carry different symbolic significance. Some have individual symbolic value, whereas others are ambiguous.

During the development of the method, a concerted effort was made to make the material as rich as possible so as to provide children with many sources of identification and symbolic expression. The toys were, and still are, collected from many parts of the world and include cannons, boats, fences, trees, and buildings of various types and sizes, and vehicles, like sports cars, trucks, police cars, and funeral cars.

There are also family figures in sets of five (father, mother, and three children). Thus, there are figures for identification regardless of the child's birth order (oldest, youngest, or middle). Other human figures include grandparents; professional figures, such as a policeman, doctor, nurse; and fantasy figures, including a king and a queen, angels, a wolf child, and a witch. Small, wooden-peg figures are also included in the collection.

Often, children with significant difficulties in the area of interpersonal relationships will select only the peg people and avoid the more human-like figures. There is a tendency for quiet children to use fewer toys and for lively children to be more creative and expansive in their play. Also noteworthy is the finding (Erikson, 1951) that it is more common for girls than boys to build household scenes with dollhouse furniture and family people. It is more common for boys, on the other hand, to use soldiers, together with cannons and explosions.

The Play Observation

When the child enters the playroom, he or she finds a sandtray filled with dry sand in the wooden frame. Another tray containing moist sand is on the floor and is partly pushed underneath the wooden frame. When the examiner feels that the child is comfortable in the situation, the following instructions are presented to the child: "In this cabinet, you can see all different kinds of things. You can take them out and build whatever you want with them in the sandtray. You can choose which things you like and build whatever you want, and you may use dry sand or the wet sand."

When the child has chosen a sandtray, the examiner sits in a place that allows observing and recording of the child's behavior without intruding into the child's play. The examiner openly makes continuous and chronological notes regarding the child's activities—what the child touches, examines, places in the sand, or avoids—as well as the child's comments, questions, facial expressions, and behavior in general.

The examiner takes the role of an active observer trying to be emphatic and available but without commenting on or interpreting the play. Questions from the child are reflected back as often as possible. These questions are frequently rhetorical in meaning, aimed at establishing and securing a relationship with the examiner rather than truly pulling for an explanation. If the child asks specific questions like "What is this?" he or she is often satisfied with "What does it look like to you?" However, if the child insists on a response, it is best to give a straightforward answer like, "I think it is a car. What do you think it is?"

As always with diagnostic observations, it is important to try to avoid entering into a therapeutic relationship with the child. The first order of business is to create a basis upon which diagnostic formulations and treatment recommendations can be made. The method of observation is nondirective in that the examiner attempts to be passive and neutral while remaining interested and supportive of what the child is doing. The examiner does not intrude with questions or suggestions. The purpose of the observation is to make the child feel free to express thoughts and feelings through the medium of the sand and toys. Thus, the method is more "toy-centered" than "relationship-centered." It is important to create a relaxed and calm atmosphere and to avoid making suggestions or giving selective support to the child's expressions or behaviors. The beginning Erica Method examiner often struggles to be nondirective, but, with experience, one usually becomes increasingly comfortable in the situation.

One should limit other tests of a verbal and directive nature during the Erica observation. If other tests and methods of observations are employed, it is usually recommended that one start with the Erica Method. The Erica materials are very attractive and enjoyable for most children and the free and spontaneous situation creates a good beginning for a diagnostic evaluation.

Although the child is operating in an atmosphere of support and acceptance, this does not mean that limits are not set. Limits are enforced as to time and use of the materials, but they are not routinely explained to the child unless there is reason to do so. Abuse or destruction of the materials and removing toys from the room are not accepted. Limits are also set on the child's handling of the sand since excessive mud play or throwing of sand is not beneficial to the diagnostic situation.

The child who starts throwing sand or breaking apart a toy animal is gently told that "The sand is not for throwing" or "The horse is not for breaking." If the child continues the destructive behavior, it is viewed as an inability to handle the stimulation of the materials. The child will be offered the use of only a portion of the toys, and the doors of the cabinet might have to be closed. In extreme situations, the child might even have to be removed from the room.

Sometimes children get so involved in the activity of creating something with the sand that they try to climb into the box. This is usually acceptable as the sandtray is constructed of heavy material and can bear the weight of most children. Although difficult to handle, all of these behaviors certainly raise many questions about the child's functioning and can provide a good basis for diagnostic impressions.

The maximum length of the observation is 45 minutes, and the examiner should carefully prepare the child for termination by announcing when there are approximately 5 minutes left in the session. If a child clearly demonstrates that he or she is ready to terminate before the 45 minutes are up, the examiner should allow it. If a child wants to put back the toys, the examiner should gently state that that is not necessary. However, if the child insists on cleaning up, it should be allowed.

When the observation is completed, the examiner proceeds to ask the child about the sand construction in a careful and nondirective manner. It is important to formulate the inquiry so that the child will spontaneously share the experience of playing in the sandtray. Comments that could be interpreted as criticism or as praise should be avoided. The inquiry always begins with broad, general questions like "What is happening here?" or "Please tell me about your world." The questions become more and more specific depending on the child's verbal capabilities and willingness to share information. While expressing a friendly attitude and sincere interest in understanding a child's play world, the examiner should not pressure the child into revealing themes with which her or she is uncomfortable or has little conscious awareness of. Young children often have difficulties in verbally describing and explaining their play, and the examiner will often have to rely on personal hypothetical and symbolic interpretations.

The observations take place during three consecutive sessions that are as closely related in time as possible. After the first observation, no detailed instructions need to be repeated. The examiner will simply say "Today you may build in the sandtray again. Would you like the dry or the wet sand?" It is to be noted that the words *play* or *toys* are deliberately not used so as to avoid influencing the child's approach to the situation. This frees children to express themselves as creatively as possible.

The use of three separate sessions allows for the observation of continuity and the repetition of themes. Comparisons and evaluations of the three observational sessions will provide information concerning the kind and the degree of pathology. The three sessions also give the child and the examiner the opportunity to view their time together from the perspective of a beginning, a middle, and an end. In regard to the need for three observations, Lowenfeld (1960) stated: "A series of worlds will display a connected line of thought, with an interior logic of its own. It is because of the rich potentialities which experience has shown to be in the extended use of the apparatus that it is essential to realize that a first world is unlikely to yield any but superficial characteristics." Children may construct a poorly organized world in the first session because of anxiety about the novel and strange situation. At later observations, when children feel more relaxed and familiar with the examiner, they are often able to create a meaningful and well-organized scene. On the other hand, a consecutive series of disorganized constructions is likely to be indicative of psychopatholgy.

All through the observation, the examiner keeps running notes on what materials the child is using and how his or her constructions or play are developing. Standardized scoring forms are used to help the examiner organize the information and make comparisons across sessions. These scoring forms are then used to summarize the observations and to help the examiner evaluate the information obtained about the child. The scoring forms also function as an aid in the formulation of the final report and of recommendations for further interventions.

SAND PLAY EVALUATION

In evaluating a child's play constructions, one must consider both formal and content aspects. In the analysis, each of the three sandtrays is evaluated separately. The final evaluation is based on the continuity and repetition of structural as well as thematic elements. It is only by analyzing both formal and content variables that the full projective picture of the child's sand play emerges.

The psychological aspects of the Erica Method of evaluation provide insight into a child's psychological functioning as projected in the play. Are the thoughts clear and easily understood, or is there fusion of thoughts and peculiarities? Can the child differentiate him- or herself from the examiner and the play objects? How is the child's reality orientation? Are there fixations and bizarre content that are not easily understood?

The observation forms can help provide an overview of such formal aspects as which sandtray (dry or wet) the children choose, how they treat the sand, or whether they use the whole surface of the tray, as opposed to building only in a corner. Information regarding how much time the children use and how they use the material is noted as well as general information regarding such behavioral aspects as relatedness to the examiner and affect level. Different columns on the scoring sheets help outline this information over the three observations and assist the examiner in formulating hypotheses and diagnostic impressions upon which the final recommendations are made. It is helpful to use an instant camera to take pictures of the child's constructions. Photos serve as invaluable concrete tools in discussions with parents or teachers. They also function well as memory supports.

Interpretation of Formal Aspects

Formal aspects of a child's play include such aspects as

1. Choice and treatment of the sand
2. Number of toys and categories used
3. Developmental level of sand play
4. Changes and corrections
5. Time limits
6. Levels of composition

They are based on relatively objective data that different examiners can be trained to evaluate in a reliable manner (Resjo, 1971).

The process of three consecutive observations is very important in the formulation of hypotheses and treatment plans. Comparisons between the three sandtrays will help the examiner assess the nature of the child's problem as well as give information as to the severity of the problem. If the three sandtray constructions show gradual improvement, it probably means that the child's difficulties are of a more reactive and transient nature. However, a series of three disorganized worlds, with no apparent recovery over the three sessions, suggest more serious psychopatholgy.

Choice and Treatment of the Sand

The soothing feeling of the sand and its fluidity as a medium give the children free rein for expressing their impulses and fantasies. Most children find the sand appealing and have the urge to touch it. Gentle stroking and smoothing of the sand is a good introduction to the task of building something in the sand. Some young children may even want to remove their shoes and socks and then climb into the sandtray. They can use their hands or any object in the tray to move the sand (a shovel is not provided as this may remind the child too much of play on the beach or in a sandbox).

In some cases, particularly with children who have been sexually abused, the rhythmic touching and stroking of the sand seem to provide sexual gratification. A child can be so stimulated by the tactile sensation of touching and stroking the sand as to become unable to move beyond this behavior and constructively use the rest of the material.

Brushing sand off hands and clothes is a normal and common behavior. However, children who are anxious about getting dirty and messy may become so upset when they get sand on them that they insist on cleaning up right away. Sometimes children are so concerned about cleanliness that they refuse to use the sand at all and will only build on the wooden ledge surrounding the sandtray.

Hiding

Children will often hide objects in the sand, and the meaning of the hiding is important. Where, what, and how is the child hiding? Does it express pleasurable, aggressive, or depressive feelings? Very young children will try to master the developmental task of object constancy by repetitiously hiding and finding objects in the sand. Other children will express depressive and maybe self-destructive impulses through hiding objects with which they identify. A small doll, symbolizing a baby brother, can be nurtured and bedded in the sand in a tender and loving manner. The same doll may be hidden in an angry and forceful way indicating a wish to get rid of the rival and thereby secure sole parental attention. Hiding can also symbolize the death or burial of real or imagined people.

Repetitive hiding may also be a child's way of dealing with separation anxiety. Children who have had trouble separating from their parents in the waiting room will often display this type of activity as a way of assuring themselves that their parent will still be there. Assessing the meaning of hiding objects in the sand is not always an easy task. Although repetitions will provide some clues, it is often advisable to ask the child some gentle, nonprobing questions. Questions like "What's happening here?" or "All covered up?" are sometimes helpful. At times, however, the child is not fully aware of the hiding or the meaning of the hiding, and the examiner then has to rely on personal interpretation.

Wet Sand or Dry Sand

The child's choice of wet or dry sand can be diagnostic. At the first observation, it is more common for children to use dry sand, which is easily moved and shifted around without resistance. Dry sand is safe and does not require a lot of effort. It often inspires children to play out fantasies about rain or snow and finding satisfaction in something that has no ending. Enuretic children will often play with the dry sand since it reminds them of water or rain. Wet sand, on the other hand, requires more effort and energy. It is often used by extroverted children who tend to play in a forceful, energetic, and sometimes aggressive way.

The level of intensity as well as the child's capacity to disconnect from activity will often indicate how deeply the child has been affected by the sand play. If the intensity builds to a level where the play is becoming too aggressive and intense, the examiner needs to provide constructive limits in a way that will not leave the child feeling hurt and criticized.

Sometimes children will use both sandtrays or switch the activity from one tray to the other. Bright and creative children may run out of space and continue their creation in the form of a lake or sea in the wet sand. On the other hand, a child who has difficulty with limits and containment might let his or her disorganization overflow into the next tray.

Often, children will shape the wet sand into some kind of construction. The complexity of the construction will depend on the child's developmental level. Young children will create primitive objects, such as mountains or isolated mounds of sand. Older children may shape the sand into more sophisticated constructions, such as a castle. The formation of the sand into round cookies may symbolize oral impulses. The expression of anal impulses will often take the form of aggressive bombings and throwing of sand. Thus, a close observation of how the child works with the sand will provide the examiner with much useful information.

The way the child uses the surface of the sandtray is often related to age. Younger children tend to perceive parts rather than the whole, but, by the age of 7, most children are able to use the whole surface. Children who leave an empty sandtray behind them may be afraid of leaving traces and be very critical of their own productions.

Empty Worlds and Crowded Worlds

On average, a child uses 50 to 70 of the 360 small objects available. If a child over the age of 5 uses less than 35 objects, it is considered to be an empty world. Charlotte Buhler found that an empty world (less than 50 objects, 5 categories, and no human figures) was often indicative of psychopathology (Buhler, 1951b).

On the other hand, selection of more than 100 objects is considered excessive. Danielson (1986) found that overproductiveness was more significant than underproductiveness. In her study of 7-year-old girls, she found that this often signified a lack of emotional maturity. Impulsive children with limited capacity to organize their play or children suffering from distorted perceptions often cannot find meaning in what they see, so they just fill up the sandtray in a haphazard way.

Developmental Level of Sand Play

Normal children discover and explore the possibilities for play quite naturally and will play according to their developmental age. Young children find satisfaction in the exploring and experimenting with the sand and with the toys, such as turning wheels or opening doors on a car. Their play is full of curiosity and surprise. A more advanced form of exploratory play is called "functional" play wherein the child attempts, for example, to drive a car back and forth but without assuming the role of the driver. Between ages 4 and 7, when children's fantasy level has expanded further, they will assume different roles. During this phase, role play increases in complexity and differentiation. After age 7, the child is more apt to create constructions. In this type of play, the task becomes goal oriented, and the need to play with the material is not as prominent as the need to produce a good end product.

Changes and Corrections

Some children create several different worlds during a session, and understanding the meaning of changes and corrections becomes important. If the changes are calm, goal oriented, and of limited frequency, they can express budding self-criticism and good reality orientation. Frequent changes, on the other hand, can signify harsh self-criticism and a feeling of not being good enough or not living up to expectations. Children who consistently avoid corrections despite expressing a wish to do so are often rigid and inflexible in their approach. If children are unaware of when objects are placed in an inappropriate way or when their constructions are poor, the diagnostician has to be alert to possibilities of perceptual difficulties or immaturities in reality testing. Infrequent changes in the play of very young children may be entirely appropriate as they follow their impulses and are content with what they have made.

Timing

There is a clear difference in the way children under and over age 7 use the 45-minute Erica Method observation. The younger children often become so involved in the play that they forget that they were actually asked to build a world. The end product is not as important as it is to the older child. This is reflected in building time. The young child often uses the maximum time, whereas the older child stops and clearly indicates when his construction is finished. Insecure and well-guarded children sometimes use very few objects but a long building time. This suggests uncertainty about where to place the objects or an inability to finish the construction and terminate the session. Extremely short building times have many causes, such as lack of fantasy and creativity or problems with concentration and attention span. Developmentally delayed children often have difficulty in combining toys and bringing meaning to the task of building a world. This can result in unusually short building times.

It is to be expected that the child will use less time for the constructions in sessions two and three. However, if the child uses much less time, it can signify a mobilization of defenses against impulses that are triggered by the materials. If the time increases, it might mean a better tolerance for anxiety and an increase in ability to tolerate and deal with conflicts.

Response latency refers to the amount of time that passes between the examiner's instructions and the child's beginning to place objects in the sand. A few minutes of looking over the available materials and then carefully choosing the toys help the child to organize the construction and approach the task in a meaningful manner. But the longer the response latency, the more likely it is that there is resistance and, maybe, underlying insecurity. Usually such children cannot continue to resist the pull and attraction of the toys, and the long response latency will often diminish over the next two sessions.

Levels of Composition

The level of composition provides important developmental information and has been found to be related both to age and to IQ (Harding, 1965). The level of composition of a child's sand world will range from chaos to a meaningful whole. The older child will try to bring order and meaning to the task of constructing a world and should be able to put the toys together in a meaningful way so as to create scenes and stories. In general, most children around the age of 7 have reached a developmental level at which they can perceive and express reality in a coherent and organized fashion. Therefore, they should be able to use the Erica materials to create a meaningful world in the sand (Danielson, 1976; Harding, 1965; Kessler, 1966).

Before age 7, however, young children will often place the toys without paying attention to what they represent. Thus, they cannot combine the toys in a meaningful manner. They do not perceive the toys as relating to outer reality, so they often place them at random in the sandtray. Most commonly, a child's sand world will represent one of the following levels of composition:

INDIFFERENT PLACEMENT.   Indifferent placements are typical of children around the ages of 2 and 3 and indicate that the child cannot perceive the relationship among the toys and is not concerned if they are placed upside-down or jumbled together in a meaningless haphazard pattern. Children at this age see reality more in terms of concrete and individual objects and have difficulty arranging memories and perceptions into meaningful constructions. Constructions in the sandtray at this age will often resemble the child's way of speaking in incomplete sentences, that is, trying to communicate through the use of one or two words. If an older child cannot go beyond this level of composition, there is reason to suspect borderline intellectual development or a high level of anxiety that impedes the child's thinking.

SORTING.   Sorting toys according to similarities, such as color or categories, is a normal behavior for children around the age of 3. A sorted category has no meaningful connection to other categories except in the way it is placed in the sand. So all the cars might end up in one corner of the box, and all the people and trees are placed in other corners. Children who simply sort the toys are often defending against underlying chaos so that the rigidity and preciseness of sorting the toys provides them with security and boundaries.

CONFIGURATION. *Configuration* refers to the formations of geometric patterns without a consideration of what the toys represent. It is a common behavior in 4-year-olds, who tend to make geometric shapes out of different objects.

SIMPLE CATEGORIZATION. Around the age of 4, the child understands the meaning of the toys and will place them together in simple ways, such as a chair next to a table or a tree next to the house. At this level, the child does not need the rigid controls evident with configuration and sorting but can start to explore and perceive the world according to more realistic principles.

JUXTAPOSING. Around ages 4 and 5, children further advance in the way they can utilize the toys to represent reality. They place individual toys together based on what they represent rather than the fact that they belong to a certain category. A typical juxtaposing scene involves a child placing wild animals and tame animals indiscriminately together in the sandtray. This suggests that the child is aware of their representational value as animals and that they somehow belong together. However, the child is still not able to distinguish among the conceptual differences between wild animals and tame animals. The juxtaposing is based on the desired content of the scene, such as trying to build a zoo. But the child just places the different animals into distinct categories, making no attempt to create a meaningful scene based on the animals' representational values.

CONVENTIONAL GROUPING. At this level, children's reality perception is such that they are able to combine form and content and make simple compositions, such as farm animals inside a fence or trees lined up around a house. Sometimes, several constructions at different levels are placed next to each other. This may indicate an unevenness in the child's development. By analyzing the three sandtrays together as well as one at a time, one may observe whether this is a stable pattern with a child.

The child who is experiencing psychological stress may produce a splintered or compartmentalized creation. This contains several different, conventional groupings that are meaningful in themselves but have no relationship to each other.

MEANINGFUL SCENE. At this level, around the age of 7, most children can create a meaningful scene that then excludes other compositional levels. The scene reflects a child's capacity to adequately relate to reality and is often a representation of the child's real-life situation. Again, the scenes can be either rather simple and primitive or highly complex and sophisticated, but the common criterion is that everything in the tray is combined together in a meaningful way.

ATYPICAL COMPOSITIONS. Even though a child is able to combine the toys in a meaningful way, the child is not necessarily free of psychopathology. It is common to see scenes in which the compositions are of poor quality with tendencies to lower levels. Many children who are referred for psychological evaluations demonstrate behaviors and symptoms that often can be found in the normal development of younger children. So a child who produces a level of composition typical of a much younger child may be showing signs of psychopathology.

In other cases, the child's compositions are so different and atypical that they cannot be understood only as regressive behaviors or fixations at earlier developmental stages. They are truly unique and difficult to interpret or understand. The following three categories (chaotic, bizarre, closed) are examples of such atypical compositions that may reflect psychological disturbance:

Chaotic grouping

A chaotic world results when the child does not have enough ego control to organize the play. The child keeps filling the sandtray with toys without any relationship between them. A child might start building a meaningful world with conventional groupings but then cannot contain this world and continues to add toys until a world is created that is difficult to understand. Such a world may consist of animals, furniture, trains, fences, and people thrown together without apparent meaning.

Often the stimulation of the material makes children lose their cognitive resources and capacity for control. It is as if the children fear what might happen if they stop and are driven by an inner need to fill the empty space. Such children will often continue until there are no more toys or space or until the examiner puts some limit on this behavior. Some children will call their chaotic world a farm or a city and appear very content and happy with the creation. Clearly, they do not have the capacity to distance themselves from their compositions and, thus, cannot see the lack of organization and meaning in what they have built.

It is important to analyze the three sandtrays since a repetition of chaotic worlds carries a different meaning from a single chaotic construction produced by a child who is very anxious during the first visit. Chaotic groupings can result from either psychological or organic etiology or a combination of both. They tend to indicate a questionable reality orientation or a strong crisis reaction following a traumatic experience.

Bizarre groupings

Bizarre groupings are strange combinations of toys about which the child cannot provide a meaningful explanation. Young children and mentally retarded children can make strange combinations that are not necessarily bizarre. Strange groupings by an older child usually have diagnostic significance. Such bizarre groupings are very rare and suggest a questionable reality orientation. However, it is important to carefully question the child about any combinations that might appear bizarre to the examiner. A child may have a plausible explanation for a composition that appears strange to an outside observer.

Closed world

In these compositions the child puts fences and walls around all the scenes, suggesting a need for control and protection. Children from chaotic home environments tend to use more fences in their sandtrays, as if they want to create safe havens without outside intrusions or disturbances. A totally closed world could also indicate intense shyness and a desire to avoid all social interactions.

Recording

The observation sheets (the Appendix) are designed to record the aforementioned aspects. Information regarding how much time the child uses is noted as well. One also assesses the child's general behavior during the play, including relatedness to the examiner and affect level. Different columns on the observation sheets clearly outline this information over the three observations and help the examiner to formulate hypotheses and diagnostic impressions on which to base final recommendations. After interpreting the formal aspects, the examiner proceeds to analyze the content of the sandtrays.

Content Analysis

Content analysis involves the examination of themes in one or several of the child's worlds and the relationships between them. The content is what the worlds are all about. Similar to popular responses on the Rorschach test, there is a tendency for certain worlds to appear more frequently in children's play, such as war scenes, cities, traffic scenes, country scenes, farms, and zoo scenes.

The child's description of the world after it is finished gives valuable information about the meaning of the creation. Some children, however, do not have the verbal capacity to explain what they have created, and the examiner then has to rely on clinical judgment. Are there repeated themes of loneliness, aggressiveness, or nurturance? Are there violent crashes or accidents? How do human figures relate to each other? Are there objects of identification? Is the child describing scary scenes from real life, or is the play a projection of wishful thinking?

Most normal children, particularly boys, will build at least one aggressive scene. So the task of the examiner is to interpret how aggressive the worlds are, that is, how intense or frequent the aggressive play is. Is the child identifying with the victim or with the aggressor; for example, is the child using active or passive soldiers? These observations provide information not only in terms of how children view aggression, but also in terms of how they handle their own aggressive feelings.

Final Analysis

After the three play sessions, the information collected on the observation sheets and from note taking is ready to be condensed and interpreted by the examiner using both the formal and the content aspects. This leads to hypotheses regarding the child's developmental level, personality, strengths, defenses, and psychological problems. Besides generating diagnostic impressions, the Erica Method play sessions are excellent opportunities for the examiner to observe the child's interpersonal relatedness and likely response to psychotherapy.

CASE ILLUSTRATION OF THE ERICA METHOD OF PLAY ASSESMENT

History

Peter, age 6, was brought for an evaluation by his parents. Peter was described by his parents as a withdrawn and shy child who manifested elective mutism and marked impairment in social functioning. Peter attended a kindergarten program within the special education program in his local public school. He was described by his teacher as nonparticipatory, extremely withdrawn, isolated, and "dead from the eyes down." He apparently enjoyed the work and did well academically but refused to talk to his teacher or the other children. Attempts by the school psychologist to test him were met with total refusal and he was described as "nontestable."

Peter was lively and talkative with his immediate family but did not speak at all to other adults or children. His early developmental history was normal. The family history revealed multiple separations from his mother. On a number of occasions she would leave her husband and two children for a few weeks at a time. The present family situation was marked by financial strain and fluctuating marital discord.

Procedure

At the first session, Peter clung to his mother, refused to speak, and demanded that his mother stay for the observation session. He understood the instructions immediately, seemed to enjoy the sand-play activity, and was able to absorb himself in the materials for the full 45 minutes without asking for his mother's attention. At the following two sessions, Peter was able to separate and stay in the playroom on his own.

Session 1. Peter took only a few seconds to look over the toys and then proceeded to pick out what he wanted to use in his construction. Initially, he lined the items up on the wood frame of the tray. Very certain in what he wanted, he did not change his plan at all during the observation. He never looked up from the play activity and did not respond to gentle comments from the examiner.

Peter used all the cars and carefully lined them up on roads he had made out of the sand. He was careful in putting sports cars with sports cars and trucks with trucks. He then proceeded to place traffic signs in appropriate places along the roads and carefully build intricate designs of trees and houses.

He used the whole surface of the tray and his "world" gave the impression of an extremely organized and well-made town. Peter took great care in placing every item just so and would often sit back and look at his construction. In the far corner of the tray, he put a father figure, a mother, and two children. The boy and girl were placed in such as way that they did not touch.

When Peter had about 10 minutes left, he started building a wall of sand around the figures and then proceeded to add fences around separate small scenes in the tray. He appeared very content with his work but did not respond to questions and was unwilling to share any thoughts about his construction.

Session 2. This time Peter separated easily from his mother and went straight to the sandtray where he immediately started to pick out toys which he put on the frame. He apparently knew exactly what he wanted to make and proceeded without interruption for 30 minutes. The first animal he picked was a black-and-white horse, which he took great care in choosing from among the available horses. At this point, Peter looked at the examiner for the first time and indicated through gestures that he wanted some water. He went on his own to the sink to get the water. He then proceeded to pour water over the sand and build a cave in which the horse was placed. Peter then used all of the wild animals and put them around the cave in an orderly and organized fashion. All the animals were sorted according to size and species, and the high fences were then used to create a wall around them.

Session 3. Peter started the third session by getting water on his own and then spending about 15 minutes in constructing what appeared to be a volcano surrounded by several smaller mountains. He then assembled all the houses and very carefully placed them on and around the mountain with some of them almost sliding down the mountain sides. Again, fences were used to surround the different small scenes within the larger one. Peter finished his construction after 25 minutes and spent the rest of the session drawing. He did not share his ideas about his world but did nod in confirmation when the examiner asked him if the high mountain was a volcano.

Evaluation of Formal Aspects

Analysis of the formal aspects of Peter's Erica Method performance revealed a bright boy with considerable strengths. He immediately became absorbed by the toys and the activity of creating a world. He approached the task in a planful, organized manner, showing goal-directed and developmentally appropriate behavior. He was able to use the whole sandtray and create a meaningful, well-integrated scene with good fine-motor coordination. This reflects his intelligence and intact neuropsychological functioning. He also demonstrated a good attention span and a certain lack of inhibition, which permitted him to use the sand in a free and expressive manner. Peter's social development, however, appeared stifled. He did not involve himself in any kind of interactive play that would be expected of a bright and healthy 6-year-old. Peter consistently refused to respond to comments or questions from the examiner. He did, however, appear to become somewhat more trusting and communicative over the sessions, as demonstrated in his willingness to stay in the playroom on his own. When he rejoined his mother after the sessions, he became more talkative and shared some of his play experiences with her. Peter's worlds were all characterized by a rigid control with all objects perfectly sorted into categories of vehicles, building, trees, cars, fences, and traffic signs. With the exception of the four family figures used in the first session, his worlds were empty of human life. The family of figures was placed in the far corner of the tray in an isolated fashion. He also avoided toys with aggressive qualities, and when he did use the wild animals, he sorted them into categories and lined them up with fences around them so as to make them harmless.

All of Peter's constructions had fences and barricades around them and were typical of a closed world. This reflects a need for protection and mirrors his anxious-avoidant symptomatology. It was as if he were saying "I will not allow other people to get close to me, and I will not give others access to my inner life and feelings."

Evaluation of Content

The content of Peter's sand constructions indicated an impairment in social/emotional functioning and unmet needs for nurturance and stability. In the first session, be built a static world with cars and trucks lined up in perfect order and surrounded by high fences. The roads were clearly outlined and cars were ready to go but were left immobilized and frozen in their positions.

In the second session, his world involved a scene with a horse seeking protection in a cave surrounded by wild animals. It was unclear whether the wild animals were trying to attack or protect the horse. Again, the toys were frozen in position. Peter's careful selection of the horse indicated that it served as an identification object, reflecting his own ambivalence in dealing with aggression and hiding behind a wall of elective mutism.

The scene created in the third session showed a volcano with houses standing on the sides of the surrounding mountains as if waiting for an eruption to occur. The content of all three worlds had an antiseptic, static, and empty quality reflecting Peter's loneliness and withdrawal from social interactions. He used few categories, and when he used human figures, they were placed apart and in isolation from each other.

The closed and empty worlds can be understood as symbolic expressions of Peter's inner feelings of emptiness, isolation, and withdrawal from interpersonal relationships. The rigid, perfectionist sorting and lining up of the toys further attest to his need to be in total control as a defense against anxiety. But as these defenses weaken, his vulnerability and need for protection are symbolically expressed in the houses resting on the upper edge of the mountains waiting to be destroyed by a volcanic eruption.

Summary and Recommendation

Peter appeared to be a cognitively advanced and neurologically intact child who currently demonstrated significant impairments in his social/emotional development. He was seen as an emotionally constricted boy who was trying to display perfect control of his inner world as well as of his environment. His social withdrawal may have been Peter's way of defending against frightening fears of abandonment.

A recommendation was made for weekly family-play-therapy sessions using the Erica Method materials. Peter adapted well to these sessions and seemed to enjoy them. They gave him an opportunity to play out feelings in a safe and accepting atmosphere. The treatment plan was to utilize his parents to facilitate the development of trust and interaction with the therapist. After a gradual building of trust, Peter began a verbal exchange with the therapist. Once he became comfortable talking to the therapist, a recommendation was made for Peter to participate in a therapeutic play group with his peers.

CONCLUSION

Besides the diagnostic information provided by the Erica Method as such, the evaluations are excellent opportunities for general clinical observations. During the course of the three sessions, the examiner will have ample opportunities to observe the child's general behavior, concentration, spontaneity, creativity, verbal abilities, fine motor functioning, and so on. The final outcome is generally a very comprehensive picture of the child.

Although the Erica Method, as described in this chapter, is a diagnostic method used for the understanding of children's feelings and behaviors, it has its origin in child therapy, and the material can readily be used for therapeutic purposes. Sand is an excellent medium for children of all ages, and, together with water, it readily lends itself to the demonstration of a large variety of fantasies.

In the process of play therapy, the therapist, according to his or her individual style, can use the Erica Method materials to communicate without words and provide the child with an opportunity to play out feelings in a safe and accepting atmosphere.

REFERENCES

Buhler, C. (1951a). The World Test, a projective technique. *Journal of Child Psychiatry*, 2, 4–23.

Buhler, C. (1951b). A comparison of the result of the World Test with teacher judgments concerning children's personal adjustment. *Journal of Child Psychiatry*, 2, 36–38.

Danielson, A. (1976). *Ericametoden*. Stockholm: Psykologiforlaget AB.

Danielson, A. (1986). *Att bygga sin vard*. Stockholm: Psykologiforlaget AB.

Erikson, E. H. (1940). Studies in the interpretation of play. *Genetic Psychology Monograph, 22*, 557–671.

Erikson, E. H. (1951). Sex differences in the play configurations of preadolescents. *American Journal of Orthopsychiatry, 21*, 667–692.

Harding, G. (1965). *Leken som avslojar.* Stockholm: Natur & Kultur.

Kessler, J. (1966). *Psychopathology of childhood.* Englewood Cliffs, NJ.: Prentice-Hall.

Lowenfeld, M. (1960). The World technique. *Topical Problems in Psychotherapy, 3*, 248–263.

Lowenfeld, M. (1979). *The World technique.* London: George Allen and Unwin.

Resjo, U. (1971). *Ericametoden.* [Erica Method] Doctoral dissertation, University of Uppsala.

Sjolund, M. (1981). Play diagnosis and therapy in Sweden: The Erica-Method. *Journal of Clinical Psychology, 37*, 822–325.

APPENDIX

THE ERICA METHOD ©

Name _____ Birthdate_____ Age_____

Examiner _____

		Dates:			
		Observations:	1	2	3
Choice of sandbox	Dry				
	Wet				
Treatment of the sand	Using the sand				
	Using a tool				
	Drizzling				
	Smoothing				
	Digging				
	Shaping to plastic construction				
	Marking				
	Trails, patterns				
	Hiding in the sand				
	Adding water, more sand				
	Explorative play				
Type of play	Functional play				
	Role play				
Changes and corrections					
Timing	Latency				
	Building time, playing time				
Building surface	The whole sandbox				
	More than half				
	Less than half				
	Outside of sandbox				
	Only outside of sandbox				
Composition	Indifferent placement				
	Configuration				
	Sorting				
	Simple categorization				
	Juxtaposing				
	Conventional grouping				
	Meaningful whole				
	Chaotic grouping				
	Bizarre grouping				
	Closed world				

Amout of Toys in Final Scene

Categories	Objects	Total	Obs 1	Obs 2	Obs 3
1. Soldiers, cowboys, Indians (48)	soldiers.	32			
	cowboys, Indians.	16			
2. People (31)	neutral figures	8			
	professions.	4			
	family members.	9			
	fantasy figures	10			
3. Wild animals (29)	full grown. . . . :.	15			
	young	12			
	defect crocodile	1			
	defect lion.	1			
4. Tame animals (57)	full grown.	17			
	young	20			
	miniatures.	20			
5. Vehicles (50)	trains.	8			
	cars, trucks	6			
	tow-truck.	1			
	funeral car.	1			
	ambulance.	1			
	fire engine.	1			
	carts	2			
	airplanes.	9			
	defect airplane	1			
	war ships	6			
	trade ships	6			
	sailboats.	6			
	rowboats.	2			
6. War objects (14)	cannons.	8			
	explosions, fires.	6			
7. Buildings (26)	large church.	1			
	small church.	1			
	mansion	1			
	cottages.	2			
	other houses	21			
8. Fences, traffic signs (47)	palisades.	20			
	fences.	20			
	railway gate	2			
	traffic signs.	3			
	gas pumps.	2			
9. Trees (33)	trees	33			
10. Interior objects (25)	furniture, telephones. . .	13			
	bed linens	12			
	TOTAL	360			

OBS 1	OBS 2	OBS 3	Average Number of Categories		Average Number of Toys	

THE ERICA METHOD

Combined evaluation of three observations

Formal Aspects

	Description	Hypothesis
Sand		
Objects and Categories		
Use of Material		
Changes		
Building-time		
Building-type		

<u>**Combinations of hypotheses founded on formal aspects:**</u>

<u>**Interpretation of content:**</u>

DIAGNOSTIC PLAY OBSERVATION

Name:

Birthdate:

Dates of Observations:

Date of Report
REASON FOR REFERRAL:

RELEVANT BACKGROUND HISTORY:

BEHAVIORAL OBSERVATIONS:
Separation

Relationship with examiner

Affect

Activity level

Verbalization

Motoric functioning

PLAY OBSERVATION:
Organization

Creativity

Age-appropriate Play

Repeated themes

Personality Traits

Unusual Observations

SUMMARY:

RECOMMENDATIONS:

CHAPTER 11

Jungian Play Therapy Techniques

GISELA DE DOMENICO

Play is of ancient, prehuman origin, and as such belongs to the primordial inheritance of the psyche which includes the emotions and the archetypal regulatory functions of the psyche.

STEWART, 1990, P. 27

INTRODUCTION

This chapter offers an introduction to the historical antecedents of current Jungian play therapy practices and an exposition of the basic metapsychological principles that govern Jungian play therapy. The emphasis is on the illustration of the Jungian play therapist's approach to various traditional play modalities.

The distinctive feature of Jungian play therapy is not a particular set of play techniques used by the therapist. Instead, it is the way in which the therapist's understanding of the nature of the psyche, the meaning of play, and the goal of the therapy influence the play therapy process. The Jungian play therapist believes the individual psyche to be capable of healing itself in a free and protected environment while in a transference relationship to a supportive therapist. Therefore, the play therapist directly supports the developmental strivings of the individual psyche. This often involves very subjective, intuitive interactions with clients. Consequently, the behaviors during the play session may vary greatly from therapist to therapist. In the six vignettes used to illustrate theory and practice, some of these different types of therapist-client interactions are demonstrated.

Because the use of diverse play therapy techniques characterizes Jungian practice, play therapy techniques are also demonstrated in the theoretical sections that describe Jung's personal play experiences. Emphasis is placed on the description of Jungian sandplay, a technique originally developed as worldplay by Dr. Margaret Lowenfeld. In sandtray work, the child, adult, couple, or family use a tray, filled halfway with either wet or dry sand, water, and/or a diverse collection of man-made miniature and natural objects to create a play, a design, a scene, or a world in this limited container, referred to as the *temenos*.

Theory

Dr. Carl Gustav Jung (1875–1961), the founder of the school of Analytical Depth Psychology, focused primarily on the human individuation process. *Individuation* involves the gradual "becoming a single, homogeneous being . . . a separate, indivisible unity . . . and embracing our innermost, last and incomparable uniqueness" (Jung, 1959, p. 275) during each developmental phase of life (Kalff, 1980; Neumann, 1973; Sidoli, 1988). Jung discovered from his own personal play experiences that play is one of the primary means to "self-realization" (Jung, 1961, p. 226). Jungian therapists base their use of creative play therapy techniques on Jung's own healing journeys into the archetypal world of play and fantasy.

While in his 80s, Jung wrote his autobiography, *Memories, Dreams, Reflections* (Jung, 1961). He recalled how during midlife he reviewed his childhood plays, dreams, and visions in search of his own unique identity that extended beyond both his persona (his social ego or outer core personality) and his highly emotionally charged personal unconscious (repressed desires, characteristics, acts, and biographical memories) to the depths of his individuality, which he called the *"Self."* Jung believed that the individuation process aimed for the constellation of a whole personality capable of balancing sociocultural and individual needs while being in contact with transcultural and transpersonal realities that provide a universal, primordial type of wisdom. To effect such a level of self-realization, his ego needed ever expanding communication with the Self (the inner central core personality). He found that playing freely in the moment gave him access to the subjectively personal stories and myths of his own individuality. Thus, he developed self-directed, spontaneous play as a therapeutic method of enhancing the expression of self and self-knowledge.

When Jung instituted regular, documented play periods for himself, he was surprised at his reluctance to follow his inner playful promptings. To surrender his adult dignity to regressive "childish plays" was difficult. There was a part of him that thought play to be foolish and nonsensical. Nevertheless, almost daily, he used twigs, stones, and mud along the lake shore to build towns and villages. He became deeply engrossed in the play. After each play period, he documented his experiences, drew or painted them, and subsequently subjected them to a psychological analysis.

Jung overcame his negative reactions, surrendered to the play, and then claimed both the process and the products of his play. Through experiencing and then reflecting on his play, he was able to confront himself:

> In the course of this activity my thoughts clarified, and I was able to grasp the fantasies whose presence in myself I dimly felt. . . . I had no answer to my questions, only the inner certainty that I was on the way to discovering my own myth. For the building game was only a beginning. It released a stream of fantasies which I later wrote down. (Jung, 1961, pp. 174–175)

The adult Jung, in search of his identity, successfully established a conscious connection to his inner world as he gave external form to his inner visions through spontaneous play. During the night, he sought refuge in his dreams, which he also saw as meaningful expressions of his inner psychic life. Slowly, his inner world yielded its secret store of images, experiences, and myths that comprised his unique individuality. In time, he connected the playful activities of his midlife with the plays of his own childhood long past. He saw in them the same impulse towards growth and development of the entire personality.

Jung remembered a secret, recurring visionary dream that made its first appearance at age 3: He visited a ritual phallus, a "man-eater," seated on a golden throne deep inside an underground room. In this vivid dream, he was "initiated into the secrets of the earth . . . and into the realm of darkness" (Jung, 1961, pp. 11–16). Jung saw this dream as an initiation into the world of the unconscious and the chthonic realms of the depth of the psyche. It was the starting point of his lifelong discovery of himself. In fact, Jung claimed that this profoundly emotional dream experience had defined the whole course of his life.

Although he did not remember the content of his prolific early childhood play, Jung knew that play had been essential in his psychological differentiation from others. Often, the play had a private, nonverbal, and intensely absorbing quality that he did not want disturbed by any intrusive adult observations or remarks: "I was deeply absorbed in my games and would not endure being watched or being judged while I played them" (Jung, 1961, p. 11).

For Jung, the inner life of childhood manifested in play was a sacred activity that others should approach only under very special circumstances and with the permission of the player. The Jungian play therapist tends to receive the play work and dream work of very young children with similar respect. Aside from assuring the safety of child, therapist, and environment, the modern play therapist tends to minimize interference with the flow of the play through judgments, giving directions, interpretations, or intruding with interactional demands.

In his memoirs, Jung also recalled memories of a turbulent latency characterized by anxiety dreams, frightening daytime visions of alternate realities, and significant alienation from family and peers. His boyhood individuality and experiences seemed at odds with the realities of living that were acknowledged by parents and others. Play served a compensatory, balancing activity:

> I was passionately fond of playing with bricks and built towers which I then rapturously destroyed by an "earthquake" . . . I was fond of playing with fire. . . . I used to tend a little fire that had to burn forever. . . . My fire along was living. . . . I drew endlessly—battle pictures, sieges, bombardments, naval engagements. (Jung, 1961, pp. 18–23)

At age 10, the boy created a ritualistic play-rite that was connected to his earlier dream of the ritual phallus. In a secret, private place in the "forbidden" attic, he placed a sacred self-made totem of his unique personality, which provided a link to his inner spiritual authority. Secretly bringing gifts to this entity soothed the anxiety and the sense of aloneness he experienced in his ordinary life. He knew well that he could not tell anyone about this play ritual. Talking would break the social taboo that required denial of this inner world. "These things belonged to that mysterious realm which I knew I must not talk about" (Jung, 1961, p. 22).

When the plays of childhood touch upon the deepest recesses of the psyche and need to be kept hidden from important others, the secret knowledge can become a formidable burden. One cannot help but wonder what the boy might have come to share with a play therapist who was initiated into this realm of human reality. Like Edith Sullwold (1987), one might also wonder where the Elders are in this society who can help guide children in their internal explorations of what it means to be a human being without sabotaging their process of psychological differentiation. The Jungian play therapist often assumes the role of such a benign elder.

For Jung, the boy, this solitary play had an intrinsic survival function. The play space gave him an opportunity to experience some measure of control (Fordham, 1970) and to actively foster his process of self-development. Pursuing his spontaneous play impulses had actually allowed him to preserve, develop, and sort out his uniquely individual thoughts, feelings, perceptions, and character. This private dialogue with himself, although a lonely preoccupation that would be understood only much later in life by his adult personality, had a calming effect. It helped the boy come to terms with his affective life as he learned how to tolerate external and internal experiences characterized by strong emotions. Play strengthened his ego and prepared him for his professional life.

By turning inward into his beingness, the child had been initiated into a numinous experiential dimension that was different from ordinary life and that seemed to be ignored by his caretakers. He practiced encountering the inner unknown, "the inescapable world of shadows that was eternal" (Jung, 1961, p. 20). Later in life, he would call this world of intrapsychic experience the "collective unconscious." In this realm are:

> inherited instincts . . . impulses that carry out actions without conscious motivations . . . and archetypes . . ., a priori forms that give rise to universal motifs in the fantasies, dreams, deliria and delusions of individuals living today. (Jung, 1961, p. 392)

Just as the ego of the personality transforms as it enters into an active relationship with the unconscious, so do societies. Jung believed that civilizations evolve as their members relate to the contents of the collective unconscious. The extent to which a society is in contact with the collective is reflected in its religions, philosophies, mythology, folklore, and cultural rites and customs (Jung, 1961, p. 209). The play therapist, following Jung's example, studies the mythological, philosophical, religious, and cultural traditions of mankind in order to be receptive to those aspects of the collective experience that emerge in a client's play, dreams, visions.

Jung observed that play creates a tension between social, familial thinking patterns and transpersonal, mythopoetic thinking patterns. From this tension arises the normal, human need to develop a personal thinking process that can bridge and encompass *both* realms, that is, that can integrate both sources of understanding. Once this connection is achieved, there arises concurrently a need to take an ethical stand in relationship to one's beliefs and to one's actions in the outer world. For Jung, this marked the beginning of the sense of responsibility and accountability that characterizes the ego of the individuating person. This moral imperative is the force that presses for change and activates the "working-through process" that results in the transformation of behavior in daily life.

As mentioned earlier, return to the sanctuary of play occurred in Jung's midlife when his professional and personal life became very difficult after the break with his mentor Sigmund Freud. Wanting relief from this crisis he instinctively resorted to play to sort out the meaning of the external events that had befallen him. As it was, he found not only answers, but solutions that provided the rationale for major professional-life decisions. "The years when I was pursuing my inner images were the most important in my life— in them everything essential was decided" (Jung, 1961, p. 175).

While maintaining a grounded relationship to his profession and his family, Jung instituted, in addition to his lakeshore play, the process of meditatively descending into the unconscious. Powerful affects and strange visions had been flooding his conscious mind. To contact their source, he would move into the affect, personify the hypnagogic images that would arise, and, thus, engage the ego- or Self-figures and activate the inner psychic archetypal structures that ensouled them. As he dialogued with them, he gave them an opportunity for expression. In this fashion, he developed active imagination or intrapsychic imaginal and verbal play.

He made the following observation:

> To the extent that I managed to translate the emotions into images—that is to say, to find the images that were concealed in the emotions—I was inwardly calmed and reassured. Had I left

those images hidden in the emotions, I might have been torn to pieces by them. (Jung, 1961, p. 177)

Many times he was afraid of the emotions and the images, especially the very negative ones. He pressed on, however, feeling he could not expect his patients to be wrestling with their inner demons and overwhelming affects if he could not dare do so himself (Jung, 1961, p. 178).

After focusing on the emotions and the experiential images that were concealed within them, he continued by painting the figures and experiences he had encountered during his journeys into the realm of darkness. By combining different creative play modalities, he would amplify the experiences even more, making them more accessible to his conscious mind.

At the age of 43 he made circular drawings, called mandalas, on a daily basis. He found that

> with the help of these drawings I could observe my psychic transformation from day to day . . . in them I saw the self—that is, my whole being—actively at work. . . . It became increasingly plain to me that the mandala is the center. . . . It is the path to the center, to individuation. (Jung, 1961, pp. 195–196)

This centering principle, also observed by Rhoda Kellogg (1967) in the spontaneous drawings of children and by Dora Kalff (1966) in the sandtray play of adults and children, was seen by Jung as the central core of the personality, the creative and self-healing force of the psyche and the meaning-making center that contains and orders the diverse and often dualistic experiences originating in the inner and outer world. Free play and play rituals allow for the gradual awakening and manifestation of the Self in both young and old. A play therapist aligns herself or himself with this center of the psyche.

Jung's encounter with the inner and outer worlds of experience evolved over the course of his lifetime. Full interpretation and integration of his play experiences did not occur until old age, for each developmental phase of life naturally provoked a reevaluation of what had gone before. Play therapy is best when its goal is to support and enhance the capacity of the individual to trust his or her own resources and to evolve during his or her entire life span, rather than to focus on the directing or interpreting of the play.

Presuppositions and Principles

Psychopathology Reflects Cultural Limitations That Impact Individuation and Socialization

Jungian therapists tend to define psychopathology as disturbances of the ego-Self relationship that activate innate strivings towards individuation and socialization. Symptoms are opportunities for growth. Sullwold (1974) sees them as "energy motivators" that bring new psychic energy and that press for new solutions on a new level of consciousness.

Most Jungian therapists believe that overt familial psychopathology, trauma, and cultural methods of raising, educating, and socializing children tend to foster ego disturbances. By minimizing or ignoring the teaching of psychological coping skills, families tend to produce children and adults who are alienated from their inner world and their true personality. People are taught that authority and sense of Self come from outside and that thinking and action need to be based on a priori principles that reside outside of themselves. Consequently, they do not know how to be in relationship to themselves (De Domenico, 1986, 1988, 1992; Kalff, 1966; Sullwold, 1974, 1987). This creates alienation from the Self and diminishes the capacity to be creative, responsible, in control, and in relationship and to make sense of unusual or socially denied experiences. It also makes it difficult for children and adults to appreciate their usefulness to others.

The breakup of the extended family, the increased mobility of the family unit, and the existing social structure do not allow children to access their elders or a family mythology that connects them to their ancestors (Sullwold, 1987). This creates alienation from the wisdom of the wise old man and the wise old woman who can share the understanding that only the experiences of a lifetime can bring. Everyone suffers from the absence of the storytellers and mythmakers that keep alive the lessons learned by those who came before. Television shows and heroic movies such as *Star Wars* offer modern myths but often do so without the critical conversational interchanges with an experienced adult viewer.

One's religious upbringing, extolling Christian virtues and damning evil thoughts and doings, supports a unidimensional, hopeless striving for perfection that fosters painful experiences of impotent inferiority and an inability to deal with the dark and shadowy side of life and human consciousness (Hannah, 1971). This creates an unrealistic view of both the nature of life and the nature of humanity. At the same time, harsh judgment and guilt often trap needed individual talents and capacities into the intrapsychic form of the *Shadow* (the unacceptable part of one's personality that is projected onto others). When religion is altogether rejected or ignored, the individual loses ready access to the spiritual dimension as a way of making human life meaningful.

Western society has not yet compensated for the decline in organized religions and still does not offer adequate rites of passage to facilitate experiencing the various stages of human physical, emotional, sexual, personal, and interpersonal development during childhood, adolescence, young adulthood, midlife, and old age (Sullwold, 1987). This prevents individuals from recognizing and adapting to the natural cycles of growth and decline, birth and death, and so on. Too often, people stand outside of life; they cannot or dare not grow into their humanity.

The vital human play instinct becomes too easily wounded as the capacity to evolve, to change, and to create from the raw materials of inner and outer possibilities is replaced by rigid copying and memorizing behaviors. The capacity to experience, order, and transform experiences symbolically is thwarted (Stewart, 1990). The Self becomes estranged and untrustworthy. Suffering psychologically, many do not know how to play nor how to use and express affects, thoughts, memories, sensations, and intuitions. Adjustment to the demands of family and society is compromised as it becomes too painful or requires too much effort. Acting-out results because neither inner nor outer experience may be utilized or trusted.

This existential dilemma expresses itself in diverse symptomotology in both young and old and is a sign of the wounding of the life force of the creative imagination (Frantz, 1979). It is not just those who were neglected, abused, and traumatized who are affected. Frequently, those who were conscientiously taken care of are equally crippled. The ego fails to thrive.

To mediate these cultural problems, Jungian psychotherapists rely heavily on the compensatory, creative function of the individual human psyche (Furth, 1988). They dedicate themselves to fostering the reawakening of the play impulse and establishing connections between the culture, the ego, the Self, and the collective unconscious. To promote healing, the Jungian play therapist strives to help the child or adult gain access to the inner realm and learn how to make use of it while being in the presence of another adult who honors and respects play, ritual, dreams, stories, and the other mythopoetic experiential expressions of the inner psyche. In fact, such activities, the appropriate therapeutic attitude of the therapist, and the development of the transference relationship carry the primary task of the play therapy healing process (Chowdorow & Stewart, 1989; Dieckmann, 1971, 1979; Humbert, 1971; Jacobi, 1959; Jung, 1961).

Play with Affect and Image: A Culturally Neglected Source of Reparation and Learning

Both the inner and the outer worlds are vital learning environments for the developing personality. Just as family and society help define *meaning* for the child, the intrapsychic collective mind (the collective unconsious) creates psychological images and mythological experiences that actually teach child and adult the meaning-making matrices of their ancestors. These universal images have a rationale of their own. They have a psychological survival value for the individual: They contain spiritual, transpersonal, and ancestral wisdom that can provide a substrate for making sense of the often incomprehensible experiences of daily life.

Edith Sullwold (1971, pp. 235–252) offers an excellent case study of a child who needed to connect his outer ethnic personality with his inner, genetic personality.

Case Illustration 1: First Session

Sullwold reports the play therapy of an aggressively acting-out 6-year-old Mexican-Indian boy who was being raised by his adoptive parents as a Jewish boy. Neither he nor his adoptive parents were aware of his origins. With Sullwold's intuitive support, the child commenced a therapy that involved the use of the sandtray, ritual tribal dances, chanting, maskmaking, heroic play, sculpting, and candle ceremonies. The psyche's goal was the reconciliation of his inner ancestral identity with his outer, social, Jewish identity.

During the first session, the boy built a sandtray: "In opposite diagonal corner, were an Indian village and a cowboy town. Between them was a body of water filled with crabs, an octopus, and poisonous snakes. Over the water was a bridge that made it possible to go from the Indians to the cowboys. On this bridge was an alligator.. . . On the water was a pirate ship and Noah's ark." As the boy handled the Indians, he said: "Indians don't like America, and, therefore, they hurt little children. . . . I'm an Indian" (Sullwold, 1971, p. 236).

Confused, Sullwold rehearsed in her mind what this child could possible mean referring to himself as an "Indian." Choosing to join him in his world, she asked him whether he had an Indian name. He said that he was "Eagle Eye" and possessed the gift of dancing. Curious about the types of dances Eagle Eye could do, she soon watched and learned how to dance the rain dance. Having been joined by an adult, Eagle Eye shared his problem: No one actually believed that he was Indian. Sullwold recalls her response: "Fortunately, I could say, out of my conviction of the efficacy of religious dance, 'I do' (Sullwold, 1971, p. 237)." She accepted the reality of the play rite.

Here was a child in search of his own inner religious rituals: Sullwold saw Noah's ark as a link to his adoptive Jewish myth and religion. She felt that the psyche was directing the boy to bridge these two cultural traditions that were dynamically alive in his inner and outer worlds of experience. Through solitary and interactional play, he was able to accomplish his task under Sullwold's care.

As this case shows, the Self activates intrapsychic experiences that tend to have a compensatory function: They tend to balance the ego's reactions to the experiences of the outer world or the imbalanced life views of family and society. Regulated by the Self, the center of the individual personality, internal experiential realities are produced. These are autonomous healing functions or the transcendent functions of the psyche. They are directly relevant to the individual's life situation. The play therapist does well to acknowledge the guiding messages of the psyche that often indicate the nature of the difficulty and the possible path of resolution. Therefore, rather than initiating the play or changing the nature of the play communication, the play therapist usually encourages the play, follows the play, and allows it safe expression during the therapeutic hour.

As the impulse to play is allowed full expression, without causing harm, the activated healing function awakens affects (Stewart, 1987). Within the matrix of affects are images. The healing function produces the images that contain life experiences and inner personalities that have not yet been lived, processed, or understood because the affect associated with the experiences was either too overwhelming or taboo. Here, Jungians find traumatic life experiences, the Shadow (same-sexed, disowned, positive, or negative qualities of the personality), the Anima or Animus (negative or often overdetermined qualities associated with the opposite sex, the bad Mother and Father, etc.). These experiential images related to the personal unconscious are contained in highly charged emotional complexes. They represent the "unfinished business" of past experiences (Jung, 1961, pp. 393–394).

Other images contain new experiences that compensate for familial and/or cultural deprivation, such as the dark-light Mother and Father, the union or coming together of female and male, the wise old man and the wise old woman, Gods and Goddesses, death, avatars, the god-child, and so on. These reparative images also mobilize certain reparative emotional states as they emerge from the collective unconscious. They tend to bring physical, emotional, mental, and spiritual balance and perspective to the personality.

Stewart (1987) described the cardinal emotions that are necessary for normal functioning as joy and curiosity. These are reactivated during the play therapy. He described the normal, often denied, existential emotions as fear, sadness, anger, shame or contempt (depending on whether it is self- or other-directed), and surprise or startle. The client learns to make use of these affective states.

Tolerating and moving into affect facilitates the revelation of the experiential images that are hidden within the affect. As Jung (1961) points out, "It is helpful, from a therapeutic point of view, to find the particular images that lie behind emotions" (p. 177). Going on to describe what happened as he found the images hidden in his strong, vital emotions, Jung stated:

As soon as the image was there, the unrest or the sense of oppression vanished. The whole energy of these emotions was transformed into interest in and curiosity about the image. (p. 177)

The play therapist supports the reality of the affect and the resulting preoccupation and elaboration of the images and fantasies that evolve during the play. The awakened interest fosters playful experimentation with the knowledge and understanding that are hidden within the problems that plague the client.

CASE ILLUSTRATION 2: MIDDLE SESSIONS

During midphase of play therapy with a physically and mentally handicapped 14-year-old girl who had been referred to me or the author for physical aggressive acting-out behavior in the classroom, the therapist and the girl created drawing-feeling stories.

This storytelling technique has the child choose an emotion and find a title for the story. After the child and therapist create the beginning point for the story, the child makes a drawing while the therapist writes down the words that go along with the drawing. The story progresses as the drawing is cut out and pasted into the storybook, receives a title, and is described in great detail. From new details, another drawing is created, which allows the story to evolve. Affect becomes increasingly magnified. New images that are hidden within the affect begin to emerge. The results are usually quite unpredictable but extremely relevant to the child's healing process.

This young girl decided to work on the feeling called "scared." The story was about a little girl who lived in an old house and who was very scared. After the patient drew a picture of the little girl, the patient and the therapist discovered that the little girl did not look scared. The patient said that that was because "the scaredness was inside her inner space. The yellow ugly ghost lived inside her." No one had any idea where the ghost lived. After the girl drew "Scary, the yellow, ugly-mouthed, blacknosed scary red-eyed ghost that went boo-boo," she said the therapist could see it, and it truly was horrid. It was traced to its home inside the girl. Soon, patient and therapist had a drawing of "Scary, the ghost locked up inside the girl's heart. The heart is ugly and evil. On the outside the heart is beautiful, but on the inside it is ugly because it is scared. . . The ghost needs to come out." Patient and therapist "need to find a secret key to unlock the heart." The key to the heart of Scary is drawn. The patient tells the therapist that, when she gets the right number, "she will open the heart, take the ugly thing out, throw it into the garbage, and we get rid of it and a lot of people will get happy and joyful." Patient and therapist experiment, find the right number and the right key, use the key, and open the heart. They "throw the ugly old beast away."

As the therapist is writing this down, she spontaneously exclaims: "Oh, the poor thing. How would you like to be the ugly old beast that gets thrown away?" The girl is silent, takes the storybook and writes: "I feel un-cuddled and un-wanted thing."

She shares how ugly she feels and how she really does not want to grow up. She feels so unlovable. Behind the experience of being scared were the images of people, including mother, father, and herself, being scared of her physical and mental deformities and wishing that they somehow could get rid of her.

In the next session, the child created a play where she was hiding, wrapped up inside a curtain. She tried to come out. She could not. The therapist had to coach her for a long time to come out. After tortuous labor, she emerged into the therapist's lap; the therapist welcomed the monster child. In play she was reborn, with the emotions of joy and curiosity, as therapist and patient explored her face, her hair, and her features and began to explore the world around her. The "beast" had been liberated from the heart. The whole child could be reborn during a reparative, spontaneous, ritual reenactment of her birth.

Although the birth of a mentally and physically disabled child is extremely difficult for parents and an experience that activates many mixed affects, the child's inner Self is fully knowledgeable and capable of tolerating all of life's experiences, including her birth, her physical deformity, her difficulty in processing information like others, and the burden of her parents' affective struggles. The Self provides for he emergence of real adaptive processes. Play explores options and different ways for the ego to heal into reality.

The Play Therapy Process: An Archetypal and Individual Thinking Process That Evolves Over Time

Play often leads to a channeling of attention. The single-minded, meditative focus of play is a manifestation of an experiential image-thinking process that clearly directs the play with the clarity and inevitability characteristic of psychological logic. It moves across temporal lines and is not a linear but a spiral process. Margaret Lowenfeld, who developed the sandplay apparatus in the 1920s, was well aware of this image-thinking process that led to the thinking through of experiences (Lowenfeld, 1935, 1939, 1950, 1964). This author prefers to call it experiential or psychological thinking—the kind of thinking that has physiological, affective, memory, verbal, and intuitive thinking components that give it the dynamic reality that characterizes human consciousness. Ego and Self are in dialogue.

During play therapy, there is a gradual evolution and expansion of content, form, affect, sensation, verbal musings, and both social and individual capacities (see later section: Evolution of Play). These follow archetypal patterns that can be more or less predictable if one looks at the play as providing the missing perspectives that, if taken into consideration, would result in a more complete picture. The uniquely individual, biographical derivatives of the archetypal experiences, including the affects associated with them, are not predictable. In the last clinical vignette, the physically and mentally handicapped child descended into her fear, which then allowed her devalued Self (Shadow) to appear, which allowed her to feel the sadness of being unloved and unwanted, which led her to rebirth herself and engage the therapist in order to constellate the experience of being welcomed into the world with her "scary crippledness" and with her "own beauty," as a total being. This played out reparative infant-mother experience allowed part of her Shadow, "the ugly old beast," to be welcomed into the world. At the same time, a new aspect of the Mother archetype (the welcoming, empathic, benign Mother) had been tapped and was now part of her experience of being human.The child's play moved her towards balance: The sadness balanced her rage towards the ones who only had eyes to see the beast. Liberating the ugly old beast from within her balanced the sweet girl that she tried to be to please Mother and Father. The benign mother, who welcomed the crippled and the conventionally congruent parts of her beingness balanced the judging, "throw the ugly old beast in the garbage" mother (and father). Her psyche was leading her to the acceptance of her own and her parents' limitations. It was also giving her the gift of seeing her mother as she was, that is, simultaneously accepting and rejecting of the girl's body, heart, mind, and spirit. The fear of the pain and the helplessness in the family needed expression.

This therapeutic play experience actually replenished the young girl's sense of curiosity and participation in the world. It was only after this experience that she seemed to become adequately receptive to the teacher's, parents', and therapist's teachings regarding interpersonal skills.

Therapeutic Channeling of the Play-Impulse into Socially Acclaimed Activities

Dora Kalff (1980, pp. 43–59) achieved a similar objective by encouraging a child to "play" by using his natural talents in socially sanctioned activities that were of direct use to the therapist. This allowed the child's ego to experience productivity and a sense of self-worth in relationship to the outer world of significant others.

CASE ILLUSTRATION 3: MIDDLE SESSIONS

Dora Kalff described the play therapy of a 9-year-old boy who was suffering from an anxiety neurosis and school truancy. After the boy had activated his play impulses through play with the sandtray, interactional dramatic play involving thieves and hide-and-seek, drawing, shooting games, vehicular play, and fighting sandtray scenes, Kalff felt that the healing forces of the psyche were stirring.

Aware of parents' and teacher's concern over the child's failures in producing schoolwork, she embarked on supporting and validating the child's ego in a different way. She encouraged the boy's "slumbering ambition" by allowing him to fix a broken electric train engine and letting him teach her about the operation of the electric train set during his session. She stated: "Because I am no good in these matters . . . I let him direct me. He obviously enjoyed this. . . . He became my teacher."

Kalff gave him other electrical projects, suggesting one to be done at home and another in the playroom. She asked him to install electric lights in her dollhouse. She chose these tasks carefully: "Because a house is a symbol for man's inner being, I wanted him to light up his inner environment" (Kalff, 1980, p. 53).

Kalff fostered the development of the child's ego, as much as she supported the awareness of his inner beingness. She created a situation in which the connection between his innate talents and his exterior behavior could grow. He experienced being a valuable person, who was allowed to make decisions, to take the lead and to be productive. He was free to choose his own approach to the play task. After these directed plays, the child resumed his free-play periods.

Integration and Transformation of Chaos and Confusion During the Play Therapy Sessions Leads to Experiences of Wholeness

The capacity to integrate different types of experiences through personal, creative efforts is seen as essential for normal growth and development of the personality no matter how old the client may be. Only then can a balanced view of life and human nature result.

No one can do such integrative work for another being; therefore, sole reliance on interpretation or directed play experiences is not advisable. At the beginning of therapy, when chaos and confusion may be the characteristics of the psychological experiences depicted in play, this integrative work is often a most difficult, often unattainable task. In fairy tales, it is the situation in which all different grains have been mixed together by a wicked person and the hero/heroine is asked to sort them out before he/she can partake of the pleasures of living (see the tales of Psyche and Cinderella). I call this the catabolic phase of the creative process—rather than experiencing form, the client is locked into the experience of the dissolution of form, disconnectedness, and much unchanneled energy. It is the primordial chaos. Fordham (1967, 1970, 1980) spoke of the deintegration phase of the constellating Self, which is illustrated in the following case.

CASE ILLUSTRATION 4: BEGINNING SESSIONS

A 9-year-old boy was brought into therapy. Shortly before coming, school phobia and carsickness, coupled with headaches and stomachaches, had made their regular appearance. He presented himself as compulsively factual, with encyclopedic bits of knowledge about his life. He seemed hurried, and burdened and appeared to need to be in control of everything. A superb student, not only did he need to be perfect, but he could not accept assistance from others. He showed no feelings of weakness. He showed no signs of needing parental support. His outer personality seemed in control. Occasionally, his inner affective world bled through into this adopted exterior facade, much to the dismay of his parents, who were helpless. They fed him the right words, but to no avail.

In therapy, he could not play. He was task oriented and needed directions from the outside. When asked to draw a spontaneous drawing (Furth, 1988), he quickly produced a person with a huge head that almost occupied the entire page. He said: "The head is 6 feet tall. He's all head. Inside the head is all sorts of stuff (drawn in lines of many different colors). The stuff makes the person's stomach sick. It is crazy and all mixed up. He is stupid. He feels weird when he can't figure out things."

Here is a child raised by parents and teachers who mean well. The boy cannot tolerate his own feelings or internal states of unknowing nor follow his own inner promptings. His head is overstuffed. His heart is inaccessible. The trunk, arms, and legs are not there; it is a very difficult way to be.

There is no external world order that can accommodate these interior feelings and thoughts. Yet, in his first sandtray, he picked a crystal church and a crystal ball that were placed in the center of a chaotic arrangement of objects that, upon close inspection, dealt with birth, death, being held, being hurt, and other common life experiences. These were half buried or fallen over. Although so much was happening everywhere, the boy already had a central, clear space.

This boy needed a safe place to carry out the business of childhood; he needed to make sense of his own observations and experiences. He needed to become reacquainted with the natural thinking processes of his inner psyche. The important people around him could not give him words or ready-made formulas for these experiences. Consequently, he would become overwhelmed and anxious. The inner security was missing. In his case, individuation was lagging far behind the process of socialization. Play therapy was to provide what he was missing in daily life.

The initial play indicated that the experience of chaos and confusion needed to be experienced. A nonverbal thinking process was required to make sense of it. The numinous spiritual realm or a place of inner clarity was accessible to the child and might provide an essential guiding principle to hold his insecurities and to eventually integrate them.

This example shows how play and active imagination are modalities that allow for transcending the split between the inner and outer World-of-Experience, the conscious and the unconscious regions of the psyche, the ego and the Self, and verbalizable and nonverbalizable experiences (De Domenico, 1992d). The boy's play demonstrated the inner chaos that was in such sharp contrast to his orderly and efficient persona. Play not only shows the nature of this discrepancy but points to possible solutions, which usually involve the balancing of onesidedness or extreme tendencies through creative, experiential explorations. The therapist protects and midwives this process.

Integration of these different spheres of human experiences creates a sense of wholeness and at-oneness with oneself and with life. This is illustrated with the final sandplay created by a young woman, who had initially started in treatment at the age of 17. In contrast to the boy's overwhelmingly chaotic World, her first World had been a very empty, subtle coastal shoreline, created from extremely compacted wet sand. She had been suicidally depressed. Her energies were trapped under the sand. Her final sandtray scene, created after many sandplays, drawings, collages, dream analyses, and verbal problem-solving sessions, depicted the following experiences:

CASE ILLUSTRATION 5: TERMINATION SESSIONS

Garlands of white flowers border the scene. In the central area, standing inside a nest, is a large peacock with wings spread out in a big display. Eight burning candles surround the nest. Eight more burning candles are dispersed around the periphery. In the lower left corner, at 7 o'clock, is a woman kneeling on a platform with a bowl of water in front of her and facing a white curled-up snake who sits on the other side of the bowl. Moving above her at 8 o'clock, towards the upper left, is an angel Smurf. At 9 o'clock is a chubby baby-toddler singing. At 11 o'clock are two nude pewter lovers kneeling in an embrace. At 12 o'clock is a mother-child pair showing the mother's face gazing into the face of her child. At 1 o'clock is a wandering woman holding a crystal ball in one hand and a staff in another. At 3 o'clock is a mother seated on a rocking stand holding up her baby in front of her assuming an en face position. At 5 o'clock is a seated woman protectively holding her baby on her lap with her dress wrapped around the child. At 6 o'clock is.a golden eye mounted on a dark blue glass surface standing up to face the peacock in the nest.

As she lit the candles, she shared the following experiences: "All of these are the same: they are all mothers and their babies; they are holding, playing, being with, and loving their babies . . . The nest is alight. It is very warm. The peacock is being born. Feel the heat . . . It's like a beautiful new creature. It radiates heat and warmth. All these women love their babies.

"This (wandering woman) is a woman in her 20s. She's feminine . . . but powerful . . . but not aggressive. She is spiritual. She holds her crystal ball to the sky. She has self-love."

"The lovers . . . they don't have a baby . . . yet, they're in love. They love each other. All these people have love."

"The little chubby baby . . . a toddler . . . I thought that he was singing . . . He is rejoicing at the birth of the peacock. He's celebrating."

"The Smurf I had to use. He's showing that this is heaven. This is a good place. . . . He is the angel looking over the others. The white flowers show that, too. The angel is a watcher, a caretaker. The eye is similar: the eye sees everything . . . it's not physically there; it knows the truth about everything . . . the eye sees everything and knows everything."

"Over there . . . the snake is no mean snake: it is a white snake and it fits with the flowers. This woman is by herself.She has lost something . . . she is sad. It's not the end of the world . . . but it IS sad when you have lost something. The snake is keeping her company. She has a water bowl for the snake."

"They all came to watch the peacock being born . . . I am the peacock!"

Recreate the images and experience the completeness of this scene, the sense of wholeness, inner strength, and beingness. There is connection on every level of experience. The patient was able to be in the moment and had choice. This heralds the emerging capacity to be spontaneous and to utilize a full repertoire of human behaviors. During the course of her therapy, many issues had been worked and resolved. When the therapist and the young woman saw this World, they both knew that she had accomplished her goals and that she was in contact with her own beingness and ready to guide herself. Sadness, love, caring, knowing, a sense of protection, warmth, birthing (rebirthing), after-death states, and loss all have a place here, along with a sense of Self, others, and numinous sources of help and knowledge. Here she could experience her own history and the right to be a unique human being.

No interpretation was necessary. For archetypal meaning matrices, one can look at the symbols and their corresponding mythology (Ryce-Menuhin, 1992, pp. 22–27, illustrates the procedure). Here is the mandala of the birth of the consciousness of being a human being, mediated by the Self and received by the ego in the presence of the therapist. It was a great moment for both.

PROCEDURE

Therapist Qualifications and Characteristics

The Jungian play therapist is trained in Jung's metapsychology and principles of psycho-therapy and in the cultural legacy of mankind. Familiarity with the nature of the collective unconscious and the archetypes comes from the therapist's personal play and dream analyses and from studies at a Jungian Training Institute. It also comes from research into comparative religion (*New Larousse*, 1989); religious mysticism and esoteric teachings (Gaskell, 1981); creation stories; mythology (Campbell, 1959, 1962, 1964); folklore (Leach, 1972); heroic epics (Campbell, 1949); cultural anthropological studies of rites, rituals, and beliefs; art and literary history; archaeology; and symbolism (Cirlot, 1971; Cooper, 1987; Moon, 1991; Sandner, 1991; Walker, 1983). Aside from the standard clinical training, which includes supervised play therapy experience, a well-rounded liberal arts and sciences education is highly desirable. Most Jungian play therapists are artists or are well grounded in art, dance, movement, and/or music therapy. All these experiential therapies are really variants of play therapy.

During their years of clinical practice, Jungian play therapists continue their research, being especially careful to know the full range of archetypal significances of symbols and props used during play. Play and dreams are known to occur within an individual, cultural, ancestral, and universal context. Ideally, the therapist understands play on all of these levels and so is capable of moving her own and the client's focus from one level of experiencing to another.

The Jungian play therapist is always encouraged to personally experience the use of various play modalities within his or her personal therapeutic context.

Client Characteristics: Indications and Contraindications

Since play is viewed as a natural healing function of the human psyche, play therapy may be indicated for clients of all ages and backgrounds. Play therapy techniques are offered to all clients to activate these healing forces of the individual psyche, thereby channeling clients' inner need to express themselves in a meaningful way. A full range of diagnostic categories have been treated with spontaneous or therapist-directed play therapy, amongst them posttraumatic stress disorder, behavioral disorders, developmental disorders, mood disorders, borderline and psychotic states, parenting problems, and occasionally couple and family problems.

Those clients who are severely defended against both internal and external experiences find free play a very difficult and painful task. They often profit from joint play, parallel play, directed play, and/or primarily verbal sessions and dream work during the initial phases of treatment. Many therapists assess the readiness of the client's ego to descend into the depths of experiences. Some exclusively trust the psyche of the client: If the client will play, that is an indication that there is therapeutic value in the play, especially if the therapist aligns himself or herself with the play by modeling a strong, healthy ego that will support and encourage the growth of the clients's fragile and wounded ego.

Contraindications to free and nondirected play may be the client's inability to play, developmental arrest at the pre-18-month level of development, and physical limitations. Here, more interactive and developmentally directive play sessions are indicated.

Logistics

Setting

Jungian psychotherapists appreciate beauty and consider the therapeutic value of environments that maximize healing. Consequently, the therapist practices not only in hospitals, school settings, clinics, and office buildings, but often in his or her home with occasional excursions to outdoor settings, like playgrounds, parks, and beaches.

Technique

To facilitate psychotherapeutic experiences, Jungian play therapists access a large array of expressive techniques, often combining them in new and different ways during the course of play therapy. Materials tend to be displayed in open view or are readily available to the client. The environment gives the sense that there is much to choose from and that others have also been here who have made use of the space and the materials. The following are some favorite techniques.

1. Verbal playfulness that moves beyond the conventional use of language
   • Active imagination and dialoguing with intangible inner "others," such as Shadow, Animus, Anima, Gods, Goddesses, Demons, and Helpers (Chowdorow & Stewart, 1989; Dieckman, 1971, 1979; Hannah, 1971, 1981; Humbert, 1971), and Voice Dialogue with inner "subpersonalities," such as the Pusher, the Lady, the Critic, the Hero, the Protector, the Controller, and the Vulnerable Child (Stone & Winkelman, 1989). These dialogues may then be further played with through use of costume play, drawing, sandplay, puppets, and so on.
   • Storytelling and storywriting (Allan, 1988; Allan & Bertoia, 1992; Spiegelman, 1988). The stories may be amplified through use of other play modalities.

2. Psychomotor play that primarily uses the physical body as a mode of expressive communication
   • Movement games that originate from spontaneous play impulses and enactment of common family and social interactional plays (peek-a-boo, hide-and-seek, etc.), mirroring

plays, and amplifications of verbal expression of internal states (De Domenico, 1988, 1991; Mindell, 1987; and Sandtray Worldplay Training, Level Four)

• Rhythm, mime, and dance (Chowdorow, 1991; Chowdorow & Stewart, 1989; Hayes, 1959; Payne, 1992; Siegel, 1984; Spencer, 1984; Whitehouse, 1979)

3. Psychomotor play that involves use of the physical body and man-made props or tools
• Art materials, such as paints, pastels, crayons, pencils, enamel, play dough, or clay (Allan, 1974, 1978, 1988; Bach, 1990: Frey-Wehrlin, 1990; Furth, 1988; Jung, 1961; Kalff, 1980; Kiepenheuer, 1991: Sullwold, 1974, 1977; Wickes, 1988)

• Play with toys, such as balls, puppets, dolls, stuffed animals, vehicles, blocks, guns, or any other toys the client enjoys (De Domenico, 1988, 1991a; Sidoli, 1989; Sullwold, 1971)

• The making of and play with masks and costumes (Sullwold, 1971)

• Play with musical instruments (De Domenico, 1991a: Kalff, 1980; Phillips, 1979)

• Play with a sandtray and a collection of miniatures (Aite, 1978; Allan, 1987; Amman, 1990; Bradway, 1979, 1985; Bradway, Signell, Spare, Stewart, & Thompson, 1989; Carey, 1990, 1991; De Domenico, 1986, 1988, 1991, 1992; Dundas, 1989; Friedman, 1991; Kalff, 1966; Kiepenheuer, 1991; Miller & Boe, 1990; Reed, 1975, 1980; Ryce-Menuhin, 1983, 1992; Stewart, 1982, 1990; Sullwold, 1971, 1975, 1977; Weinrib, 1983; Vinturella & Vinturella, 1987)

• Dramatizations and the creation of rites and rituals inside the sandtray, in the therapy space, and in nature (De Domenico, 1992d; Jung, 1961, Sidoli, 1986; Sullwold, 1971)

4. Psychomotor play involving the physical body and/or natural elements and nature
• Ritual or exploratory play with earth/sand/mud, water, fire, and air (De Domenico, 1987; Friedman, 1991; Kalff, D., 1966; Kalff, M. & Hood-Williams, 1988; Sidoli, 1986).

Schedule

A client in Jungian play therapy may be seen as frequently as five times per week, if treatment is conducted as an in-depth analysis. Jungian therapists tend to be flexible and follow the needs of the psyche. It is not uncommon to conduct play therapy once weekly, bimonthly, or on an "as needed" or "as possible" basis. Intermittent therapy is not necessarily seen as being counterproductive to the psyche's strivings towards healing. A brief, short-term therapy may be welcomed as a special opportunity for the psyche to work on current growth and adjustment issues.

Specific Strategies: Play Therapist Behaviors

Creating the Free and Protected Space

Because the Jungian psychotherapist works with the innate healing force of the individual psyche, play therapy is usually nondirective. The therapist provides the tools, the freedom, the safety, and the conscious but nonjudgmental presence. When the *temenos* (safe container that allows for optimal freedom, or the free and protected space) has been constellated through the direct efforts of the therapist, the healing force is activated and can express itself freely through play, dreamwork, and interpersonal interactions with the therapist.

The therapist aims to trust the play expressions of the psyche and assumes that the client will eventually connect with the healing forces of his or her psyche without being pushed or confronted by the therapist. (For exceptions to this practice, see Dr. Allan's case of Lucy [Allan, 1988: Chowdorow & Stewart, 1989]). The push comes from the impulses and images that emanate from the Self and that find a primary channel of expression in the play, rather than in nonplay-related verbal interactions with the therapist. The therapist welcomes and nurtures this healing force, guards against thwarting its safe expression, and tries to stay out of its way.

Dora Kalff (1971) describes the atmosphere as a "free and sheltered space." The aim is to create an ambiance in which inner- and outer-world experiences may be expressed with their concomitant affects without judgment or undue constraints and interventions. The therapist is empathic. Chowdorow describes the therapist's state as an "empathic mirroring" (Chowdorow & Stewart, 1989). The therapist needs to be "moved" by the play without being overwhelmed or too detached. The therapist essentially tries to create "the good-enough mother" for the client and constellate a therapist-client participation mystique that allows the uniquely individual emanations of the client's Self to emerge. Edith Sullwold described this function when she said: "I have the responsibility to provide a surrogate lap" (Sullwold, lecture, 1975).

The therapist's role is to ensure that the fantasies are expressed in a way that is not overwhelming or physically hurtful. The therapist's ego watches that the client's surrendering to unconscious impulses, archetypal images, and the accompanying emotions, creative plays, memories, and insights can occur in a constructive rather than hurtful way. *Constructive* implies movement towards the client's eventual capacity to integrate these experiences on the sensation, feeling, thinking, and intuiting levels.

Joining the Play-Activities

Although the therapist generally does not direct the play, at times it is helpful to join the play activities when invited by the child or adult. This validates the existence of the inner images and fantasies that are depicted in the play and provides for an avenue of cooperative sharing and/or play.

The Healing Influence of the Transference

Most Jungians believe that the constellation of a transference relationship is an essential ingredient of a successful play therapy. A participation mystique needs to be constellated in the transference, which results from the empathic being-with-the-client and from the therapist's understanding of the symbolic, archetypal meaning of the play.

The "Silent Holding" of the Interpretation

The play therapist follows the play over time. As the play proceeds, the therapist silently interprets the emerging symbols and rites to himself or herself by accessing his or her knowledge of the collective experiential imagery of mankind. It is primarily in collegial case presentations or in professional writings that the therapist gives voice to interpretations of the play process. During the session, the therapist places the context of the individual play into the meaning matrix of the archetypal or universal and quietly holds this "silent knowing." This creates a certain

> ... participation ... whereby, under certain circumstances, the situation ... of mother-child unity is restored and exerts its healing influence. . . . This therapeutic effect occurs even though the insight of the analyst is not communicated to the child in words. (Kalff, 1966, p. 178)

The therapist's trained understanding provides both a security and a support that gives a sense of interpersonal, interpsychic relatedness that is optimal for the healing factors to exert their influence during the play therapy.

Many Jungian therapists, with notable exception of Fordham's London-based group (who have integrated the methods of the British psychoanalytic school into their practice), do not actively interpret the play activities of their clients. They will, however, at times create a verbal link between the play content or the play experience and the person's daily-life situation. This may bring about a "coalescence of awareness of inner and external problems, which is so significant that a next step in development can be achieved" (Kalff, 1966, p. 178).

Interpretive Myth—and Storytelling During Play Therapy

Frequently, therapists choose to relate a myth, a fairy tale, or bits and pieces of religious and spiritual practices the meanings of which correspond to the content of the types of human experiences depicted in the play. This helps amplify the psychotherapeutic efforts of the healing functions of the psyche by providing an external source of cultural valida-tion that will facilitate a more conscious understanding of the nature life's ordinary and not so ordinary experiences.

The author experienced this directly with Dora Kalff during a sandplay session.

CASE ILLUSTRATION 6

When working with Dora Kalff, I created a sandtray, divided diagonally by a roadway lined with trees. On the upper left was a castle with a man standing by the door. On the lower right was a wandering woman moving towards the castle. On the lower portion of the diagonal were a beautiful lake in a wooded setting and a man catching fish. Nearby was a woman with her child. On the upper portion of the diagonal was an elevated mound, vegetation, and an imposing male god.

As I experienced the result of my play, I was flooded by a great wave of sadness. Tears emerged as I gazed at the man catching fish for his wife and child. I was experiencing the lack of this nurturing relationship in my own life. I moved into a deep state of mourning.

Gently, Frau Kalff redirected my attention by pointing out that the psyche had presented more for me to experience. My attention went to the God, whom I experienced as a kind and protective male figure. To deepen my experience of this divine, nurturing, protective male figure in the tray, she told me who this mythological figure was: It was a Japanese rice god, who lived in the mountains . Every year, when the people had prepared their rice fields, flooded them, and sowed their seeds, this God would come down from the mountain. He would stand guard by the little seeds and seedlings and protect them for the people until the plants were strong enough to grow on their own. Although the God did not provide the people with the food directly, he saw to it that their efforts to grow their own would be fruitful.

Frau Kalff's story moved me through the bitter sadness that had prevented me from experiencing the dynamic reality of the compensatory, archetypal, nurturing husband and father (the fisherman) with which my psyche had gifted me. For a moment, I became connected to the archetypal caring Father-God who would descend from his godly realm to assure the well-being of his people by guarding their potential harvest. An energy was moved deep within me that allowed me to receive this experience more fully. The therapist had taken me from the personal, factual experience to the archetypal realm.

An interpretation of my inability to respond to a positive, caring, nourishing male and my entrapment with a negative animus was not necessary during the session. Instead, while I, as the client, focused on the reliving of the biographical trauma, the therapist aligned herself with the archetypal, universal theme in the play. This supported my capacity to hold the emotion generated by the reparative human counterpart (the fisherman) in the play.

By supporting the imagery in the tray, rather than the affective abreaction it evoked, she helped me experience the totality of this World in a conscious way. My ego attitude changed: During the same week life presented me with an opportunity to tolerate and welcome the emotions generated when a heretofore difficult male relative approached me in a caring and supportive way. The work accomplished in the playroom could then be done in daily life.

Amplification of Play During the Session

In current Neo-Jungian practice, attempts are often made to amplify (make more conscious through playful and verbal elaborations) the experiences contained in the play. The client is asked to use the amplification techniques of active imagination to play out his or her experiences of the play and/or his or her reactions to the play and to create these states "inside" the therapist. This creates a conscious mutual experiencing that becomes accessible to conversation. This type of postplay, reflective sharing with the therapist often creates a mutual client therapist dialogue of shared meanings. The client begins to find words for some of his/her own experiences. This helps the client develop the capacity to "interpret" the play and explore its relationship to past, present, and anticipated future situations. It also prepares the client for managing the vicissitudes of living without the help of a therapist (De Domenico, 1988; Level 2-5 Sand tray World play and Playtherapy Trainings; Mindell, 1987).

Reviewing the Play Processes That Occurred During the Play Therapy

Jungian play therapists tend to photographically document the productions of play, particularly sandtrays that have been created during the course of therapy. Questions arise as to whether to share these documents with clients and, if so, when. This remains the decision of the individual therapist. In fact, there is a lively debate and difference of opinion as to the timing and the efficacy of interpretations and client-therapist dialogue concerning the play process, or the review of the meaning of play episodes. This is particularly true for therapists who utilize the sandtray (De Domenico, 1988, 1992a, 1992b; Kalff, 1980; Ryce-Menuhin, 1992; Weinrib, 1983). Some review previous work at any time, others during termination, and some only when they feel the client has completely worked through their presenting problems. This may actually be many years after the completion of the play therapy.

Phases of Treatment and Thematic Evolution of Play

Initial, Orientation Phase

The therapist welcomes the client into the therapeutic environment, meeting him or her without reservation and with positive regard. It is during this time that the free and protected space is created. All efforts are made to allow the client to create a therapeutic alliance to the therapist and to approach the play process with freedom and trust.

The Struggling Phase: Negative Reactions and Limit Setting

Whenever the Shadow or negativistic aspects of the client's personality appear in the playroom, the therapist acknowledges and welcomes this way of being. The degree to which socially unacceptable behaviors are tolerated varies with the individual therapist. It is important that the therapist be at ease and safe with whatever limits he or she has set for the playroom. To extend the limits of behavioral and play expressions when the therapist is actually uncomfortable or is hurt does not help the client. Dora Kalff, in one of her lectures, once stated: "If you (the therapist) believe a play is therapeutic, it will eventually be therapeutic" (Santa Cruz, late 1980s).

Therapists recognize that many teachers and parents do not allow children to express their "bad" selves, their bad emotions, and their bad desires. These bad aspects need to find expression in the play therapy room so they may eventually become useful to the client.

Negative behaviors and projections onto the therapist are seen as manifestations of fragmentation, woundedness, negative internalized experiences of the past, and yet unshaped and unutilizable empowerments of the true personality. The therapist encourages safe expression of these states so that they may become available to the ego and be allowed to evolve through practice of expression. The Shadow or dark side of the client, which is the hidden, unvalued aspect of the personality, is potentially a source of great strength and uniqueness. The monstrous, destructive, and catabolic elements of the personality need free expression while being securely held by the therapist in a benign, nontraumatizing way. Socialization will eventually come without damaging the personality.

Working-Through Phase: The Transformative Process

The entire psychotherapeutic journey involves the process of working through the client's internal- and external-life experiences within the framework of the life cycle of disintegration and chaos and emergence and integration. This results in the active transformation of the personality. Working through tends to occur first by playing out the full situation, then by incubating the old and new possibilities intrapsychically, and finally by practicing observing the effects when using a mixture of old and new ways in daily life. The relativization of the ego that occurs with the activation of the Self during play always provides for the eventual appearance of new options and new directions.

It is important to view the play therapy process as activating human experiences of the natural cycles of life and of human nature. Although the evolution of the client-therapist relationship clearly goes through various predictable phases, the evolution of the actual play content does not occur in strictly linear phases.

The Jungian play therapist is very attentive to the thematic content, that is, the experiential content of the play, because the experiencing of the play reality facilitates social and individual growth and development in a natural way: Development occurs through the exposition, the polarization, and the subsequent weaving together of human experiences. At different times in the therapy, various themes, dilemmas, and human existential conditions are experienced. These experiences need to be worked through physically, emotionally, mentally, and spiritually by being placed within a personal, interpersonal, and transpersonal context.

Cycles of Integration, Disintegration, and Transformation of Experiential Realities

Play motifs seem to readily fit into cyclical processes of creation and destruction that regulate the life cycle of being and becoming. In play, the ego learns the laws and principles that govern being human. Each person who plays begins at the point of the cycle where they are. There is no right or wrong way of being in the transformative cycle of play. Those who cannot play cannot follow their cycle. Their energy does not flow. They need playful developmental remediation (Allan, 1974; De Domenico, Play Therapy Trainings).

Below is a listing of common experiences that are part of the play cycle and that need to be tolerable for individuation and socialization to proceed fully:

1. *Playing out of current and past biographical trauma.* Frequently this involves partial and/or complete dramatic reenactments; confrontations with parents, perpetrators, or fate; and experimentation with ways of dealing with potentially traumatizing events. The reworking may happen at any phase during the therapy or at any time.

2. *Acting-out of chaos, death, and destruction.* This may appear as the presence of overwhelming, engulfing, devouring forces; being buried, drowned, or submerged; experiencing different aspects of primordial body experiences (alimentary body awareness: focus on mouth/alimentary canal/anus; gender awareness: focus on vagina/ovaries/breasts/penis); being lost in the darkness; energy moving/exploding in all directions.

It appears as if there is no unifying theme, yet the unifying theme is chaos, dissolution, and unrefined energy. These experiences often mark the descent into the intrapsychic depths.

3. *Depictions of emptiness, stasis, and/or anticipatory nothingness.* This may appear as little or no action and movement, desolation, hopelessness, barrenness, and/or fruitlessness. Sometimes all is frozen, flooded, or wiped out with no trace of life. Sometimes all is in the black hole, that is, the great void that will eventually transform into the womb of creation.

Initially, there is often a sense of depression and depersonalization as conditions of unresponsive parenting, abandonment, or neglect during early symbiotic life development are recreated.

4. *Scenes that show differentiation, divisions/barriers and/or blocked movement, disconnectedness, isolation.* This may appear as the juxtaposition of opposing forces and/or imminent or acted-out conflict; warring between two or more forces, roles, and viewpoints, such as good and evil; formidable impasses; or protective isolation.

Such play creates much tension and polarization that may move either towards harmony or conflict, depending on the direction of movement.

5. *Emergence of aggressively untamed animals and of nature forces and fighting warriors.* This may appear as wild animals, emerging instinctual physical/sexual energies; prehistoric animals, monsters, dragons; wild and untamed elemental forces such as earth, air, fire, and water or different geological niches that can be beneficial or overwhelmingly dangerous and lethal. Themes of living through killing, forcefully claiming one's space, and learning to use one's power abound.

Such play creates a sense of power, prowess, and fatalism and readily concerns itself with the food chain, procreation, death, survival, and so on.

6. *Appearance of vegetation and domesticated animal life.* Here are often seen woods, grasses, jungles, cultivated fields, and different forms of animal life. Such play may create

a sense of comfort, protection, privacy, nourishment, friendliness, darkness, a place of incubation, and so on. It often leads into the acceptance of life itself and abundance.

7. *Scenes of digging, construction, making connections, and rebuilding.* Here energy and force are used for finding and building anew; experimentation with the regulation, the control, and the subtle ranges of energy, movement, power, and force; creation of roads, connected habitats, and communities. Such play often evokes a sense of moving, controlling, relating, and connecting different energy patterns and is reminiscent of a toddler's exploratory play with the world and the caretaker.

8. *Depiction of harmonious coexistence and/or joining of opposites.* Here is the *coniunctio,* or coming together, of the opposites such as male-female, mother-father, lion-lamb, hero-monster. This leads deep into the unknown; generates much tension; often involves a sacrificial, transformational death; and brings many beneficial surprises in the form of new attitudes and increased freedom.

9. *Manifestation of the center, the circle, the square, the ellipse, and the spiral.* Here is experienced the centering principle (Self), from which diversity proceeds and which can contain all states of being without judgment. It is the Mandala. Often it contains treasures or beneficial attributes. It may contain maps of the journey from life into death. The central area may be a circus ring, a racetrack, a multibridged island, a round sea, a sphere, a Mother-Father God, and so on.

The place of integration is often referred to as the constellation of the Self (Jung, 1959; Kalff, 1966; Kellogg, 1967). This creates a sense of security, sacredness, warmth, strength, and faith.

10. *Scenes depicting fecundity, creative experimentation with new attitudes and possibilities.* Characters from the magical planes are often met; themes are of conception, incubation, and rebirth/birth/renewal, nourishment, and/or holding; the world has hope and possibility. This frequently creates a sense of wonder and freedom. Frequently, beginning experimentations with problem solving and curiosity about the laws of cause and effect start here.

11. *Creation of a special, private space where one is at first taken care of by a benign Mother-Father-Fairy godmother/Fairy godfather, and later is completely self-contained and self-sufficient.* Food, drink, and housing are provided. Others may come to visit. This may create a sense of turning inward, finding security and faith, being in control, and just beingness. This often is a time for cutting the umbilicus to the Mother, letting go of the family, and becoming ready to grow from within. The safe place of solitude is essential.

12. *The experience of joy and pleasure.* Here are humorous episodes that evoke belly laughter and a sense of fun. Such play is often coupled with naughtiness and a deliberate play with conventional and family rules, and it often sees the emergence of the cleverness of the trickster. This usually creates a sense of spirit, aliveness, potency, and a benign way of having impact on others and being noticed.

13. *Experiencing something numinous beyond birth/death.* Here may be encountered spiritual sources of knowing and being, such as Gods; universal, transcendent forces, and planetary guides, who offer teachings and a helping presence. This usually gives rise to a sense of inner security, inner wisdom, inner guidance and faith, and speculations about what life is about.

14. *The journey.* Frequently children and adults commence a journey of curious exploration, visiting foreign lands and/or having strange new encounters. This promotes

a sense of a readiness to deal with the unexpected and an emergent willingness to take a chance. The journey has many different features that will inevitably appear quite spontaneously over the course of a play therapy:

1. Experiencing a stasis and a need to change the status quo.

2. Finding wise helpers and comrades, trusting them, and practicing a willingness to try a different way. This cultivates trust and empathy. It usually represents a reparative motif.

3. Overcoming obstacles, demons, and monstrous guardians, slaying of dragons, and descending into the abyss and other strange dimensions. This cultivates courage, assertiveness, strength, willingness to defend one's turf and life, and the capacity to confront evil.

4. Finding a special treasure, special knowledge, special gifts that will increase the scope of freedom and self-expression. This gives a sense of value, meaningfulness, and uniqueness. It returns one to the preciousness of life and often is experienced as a second birth.

5. Losing the special gifts through carelessness, inattentiveness, weakness, and naiveté. This gives the sense of pain, despair, futility, ignorance, and being wronged by others.

6. Searching for and rediscovering the lost treasure after much hardship, persistent hard work, and a bit of luck. This gives a sense of hope, renewed strength, longing, and overcoming the loss. It teaches the process of working through to completion through self-realization. Major defense mechanisms, such as denial and repression, may be overcome here.

7. Learning how to protect the special treasure. This gives a sense of value, boundary, self-protection, and entitlement. It further cements the connection between the Self and the ego.

8. Sharing the benefits of the journey, such as treasure and powers, with others. This gives the sense of being of benefit to others; of sharing, communion, friendship, and friendliness; and of usefulness to others. From the descent into the depths of the inner world, the client begins to ascend to daily life and community.

This archetypal developmental cycle is activated and expressed during the play therapy process. It has been described in great detail in the cultural collective experience of every society in mythology, heroic legends, and religious traditions. Familiarity with these universal themes through readings and one's own personal play therapy will help the therapist understand their value and support their expression during the therapeutic hour. This is especially important during interactive play or during the creation of play rituals or ceremonies in which the therapist participates in structuring the play. The Jungian play therapist frequently conceptualizes this cycle of archetypal growth and development as the trickster's, the hero's, and/or the initiate's journey (Allan, 1974, 1978, 1982, 1988: Allan & Bertoia, 1992; Campbell, 1949, 1959, 1962, 1964; Henderson, 1967; Jung, 1924, 1953, 1958, 1959; Kalff, 1966; Neuman, 1955, 1973).

It is important that the therapist not pathologize various segments of the journey, such as chaos, fighting, and destruction, because they are part of the cycle of real life that needs to be mastered, endured, and worked with. When allowed full expression within the safety of the therapeutic setting (the temenos), those segments will eventually connect with the other aspects of the integrative cycle, such as harmonious coexistence, finding a treasure, and rebirth. Jung (1953) likened this process to the alchemical transformative process of individuation and the evolution of consciousness.

Although attempts have been made to delineate definite linear stages in this rather cyclical process (Kalff, 1980; Neumann, 1955; Ryce-Menuhin, 1992), this author has not found them helpful. It is not a matter of sequence of experiences. It seems to be more a matter of being initiated into a sufficient number of the different types of experiences that belong to the cycle of life. All the different experiential stages may actually be existing simultaneously, both in the inner psychic world and in the outer world of daily life. During certain play periods, the theme of chaos and disintegration of the existing structure simply predominates over the theme of unity of structure, which at that point in time may only be dimly discernible, much like in the sandtray of the 9-year-old boy that was described previously. In his World, chaos seemed to reign, yet an ordering principle was already emerging in the center of his World. One experiential state readily gives rise to the next one. A large value of play therapy might lie in the fact that it helps one to learn how to transition from one type of experience to another type of experience, rather than to discover each phase in a given order. To be able to transition from one experience to another without evoking splitting, denial, projection, and the host of other nonintegrative ego defense mechanisms that ultimately further becoming more, rather than less unconscious and without being overwhelmed by the content of reality seems to this author to be the great achievement of a play therapy process.

Although they may appear in any play form, these themes are most readily traced in the sandplays of both children and adults. The sandtray, because of its limited dimensions, tends to focus these developmental themes in a more concentrated form. Dora Kalff (1980) felt quite strongly that the limited container actually fine-focuses the scope of the fantasy that is expressed in the play. The fantasy is not as readily diluted as it is in floor play.

Termination Phase

Since the Jungian play therapist places much emphasis on being guided by the individual psyche, the play therapist tends to consider the play content, the evolution of the diversity of the play content over time, and the expressed wishes of the client (including child clients) to determine when it is time to terminate the therapy (see Case Illustration 6).

During the termination process, some therapists review preserved pieces of creative play, such as drawings, sculptures, dream journals, sandplays, musical recordings, and/or videos. Termination stories that encapsulate the therapeutic journey are often told by the therapist or are created jointly by client and therapist.

It is generally accepted that the client is not "fixed." Instead, it is assumed that the client has the creative resources to continue to grow and develop as an individual and as a social being within the context of family, peers, and society. Often, the client has already developed outside hobbies and special interests. Children, who often eagerly awaited their sessions, would actually rather play with their friends and see the therapist as being in the way of their daily life. Feeling secure within themselves, clients know they can manage their own affairs now and look upon the therapeutic playroom as a place they can revisit should the need arise some time in the future.

CONCLUSION

C. G. Jung believed that a healthy individual and social life can arise only from the knowledge that is gained from active, dynamic experiencing in the inner and outer realm of experience. This experiencing process can be reawakened by expressive play, whether this play be called dramatics, movement, art, active imagination, or any other name. He believed expansion of the personality, the capacity to find personal solutions to life's daily problems, psychotherapeutic healing, and independence from the psychotherapeutic transference to the therapist occur as the ego develops an experiential relationship to the contents of the unconscious without being overwhelmed by them (Jung, 1961; Hannah, 1981).

Play, dreams, and fantasies are considered the royal road to the unconscious. At first, the asocial and idiosyncratic nature of play material led to fears of inducing psychotic or inflated ego states. Since then, it has been shown that play and creative active imagination, coupled with appropriate therapeutic action on the part of a therapist, can help those psychotics who can participate in play communicate the nature of their experiences (Allan, 1988; Allan & MacDonald, 1975; Chowdorow & Stewart, 1989; Frey-Wehrlin, 1990: Sidoli, 1986). Appropriate therapeutic counseling can help the client utilize the often bombastic energy that is released during play in daily life in a beneficial, rather than harmful, way (De Domenico, 1988; Weinrib, 1983).

Jung consistently sought to give his adult clients access to creative play as a way of getting to know themselves both as social beings and as unique individuals. Whenever he himself felt blocked or faced a difficult life transition, he would again resort to the use of playful, creative activities, particularly painting and sculpting (Jung, 1961).

Followers of Jung who have worked with both children and adults have had little difficulty incorporating experiential play therapy techniques, often borrowed from other therapeutic traditions, into their psychotherapeutic practice. While adhering closely to the general principles of analytical psychology, Jungian play therapists each tend to develop a unique style of integrating play activities into the analytical setting.

The attempt has been made to report on the richness and diversity that characterize Jungian play therapy techniques and the depth of experience that may await clients of any age who enter the play therapy room.

REFERENCES

Adamson, E. (1990). *Art as healing.* Boston: Coventure, LTD.

Aite, P. (1978). Ego and image: Some observations on the theme of "sand play." *Journal of Analytical Psychology, 23,* 332–338.

Allan, J. (1974, April 6-7). *Alchemical drawings in individual process.* Lecture presented at University of California, Santa Cruz. (Cassette recording available from C. G. Jung Institute Library, 2040 Gough St., San Francisco, CA 94109.)

Allan, J. (1978). Serial drawing: A therapeutic approach with young children. *Canadian Counsellor, 12,*(4), 132–137.

Allan, J. (1982). *The Child's Journey.* Lecture. (Cassette recording available from C. G. Jung Institute Library, 2040 Gough St., San Francisco, CA 94109).

Allan, J. (1987, April). Sandplay. *Elementary School Guidance and Counseling,* 300–306.

Allan, J. (1988). *Inscapes of the child's world.* Dallas: Spring Publication.

Allan, J., & Bertoia, J. (1992). *Written paths to healing: Education and Jungian Counseling.* Dallas: Spring Publication.

Allan, J., & MacDonald, R. (1975). The use of fantasy enactment in the treatment of an emerging autistic child. *Journal of Analytical Psychology, 20,* 57–68.

Amman, R. (1990). *Healing and transformation in sandplay: Creative processes become visible.* La Salle, IL: Open Court.

Bach, S. (1990). *Life paints its own span. On the significance of spontaneous paintings by severely ill children.* Zurich, Switzerland: Daimon Verlag.

Bradway, K. (1979). Sandplay in psychotherapy. *Art Psychotherapy, 7,* 85–93.

Bradway, K. (1985). *Sandplay bridges and the transcendent function.* San Francisco: C. G. Jung Institute of San Francisco.

Bradway, K. (1992). Sandplay in preparing to die. *Journal of Sandplay Therapy, 2* (1), 13–19.

Bradway, K., Signell, K., Spare, G., Stewart, C., & Thompson, C. (1989). *Sandplay studies: Origins, theory and practice.* Santa Monica: Sigo Press.

Campbell, J. (1949). *The hero with a thousand faces.* (Bollingen Ser. XVII). New York: Pantheon Books.

Campbell, J. (1959). *The masks of God: Primitive mythology.* New York: Viking Press.

Campbell, J. (1962). *The masks of God: Oriental mythology.* New York: Viking Press.

Campbell, J. (1964). *The masks of God: Occidental mythology.* New York: Viking Press.

Carey, L. (1990). Sandplay therapy with a troubled child. *The Arts in Psychotherapy, 17,* 197–209.

Carey, L. (1991). Family sandplay therapy. *Arts in Psychotherapy, 18,* 231–239.

Chowdorow, J. (1991). *Dance therapy and depth psychology. The moving imagination.* New York: Routledge.

Chowdorow, J., & Stewart, L. (1989). *Active imagination and the creation of personality.* (Cassette recording available from C. G. Jung Institute Library, 1040 Gough St., San Francisco, CA 94109).

Cirlot, J. (1971). *A dictionary of symbols.* New York: Philosophical Library.

Cooper, J. (1987). *An illustrated encyclopedia of traditional symbols.* London: Thames and Hudson.

De Domenico, G. (1986). *Lowenfeld World Apparatus: A Methodological Contribution Towards the Study and Analysis of the Sandtray Play Process.* Unpublished doctoral dissertation, Pacific Graduate School of Psychology, Menlo Park, CA. UMI #8717059.

De Domenico, G. (1987, November). *The use of sand, water, and fire in the sandtray play.* Lecture given at Vision Quest into Symbolic Reality, Oakland, CA.

De Domenico, G. (1988). Sandtray Worldplay: Comprehensive guide to the use of the sandtray in psychotherapy and transformational settings. Oakland, CA: Vision Quest into Symbolic Reality.

De Domenico, G. (1991a, June and September). Applications of the Lowenfeld World Technique. *Association for Play Therapy Newsletter, 10*(2).

De Domenico, G. (1991b). *Sandtray with couples: Applications and techniques.* Oakland, CA: Vision Quest into Symbolic Reality.

De Domenico, G. (1992a). *Introduction to sandtray worldplay: Teaching video #1* [videotape]. (Available from Vision Quest into Symbolic Reality, 1946 Clemens Rd., Oakland, CA 94602)

De Domenico, G. (1992b). *Introduction to sandtray worldplay: Teaching video #2* [videotape]. (Available from Vision Quest into Symbolic Reality, 1946 Clemens Rd., Oakland, CA 94602)

De Domenico, G. (1992c). *Introduction to sandplay: A variety of sandtray images: Teaching video #3* [videotape]. (Available from Vision Quest into Symbolic Reality, 1946 Clemens Rd., Oakland, CA 94602).

De Domenico, G. (1992d). *Sandtray worldplay: A psychotherapeutic technique for individuals, couples and families.* Oakland, CA: Vision Quest into Symbolic Reality.

Dieckmann, H. (1971). Symbols of active imagination. *Journal of Analytical Psychology, 16* (2), 127–148.

Dieckmann, H. (1979). Active imagination. In H. Dieckmann (Ed.), *Methods in analytical psychology: An introduction.* Wilmette, IL: Chiron Publications.

Dundas, E. (1989). *Symbols come alive in the sand.* Santa Monica, CA: Sigo Press.

Edinger, E. (1990). *The living psyche. A Jungian analysis in pictures.* Wilmette, IL: Chiron Publications.

Fordham, M. (1967). Active imagination—deintegration or disintegration? *Journal of Analytical Psychology, 12,* 51–66.

Fordham, M. (1970). *Children as individuals.* New York: C. G. Jung Foundation, Putnam's.

Fordham, M. (1980). The principles of analytic psychotherapy in childhood. In Ian F. Baker (Ed.), *VII International Congress of the International Association for Analytical Psychology: Methods of Treatment in Analytical Psychology.* Dallas: Spring Publications.

Fordham, M. (1988). The emergence of child analysis and principles of child analysis. In M. Sidoli & M. Davies (Eds.), *Jungian child psychotherapy: Individuation in childhood* (pp. 19–51). London: Karnac Books for the Society of Analytical Psychology.

Frantz, G. (1979, January 24). *Approaching the unconscious through play.* Lecture presented at San Diego Friends of Jung. (Cassette recording available from C. G. Jung Institute Library, 2040 Gough St., San Francisco, CA 94109)

Frey-Wehrlin, C. T. (1990). *The psychotherapy of psychosis from a Jungian perspective.* Lecture presented at C. G. Jung Institute, San Francisco, CA. (Cassette recording available from C. G. Jung Institute Library, 1040 Gough St., San Francisco, CA 94109)

Friedman, H. (1991, September 21–22). *A heritage rediscovered: A journey through the five elements.* Lecture presented at C. G. Jung Institute Conference: Earth, air, fire, water. Transformation in sand, San Francisco, CA. (Cassette recording available from C. G. Jung Institute Library, 2040 Gough St., San Francisco, CA 94109)

Furth, G. (1988). *The secret world of drawings. Healing through art.* Boston: Sigo Press.

Gaskell, G. (1981). *Dictionary of all scriptures and myths.* New York: Avenel Books.

Hannah, B. (1971). *Striving towards wholeness.* Boston: Sigo Press.

Hannah, B. (1981). *Encounters with the soul: Active imagination as developed by C. G. Jung.* Boston: Sigo Press.

Hayes, D. (1959). Considerations of the dance from a Jungian viewpoint. *Journal of Analytical Psychology, 4,* 169–181.

Henderson, J. (1967). *Thresholds of initiation.* Middletown, CT: Wesleyan University Press.

Humbert, E. (1971). Active imagination: Theory and practice. In *Spring: An annual of archetypal psychology and jungian thought* (pp. 101–114).

Isaac-Kassof, R. (1981). *Guided picture series and the role of the helper as midwife.* Unpublished diploma thesis, C. G. Jung Institute, Zurich, Switzerland. (Available from C. G. Jung Institute Library, 2040 Gough St., San Francisco, CA 94109)

Jacobi, J. (1959). *Complex, archetype, symbol in the psychology of C. G. Jung* (R. Manheim, Trans.). New York: Princeton University Press.

Jung, C. G. (1924). *Psychological types: Or the psychology of individuation.* H. G. Baynes, (Trans.). New York: Harcourt Brace.

Jung, C. G. (1953). *Psychology and Alchemy.* H. Hull, (Trans.), Collected Works (Vol. 12). New York: Pantheon Books.

Jung, C. G. (1958). *Psyche and symbol.* (V. Staub de Lazlo, Ed.). Garden City, NY: Doubleday Anchor Books.

Jung, C. G. (1959). *The archetypes and the collective unconscious: A study in the process of individuation.* H. Hull (Trans.), Collected Works (Vol. 9. Part I). New York: Pantheon Books.

Jung, C. G. (1961). *Memories, dreams, reflections.* New York: Vintage Books.

Jung, C. G. (1969). *Aion: Researches into the phenomenology of the Self.* H. Hull (Trans.), Collected Works (Vol. 9. Part II). New York: Pantheon Books.

Kalff, D. (1966). The archetype as a healing factor. *Psychologia, 9,* 177–184.

Kalff, D. (1971). *Sandplay: Mirror of a child's psyche.* San Francisco: Browser Press.

Kalff, D. (1980). *Sandplay.* Santa Monica, CA: Sigo Press.

Kalff, M., & Hood-Williams, J. (1988, January 2). *Sandtray workshop: Jungian sandplay and Lowenfeld World Technique: Two case presentations.* John F. Kennedy University, Orinda, CA. (Videotape available through Counseling Program Faculty Department.)

Kellogg, R. (1967). *The psychology of children's art.* San Diego, CA: CRM Random House.

Kiepenheuer, K. (1991). *Crossing the bridge.* La Salle, IL: Open Court.

Leach, M. (Ed.). (1972). *Funk & Wagnalls dictionary of folklore, mythology, and legend.* New York: Harper and Row.

Lowenfeld, M. (1935). *Play in childhood.* London: Gollancz.

Lowenfeld, M. (1939). The world pictures of children: A method of recording and studying them. *British Journal of Medical Psychology, 18,* 65–101.

Lowenfeld, M. (1950). The nature and use of the Lowenfeld World Technique in work with children and adults. *Journal of Psychology, 30,* 325–331.

Lowenfeld, M. (1964). *The study of preverbal thinking and its relationship to psychotherapy.* Paper presented at the 6th International Congress of Psychotherapy, London, England.

Lowenfeld, M. (1979). *The World Technique.* London: George Allen & Unwin.

Miller, C., & Boe, J. (1990). Tears into diamonds: Transformation of child psychic trauma through sandplay and storytelling. *The Arts in Psychotherapy, 17,* 247–257.

Mindell, A. (1987). *Working with the dreaming body.* New York: Routledge and Kegan.

Moon, B. (Ed.). (1991). *An encyclopedia of archetypal symbolism.* Boston: Shambhala Publications.

Neumann, E. (1955). *The origins and the history of consciousness.* (R. Hull, Trans.) (Bollingen Ser. XLII). New York: Pantheon Books.

Neumann, E. (1973). *The child.* New York: C. G. Jung Foundation.

New Larousse Encyclopedia of Mythology. (1989). (R. Aldington & D. Ames, Trans.) New York: Crescent Books.

Payne, H. (Ed.). (1992). *Dance movement therapy: theory and practice.* New York: Routledge and Kegan.

Phillips, K. (1979). *Music: A Jungian insight into the listening process* [Audiocassette]. Available from C. G. Jung Institute Library, 2040 Gough St., San Francisco, CA 94109.

Reed, J. (1975). *Sand magic, experience in miniature: A non-verbal therapy for children.* Chicago: Sterns Book Service.

Reed, J. (1980). *Emergence: Essays on the process of individuation through sandtray therapy, art forms and dreams.* Chicago: Sterns Book Service.

Ryce-Menuhin, J. (1983). Sandplay adult Jungian psychotherapy. *British Journal of Projective Psychology and Personality Study, 28,* 13–21.

Ryce-Menuhin, J. (1992). *Jungian sandplay: The wonderful therapy.* New York: Routledge and Kegan.

Sandner, D. (1987). The split shadow and the father-son relationship. In L. Mahdi, S. Foster, & M. Little (Eds.), *Betwixt & between: Patterns of masculine and feminine initiation* (pp. 175–188). La Salle, IL: Open Court.

Sandner, D. (1991). *Navajo symbols of healing: A Jungian exploration of ritual, image and medicine.* Rochester, VT: Healing Arts Press.

Sidoli, M. (1986). The volcano and the iceberg: The analysis of an eleven-year-old boy. *Journal of Analytical Psychology, 31,* 135–152.

Sidoli, M. (1988). Deintegration and reintegration in the first two weeks of life. In M. Sidoli & M. Davies (Eds.), *Jungian child psychotherapy: Individuation in childhood* (pp. 53–69). London: Karnac Books for the Society of Analytical Psychology.

Siegel, E. (1984). *Dance-movement therapy: Mirror of our selves: The psychoanalytic approach.* New York: Human Sciences Press.

Singer, D., & Singer, J. (1990). *The house of make-believe; Play and the developing imagination.* Cambridge, MA: Harvard University Press.

Spencer, M. (1984). Amplification: The dance. *Journal of Analytical Psychology, 29,* 113–123.

Spiegelman, M. (1988). *Active imagination and story writing.* Lecture presented at C. G. Jung Institute of Los Angeles. (Cassette recording available from C. G. Jung Institute Library, 2040 Gough St., San Francisco, CA 94109)

Spiegelman, M. (1989–1990). Active imagination and storywriting: Individuation and art. *Harvest, Journal for Jungian Studies, 35,* 121–133.

Stewart, L. (1982). Sandplay and Jungian analysis. In M. Stein (Ed.), *Jungian analysis,* (pp. 204–218).

Stewart, L. (1987). Affect and archetype in analysis. In N. Schwartz-Salant & M. Stein (Eds.), *Archetypal processes in psychotherapy* (pp. 131–162). Wilmette, IL: Chiron Publications.

Stewart, L. (1990). Play and sandplay. In S. Sternback (Ed.), *Sandplay studies: Origins, theory and practice* (pp. 21–39). Boston: Sigo Press.

Stone, H., & Winkelman, S. (1989). *Embracing ourselves: The voice dialogue manual.* San Rafael, CA: New World Library.

Sullwold, E. (1971). Eagle eye. In H. Kirsch (Ed.), *The well tended tree* (pp. 235–252). New York: Putnam's.

Sullwold, E. (1974). *Healing through the symbolic process.* Paper presented at the Conference for the Center of Healing Arts, San Francisco. (Available from C. G. Jung Institute Library, 2040 Gough St., San Francisco, CA 94109)

Sullwold, E. (1975). *Therapy with children.* (Available from C. G. Jung Institute Library, 2040 Gough St., San Francisco, CA 94109)

Sullwold, E. (1977). Jungian child therapy. In B. Wolman (Ed.), *International encyclopedia of psychiatry, psychology, psychoanalysis and neurology.* New York: Aesclepius Publishers.

Sullwold, E. (1987). The ritual-maker within at adolescence. In L. Mahdi, S. Foster, & M. Little (Eds.), *Betwixt & Between: Patterns of masculine and feminine initiation* (pp. 111–114). La Salle, IL: Open Court.

Vinturella, L., & Vinturella, J. (1987). Sandplay: A therapeutic medium with children. *Elementary School Guidance Counseling, 21,* pp. 229–238.

Walker, B. (1983). The woman's encyclopedia of myths and secrets. San Francisco: Harper and Row.

Weaver, R. (1964). *The old wise woman.* London: Vincent Stuart.

Weinrib, E. (1983). *Images of the Self: The sandplay therapy process.* Boston: Sigo Press.

Whitehouse, M. (1979). C. G. Jung and dance therapy: Two major principles. In M. Whitehouse (Ed.), *Eight theoretical approaches in dance/movement therapy.* Dubuque, IA: Kendall & Hunt.

Wickes, F. (1988). *The inner world of childhood. A study in analytical psychology.* Boston: Sigo Press.

Bibliography of Case Studies of Jungian Play Therapies

To help guide the reader in the further explorations of the frontiers of Jungian play therapy methods and techniques, the reader is directed to the following sources that offer good case material:

The Preschool Child

1. J. Allan and R. MacDonald: *The Use of Fantasy Enactment in the Treatment of an Emerging Autistic Child.*
2. G. De Domenico: *The Lowenfeld Apparatus: A Methodological Contribution towards the Study and the Analysis of the Sandtray Play Process.*
3. G. De Domenico: *Application of the Lowenfeld World Technique.*
4. G. Furth: *The Secret World of Drawings. Healing through Art.*

The Latency Child

1. L. Carey: *Sandplay Therapy with a Troubled Child.*
2. D. Kalff: *Sandplay.*
3. C. Miller and J. Boe: *Tears into Diamonds: Transformation of Child Psychic Trauma Through Sandplay and Storytelling.*
4. J. Reed: *Sand Magic, Experience in Miniature: A Verbal and Non-Verbal Therapy for Children.*
5. M. Sidoli: *The Unfolding Self. Separation and Individuation.*
6. E. Sullwold: *Eagle Eye.*

The Adolescent

1. E. Dundas: *Symbols Come Alive in the Sand.*
2. K. Kiepenheuer: *Crossing the Bridge.*
3. J. Ryce-Menuhin: *Jungian Sandplay. The Wonderful Therapy.*
4. E. Sullwold: *The Ritual-Maker Within at Adolescence.*

The Young Adult:

1. C. Frey-Wehrlin: *The Psychotherapy of Psychosis from a Jungian Perspective.*
2. D. Sandner: *The Split Shadow and the Father-Son Relationship.*
3. M. Woodman: *From Concrete to Consciousness: The Emergence of the Feminine.*

Adult in Midlife

1. E. Adamson: *Art as Healing.*
2. E. Edinger: *The Living Psyche. A Jungian Analysis in Pictures.*
3. B. Hannah: *Encounters with the Soul: Active Imagination as Developed by C. G. Jung.*
4. K. Kiepenheuer: *Crossing the Bridge.*
5. M. Spiegelman: *Active Imagination and Story Writing: Individuation and Art.*

Adult in Old Age

1. K. Bradway: *Sandplay in Preparing to Die.*

CHAPTER 12

The Good Feeling-Bad Feeling Game

A Technique to Facilitate Attachment, Communication, and Therapeutic Process Between Foster Parents (and Parents) and Children

SUE AMMEN

INTRODUCTION

The Good Feeling-Bad Feeling Game is a technique originally developed for use with seriously disturbed foster children living in therapeutic foster-care settings. Since its origin, it has been used with any parent-figure-and-child dyad for whom attachment and/ or affective communication are seen as important therapeutic goals. This technique combines elements of attachment theory, play therapy, family therapy, and cognitive-therapeutic problem-solving approaches. It can be used to structure the entire therapy session in order to facilitate attachment between the parent-figure and the child and to provide a format for communicating about feelings and problems. Over time, the child is able to use the strengthened relationship with the parent-figure and to use the structure of the sessions to process therapeutically his or her present distress and past traumas. This technique involves a talking component, a dyadic play component, and a free play component. It is usually used as an adjunct to individual play therapy, family therapy, day treatment, and so on, but it may be used alone as well.

Theory

Attachment

Bowlby (1988) used the concept of a *secure base* to define a healthy attachment between a parent and a child. The key criterion of attachment is the experience of security and comfort obtained from this relationship. This security allows the child to move off and explore the world and to establish healthy social relationships with others. Bowlby (1982) identified two parental variables as significantly related to the development of positive attachment behavior: (a) responsiveness to the child's signals of his or her feelings and needs; and (b) mutually enjoyable social interactions. "What is believed to be essential for mental health is that the infant and young child should experience a warm, intimate and continuous relationship with his [or her] mother (or permanent mother-substitute) in which both find satisfaction and enjoyment" (Bowlby, 1982, pp. xi–xii).

Over time, this parent-child relationship typically develops into what Bowlby (1982) called a "goal-corrected partnership." As the child develops more sophisticated cognitive

This chapter could not have been written without the creative participation and insights of P. B., foster mother, in developing the Good Feeling-Bad Feeling Game, nor without F. V. H., who, between the ages of 8 and 11, played the Game with incredible courage and a desire to heal. This chapter is dedicated to them.

and language abilities, he or she is able to acquire insight into the parent-figure's motives and feelings. The more the parent-figure takes the child's viewpoint into account when dealing with him or her, the greater the rate of development of a child's capacity to grasp the viewpoint of the parent-figure (Light, 1979). Put another way, the parent-figure who is as much concerned with a child's feelings and intentions as with the child's actual behavior and who is prepared to make reasonable concessions when the situation warrants it promotes the development of a child who is capable of taking account of another's goals and feelings, that is, a child who is capable of experiencing empathy. At this point, the child and the parent are capable of sharing common goals and experiencing a sense of common purpose, which strengthens the security of the relationship and assists the child in experiencing himself or herself as competent and valued.

Several authors have recognized parent-child attachment disruptions or distortions in the attachment relationship as a major contributor to emotional disturbances in children and adults (e.g., Ainsworth, 1989; Bowlby, 1982, 1988; Hartup, 1989; Stern; 1985, Tronick, 1989). In particular, children with problems in their attachment relationships tend to have difficulty relating to others, regulating their emotional states and their behavior, and communicating their feelings.

Affective Communication

Tronick (1989) identified the degree of interactive coordination in the affective communication system between an infant and a caretaker as crucial to the development of that child's ability to interact with others, regulate his or her emotional states, and communicate effectively. He identified the caretaker's role as critical in regulating the infant's emotional communications so that the child's experiences of negative affect are successfully transformed into experiences of positive affect. When the parent-figure and the child have developed a coordinated affective communication system, the child develops a sense of himself or herself as effective and the parent-figure as reliable and secure. This is consistent with Bowlby's description of the responsive parent-figure facilitating secure attachment.

When the parent-figure is unavailable and/or less than adequately responsive to the emotional signals from the child, the child is likely to develop problems with his or her ability to regulate emotional states and communicate effectively. A common goal of many therapeutic approaches with emotionally disturbed children is the development of the child's ability to manage feelings and affective material appropriately. Three subskills have been identified as necessary to the development of this ability (O'Connor, 1983, p. 251): (a) an awareness of the variety of affective states; (b) the ability to relate those affects to situations in one's own life, and; (c) verbalizing affects in appropriate ways.

The Good Feeling-Bad Feeling Game provides a structure that facilitates both affective communication and the attachment relationship between a parent-figure and a child. Specific goals of the Game include:

1. The child (and the parent-figure) will learn to identify positive and negative affective states.

2. The child (and the parent-figure) will relate these affects to situations in his or her own life, both past and present.

3. The parent-figure will learn to respond to the child's negative affects in a responsive. supportive manner, such that the child's experience of a negative affect is transformed into an experience of being understood and accepted.

4. The parent-figure and the child will learn to use a problem-solving strategy.

5. The parent-figure and the child will learn to participate in mutually enjoyable social interactions with each other.

6. Within the security of the attachment with the parent-figure and with the development of affective communication skills, the child will be able to address and work through past traumas and conflicts.

The Good Feeling-Bad Feeling Game consists of three components:

1. *Talking:* The parent-figure and the child talk about feelings and problems in a semistructured format.

2. *Dyadic Play:* The parent-figure and the child participate in some play activity together.

3. *Free Play:* The child engages in free play.

In the following sections, each of these components of the Good Feeling-Bad Feeling Game is described in detail, including a description of the role of the therapist and the developmental changes observed in each component over time. Finally, a case example is presented to illustrate both the therapeutic use of this technique and the dynamics of a child in foster care for whom this technique was particularly useful.

PROCEDURE

Therapist Characteristics

The therapist should have skills in family therapy, marital therapy, or group therapy such that he or she can facilitate dyadic processes. Experience in play therapy is needed to facilitate the dyadic play and free play components. Play therapy approaches that are particularly helpful in addressing the dyadic play include Theraplay (Jernberg, 1979), Family Play Therapy (Griff, 1983), and Conjoint Play Therapy (Safer, 1965). A solid understanding of children's social-emotional development (e.g., Harter, 1983; Wood, Combs, Gunn, & Weller, 1986) is also useful. Finally, a good understanding of the importance of attachment as a therapeutic goal (e.g., Bowlby, 1988) is seen as vital.

Client Characteristics

Child

The Good Feeling-Bad Feeling Game was initially developed for use with foster children and their foster parents. Since then, it has been used with any parent-figure-and-child dyad where early attachment problems were seen as contributing to the current difficulties. Early attachment problems may be due to any combination of: (a) child factors, such as neurological deficits that interfere with the attachment process; (b) parent factors, such as parents whose emotional problems interfere with their ability to be a consistent "secure base" for the child; or (c) environmental factors, such as illness of a sibling or death of a parent. Thus, this technique is appropriate for any child in which the therapeutic goals include facilitating the ability to communicate feelings and strengthening the attachment relationship between that child and a parent-figure.

This technique requires a certain level of associative and logical thinking, so very young children (less than 5 or 6 years old) might have difficulty participating, as might a psychotic child. However, it has been used with some success with a high-functioning autistic child. It is probably most useful with children who are between the ages of 6 and 12 but whose social-emotional functioning is younger than their chronological ages. In most cases, these children have difficulty regulating their emotions, managing their behavior, relating to others, and/or communicating their feelings. The structure of the Game seems to be particularly useful for children with hyperactivity, impulse-control problems, or attention deficits.

Parent-Figure

The parent-figure participant should be able to listen and reflect at a very basic level. Many foster parents, especially those from therapeutic foster homes, already have these basic communication skills. The emphasis then is on establishing a relationship of trust between the foster child and the foster parent. With other parents even if they possess basic communication skills, the task is in some ways more difficult because the child and the parent have a history with each other. This history often includes an already established pattern of communication that is dysfunctional. The emphasis then becomes addressing the dysfunctional communication in the dyad. In addition, the parent may have cognitive, personality, and/or emotional limitations that interfere with his or her readiness to participate. In this situation, individual collateral sessions with the parent may be required before initiating the conjoint sessions.

Logistics

(*Note:* In the following discussion of the Good Feeling-Bad Feeling Game, the term *parent* will be used to refer to the many variants of parent-figure, including biological, adoptive, and foster parents, grandparents, and other caretakers.)

Talking

PROCEDURE.   The parent and the child sit facing each other, facilitating direct eye contact. One person starts the Game by asking the other person "What happened this week that felt good?" or "What happened this week that felt bad?" It does not matter which is first, but if "good feelings" are discussed first by one member of the dyad, then "good feelings" should be discussed next by the other member. Thus, if the child starts out by asking the father about "bad feelings," then, after answering, the father should ask the child about "bad feelings." The focus is on identifying the feelings and linking them to events, rather than on the problems these events may represent.

Once each member of the dyad has talked about good feelings and bad feelings, then problems identified during the discussion may be addressed. At this point, some sort of problem-solving procedure should be used to provide structure for the parent and child. One example is the following procedure extrapolated from the four-step-problem-solving strategy described by O'Connor (1991):

1. The problem is defined both from the perspective of the child and from the perspective of the parent. This reduces the child's experience that he or she is in trouble or being criticized.

2. Both child and parent brainstorm solutions.

3. Child and parent reach a mutually agreed upon plan to address the problem in the future.

4. They implement the plan and evaluate the proposed solution in later sessions. In addition to problems that may have come up during the discussion, any other concern(s) identified by the child, the parent, and/or the therapist may be addressed at this time.

THERAPIST ROLE.   Initially, the therapist may need to provide considerable structure for the child and the parent. For many emotionally disturbed children, learning to label feelings and link them to events is a difficult task. If the child is unable to identify an event, the parent is asked to assist the child. In addition, many children are only able to identify very basic feelings, such as sad, happy, angry, scared, and lonely. Thus, in many of the early sessions, the therapist may focus on educating the child about how to identify and talk about his or her feelings.

Many parents find it difficult to talk about events involving the child that have evoked negative feelings without being critical and/or focusing on the problem behavior of the child. Thus, the therapist may initially need to assist the parent in focusing only on how the event made him or her feel, rather than on the problem. Knowing that the problems will be addressed eventually seems to help. The therapist's ultimate goal is to facilitate the parent's ability to be responsive to the child's feelings and motivations in such a way that the child experiences the parent's responses as supportive. In a healthy parent-child relationship, the child is able to express both positive and negative emotions with the parent, and the parent is able to join with the child's experience and assist him or her in coping with those emotions.

Although this exchange of feeling experiences may feel like a task initially, it is the therapist's role to transform the experience for the parent and the child into a constructive and, as much as possible, enjoyable experience, that is, to make it into a game. The idea of this task being perceived as a game is important for several reasons. Games are time-limited, with beginnings and endings. Thus, the child can experience a sense of control over this discussion of feelings and events in his or her life. Games are played with someone; thus, the parent is seen as a coparticipant in this activity with the child. Finally, although games can be challenging and frustrating at times, ultimately the participants should experience a sense of positive participation and/or accomplishment.

Once the parent and the child become comfortable and proficient with the game, the child seems to appreciate and look forward to the opportunity to talk about things that happened during the week that were difficult for him or her. The game becomes a safe place to talk about even those times when the child did things that made the parent angry or disappointed, and it is hoped that both parent and child leave the experience with a feeling of resolution. For emotionally disturbed children, even hearing positive emotions from the parent regarding the child's behavior can be difficult, as they tend to view themselves as bad or unworthy of these positive attributes. Thus, helping the child to express and accept positive feelings is as important as helping them to cope with the negative affective experiences.

The problem-solving component provides an opportunity for the parent to assist the child in reaching a mutually agreeable solution to the problem. The therapist should assist the parent in communicating clear expectations for appropriate behavior, while affirming that the child is still valued. Further, the child needs to hear that the parent feels optimistic that they can develop a plan to deal with the problem. Through this process, the child feels hopeful about the problems and about his or her parent's ability to be of assistance. It is the therapist's role to assist parent and child in developing the skills and relationship such that the problem-solving process is experienced constructively. This may require specific behavioral instructions, modeling, structuring, gentle feedback, and guidance of the process.

It is important throughout this procedure that the therapist create a safe space for the child to talk about feelings and problems. This will not occur if the process is experienced as critical or if the child experiences himself or herself as a bad person. It is important that the child learn to differentiate *feeling bad* and/or having a parent who is *feeling bad* because of something the child did or did not do from *being a bad person*. At the same time, the parent needs to feel safe and validated as a parent. Thus, the structuring and feedback to the parent must be done in a supportive and empowering manner.

The therapist's role during the feeling dialogue and the problem-solving component is, in many ways, similar to that of a family therapist. The therapist must focus on the process between the two participants, while keeping each individual participant's needs and abilities in mind. In individual therapy, the therapist would assist the child in communicating his or her negative feelings. Although the therapist may need to model this, the therapeutic goal is to facilitate the parent's ability to assist the child in affective communication. The same is true for the problem solving. Although the therapist may need to model the process, the goal is teaching the parent and child to mutually accomplish the problem solving.

Once the dyad is able to "play the game" in a constructive manner, the therapist can decrease his or her focus on structuring and can focus more on facilitating the communication and therapeutic process.

Dyadic Play

PROCEDURE.   The parent and the child then participate in some play activity together, such as drawing a picture, playing with clay, or drawing a squiggle (Claman, 1980). (Drawing squiggles is an easy interactive game where one person draws a meaningless squiggle, or wavy line. The next person turns the squiggle into something, and the picture continues through some set number of turns or until the squiggle is saturated. It is useful to have the parties involved use different colored pens or crayons.) Initially, the therapist may need to participate in the activity to provide modeling for the parent. The activity is chosen by either the therapist, the parent, or some consensus between parent and child.

THERAPIST ROLE.   Initially, the therapist chooses the activity and structures the process enough to guarantee that the child and the parent experience the activity as enjoyable. This is particularly important for two reasons: First, the parent and the child may have just finished talking about some difficult topics and need an opportunity to interact with each other in a positive manner, which affirms the child's positive value in spite of negative feelings and behaviors. Secondly, when a parent and a child find mutual enjoyment in each other's company, this strengthens the emotional attachment between them.

Over time, allowing the parent to identify an activity empowers him or her and provides an opportunity for the therapist to observe the parent's ability to choose appropriate activities and to engage the child. Finally, parent and child should be able to mutually agree upon an activity.

Free Play

PROCEDURE. The child is free to play with whatever he or she chooses, within the limits of the playroom setting. This may or may not involve the parent and/or the therapist. The key component at this point is that it is the child's choice.

THERAPIST ROLE.   Initially, the free play is a reward. Thus, there should be activities available that motivate and that are of interest to the child. For many children, playing alone is their preference, especially after the forced interaction around affective material. If this is the case, then their need for this space should be respected. Other children prefer interaction with either the therapist or the parent or both while enjoying the fact that they get to choose the activity. Over time, the children tend to use these activities to continue whatever issues were addressed or identified in the earlier part of the session. At these times, it is important that the therapist affirm the child's process and, when appropriate, provide interpretations.

Stages of Treatment

As the therapy progresses, the child gradually moves from superficially identifying feelings to using the structure of the game as a place to talk about very difficult feelings and events, both present and past. The process observed most often with resistant, socially isolated children in foster care was that the children at first resisted both talking about feelings and play that involved another person. They tended to prefer isolation in free play. Later, as the children developed a relationship with the foster parent, they chose to include the foster parent in free play of their own choice or to expand on the dyadic activity. Finally, they began to use the talking component as a safe place to talk about very difficult feelings and events, both past and present, oftentimes using virtually the whole session for this. With other children who were not so socially disengaged, they tended to choose activities involving the therapist and/or the parent during the free play component, while enjoying the fact that they got to choose the activity.

Although the child must participate in the feeling dialogue to get to the free play, it is important that the talking component not take up the whole session. The therapist should structure the session, if possible, so that the child has at least 5 minutes of play, whether it be alone or with the parent, if this is rewarding for the child.

There are three potential situations that may interfere with including play in the session:

1. The child has been resistant to participating in the talking and/or dyadic play. In this situation, the therapist should try to structure the session somehow so that these components are successfully accomplished; for example, the therapist can get the parent to talk about what he or she imagines the child felt about a certain situation and then ask the child for clarification and/or confirmation, while rewarding the child for even brief participation in the discussion.

2. The parent may want to expend considerable energy and time focusing on the problems with the child that have been occurring at home. In these situations, the focus on the problems interferes with the opportunities for positive social interaction (play) between the parent and the child. This is likely a replication of what occurs at home, where there is so much focus on the problems that there is little time to enjoy each other as a family. Consequently, the therapist must provide some structure to ensure that the dyadic

play component is included. Depending on the sophistication of the family, this may include setting a limit on the time spent problem solving, educating them as to the importance of the dyadic play, and/or interpreting the pattern as similar to the pattern of interacting at home.

3. The child begins to use the structure of the game as a place to process difficult feelings and events in his or her life, and this process may take up most of the session. In that case, it is helpful to have a brief period at the end of the session that focuses on either mutual enjoyment (e. g., drawing a squiggle) or positive nurturing from the parent (e. g., holding the child and telling the child how brave he or she was to talk about the things he or she had shared). Without this, the child may experience the talking process as too intense and may be resistant or anxious when asked to play again.

CASE ILLUSTRATION

Background

Phillip entered the foster-care system at approximately 7 years of age. His mother had been severely depressed and emotionally unavailable to him most of his life. She died in an accident when he was 4, and during the next 3 years, he lived with his father, who physically and sexually abused him. Phillip was so aggressive towards property, animals, peers, and adults when first detained in foster care that he failed in several homes before finally being placed in a therapeutic group home where he lived for the next 3 years.

During those 3 years, Phillip was provided with extensive psychotherapeutic services using an ecosystemic model that addressed the child from within the context of the child's ecosystem (O'Connor, 1991). Within this model, children are seen as part of a larger community, that must be recognized and often restructured to facilitate the therapeutic growth of the child (Knitzer, 1982). Consequently, in addition to his placement in the therapeutic group home and a special day class for emotionally disturbed children, Phillip participated in an afterschool day treatment program, individual play therapy, conjoint therapy with the foster mother, and a boy's sexual abuse treatment group. In addition, frequent collateral contacts were maintained with the group home, school, and Child Protective Services, with the goal of maintaining the stability of his placement. It was within the conjoint sessions with the foster mother that the Good Feeling-Bad Feeling Game evolved.

The idea of meeting with Phillip and his foster mother together resulted because the therapist's supervisor at the time was a staunch family therapist who felt that if no family was available for this child, perhaps the therapist (this author) should work to create one for him. That is, in large part, what occurred during those next 3 years.

For Phillip, as for most foster children, there had been a significant disruption of the crucial process of attachment and the establishment of basic trust (Gries, 1986). Initially, he experienced unresponsive mothering, then traumatic loss, then abuse and betrayal of trust, followed by more loss. It is not surprising that Phillip was unable to regulate his emotions and behavior, and he tended to avoid rather than approach genuine social contact. He either acted in ways that alienated others through his aggressive behaviors or socially isolated himself. His emotional states were labile, with several tantrums a day, even in very structured settings. He was unable to identify any feelings and tended to act out his feelings impulsively. He had no secure base.

Bowlby (1988) has identified the role of the therapist as that of an attachment figure who, by inspiring trust, can provide a secure base from whence the child may participate in the therapeutic process. However, this child needed a secure base with someone who was available for more than one hour a week. Ruff, Blank, and Barnett (1990) have identified the role of a stable, responsive caregiver as critical for the positive development of foster children. They stated:

> Rather than assigning a professional to be responsible for a "special intervention" with the child while the foster parent is viewed as a "routine caretaker," it is preferable to make the foster parent the major force in the intervention. Professionals can facilitate this process by supporting the foster parents through the initial development of a relationship with the child. (p. 267)

Although the role of the primary therapist in this case was more extensive than envisioned by Ruff et al., the basic premise was the same. Thus, this author began to meet weekly with Phillip and his foster mother, with two goals: (a) stabilizing his behavior in the group home so that he did not again experience a rejection, and (b) facilitating the development of a trusting relationship between the foster mother and Phillip to provide a secure base for therapy. The first goal was accomplished by helping the foster mother to understand why he behaved as he did while supporting the excellent behavioral management program already in place at the group home. The second goal was accomplished through the Good Feeling-Bad Feeling Game.

Evolution of the good feeling-bad feeling game

Since this author had not yet developed the Good Feeling-Bad Feeling Game, initial sessions with Phillip and his foster mother were unstructured. Phillip's play was repetitive and compulsive, building forts (places of safety) then tearing them down. He resisted interaction with either the therapist or the foster mother. After a couple of months, his behavior had stabilized to some degree at the group home, and he began to seek out the foster mother at times for support and nurturing. However, he had almost no skills for identifying and talking about feelings. His language was limited, he became extremely anxious, and his attention span was short. After 6 months of conjoint therapy and play therapy, he still was using play and language in very limited ways. Thus, a decision was made to incorporate more structure into the sessions, using the relationship he was developing with the foster mother. The goal was to improve his capacity to put his feelings into words within a context. The Good Feeling-Bad Feeling Game was born.

During the first session, Phillip identified feeling happy about playing with kids at school and feeling sad but he did not know why. Finally, with assistance, he identified that he felt sad/angry because he had to talk instead of play. During the second session, he stated that he did not want to talk about feelings, but he did not resist the game. With the foster mother's help, he was able to talk about some sadness over the recent death of an adult friend of the group home. During the third session, he was able to identify his negative feelings *and* the circumstances (he was mad because he had been suspended from the bus for fighting). Problem solving was introduced at this point.

During the next 2 months, the talking and dyadic play were activities he had to complete so that he could have free play, though he clearly expressed enjoyment during the dyadic play activities. Most of the feelings he identified were linked to anger and sadness about people leaving. By this time, the foster mother was actively participating in the sessions as a cotherapist. She began to introduce puppet play into the dyadic play time, which continued some of the topics and feelings identified during the talking time. Phillip responded positively to this and began to use his free time also to reenact these themes. He began to incorporate the foster mother into his free play time.

Over the next 6 months, Phillip increasingly used the structure of the sessions to process current feelings and experiences. On one occasion, he stated that he had felt sad and angry the day before when he went to school because his teacher from last year was not there. He then stated that he had felt like having a temper tantrum but instead had gone home and gone to his room and slept. This demonstrated considerable improvement in his awareness of his feelings, his ability to relate them to situations in his life, and his ability to think about those feelings and cognitively choose an alternative to acting-out.

Phillip's relationship with the foster mother was much like that of a preschool child with a parent. He sought frequent nurturing, was spontaneous in expressing affection, worked very hard to control his behavior and talk about feelings with her assistance, and felt unsafe when she was unavailable or absent from the group home. During the next year, Phillip used the Good Feeling–Bad Feeling Game to begin to process his past history. There were several sessions when he participated in talking during most of the session. Often he initiated and maintained the topics, though he still required the therapist and foster mother to initiate the Game.

Then one day, Phillip walked into the room and said, "We have to talk about the bad feelings now." The previous week, we had talked about his father's sexual abuse of him and, after the session, Phillip had injured a small animal at the group home. During this session, he was able to relate that he had been thinking about his father's abuse of him while holding the animal and had felt so angry that he just squeezed the animal. Now he felt that he was a very bad person and that the punishment he had received from the foster mother was not severe enough. The session focused on helping him to understand that he was not a bad person, that being angry about his father's abuse made sense, but that there were better ways to deal with it, and that they could make a plan for when he had these feelings in the future. For Phillip, the Good Feeling–Bad Feeling Game had evolved from making him angry that he had to talk about feelings to a safe place for him to talk about very difficult feelings.

Unfortunately, there were external factors that began to interfere with the therapeutic process. A biological child of the foster mother developed a serious illness, requiring significant periods of absence on the part of the foster mother. Though Phillip was able to tolerate her absences without significant loss of behavioral control, he had great difficulty continuing the therapeutic work during those times. As Phillip became more in touch with his past pain and grief, he became very depressed and at times suicidal. In addition, Phillip was growing older and larger. When he did lose control, his behavior was more dangerous to those around him, and his needs for control began to exceed those of his current group-home placement. Thus, in the middle of his therapeutic work on his past losses, he needed to be prepared for a move to a residential placement that could more appropriately keep him safe from hurting himself or others. This was extremely difficult for him to understand and accept.

Ainsworth (1989) has noted that attachment to parent surrogates is especially important in the case of children who find in these relationships the security that they could not attain with their own parents. One of the dilemmas for children in foster care for any length of time is their need for such a parent-surrogate relationship with the foster parent. But there is a risk in this attachment because of the possibility of future separation, an event that is likely to cause pain to both child and foster parent(s) (Ruff, Blank, & Barnett, 1990).

After 3 full years in the therapeutic group home that had become "home" to him, Phillip was transferred to a residential treatment program. The foster mother continued to be identified by him as his primary attachment object, and he spent holidays and birthdays with the foster family when his behavior was appropriate.

CONCLUSION

The Good Feeling-Bad Feeling Game was developed by this author as a way to strengthen the attachment relationship between a parent and a child and to increase the child's ability to talk about feelings and problems. It provides a structure and a secure base for the child to participate in the therapeutic process. It is a useful technique with any parent-figure and child where strengthening the attachment relationship is an important therapeutic goal. The relationship is strengthened by creating a situation through which the parent-figure becomes more responsive to the child's feelings and needs and the parent-figure and the child learn to engage in mutually enjoyable social interactions, that is, play. For foster children in foster care for any length of time, it is vital that they develop a positive surrogate attachment relationship with the foster parent and/or strengthen the attachment relationship with the biological parents, if available. The need for secure attachment relationships is a lifelong human need.

REFERENCES

Ainsworth, M. D. S. (1989). Attachments beyond infancy. *American Psychologist, 44*(4), 709–716.

Bowlby, J. (1982). *Attachment* (2nd ed.). New York: Basic Books.

Bowlby, J. (1988). *A secure base: Clinical applications of attachment theory.* London: Routledge.

Claman, L. (1980). The Squiggle-Drawing Game in child psychotherapy. *American Journal of Psychotherapy, 34*(3), 414–425.

Gries, L. T. (1986). The use of multiple goals in the treatment of foster children with emotional disorders. *Professional Psychology: Research and Practice, 17*(5), 381–390.

Griff, M. D. (1983). Family play therapy. In C. E. Schaefer & K. J. O'Connor (Eds.), *Handbook of play therapy* (pp. 65–75). New York: Wiley.

Harter, S. (1983). Cognitive-developmental considerations in the conduct of play therapy. In C. E. Schaefer & K. J. O'Connor (Eds.), *Handbook of play therapy* (pp. 95–127). New York: Wiley.

Hartup, W. W. (1989). Social relationships and their developmental significance. *American Psychologist, 44*(2), 120–126.

Jernberg, A. (1979). *Theraplay.* San Francisco: Jossey-Bass.

Knitzer, J. (1982). *Unclaimed children: The failure of public responsibility to children and adolescents in need of mental health services.* Washington, DC: Children's Defense Fund.

Light, P. (1979). *Development of a child's sensitivity to people.* London: Cambridge University Press.

O'Connor, K. J. (1983). The Color-Your-Life technique. In C. E. Schaefer & K. J. O'Connor (Eds.), *Handbook of play therapy* (pp. 251–258). New York: Wiley.

O'Connor, K. J. (1991). *The play therapy primer: An integration of theories and techniques.* New York: Wiley.

Ruff, H. A., Blank, S., & Barnett, H. L. (1990). Early intervention in the context of foster care. *Developmental and Behavioral Pediatrics, 11*(5), 265–268.

Safer, D. (1965). Conjoint play therapy for the young child and his parent. *Archives of General Psychiatry, 13*, 320–326.

Stern, D. N. (1985). *The interpersonal world of the infant. A view from psychoanalysis and developmental psychology.* New York: Basic Books.

Tronick, E. Z. (1989). Emotions and emotional communication in infants. *American Psychologist, 44*(2), 112–119.

Wood, M., Combs, C., Gunn, A., & Weller, D. (1986). *Developmental therapy in the classroom* (2nd ed.). Austin, TX: Pro-Ed.

PART 4

Play Therapy Applications

CHAPTER 13

Play Therapy for Psychic Trauma in Children

CHARLES E. SCHAEFER

INTRODUCTION

In recent years, researchers have given growing attention to the treatment of adults' reactions to severe trauma. However, the literature contains relatively few published accounts of children's reactions to psychic trauma. Particularly lacking are detailed treatment approaches. This chapter will examine childhood trauma resulting from isolated incidents as opposed to trauma related to chronic situations. Common childhood reactions to disaster, spontaneous posttraumatic play, play therapy interventions, and clinical issues related to the treatment of traumatized children will all be addressed.

Psychic trauma is a term used to describe the effect on a person of an extremely stressful life event. It refers to an external event that is outside the range of usual human experience and that would be markedly distressing to almost anyone. According to Eth and Pynoos (1985), psychic trauma results when an individual is exposed to an overwhelming event and is rendered temporarily helpless and unable to use ordinary coping and defensive operations of the ego in the face of intolerable danger, anxiety, or instinctual arousal. Events that people perceive as uncontrollable and/or unpredictable are more stressful to them. Sources of psychological trauma for children include natural and man-made disasters, life-threatening diseases, injuries, war-related trauma, physical and sexual abuse, and murder/suicide of a loved one.

Posttrauma Reactions

The fact that exposure to extreme adversity can lead to the development of psychopathology has been recognized since Janet (1925) and others reported on their studies of hysteria. Researchers have confirmed that individuals who have experienced frightening external events, such as natural disaster, accidents, sexual abuse, and combat, are prone to develop a distinct syndrome labeled *posttraumatic stress disorder* (PTSD) (Rothbaum & Foa, 1991). PTSD was first introduced as an anxiety disorder in the *Diagnostic and Statistical Manual of Mental Disorders* (DSM-III) (APA, 1980) and is characterized by three groups of symptoms in the 1987 revision of DSM-III (DSM-III-R): (a) reexperiencing, such as nightmares and play reenactments; (b) emotional distancing and psychic numbing, such as avoidance of thoughts or situations that remind one of the trauma; and (c) heightened arousal, as seen in difficulty sleeping, hypervigilance, and irritability.

Only recently have researchers begun to study the posttraumatic responses of children. In 1987, the American Psychiatric Association listed in DSM-III-R symptoms of PTSD that are specific to children. Preschool children are likely to report nightmares of monsters, of rescuing others by superhuman powers, and of threats to self and others. They also tend to relive the trauma in their play without realizing they are doing it. Regressive behaviors (encopresis, enuresis) and somatic complaints (headaches, stomachaches) are also common.

School-age children often exhibit a constriction of affect and reduced interest in customary activities. A foreshortened sense of the future may be expressed (not expecting to marry or have a career), as well as *omen formation* (belief in the ability to predict future calamities). Specific fears and an impaired capacity to trust may also be exhibited (Yule, Udwin, & Murdoch, 1990). Expected responses of adolescents include increased time spent with peers, increased drug or alcohol use, and fighting with parents or siblings.

Based on extensive work with child victims of trauma, Terr (1991) observed several common childhood reactions to disaster. She described four characteristics that children exhibit after exposure to a traumatic event: (a) strongly visualized or otherwise repeatedly perceived memories of the trauma; (b) repetitive behaviors; (c) trauma-specific fears; and (d) changed attitudes about people, aspects of life, and the future. The first characteristic is also experienced by adults, but in a very different form. Adults reexperience memories of a traumatic event in an intrusive, abrupt, and disrupting form. Children, on the other hand, tend to reexperience their memories during relaxing times of the day, perhaps when they are playing or watching TV.

Repetitive behaviors typically take the form of either reenactment or posttraumatic play. The main difference between the two is in whether or not the behavior is perceived as fun by the child. Reenactments are *not* perceived as fun, while posttraumatic play is reported to be fun and entertaining.

In describing trauma-specific fears, Terr (1991) used the example of a dog phobia. A non-trauma-specific dog-phobic child would be afraid of *all* dogs, while a trauma-related phobia would be specifically triggered by the kind of dog involved in the original trauma.

The final characteristic that Terr observed involves changed attitudes about people, life, and the future. not only do traumatized children see themselves and others as more vulnerable and helpless, but they view their futures as extremely uncertain and feel as if they are powerless to prevent future calamity (Terr, 1991).

Terr (1991) categorized psychic traumas as either Type I (single, sudden, and unexpected stressor) or Type II (longstanding and repeated ordeals). Based on clinical experience, Terr noted that children suffering Type I traumas do not appear to exhibit the massive denial, psychic numbing, dissociation, depersonalization, rage, or personality disorders that characterize the Type II traumas. This chapter focuses on Type I traumas in children.

PTSD symptoms in children and adolescents tend to be serious and enduring. Without treatment, they are likely to be present for years. Symptoms usually begin immediately or soon after the trauma; but they might only surface several months or even years later.

Risk Factors for Childhood Trauma Reactions

In general, children have been found to be more prone to developing PTSD than adults (Frederick, 1982). Block, Silber, and Perry (1956) studied children's emotional reactions after a tornado. Their investigation revealed that 49.5% of the children showed emotional disturbance immediately after the disaster. Even the children who did not show a major emotional disorder did show signs of regressive behavior, clinginess, and low frustration tolerance. Applebaum and Burns (1991) investigated PTSD in surviving siblings who had lost a brother or sister to accidental death or homicide. All the surviving siblings reported PTSD symptomatology, with 45% meeting the full psychiatric criteria for the disorder.

The following factors have been found to increase the risk that a particular child will develop PTSD:

1. Lack of social support when experiencing the trauma. The absence of the child's parents is particularly stressful. In a study that has become a classic, Freud and Burlingham (1944) studied the effects of German air raids during World War II on London's children. They found that the children were more disturbed by separation from their parents than they were by fear of the objectively more dangerous consequences of the bombing of London.

2. Traumas that are man-made versus natural disaster.

3. Traumas involving human aggression. Child or spouse abuse, for example, are especially upsetting to children.

4. Traumas that are life-threatening or involve great destruction of property.

5. Parental distress or inability to parent after the trauma. If parents show severe emotional distress after the trauma (PTSD), the children are likely to do the same. It seems that children's ability to maintain a barrier against psychic trauma is dependent upon their parents' reaction to the event.

6. The degree to which the child perceived significant others (e.g., parents) to be in physical danger.

7. Lack of parent-child communication about the trauma. Parents often find it difficult to talk with their children about a trauma. Many parents believe children will become confused and upset by discussing a recently experienced trauma. However, Block et. al. (1956) observed that when parents are better able to discuss the disaster openly and frankly, children become less anxious.

8. Children who just experienced previous stress-trauma or were emotionally disturbed prior to the trauma.

9. Significant, firsthand exposure to the trauma. The greater the degree of exposure to the trauma, the greater the severity of PTSD. Nader, Pynoos, Fairbanker, and Frederick (1990) studied elementary school children exposed to a sniper attack at school a year earlier. As evident with adults, proximity to the violence and degree of life threat were the primary predictors of continued PTSD reactions. There was a rapid diminution of symptoms in those less exposed. Primary victims are those who experienced firsthand the effects of a disaster. A secondary level of victimization is comprised of those individuals who witnessed the disaster, but did not experience the actual impact directly.

Assessment of Childhood Trauma Reactions

A wide variety of instruments are now available to assist the clinician in the diagnosis and assessment of PTSD in children. A description of a number of the more commonly used measures follows. Noteworthy is the fact that these measures are in their infancy stage of development, and psychometric properties remain to be established for all scales.

Child PTSD-Parent Inventory

The Child PTSD-Parent Inventory is a structured interview for obtaining a parent's perception of the child's PTSD response to a traumatic event (Pynoos & Nader, 1987). In addition to a focus on the child's general personality characteristics and adjustment prior to an event, the interview specifically addresses parental perception of current PTSD symptoms in the child.

Childhood PTSD Reaction Index

Frederick's (1985) Childhood PTSD Reaction Index is a 20-item questionnaire administered in an interview format. Patterned after DSM-III-R diagnostic criteria for PTSD, the items inquire about the child's specific reactions to the traumatic event. Degree-of-severity ratings range from very severe to doubtful.

Children's PTSD Inventory

The Children's PTSD Inventory is constructed on the basis of the DSM-III-R criteria for the PTSD syndrome. It can be used to identify acute PTSD using children's self-report (Saigh, 1989).

State-Trait Anxiety Index for Children (STAIC)

The STAIC (Spielberger, Edwards, Montuori, Lushene, & Platzek, 1971) consists of two 20-item self-report questionnaires for primary-grade children measuring state (A-state) and trait (A-trait) anxiety. The child's response set for the A-state scale is in terms of how he or she feels at that moment; for example, the child is asked to choose among the responses: *very calm, calm,* or *not calm* to complete the statement "I feel..." For the A-trait measure, the child's response set is in terms of how he or she generally feels.

Crisis Behavior Rating Scale (CBRS)

The CBRS is a 12-item rating scale to be completed by teachers. Items list behaviors that children might show in crisis situations, such as crying, arguing, or seeking attention. Teachers rate the frequency of occurrence of each behavior for the preceding 2 weeks on a 4-point scale. High scores indicate more acute, recent symptoms (Felner, Norton, Cowen, & Farber, 1981).

Children's Impact of Traumatic Events Scale Revised (CITES-R)

The CITES-R was developed by Vicky Wolfe and Carole Gentile at the University of Western Ontario to assess the effect of sexual abuse from the child's perspective. The 77-item CITES-R contains 10 scales that tap 4 dimensions: PTSD (intrusive thoughts, avoidance, hyperarousal, and sexual anxiety); Social Reactions (negative reactions from others and social support); Abuse Attribution (self-blame and guilt, empowerment, vulnerability, and dangerous world); and Eroticism.

Impact of Events Scale

This 15-item scale was developed by Horowitz, Wilner, and Alvarez (1979) to measure the two most characteristic aspects of PTSD, namely the strength of unpleasant, intrusive thoughts and the energy spent in trying to block them out of consciousness (avoidance). It is currently the most widely used instrument in the study of PTSD in adults. In recent years, it has been found suitable for use with traumatized children ages 8 to 16 years (Yule & Williams, 1990).

Play and Drawing Assessment

Since children tend to cling and to suppress anxiety after a trauma, it is often difficult to assess symptoms by self-report or parent-teacher questionnaires. Play and drawings have been found to be extremely helpful in assessing psychic trauma in children. The child's unconscious preoccupations and anxiety often emerge in play and drawings. In a play/ drawing assessment, a child is asked to play with toys that are similar to the trauma and/ or to draw a picture of the trauma and tell a story about it. Later, the child may be requested to play out or draw pictures of the worst part of the trauma as well as of wish-fulfilling fantasies related to the event. Such ongoing assessment in the playroom will often yield valuable clues as to how well the child is controlling trauma-related cognition, emotions, and behaviors. Evidence for intrusive symptoms includes drawings and repetitive play involving traumatic themes. Avoidance responses can be identified when the children are unable to become involved in activities that remind them of the trauma and may be inferred when superficial happy themes predominate in a traumatized child (Lipovsky, 1991).

Curative Powers of Abreactive Play

It is well known that adults naturally try to get over the shock of unpleasant experience by telling and retelling the minute details of the stressful event (e.g., an operation) to anyone who will listen. The concept of *abreaction* is based on the strong inner drive in all human beings to recreate their experiences in order to assimilate them. After a passive helpless experience of trauma, children have a compelling need to actively rework the dramatic elements of the trauma in their play. Adults like to talk out their stressful experiences, while young children are prone to play out these experiences. Coping strategies that confront rather then avoid the event seem to be most effective in resolving trauma symptoms.

Abreaction, a concept used by Sigmund Freud (1920) to help explain how trauma victims resolve the experience, is a mental process in which repressed memories are brought to consciousness and relived with appropriate release of affect. At the turn of the century, Josef Breuer observed that clients who were able to recall the origins of their symptoms and to give free reign to the expression of the accompanying emotions were relieved by this process and generally showed improvement.

In applying the concept of abreaction to children, Freud (1920) noted that play offers young children a unique opportunity to work through traumatic events. He stated that, in their play, children repeat everything that has made a great impression on them in real life and that, in so doing, they abreact the strength of these impressions and make themselves master of the situations. Active reenactment of the trauma in play, as opposed to the passively experienced real-life event, facilitates the mastery feeling. According to Erik Erikson (1950), to play it out is the most natural self-therapeutic process childhood offers. The child uses play to come to terms with defeats, sufferings, and traumas.

Abreaction is greatly facilitated through the act of repetition. Freud was the first to discuss the "repetition compulsion" that reflects the need to relive again and again a painful memory. Freud (1914, 1958) maintained that children unconsciously recreate in their play, situations related to the original traumatic event and that the frequency of these reenactments is related to the intensity of the trauma. Every new repetition in play seems to weaken the negative affect associated with the trauma and strengthens a sense of mastery of the event in the child.

Ekstein (1966) also discussed the concept of abreaction and stated it is an active process by which children resolve passively experienced traumatic events of the real world by actively repeating them in the microcosmic play world. He asserted that several therapeutic elements are at work in the play process, namely, the miniaturization of experiences by use of the small play objects, the active control and domination of events that are possible in play, and the piecemeal assimilation of a traumatic event by repetitiously playing out that event.

Other eminent theorists have emphasized the value of abreactive play for children. According to Erikson (1950), children in play reconstruct, reenact, and reinvent their stressful experiences in order to understand them, assimilate their reality, and achieve mastery over them. Through play, children can adopt roles that were not part of real experiences, transform passivity into activity, and, thus, master difficult life situations.

Piaget (1962) maintained that play is assimilative rather than accommodative; that is, play enables the child to relive past experiences and allows for the satisfaction of the ego rather than for its subordination to reality. Piaget observed that, in play, children work through and, thus, assimilate and gain control over future or past stresses. In play, children reenact traumatic events in an effort to gradually mentally digest and gain mastery over them. This is a slow healing process by repetition.

Piaget (1962) identified two categories of play that serve this healing function: compensatory combinations and liquidating combinations. *Compensatory combinations* are play behaviors that distort reality to fit the child's desire and transform a negative emotional experience so as to make it more pleasant (e.g., child adopts a hero role in reenacting the trauma in play). *Liquidating combinations* are play behaviors designed to neutralize and derive pleasure from strong emotions elicited by trauma, (e.g., child pummels a baby doll to release angry feelings).

Apart from these compensatory and liquidating functions, play facilitates abreaction by giving children needed distance from the actual trauma so that they can express their inner feelings and still feel safe. The following properties of play allow the necessary sense of distance from the traumatic event:

Symbolization. The child can use a toy snake to represent a feared father figure.

"As If" Quality. The pretend quality of play permits children to act out events as if they are not real life.

Projection. Children can project their angry feelings onto the puppets who can then safely act out these feelings.

Displacement. Instead of exposing negative feelings toward their siblings, children can displace these feelings onto dolls.

Self Initiated Abreactive Play

There is abundant evidence that children use play activities to adaptively work out their fears and anxieties about a specific traumatic event, with little or no assistance from others. When they engage in this play, they tend to become deeply engrossed and emotionally expressive (Saylor, Swenson, & Powell, 1992). Although pervasive and powerful, abreactive play in childhood often goes unnoticed by parents and professionals. Examples of self-initiated mastery play follow:

- After the death of a parent, preschoolers often seek relief from anxieties by throwing themselves into play activities. Their games of playing "dead" or "funeral" are efforts at gaining mastery or control over the real-life experience.
- A young girl endured a frightening ride to a hospital during which she feared that

ambulances and rescue teams arrived in a timely manner in disaster after disaster and took the injured to the hospital for treatment.

- A 3-year-old girl with ataxia repeatedly placed a doll on a chair and knocked it off. The child's medical history documented her balance problems and her frequent experience with being knocked over (Peller, 1978).

- In 1982, A PanAm plane crashed shortly after takeoff from New Orleans, killing 146 passengers and 8 people on the ground. Children who lived near the crash area exhibited reenactment play (fire setting and plane crashing) with siblings and others (Sugar, 1989).

- A preschool class observed a worker fall 20 feet from a school roof and sustain serious injury. He was given first aid on the spot and then taken to the hospital by ambulance. Quite upset by this accident, the children frequently and almost compulsively engaged in dramatic play related to the event. The dominant themes in their play were falling, injury and death, and ambulances and hospitals. After several weeks, the frequency of such play diminished, and the children no longer appeared bothered by the accident.

- Block et al. (1956) studied children's reactions to a tornado in Vicksburg, Mississippi. Even the children who did not show emotional disturbances immediately after the disaster were described as irritable, sensitive, and prone to repeatedly play out a tornado game.

- Erikson (1950) described an episode involving a 4-year-old boy shortly after the child had an operation. Using simple play materials, the child reduced his traumatic reaction by playing out the role of the doctor. In fantasy, he became master of the situation that in reality had made him a helpless victim.

- A 13-year-old girl who discovered her father shot dead after a robbery played at sawing a robber's body apart very slowly, starting at his feet, so he could feel the pain and see himself bleed to death as she saw her beloved father (Pynoos & Nader, 1987).

- After the San Francisco earthquake in 1989, a group of preschoolers at a school playground played earthquake by having one child be "it" and shout "Earthquake!" and having all the other players duck and take cover. The last player to duck and take cover became "it" for the next round of play.

- Also, in 1989, children at the Cleveland Elementary school in Stockton, California, experienced a trauma in which Patrick Purdy used a semiautomatic assault rifle to shoot first- and second-graders on the playground. After the 7-minute attack, 5 children lay dying, while a teacher and 29 more children were wounded. Purdy then turned the gun and shot himself in the head. The children's safe haven had become a killing field. After the trauma, the children started playing the game "Purdy." In the game, Purdy shot schoolchildren, but the children often changed the ending so the Purdy is killed by them.

- Following a sniper attack at her school, a girl played the role of a nurse who aided the victims. By playing such an active role in the play, she experienced a sense of relief from anxiety.

- After hurricane Hugo devastated Charleston, South Carolina, in 1989, parents reported their young children would play "Hurricane" over and over until they felt safe. They would make noises like a loud wind while toppling play houses and then would pretend to be working repairing the homes. After this play, the parents noted that the children seemed calmer "as if they had let go of something" (Saylor, et al, 1992, p. 145.)

- In *War and Children*, Freud and Burlingham (1944) contrasted adult reactions with the way children expressed their reactions to the bombing of London. Following an air raid, adults told and retold their feelings of terror. Children who suffered through the same traumatic experience almost never talked about it. Their fearful reactions were expressed through their play. The children constructed houses out of blocks and dropped bombs on them. Buildings were destroyed, sirens wailed, and people were killed and injured. These play reenactments continued for several weeks.

Typically, children's spontaneous mastery play includes changes that represent wish-fulfilling fantasies or that give new meaning to the event. James (1989) noted that children often cope with life's stresses by playing the role of a hero who has supernatural strength and magic powers. By role playing, the child can overcome anxieties and resolve conflicts. In play, the child can surmount feelings of helplessness, deprivation, and dependency by playing the role of a powerful superhero, wealthy king, or domineering general.

For children with mild stress reactions to a trauma, these self-initiated play re-enactments can prove curative. They offer a child both a sense of active control over the trauma and piecemeal assimilation of it. However, children with moderate to intense reactions to the trauma will likely need to receive play therapy because they need external aid in resolving such symptoms as retraumatizing play, play disruption, and dissociation.

Retraumatizing Play

Reenactment of a trauma in play can either lead to mastery or a retraumatizing experience. Retraumatizing play involves the repetitive and compulsive reenactment in play of episodes of the trauma or the repetition in play of traumatic themes. Terr (1981) observed that retraumatizing play fails to provide resolution for the child and creates rather than relieves anxiety. It tends to retraumatize the child by stirring up feelings of helplessness and terror. Retraumatizing play can be repeated endlessly without relief of anxiety related to the event. Children who play this way are fixated on the trauma and cannot move forward on their own to resolve it (Green, 1983).

There is a driven quality to retraumatizing play. The child is not in control of the play but seems driven by a compulsion to play in a way that produces the same terrifying outcome. Such play is very literal, devoid of enjoyment or variety, and lacks freedom of expression. This play reflects a compulsion for traumatized children to repeat the repressed experience. There is a need on the part of the psyche to force repressed memories into consciousness and to relive them (Chu, 1991). Otto Fenichel (1945) described traumatic repetitions as attempts at belated mastery that fail so that the child is placed again and again in the role of victim.

Terr (1983) observed that children involved in the Chowchilla bus kidnapping often engaged in secret repetitive play centered on their experience of this incident. They continued this play for years without managing to obtain a sense of mastery. In these cases, the therapist must be an active mediator in the play reenactment to produce a sense of control and mastery in the child.

The cycle of retraumatizing play must be broken by active intervention from a therapist who directs the trauma play so as to create a sense of mastery. Reenactment of a trauma can become mastery rather than retraumatizing play when the child does the following:

1. Feels in control of the outcome of the play.
2. Plays out a satisfactory ending to the play.
3. Feels free to express and release negative affect.
4. Exhibits a cognitive reappraisal of the event.

Play Disruption

Sometimes a child feels so threatened that she or he will not attempt to play out a trauma reenactment; or sometimes the child's level of anxiety becomes so unbearable that she or he will abruptly stop playing. This play disruption signals a breakdown in the child's defenses and an inability to express, even indirectly in symbolic play, thoughts and feelings related to the trauma (Ekstein, 1966). Erik Erikson (1950) was the first to describe the phenomenon of "play disruption" in children. He defined such highly anxious behavior as follows:

> This phenomenon of transference in the playing child, as well in the verbalizing adult, marks the point where simple measures fail — namely, when an emotion becomes so intense that it defeats playfulness, forcing an immediate discharge into the play and into the relationship with the play observer. The failure is characterized by what is to be described here as play disruption — i.e., the sudden and complete or diffused and slowly spreading inability to play. (p. 357)

To avoid disruption, the therapist needs to structure the play so that the child plays out only a part of the trauma and, thus, releases only a small amount of repressed feelings. The danger of play disruption is that the fearfulness can be so overpowering that it confirms for the child the danger of expressing buried feelings. This leads to a strengthening of defenses (Stachey, 1934). With play disruption, the therapist should not try to storm or to sneak through the child's defenses, but should rather launch a prolonged siege to gradually weaken the defenses (Reich, 1960).

Dissociation

As previously indicated, children who experience Type II trauma often dissociate from the traumatic events. Dissociation involves psychological detachment from one's surroundings and a distancing of self from situations, thoughts, or emotions. It also alters perceptions of time and identity, often resulting in memory gaps. The child spaces out, which allows him or her to mentally escape the memory of the traumatic event.

In a widely publicized court case that ended in 1991 with a conviction, a 28-year-old woman claimed she suddenly remembered witnessing her father murder one of her playmates 20 years earlier. The woman, who said she was repeatedly raped by her father as a child, recalled the murder when she looked into her own daughter's eyes and realized that they resembled the murder victim's eyes. The memory surfaced after the father made sexual advances to the woman's daughter.

Many adult survivors of child abuse do not remember the abuse until well into adulthood. With these late presenters, buried memories can be triggered by almost any-thing, and, once they come flooding back, there is not much the victim can do to suppress them. The defenses of denial and dissociation do not work anymore.

In treating dissociation, Gil (1991) recommends explaining to the child that sometimes when things are scary, people space out and that this is all right but there are likely to be better ways to cope. It is usually better to remember the trauma and express one's thoughts and feelings toward the event in play. Therapy for dissociative reactions often involves a long and difficult course.

PROCEDURE

Historical Roots of Mastery Play Therapy

The usual adult reaction to children of trauma is to deny or minimize the impact of an event that would overpower most people. Parents and teachers are prone to help the child bury all memory of the event. Often, the child's attempts to play out or talk about the incident are discouraged. Some adults do this because they believe that the less attention paid to the event, the quicker the child's upset will abate. Others want to avoid the topic to prevent emotional upset in the child or because they feel guilty over not protecting the child from stress. Still others find recall of the event too painful for them to possibly bear. Because of these reasons, most childhood victims of psychic trauma do not receive treatment. There is, however, an emerging consensus among child therapists that it is dangerous to leave the children unsupported in their efforts to master the experience of trauma. Following a psychic trauma, a child may appear to get better without professional intervention when in fact what is happening is that coping defenses are being built up while the underlying trauma reactions are affecting the child's personality and character. Thus, Terr (1991) concluded that "untreated, all but the mildest of childhood traumas last for years" (p. 14).

Indeed, most Holocaust survivors who have tried sealing off memories of the awful experience report that they think of it every day and that it adversely affects their emotional well-being even 50 years later.

Rather than shielding children from the painful memories of the trauma, adults should help them to confront these thoughts and feelings. This confronting process is essential if psychic integration and mastery of the trauma are to occur. Quick therapeutic intervention is needed for children of trauma in order to reduce the immediate distress and to prevent long-term psychological disturbance. If children experiencing psychic trauma do not receive therapeutic intervention, Galante and Foa (1986) report that three-quarters of the children will still exhibit symptoms 2 years after the traumatizing event. Few young children (ages 2 to 10) will be able to sit and talk directly about their traumatic experiences, even at a superficial level. As a result, play therapy is likely to be the treatment of choice for these children.

Release Therapy

Levy (1938) developed a play technique called *release therapy* to help children adjust to stress or trauma. In this structured play therapy approach, the therapist uses toys and play materials to create a situation containing many of the elements of the recent trauma experienced by the child. The presentation of play objects similar to those in the traumatic event generally leads to replication and reenactment of the trauma, thus avoiding hours of diffuse, unproductive play activity. The therapist is generally permissive, but may assist with some simple interpretations.

To be effective, release play therapy necessitates direct handling of the play objects by the child, the child's becoming so absorbed that he or she becomes oblivious to the surroundings, and playing out fears fully by repetition of the play scene. According to Levy (1938), the therapist must gauge the right moment to introduce the experience and the amount of dilution of the experience in order not to exceed the child's tolerance level. Pynoos and Nader (1987) found that children's tolerance levels for directly reenacting traumas in play are high, especially within the first 3 months after the traumatic event.

In selecting cases suitable for release therapy, Levy (1938), used the following criteria:

1. The child should be between 2 and 10 years of age.
2. There should be a definite reaction pattern triggered by a specific stressor (e.g., a frightening experience, birth of a sibling, death of a parent).
3. The problem should not be long-standing.
4. The traumatic experience should be in the past, that is, not continuing at the time of referral.
5. The child should be from a relatively normal family situation.

If these five conditions were present, Levy believed there was little need to involve parents in the therapy other than for information about the trauma and the child's reaction.

Levy (1938) contended that children between the ages of 2 and 5 do not have to know the nature of their difficulties or of their relationship to the therapist in order to improve. He stated that emotional release and a positive therapeutic relationship are the two basic therapeutic elements leading to resolution of the trauma. If a child seemed relieved when sessions ended, Levy regarded it as a sign of progress.

MacLean (1977) described a release-play-therapy case involving a 4-year-old boy who had been mauled by a leopard in a pet shop. His symptoms encompassed sleep disturbances, clinging, fearful behaviors, and separation anxiety. During 24 play sessions over an 8-month period, he reenacted the trauma during every session by using miniature play objects, including a toy leopard.

Solomon (1938), who advocated a more directive and active role for the therapist than Levy did, developed a technique called *Active Play Therapy*. He maintained that child therapists tend to be too passive and wait too long for things to happen with traumatized children. Solomon advocated three ways to move things along.

1. The therapist should be active and keep the conversation in the third person to provide anonymity and reduce defensiveness.

2. The therapist should actively play out the scene with the child, thus helping the child become less frightened because he has a partner to help him master the stress.

3. The therapist should actively direct the child's play, thus helping to uncover the child's inner fantasy life.

Anxiety generated by this active approach can be handled by introducing a therapist doll upon which the child can release his feelings.

Solomon (1938) also suggested developing children's sense of time by teaching them to differentiate fears over past trauma and future calamities from the reality of their current life situation. In addition, he would wait to establish a trusting relationship with a child before he attempted his direct and intrusive approach. At the end of a session, he would allow free play so the child's arousal level could diminish before leaving the playroom.

Trends in Mastery Play Therapy

In recent years, there has been a growing realization that successful therapy for trauma victims usually combines several therapeutic strategies. The prevailing treatment approach best fits an eclectic paradigm. A technical eclectic approach (Norcross & Prochaska, 1988) is often employed wherein there is a combination of therapeutic strategies and common factors without an attempt to integrate the theoretical foundations of the techniques.

Currently, child therapists are combining abreaction, cognitive reappraisal, a supportive relationship, and crisis-intervention principles in their play therapy approach to psychic trauma.

Crisis Intervention

A crisis-oriented intervention approach for children of Type-I psychic trauma seems warranted. This means therapy should be brief, focused, and directive. The crisis-intervention literature indicates that persons in crisis need immediate, active, and intensive therapy from a trained helper. It is generally believed that therapy for psychic trauma should occur relatively soon after the trauma (i.e., within the first 3 months) and that therapy should be relatively short (less than 15 sessions) and focused on helping the child master the troubling memory.

Crisis counselors report that most crises are resolved for better or worse within 6 to 8 weeks. Of course, if the client has personal and/or family problems as well as PTSD, longer term treatment will be required since a return to the pretrauma level of functioning will not suffice. Individual psychotherapy is likely to be the cornerstone of therapy, but group and family therapy as well as medication are often included as part of the intervention.

Abreaction

Sigmund Freud's (1920) abreaction approach remains the key strategy in mastery play therapy. According to Freud, the posttraumatic anxiety can only be resolved if the therapist is able to get the child to relive the trauma with appropriate release of effect. One must face the painful event and slowly assimilate it. According to Stiles et al. (1991), assimilation of problematic experiences follows a predictable series of stages. Initially, the client wards off thoughts and feelings associated with the trauma; then these unwanted thoughts enter into vague awareness, which leads to problem statement/clarification, then understanding/insight, which in turn contributes to application/working through; and finally the thoughts are mastered and integrated into a cognitive schema.

According to the assimilation model, children need to gradually assimilate a traumatic experience into a schema (frame of reference, narrative, metaphor, script) that is developed during therapy. A child's schema gradually changes in therapy to accommodate the traumatic experience so as to take it in—integrate, explain, and incorporate it into the mind's system of associations. This model implies that there is no one best way for a child to structure the experience as long as the schema relieves the distress.

In abreaction, the child has to do the opposite of what he or she wants to do, namely avoid processing the trauma. Avoidance can take place on a number of levels: (a) avoidance of knowledge of the event (amnesia), (b) avoidance of affect (numbing), (c) avoidance of behavior (phobic responses), and (d) avoidance of any communication about the event. The problem with an avoiding defense is that one cannot process the traumatic experience unless one comes to grips with it. The child must switch from passive avoidance to active confrontation.

A common principle for the treatment of avoidance has emerged across schools of psychotherapy: the principle of exposure. One needs to confront and face up to the disturbing event. Many studies support the efficacy of exposure techniques (Foa & Kozak, 1986). In effective exposure therapy, the child initially shows anxiety responses to the trauma stimulus, and these reactions gradually decrease (habituate) within a single session and over repeated sessions.

The best way to expose a young child to traumatic memories is through structured play. In the playroom, the therapist can present the child with miniature play objects representing the trauma scene and can encourage the child to play out the trauma. For children to benefit from play reenactment of past traumas, a number of therapeutic processes must be present. The curative processes of abreactive play therapy include: power and control, insight, cognitive reappraisal, emotional release, repetition, and social support.

Power and Control

In marked contrast with the sense of helplessness children experience during a disaster, play affords them a strong sense of power and control. The child towers over the play materials and determines what and how to play during the therapy session. Eventually, this competing response (power) helps overcome the child's feelings of insecurity and vulnerability.

Wish fulfillment in play is one aspect of power and control. Preschoolers may play out a scene in which a superhero comes to the child's rescue. Older elementary school children tend to prefer to play out more realistic solutions to the trauma, for example, one's father shooting the vicious dog or oneself comforting wounded classmates during a sniper attack (Pynoos, Frederick, & Nader, 1987). To this end, the therapist should ask the child to play out what he or she would have liked to have happened during the trauma; for example, the therapist might suggest, "I imagine you wished . . ." and then help the child play out the different ending. A therapist might suggest that a young child reenact the trauma in play with himself or herself this time playing the role of an invincible person who is master of the event. Thus, the therapist might initiate a play session by giving the following direction (James, 1989):

> Today you are going to direct a puppet show about a girl who went to the hospital when she was very sick. A wonderful thing happened when she got to the hospital: She found she was just like She-Ra, Princess of Power, and she was able to tell everyone in the hospital what to do. You be the girl, what puppet do you want me to be?

Insight

Once children reenact the traumatic event through play, they are more likely to directly acknowledge their own feelings, ideas, and behaviors about the real trauma. To facilitate this, a helpful technique is interpretation; for example, a therapist might ask a child, "I wonder if you ever felt you were going to die during the hurricane, like this baby doll just did?" This opens the door for children to speak openly about their past reactions to the trauma and to connect present behaviors with it.

Interpretations help children acknowledge and accept the reality of the trauma and their response to it. According to Horowitz and Zelber (1983), the child must integrate the experience of a traumatic event into a new model of the world that includes a sense of reality about what happened. They stated that one should help the child accept as real what tends to be experienced as unreal. This moves a child from a state of denial toward actively dealing with the trauma and its pain.

Emotional Release

After a trauma, children may defend against overwhelming feelings by numbing themselves to all emotions. Although this blunts the emotional pain, it leads to other problems. Pennebaker (1985), for example, noted that the inhibition of the expression of feelings about stressful events often leads to psychosomatic disease. Emotional expression is clearly preferable to blunting. According to Nichols and Efran (1985), catharsis involves completing a previously inhibited or interrupted emotional reaction. The emotional expression is the one that would have occurred as a natural reaction to the experience had that expression not been thwarted. Tears or angry outbursts are usually involved in the cathartic expression. Therapists need to explicitly encourage children to express the feelings they would have liked to express during the trauma but did not. Children also need to express blocked actions, not just feelings.

Reenactment play with no emotional expression by the child will not be effective. Similarly, adults who fail to express their thoughts and feelings about a traumatic experience have been found in a number of studies to be more likely to experience physical illness and subjective distress (Pennebaker, 1989). Two possible reasons for this finding are (a) that actual inhibition of one's thoughts, feelings, and behaviors requires psychological work and (b) that inhibition prevents the person from processing the event fully and, thus, from understanding and assimilating it.

Cognitive Reappraisal

There is growing recognition that traumatized children must not only release repressed emotions about the event but must also change dysfunctional thoughts and beliefs. Cognitive restructuring requires exploring the child's belief systems and cognitive misinterpretations and offering the child alternative cognitions that are more adaptive.

With regard to a traumatic event, children are prone to develop confusion and distortion that can be corrected with clarification and explanation. Victims of a trauma tend to make a "formulation" of the trauma experience in an attempt to understand it. Often, the child's cognitive appraisal of the event is an oversimplification or generalization; for example, "Every time there is a thunderstorm, lightning is likely to strike the house and kill us" or "All dogs are vicious and apt to bite" or "I'm responsible for the death of my father." Play gives the therapist an opportunity to correct cognitive distortion. Thus, a therapist might state, "It is very unlikely that lightning will harm your house during future thunderstorms."

Also children with PTSD often need help from the therapist to obtain a more positive outlook on the way they handled the trauma experience. Reframing involves offering children a different perspective for viewing their response to the trauma. Reframing often involves the therapist attributing positive qualities to the child or the experience. In addition, the therapist can help a child problem solve how to prevent or cope with such a trauma in the future. In this case, the child may feel a greater sense of power and control over his environment.

Repetition

Abreaction involves integrating the terrifying event a little at a time. A child may repetitively play out a particular aspect of the trauma until a sense of mastery and control is achieved. In later play sessions, different distressing details of the trauma are likely to be emphasized until, piecemeal, the event is brought into complete awareness and the reality of it accepted and integrated into the psyche.

There is a slow working-through process by repetition. As more and more pieces of the traumatic memory are integrated into the self, defense mechanisms are needed less and intrusive symptoms disappear. Unless the trauma is slowly processed and assimilated, the unconscious is likely to bring the event back into awareness at some time.

Supportive Relationship

A trusting relationship with a therapist is needed to help a child feel safe enough to reenact the trauma in play. The child often needs a therapist who is an active participant in the child's fantasy play and who models not becoming fearful or overwhelmed by play enactments. It is a tremendous relief for a child to have a therapist act as an alter ego while he reexperiences the trauma in play.

Numerous studies have indicated that social support lowers the risk of psychological disorders in individuals involved in severely stressful experiences (Caplan, 1981). Social support helps a child to allow painful thoughts and feelings to emerge, despite the psychic pain involve. The therapist assuages the child's pain by expressing concern, empathy, acceptance, and understanding.

In regard to the importance of an understanding listener, Figley (1992) stated, "When you look across the landscape of trauma, from the Holocaust through Hurricane Andrew and on down, talking it over helps you see that your reactions, no matter how extreme at the moment, were normal or understandable given what happened.

Clinical Issues

Among the many clinical issues that must be addressed in mastery play therapy are countertransference, inappropriate cases, booster sessions, and termination. Countertransference issues are common in treating traumatized children and include overidentification with the helplessness of the child and the unfairness of the circumstances, denial, excessive distancing, and "vicarious traumatization." Therapists must seek to remain sympathetic, empathic, and objective throughout the therapy, despite the difficulty of doing so. Therapists should continually monitor these common reactions and seek supervision to ensure that their personal feelings do not interfere with therapy.

In regard to case selection, mastery play therapy seems inappropriate for child trauma cases who are severely depressed, persistently resist play reenactment, show no negative affect in play reenactment, exhibit no diminution of fear reaction over the course of an exposure play session, exhibit overvalued ideation (i.e., believe their fears are realistic), or have a history of heart disease.

As children of trauma mature, they will likely need to periodically rework their understanding of the trauma to fit their current level of cognitive development. This means booster sessions must be held when the youths face different developmental tasks (e.g., industriousness, identity, intimacy).

At what point should a therapist consider a child's trauma reactions resolved? According to Caplan (1981), the therapist will know when mastery play has been successful when two considerations are met:

1. The mastery play reduces to tolerable limits physiological and psychological manifestations of emotional arousal during and shortly after the stressful event.

2. The mastery play mobilizes the child's coping resources so that he or she can reduce the threat and find substitute sources of gratification for what was lost in the trauma.

To assess whether emotional processing is complete during or following therapy, Rachman (1980) suggested the use of "test probes," that is, the presentation of relevant trauma stimuli in play or conversation in an attempt to evoke an emotional reaction. If a strong negative response is elicited, it indicates that emotional processing has not been successfully completed and further sessions are needed before termination.

CASE ILLUSTRATIONS OF MASTERY PLAY THERAPY

Case 1. Wallick (1979) treated a toddler with posthospital fearfulness. Hospitalized for major chest surgery, 20-month-old Sally was given no preparation for or subsequent explanations of the experience or the resulting scar. After the hospitalization, she changed from a happy, outgoing, affectionate toddler to a withdrawn child who was excessively fearful of doctors, of strangers, of noise, and of faces on television. Although her parents were very nurturing, Sally continued to cry hysterically and tremble when in contact with doctors. Since she needed frequent medical visits, Sally was referred for therapy 4 months after hospitalization to reduce her fears of doctors and hospitals.

After three rapport-building sessions, Sally's therapist gave her weekly release-play-therapy sessions. She was encouraged to play with the following: a doll with an adhesive bandage on its chest, "doctor" equipment for pretend play, and books about going to the doctor. Initially, Sally was anxious and resistant. The therapist accepted and verbalized her feelings, which resulted in her anxiety gradually lessening over the next month. Later, in vivo desensitization sessions were scheduled in which the therapist accompanied her on visits to the periodontist's office. Since a ride on the elevator triggered terrifying memories of her hospital stay, Sally was given play sessions in which "mother" and "therapist" dolls rode an elevator constructed of blocks. Soon they were joined by the "little girl" doll on elevator rides that had happy endings. Sally added variations on the play theme, which soon involved a "daddy" doll as well.

Outdoors, an "elevator game" was played with a basketball, a 5-foot-high basketball goal, and an imaginary elevator button. Sally pressed the button and made sounds suggestive of an elevator when lifted to the goal by her therapist.

After 4 weeks of elevator play, along with doctor play with a bandaged doll, Sally and her therapist returned for a second visit to her periodontist. This time, Sally rode the elevator without fear. She did ask to be held by her therapist during the ride up but laughed with animation as she pushed the elevator buttons for the eight floors. On the ride down, she stood alone in the elevator and counted aloud as the floor numbers lit up. On her next visit, she allowed her doll to sit in the periodontist's chair as it went up and down. Then, while sitting on her therapist's lap, she rode up and down on the chair and let the dentist examine her teeth. At the next visit, she eagerly rode the elevator without fear and sat alone in the dental chair. After 4 months of therapy, she was able to visit her pediatrician and pediatric surgeon without fear. As the initial fears were overcome, her fears of noises and strangers also disappeared. The desensitization of her fear by play and in vivo exposure was maintained over 2-year follow-up sessions.

Case 2. Galante and Foa (1986) investigated the effects of a severe earthquake on Italian children. Over 4,000 people died as a result of the quake on November 23, 1980, and tens of thousands lost their homes. The villages were relatively isolated, and several days passed before help could be mobilized. Galante and Foa studied the psychic trauma that these children experienced and described treatment interventions. For 1 year, play therapy interventions to encourage expression of thoughts and feelings about the disaster were implemented with children in the first through fourth grades of a selected village (considered to have the greatest number of at-risk children). The play sessions began with children drawing while listening to stories about earthquakes and stories about children being afraid to speak openly about their fears. Middle and later sessions focused on role-playing the disaster with a particular emphasis on coping skills. Open discussion was encouraged after all sessions.

At first, the children's drawings were filled with threatening images, even though they did not actually draw the earthquake or the damage to their village. Soon however, some children began playing out scenes related to their losses from the quake. In playing the "earthquake game," they would simulate an earthquake by shaking a table, a simulation of the rumble of the earthquake. After they reenacted the quake that destroyed the village and killed so many people, the children would reconstruct the village in their play. Thus, they played out a two-step process of destruction and reconstruction.

Over the course of the seven group sessions, the frequency of reenactment of earthquake stories in the play declined, and fear of recurrence and other fears declined dramatically after the fourth session. The children evidenced a strong need for the therapy sessions and often had to be asked to leave at the end of each session. They clearly wanted to work through feelings that were not expressed in routine retelling of earthquake stories. The concrete reenactment of the quake in the play seemed to release more unconscious images and feelings than was possible in verbal exchanges. Because this was a widespread trauma, group play sessions seemed to work best. In this approach, group therapeutic factors were added to the curative powers of play.

Case 3. In another study of psychic trauma in children, Rigamer (1986) described the psychological reactions of American children in Afghanistan and Pakistan to the assassination of an American ambassador in 1978 and the subsequent trauma related to this event. The children's parents had requested professional help in dealing with their children's responses to the crisis. Rigamer found that the parents were denying or minimizing the children's reactions to the event. They were trying to quiet the children and make light of the situation, and that did not reassure the children. Teachers also needed encouragement to assist the children in voicing their fears and teaching them more effective ways to cope.

Rigamer (1986) stated that young children who were not very verbal were helped to express their anxieties through drawings and play. The author concluded that these activities were necessary to restore the children's emotional balance. It is apparent from Rigamer's discussion that parents and teachers need to be taught how to effectively implement these play techniques in crisis situations.

Case 4. Seroka, Knapp, Knight, Silmon, and Starbuck (1986) pointed out the differences between the postdisaster treatment needs of younger children and those of older children. These researchers conducted a study examining community reactions following a tornado in Marion, Illinois (May 29, 1982). While primary interventions for junior and senior high school groups centered around discussion of the disaster, elementary level interventions included art therapy, role-playing, and storytelling. Preschool interventions also focused on play materials such as a tornado coloring book and a tornado storybook. Parents were provided with information to assist them in handling and facilitating their children's reactions.

Case 5. On June 11, 1985, a train collided with the first of four school buses that were transporting a group of seventh graders on a field trip in Petach Tikva, Israel (Klingman, 1987). There were 22 deaths and 15 critical injuries. Students in the other three buses watched as the crash occurred. After the initial emergency stages of intervention were set in place, mental health professionals attempted to determine which individuals were most at risk for psychological disturbance. Attention was then given to possible interventions for these individuals. While class discussions and verbalization of feelings related to the accident were encouraged for all students, some refused to participate by withholding speech. Klingman reports that these children were referred to the "creativity room," where they were encouraged to draw, make collages, and write poems as an alternative mode of expression of thoughts and feelings related to the crash. A year later, Toubiana, Milgram, Strich, and Edelstein (1988) published an article discussing the interventions used in this same crisis. They presented a theoretical model for coping with adversity that closely resembles that used with soldiers suffering from PTSD reactions. They state that "In both cases, treatment is short-term, oriented to the present anguish and to heroic coping behaviors, encouraging the ventilation of feelings, especially depression or anger, and permitting abreaction of emotions associated with the stressful experience" (p. 234).

Case 6. Sugar (1988) presented a case report of a 4 1/2-year-old child who witnessed the crash of PanAm Flight 759 in New Orleans on July 9, 1982. The plane went down approximately 75 feet from the child's home. The child was given access to toys related to the crash and was allowed to choose whatever he desired to play with in each session. Initially, he played with cars and airplanes and showed the therapist how the crash occurred. Sugar noted that the boy was obsessively repetitive about playing out the crash and his anxiety seemed to increase until the 20th session. At this point, the child seemed to have "massive abreaction" about the crash and repeated the events in painstaking detail. One month later, he experienced another massive abreaction, and then his play began to become less aggressive and less anxious. Sessions 30 to 34 were described as filled with much less anxiety. The child was still playing with airplanes at termination, but now his airplanes managed to avoid crashing — indicating that a sense of mastery and trust had been reestablished.

Lenore Terr (1989) has also found play therapy to be a particularly useful intervention with families of young children who have experienced trauma. "If the entire family has gone through a traumatic experience together, the members will most likely benefit from being brought together for ventilation, abreaction, and interpretation. The symbolic elaborations with which the separate family members eventually portray their own ordeal may come to light when standard family-therapy techniques are combined with some play, drawing, or poetry making" (p. 18).

Terr (1983) also described "corrective denouement" play in which the therapist assists the child in a cognitive restructuring of his or her thoughts related to the traumatic situation. The child is helped to understand that there was nothing he or she could have done to keep the disaster from happening because he or she did not know how: the child is also helped to discover coping skills that could be used in the future to deal with a similar crisis. Terr has found this form of play therapy to relieve the child's anxieties and guilt feelings.

SUMMARY AND CONCLUSION

Adjusting to traumatic events is difficult for everyone, especially children. Traditionally, adults have tended to deny or minimize the psychological impact of traumatic events on children and shielded them from painful recollections. Almost all children will exhibit posttrauma reactions involving signs of anxieties, regression, and dependency. Responding to an inner need to reenact the traumatic event so as to assimilate it, children will naturally engage in play behaviors related to the recent trauma. This repetitive replaying of stressful events has been termed the most natural self-curative process in childhood. For mild cases of psychic trauma, playful reenactment of a recent event can facilitate a sense of mastery and amelioration of symptoms. However, when a Type I trauma is moderate to severe in intensity and/or if there are aggravating personal and family difficulties, children are likely to need therapeutic intervention in the form of mastery play therapy.

Mastery play therapy seems to be the treatment of choice for young children with PTSD. The mastery-play-therapy approach should be comprehensive and utilize such strategies as crisis intervention, abreaction, affective expression, exposure techniques, cognitive reappraisal, and social support. Mastery play therapy is an active, directive approach that follows a strategic eclectism model and is adaptable to individual, group, and family therapy modalities. Only by combining several therapeutic factors does this treatment become powerful enough to enable children to overcome the extraordinary emotional ordeal they experience in the wake of a trauma. It is expected that the next decade will witness a continued refinement of play therapy methods for assisting traumatized children.

REFERENCES

American Psychiatric Association. (1980). *Diagnostic and statistical manual of mental disorders* (3rd ed.) Washington, DC: Author.

American Psychiatric Association. (1987). *Diagnostic and statistical manual of mental disorders* (3rd ed., rev.). Washington, DC: Author.

Applebaum, D. R., & Burns, G. L. (1991). Unexpected childhood death: Post traumatic stress disorder in surviving siblings and parents. *Journal of Clinical Child Psychology, 20,* 114–120.

Block, D. A., Silber, E., & Perry, S. E. (1956). Some factors in the emotional reactions of children to disasters. *American Journal of Psychiatry, 133,* 416–422.

Caplan, G. (1981). Mastery of stress: Psychological aspects. *American Journal of Psychiatry, 138,* 413–420.

Chu, J. A. (1991). The repetition compulsion revisited: Reliving dissociated trauma. *Psychotherapy, 28,* 327–332.

Ekstein, R. (1966). *Children of time and space, of action and impulse.* New York: Appleton-Century-Crofts.

Erikson, E. H. (1950). *Childhood and society.* New York: Norton.

Eth, S., & Pynoos, R. S. (Eds.). (1985). *Post-traumatic stress disorders in children.* Washington, DC: American Psychiatric Press.

Felner, R. D., Norton, P. L., Cowen, E. L., & Farber, S. (1981). A prevention program for children experiencing life crisis. *Professional Psychology, 12,* 446–452.

Fenichel, O. (1945). *The psychoanalytic theory of neurosis.* New York: Norton.

Figley, C. (1992, October 6). *New York Times,* p. C2.

Foa, E. B., & Kozak, M. J. (1986). Emotional processing of fear: Exposure to corrective information. *Psychological Bulletin, 99,* 20–35.

Frederick, C. J. (1982). *Children of disaster.* Paper presented at the meeting of the International Association of Child and Adolescent Psychiatry in Dublin, Ireland.

Frederick, C. J. (1985). Children traumatized by catastrophic situations. In S. Eth & R. S. Pynoos (Eds.), *Post-traumatic stress disorder in children.* Washington, DC: American Psychiatric Press.

Freud, A., & Burlingham, D. (1944). *War and children.* New York: International Universities Press.

Freud, S. (1920). Beyond the pleasure principle. In J. Strachey (Ed.) (Vol. 18) *The standard edition of the complete psychological work of Sigmund Freud* (SE). London: Hogarth Press.

Freud, S. (1958). Remembering, repeating, and working through. In J. Strachey (Ed.), *The standard edition of the complete psychological work of Sigmund Freud.* (Vol. 12, pp. 147–156). London: Hogarth Press. (Original work published 1914)

Galante, R., & Foa, D. (1986). An epidemiological study of psychic trauma and treatment effectiveness for children after a natural disaster. *Journal of Child and Adolescent Psychiatry, 25,* 3357–3363.

Gil, E. (1991). *Healing power of play.* New York: Guilford Press.

Green, A. H. (1983). Dimension of psychological trauma in abused children. *Journal of Child Psychology, 22,* 231–237.

Horowitz, M. J., & Zelber, N. (1983). Regressive alteration of the self concept. *American Journal of Psychiatry, 140,* 284–289.

Horowitz, M. J., Wilner, N., & Alvarez, W. (1979). Impact of events scale: A measure of subjective stress. *Psychosomatic Medicine, 41,* 209–218.

James, B. (1989). *Treating traumatized children: new insights and creative interventions.* Lexington, MA: Lexington Books.

Janet, P. (1925). *Psychological healing* (Vols. 1, 2). New York: Macmillan. (Original work published in France, 1919).

Klingman, A. (1987). A school-base emergency crisis intervention in a mass school disaster. *Professional Psychology: Research and Practice, 18,* 604–612.

Levy, D. M. (1938). Release therapy in young children. *Psychiatry, 1,* 387–390.

Lipovsky, J. A. (1991). Posttraumatic stress disorder in children. *Community Health, 14,* 42–51.

MacLean, G. (1977). Psychic trauma and traumatic neurosis: Play therapy with a four-year-old boy. *Canadian Psychiatric Association Journal, 22,* 71–76.

Nader, K., Pynoos, R., Fairbanks, G., & Frederick, C. (1990). Children's PTSD reactions one year after a sniper attack at their school. *American Journal of Psychiatry, 147,* 1526–1530.

Nichols, M.P., & Efran, J. S. (1985). Catharsis in psychotherapy: A new perspective. *Psychotherapy*, *22*, 46–58.

Norcross, J. C., & Prochaska, J. O. (1988). A study of eclectic and integrative views revisited. *Professional Psychology: Research and Practice*, *19*, 170–174.

Peller, L. (1978). Theories of play and survey of development. In E. Plank (Ed.), *On development and education of young children*. New York: Philosophical Library.

Pennebaker, J. W. (1985). Traumatic experience and psychosomatic disease: Exploring the roles of behavior inhibition, obsession, and confiding. *Canadian Psychology*, *26*, 82–95.

Pennebaker, J. W. (1989). Confession, inhibition, and disease. *Advances in Experimental Social Psychology*, *22*, 211–244.

Piaget, J. (1962). *Play, dreams and imitation in childhood*. New York: Norton.

Pynoos, R. S., Frederick, C., & Nader, K. (1987). Life threat and post-traumatic stress in school-age children. *Archives of General Psychiatry*, *44*, 1057–1063.

Pynoos, R. S., & Nader, K. (1987). *The childhood post-traumatic stress disorder-parent's questionnaire*. Unpublished manuscript.

Rachman, S. (1980). Emotional processing. *Behavior Research and Therapy*, *18*, 51–60.

Reich, W. (1960). *Selected writings*. New York: Noonday Press.

Rigamer, E. R. (1987). Psychological management of children in national crisis. *Journal of the American Academy of Child Psychiatry*, *25*, 364–369.

Rothbaum, B. O., & Foa, E. B. (1991). Exposure treatment of PTSD concomitant with conversion mutism: A case study. *Behavior Therapy*, *22*, 449–456.

Saigh, P. A. (1989). The development and validation of the children's post-traumatic stress disorder inventory. *International Journal of Special Education*, *4*, 75–84.

Saylor, C. F., Swenson, C. C., & Powell, P. (1992). Hurricane Hugo blows down the broccoli: Preschoolers post-disaster play and adjustment. *Child Psychiatry and Human Development*, *22*, 139–149.

Seroka, C. M., Knapp, C., Knight, S., Silmon, C. R., & Starbuck, S. (1986). A comprehensive program for postdisaster counseling. *Social Casework*, *36*, 37–44.

Solomon, J. C. (1938). Active play therapy. *American Journal of Orthopsychiatry*, *8*, 479–498.

Spielberger, D. C., Edwards, C. D., Montuori, J., Lushene, R. D., & Platzek, D., (1971). *Manual for the State-Trait Anxiety Inventory for Children*. Palo Alto, CA: Consulting Psychologist Press.

Stachey, J. (1934). The nature of the therapeutic action for psychoanalysis. *International Journal of Psychoanalysis*, *15*, 117–126.

Stiles, W. B., Morrison, L. S., Haw, S. K., Harper, H., Shapiro, D. A., & Firth-Cozens, H. (1991). Longitudinal study of assimilation in exploratory psychotherapy. *Psychotherapy*, *28*, 195–206.

Sugar, M. (1988) A preschooler in a disaster. *American Journal of Psychotherapy*, *62*, 619–629.

Sugar, M. (1989). Children in a disaster: An overview. *Child Psychiatry and Human Development*, *19*, 163–179.

Terr, L. C. (1981). Psychic trauma in children: Observations following the Chowchilla school-bus kidnapping. *American Journal of Psychiatry*, *140*, 1543–1550.

Terr, L. C. (1983). Play therapy and psychic trauma: A preliminary report. In C. Schaefer & K. O'Connor (Eds.), *Handbook of play therapy*. New York: Wiley.

Terr, L. C. (1989). Family anxiety after traumatic events. *Journal of Clinical Psychiatry, 50* (Suppl.), 15–19.

Terr, L. C. (1991). Childhood traumas: An outline and overview. *American Journal of Psychiatry*, *148*, 10–20.

Toubiana, Y. H., Milgram, N. A., Strich, Y., & Edelstein, A. (1988). Crisis intervention in a school community disaster: Principles and practices. *Journal of Community Psychology*, *16*, 228–240.

Wallick, M. M. (1979). Desensitization therapy with a fearful two-year-old. *American Journal of Psychiatry, 136*, 1325–1326.

Yule, W., Udwin, O., & Murdoch, K. (1990). The "Jupiter" sinking: Effects on children's fears, depression and anxiety. *Journal of Child Psychology, Psychiatry, 31*, 1051–1061.

Yule, W., & Williams, R. A.. (1990). Post-traumatic stress reaction in children. *Journal of Traumatic Stress, 3*, 279–295.

CHAPTER 14

Play Diagnosis and Play Therapy with Child Victims of Incest

JAMSHID A. MARVASTI

INTRODUCTION

In this chapter, the author will demonstrate the technique and process of play therapy with sexually abused children and, in particular, with victims of father-daughter incest. *Father*, as it is used in this chapter, refers to any father figure, such as a stepfather, foster father, mother's boyfriend, or anyone who may be considered a paternal surrogate. Further, for the sake of simplicity, a female pronoun is used for the victim and a male pronoun is used for the offender. This is not meant to imply that there are never female offenders or male victims (Marvasti, 1986a). The treatment procedures are divided into four types for the sake of clarity. These procedures are explained in detail and are as follows: (a) play diagnosis, (b) forensic play interview, (c) play therapy, and (d) collateral therapy.

Clinical literature recognizes the likely development of psychopathology in victims of incest (Sgroi, 1982). The healing power of play therapy with mistreated children has been documented (Gil, 1991; Marvasti, 1989). In fact, play therapy is considered the treatment of choice for maltreated children. The play therapy technique described in this chapter may be used with any child, male or female, who is the victim of incest or extrafamilial sexual abuse. Within play therapy, a traumatized child is allowed to integrate and heal her assault through the metaphoric images of the dollhouse, puppets, and drawings. The externalization of the victimization and revictimization onto the play materials allows the child a safe distance to work without retraumatization (Mills & Allan, 1992).

Definition of Incest (Sexual Abuse)

From a legal point of view, *sexual abuse* is defined as a sexual offense against a child. From a clinical point of view, the definition of *sexual abuse of children* is controversial and subject to the culture, the time period, and the clinician's ideology and upbringing. It may be considered to be any interaction or contact between a child and adult in which the child is being used for the sexual stimulation of the perpetrator or another person (Broadhurst, 1979). Some clinicians prefer the term *sexual exploitation* or *sexual misuse* of children to explain the exposure of a child to sexual overstimulation that is not age-appropriate (Brant & Tisza, 1977). Ward (1984) prefers the label *father/daughter rape,* whereas Summit and Kryso (1978) define a progression of categories of sexual involvement with an ascendancy of harmfulness, from *incidental sexual contact* and *ideological sexual contact* to *child rape* and *perverse incest*. In this chapter, *sexual abuse* is defined as "the sexual use of a child by an adult for the sake of the adult's sexual gratification without consideration of the child's psychosexual stage" (Mrazek, 1981).

Incest is any sexual contact (including eye contact) between a child and a family member or parent surrogate. These sexual contacts vary from intercourse to exhibitionism and voyeurism. Unprescribed, frequent enemas are also considered sexual abuse if they create sexual arousal in the child or if they are administered for the sake of parental sexual gratification, that is, if the child's perception of the event or the parent's motivation is sexual.

Incest is a violation of the *interpersonal relationship* created through the vehicle of *sex*. It is not surprising that the resulting symptoms will often occur in *object relationships* and *sexuality*.

Incest is a taboo in almost all cultures; *taboo* is defined as "a necessary proscription that would regulate the behavior of community members."

Unfortunately, discussing incest has also become a taboo. Professionals need to overcome this communication barrier. Self-exploration may enable professionals to look beyond the chief complaints of their patients and, consequently, to more readily make the diagnosis of incest.

Incest is generally considered traumatic to children by a majority of clinicians. Mudry (1986) has labeled it as "a developmental dystopia" and explains that "dystopia" is the opposite of utopia. Sexual abuse of children by parents originally was reported exclusively in dysfunctional families, such as those having parents suffering from alcoholism, psychoses, or other severe disturbances. However, it was eventually discovered that these dysfunctional families did not have enough resources to keep the secrecy of incest intact, especially when they had close contact with the social system, that is, the hospital emergency room, social services, or police, (Marvasti, 1985).

Incest as Trauma

Trauma has been defined in psychiatric literature as "a breakdown or disruption in a person's coping/defense mechanism due to a stimulus (either from within or from without) that is powerful enough to break the *protective shield*." A victim of trauma is not able to assimilate or integrate the traumatic events; the ego is overwhelmed, and a state of helplessness, powerlessness, and submissiveness results. Incest has been considered harmful and a "psychic trauma" by a majority of professionals. Summit and Kryso (1978) stated, "We are convinced that incest is a specific variant of child abuse." However, a minority of clinicians believed that occasionally the incestuous action may be perceived by the child as nuturant and caring behavior affording the child psychic gratification and physical pleasure; this would be especially true for a deprived and neglected child (Butler, 1978; Yates, 1982). In the author's opinion, the effect of incest is very much connected to the child's perception and interpretation of it, her ego-strength, and her coping mechanisms; in a few cases, it may have been perceived as not harmful. In other cases, it may result in anything from an affective response (panic/anxiety) to the shattering of self, dissociation, and a blow to the child's sense of omnipotence, invulnerability. and feelings of safety (Ulman & Brothers, 1988). It may cause posttraumatic stress disorder (PTSD), a change in the victim's "world view," traumatic neurosis, and personality disorder.

Child's Perception of Trauma

Diversity of reaction, symptom formation, and resolution of the trauma prevent any generalization of the effects of incest. The victims of incest and child abuse perceive the trauma and react to it in an individualized way: One incest victim may become, in adulthood, a healthy woman with normal sexuality; another may become a prostitute (going toward sex to overcome her fear of sexuality); and a third may became a nun (going away from sex and avoiding sexuality). All three experienced the same trauma, but the way they reacted, adjusted, compromised, and resolved the trauma was different.

The child's perception and interpretation of incest is the most important element in determining the impact of the abuse and its contribution to psychopathology in the child.

CASE ILLUSTRATION

Michelle, a 4-year-old child, was molested almost every other night by her father. Her mother worked at night and slept during the day; and she was a depressed woman who was unable to give enough attention or affection to her child. After the disclosure of incest, the father was prohibited from living in the home. During the play therapy sessions, the therapist felt that the child interpreted the sexual molestation as a sign of affection and attention. The child was angry at her mother because she did not come to her bed every other night to kiss her, touch her, and fondle her the way her father had done. This interpretation became evident when the child played out a scenario with the dollhouse: a monster came and took the father doll out of the home and put him in jail. Later on, the girl doll went to the monster and asked him if he could give back her father and take the mother instead.

The illustration reveals that Michelle's interpretation of the sexual abuse was markedly different from the interpretation of adults and of the justice system (Marvasti, 1989). However, these rare examples cannot nullify the overwhelming data in regard to the negative impact of incest on the victim.

THERAPIST CHARACTERISTICS

Qualifications of a Therapist in the Treatment of Abused Children

Some clinicians have documented certain desirable personality characteristics in therapists who work with incestuous families and abused children. These characteristics include:

1. The ability to be both *warm* and *authoritative, kind* and *firm.* "A permissive attitude is not consistent with the therapeutic needs of clients from sexually abusive families" (James & Nasjleti, 1983).

2. Being comfortable with one's own sexuality, feeling equal to the cotherapist of the opposite sex.

3. Having the ability to resolve his or her past trauma of abuse (if any).

4. Assertiveness, a good sense of humor, the capacity to assume power/control/limit setting and flexibility in techniques. One must be a "team player" and be able to ask for a consultation and second opinions.

5. Ability to overcome cultural fallacy (e.g., homophobia, stereotyped gender behavior, chauvinistic attitude) and society's prejudice (e.g., blaming the victim, considering sex as "dirty").

6. Capacity to cope emotionally in spite of having seen clients with black-and-blue marks and scars and bruises.

7. Able to work out the issue of incest in himself and herself and to see beyond the patient's "chief complaint."

8. Resistant to the "burnout phenomenon": Burnout may be a realistic reaction to the reality of working with abuse cases; and, generally, it is due to a problem with the system rather than clients. However, in some therapists who have a past history of childhood abuse, not burning out may be more of an example of countertransference than burning out. This countertransference reflects the therapist's strong need to rescue the child from an abusive family situation. On the other hand, by openly helping the patient to recover from trauma, the therapist is also indirectly and unconsciously solving his or her own personal childhood conflicts. In this situation, one may be immune to burnout, because growth is unlimited for the therapist and the gratification of childhood wishes is substantial (Marvasti, 1992a).

McCann and Pearlman (1990) explained that therapists, in working with abused children might initially picture themselves as effective people who can help children to resolve the negative impact of abuse. But, over time, they learn that the ability to be helpful depends at least as much upon the family, the judicial system, and the social services system as upon the therapist's own compassion and skills. Furthermore, as therapists struggle to make sense out of an often violent and unpredictable world, they may lose their faith that such a world can be just and kind.

In the field of treatment/evaluation/intervention of sexually abused children, there may be an indication that people who get interested in working with these cases may fall into a "special population" with a "special childhood history." The wide variety of child protective workers' reactions to similar cases is an indicator of countertransference rather than differences in the education and experience of these workers. In the author's opinion, it is acceptable and legitimate for a therapist to help a child resolve a trauma while simultaneously helping himself or herself to resolve a similar conflict from his or her own childhood. The question of "who is the patient" in these situations is irrelevant. Therapists who grew up in dysfunctional families can get satisfaction by focusing on their parental needs and rescue fantasies. They may fulfill a desire to be helpful and nurturant and to be a healer to the needy child. These therapists lacked someone with these qualities in their own childhood.

Therapists also may compare themselves to the parents of their patients and believe, as they soothe the child's pain, that they care more than the child's parents do. The therapist may overidentify with the patient: see himself or herself in the child or see the child in himself or herself. In other cases, countertransference may develop when the therapist sees the child's parents as his or her own parents or sees himself or herself as the child's parent; for example, the therapist who sees part of the incestuous parent in himself may excessively defend against this unacceptable feeling and, thus, view the father/daughter sexual excitement as an "unbelievable" and "crazy" phenomenon, rather than as a sexual reaction, outside the scope of cultural approval. On the other hand, if the therapist accepts the incestuous feelings, he may see incest as a universal phenomenon because he has seen it in at least two people—his patient and himself.

Subjectivity in Professionals

In recent years, two distinct professional groups challenged each other in regard to the negative effects of incest and sexual contact between child and adult. Subjectivity or countertransference is influential in the outcome of any study and in the relationships of professionals with victims. Some of the research on the subject of incest and its consequences, for example, has been done by professionals who have strong cultural ideologies and social beliefs (i.e., "liberal," "conservative," "feminist"). Although they have done some of the most enlightened work, they may be criticized as having had a preconceived idea as to the cause and effect of incest; that is, their findings were colored by their political and philosophical orientation. Terr (1985) commented on researchers who studied children's attitudes toward the threat of nuclear war and who were themselves concurrently active in antinuclear political movements. Clinicians with a history of incest themselves (especially those giving court testimony) have been indiscriminately singled out as having biased findings and impressions. The author's experience based on his supervision or treatment of several psychotherapists who were incest survivors does not confirm the indiscriminate labeling of bias. However, it is necessary to be aware of clinicians who are more interested in "finding and confirming" rather than "exploring and researching" in regard to any negative effect of incest (Marvasti, 1993a). "Search" is not "research."

There is a possibility that clinicians may project their subjectivity onto their patients. On the other hand, patients also have the capacity to perceive what their therapists are looking for and may please them by presenting it. The problem of finding too much or of not bothering to confirm the effect of incest has been seen in clinical literature. Freud was criticized in his analysis of Wolfman because he ignored his patient's history of incest with his older sister (Miller, 1984, p. 166). Other elements of Wolfman's childhood were considered more pathogenic than the sexual victimization. Miller claimed these "other elements" were Freud's childhood conflicts. Stolorow and Atward (1979) explained the subjectivity in personality theory of several outstanding psychoanalysts, including Freud and Jung. Warner (1978) found that professionals tend to label men as antisocial and women as hysterical, even when they had identical features.

Incestuous families are multiproblem families in which any of these problems and dysfunctions could be considered a variable in causing psychopathology. Therefore, if one believes that sexual abuse and incest per se are the central cause of psychopathology in victims, certainly many patients may provide proof if the therapist looks for it. However, if another clinician believes that it is not the incest itself but the makeup of the incestuous family (and its dysfunctional character) that is pathogenic, then many victims will provide enough evidence for the clinician to construct a cause/effect relationship on the basis of his or her preconceived ideas.

PROCEDURE AND TECHNIQUE

Modality of Referral

Sexually abused children may be referred to a play therapist under several circumstances:

1. Incidents of sexual abuse are confirmed. In such a situation, the validation of the allegation has been done by someone else; the child is only is need of therapy due to the negative effect of incest.

2. The child has partially disclosed the issue of incest to someone. This child is referred for forensic evaluation, and validation of the incest.

3. The child has affective or behavioral complaints including mood disorder (e.g., depression, anxiety), somatic disorder (e.g., bed-wetting, somatic pain), and behavioral abnormality (e.g., aggression, attachment disorder). Such a child may, during the stage of clinical diagnosis or therapy, disclose the incest.

The therapist should not assume that sexually abused children would talk about it without prompting and clues from the clinician. Incest is a sexual phenomenon and, due to its nature, is secretive and shameful. Disclosure of it constitutes the betrayal of a family member (offender). These characteristics inhibit children from talking freely about incest. In addition, some children may dissociate, thereby developing amnesia in regard to incest; by the same token, the incest offender also may have dissociation, not remembering it even if the therapist asks directly about it.

Psychopathology in Sexually Abused Children

The effective treatment of the child victim is associated with comprehension of the significant impact of victimization upon the victim. In other words, therapy is the treatment of the negative impact of sexual assault. Porter, Blick, and Sgroi (1982) identified 10 impacts and suggested special treatment approaches for each of them. These 10 impacts are:

1. "Damaged goods" syndrome
2. Guilt
3. Fear
4. Depression
5. Low self-esteem and poor social skills
6. Repressed anger and hostility
7. Impaired ability to trust
8. Blurred role boundaries and role confusion
9. Pseudomaturity coupled with failure to accomplish developmental tasks
10. Self-mastery and control

The last five impacts are more exclusive to intrafamily child sexual abuse cases, whereas the first five are likely to affect all sexually abused children regardless of the identity of the perpetrator.

The long-term negative consequences of incest and child sexual abuse have been explained in the professional literature. Sexual abuse of children has been associated with disorders and symptomatic behavior such as posttraumatic stress disorder (Gelinas, 1983), alexithymia (Marvasti, 1991), sexual dysfunction (Meiselman, 1978), prostitution (James & Meyerding, 1977), anorexia nervosa (Marvasti, 1987; Oppenheimer, Howells, Palmer, & Challoner, 1984), depression (Summit & Kryso, 1978), and borderline personality disorder (Stone, 1990; Sepahbodi & Marvasti, 1986). These disorders have all been detected in some victims years later and are possibly associated with their victimization. Such disorders, if present, need to be addressed during therapy in a gradual manner.

Play Diagnosis

In play diagnosis, the clinician encourages the child to interact with dolls, toys, and other play materials; these may help the child to express her emotional conflicts in a symbolic and metaphoric way. During the session, the diagnostician is active, engaging, supportive, and warm. If needed, anatomical dolls also may be used during the play diagnosis; however, one needs to differentiate between this clinical play diagnosis session and a forensic play interview. In the latter one, the clinician needs to demonstrate a completely different technique and attitude.

During play, the child reveals her internal conflicts, wishes, and family dynamics and her perception of her trauma by using ego defense mechanisms; these include *projection, displacement,* and *symbolization.* The child, without knowing that she is talking about her own life, will displace her trauma and family conflict onto the dolls and puppets. The dollhouse becomes her house, and, in that environment, the child may become Cinderella with her victimization, a cowboy with his anger, or a monster with its mischief.

CASE ILLUSTRATION

Laura, sexually molested by her father for a couple of years, kept the secret for 2 years. She did so because her father warned her that, if she told anyone about "their secret," he would kill himself by jumping out the third-floor window (the window in Laura's room); then she would be without a father, and her mother would cry forever because of losing him. Eventually, Laura's father abused a neighbor's child and was arrested. At that time, Laura disclosed his abuse of her to her mother. As a consequence of the disclosure, the child was referred for therapy.

During the play therapy session, Laura arranged for a family of dolls to live in the dollhouse. At the beginning, Laura compulsively placed a lot of furniture in the front of the dollhouse windows. These window were sealed by the girl doll, and the father doll was placed on the first floor so, as Laura said, "he can't jump out of the window and hurt himself." Eventually, a neighbor doll forced herself into the dollhouse and yelled, "I kill. I like to kill." She held the father doll, brought him to the second floor, removed the furniture from a window, and threw the father doll out of it. However, the father doll was not hurt because his daughter jumped out and held him in the air before he hit the ground. This scenario was repeated several times, during which "doing" and "undoing" were present.

THERAPIST PUPPET: Oh, this child has a lot of power; she takes care of her father and rescues him.

LAURA: Yes, she can do everything.

THERAPIST PUPPET: Yes, she also has the power to let her father fall and get hurt.

LAURA: She never lets her father get killed

THERAPIST PUPPET: Tell me more about this little doll girl. Someone gave a big job to her. She is a little child and is doing things that are an adult's responsibility, like rescuing her father.

LAURA: This little girl is upset. She hurt her parents. She is scared that something bad is going to happen in her home.

Eventually, the neighbor doll (who had forced herself into the house) threw the father doll out of the window, and he hit the ground. All the dolls then jumped out of the dollhouse to see what happened to the father doll.

LAURA: Someone did a magic.

THERAPIST PUPPET: What is the magic?

LAURA: See, this is not the father who hit the ground; this is the other girl who was pushing him out the window. This time she herself fell and got killed.

Later on in this session, the therapist puppet interviewed the daughter doll and told her she could tell all the secrets to the puppet. The girl doll told the puppet her life story, which was similar to Laura's life as she perceived and comprehended it.

In this play vignette, Laura is more preoccupied by her father's possible death than she is by her sexual molestation. Possibly, the loss of her father may be more traumatic for Laura than the sexual molestation. Also, she may be aware of society's attitude that sexuality is "secret" and not a subject for discussion. In addition, Laura's perception of sexual molestation could be that it is not an abusive painful act—since she is not preoccupied with it, it is not projected into the play.

Laura's ambivalent feeling toward her father, her role at home as a parentified child (one who is empowered to the point that she feels responsible for her father's life), is evidenced in this play. Laura also symbolically expressed her wish (by killing the neighbor's doll) that the sexual abuse would not be disclosed and that her father would not die. The self-blame, the guilt feelings, and an image of a "frightened child" that were all projected into the play were Laura's own feelings and emotional conflicts. In this play, Laura had a *solution* for the situation: her wish that the neighbor would not disclose the abuse. Conceivably, the neighbor doll's anger and murderous wishes toward the father doll are the displacement of Laura's resentment toward her father, that is, anger at the father who makes her responsible for his life and death. Such a task, which imposes upon a child the responsibility of life and death of her father, is overwhelming and inappropriate to a child's developmental stage and is beyond her level of maturity.

During the play diagnosis, the child is encouraged to displace and project her feelings onto the dolls and puppets. Thus, in a symbolic way and in disguise, she can play out her life scenario in the dollhouse or in the puppet game. The therapist observes the child's play and participates in it without contamination. The therapist is a follower who asks the child to assign a role to him or her. However, at times, the therapist's puppet becomes very nosy and wants to know a lot about the doll's feelings and what is bothering the doll. The therapist puppet may ask such questions as "Where is the favorite room for this girl in this dollhouse?" "Where is the scary place for her?" "What is happening in the bathtub that makes this little doll scared to be there?" Or it may make statements such as: "I wish that this little doll would talk because when people talk about bad things that happen to them, they feel better."

Generally, at the beginning, the clinician may view more family violence and physical abuse in the dollhouse rather than sexual abuse. A good number of incestuous families (father/daughter incest) have other problems, such as alcoholism, battering, and aggression. As previously mentioned, the dollhouse is a miniature of the child's house in the way that child perceives it or wishes it would be (Marvasti, 1993b).

In play diagnosis, the examiner, by observing the child's play, may elicit knowledge of the child's feeling and her trauma, which may be summarized as follows:

1. Diagnostic play may provide knowledge about the child's perception of herself and her role in the family.

CASE ILLUSTRATION

Eight-year-old Julie was her father's favorite, so much so that there were incidents of incest between them. Julie, during one of the early diagnostic interviews, played out a scenario in the dollhouse: A father doll wanted to go on a trip and selected his daughter, rather than his wife, to accompany him. When the therapist puppet asked, "Where is the mother?" the child brought up the mother doll, who said, "I gave in; everyone knows my daughter is better than me."

This piece of play reveals the child's perception of herself, as well as indications of Oedipal victory over her mother and possible wishes that her mother will "give in" rather than retaliate.

2. In play diagnosis, the child's perception of others, especially significant family members, is projected into play material.

CASE ILLUSTRATION

Jimmy was a 6-year-old boy whose stepfather did not want to adopt him because he had no interest in this child. His mother was somewhat overprotective of him, whereas his stepfather was emotionally abusive to both Jimmy and his mother. During the play, Jimmy played out a scenario in which there was a farm with animals of all ages. Everyday, a baby animal would wander around and then disappear. When the mother ran toward the father to ask for help in finding the lost child, the father would say, "I don't care about him; he is not mine." The next day, another animal child was wandering around, and the father repeated the same story. "It is not mine. I don't care." The father repeated this every time a child got lost. This play reflects Jimmy's perception of his stepfather's rejection of him.

3. In play diagnosis, the child's compulsion to repeat the trauma in a symbolic way may be present.

The child who has been traumatized may repeat the traumatic events over and over. Freud (1920) has said that such play is sometimes repetition compulsion; however, it is also an active attempt at problem solving, a visible externalization of impulses causing both pleasure and pain in a search of resolution. Overwhelmed by the trauma, the child will reenact it in the play in order to gradually digest it and to acquire ego mastery over it.

CASE ILLUSTRATION

Melody, a 9-year-old child, witnessed her mother being raped in their home. The rapist broke into the house by breaking the door's lock. During play session, Melody repeated over and over a scenario in which a man breaks the dollhouse door, goes in, hurts the mother doll in "her belly," and runs out. This pattern of play was repeated several times, and, gradually, Melody found a solution to the helplessness of the mother doll. Once the doll called the police; another time, the rapist sat on the mother's bed, where a hidden knife went into his body, causing his death. Gradually, the helplessness, powerlessness, and passivity of the play decreased, and "help came soon."

During play diagnosis, the child may repeat the trauma, but she may modify the end of it, creating more hopefulness and optimism than the helplessness and victimization that she once passively experienced.

CASE ILLUSTRATION

Nadia was going to court because of sexual molestation by her father. Court was traumatic for her because she was somewhat shy and nervous. During several play therapy sessions, she played out the court sessions in the dollhouse by placing a monkey as the judge. She also had several other dolls and animals playing the roles of the attorneys. This play was repeated frequently, and, every time, the passive, shy child became more strong and powerful. Eventually, it was the child who would order the court to recess, and the judge to go home to rest and to come back the next day. Her order to the lawyers was, "You should not fight because it scares people."

4. During the play diagnosis, the child's conflicts and her coping and ego defense mechanisms can be noticed.

CASE ILLUSTRATION

Sabrina, who was sexually molested by her father, had negative and positive feelings toward him. After the molestation was disclosed, he was arrested. The child's conflict was due to sadness at losing the father whom she loved and, yet, being expected to be angry at the same father. Her mother asked for a divorce and tried to create negative feelings in her child. Sabrina's conflict began when she tried to satisfy her mother's need by believing that "Daddy is a bad guy." Conflict was demonstrated during the play as the doll was torn by her ambivalence toward her father. During the play, she developed a magical solution to the conflict. The doll had two fathers: one who was loved and loving, and one who hurt her and at whom she was angry. The child's ambivalence toward her father was projected on to the two father dolls. In some ways, splitting had helped her to be able to love her father and also to be angry at him.

5. During the diagnostic play, the child may exhibit her perception of the world and of her life.

A child who was abused sexually and emotionally for years by both parents revealed during the play her perception that the world is abusive and unfair. She believed that everything was hard—that baby cows die because of snow and sand storms. There was no help and no hope for rescue. This play revealed the child's perception of her world as abusive, cold, and uncaring.

6. During the diagnostic play, the family dynamic may be revealed.

CASE ILLUSTRATION

Jackie played out a story of a father and a mother who were constantly fighting with each other. The mother threw the father out, but the baby sister picked up the father and brought him back home. In reality, Jackie's parents had fought with each other many times. They would separate, but, within a short period, they would get back together because they had something in common—Jackie's baby sister. Jackie, from a previous marriage of the mother, was not considered a "common point" with the parents.

7. During diagnostic play, the feelings and attitudes that the child directs toward the therapist may have the quality of transference and may reveal the child's experience with her significant family members.

CASE ILLUSTRATION

Tina, a "daddy's girl," was singled out by her father and became his favorite and the target of his sexual feelings. During group therapy, Tina expressed feelings and ideas about the male therapist such as: "I know he loves me, I love him." Later on, she told her mother that she was surprised that the therapist had not yet touched her.

8. During the play diagnosis, the diagnostician needs to give attention to differential diagnosis and rule out any indication of major psychiatric symptoms.

CASE ILLUSTRATION

Judy, a 7-year-old Hispanic child, was brought to the hospital because, after a severe argument between her grandmother and her drug-abusing mother, Judy told her grandmother that she felt like jumping out a window. Judy had been placed in her grandmother's custody since age 2 ½ because of her mother's drug abuse and neglect. Between the ages of 4 and 5 years, Judy was sexually abused by several men with whom her mother had left her. During the play interview, Judy expressed a fear of returning to her home because of the fighting between her grandmother and her mother. She reported auditory hallucinations. Judy "heard" up to five voices of males and females from "inside" her head. She also explained having a "little mother" named "little Joanna" who lives inside of her and who sometimes can come out. She had told her friends about being able to see her little mother. In regard to fighting between her family members, Judy mentioned it scared her so much that she hid and pulled out her hair and then "felt better." During the interview, Judy's voice and behavior sometimes became regressive. At times, she would stare at the therapist, and a few times, abrupt changes in her speech, behavior, and affect occurred. Additionally, there was a history of a head injury at age 3.

The therapist felt the differential diagnosis among the following disorders should be established: (a) multiple personality disorder; (b) posttraumatic stress disorder; (c) dissociative disorder, N.O.S. (not otherwise specified; (d) partial complex seizures (psychomotor epilepsy); and (e) psychotic disorder, N.O.S.

The clinician felt that the hallucinations Judy had experienced since age 4 or 5, which Judy described as "inside" her head, are probably "traumatic" in origin (as opposed to voices described as "outside," which are usually "psychotic" in origin). Further study, such as psychological testing, neurological evaluation, and completion of a structured question-naire for diagnosing dissociative disorder, and interviews with Judy's family and teacher were arranged.

Forensic Play Interview

In this modality, the play is being used as a medium to decrease the child's anxiety and to develop a relationship. With the use of this technique, the play material may not need to have symbolic or metaphoric meaning (e.g., monster, princess, Indian, cowboy), and the assessment is based generally on the verbal interview rather than on the analysis of the symbolic meaning of the child's play.

Generally, professionals have identified the following information as important factors to extract from the child during an interview (Sgroi, 1982):

1. A *description of the abusive behavior*, with the consideration that young children may have a blurred memory of the peripheral details of the act (Goodman & Reed, 1986). The core and central issue of victimizing, however, is reported accurately by the child; for example, when Mary was asked about the color of her offender's shirt, she told her therapist it was red. Yet, a week before, she had reported to a detective that the offender was naked and wore no clothes. Very young children may distort the details of a victimiza-tion and report it differently to different people, but the main issues of the victimizing act remain fairly stable in the children's reports.

2. Information regarding the *nature of the abusive act*. Was there an element of force or threat? Was there penetration involved? The child may present this information verbally or through demonstration with anatomical dolls.

3. The *child's perception of and the reaction to the abusive act*. Was sexual molesta-tion playful and entertaining or painful and traumatizing?

4. *The performer of the abusive act* Was there anyone else involved in the abusive act? How often had the abusive act occurred? Over what period of time did it occur?

5. The precipitating factor or *motivation in disclosing the abuse at this time*. Was there any secret involved? Does the child fear the offender? Is there evidence of self-blame by the child? To whom did the child initially disclose the abuse?

6. Any indication of *false allegation of incest*. Are the parents in a nasty divorce/custody fight? Was the sexual abuse allegation elicited during the parental fights? Does the child deny any sexual abuse by father in individual session, but talk about it only when her mother is present?

7. *Whether the child is safe* at the present time. Is the alleged offender still living with the child, or does he have access to the child? Does the child say that she was threatened by him?

When the play interview is being done for the purpose of the validation of abuse for a legal proceeding, it is advisable for the interviewer to ask the child the following questions near the end of the interview:

1. Has anyone told you what you should tell me today? The questioning could proceed as in the following sample dialogue:

DOCTOR: Does anyone know about what you are telling me today?

CHILD: Yes, my mother knows.

DOCTOR: How does she know?

CHILD: Because she told me to tell you these things today.

DOCTOR: Tell me exactly what she told you to tell me?

CHILD: She told me to tell the truth to the doctor and not to be afraid of anything.

DOCTOR: What is the truth?

CHILD: The truth is what I told you just now.

DOCTOR: How did your mother know about the truth?

CHILD: Because I told her.

DOCTOR: What did you tell her?

Child: We were watching TV, and someone was rubbing himself up to a girl's body and so I told my mother that Uncle Jim does the same thing with me. We call it a touching game.

It is important to inform the child that the interviewer is only interested in knowing the child's experience and knowledge, not what adults have talked about.

2. Do you know the difference between the truth and a lie? What is the difference between a dream and what truly happens in real life? The following is a sample dialogue:

INTERVIEWER: If I had eggs for breakfast, but I tell you I had cereal, what do you call that?

CHILD: Lie, not truth.

INTERVIEWER: What things are truth?

CHILD: The things that really happen.

INTERVIEWER: How do you know that what you told me was not in your dream?

CHILD: I know because it happened first in his home: then I came to my home, very upset. I slept, then it happened again in my dream."

3. During the play interview, the examiner may need to give attention to ruling out any indication of delusional thinking or psychotic symptoms. If the examiner is subpoenaed by the court, he or she may be asked questions such as:

- Does the child know right from wrong?
- Has the child developed any ethical/moral capacity?
- Does the child fantasize excessively?
- Could this child's recanting be due to false allegations?
- Does this child have the capacity to falsify or confabulate?
- Did you measure the child's suggestibility?
- Is the child's testimony credible?
- Has anyone assessed the child's credibility?
- Is this child, at this age, capable of understanding abstract concepts?
- At what age did this child first learn about good touch and bad touch?

- Does this child have any friends who have been sexually abused?
- Could guilt feelings in this case be connected to falsely accusing this child's father of abuse?
- Are you aware of nonabused children's behavior with anatomical dolls? Where did you train using anatomical dolls?
- What is the reliability of your questionnaire data?
- Does the child understand why truth is important in court?
- Are you aware of the latest studies on false allegations during divorce and custody procedures?
- Is play therapy a scientific entity or a subjective one?

In discussion on the following pages, the potential responses to and issues surrounding these questions will be examined.

How Professionals Confirm the Incest

Psychiatric literature, in recent years, has given significant attention to the criteria and circumstances that indicate the presence of incest and child sexual abuse. The process of validating a sexual abuse allegation is multiphasic and requires a constellation of evidence. This is obtained through forensic play interview, past and present medical and psychological history, an interview with the alleged incest offender, an interview with the nonoffending parent, and an interview with the person to whom the child initially disclosed the abuse. A clinician may use anatomical dolls to increase the level of communication. In addition, it is necessary to obtain the details of the abuse by enhancing the child's memory and, if possible, by seeing the child and her alleged offender together. Professionals should always consider the possibility of false allegations of incest, even if it is a statistically rare occurrence (Marvasti, 1992b).

Indicators of Possible Incestuous Sexual Abuse

Indicators of possible sexual abuse may be divided into sexual symptoms, medical symptoms, and behavioral symptoms. Thus far, professionals have not determined any symptom that is specific to incest. Examples of sexual symptoms are excessive and compulsive masturbation, excessive sexual play with peers and adults, sexual aggression toward children, seductive behavior, and excessive sexual knowledge beyond what is expected for a child's developmental state (Faller, 1990). Such *medical symptoms* as bed-wetting, urinary retention, abdominal pain, eating disorders, sleep problems, and urinary infections, may be considered possible indicators of sexual abuse. Broad *behavioral problems*, such as affective disorder, aggression, interpersonal problems, hyperactivity, conduct disorder, and running away from home, may indicate the possibility of sexual abuse.

What makes the sexual abuse allegation valid is the cohesion of several symptoms and statements that are consistent with child victimization. It is possible that the act of sexual abuse may not result in any noticeable disorder at the time of evaluation. In one study, 21% of sexually abused children were, at the time of evaluation, initially asymptomatic (Conte & Berliner 1988).

Use of Anatomical Dolls

At this point, if the clinician wants to facilitate communication and enhance the child's memory, he or she may use the anatomical dolls. Anatomical dolls are introduced only *after* the child has disclosed the abuse.

With the help of the child, the evaluator will undress the female doll (if the victim is female) and complete "a body inventory." This includes the naming of parts and organs of the doll, including the genital area. The purpose of this is to understand the child's terminology for the genital area. After the general body inventory, the evaluator may ask the child to identify the doll as either a girl or a boy or may ask the child to show the therapist the private parts of the doll. Some very young children may mistakenly identify a girl doll as a boy and vice versa. In the same way, the male doll is then introduced, if the offender is male.

EXAMINER: Mary, tell me if this doll is a girl or boy.

MARY: It's a girl.

EXAMINER: How do you know it is a girl?

MARY: Because she has a lot of hair on her head.

EXAMINER: Let me cover her hair (the therapist puts his hand over the head of the doll). Now how do you know if it is girl?

MARY: She is a girl because she has gina. (Points toward the vagina of doll)

When anatomical dolls are utilized, an "informed consent" from the parents may be necessary, which would explain the benefit and side effects of using these dolls in validation interviews. The interviewer may explain to parents that some defense attorneys may believe that these dolls elicit "sexual stimulation" and "sexual play" from children and may contaminate the interview. Parents also need to be told that some clinicians may obtain the same results with ordinary fashion dolls and that a minority of children may show a frightened reaction when they are exposed to a naked doll (flashback of PTSD). During play therapy, anatomical dolls may be utilized for sex education, facilitating communication, enhancing the child's memory, and reenacting the rape trauma. Anatomical dolls may be used as a substitute for the therapist, that is, as a pretend therapist, when an overstimulated child is obsessed with the desire to touch the therapist's genital area (Marvasti 1994b).

In some cases, there is no need for an anatomical doll because a regular naked fashion doll may be used, as is evidenced in the following dialogue:

CLINICIAN: You told me that you saw a policewoman yesterday. Could you tell me what she wanted to know?

CHILD: She asked me about what Paul did to me.

CLINICIAN: Can you tell me?

CHILD: He touched me there. (Pointing toward her genital area)

CLINICIAN: Can you show me on this doll where "there" is that he touched you?

CHILD: (While touching between the thighs) Here, he touched me here.

CLINICIAN: How did he touch you?

CHILD: He did.

CLINICIAN: How?

CHILD: He did it. He touched.

CLINICIAN: Maybe it is easier for you to show me. Let's pick up a doll that looks like Paul and a doll that is a girl like you. Now show me what you told me.

CHILD: (Taking the hand of the male doll and rubbing it in genital area of the female doll, front and back) See, See!

Memory is a "state dependent" phenomenon. A child's memory is enhanced when the child is exposed to the state and circumstances that registered the event. Anatomical dolls, with explicit genital areas, may enhance the child's memory; and the child may be able to show how a male doll with his penis lies down on a female doll and moves front and back or up and down (Marvasti, 1986b).

In a forensic evaluation, anatomical dolls are considered tools rather than toys. But in play therapy and play diagnosis, anatomical dolls may be used like any other play material. An anatomical doll is also used in therapy for sex education or for other therapeutic purposes, such as repeating the sexual abuse act with dolls, ventilating the trauma, or kicking the male doll's penis. An advantage of these dolls is that the child may explicitly demonstrate if there was any bodily penetration. It also may be used under the following circumstances:

JUNE: Can I touch your do-do? (Pointing toward the therapist's genital area)

THERAPIST: I don't like to be touched by children, but I can give you this special doll, and you may pretend it is me and do whatever you want with it.

JUNE: Is your do-do just like this one?" (Pointing toward the doll's penis)

THERAPIST: Yes, I have a boy's and men's do-do. Girls also have something called a vagina. You may see it by looking at the other doll. (The therapist hands June the anatomically correct female doll.)

During the forensic evaluation, the examiner should remain neutral with no feedback (verbal or nonverbal) to the child in regard to the child's performances or the therapist's interest. The forensic evaluator should not give the child the impression that he or she is only interested in the genital area of the dolls.

Play Therapy

For children, play is considered as important as words and communication are for adults. It is a child's natural vehicle for expressing trauma in a symbolic way, rehearsing it for the purpose of mastering the trauma and working through conflicts. Play and art therapy have been used to help traumatized children ventilate and integrate trauma. Children are encouraged to express anger and hatred through play therapy in the safe and nonjudgmental environment of the therapist's office. The major goal of play therapy is to help children in overcoming the negative impact of incest, to empower them, and to release the mental energy that is being used to suppress the trauma so that it is available to support their emotional growth.

During play sessions, the therapist communicates with the child through the help of play material. Play therapy sessions may help the child find a better solution for emotional conflicts. In young children, the communication can be done entirely through the dolls.

The solution is for the dolls, not for the child. So the interpretation, suggestion, support, and correction may remain on the level of the dolls and puppets (Marvasti, 1990). However, with older children, one may go beyond the dolls, bringing up the similarities between the doll's life and the child's life, between the puppet's feelings and the child's feelings. This results in the ego defense mechanisms, such as displacement, projection, and symbolization, gradually being neutralized and removed. In play diagnosis, the child is encouraged to use these defense mechanisms. Yet, in play therapy, the reverse phenomenon is elicited, and the child is being directed to face the conflict and to eventually find a better solution for the child, rather than for the doll. Many play therapists believe that there is no need for the therapist to entirely understand and interpret the child's play and symbolism directly. The child's learning or insight into the doll's behavior may be enough to create change in the child (Marvasti, 1994a).

The sexually abused child in an incestuous family may present a variety of unwanted characteristics and behavior during the play sessions; these become the issues being addressed and/or corrected in therapy. These issues are very individualized and are related to the child's perception of incest, her coping mechanism, and the extent of incest/trauma. However, the majority of children in father/child incest present some common behavioral attitudes and feelings as a reflection of growing up in a dysfunctional family. These are:

1. Distrust in grownups and feelings of betrayal
2. Shame, guilt, and self-blame
3. Inability to express anger
4. Presence of anger toward both parents, but particularly toward the mother
5. Secrecy, loyalty to family, a sense of being special, and, at times, "islands of amnesia" and recanting in regard to the abusive incidents
6. Sexualizing behavior, seductiveness, and overstimulation behavior
7. "Parentified behavior," pseudomaturity
8. Low self-esteem and poor self-image and, sometimes, paradoxically, pseudograndiose feelings
9. Depression, anxiety, and explosiveness
10. Emotional distancing/intimacy problems: In some incestuous families, the child is not allowed to socialize with outsiders; all emotional satisfactions and connections must be within the family. Such a situation denies the child the experience of a close relationship with individuals other than her family members. The presence of secrets also prevents the child from getting close to a peer group or an adult.

Treatment Levels

Psychotherapy with the incest victim and her family may be conducted in three categories or levels. Each level has special therapeutic goals. These levels reflect an arbitrary delineation and may frequently overlap each other.

• *Therapeutic goals in Level 1:* Play diagnosis, developing rapport, using anatomical dolls (if necessary), and assessing the psychopathology.

• *Therapeutic goals in Level 2:* Dealing with the conflicts and symptoms that were identified in Level 1 (diagnostic play). The therapist tries to help the child explore emotional conflicts and to offer a more adaptive solution to the trauma. Some of the child's defense mechanisms are neutralized.

• *Therapeutic goals in Level 3:* Therapeutic interactions that deal with the possible presence of dissociation, posttraumatic stress disorder, posttraumatic play, reuniting the family, collateral therapy, and the termination process

These three levels of treatment goals are explained in detail in play therapy, with a child victim of incest, as follows:

Level 1

Diagnostic play, developing a rapport, decreasing the separation anxiety/stranger anxiety and having fun together with the child are the goals of the therapeutic interaction. In some cases, during the first session, limit setting and boundaries are explained.

At this level, the purpose of the child meeting with the therapist is explained, although many children have already been told by adults the reason that they are going to see a therapist. Any misperception, miscommunication, or confusion in regard to the child's understanding of the therapeutic meeting needs to be cleared.

DOCTOR: I wonder if anyone explained to you the reason that you are meeting with me here.

CHILD: There are two kind of doctors; one is a "needle and pill doctor," and the other is a "worry doctor." When I get sick, I go to the "pill" doctor; but when I feel scared and upset, I see the other one.

During this phase of therapy, the child's behavior and mood are assessed: Is the child hyperactive? Is the child excessively shy and inhibited? Is the child avoiding physical contact with the therapist during play? Is the child touching her genital area? Is the child aggressive, controlling, bossy, and demanding? Language development, intelligence, and the child's maturity level may be explored in the first few sessions. The child is being encouraged to play and to project and displace feelings in a symbolic way onto the dolls and puppets.

At Level 1, the therapist is interested in finding out from the child as much information as possible about the family dynamics and the child's perception of the trauma. The therapist should also try to see the world as the child sees it. It is possible that the therapist will find, from the child's point of view, that sexual abuse, per se, is not the most traumatic event in the child's life. The child may reveal a preoccupation with other painful elements: the fear of losing a parent; the fear of bodily harm by the offender; and losses and painful events that happened prior to the sexual molestation. Contrary to the forensic play interview, in play therapy, the clinician initially may focus attention on negative elements of the child's life other than the incest (Marvasti 1986c).

CASE ILLUSTRATION

Ted, an 8-year-old child born out of wedlock, had been placed in several foster and group homes. At Ted's last placement, it was revealed that he had been sexually molested by a male teenager for over a year. During play therapy, Ted became involved with the dollhouse and a monster who could fly, going from one dollhouse to another. When the monster entered the dollhouse, the grownups fed him, then threw him out of the house, saying: "We don't want you, bastard."

THERAPIST'S PUPPET: Poor monster, nobody wants him.

TED: Yeah, because he is bad.

THERAPIST'S PUPPET: What has he done that you call him bad?

TED: He is a monster; he eats everyone's cookies; when he gets angry, he eats people, but everyone is giving him food so he does not eat them.

THERAPIST'S PUPPET: I feel bad for this monster. Tell me, where are his parents?

TED: He is a bastard and is up for adoption; his parents are dead. I think the monster killed his parents.

THERAPIST'S PUPPET: Does he have any friends? Does anyone like him?

TED: Yeah, only one dude and he is in jail. The monster is going to take him out of jail, but first he's going to kill a policeman; then they will both fly away.

Eventually, it was evidenced that the monster represented the "angry Ted," and the "dude" was the teenage sex offender. It seemed, from Ted's point of view, that sexual molestation was considered a sign of caring and nurturing.

At this level, the therapist should supplement the material that he or she has gathered during the play diagnosis. One example of this occurred when, during play diagnosis, a child revealed that she was molested by her male baby-sitter. She demonstrated this on the anatomical dolls, expressing negative feelings toward him. During the play, the therapist gathered information such as the child's ambivalent feelings toward the baby-sitter. She especially expressed positive feelings and a desire to see him, "if he promises he wouldn't do it anymore." In addition, the therapist found several episodes of family violence in the dollhouse, in which the father doll hit the mother doll, and then the whole family got together and cried, including the father. Later on, the therapist's speculation in regard to family violence in the child's home was confirmed by the state protective services agency.

At this level, the child's view of the world, the child's perception of self and family, and the child's wishes, conflicts, and feelings are all displaced onto the dolls and puppets. *Therapy* and *diagnosis* are together side by side; for example, when the therapist found that the doll was being punished because he was angry at his teacher, the therapist's puppet started *therapy* by suggesting that anger is an ordinary feeling of any person and that it is okay to be angry, even at grownup people.

During this phase of therapy, projective techniques may be used to elicit more information about the child's conflicts. These include drawing pictures; kinetic family drawing; the house-tree-person (HTP); Winnicott's squiggles game (Winnicott, 1971); fable tests; and dreams. If the child does not have any dreams, the child can be asked to make up a dream. The content of such dreams, or "pretend dreams," is a step in obtaining insight into the child's fantasy life.

Level 2

The second level of play therapy may begin when the therapist decides to remove the child's ego defense mechanisms. This may be done for examples, by presenting the similarities between the doll's life and the child's life and between the monster's anger and the child's anger toward her parents. The therapist may use clarification, interpretation, education, and persuasion. As the therapist offers alternative ways of handling the conflict and offers support to the child, gradually some of the therapeutic goals will be accomplished. These therapeutic goals are as follows:

1. Enhancement of ego skills in coping with trauma
2. Establishment of a therapeutic relationship (working alliance)
3. Ventilation of pent-up feeling and old injuries
4. Reworking the trauma and integration of the trauma
5. Making sense and meaning of victimization/trauma, finding some explanation for the abusive behavior
6. Creating the corrective emotional experiences
7. Resolving the developmental fixation, which resulted from incest and growing up in a dysfunctional family
8. Establishment of healthy boundaries
9. Creating a "holding environment" and "good enough mothering" milieu (Winnicott, 1965)
10. Removal of "damaged goods" syndrome (Sgroi, 1982)
11. Facilitating grieving the loss of parents and/or friends or the loss of virginity
12. Preventing transference of victimization/helplessness to a sibling or to the next generation
13. Enhancing the child's self-esteem/self-image/self-worth
14. Clarification of negative life events other than incest (e.g., divorce, family violence, incarceration of parent)
15. Channeling the child's psychological energy into more adaptive functions

During the play therapy, the child may give surprisingly strong indications of self-blame and guilt feelings, despite the fact that the child has been a victim of rape and had nothing to do with the offender's action.

Self-blame, which is almost a universal phenomenon in trauma victims, has been attributed to the victim's need to feel in control. In incest victims, self-blame has been attributed to the egocentricity of the child or, at times, to the possibility that the child "enjoyed" the sexual activity and his or her unconscious wishes about it. However, studies of children who were subjected to the trauma of parental loss revealed that self-blame may be less threatening to the child than is the alternative view of the self as helpless to control life events. There are indications that self-blame may have an adaptive value and that it is a phenomenon that may decrease the fear of helplessness, powerlessness, and passivity in traumatized victims. In paralyzed accident victims, self-blame was found to be a predictor of good coping ability (Bulman & Wortman, 1977). Clinicians have identified two types of self-blame: adaptive and maladaptive. In the maladaptive type, the victim feels she "deserved it" because she is a bad person and justifiably subject to victimization and punishment. In treating sexually abused children, it was proposed that clinicians refrain from telling them that the experience of abuse was not their fault, because it can diminish the sense of power and control that children may feel in addition to their guilt (Lamb, 1986). In incest victims, often self-blame is a symptom of depression. However, in a few, self-blame is an adaptive measure that is present with its "reassuring" and "controlling" quality; for example, a child who had been molested by her father and was told "this is a game that fathers and daughters play" blamed herself for the molestation:

"I was stupid." She reassured herself by repeating that "it will never happen to me again, now that I know it is not a game." In this situation, the therapist might focus on the underlying dynamics of the child's need for self-blame, for example, "I know you blame yourself for what happened that night, but you are definitely not responsible for a grown-up's bad behavior. It seems that, by believing you were responsible, you feel safer and more secure because you are in control. Let's talk about your need to be in control and your feelings of insecurity since this incident happened."

During play therapy, the abused child becomes freer within the experience; she develops relationships within which interpersonal patterns can be reexamined and relived and gains a deeper awareness of her potential. Eventually, the child needs to experience affect and emotions in a reasonable fashion.

Level 3

The third level starts when the diagnostic play has been completed, the finding has been addressed, the child is gaining insight about her conflicts (or the doll's conflicts), and improvement is seen in her symptoms and interpersonal problems. The child is getting in touch with her deep feelings, is verbally experiencing the details of her trauma, is mourning for the losses (including loss of a protective father that she never had), and getting in touch with the bitter reality of her life and her dysfunctional family. At this time the child may develop posttraumatic stress disorder as a result of getting in touch with her victimization/trauma, although PTSD may present itself at any level of therapy, including the first session of diagnostic play. During the therapeutic session, an abused child may demonstrate dissociation and possibly multiple personality disorder. These include abrupt changes in tone of voice or affect, irrelevant answers to questions, and changes of right/left domination (e.g., using the right hand during most of the session, but changing voice and affect accompanied by using the left hand to scratch her face).

In this level, the therapist deals with signs/symptoms of PTSD (if any) and will address the posttrruamatic play of the child (if present). *Posttraumatic play* may be described as "repetition of the same play over and over during the session." In a majority of cases, the repetition of traumatic events through play is beneficial and is a way for ego mastery of events and integration of trauma to the conscious level of psychic constellation. In a minority of cases, it may have no positive effect and may need to be stopped with the therapist's intervention. Terr (1985) explained these kinds of play as monotonous, at times possibly dangerous, and of no help to the child in gaining ego mastery. This latter type will be further discussed later in this chapter.

Johnson (1989 p. 119) suggested that important goals in posttraumatic treatment are "re-experience, release, and reorganization." These goals may be achieved during the therapy in Levels 2 and 3.

Difficult Moments and Stumbling Blocks in Psychotherapy with Incestuous Children and Their Families

These "difficult moments" may be summarized as follows:

1. EMERGENCE OF SEVERE PTSD IN THE VICTIM OR THE THERAPIST (who is an exvictim). Many victims of child abuse are unable to feel safe in their body because the body was the entity that received pain and forbidden stimulation. Some children show terrifying psychophysiological reactions during the play therapy when naked dolls are introduced or when sexual encounters are discussed. Clinicians have labeled some of these reactions as

also indicative of PTSD. In these situations, the therapist may reassure the child and her family that these are normal reactions to abnormal events and are a coping mechanism toward repressed trauma. From the beginning of therapy, the parents, and possibly the child, need to be prepared to know that some children, midway through therapy, may become troubled by nightmares and flashbacks of their traumatic events: "You will tell me when it happens and together we will deal with it." It is important to reassure them that "therapy is working" and they are not "going crazy or getting worse."

The emergence of severe PTSD in patients is not necessarily indicative of "overdose of therapy," "premature removal of amnesia, " or excessive "flooding" with repressed painful events. However, severe PTSD, such as constant nightmares and sleep deprivation, can indicate a need for a slowdown in therapy and the possible use of medication to shorten the stages of sleep that include the most frightening nightmares (REM sleep). PTSD may need to be explained, in analogy, as similar to a fever, that is, a normal body reaction to infection intended to fight the invading germs. But when the fever becomes too intense or prolonged, then it becomes more disadvantageous than advantageous and needs to be decreased to the point that the person can tolerate.

In any kind of psychotherapy for a trauma victim, as explained by Ochberg, 1991, the following four therapeutic principles should be considered: (a) normalization, e.g., your flashback/nightmare is a normal reaction to an abnormal situation or to a traumatizing event; (b) empowerment; (c) integration of the trauma into consciousness and reduction of amnesia; (d) and the individuality principle, which implies every individual has a unique pathway to recovery (Ochberg. 1991).

PTSD may also involve the therapist who is a survivor or an exvictim. The patient's description of her victimization and sexual molestation may trigger a reawakening reaction in the therapist and old injuries (which have not been completely worked out) will come to the conscious mind through flashbacks, visions, and nightmares. The therapist's deep-seated conflicts and leftover issues, in regard to her past victimization, may emerge and surface, preventing the therapist from exploring the patient's victimization. In this situation, the clinician needs immediate involvement with personal psychotherapy; and her or his therapist or supervisor may eventually recommend that the patient be referred to another therapist.

2. RECANTING OF SEXUAL ABUSE. Several clinicians who have worked with sexually abused children have explained a *tardive disclosure phenomenon*, which may be named the "no, maybe, sometimes, yes" syndrome. In incest cases, the same syndrome may be present at the beginning and eventually may change to a "tardive recanting" and reversal. This means that after the victim of incest discloses the sexual abuse, in a vague, gradual, doubtful, piece-by-piece, pulling-of-teeth way, the victim may reverse and recant it after finding that disclosure brought more pain to her family and guilt feelings to herself. She may get the message from her family members that recanting may bring back the family equilibrium and make everyone happy. Eventually, the child may give a statement to the therapist such as "Maybe it didn't happen" or "I wonder if it happened only in my dream."

The recanting may also be partial. The child may have alleged that the abuser was her father but then she "discovered" that the abuser was someone else. She may say something like "I know my father loves me; he would never do something like that to me" or "My grandmother told me maybe someone else did it to me; I mistook him for my father; no I remember more and more that it was not my father."

Recanting, which is called "normal" by many clinicians (Summit, 1983), may deceive the therapist and divert his attention from incest to other subjects. Now the therapist is actively participating in the "conspiracy of silence" and becomes a part of the family system's denial (Sukosky & Marvasti, 1991). One of the therapeutic tasks is to affirm the incest: "Yes, it happened; let's talk about it."

3. PLAY DISRUPTION.   Erickson (1950) defined play interruption as "a break in the continuity of the child's play when the play is bringing up conflictual material significant enough to increase the child's anxiety."

CASE ILLUSTRATION

Tanya, a 7-year-old girl who was sexually abused by her stepfather, was involved in play therapy. During a session, she left a girl doll and father doll together in the bedroom. The therapist asked, "Let's see what's going on in this bedroom." Tanya immediately stopped playing, became somewhat pale, and asked to see her mother.

4. EMERGENGE OF POSTTRAUMATIC PLAY (PTP), NEGATIVE TYPE.   PTP is a frequent type of play seen in traumatized children; it is a repetition of traumatic events, in a symbolic way, for the purpose of ego mastery, which may be labeled as *positive type* (Marvasti, 1993c). However, Terr (1990) described a kind of PTP that is detrimental to the child's well-being—*negative type*. During this kind of play, the child compulsively repeats the traumatic events, but play itself fails to relieve any anxiety or to create ego mastery. It is a monotonous, repetitive play that, at times, may be dangerous because it may create more terror (Terr, 1985) and may need to be interrupted by the therapist. Gil (1991) explained that after observing that the PTP remains static for a period of time (8 to 10 times), she attempts in intervene by asking the child to make physical movements, take deep breaths, to take a specific role, and to differentiate between the posttraumatic event and current reality. The therapist may manipulate the dolls, moving them around and asking the child to respond to "What happens if . . ." Eventually, the purpose of interrupting the PTP (negative type) is to generate a healthier alternative that might promote a sense of control, safety, and empowerment in the child. Repetition of a trauma in a play session, without resolution and emerging ego mastery, may reinforce the child's sense of helplessness, passivity, and lack of control (Gil, 1991).

5. EMERGENCE OF ACTING-OUT BEHAVIOR IN THE PLAYROOM OR OUTSIDE.   *Sexual acting-out* means "the expression of sexual trauma through action rather than in words or play during psychotherapy." The child repeats a sexual act without becoming aware of the meaning of the act. In general, the traumatized child should bring early trauma into consciousness; therefore, through play, the trauma can be worked through rather than acted out (Mills & Allan, 1992). Some of these children become sexually involved with other children as a coping mechanism and reaction to their victimization. The child may also demonstrate oversexualized behavior toward the therapist, such as having an obsession to touch the therapist's genital area, asking the therapist to touch the child, or having a compulsion to take her clothes off and expose herself. Each therapist develops a unique way of handling this excessive sexualized behavior related to how comfortable he or she feels about sex and sexuality.

CASE ILLUSTRATION

Neda, an 11-year-old girl who was a victim of chronic sexual molestation and vaginal stimulation, frequently sat on the edge of a chair and rolled her vaginal area on the chair during play sessions. The therapist did not comment or intervene in this behavior. Neda continued masturbating with different objects during the play; for example, one of her hands was in the dollhouse manipulating the dolls or moving the puppets, while her other hand was rubbing her genital area with a wooden ruler. Eventually, Neda asked the therapist to scratch and touch her genital area. First, the therapist commented on Neda's pleasure in touching her genital area and her desire that the therapist would also give her the same stimulation. He explained that this may be a "very normal" reaction by children who have been frequently touched in their genital area by "grown-up people" without the children's permission or consent. The therapist added that he does not feel comfortable touching children's "private parts," although he knows that when he touches his own private part it is pleasurable; that, he added, is something to be done in the privacy of his room and not in front of people. The therapist brought an anatomical doll with fingers and a penis, gave it to Neda, and suggested she might pretend this is the therapist and direct the doll to do what she wished the therapist would do to her. However, when the child tried to pull down her pants and rub the doll to her genital area, the therapist felt uncomfortable (being exposed to a child's genital area) and asked her to pretend that she was naked; "One of our playroom rules is that we can't be naked, but we can make the dolls naked and we can pretend that we are naked."

6. PSEUDOHEALTHY, PSEUDOMATURE ATTITUDE with superficially pleasant mood and "in control" gestures, which some of these "parentified" children may demonstrate during the evaluation. These pseudoadult behaviors may deceive the therapist into believing that the child is mature and all right, without need for therapy.

7. POSITIVE FEELINGS TOWARD THE OFFENDER, which may be a kind of reaction formation or, most likely, a reality of being exposed to positive and negative qualities in the offender. The clinician may give up dealing with the issue of incest because he or she cannot comprehend how an abused child may love her abusive father.

8. THERAPIST PITFALLS, such as overidentification with the victim (or offender), projection of the therapist's subjectivity onto the patient, preconceived ideas, and lack of limit setting and boundary defining. These "therapeutic pitfalls" are very much connected to the therapist's countertransference and may need to be identified and addressed in consultation, supervisory, or personal psychotherapy sessions.

Collateral Therapy

O'Connor (1991) suggested that a therapist must consider the child's entire *ecosystem* when planning and implementing a course of play therapy. He defined this play therapy technique, an integrated model that is parallel to the meaning of the term *ecology,* as the totality or pattern of relations between child and environment. The ecosystemic approach emphasizes the necessity of considering multiple systems of which the child is a part (O'Connor, 1991). Maybe the most important individuals or "system" in children's lives are their parents and their family organization. *Collateral therapy* in this chapter denotes therapeutic work with parents in group, individual, or family settings. In father-daughter incest, the purpose of involvement with every member of the family is multifold:

1. To assess the possibility of abuse in siblings.
2. To evaluate and, if needed, rehabilitate mother/child relationship. It is documented

in clinical literature that the mother (in father-daughter incest) may be distant, cold, depressed, or overwhelmed. The child has a certain amount of anger toward the nonoffending parent any may feel neglected by her.

3. To support the mother, empower her, and help her to arrive at a conclusion in regard to her marriage; to identify if she is a "battered wife."

4. To evaluate the offender (father) in regard to his willingness to apologize to his victim and to take total responsibility for incest. Fathers generally are involved in treatment for their sexual offense in a special treatment program. It is desirable to have consent from the father for communication with his therapist at the time of reuniting the family. Risk factors need to be assessed thoroughly in regard to reunification of the family.

5. To evaluate the possibility of conducting family therapy as an adjunct to play therapy with the child victim.

The incestuous family frequently will try to involve the therapist in their familiar interactions as they struggle to rebalance the family dynamics in order to recreate the pattern that was present before the disclosure of incest. In this situation, the treatment of family members is essential and a homogeneous group therapy may be the best modality for mothers.

Group Therapy with Mothers of Victims

In order to facilitate the reestablishment of the mother/daughter relationship, a support group for mothers may be beneficial. Frequently, it is found that the mother/daughter bond has either not been formed or has been broken during the incest process (Prewo, Mudry, & Marvasti, 1984). Mothers of victims often appear passive, dependent, and depressed. If forced to decide between the husband or the child, some may choose the husband because of strong dependency needs. Within the group, feelings of guilt and shame are ventilated, hurt and anger are expressed, and the sense of isolation is diminished. The mothers begin to view their own feelings of helplessness, sometimes recall their own past childhood sexual trauma, restructure their self-image, reevaluate their strengths and weaknesses, come to understand the factors contributing to their remaining in the relationship, express feelings of powerlessness, and explore their fear of rejection. She is then free to reestablish the mother/daughter relationship and husband/wife relationship or to end the marriage and look for more appropriate choices.

The mothers' group is particularly important during the legal/court proceedings. Support is vital. They need to understand their role and their rights and to have realistic expectations.

Family Therapy with Incestuous Families

Clinical literature has documented characteristics of "healthy" families, for example, (a) a strong parental coalition, with explicit boundaries between generations; (b) open and clear communication; (c) capacity to share feelings openly with predominance of positive affect; and (d) respect and tolerance for growth and autonomy among family members (Lewis, Beavers, Gossett & Austin Phillips, 1976). Incestuous families lack these qualities and are generally considered a dysfunctional system in which sex is being used within the family to cope with fear of separation, powerlessness, and shattered masculinity. Incestuous families are a heterogeneous population, and each may have their specific characteristics. However, in a classical case of father/child incest, there are similarities and common qualities that one may detect in evaluation, for example, boundary disturbance and role confusion among family members.

Family therapists have divided the nuclear family into three subsystems: (a) the parent/child subsystem; (b) the husband/wife subsystem; and (c) the parents/family of origin subsystem.

Family therapists have demonstrated how the disorders and symptoms in one subsystem may be a reaction to conflicts pertaining to the other; for example, disorders in the third subsystem frequently have a substantial impact on the other subsystems (Zuelzer & Reposa, 1983). The current marital/family problems are usually considered to be extensions of relationship difficulties of parents in their original families. The family of origin is an arena of individuation and growth, a learning milieu for intimacy and boundaries (Framo, 1974). In other words, the past is being perpetuated in the present and the future. In the family treatment of incestuous families, one needs to explore the conflicts between parents and their families of origin in order to understand the present interaction between parents and children and also between parents themselves.

Family therapy of an abusive family, especially in the case of father/daughter incest, is a controversial issue among clinicians. There is evidence that countertransference is highly influential in this modality of treatment. There are clinicians who believe that the victim *does not need this kind of father* and that permanent separation is beneficial for the child. However, there are other clinicians who are concerned that permanent separation causes losses for the child. Since these fathers are not abusive 24 hours a day and may have some attractive qualities, the children may have some positive feelings and attachment toward them.

Some feminist therapists suggest that family therapy in father/daughter incest is contraindicated because they feel the father would manipulate his way back into the family and gradually regain his abusive power and authority. There are also clinicians who believe it is the family members themselves who should decide if they want to remain intact or go through separation. The victim's wishes should be respected if she does not want to accept her father as a father; however, it is important to help her to identify her ambivalent feelings toward him.

During family sessions, the following issues frequently surface and are addressed: role reversal (parentification of victim); enmeshed and symbiotic relationship; difficulty in separation/individuation process; inappropriate distribution of power; lack of protection; lack of limit setting (in offender and victim); family isolation; blurred boundaries; lack of empathy; neediness; abuse of power; the victim's role as rescuer/peacemaker, and, as Sgroi (1982) mentioned, divided loyalty (family members ally with either the offender or the victim).

CONCLUSION

Play is considered the child's natural medium for rehearsing new developmental skills, for mastering them, and for working through conflicts. For young children, verbal psychotherapy, which is dependent upon abstract symbolic thinking with language, is not a very useful way of learning new emotional responses and behavioral skills (Walker & Bolkovatz, 1988).

Play diagnosis and play interview are techniques that enable the traumatized child to express her suffering and to reenact her trauma. Externalization of the "child's issues," which eventually become the "doll's issues," will give the diagnostician the opportunity to discover the child's conflicts and her perception of trauma. In a forensic play interview, the anatomical dolls are used *only after* the child discloses information about her victimization. However, in clinical play diagnosis, these dolls may be used in the same way as any other dolls, before or after the child's disclosure of incest.

Not every child who is involved in incest is damaged, traumatized, or victimized; and not every traumatized child needs play therapy. Some of the psychopathology seen in victims (years later) may be the result of genetic factors, emotional neglect, or growing up in a dysfunctional family, rather than incest itself. In victimized children, sometimes a homogeneous play group therapy may be more beneficial than any individual session, especially if group therapy includes male and female cotherapists (Marvasti, 1994c).

In psychiatry (unlike surgery), injuries may not result in scarring. Children may overcome a traumatic event that they have encountered and may even become stronger or more resistant to future trauma.

Play therapy with a child in the posttrauma stage may follow the same principles that are taken in psychotherapy with any posttrauma patients: (a) normalization; (b) empowerment; (c) integration of the trauma into consciousness; and (d) individuality principle, which implies every individual has a unique pathway to recovery after traumatic stress (Ochberg, 1991).

In this chapter, posttraumatic play (PTP) is divided into positive and negative types (Marvasti, 1993c). The positive type of PTP is demonstrated by the child's compulsion to repeat the trauma during play, psychodrama, and storytelling. In this symbolic recreation of the trauma, the child's memories and associated affect emerge; this may result in ego mastery of the old traumas. The negative type of PTP is a kind of repetitive play, with no accomplishment in ego mastery or reduction in anxiety (Terr, 1990). This repetitive, monotonous play needs intervention and interruption by the therapist.

Play therapy, for the child victim of incest, is only one of the components of the comprehensive treatment program for these members of dysfunctional/multiple-problem families. The empowerment of the mother in father/daughter incest and the restoration the mother/child bond are essential. The reuniting of the family should not be based solely on the improvement of and/or change in the offender (father). (This author has never seen any incest offender who did not improve or change after the arrest and court-ordered counseling.) Improvement or change needs to be documented in the victim and in her nonoffending parent before recommending any family therapy or considering reunification.

REFERENCES

Brant, R. S. T., & Tisza, V. B. (1977). The sexually misused child. *The American Journal of Orthopsychiatry, 47*(1), 80–90.

Broadhurst, D. (1979). The educator's role in the prevention and treatment of child abuse and neglect. (DHEW Publication No. OHDS 79–30172). Washington, DC: U.S. Department of Health, Education and Welfare.

Bulman, R., & Wortman, C.B. (1977). Attributions of blame and coping in the "real world": Severe accident victims react to their loss. *Journal of Personality and Psychology, 35*, 351–363.

Butler, S. (1978). *Conspiracy of silence.* New York: Bantam Books.

Conte, J., & Berliner, L. (1988). The impact of sexual abuse. In L. E. A. Walker (Ed), *Handbook on sexual abuse of children* (pp. 79–93). New York: Springer.

Erikson, E. H. (1950). *Childhood and society.* New York: Norton.

Faller, K. C. (1990). *Understanding child sexual maltreatment.* Newbury Park, CA: Sage Publications.

Framo, I. L. (1974). Family of origin as a therapeutic resource for adults in marital and family therapy: You can and should go home again. *Family Process, 15,* 2.

Freud, S. (1920). Beyond the pleasure principle. In *The standard edition of the complete psychological works of Sigmund Freud* (Vol. 19, pp. 3–64). London: Hogarth Press.

Gelinas, D. J. (1983). The persisting negative effect of incest. *Psychiatry, 46,* 312–332.

Gil, E. (1991). *The healing power of play.* New York: Guilford Press.

Goodman, G. S., & Reed, R. S. (1986). Age differences in eyewitness testimony. *Law and Human Behavior, 10,* 317–332.

James, B., & Nasjleti, M. (1983). *Treating sexually abused children and their families.* Palo Alto, CA: Consulting Psychologist Press.

James, J., & Meyerding, J. (1977). Early sexual experiences and prostitution. *American Journal of Psychiatry, 134,* 1381–1385.

Johnson, K. (1989). *Trauma in the lives of children.* Claremont, CA: Hunter House.

Lamb, F. (1986). Treating sexually abused children: Issues of blame and responsibility. *American Journal of Orthopsychiatry, 56,* 303–307.

Lewis, J. M., Beavers, W. R., Gossett, J. T., Austin Phillips, V. (1976). *No single thread: Psychological health in family systems.* New York: Brunner/Mazel.

McCann, L., & Pearlman, L. A. (1990). Vicarious traumatization: The emotional costs of working with survivors. *The Advisor, 3*(4).

Marvasti, J. A. (1985). Fathers who commit incest, jail or treatment? The need for a "victim oriented law." *American Journal of Forensic Psychiatry, 6*(3), 8–13.

Marvasti, J. A. (1986a). Female sex offenders, incestuous mothers. *American Journal of Forensic Psychiatry, 7*(4), 63–69.

Marvasti, J. A. (1986b, May). *Using dolls in interviewing sexually abused children.* Paper presented at Fourth National Conference on the Sexual Victimization of Children, New Orleans, LA.

Marvasti, J. A. (1986c, January). *Play therapy and the child victim: Making the correct interpretation.* Paper presented at Thirteenth National Conference on Juvenile Justice, New Orleans, LA.

Marvasti, J. A. (1987, April 6–10). *Eating disorder as a consequence of incest and child sexual abuse.* Paper presented at First European Congress on Child Abuse and Neglect. Rhodes, Greece.

Marvasti, J. A. (1989). Play therapy with sexually abused children. In S. Sgroi (Ed.), *Vulnerable population* (Vol. 2, pp. 1–41). Lexington, MA: Lexington Books.

Marvasti, J. A. (1990, June 21–24). *Is father a snake, is mother a monster? Play therapy with child incest victim.* Paper presented at Seventh Annual International Play Therapy Conference, Association for Play Therapy, University of British Columbia, Vancouver, British Columbia, Canada.

Marvasti, J. A. (1991). Dysfunctional mothering in survivors of incest. *American Journal of Forensic Psychiatry, 12*(4), 39–47.

Marvasti, J. A. (1992a). Psychotherapy with abused children and adolescents. In J. R. Brandell (Ed.), *Counter-transference in psychotherapy with children and adolescents* (pp. 191–214). Northvale, NJ.: Jason Aronson.

Marvasti, J. A. (1992b, April 2–5). *False allegations of child sexual abuse.* Paper presented at Tenth Annual Symposium of American College of Forensic Psychiatry, San Francisco, CA.

Marvasti, J. A. (1992c, October). *Play interview technique with sexually abused children.* Paper presented at Ninth Annual International Play Therapy Conference, Association for Play Therapy, Nashua, NH.

Marvasti, J. A. (1993a). Psychopathology in adult survivors of incest. *American Journal of Forensic Psychiatry, 14*(2), 61–73.

Marvasti, J. A. (1993b, May 20–22). *Play interview techniques with sexually abused children.* Workshop presented at 1993 National Children's Mental Health Conference, Family Psychological Consultants, Seattle, WA.

Marvasti, J. A. (1993c). Please hurt me again: Posttraumatic play therapy with an abused child. In T. Kottman & C. Schaefer (Eds.), *Play therapy in action: A casebook for practitioners*, (pp. 485–525). Northvale, NJ.: Jason Aronson.

Marvasti, J. A. (1994a, May 4–7). *Therapeutic use of play with sexually traumatized children.* Paper presented at Second National Colloquium, American Professional Society on the Abuse of Children, Cambridge, MA.

Marvasti, J. A. (1994b, June 10–12). *Forensic play diagnosis with sexually traumatized children.* Workshop presented at Believe the Children's Second Annual National Conference, Ritual Child Abuse, Disclosures in the 80's, Backlash in the 90's.

Marvasti, J. A. (1994c). Play group therapy with sexually abused children. In S. Sgroi (Ed.), *Handbook of clinical intervention in child sexual abuse.* New York: MacMillan Free Press.

Meiselman, I. K. (1978). *Incest.* San Francisco, CA: Jossey-Bass.

Miller, A. (1984). *Thou shalt not be aware.* New York: Farrar, Straus, Giroux.

Mills, B., & Allan, J. (1992). Play therapy with the molested child: Impact upon aggressive and withdrawn patterns of interaction. *International Journal of Play Therapy, 1*(1), 1–20.

Mrazek, P. B. (1981). Special problems in the treatment of child sexual abuse. In P. B. Mrazek & C. H. Kempe (Eds.), *Sexually abused children and their families* (pp. 159–166). New York: Pergamon Press.

Mudry, S. (1986). Incest: A developmental dystopia. *The Journal of Specialists in Group Work, 11*(3), 174–179.

Ochberg, F. M. (1991). Posttraumatic therapy. *Psychotherapy, 28*(1), 5–15.

O'Connor, K. J. (1991). *The play therapy primer.* New York: Wiley.

Oppenheimer, R., Howells, K., Palmer, R. L., & Challoner, D. A. (1984, September). *Adverse sexual experience and clinical eating disorder.* Paper presented at Fifth International Congress on Child Abuse and Neglect, Montreal, Canada.

Porter, F. S., Blick, L. C., & Sgroi, S. M. (1982). Treatment of the sexually abused child. In S. Sgroi (Ed.), *Handbook of clinical intervention in child sexual abuse* (pp. 109–146). Lexington, MA: Lexington Books.

Prewo, K., Mudry, S., Marvasti, J. A. (1984, September). *Establishing a sexual trauma center.* Paper presented at the Fifth International Congress of Child Abuse and Neglect, Montreal, Canada.

Sepahbodi, T., & Marvasti, J. A. (1986, April). *Past history of sex abuse and victimization in patients with borderline personality disorder.* Paper presented at Fourth Annual Symposium in Psychiatry and Law, American College of Forensic Psychiatry, Sanibel Island, FL.

Sgroi, S. (1982). *Handbook of clinical intervention in child sexual abuse.* Lexington, MA: Lexington Books.

Stolorow, R.D., & Atward, G. C. (1979). *Faces in a cloud: Subjectivity in personality theory.* New York: Jason Aronson.

Stone, M. H. (1990). Incest in the borderline patient. In R. P. Kluft (Ed.), *Incest related syndromes of adult psychopathology* (pp. 183–204). Washington, DC: American Psychiatric Press.

Sukosky, D. G., & Marvasti, J. A. (1991). Comparative overview of child and elder abuse: Relevance for the forensic professional. *American Journal of Forensic Psychiatry, 12*(1), 23–39.

Summit, R. (1983). The child sexual abuse accommodation syndrome. *Child Abuse and Neglect, 7,* 177–193.

Summit, R., & Kryso, J. (1978). Sexual abuse of children: a Clinical spectrum. *American Journal of Orthopsychiatry, 48* , 237–251.

Terr, L. C. (1990). *Too scared to cry.* New York: Harper & Row.

Terr, L. C. (1985). Psychic trauma in children and adolescents, *Psychiatric Clinics of North America, 8(4),* 815–835.

Ulman, R. B., & Brothers, D. (1988). *The shattered self.* Hillsdale, NJ. The Analytic Press.

Walker, L. E. A., & Bolkovatz, M. A. (1988). Play therapy with children who have experienced sexual assault. In L. E. A. Walker (Ed.), *Handbook on sexual abuse of children* (pp. 249–269). New York: Springer.

Ward, E. (1984). *Father-daughter rape.* New York: Grove Press.

Warner, R. (1978). The diagnosis of antisocial and hysterical personality: An example of sex bias. *Journal of Nervous and Mental Disorders, 166,* 839–845.

Winnicott, D. W. (1965). *Therapeutic consultations in child psychiatry.* New York: Basic Books.

Winnicott, D. W. (1971). *The maturational processes and the facilitating environment.* New York: International Universities Press.

Yates, A. (1982). Children eroticized by incest. *American Journal of Psychiatry, 139(4),* 482–485.

Zuelzer, M. B., & Reposa, R. E. (1983). Mothers in incestuous families. *International Journal of Family Therapy 5(2),* 98–110.

CHAPTER 15

Play Therapy with Mentally Retarded Clients

JOOP HELLENDOORN

INTRODUCTION

Play therapy has only recently been recognized as an appropriate form of treatment for emotionally disturbed retarded persons. This development is closely linked to another recent and quite fundamental change of view in the field of mental retardation: the acknowledgment of mental illness and emotional disturbance as real phenomena among retarded persons. All too often, the atypical or abnormal behavior of mentally retarded adults and children has been ascribed to their retardation, instead of to possible emotional causes. Consequently, as Menolascino (1990b) stated, for a long time "treatment nihilism" reigned. There was an almost exclusive emphasis on medication and behavioral control. Treatment guidelines based on careful diagnostic considerations and on an individualized clinical picture were seldom, if ever, considered.

There is now a growing awareness that persons with a mental handicap can and do suffer from emotional disorders. Estimates of incidence of psychological problems among retarded persons range from 23% to over 50% (Dosen, 1983; Gunzburg, 1974; Menolascino, 1990a, 1990b), dependent on the definition used. Depression, low self-esteem, and socialization problems are the most common symptoms (Dosen, 1990; Menolascino, 1990a). This is no surprise because all children with mental retardation (from mild to severe) frequently experience situations in which they fall short of expectations and in which they feel, or are made to feel, their cognitive and social limitations. Very little is known as yet about the attachment processes in retarded children and their families, but, especially in the case of more severely retarded children, it is almost certainly more difficult for parents to be the sensitively responding adult a child needs in order to develop a secure attachment. Moreover, all those retarded persons who have been placed outside their parental home and natural environment have experienced losses in basic security and in family ties. These psychological problems, which are specifically related to retardation, can be confounded by other stressful life events (accidents, illness, loss of near relations or other important persons, and so on) that are related to life in general and could be encountered by anyone, regardless of any handicap. The use of the *Diagnostic and Statistical Manual of Mental Disorders*, third edition, revised (DSM-III-R) (American Psychiatric Association, 1987), which arranges psychiatric syndromes and concurrent mental retardation on different axes, has facilitated "dual diagnosis" of retarded persons. It is especially important to reexamine the disturbances

The author wishes to express her indebtedness to therapist Annemieke Biessels for her in-depth comments on an earlier draft of this paper and for her permission to present one of her cases. Thanks also to students Trees van Eijden, Ellen Hansen, Sonja van Heumen, Marjan Lanser, Wilma van der Jagt, Mary Kwint, and Detsje Rienks for their contributions to the evaluation project. Lastly, this chapter could not have been written but for the intense and keen participation of many therapists.

more frequently reported in the *nonretarded* population (e.g., adjustment disorders and crisis situations) and to question why these are still so rarely seen in the retarded population (Menolascino, 1990b).

With the recognition that mental health is just as much (and sometimes even more) at risk in retarded as in nonretarded persons, the way has been paved for treatment. If the same sort of disturbances can be diagnosed retarded as in nonretarded persons, might not the same kinds of treatments be applicable? Play therapy is one of the most widely used forms of psychological treatment for children in the age range of 2 to 11 years. Could it perhaps also be used for retarded people with a comparable *mental* age range?

Pioneers in the field have tested different methods of play therapy. They argued that play might be particularly useful as a vehicle for therapy for retarded children and youth because it provides them with a relatively free and safe environment in which to express experiences and problems and that is tuned to their mental level (e.g., Hellendoorn & Hoekman, 1992; Li, 1981; Scholten, 1985). Leland and Smith (1965) have written a very useful overview of the different possibilities of play therapy for retarded children (see also Leland, 1983). Their division of play treatment into four groups, dependent on the degree to which the materials and the therapeutic approach are structured, as well as their emphasis on the need for directiveness on the part of the therapist, have clarified the field considerably. However, their main goal was behavioral change, whereas this chapter will deal primarily with play therapy as a treatment for emotional problems, an approach that comes nearest to Leland and Smith's S-U variant (structured material, unstructured approach).

In a survey in the Netherlands, Lamers-Osterhaus and van Santen (1985) found that, in about 40% of the residential centers for retarded persons, play therapy was practiced, with children as well as with older retarded persons. However, very little is known as yet about the therapeutic process and its effects (Bernhardt & Mackler, 1975; Hellendoorn, 1990; Li, 1981). The results of the few existing studies are ambiguous. Mehlmann (1953) and Subotnik and Callahan (1959), for instance, found no significant improvement after play therapy. Others (Leland, Walker, & Taboada, 1959; Morrison & Newcomer, 1975) observed some improvement in cognitive but not in social functioning. One of the main problems with such studies is that they all use standard tests as outcome measures. Because the limited sensitivity of these tests to clinical change makes them already too coarse a sieve in outcome studies with nonretarded children, this may be even more problematic with retarded clients. Individual case studies *do* show positive effects that do not seem purely incidental (e.g., Biessels-Smulders & Wagenborg, 1990). Therefore, it may well be that more individual goals and outcome measures are needed. Then again, effect studies are rather premature given that the therapeutic process is an almost unknown entity (Kazdin, 1988).

In the Netherlands, a group of play therapists, organized in a special section of the Dutch Association for the Study of Mentally Retarded People, had a pioneer role in bringing together colleagues who were trying to develop play therapy methods specifically geared to their group of clients. By meeting regularly to discuss their cases and to strengthen their theoretical background, they have played a prominent part in putting play therapy on the treatment program of many residential and day-care institutions in their country. They also paved the way for a change in attitude on the part of the vested therapeutic schools. Until recently, the general attitude towards therapy for retarded persons was slightly disdainful. The large audience at the first Symposium, organized by the Dutch Section of Play Therapists in 1990, and the success of their practice-oriented book (Biessels-Smulders & Wagenborg, 1990) bear witness to the growing interest in the possibilities of play for the treatment of retarded persons. On the other hand, the therapists themselves became aware of their need for further research on their explorative work. In all, this proved a fertile field to start an evaluation study.

In close cooperation with the therapists themselves, the following research questions were formulated:

1. What indications for play therapy are used by the therapists?
2. What (therapeutic) goals are formulated?
3. What specific features and/or problems characterize play therapy with mentally retarded children as compared with nonretarded children?
4. On what grounds and in what ways do therapists plan their interventions?
5. What results and developments can be perceived in the client, short-term as well as long-term?

Since the literature in the field suggests no reason to think that the research questions or the sort of data gathered in this study are invalid for the situation in countries other than the Netherlands, its results will be reported throughout this chapter.

PROCEDURE

Participating Clients and Therapists

Participants in this evaluation study were 13 Dutch play therapists, all female, working all over the country in day-care and residential centers and (one therapist only) in a special school. They all had professional training in special education, and most of them had some additional training in play or play therapy. Usually, doing therapy was only part of their duties. With one exception, they all participated actively in the pioneer organization of therapists previously mentioned, regularly meeting and discussing their cases.

Since so little is known as yet about the therapeutic process, the researchers chose a descriptive process approach that was designed as a multiple-case study. To this purpose, the participating therapists were asked to keep a detailed file on each of their clients. Again, in close cooperation with the therapists, standard forms were constructed to record different aspects of therapy. Most forms consisted of open-ended questions in order to minimize experimental constraint on the natural situation of a therapist reporting about clients. Before the start of therapy, forms were filled out listing personal data and indications and goals for therapy. In addition, a list of behavioral symptoms at referral was completed by one or more primary caregivers. This list contained 48 behavioral symptoms to be scored on frequency of occurrence (often, occasionally, rarely) and on problem importance. During therapy, all play sessions and interviews with caregivers were recorded. Moreover, every second month, the therapy process was summarily evaluated by the therapist. Every 6 months, the behavioral symptom list was repeated, if possible by the same scorer(s). At termination, the results of therapy were evaluated by the therapist and the primary caregivers.

From the first, the researchers were delighted by the consistency and conscientiousness with which the therapists sent in their (anonymized) data. From experience with other studies, much more resistance had been expected on the part of the participants to share their often frustrating and difficult work. The researchers tried to keep the therapists' motivation on a high level by replying personally to each consignment of material.

Sixteen therapists participated in the preparatory work for this study. Because of illness and/or long absence from work, three of them stopped their regular reports. No data on these therapists or their clients have been included. However, there is no reason to believe that their exclusion distorts the results of this study because, during the time they did participate, no specific differences were found between them and the other therapists and clients.

The group of 20 clients on whom the remaining 13 therapists reported consisted of 9 males, with chronological ages from 5 to 25 years and mental ages from 2.2 to 7.0 years, and 11 females with chronological ages from 4.3 to 65.0 years, and mental ages from 1.8 to 6.0 years. Of the 10 clients under 16 years of age, seven were living at home and visiting a day-care center or a special school, and three lived in a residential center. Among the 10 clients older than 16, only one (a 27-year-old woman) was living in the parental home. The others lived in residential homes, usually with day activities on the premises or nearby.

Although all the therapists in the sample presented themselves as "play therapists," they were flexible in using other techniques besides play, depending on the theoretical framework to which the individual therapist adhered and also on the specific abilities and interests of each client. Most widely used by the therapists were the hermeneutic method (Lubbers, 1988; Mook, 1994) and Imagery Interaction Play Therapy (Hellendoorn, 1988). In both therapy methods, the emphasis is on understanding the personal significance and the personal meaning of the client's actions. Everything the client plays, paints, says, or shows has "image quality:" it conveys something specific about the client's experience of the world. The therapist tries to join in that experience, thus closely approaching the client's thoughts and feelings. This special way of empathizing also helps the therapist to understand the client's personal meanings and, thus, forms the basis for providing therapeutic interventions. This is one of the two main reasons why therapists generally feel that play or related (often imaginative) forms of communication have a special value in the interaction with retarded clients, who are often difficult to understand otherwise. The other reason is that play interaction minimizes demands on the clients' cognitive and verbal development but does provide them with a means for expressing their feelings and needs that is much better geared to their communicative abilities.

INDICATIONS AND GOALS*

To acquire an overview of the indications and goals for therapy as formulated by the therapists, the completed forms listing personal data and indications and goals were studied. Because of the qualitative nature of the responses, a content analysis of "referral problems" and "therapy goals" was performed by two judges. The categories they inductively and independently formulated showed remarkable similarity, and their agreement on the scoring of separate items in these categories was about 80%.

---

*In a previous paper (Hellendoorn, 1990) on this subject, data on 16 clients from this same sample were presented.

Indications and Contraindications

Referral problems as stated by the theapists were classified in 6 categories and 10 subcategories (see Table 15.1). As could be expected, maladaptive behavior was a major category of referral problems. Reduced or inhibited social and emotional competence, and manifest anxieties, as well as traumatic experiences, were also often considered an indication for play therapy.

In the majority of the clients, the problems were long-standing. Usually, many other efforts had been undertaken to help the clients. Frequently, behavior modification procedures had been attempted and totally or partially failed. Indeed, it seemed as if play therapy was often seen by the referring caregivers or professionals as a last resort rather than as a distinctive and specific way of helping that might be indicated in the case of specifiable emotional problems.

What kind of diagnostic material did the therapists use to decide on play therapy as a suitable form of treatment? In all cases, the existing record files were used, including reports of parents or caregivers on present and past experiences and behavior. In three cases, a case conference with other professionals was a decisive factor. Developmental or intelligence test data were used in 12 cases. The Wechsler Intelligence Scale for Children–Revised (WISC-R) and the Snÿders-Oomen Nonverbal Intelligence Test (SON 2 1/2–7, a Dutch nonverbal test for young children) were the most popular developmental tests. However, most of the test data were not recent. Traditionally, psychological assessment never had a prominent place in the care for mentally handicapped persons, particularly with regard to elder persons for whom daily living experiences were deemed more important than objective knowledge about their level or their way of thinking and feeling. Then again, standard tests might yield a very limited reflection of a retarded person's state of mind. Often, too, retarded clients have been considered untestable. Consequently, many of the therapists set up a standard procedure of one to four observation sessions in the client's living environment or day activity group. This was part of the assessment process for 13 clients. Not unnaturally, play observation was a favorite indicator, used in 17 of 20 cases. Even with this, therapists often felt they did not really know enough about their clients to be sure about their goals. For this reason, they often mentioned that their first sessions would have a diagnostic purpose. This point will be raised again in the section on therapeutic goals.

TABLE 15.1. Indications for Play Therapy (Referral Problems) as Stated by Therapists (No. of clients: 20)

	Referral problems	No. of cases
Behavioral:	• Specific maladaptive behaviors	18
Social:	• Lack of social contacts and initiatives	12
	• Inability to communicate emotional experiences	9
Emotional:	• Inability to handle/differentiate emotions	14
	• Manifest anxieties	13
	• Lack of basic acceptance/trust	6
Cognitive:	• Inability to cope with emotional (traumatic) experiences in life history	9
	• Inability to deal with daily experiences/low self-regard/low confidence	9
Developmental:	• Developmental blocks	6
Other:	• Problems with parents, sexual problem, no pleasure in life, and so on	2

Another problem was the respective positions of the caregivers and the therapist in the *referral* process. Although the referral problems are part and parcel of daily life (at home, in the day-care center, the special school, or the residential center), the contribution of caregivers and parents to the decision process seemed limited and sometimes almost absent. Usually, it was not the care staff or the parents but the professional staff that decided on any special help for clients. With a view to the need for the daily caregivers to become involved in the therapy and the change process, it seems advisable to give them a stronger voice in the referral phase. Another possible pitfall was the decision-making power of the therapists themselves. Therapists with a high level of training and a heavy caseload usually held a strong staff position and, consequently, had a strong voice in the decision as to whether to provide play therapy to a given client. Especially in some of the larger residential centers, play therapists with less specific training and a small therapeutic caseload were largely dependent on the decision-making power of others. Some of them did not even have a right to veto a decision for therapy or a decision to terminate!

In all but one of the cases, clients seemed motivated for therapy in the sense that they liked to come. One client was unable to take any initiative at all because of an acute crisis. In that case, the therapist went to the client in order to try patiently and carefully to establish a first contact; that was the exception. The free and easy aspect of play was generally described as a powerful stimulant for the clients to express themselves in a way that respected their anonymity, that did not seek to break through ritualistic behaviors, and that did not demand too much of their integrative powers. Many therapists felt they themselves could help the integrative process by initiating transfer and by informing and consulting with caregivers. Therefore, a cooperative attitude on the part of primary caregivers was considered crucial to effective therapy.

In two cases, an unfavorable living environment was considered a possible contraindication for therapy. In three cases, the therapist thought that play therapy might be too anxiety provoking, in which case more structured ways of working with the client (e.g., one of the variations proposed by Leland, 1986) might be favored over play therapy. Other contraindications mentioned were uncertainty about the suitability of *play* techniques (too little imagination? play not really suitable, that is, too childish, for a client?), and possible organic causes for a client's maladaptive behavior. Of course, since all these clients were already admitted to therapy, the possible contraindications might be regarded more as a warning than as a reason to reconsider the decision for treatment.

To conclude, there was still a lot of uncertainty about the indications for play therapy and about the assessment process needed. This will come up again when the therapeutic goals and the stages of therapy are discussed. Also, the contribution and decision making power of the caregivers and the therapist herself seemed in many cases too limited in view of their respective responsibility for the therapeutic and change process.

Therapeutic Goals

Next, therapists were asked to formulate therapy goals for each individual client, as well as goals for the counseling of the caregivers. In general, the client goals were much clearer; therefore, only the client goals will be reported. Using the same methodology as was used to study the referral problems, the client goals were qualitatively separated into 13 categories, in 6 clusters, as shown in Table 15.2. The number of goals for each client varied from three to seven (for the caregivers, from one to three).

TABLE 15.2.   Goals for Play Therapy Clients as Stated by Therapists
(No. of clients: 20)

	Therapeutic goals	No. of cases
Intermediate:	• Establishing a therapeutic relationship	13
	• Getting a clearer view of problems and symptoms	6
Behavioral:	• Promoting specific adaptive behaviors	6
	• Reducing maladaptive behaviors	7
Social:	• Better/stronger social contacts and initiatives	9
	• Learning to communicate emotional experiences	9
Emotional:	• Differentiating/better handling of emotions	9
	• Reducing anxieties	7
	• Promoting feeling of being accepted/loved	5
Cognitive:	• Coming to terms with emotional (traumatic) experiences in life history	10
	• Better dealing with daily experiences/promoting self-regard and self-confidence	9
Developmental:	• Reducing blocks/facilitating development	6
Other:		2

The intermediate goal, establishing a therapeutic relationship, was the one most frequently named. Even though the relationship should, by definition, be temporary—and, thus, cannot be a final goal of therapy—it was evidently seen as most important. Interesting is the fact that, in some cases, the relationship was *not* specifically mentioned. In those cases, the clients may have established contact so easily that there was no need for special attention on that point. The second intermediate goal mentioned was diagnostic: that, through therapy, therapists hoped to get more insight into the problem behavior and problem experiences of their clients. The other goals can be categorized either as "substantial," that is, pertaining to general ways of thinking, feeling, and acting, or as "functional," that is, pertaining to the way a person actually copes with everyday problems (Schmidtchen, 1978): better dealing with emotions, with emotional experiences and life events in one way or another; better coping with past and present occurrences; more and better social contacts. It is interesting that no goals were formulated in terms of "giving the client better insight into his or her own problems," such as might often be found in therapy with nonretarded persons.

Comparing Tables 15.1 and 15.2, some differences emerge. Naturally, the "intermediate goals" in Table 15.2 were not present in Table 15.1. For although social relationships in general were an important referral problem, the therapeutic relationship is limited to therapy itself. And even though uncertainty about the causes of behavior and about what exactly activated a client's problem prompted the need for "a clearer view of problems and symptoms" to be mentioned six times in connection with therapeutic goals, this was not (and should not be) an indication for treatment. Indeed, in such cases there is a need for better assessment, not for therapy.

A more interesting difference concerns the behavioral categories. Although maladaptive behavior was the main cause for referral, the play therapists—as opposed to behavior therapists—were not primarily concerned with the reduction of maladaptive behavior and/or the formation of specific adaptive behaviors. Rather, they focused on establishing a therapeutic alliance, on working through emotional and social problems, and on advancing emotional development.

THE THERAPY CONTEXT

Is play therapy for children with a mental handicap organized differently than therapy for nonretarded children? The therapists were asked about the frequency and the duration of sessions, about how their clients came and went, and about their playroom. In play therapy with nonretarded children, a frequency of once or twice a week is usually recommended. From the meager literature on this topic, one might expect a higher frequency for retarded clients because of their limited capacity to learn independently. However, among the 20 clients in the study, once-a-week sessions prevailed, although in the starting phase twice a week was not uncommon. Frequency was not related to mental age or to mental level. Rather, the therapist's other commitments and schedule seemed a more powerful criterion. The same was true for session duration. The customary session duration, as in therapy with nonretarded children, was 45 to 60 minutes.

All clients in the sample were treated in the context of their special school, day-care center, or residential center and not, as is usual for nonretarded children, in a counseling agency. There, clients are usually brought to session by their parents. The retarded clients were either ferried to and fro by the therapist, or they came on their own. Ferrying by the therapist had the advantage that the preparation and end phase of each session could take place in transit. Moreover, when taking a client out of a group, the therapist usually had a brief informal contact with the caregiver or teacher. When clients came on their own, these advantages were missed, but this left more time to spend on the session itself. Moreover, when the distance is not far and the route not dangerous, coming on his or her own may strengthen a client's feeling of self-esteem.

All therapists in the study appointed a fixed day and time for each client. The security and structure this provided were unanimously seen as essential conditions for retarded clients. However, this was not always tenable when therapists had to share a room with other professionals. Particularly when their room was claimed by a physician or other (para)medic, play therapists often had to yield precedence and find another room in which to play. On the other hand, some therapists found wonderfully creative solutions for sharing a room and still keeping it a client-friendly place with all the necessary toys easily accessible. Sometimes, too, appointments with physician or dentist were made on (or just before) the therapy hour. Such occurrences, of course, tended to seriously disturb that particular session.

Most playrooms were reasonably well equipped with materials. With one exception, sandtable and water basin were available. All rooms had a choice of different toys. Interestingly, in only about half of the playrooms were fighting toys, such as toy guns, soldiers, cowboys, or tanks, present. In playrooms for nonretarded children, these toys are considered almost obligatory for expressing anger and other negative feelings. It seems possible that the therapists had some reservations with regard to these toys because of the limited ability for stimulus selection and impulse control, and the greater suggestibility, of retarded clients.

Interesting, too, was the presence of food and drink in all but two of the playrooms. It seemed rather common to start or end a session with a drink and a cookie. In the literature on play therapy in general, opinions on this topic are divided. Some authors characterize the presence of food and drink as necessary for oral satisfaction (e.g., Ude-Pestel, 1975). Others tend to judge a liberal use of food and drink as a misguided attempt on the part of the therapist "to present herself as the all-giving, good, and nurturant parent" (e.g., Haworth & Keller, 1964). In this study, many clients were adults. Therapists often felt that a regular welcoming ritual with a drink and a snack might help to structure the therapeutic situation. Further research is needed on the question of whether food and drink can be used as an explicit therapeutic strategy and with what purpose.

THERAPEUTIC TREATMENT STAGES

The First Stage: Establishing a Relationship

As could be expected, most therapists reported slow progress. The focus during the first phase of therapy was usually on the intermediate goals: further assessment and establishing a therapeutic relationship. This was not an easy task because many retarded clients have acquired some kind of basic distrust. In the course of their lives, many different people can be appointed to their care. The large personnel turnover in all institutes for retarded people is undoubtedly responsible for an enormous challenge to their limited adaptive powers. When one or two different placements are added (not at all an unusual occurrence), the numbers expand even more. Perhaps the distrust many retarded clients show is not such an unhealthy sign as it may seem. Rather, it may be the most sensible way of meeting an uncertain and constantly changing environment.

The therapist, at first, is just another person who seems to care. But how trustworthy will he or she prove to be? Being there, week after week, sometimes twice a week, in the same interesting and attractive playroom, may help the client to settle in this new situation. Therapists tend to feel that the relationship they establish with their clients might be exemplary for other possible relationships for the client. But, in view of the temporariness of therapy, their relation with the client can, of course, never be permanent. Therefore, its gradual termination needs much specific care.

Once therapist and client get to know each other and establish a working alliance, play may have a larger or smaller role in the therapeutic process. Play is important because of its inherent freedom of expression. Even the much older clients in the sample seemed to enjoy manipulating and playing with all kinds of toys and other creative materials. As explained earlier, in the therapeutic methods most used in this group of therapists, Hermeneutic Therapy and Imagery Interaction Play Therapy, the therapist tries to discern the personal meaning of all (play) activities, to join in that experience, and to intervene, as much as possible, in the client's own (play) language.

Two examples illustrate what the therapist can do to establish the relationship. The first is the start of the therapy process with Rose, an institutionalized female client. In the second example, the working relationship also took a lot of the therapist's attention, but proved much easier to establish.

Case Illustration—Rose

Rose was 22 years old, with a mental age estimated at about 3 years. Her main referral problem was her extreme compulsiveness and her social problems. In the living group, attempts to counteract her compulsiveness by behavior modification had failed. In despair, the help of the play therapist was sought. The play therapist felt that perhaps in trying to modify Rose's annoying and troublesome compulsions, too little attention had been paid to the *meaning* of that behavior. Rose's history was characterized by illness, physical abuse, and different living environments. Because of her difficult behavior, she had been placed outside her parental home at the age of 10 and had since been relocated twice.

Repeating the same actions over and over again may well have provided her with the basic security she sorely missed. Therefore, the therapist's first strategy was *acceptance* of the compulsion.

In the playroom, Rose started every session by selecting a small toy house and carefully arranging and rearranging all the furniture. At first, this took the whole session. The therapist was not allowed to take part, but, once in a while, Rose would look at her, as if to convince herself that the therapist was still there. The therapist watched her acceptingly and verbalized what Rose did. At the end of the session, after finishing her play, Rose wanted to sit near the therapist and sing together; so it seemed that she did not reject the therapist but was still unable to include her in any play activity. This pattern remained the same during the first six twice-weekly half-hour sessions. Each time, the therapist tried cautiously to see whether Rose could accept more involvement on her part. In this, she did not succeed, but each session ended positively with Rose and the therapist singing together. During sessions 7 through 12, little by little, Rose permitted the therapist to come nearer and to involve herself more: first, by sitting nearer; next, by helping Rose carry some playthings; then, by offering a simple suggestion; and so on. Whereas, at first, Rose appeared to separate her play from her relationship with the therapist, gradually these two features of therapy became more of a unity, which opened the way for further therapeutic work.

CASE ILLUSTRATION—NELL

Nell was 27 years old, with an estimated mental age of 5 years. She lived with her parents and visited a day-care center. Nell was referred for therapy because of an extremely low self-image, sleeping problems, anxieties, and bizarre disturbing behavior like stumbling, tongue-clacking, and sneezing. In her first sessions, her anxiety was strong; also, Nell indicated that she felt "different." In the very first session she told the therapist that "she was born with her mouth shut" and that, because of this, she could not talk well. As usual, her therapist tried to structure the therapeutic situation in such a way that Nell could feel safe. The therapist created a very quiet atmosphere and, since she knew Nell was interested in drawing and painting, selected some attractive drawing materials. This worked very well. In her drawings, Nell quickly started to express her night terror and her feeling of menace. The therapist took the opportunity (in session 4) to work on these directly, by telling Nell a fairy tale about Little Red Ridinghood, who got lost in a dark wood; but, in her pocket, she carried some matches (a theme from another fairy tale, *The Little Matchgirl*) so that she could light her way. Later in that session, Nell drew a girl in a garden, next to a house with its windows all dark. The therapist suggested she might paint a lantern on the side of the house. Nell at once agreed to do so.

In the therapist's own view, two aspects helped Nell to involve herself affectively in the therapeutic work in this early stage: the first was the quite appealing metaphoric fairy-tale character of the story; the second was the tactile quality of the painting work. As the therapist herself commented: "What it comes down to is that I was telling fairy tales to a confused woman with the mental grasp of a little girl. To my mind, it was the imaginative power of the metaphor which touched and affected her way of feeling about the world around her—and later helped to differentiate her ways of feeling."

In this case, the therapist also had regular contacts with Nell's parents. She suggested that it might be a good idea to give Nell a bedroom light. This, combined with Nell's imaginative coping with the dark, resulted in a quick reduction of the night terrors after only six sessions. And although a lot more work had to be done, therapy at this early stage was already well under way.

The therapeutic process is, of course, different for each individual client because it is their personal experiences with which one works. The difference in mental capacity from client to client also causes large differences in the forms of play that can or cannot be attained: for instance, for clients with a mental age (MA) under 2 years, symbolic play in any form is virtually unattainable. This limits the possibilities of play therapy. However, the results of treatment seem not so much dependent on mental level particularly as on the client's ability to relate to the therapist and on the speed with which the client engages in meaningful (play) activities. In a comparative study of five therapies that were successful in the relatively short time of less than 1 year (of which Nell was one), with four other therapies that were prematurely terminated, it was found that, in all these successful therapies, the therapeutic process got quickly under way: these clients related easily, and, from early in therapy, their main problems became clear, which greatly helped formulating treatment goals. There was no long diagnostic struggle to get through to the client's main life themes, and these themes could be worked through without great interference from other sources. In contrast, in the four prematurely terminated therapies the relationship remained uncertain, and no clear image of the client's problems emerged. Moreover, all of these therapies suffered from different external interferences. Here is a striking example of such a case:

Case Illustration—Tina

Tina, a 9-year-old girl with a mental age of 1.8 years, having lived for 8 months in a residential center, was referred for play therapy because of extreme changes of mood, hypersensitivity to stimuli, social problems, and strong anxiety. For the previous 2 months, she visited a special school for a few hours each day. Play therapy was recommended as a last resort: No other form of treatment seemed to work, and it was clear that she needed more individual attention. Thus, the indication was vague. During an observation period of six play sessions, the therapist focused on Tina's way of establishing contact and her handling of toys. Imitation appeared to be Tina's strong point; she picked up new actions quickly and seemed able to retain these. A possible problem the therapist noticed was that, among the care staff, opinions about Tina and the necessity of therapy differed. Still, because of Tina's apparent pleasure in imitative play, the therapist decided to give therapy a try. Because of the therapist's other commitments, therapy started 3 months later.

During the first two sessions, Tina was disappointingly restless and chaotic. When the therapist brought Tina back to the living group after the second session, she was informally told that the staff planned to put Tina on a full-time school program, an unexpected and unpleasant surprise for the uninformed therapist. When she asked the school for more information, it appeared that there had recently been a lot of personnel illness and turnover and that Tina had reacted strongly to the ensuing changes. Still, the pressure of the group staff to have Tina in school (and not under their care) during most of the day became so strong that the team as a whole (including the consulting psychologist who had also been instrumental in the decision for therapy) had decided to go along with this. To let the play therapy go on, too, Tina would be kept home only one-half morning a week.

As agreed, Tina stayed at home for session 6, which took place shortly after the change in school hours. But since she had to miss out on swimming, the school asked for a change in the therapy hour. And although the therapist went along with this request, she found that Tina was away at school when she came to the group to fetch her for the next session.

By now, the therapist thoroughly doubted the motivation of care staff and school for therapy. Consequently, though reluctantly, she decided to discontinue therapy. She considered the conditions for therapy so poorly fulfilled that the chances were she would have had to break off anyway sometime soon. Therefore, she decided to do it before Tina and she herself had really started to invest in their relationship.

Apart from establishing the relationship, the first stage of therapy often serves yet another purpose: getting more insight in the client's problems. When the indication for treatment was mentioned earlier, the scarcity and inadequacy of diagnostic material and of standard tests was mentioned. Therefore, as an intermediate goal, many therapists felt the therapy might also yield more information about the real thoughts and feelings of the client. Consequently, the investigators expected to find in the therapists' reports some sort of conclusion to this first diagnostic phase of therapy, marked by reflection about play therapy as a suitable form of help or about its goals. However, this occurred only in a few cases. In fact, it seemed that the diagnostic goal receded as therapy progressed, with an almost imperceptible transition from the assessment stage to treatment proper.

The Working-Through Phase (and Subsequent Termination)

As mentioned earlier, all clients pass through their own individual process. In general, one can say that the working-through phase starts when there is a working relationship between client and therapist and when the client has shown something of his or her main life themes. In this section, the therapeutic process of two clients presented before, Nell and Rose, will be described. In both these cases, the main phase of therapy blended so continuously into termination that this last period will be incorporated in this paragraph.

CASE ILLUSTRATION—NELL

With Nell, the working-through phase started quickly, as previously stated. After session 4, the therapist already reported that Nell made much more eye contact as well as physical contact. Moreover, another major theme had come up: the original sleeping problems seemed to have a strong erotic component. The therapist interpreted this as an expression of Nell's yearning for tenderness. Talking this over with the parents, the therapist discovered that there had been one or two (rather recent) incidents of sexual abuse in Nell's life. Hearing about this had been a great shock to the parents, which may have caused or strengthened their rather rejecting attitude toward sensuality and possible sexuality with regard to their daughter. Their acceptance of Nell's retardation had, earlier, already been jeopardized by careless workers with little real concern about the parents' feelings. Therefore, the therapist took a lot of time to establish a working relationship with them, too. Next, she tried to help the parents understand that sensual desires are a normal aspect of human existence, in retarded persons as well as in others. Slowly, the parents became able to see things more from Nell's point of view instead of just from their own.

Even though the parents were still doubtful, the therapist felt that Nell's sensual desires, combined with her anxiety about these unpermitted feelings, needed to be worked through and put into a "natural" perspective. She chose a nonthreatening way of doing this. First, she took Nell with her on a walk outside and spent some time looking at animals and plants, emphasizing the natural processes to be seen there, such as life and growth. Next, she helped Nell sow some seeds and plant bulbs, which could remain in the playroom until they should grow. Nell showed interest and asked for information.

Then, in session 13, while kneading some clay (a tactile activity that often helps to elicit new imagery), Nell suddenly said, "I can't help being different." She connected this with feeling physically unwell, having flu, having small injuries, and so on. This gave the therapist the opportunity to work on another important goal with regard to her self-image. In the next session, the therapist read the story *The Ugly Duckling*, in which she emphasized the duckling's feeling of being different and wanting to belong. Nell listened attentively and asked for the story to be read again.

During the following sessions, this theme of being different was elaborated by Nell in a series of paintings. First, she painted a duck with a clown's face and spectacles. Later, she added some other ducks (his family), a smart cat, and a beautiful peacock. With these three figures (duck, cat, and peacock), she seemed to differentiate various aspects of her (ideal) self. At the same time, she indicated clearly how important physical appearance was to her. Work on these paintings, by the way, was regularly interlaced with Nell telling about significant experiences and her feeling/s about them, such as the death of her uncle and her yearning for love and nurturance; for example, she told a dream about a female caregiver who loved and kissed her and another, more disturbing dream with a distinct sexual side, about a man who approached her. Briefly, during this period, the night terror returned.

The therapist tried to work towards integration of the three self-images (duck, cat, and peacock) by suggesting to Nell that they might live in the same house. But this idea did not work: Nell drew separate tents for all three. But she initiated another image: "a strange bird who forgot his alphabet" and who had to be helped with everything (just like Nell herself). The therapist followed this up by telling the fairy tale *The Princess and the Pea*, about a princess who had to be helped to prove her identity, to be acknowledged as the person she was. In session 24, Nell took a lot of time painting the beautifully dressed princess. The therapist saw a chance here to approach Nell's body image and the physical side of life in a positive way and suggested that she might also like to paint a picture of the princess with no clothes on. After some hesitation, Nell started to do so in the next (25th) session. Her way of drawing, though, was noticeably clumsy as compared to her earlier drawings. Throughout the drawing process, the therapist emphasized the "normality" of the female figure, with breasts and nipples, as well as armpit and pubic hair.

In the session following this, Nell did not want to draw or do anything else. Therefore, the therapist drew the princess for her, from the front and from the back. Looking on, Nell was somewhat self-conscious and embarrassed but also clearly interested. Incidentally, during these last sessions the tongue-clacking (one of the referral problems) had disappeared completely. The night terror also decreased again.

In the next session, Nell stated that she had not wanted to come, that she was confused, because she wanted to think about her dreams whenever she was with the therapist. The therapist felt Nell needed to share this confusion and asked her to draw her dream. It became a man in a swimming pool, "a man with no clothes on." In some detail, she drew, colored, and told about this man's beard. Next, the therapist asked about his penis, which Nell said she could not draw. However, she allowed the therapist to do this, and she explicitly approved of the therapist's attempt. This session was closed by looking at the photos and illustrations in a sex education book. Nell agreed that her princess and her man both looked like real people.

After a pause during the holidays, the therapy (in session 28) resumed with looking at all the paintings and drawings Nell had made. Since she was clearly much more interested in the drawings of the princess and the man than in those of the animals, the therapist decided to continue with the sex education aspect. By now, Nell's parents also agreed that this might be a good idea. Three sessions were devoted to looking at and talking about all kinds of physical functions, including having babies. Nell seemed specially interested to hear that these functions were the same for all women, including herself and the therapist. In the last of these sessions, Nell's interest gradually receded. Instead, she talked about a recent fight with another member of her day-care group and made a drawing of this event in quite a normal and not overemotional way. An interview with the caregivers confirmed that Nell was now much quieter, and the sudden changes of mood much less frequent, while disturbing behavioral symptoms had disappeared. Moreover, the care staff felt they could now talk to Nell about things that might bother her.

The next session, session 32, was to be the last. Therapist and Nell together looked at all her drawings and talked playfully about the ugly duckling, the strange bird, and the beautiful princess and about how they were now able to live together. The therapist then mentioned possible changes in Nell herself, which she termed as "not being confused any more." Nell reacted positively and did not seem unduly distressed to part from the therapist. This last session ended with a walk in the park, where together they looked at the autumn colors.

In this therapy, two main lines could be distinguished: First, there was Nell's feeling of being different (i.e., incompetent); second, there was her desire to be loved and the confused feelings about this desire, aggravated by the abuse experiences and her parents' restrictive position. The night terror, which briefly reoccurred during the working through of the second theme, seemed closely linked with the guilt feelings it evoked. Therefore, the therapist approached this physical (sensual, and partly sexual) theme mainly by emphasizing the normal and natural functioning of the body. Cognitive information was coupled with the emotionally important drawing. By sharing her confused feelings with the therapist, and undoubtedly greatly helped by her parents' growing acceptance of this part of her life, Nell gradually became able to integrate these experiences. At the same time, talking about the female body may have helped her to discover that she was not all that different. And her quieter and less changeable behavior made it easier for caregivers and parents to approach her in a more loving and accepting way.

In this case, the termination phase was very brief. Because of Nell's deepening relationship with her parents and the caregivers at the day-care center, the therapist considered that Nell would not feel the end of the therapeutic relationship as a specific loss.

With Rose, a young woman of about the same age as Nell, but with a much lower mental level (MA 3 years), the introductory phase lasted much longer, as described in the previous section. Before starting therapy, the therapist formulated the following goals: (a) (intermediate goal) establishing a trustful relationship; (b) working through Rose's traumatic experiences, diminishing anxiety; (c) decreasing compulsive behavior; and (d) better coping with daily life. To attain these goals, the therapist chose as her strategy: accepting the compulsive behavior (as described before), gradually suggesting variations in play by introducing new materials or new actions, and frequently verbalizing play actions with their accompanying emotions. Especially with a nonverbal client like Rose, verbalizing by the therapist could be of great help in structuring the client's world, which she herself was almost unable to do.

CASE ILLUSTRATION—ROSE

The therapist quickly discovered that Rose needed time to accept her as a co-player. In the early sessions, suggestions by the therapist did not work at all. Indeed, almost anything the therapist did seemed too intrusive. During this period, in her comments on her own work, the therapist often noted that she was unsure of the amount of suggestiveness and directiveness she could afford. If she did not interfere, would Rose then continue to ignore her, or would it help to establish trust? With the help of her supervisor, she decided to keep her distance and to limit her active involvement to the physical nearness and the singing Rose herself initiated at the end of each session. Gradually, Rose seemed to get used to the therapist and to accept her help. After session 12, they appeared to have found some common ground. The more the therapist followed and joined Rose's play, the easier it became for Rose to accept small interventions, such as the offering of new materials *within* her house play.

Next, Rose began to show interest in other playthings, such as the sandbox and the nursing bottle, which she filled and then emptied. In doing this with the bottle, she squeezed hard. This gave the therapist more opportunities to join in by also shoveling sand or squeezing a bottle. Such joint tactile play could now be enjoyed by Rose. Another new and positive sign was the changing reaction to unexpected incidents (e.g., a toy falling); during the first sessions, such an occurrence made her angry or apathetic, but now Rose could laugh about it. This gradual variability was reflected in the fixed ritual of singing at the end of each session, which now was becoming optional: Sometimes Rose asked for it, sometimes she did not. Sometimes, too, the therapist could suggest that they sing together.

The emphasis of the therapeutic work, up to about session 16, was on goals (a) and (c): the relationship and the decrease in Rose's compulsive behavior. Goal (b), the working through of traumatic behavior, seemed as far off as ever. By now, the therapist considered that perhaps this goal was not really workable. She was not quite sure herself what those traumatic experiences had actually and precisely been. Rose's personal file was vague about her past. And Rose herself provided no clues on this point because of her nonverbal tendencies and her very limited imaginative ability. On the other hand, her anxiety and inability to express (particularly negative) feelings clearly needed to be addressed. Therefore, the therapist formulated an alternative goal—goal (b): ability to express emotions in an understandable way.

She then proceeded to work on this goal (b), for instance, by verbalizing the feeling of nearness when Rose sat with her or had physical contact with her. Another opportunity was offered by Rose's play with sand. Here, tactile experiences could be verbalized with regard to the softness (or hardness) of the sand, about how you can feel it slip through your fingers, and so on. Still another point came up from session 17 onward. Rose seemed to experience some sort of emotional catharsis from flinging material about (sand, toys), from squeezing things, and also from banging toys together. The therapist often verbalized this feeling of "doing something really hard," the "loud noise," and the feeling of "being able to do this yourself."

Interestingly, in an interview with Rose's parents shortly after this change in therapy strategy, Rose's mother expressed her surprise at the sandplay because Rose had always rejected this as "dirty." The parents also noticed Rose's behavior had become less compulsive. She seemed less involved in her own small world and somewhat more interested in things outside. The same was mentioned by the care staff of the institution where Rose lived. There, she also showed more interest in social contacts with her coresidents (although she did not take any initiative in this respect).

In sessions 21 to 24, these developments continued. Consequently, the therapist decided to decrease session frequency to once a week. At first, Rose reacted to this with renewed withdrawal and rejection of whatever the therapist did, but that did not last long. From session 27 on, the therapist was surprised by Rose using much more space, being more cheerful, and laughing a lot. Once or twice, Rose even forgot to start a session with her ritual house play! A brief relapse after a vacation, in which 3 weeks went by without therapy, was quickly overcome.

During the next 4-month period, sessions were much less frequent because of illnesses of both the therapist and Rose herself and because of holidays. Even so, play seemed to stabilize. Rose was relaxed and much better able to cope with the disorder she sometimes created in the playroom. Outside the playroom, too, her compulsive behavior had decreased to a more acceptable level. The therapist even considered working towards termination of therapy and further decreasing session frequency.

Unfortunately, at this stage, conflicts cropped up among the staff who cared for Rose's living group. To these outside disturbances, Rose immediately reacted with frequent and strong compulsive behavior. This, naturally, did nothing to help stabilize the group climate. On the urgent request of Rose's parents, the therapist decided to keep session frequency at once a week for as long as the staff's problems continued. As one of the institution's psychologists, the therapist also took an active part in helping to work out the trouble. This took some time.

With Rose, this required more attention to goal (d): helping her to take more initiatives and to strengthen her coping ability. During the last 16 sessions of her therapy, goal (d)— adequate expression of emotions—remained primary. This therapy took a total of 52 sessions over a period of 1 ½ years.

At termination, therapist, care staff, and parents concluded that Rose was now able to express emotions more understandably and that her compulsive behavior had decreased considerably, although it had by no means disappeared. In daily life, Rose had become somewhat less vulnerable. she took more initiatives and knew better how to hold her own in the group as well as other social contacts. Moreover, she seemed better able to make clear what she did and did not want.

In all, the therapy goals seemed attained as far as possible, with the proviso that goal (b), working through of traumatic experiences, had proved unworkable and had been changed to a less pretentious goal, which fit more adequately with her actual problems, her mental level, and her capacity for change. All the people concerned were reasonably satisfied about the result. However, the therapist still expressed some doubt about Rose's ability to retain these changes, especially in the face of personnel changes and other such disturbances.

In both these therapies, different though they were, as well as in most other cases in this sample, the investigators were especially struck by the resourcefulness of the therapists in devising strategies and techniques to approach the specific problems of each individual client. Often, and very honestly, therapists expressed their doubts about their ways of working with a particular client or about the best way to relate. Should one be nurturant and caring or more distantly involved? Should one leave the initiative to the client or should a more directive approach be used to help the client to overcome his or her passivity or resistance? Of course, there are no simple answers to those questions. Rather, they ask for a systematic reflective approach in which the why and wherefore of one's actions are constantly reviewed.

PROGNOSIS, DURATION, AND RESULTS

For the whole sample of 20 cases, the therapists' prognosis for duration of therapy ranged from 6 months to several years, although for most cases a length of between 1 and 2 years was prognosticated. One could hypothesize that younger clients and/or more mildly handicapped clients might be easier to help. However, as can be seen in Table 15.3, no relation was found between estimated length of treatment and client age or mental level.

Four therapies were ended prematurely, after 6 to 22 sessions (6 weeks to 5 months). In two of these, there had been some progress towards the therapy goals, whereas the other two were broken off without noticeable positive change (as in Tina's case). In one other case, there was so little positive change after 9 months (28 sessions) that the therapist decided to terminate. Factors common to a majority of the terminated cases, which may have been instrumental in their negative result, were (on the side of the therapist) lack of clarity with regard to indications and goals, (on the side of the client) limited ability to become a partner in the relationship or recurrent illness and in three cases, (on the side of the therapy context) motivation problems in parents and/or staff or care staff conflicts.

Three therapies were still in progress at the time of this report. Two of these long-term therapies were past their 90th session; this was in accordance with the prognosis ("probably more than 2 years"). One therapy started later and was still amply within its prognosticated duration of 2 years.

Actual treatment length for those 12 therapies that ended naturally ranged from 5 months (14 sessions) to 2 ½ years (93 sessions). According to the therapists and the care staff, therapy was successful in eight cases (as in the case of Nell), whereas in four cases, there were some reservations about the results (e.g., Rose's case). In Table 15.3, the result of therapy is related to duration of treatment, sex, age at start of treatment, and mental level of the client. It is clear that mental level, sex, or age had no relation to therapy success, and that the successful therapies were definitely shorter. This, of course, is understandable. When one is not yet quite sure about the result, one tends to work on with that client. It is much easier to terminate when all the people concerned judge the therapy as successful. Still, one very long therapy (with a 20-year-old male client with the relatively high mental age of 7 years) ended with good results.

In the successful therapies, the goals were usually fairly clear, and a good working relationship could be established, although not always smoothly and not without ups and

TABLE 15.3. Overview of All Therapies, with Results Taken as Point of Reference

Result	Duration	No. of sessions	Mental level*	Sex	Age at start
+	5 mo	14	Low	f	45 yrs
+	7 mo	21	Low	m	25 yrs
+	1 yr	32	Higher	f	27 yrs
+	1 yr	34	Higher	m	5 ½ yrs
+	1 yr	40	Low	f	46 yrs
+	1 ½ yr	37	Higher	m	6 yrs
+	1 ½ yr	49	Higher	m	8 yrs
+	2 ½ yrs	92	Higher	m	20 yrs
±	1 ½ yr	52	Low	f	22 yrs
±	1 ½ yr	68	Higher	m	5 ½ yrs
±	2 yrs	80	Higher	m	27 yrs
±	2 ½ yrs	93	Low	f	17 yrs
−	9 mo	28	Higher	m	5 yrs
p.t.**±	7 weeks	7	Higher	f	4 ½ yrs
p.t.±	4 ½ mo	12	Low	f	65 yrs
p.t.−	6 weeks	6	Low	f	9 yrs
p.t.−	5 mo	22	Low	f	20 yrs
Going on	15 mo	49	Higher	f	12 yrs
Going on	2 ½ yrs	95	Higher	f	10 yrs
Going on	3 yrs	101	Higher	m	5 ½ yrs

*Mental level low = IQ < 35; or, in clients above 16 years, MA ≤ 5.0 years
Mental level higher = IQ ≥ 35; or, in older clients MA > 5.0 years
**p.t.: prematurely terminated

downs. The problems most amenable to treatment were actual problems (e.g., current anxieties), traumatic life events from the recent past (e.g., death of an older parent, abuse by a group member), feeling incompetent, and feeling "different." Concurrently, although this was often not a specified working goal, many maladaptive behaviors decreased or even disappeared, and more adaptive behaviors developed.

CONCLUSIONS AND GUIDELINES FOR PRACTICE

Play psychotherapy with mentally retarded clients is only a recent addition to the treatment program of many institutions. Consequently, its practice is, in general, still in the pioneering stage. Much more research on all aspects of therapy with this group of clients is needed to create a theoretical and knowledge base for therapeutic action and process and to investigate its short- and long-term effects. However, some preliminary conclusions can be drawn on the basis of the evaluative material reported in this chapter.

First and foremost, play psychotherapy seems a valuable form of treatment for clients with mental retardation who experience emotional problems. In particular, clients with reduced or inhibited social and emotional competence and manifest anxieties, as well as (recent) traumatic experiences, appear to benefit from this form of help.

However, it is important that, in each case, the indications are carefully considered. The assessment procedures still leave a lot to be desired. An important development in this respect is the implementation of more systematic observation procedures by some therapists and some institutions. The contributions to the referral and decision process by the daily caregivers (including the parents, if they are involved with their child) and by the therapists themselves can still be expanded in many ways. Even though their professional staff status may not be high, the heavy responsibility therapists carry for the change process should be more clearly recognized.

At the start of therapy, many therapists may feel a need for further assessment. If so, it might be fruitful to insert a diagnostic phase of a specified number of sessions (say, 6 or 10 or 20, dependent on the complexity of the problems) with a distinct observational and evaluative purpose. Probably, such a phase will yield the best results if it ends in a deliberate reflection of and explicit formulation of the indications/contraindications and goals for therapy. In particular, the ability of the client to relate to the therapist and the gist of the client's main life themes should become clearer. If the therapist's position calls for his or her decisions to be confirmed by other responsible staff members, this reflective process should be shared by them. This, combined with the data already available, should lead to an individualized clinical picture, to a definite indication for therapy, and to clear-cut therapeutic goals, thus, providing a stronger working base for therapy itself.

Another point, which seems self-evident, is that emotional growth can only take place against the background of a "good enough" emotional climate in the client's living environment. But this is not always easy to attain. In some of the cases in the study, very little contact between the therapist and parents or other caregivers was possible. In others, staff conflict seemed to play a large part in stagnation of therapy and even premature termination. A stronger active participation of parents and caregivers, both in terms of coformulating indications and goals and in terms of being counseled during the therapy process, might, in the investigators' view, still contribute essentially to the therapeutic process (see also Brack, 1982). However, all those with some experience in working with the mentally retarded will recognize how difficult it can be, particularly in larger institutions, to "beat the system"!

The therapeutic goals are, of course, individualized. In formulating them, account is taken of the referral problem, of the diagnostic data (including the problem experience of the client himself or herself), and of the age and mental ability as well as the integrative ability of the client. In doing so, therapists should especially consider the attainability or workability of these goals; for instance, the working through of diffuse childhood experiences by a severely retarded middle-aged client seems an unattainable goal that can only add frustration to a therapy process that is difficult enough in itself. It may be more fruitful for both therapist and client to focus on actual emotional and social problems, on anxieties that crop up in the here and now, and/or on experiences from the more recent past.

Most of the conclusions of this study, which was designed to support therapists in their continuing struggle for more effective and systematic methods of helping their clients, were already shared with the therapists. This was not always easy. Having generously allowed the investigators to look over their shoulders, the therapists felt naturally vulnerable when it came to the remarks and suggestions ensuing from this study. On the other hand, throughout this investigation, their positive motivation has been a powerful stimulant. And indeed, in their regular meetings, they have already taken up some of these points, and it is hoped that they will continue to work these out with a view to their own particular clientele.

One last remark: During this study, the investigators have unsuccessfully tried to discern specific patterns or subgroups among the clients. Instead, it was the diversity of problems and goals, as well as the variability in age and mental level, that were striking. There was no clear relation between any of these variables and the success or failure of therapy. From this material, *the classic* mentally retarded play therapy client did not emerge. In fact, such a generalized client description probably does not exist. The group of clients seemed as heterogeneous as any group of nonretarded persons, requiring the same individualized approach.

REFERENCES

American Psychiatric Association. (1987). *Diagnostic and statistical manual of mental disorders* (3rd ed., rev.). Washington, DC: Author.

Bernhardt, M., & Mackler, B. (1975). The use of play therapy with the mentally retarded. *Journal of Special Education, 9,* 409–414.

Biessels-Smulders, A. M., & Wagenborg, P. (Eds.). (1990). Variaties in een speelveld: Speltherapie met geestelijk gehandicapten [Variations in a playing field: Play therapy with mentally handicapped people]. Amsterdam/Lisse, The Netherlands: Swets & Zeitlinger.

Brack, U. B. (1982). Eltern als Co-Therapeuten von retardierten Kindern: Probleme des Anleitung und Motivierung [Parents as co-therapists for retarded children: Indication and motivation problems]. *Psychologie in Erziehung und Unterricht, 29,* 41–48.

Dosen, A. (1983). *Psychische stoornissen bij zwakzinnige kinderen* [Psychological disorders in mentally retarded children]. Lisse, The Netherlands: Swets & Zeitlinger.

Dosen, A. (1990). *Psychische en gedragsstoornissen bij zwakzinnigen* [Psychological and behavioral disorders in the mentally retarded]. Meppel, The Netherlands: Boom.

Gunzburg, H. C. (1974). Psychotherapy. In A. M. Clarke & A. D. B. Clarke (Eds.), *Mental deficiency: The changing outlook* (3rd ed., pp. 708–728). New York: Free Press.

Haworth, M. R., & Keller, M. J. (1964). The use of food in therapy. In M. R. Haworth (Ed.), *Child psychotherapy: Practice and theory* (pp. 330–338). New York: Basic Books.

Hellendoorn, J. (1988). Imaginative play technique in psychotherapy with children. In C. E. Schaefer (Ed.), *Innovative interventions in child and adolescent therapy* (pp. 43–67). New York: Wiley.

Hellendoorn, J. (1990). Indications and goals for play therapy with the mentally retarded. In A. Dosen, A. van Gennep, & G. J. Zwanikken (Eds.), *Treatment of mental illness and behavioral disorder in the mentally retarded* (pp. 179–187). Leiden, The Netherlands: Logon Publications.

Hellendoorn, J., & Hoekman, J. (1992). Imaginative play in children with mental retardation. *Mental Retardation, 30,* 255–263.

Kazdin, A. E. (1988). *Child psychotherapy: Developing and identifying effective treatments.* New York: Pergamon Press.

Lamers-Osterhaus, M., & van Santen, M. (1985). *Spelend werken aan bevrijding: speltherapie in de zwakzinnigerzorg* [Working toward freedom through play: Play therapy for the mentally retarded]. Utrecht, The Netherlands: NGBZ.

Leland, H. (1983). Play therapy for mentally retarded and developmentally disabled children. In C. E. Schaefer & K. O'Connor (Eds.), *Handbook of play therapy* (pp. 436–454). New York: Wiley.

Leland, H., & Smith, D. (1965). *Play therapy with mentally subnormal children.* New York: Grune & Stratton.

Leland, H., Walker, J., & Toboada, A. N. (1959). Group play therapy with a group of post-nursery male retardates. *American Journal of Mental Deficiency, 48,* 53–60.

Li, A. K. F. (1981). Play and the mentally retarded children. *Mental Retardation, 23,* 121–126.

Lubbers, R. (1988). *Psychotherapie door beeld- en begripsvorming* [Psychotherapy by imagery and concept formation]. Nijmegen, The Netherlands: Dekker & Van de Vegt.

Mehlmann, B. (1953). Group play therapy with mentally retarded children. *Journal of Abnormal and*

Social Psychology, 48, 53–60.

Menolascino, F. J. (1990a). Mental retardation and the risk, nature and types of mental illness. In A. Dosen & F. J. Menolascino (Eds.), *Depression in mentally retarded children and adults: An update for clinical practice* (pp. 11–34). Leiden, The Netherlands: Logon Publications.

Menolascino, F. J. (1990b). Mental illness in the mentally retarded: Diagnostic issues and treatment considerations. In A. Dosen, A. van Gennep, & G. J. Zwanikken (Eds.), *Treatment of mental illness and behavioral disorder in the mentally retarded* (pp. 21–36). Leiden, The Netherlands: Logon Publications.

Mook, B. (1994). From interpretation to intervention. In J. Hellendoorn, R. van der Kooij, & B. Sutton-Smith (Eds.), *Play and intervention* (pp. 39–52). Albany, NY: SUNY Press.

Morrison, T. L., & Newcomer, B. L. (1975). Effects of directive vs. nondirective play therapy with institutionalized mentally retarded children. *American Journal of Mental Deficiency, 79,* 666–669.

Schmidtchen, S. (1978). *Handeln in der Kinderpsychotherapie* [Acting in psychotherapy with children]. Stuttgart, Germany: Kohlhammer.

Scholten, U. (1985). *Spel en speelgoed bij geestelijk gehandicapte kinderen* [Play and toys for mentally retarded children]. Nijmegen, The Netherlands: Dekker & Van de Vegt.

Snÿders, J. T., & Snÿders-Oomen, N. (1975). *Snÿders-Oomen Niet-verbale Intelligentieschaal SON 2 1/2–7.* Groningen, The Netherlands: Tjeenk Willink.

Subotnik, L., & Callahan, R. (1959). A pilot study in short-term therapy with institutionalized educable mentally retarded boys. *American Journal of Mental Deficiency, 63,* 730–735.

Ude-Pestel, A. (1975). *Protokoll einer Kinderpsychotherapie* [Protocol of a child psychotherapy]. Stuttgart, Germany: Deutsche Verlag Anstalt.

CHAPTER 16

Filial Therapy for Adoptive Children and Parents

RISË VAN FLEET

INTRODUCTION

The decision to adopt a child has far-reaching implications for the parents as well as for the child. Whereas adoption often fulfills a couple's long-time desire for a child, it also presents many adjustments and potential problems for the new family to face. These challenges frequently extend beyond the usual demands of family life, and they can result in additional stress for the adoptive family. This chapter describes the special characteristics and needs of adoptive children and parents and the developmental and relationship problems that sometimes arise. The use of filial therapy to prevent or to intervene in those problems and to strengthen adoptive parent-child relationships through the use of special play sessions is then described.

Characteristics and Needs of Adoptive Families

Adoptive Children

Adoptive children vary widely in their psychosocial characteristics as well as in their needs. The age at which they are adopted, their individual temperament and coping resources, the circumstances surrounding their adoption, and their prior life experiences in general can have a profound effect on their adjustment to adoption. One feature shared by adoptive children is a disruption in the developmental sequence, which has the potential to interfere with children's individual development, personal security, and capacity to form satisfying, intimate family relationships (Ginsberg, 1989).

Other characteristics found in adoptive children include attachment difficulties; unresolved feelings about past rejections, abuses, or losses; uncertainty about personal boundaries and safety; and insecurity about their environment and the future (i.e., a sense that everything is "temporary". Some may have lived with a number of different relatives or foster families prior to adoption, and feelings of rejection or helplessness might be intensified. Adoptive children are likely to have questions and confusion about their biological parents and the meaning and role their adoptive parents play in their lives. Separation from the potential bonding and support of siblings can also be difficult. Although these characteristics certainly do not appear in all adoptive children, clinicians and educators who work with adoptive children must be aware of them as possibilities.

The research on the impact of adoption on the psychological functioning of children is not definitive. In a review of the literature, Ginsberg (1989) described comparative studies that suggested greater maladaptation in adoptive children than in nonadoptive children, as well as research that found no difference in psychiatric diagnoses between adoptive adults and nonadoptive adults. Brodzinsky, Radic, Huffman, and Merkler (1987), in a study comparing 6-to-11-year-old adopted and nonadopted children, suggested a higher degree of hyperactivity in adopted boys and girls, greater uncommunicativeness in adopted boys, and more depression and aggression in adopted girls than in their nonadopted counterparts.

More research is needed before conclusions can be drawn about the psychological risks of adoption for children. Adoption is confounded with many other variables that might influence adjustment, for example, history of abuse or neglect, number of disruptions or foster placements, quality of prenatal care, age at adoption, and length of adoption. Studies that tease apart the relative contributions of these various factors to children's adaptation to adoption are needed.

Adoptive Parents

Adoptive parents face a number of unique personal and parenting issues. Reasons for adopting a child are quite varied, but couples who have been unable to conceive their own child may need to resolve possible feelings of guilt, anger, or loss. Adoptive parents might experience frustration with the length and uncertainties of the adoption process. There are also potentially painful situations, such as when a child is placed with adoptive parents only to be removed when the biological parents change their minds and decide to keep their baby.

The child's arrival is usually a joyful occasion, but it can happen suddenly and unpredictably, requiring rapid modifications of the couple's plans and life-style — perhaps positive stress, but stress nonetheless. While the experience of pregnancy usually sets some life-style changes in motion, such as the need to decrease working hours, the adoption process does not necessarily do this. Although adoptive parents can plan for the child's arrival, the uncertain timing may result literally in overnight disruption of home and career.

Adoptive parents are likely to have questions and concerns about the meaning and role of the biological parents in their adoptive children's lives. They also need to decide how, when, and what to tell the children about their biological parents and adoption. Child- and family-identity issues, such as name changes, can be problematic as well.

Another area of concern for adoptive parents sometimes is the lack of information about the child's medical and psychosocial history. Their high hopes for a healthy, responsive child can be dimmed if the child experiences unforeseen attention deficit, neurological, learning, or behavior problems. It can be extremely disappointing for parents to learn that their love alone is not always sufficient to help a child with limited emotional responsiveness or mental health problems.

Although the literature is inconclusive about the impact of adoption, it is clear that some adoptive children and families do experience psychosocial adjustment problems that require therapy. Other children and families might be considered at risk for developing social or emotional difficulties, and early intervention might prevent or reduce the severity of their problems. Finally, there are many adoptive families who adjust satisfactorily on their own, but who might benefit from preventive, educational programs that could facilitate and support their development as a family. Filial therapy is an intervention that can be used to remediate the problems of adoptive children and families, and it is a preventive approach to strengthen parent-child relationships following adoption.

Filial Therapy

Filial therapy seems ideally suited to the special needs of adoptive children and parents. It was developed in the early 1960s by Drs. Bernard and Louise Guerney as a treatment for children with a variety of emotional and adjustment problems (Guerney, 1964; Guerney, 1976a; Guerney, 1983). The approach uses a psychoeducational, skills-training model and involves parents as the primary change agents for their own children. Filial therapists teach parents how to conduct child-centered play sessions, supervise the parents during the play sessions with their children, help the parents deal with their own issues and concerns, and train parents in a comprehensive set of parenting skills. Parents eventually transfer the special play sessions to the home setting and learn how to apply the skills to a wide range of parenting situations.

Filial therapy is applicable to adoptive families for several reasons. First, it is developmental in focus, a factor of importance for children and families whose development has been disrupted by the circumstances leading to the adoption as well as by the adoption itself. Filial therapy creates a nonthreatening atmosphere that encourages the growth of both children and parents. Filial therapy uses a child-centered play therapy approach that allows children to develop and adjust at their own pace.

Second, a major purpose of filial therapy is to strengthen parent-child relationships. This usually fits nicely with the goal of adoptive parents to build healthy, caring relationships with their adoptive children. The entire family is involved. By using parents as the primary change agents for their adoptive children, filial therapy helps parents to understand their children's needs more fully and to create a nonjudgmental climate in which children can feel free to express and be themselves. Furthermore, adoptive children, who often have had to form relationships with many different caregivers prior to their adoption, can receive therapeutic help through their parents, avoiding the need for them to establish yet another primary relationship with a therapist.

Third, the psychoeducational, skill-development orientation of filial therapy offers adoptive families the opportunity to learn healthy interaction patterns and parenting skills that they can use as their relationships develop throughout their lives. It serves a preventive function by empowering families to strengthen themselves.

Fourth, filial therapy can provide therapeutic benefits to adoptive children and parents alike. The child-centered play sessions with their parents provide children with the same benefits as play therapy with a therapist: the ability to express themselves without fear of rejection, the development of a sense of independence and mastery of their environment, strengthened self-esteem and confidence, and the development of feelings of security within clear boundaries (Axline, 1947, 1969). As the adoptive parents interact with their children during the play sessions, adoption and family issues often arise. When filial therapists meet with the parents to discuss the play sessions, they encourage them to discuss and resolve their own reactions and concerns as well as those of their children.

Efficacy of Filial Therapy

Research (Stover & Guerney, 1967) and clinical experience have shown that parents can learn to conduct child-centered play sessions with a degree of competence that compares with that of professional play therapists. The effectiveness of filial therapy in reducing child problems and in increasing parental acceptance of their children has also been shown

(Guerney & Stover, 1971; Sywulak, 1977). Sensue (1981) demonstrated in a comprehensive follow-up study that therapeutic gains from filial therapy are maintained for at least 3 years.

PROCEDURE

Therapist Characteristics

Filial therapy is based upon a psychoeducational, competence-based framework, and therapists tend to think of themselves as clinician-educators. Because they believe that many of the problems facing adoptive families arise from the newness of the relationships, from a lack of learning or understanding, or from insufficient coping, parenting, or interpersonal skills, filial therapists spend much of their time teaching families the skills they need to solve their own problems more effectively and independently. It would be difficult to be a filial therapist without a belief that most families are competent to manage themselves, provided they have the proper resources and tools. A commitment to family empowerment is essential.

Play therapists often derive satisfaction from working directly with children in the playroom. Filial therapists, who work less directly with children, must shift their sources of satisfaction to the family's growing relationships with each other. Filial therapists believe that most parents are capable of conducting play sessions competently, and they facilitate the children's development through their interventions with the family. This is particularly true in the case of adoption—the focus needs to be on the *relationships* among family members rather than on any individual family member. Filial therapy can be very rewarding, but it does require a shift in orientation from some traditional approaches.

Filial therapists must be competent and experienced as child-centered play therapists because they demonstrate play sessions for the parents and then train and supervise parents as they learn to conduct them. In other words, filial therapists must be able to "practice what they preach." They must also be well versed in child and family development, family therapy, and training and teaching skills.

Client Characteristics

Filial therapy is most useful for children 3 to 12 years of age. At the younger end, children should be moving into imaginary play. At the upper end, if children have outgrown the play session toys, parents can add some toys for older children or hold special times with the children, using many of the play session skills but with a wider range of activities.

Filial therapy is appropriate for adoptive children experiencing a variety of adjustment problems, such as insecurity or abandonment fears, attachment difficulties, depression, aggressive or acting-out behaviors, discipline problems, peer or social relationship issues, or school problems. It can be a supportive therapy for adoptive children with attention deficits and low self-esteem. It can also be used in cases of abuse or neglect, assuming that the perpetrator is not one of the adoptive parents.

Adoptive families who are not experiencing any clinically significant problems but who wish to strengthen their relationships and reduce the chances of future problems also find filial therapy to be useful. Its educational approach lends itself easily to family enhancement efforts.

Logistics

The Playroom

A filial therapy playroom is set up in the same manner as a child-centered play therapy playroom. There needs to be enough space so that children can engage in some rough-and-tumble play (e.g., knocking a bop bag around). The room needs to be able to withstand water spills as well.

Filial therapists need an area from which they can supervise the parents' play sessions with their children. An observation booth with a one-way mirror is ideal. When that is unavailable, the therapist can watch from a location just outside the playroom door (e.g., from a small anteroom). If that, too, is not possible, the therapist observes from an unobtrusive location within the playroom. The arrangement of the playroom furniture can help divide off a small section for this purpose.

The toys used in the playroom are selected for their ability to evoke affective expression on a variety of themes. They include toys that can be used to express aggression, nurturance, family and social relationships, control, mastery, and themes that are likely to have significance for the child. In general, playroom toys include an inflated bop bag, dart guns with darts, a 6-foot length of rope, a deck of cards, play money, a container of water, bowls, baby bottles, a doll family (mother, father, brother, sister, baby), a house or box with doll furniture, a puppet family, crayons/markers with drawing paper, kitchen dishes, a blackboard, blocks or construction toys, plastic soldiers, and play dough. (Guerney, 1976b).

There are three main considerations when deciding whether or not to include a toy in the playroom, such as when adding toys for older children: (a) the toy's safety; (b) the toy's ability to encourage the expression of children's feelings; and (c) the toy's ability to be used in an imaginative or projective way by children. Toys that have narrowly defined uses or that require many directions are usually not good candidates for filial therapy playrooms.

Session Logistics

After they have been trained, parents conduct child-centered play sessions with their own children. Each play session involves one parent and one child so that individualized attention takes place. The parents take turns holding sessions with all of the children in the family, adopted and nonadopted alike. This is done to prevent singling out the adoptive child, to maintain the family focus, and to ensure that all children in the family benefit. If the adoptive child is the only child in the family, the parents take turns holding play sessions with him or her. Adolescents take part in special times in which the parents, one-on-one, give their undivided attention to them as they share in activities of the adolescent's choosing, within a reasonable range, such as playing games, taking a hike, bowling, or going out to eat.

Parents conduct play sessions or special times once a week for one-half hour with each of their children. Initially, the filial therapist supervises parents as they conduct the play sessions in the therapist's playroom. When bound by a 1-hour session length, the therapist observes one 30-minute play session and then discusses it with the parents for the remaining time, alternating parents each week. Sessions of 1 ½ to 2 hours permit therapist observations of both parents' play sessions, but this time frame is not always possible.

Eventually, the therapist helps the parents transfer the play sessions to the home setting, meeting with the parents regularly to discuss the play sessions. The logistics of that transition are covered in a later section.

Frequency and Duration of Therapy

Filial therapists usually meet with parents on a weekly or biweekly basis in order to maintain continuity from one session to the next. After the parents have successfully made the transition to home play sessions and progress is noted, therapists gradually meet less frequently with parents as therapy is phased out.

When used for family enhancement purposes, filial therapy can be conducted in as few as 10 sessions (Coufal & Brock, 1983; Ginsberg, 1989). When filial therapy is used to address child or family difficulties, its duration varies in accordance with the nature and severity of the problems. In general, filial therapy with an individual family takes 3 to 6 months. It is possible to use filial therapy in a small-group format and this typically takes 6 to 9 months.

Sequence and Strategies of Filial Therapy

Filial therapy procedures have been detailed elsewhere (Guerney, 1983; VanFleet, 1994), but each phase is described briefly in the sections that follow.

Sequence

The basic sequence of filial therapy is the following:

1. Initial assessment of the child and family using interviews, family play observations, and measures of parent-child behaviors, attitudes, and skills.

2. As appropriate, recommendation of filial therapy to parents, including full discussion of its rationale, content, and process.

3. Therapist demonstrations of child-centered play sessions with the children as parents observe.

4. Training period for parents to learn play session skills; includes skills-training exercises and mock play sessions with therapist feedback.

5. Office-based parent play sessions with their own children, followed by supervisory feedback from the filial therapist.

6. Ongoing home-based play sessions, followed by regular therapist-parent meetings to discuss play themes, parents' concerns, additional parenting skills, and generalization of skills.

7. As needed, and prior to discharge, follow-up office-based play sessions with live supervision by the therapist for maintenance.

8. At discharge, evaluation of filial therapy by parents and therapist; post-therapy assessment of parent-child behaviors, attitudes, and skills.

Therapist Behavior

Throughout the course of filial therapy, the therapist models for the parents the various skills and attitudes that they are to use with their children. The therapist is honest and direct with parents, fostering a team approach. The therapist listens empathically and patiently to all parent concerns, including doubts they may have about filial therapy or the therapist. Parents receive unconditional positive regard from the therapist, just as they are expected to show it to their children.

Filial therapists use other behavioral principles to help parents learn new skills and deal with child and family therapeutic issues. Shaping is used when setting expectations of the parents. Therapists challenge parents to try new behaviors with their children, but they do not push them to the point of frustration. They provide regular feedback to parents, recognizing their gradual steps toward skill mastery. Filial therapists also use reinforcement a great deal. They praise parents' efforts in conducting the play sessions and in eventually using parenting skills more effectively at home. They also praise parents for dealing with difficult therapeutic material. Role-play and behavioral rehearsal are an integral part of the parents' training in play sessions and parenting skills.

Assessment

When assessing adoptive children and families for filial therapy, a three-step process works well. The therapist first meets with the parents alone to obtain thorough social and developmental histories and a description of the presenting problems. Information about the child prior to the adoption sometimes is sketchy, but the therapist works with the parents and agencies involved to obtain as much information as possible.

The second step of the assessment process involves a family play observation. The therapist watches as the entire family plays together in the playroom, noting the adoptive child's behavior and the interactions among all family members. The therapist then inquires of the parents as to whether the interactions during the play were typical when compared with those at home.

The final step involves a meeting between the therapist and the parents in which the recommendation for filial therapy is made, if appropriate. Recommendations for further assessment, other interventions, or referral to another therapist might occur at this step as well. When therapists recommend filial therapy, they describe its rationale, methods, and possible outcomes in detail, answering whatever questions parents might have as accurately as possible.

Therapists might also want to administer behavior rating scales, parental attitude measures, or other questionnaires to use as a baseline to determine later progress. Schaefer, Gitlin, and Sandgrund (1991) have detailed play diagnostic and assessment approaches that are very useful.

Play Session Training

After the parents and the therapist decide to use filial therapy, the training in play session skills begins. Parents learn four basic skills.

1. The *structuring skill* helps children understand how the play sessions work. Parents learn how to explain the sessions to their children, what to say upon entering the playroom, and how to handle room departures. The therapist prepares the parents to handle resistance from the child, particularly at the end of play sessions.

2. The *empathic listening skill* helps parents show greater understanding and acceptance of their children's needs. The therapist teaches the parents to rephrase aloud the child's main thoughts and feelings and to convey interest in the child by their nonverbal behavior. Parents learn how to refrain from leading or directing the child's play.

3. The *child-centered imaginary play skill* helps parents engage in pretend play in a manner consistent with the child's wishes. They learn to act out different roles the child might assign. Sensitivity to the child's ideas about how the imaginary play should go is paramount so that the themes of importance to the child can emerge.

4. The *limit-setting skill* helps parents enforce the few rules of the play sessions and helps children understand their boundaries. Rules, such as "No writing on the walls with crayons" and "No pointing the dart guns at people when they're loaded", and personal limits of the parents are covered. The therapist teaches the parents to use a three-step process for handling broken limits: (a) state the limit clearly when it is first broken and redirect the child to other play; (b) give the child a warning on the second infraction of the same limit, telling him or her what the consequence will be the next time; and (c) enforcing the consequence on the third infraction (i.e., ending the play session).

The filial therapist teaches each of the basic skills using brief lectures, demonstrations, modeling, role-playing, skills exercises, feedback, and reinforcement. Parents observe while the therapist demonstrates play sessions with their children; then the parents participate in mock sessions in which the therapist plays the part of the child and the parent practices the four skills. The therapist tailors two or three mock play sessions to each parent's skill level, gradually increasing the challenges as the parent's competence develops. The skills-training period usually takes only a few sessions with a single set of parents and about 2 months with filial therapy groups of six to eight parents (Guerney & Guerney, 1987).

As much as possible, filial therapists prepare adoptive parents for children's play themes that might be difficult for them to understand, such as those reflecting the child's yearnings to be accepted by the biological parents. The therapist helps adoptive parents understand that themes about biological parents, foster parents, and adoptive parents are common for a child who is trying to sort out his or her identity, roles, and relationships. When adoptive parents realize that it is common for an adoptive child to explore issues about his or her biological parents in fantasy and play, they are less likely to feel threatened by the child's play and more likely to be accepting of it, thus, ultimately being more helpful to the child.

Similarly, filial therapists make certain during the training phase that adoptive parents are able to listen empathically during play sessions to negative feelings that their children might express: anger, aggression, fear, depression, and so on. This includes anger that might be directed at the adoptive parent; for example, after a parent sets a dart gun limit during a play session, the adoptive child might become angry, saying, "You're no fun. My *real* dad would have let me do that." Through training, parents learn to recognize this as an expression of anger rather than a true comparison of biological and adoptive parents, and they then reflect the feeling behind the word: "You're mad because I won't let you shoot the dart gun at me."

Filial therapists usually have some ideas about how the children might react in the playroom based upon the parents' earlier descriptions, the family play observation, and the play session demonstrations. The therapist first discusses potential reactions and issues with the parents and then plays them out during the mock play sessions so that the parents are trained to handle them if they occur during an actual play session.

Supervised Play Sessions

When parents have learned the basic skills and have applied them satisfactorily during the mock play sessions, they are ready to begin actual play sessions with their children. Initially, this occurs under the direct supervision of the therapist, who sits behind a one-way mirror or in an unobtrusive place within sight of the playroom. Each parent conducts a 30-minute play session with one of the children, after which the therapist provides feedback. The filial therapist asks for the parent's reactions to his or her own session, provides reinforcement, and makes suggestions for skills that need further work.

After providing skill feedback, the therapist encourages discussion of the child's play and possible meanings of thematic material. Through this process, parents learn to recognize thematic play and to understand its symbolism. Parallels to real-life issues are also explored. It is during this discussion period that parents' own issues often arise and are handled in an empathic manner by the therapist.

CASE ILLUSTRATION

After one adoptive mother held a play session during which her 6-year-old adopted son of one year asked her to play his "real mother," the adoptive mother expressed her own intense concerns to the therapist. She said that she constantly worried that her adoptive son might never accept her as a "real mom," and she did not feel comfortable when he asked questions about his biological parents. The therapist was able to help the mother better understand her son's play, to reassure her and reframe the way she thought about her own role, and to provide her with some ideas on how to answer her son's questions about his biological parents and his adoption. In this case, the boy's play theme triggered dynamic issues for the adoptive mother and the therapist consequently was able to intervene.

As parents begin play session with their children, other adoption-related themes often emerge. Parents sometimes become upset when their children choose solitary types of play and do not engage the parents during the play sessions. In many cases, such play is simply the child's preference at the time, as it sometimes is with nonadoptive children. At these times, the therapist reassures the parents that individual play that does not involve them all the time is normal and helps them realign their expectations of their relationships with their adoptive child. It can be confusing for parents to determine the optimal levels of dependence, independence, and interdependence, especially in adoptive families, and filial play sessions frequently trigger discussions of these topics. A sensitive therapist can help parents put these issues in perspective by listening carefully, by sharing sound child- and family-development information, and by guiding and supporting the family as it explores alternatives.

At other times, the child might exhibit actual attachment difficulties or abandonment fears during the play sessions and at home. In these cases, the filial therapist encourages the parents to show acceptance and to give the child time to feel safer and more trusting, something the child-centered play sessions are likely to provide. The therapist then helps the parents to express and work through their own fears and disappointments about their child's behavior and their relationships with him or her. (In cases of serious attachment problems or extensive past abuse, other interventions or types of play therapy may be needed, but this is usually determined during the assessment period and typically is not an issue at this phase of filial therapy).

In summary, filial therapists are involved in two main interventions as parents begin play sessions with their own children: (a) refinement of parents' skills and confidence through supervision and feedback, and (b) support and therapeutic guidance for parents as they react to their children's play and raise their own concerns and issues.

Home Play Sessions

When parents have become competent and confident in conducting play sessions, usually after four to six supervised sessions, the filial therapist helps them transfer the sessions to the home setting where parents continue to hold play sessions with their children each week. The therapist uses one session to help parents decide where they will hold the play sessions in their home, how they will schedule them with their own and their children's needs in mind, how they will handle interruptions that might occur during the play sessions, how the other children will be occupied during the play sessions, ways to obtain the needed toys as inexpensively as possible, and any other logistics.

After beginning their home play sessions, the parents meet with the therapist on a weekly or biweekly basis to discuss the play sessions and the children's play themes. Parental issues continue to be covered, and the focus shifts from skill development to the therapeutic goals. The therapist also helps the parents apply the play session skills to a wider range of parenting situations and teaches them additional parenting skills, such as setting realistic expectations, parent messages, and the use of reinforcement. If therapists suspect difficulties with the home play sessions, they can ask to observe the play sessions directly again as needed.

As the play sessions progress at home, issues of therapeutic importance continue to arise, and the therapist monitors progress carefully. There is wide variation in adoptive children's play, depending on their ages, their histories, and the nature of their adoption. Their play themes often reflect aggression and anger, sadness and loss, boundary testing, control, abandonment and trust, mastery and coping, and family and peer relationships. Through the symbolism of play, the children express their feelings and dilemmas and experiment with ways of solving their problems.

The play sessions continue to raise issues for the parents as well. During their regular meetings with parents, filial therapists discuss the home play sessions and ask parents to describe possible connections between the children's play and events in real life. They listen while parents talk about their concerns; they help parents understand the developmental, psychosocial, and family contexts of their own and their children's reactions; and they assist them in finding more satisfactory ways of dealing with the problems that arise for the family. Through this process, they help parents apply the play session and other parenting skills more effectively in broader contexts, thus helping parents generalize what they have learned.

Discharge

The decision to end therapy is made jointly by the filial therapist and the parents, and it occurs when presenting problems have been resolved and therapeutic goals have been met. A phased-out discharge process is often used. The therapist directly observes a final play session with each of the children, ensuring that gains have been made and that parents are still using their skills well. Post-therapy assessment measures can be administered at this time.

Home play sessions continue as long as the children show interest in them. The therapist teaches parents how to change the play sessions into special times when the children's interest wanes. During special times, the child chooses from a wider range of activities, such as going to the park or playing games, and the parent continues to use empathic listening and other play session skills to create an understanding, child-centered atmosphere. Special times are recommended for at least one-half hour per week.

The therapist plans one or two follow-up meetings with the parents, often at 1 or 2 months after the decision to terminate. If things have continued to go well, discharge is finalized.

CASE MATERIAL

In order to protect client privacy, the case material that follows is a composite of several different families, and identifying information has been changed. The clinical problems, family dynamics, and treatment strategies realistically illustrate the application of filial therapy to adoptive families, however.

CASE ILLUSTRATION: THE MARTINS

Five-year-old Chris Martin and his adoptive parents, Wendy and Tom, were referred for therapy by the children's agency that had been involved in Chris's placement. The Martins were assessed for filial therapy approximately 3 months after Chris's adoption had been finalized.

Wendy and Tom had been happily married for 6 years; they had unsuccessfully tried to conceive for 4 years. Tom was an architect, and Wendy was a substitute teacher. They had been very eager to adopt Chris. Chris had a history of physical abuse in the form of hitting and extensive neglect by his biological parents and other relatives for much of his life, although details were sketchy. He had been in three different placements in the 2 years prior to his adoption. Earlier placements had been difficult because of his rather wild acting-out behaviors, including kicking, pinching, and spitting on strangers in public for no apparent reason.

In addition to his acting-out behavior, Chris seemed to lack personal boundaries and would sit uncomfortably close to or on others, including strangers. Upon first meeting the therapist, he immediately jumped up on her lap and began touching and trying to lick her face until she set a limit. He seemed to attach more readily to objects than to people and was rather flat in affect much of the time. He interacted with Tom and Wendy, but it seemed that he was just going through the motions. He did turn to them when something frightened him, and he seemed to enjoy playing with them, although his focus was primarily on the toys.

During the assessment, Tom and Wendy expressed their desire to "erase and make up for Chris's awful past" by giving him a loving home. They viewed his crawling all over them as a sign of his affection for them, and they seemed unaware of possible boundary issues. Against the advice of the children's agency and their pediatrician, they had changed their son's first name from Johnny to Chris at the time of his adoption, and they were somewhat troubled that he didn't always respond to his new name. They also described a great deal of fearful behavior at home. They were most concerned with his inappropriate behavior in public, and they were interested in building their relationship with Chris as quickly as possible.

After a comprehensive assessment, the therapist recommended filial therapy to help Chris with his fearfulness, boundary issues, and attachment difficulties and to help Wendy and Tom develop more realistic expectations of Chris and strengthen their relationships with him.

Tom and Wendy learned the play session skills in three training sessions, and they began play sessions with Chris under the therapist's supervision in the fourth session. The parents alternated playing each week so that each of the supervised sessions involved a 30-minute play session between Chris and one parent, followed by the therapist's feedback to Wendy and Tom about the play session just observed.

Chris's early play sessions were characterized by exploratory play and limit-testing. Wendy had difficulty setting limits with him, and, as he poured the entire container of water over her head, she said with a horrified look on her face, "Chris, I'm not sure if you should be doing this, Honey." During the supervisory feedback period, she expressed her frustration at his water-dumping behavior but also her fear that Chris would see her as another abusive adult if she set limits and enforced consequences with him. The therapist empathically listened to her concerns and then explained how Chris needed appropriately set boundaries in order to feel secure while exploring his world and to learn to control his behavior better. The therapist also gently pointed out the mixed messages of Wendy's facial expression and her statement of the limit. Wendy had not thought of limit-setting in terms of Chris's feelings of security or the inconsistency of her message to him, and this discussion provided a framework that made it easier for her to set limits.

During the first four play sessions, Chris showed considerable fear of the clear-faced masks in the room. He whined, pointed at them, and shook his head, saying, "I don't like those!" The first time this happened, Tom was playing with him and reflected Chris's feelings very well: "You don't like those. They're kind of scary to you." Chris watched Tom for a minute, as if waiting for him to do something with the masks, and again Tom reflected his feelings accurately."You want something done with those masks that scare you." After this, Chris directed Tom to put the masks on top of a cabinet in the room, up high where he could not see them. The therapist reinforced Tom's excellent empathic listening during the feedback period.

This sequence occurred in all four sessions whether Chris was playing with Tom or Wendy. After he directed his parent to place the masks out of sight, he continued with his play. Much of his play was aggressive during this time, punching the bop bag, shooting the dart guns, and pretending he was a champion boxer. Wendy improved her limit-setting, and Chris responded well to limits from both parents during the play sessions. He rarely involved them in his play, but he seemed to enjoy telling them where to sit or stand.

When he entered the playroom for his fifth play session, Chris walked over to the masks and picked them up. He handed one to Tom and told him to put it on. After laughing at his father, he put the other mask on himself. After laughing at himself in the mirror, he put aside the masks and went on to other play, apparently having overcome his fears.

Tom was eager to discuss the session afterward. He commented that the play sessions seemed to work like "magic." The therapist asked if they had any theories about what had happened. Wendy said Chris may have been able to overcome his fears by exerting some control, taking action by directing Wendy and Tom to place them on the cabinet; the therapist agreed. Prior to this time, Tom had had some difficulty refraining from directing Chris's play. He was so impressed with Chris's ability to solve his own problem with the masks that he renewed his efforts to let Chris lead the way during the play sessions.

By this time, Wendy and Tom were conducting the play sessions very competently, and most of the post-play-session discussions centered on Chris's play themes and their own concerns as adoptive parents. While they found the play sessions enjoyable and interesting, they were frustrated that Chris still did not involve them in his play or respond to them as intimately as they had hoped. They began to realize that Chris had some problems, and they expressed doubts about their ability to help him and to ever have a close relationship with him. The therapist listened empathically to their fears and concerns before helping them reframe the problem. She emphasized for them a number of the signs that Chris had begun to bond with them (e.g., his turning to them for solace when frightened), reinforced their excellent play session efforts to date, and encouraged them to be patient with the process.

The therapist and the parents jointly decided that they were ready to transfer the play sessions to the home setting. A sixth play session was held in the therapist's playroom, and then the therapist planned to meet with Tom and Wendy alone for one session to work out all of the logistics of home play sessions.

During that sixth play session, the nature of Chris's play changed. He was playing with Wendy, and the tone was quieter and less aggressive. Midway in the session, he filled one of the baby bottles with water, took it with him as he sat on Wendy's lap, and then asked Wendy to sing him "baby songs." As she sang lullabies to him, he closed his eyes and sucked on the bottle. Both parents recognized this play sequence as a possible nurturance theme emerging, and they said Chris had also been engaging in a lot of baby talk at home.

After they began home play sessions, the Martins met with the therapist on a biweekly basis. They held the home play sessions in their large kitchen, and they reported that the transition had gone smoothly. They each held a 30-minute play session with him every week.

During his next two play sessions with Wendy, Chris requested that she rock him in her arms and sing lullabies again for nearly the entire session. Both parents indicated that he had been accepting and showing more affection in other ways, such as curling up next to them and cuddling while watching television rather than crawling all over them and the furniture. Although his play with Tom remained somewhat aggressive, he began to involve Tom more in some imaginary boxing scenarios. He cast Tom in the role of the announcer who told the imaginary audience what a great champion boxer Chris was.

The therapist began to help the Martins generalize the play session skills by teaching them to use empathic listening and limit-setting with Chris outside the play sessions. They had seen that the skills had worked well in the play sessions, so they willingly adapted them to other situations.

Meanwhile, Chris began to show more affection during the play sessions. He once switched roles with Wendy, rocking her and singing to her. His level of aggressiveness gradually decreased, but his play continued to reflect many control themes. Initially, Chris placed himself in the role of the "bad guy" who hurt and yelled at other people, possibly reflective of some abuse issues. He eventually chose the parts of policemen and superheroes who helped those in trouble.

During each meeting with Wendy and Tom, the therapist reviewed their play sessions from the previous 2 weeks. They discussed their use of the skills, questions they had, and the themes in Chris's play. They covered possible meanings of his play themes and how they related to other things that were happening in their lives. It was during these discussions that many of the Martins' concerns surfaced and were dealt with in a sensitive manner by the therapist. The therapist also taught them additional parenting skills.

Chris's behavior continued to improve as the home play sessions continued, and Tom and Wendy were pleased with the way their relationships with Chris were developing. Most of the presenting problems were resolving, and the Martins seemed capable of continuing the play sessions on their own. They seemed to have more realistic expectations of Chris and his relationships with them, also. The therapist directly observed one more play session each with Wendy and Tom in anticipation of discharge.

Chris's play during each of these play sessions confirmed the progress the Martins had reported. The play sessions were interactive, and Chris was actively using imaginary play. Family themes predominated. Chris "played house" in the kitchen area with Wendy and involved Tom in some puppet-family play. His play reflected family members completing daily chores and doing enjoyable things together. The activities depicted paralleled those in which the Martins engaged in real life. When he played with the dart guns, he set up a competition with Tom and was pleased when he could beat Tom.

Throughout the play sessions, Chris's affect seemed appropriate to the situation, no longer flat. His behavior with the therapist was open and friendly but not intrusive. Reports from the pediatrician and the school were positive.

The therapist met with the Martins 6 weeks later. They were continuing with the home play sessions and still were pleased with the way in which their new family was evolving. The therapist assured them of her availability should other problems arise in the future. Filial therapy with the Martins lasted for 19 sessions spanning 6 months. A follow-up contact 6 months later with the Martins and the school revealed that they were still doing well.

CONCLUSION

Adoptions are usually happy occasions uniting a couple's desire to have a child with a child's need for loving, caring parents. The process of adoption, both prior to the child's placement and as the family begins its life together, is not an easy one, however. By its very nature, adoption represents disruption. A child's life with his or her biological parents has been disrupted for any number of reasons, and the lives of the adoptive parents often change suddenly and dramatically. There are many adjustments for the new family to make, and sometimes the child has unforeseen special needs requiring the family's care. Even with established adoptive families, questions arise periodically about the biological parents and the meaning of the adoption, and this can be difficult for the adoptive child and parents alike. Overcoming the effects of past negative experiences or abuse is something that adoptive families sometimes must face together.

Through all this, the central challenge for adoptive children and parents is to build their relationships with each other in such a way that each family member's psychosocial development is fostered. Filial therapy, in which parents conduct child-centered play sessions with their own children under a therapist's supervision, can help families meet that challenge. It provides an opportunity for adoptive families to understand each other better, to solve their problems more effectively, to strengthen their relationships with each other, and simply to have an enjoyable time together. Filial therapy's skill-development approach permits its use both as a short-term educational program to help adoptive families prevent parenting and relationship problems as well as an intervention to help families experiencing significant difficulties. Filial therapy offers a straightforward, flexible, nonthreatening approach for practitioners who wish to empower adoptive families by enhancing their relationships with each other and their abilities to support one another.

REFERENCES

Axline, V. M. (1947). *Play therapy*. Cambridge, MA: Houghton-Mifflin.

Axline, V. M. (1969). *Play therapy* (rev. ed.). New York: Ballantine Books.

Brodzinsky, D. M., Radic, C., Huffman, L., & Merkler, K. (1987). Prevalence of clinically significant symptomatology in a nonclinical sample of adopted and nonadopted children. *Journal of Clinical Child Psychology, 16*, 350–356.

Coufal, J. D., & Brock, G. W. (1983). *Parent-child relationship enhancement: A 10-week education program*. Menomonie, WI: Coufal & Brock.

Ginsberg, B. G. (1989). Training parents as therapeutic agents with foster/adoptive children using the filial approach. In C. E. Schaefer & J. M. Briesmeister (Eds.), *Handbook of parent training* (pp. 442–478). New York: Wiley.

Guerney, B. G., Jr. (1964). Filial therapy: Description and rationale. *Journal of Consulting Psychology, 28*, 303–310.

Guerney, B. G., Jr., & Stover, L. (1971). *Filial therapy: Final report on MH 1826401* [Monograph]. State College, PA: Pennsylvania State University.

Guerney, L. F. (1976a). Filial therapy program. In D. H. Olson (Ed.), *Treating relationships* (pp. 67–91). Lake Mills, IA: Graphic Publishing.

Guerney, L. F. (1976b). Training manual for parents: Instruction in filial therapy. In C. E. Schaefer (Ed.), *Therapeutic use of child's play* (pp. 216–227). New York: Jason Aronson.

Guerney, L. F. (1983). Introduction to filial therapy: Training parents as therapists. In P. A. Keller & L. G. Ritt (Eds.), *Innovations in clinical practice: A source book* (Vol. 2, pp. 26–39). Sarasota, FL: Professional Resource Exchange.

Guerney, L. F., & Guerney, B. G., Jr. (1987). Integrating child and family therapy. *Psychotherapy, 24*, 609–614.

Schaefer, C. E., Gitlin, K., & Sandgrund, A. (Eds.). (1991). *Play diagnosis and assessment*. New York: Wiley.

Sensue, M. (1981). *Filial therapy follow-up study: Effects on parental acceptance and child adjustment*. Unpublished doctoral dissertation, The Pennsylvania State University, University Park, PA.

Stover, L., & Guerney, B. G., Jr. (1967). The efficacy of training procedures for mothers in filial therapy. *Psychotherapy, 4*, 110–115.

Sywulak, A. E. (1977). *The effect of filial therapy on parental acceptance and child adjustment*. Unpublished doctoral dissertation, The Pennsylvania State University, University Park, PA.

VanFleet, R. (1994). *Filial therapy: Strengthening parent-child relationships through play*. Sarasota, FL: Professional Resource Press.

CHAPTER 17

Play Therapy with Children of Alcoholics and Addicts

MARY HAMMOND-NEWMAN

INTRODUCTION

At the turn of the 20th century, addiction was a hidden disease. Children were to be seen and not heard. Children of alcoholics and addicts (COAs) were better off neither seen nor heard. As the decades passed, medical and psychiatric professionals continued to be baffled by their patients' recurring battles with the bottle and continued to look for the reasons in alcoholics' lives for their drinking or use of other addictive substances. In 1935, addicts were considered sinners, not patients. With the establishment of Alcoholics Anonymous (AA) by Dr. Bob and Bill W., alcoholics took the treatment of their disease into their own hands (Alcoholics Anonymous World Services, 1957, 1976). The children of alcoholics, however, remained forgotten (Cork, 1969).

Soon after the beginning of AA, hospital programs were developed that followed AA principles and used a specialized model of treatment that effectively confronted denial (Johnson, 1980). The treatment of alcoholics was greatly legitimized when AA's premise that alcoholism is an "allergy of the body and an obsession of the mind" (Alcoholics Anonymous World Services, 1976) was substantiated by neurological and metabolic research, and alcoholism was designated as a disease by the American Medical Association in 1954 (Hoffman, 1986; Milam, 1981). However, drug addicts still wandered in and out of prison gates until they entered the final gate: death. Their children often followed in their footsteps.

Al-Anon Family Groups (1986) were established by Bill W.'s wife, Lois, in the late 1940s. Alateen (Al-Anon, 1973), for alcoholics' children ages 12 through 18, later grew out of the Al-Anon organization. For decades, these groups were the only acknowledgment that children of alcoholics needed help; but children under 12, the most vulnerable, were excluded.

The emergence of community mental health centers and the addition of public school counselors expanded services for alcoholics and their families. These practitioners continued, however, to look for the external reasons for alcoholism and to treat its symptoms. As a result, many alcoholics died unnecessarily.

Children of alcoholics and addicts also received help only for their symptoms that were the result of alcoholism in the family—for anxious and aggressive behavior, for avoidant and withdrawn behavior, and for depression. The children did not mention the drinking going on at home. The counselors did not ask. The parents convinced the counselors that their stress was caused by the children's behavior. The counselors colluded with the family's distortion of the family's problem. Many children of alcoholics were lost unnecessarily. The achieving, superresponsible child was particularly ignored. This child seemingly had no problem. Families, schools, and communities were baffled and shocked when their "star" committed suicide.

The early 1960s saw a revolution in the use of illicit drugs and a rise in the use of alcohol. Abusive drug and alcohol use became the norm. By the late 1960s, clinics such as Haight-Ashbury in San Francisco began treating the first casualties of the revolution, and Narcotics Anonymous (NA) (Narcotics Anonymous World Services, 1986) was well established. Children raised in this era either joined their parents in drinking and drug using or denied this life-style and created a world of illusion that carried them to adulthood. When, as adult children of alcoholics and addicts (ACAs), they attempted to live this illusion, many fell into the abyss of depression and panic. When ACAs sought help, medical and psychiatric professionals were similarly baffled by their presenting somatic symptoms and their ongoing battles with compulsive behavior, depression, panic disorder, and numerous other disorders (Hammond-Newman, 1993).

In the early 1980s, a few courageous ACAs gathered together and, in the spirit of the two generations of AA before them, decided that they, too, should take their treatment into their own hands. The Adult Children of Alcoholics movement, founded originally in New York and Los Angeles, soon spread throughout the country (Black, 1981). However, their own children, the grandchildren of alcoholics, were forgotten (Smith, 1988).

Immediately following the emergence of the ACA movement, the federal government allocated funds specifically for prevention and treatment for COAs. Through school prevention programs, the last decade has brought considerable progress in outreach to COAs. (Lerner & Naditch, 1984).

A literature search in late 1982 documented a few articles and one book regarding young COAs. Only one article was located that reported the use of play therapy with COAs (Brown & Sunshine, 1982). A decade later, a National Clearinghouse for Alcohol and Drug Information literature search documents over 100 articles and over a dozen books on young COAs, indicating high risk for emotional, mental, and physical health problems for COAs (Woodside, 1988a). In addition, several hundred articles and books have been produced regarding fetal alcohol syndrome, fetal alcohol effect, and fetal drug effect. The recently published *The World of Play Therapy Literature* (Landreth, Homeyer, Bratten, 1993) from North Texas University, boasting 1,200 references, lists one title that includes "children of alcoholics" (Hammond, 1985) and a few scattered references in other writings (O'Connor, 1991). Kinetic family drawings of COAs were studied at George Washington University and found to be both diagnostically and therapeutically effective with COAs (Gardano, 1988).

Discoveries about alcoholism and addiction (chemical dependency) and about ACAs have increased significantly over the last several decades (Brown, 1985, 1988). During the same time, the developmental approach to play therapy with traumatized children other than COAs has been increasingly documented. There is still much to learn regarding the children affected by addiction, as the children-at-risk literature indicates (Blaine, 1988; Woodside, 1988).

This chapter will document this therapist's experience with COAs in developmental play therapy.

The Developmental Approach to Play Therapy with Children of Alcoholics

The disease of chemical dependency renders young children powerless in their own homes. It is this author's position that developmental play therapy empowers COAs and, in the spirit of the previous generation of recovering adults, makes it possible for them to take their treatment into their own hands. The children-at-risk literature further supports programs that use developmental models (Johnson & Rolf, 1990) and programs that provide choice and empower COAs (Oliver-Diaz, 1988).

In child-development and play-theory training, the diagram in Figure 17.1 is presented to describe the developmental approach to the whole child.

In alcohol and drug treatment hospitals and training programs the model in Figure 17.2 is presented for the developmental disease/recovery process.

Clearly, the developmental approach to the treatment of addiction also applies to the COAs. Alcoholism treatment is largely written and verbal, the accepted form of expression for adults. Children's treatment traditionally is largely play and art, the accepted form of expression for children.

Play theory and play therapy training are the bridge to working with COAs. The literature regarding child-centered classrooms where children can explore their natural cognitive, creative, emotional, and social abilities creates the theoretical foundation for developmental change for this therapist's work (Goodlad, 1984; Schweinhart & Weikert, 1980; Wadsworth, 1971). These Piagetian, child-centered environments are a natural entrée into the Rogerian world of Virginia Axline's play therapy (Axline, 1969; Rogers, 1961).

Clark Moustakas (1992) and Garry Landreth (1991) described the importance of the relationship between the therapist and child. Moustakas (1992) said,

> The creative relationship in play therapy is not the external butterfly, the fleeting life of Buber's I-Thou, but is an enduring and sustained mutuality, a oneness of continuing substance. It is an experience between two persons—not experiencing each other, but relating as persons. It is an experience of participation, a meeting of real persons—not a transitive managing or perceiving of something or someone. (p. 104)

Blending the relationship with the science of play therapy is the art of play therapy.

The bridge from early childhood teacher to play therapist more closely follows Violet Oaklander's footsteps than the other theorists. Specific uses of her gestalt projective

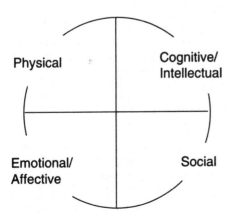

Figure 17.1. Developmental aspects of the child.

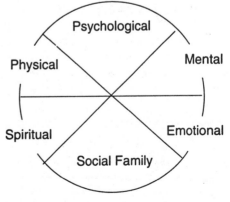

Figure 17.2. Developmental disease/recovery process.

technique in play and art are very beneficial with older children and teens to intervene with denial and to explore the child's perceptions of the alcoholic or the addicted family (Oaklander, 1978).

Developmental play therapy is built on the premise that children have an inherent ability to heal themselves in an interactive therapeutic play environment with supportive adults. The child's innate powers of healing lie dormant and repressed in the addictive family until help and hope are offered.

They inherently know they need someone to watch and listen as they play out their hurts, their fears, and their disgust with the drinking, the drug using, and the accompanying behaviors in their families.

They reveal their hurts as they bandage the dolls; they reveal their fears as the characters of their dramas change unpredictably; they reveal their anger through war scenes and battered block structures. As the therapist watches and listens attentively over many weeks, their hurts, fears, and anger begin at first to lose intensity and then, eventually, to transform.

PROCEDURE AND TECHNIQUES

Inspired by COAs' play, by the work of professional forerunners, and by colleagues who have traveled this path while assisting young children and teens to cope with the pain of family addiction, this therapist's chosen model became developmental play therapy (White & Hammond, 1983).

The last decade brought more than 200 young children and teens of alcoholics and addicts through the playroom doors and into individual or group therapy. In addition, this therapist has supervised other therapists and consulted with programs serving thousands of young children and teens of alcoholics and addicts and adult children of alcoholics. In child-development and therapy settings, this therapist has worked with another 2,000 children and families who were not identified as addictive families, although in retrospect many were. They had a potpourri of issues: divorce, blended family, hyperactivity, depression, anxiety, anger, perfectionism, control, and abuse. More than 1,000 adult children affected by addiction have also found healing in the rooms of toys and art materials. Their *children within* have contributed enormously to this therapist's understanding of their younger counterparts' lives and needs.

The young COAs this therapist has worked with have ranged in age from 2 to 19 years and were approximately 60% male and 40% female. The predominantly Caucasian northwest United States has brought only a 15% racial mix of Hispanic, American Indian, and black children to this therapist's treatment settings. An Hispanic group with a Spanish-speaking cotherapist and one group for severe fetal alcohol effect (FAE), fetal drug effect (FDE), and mild fetal alcohol syndrome (FAS) children were conducted.

Frequency and Duration of Treatment

COAs came to individual play therapy for 1 hour per week and/or group therapy for 1 1/2 to 2 hours per week. They stayed in therapy for 3 months to 18 months depending on the severity of their symptoms and the degree of family chaos or stability. Some came to chemical-dependency treatment centers where their parents were in treatment for addictions and codependency. Often, those still living with parents practicing their addictions were seen in school settings. Some were referred by their recovering family members, others by Children's Services Division (protective services), mental health agencies, and schools to COA play therapy.

The Setting and Materials

The children were fortunate to work in large, well-equipped rooms. Their therapist would not stand for less! The space in which they played out the dramas of addictive families is a warm, carpeted, 21 ft × 15 ft room. In the tradition of early childhood training, there are areas that suggest soft and hard, wet and dry, noisy and quiet. There is a dramatic-play area equipped with a kitchen corner complete with pots, pans, dishes, and "pretend" food (sometimes real food for hungry after-school snackers.) The kitchen corner also includes a "bar" with beer cans, wine and whiskey bottles, and drug paraphernalia. There are costumes, hats, masks, dolls, and baby bottles. There are binoculars, flashlights, and sunglasses to better "see" the reality of their worlds. There are guns and knives to play out the torture and anguish in their addictive families. There are small ornamental bottles that invariably become the magic potion that carries out the wishes of the child's magical thinking (Pearce, 1980).

There is a creative art center with an 8 ft × 8 ft sheet of acrylic plastic on the wall, which is routinely painted, squirted, and attacked with play dough. There are materials for sculpting, painting, drawing, and collage making that appeal equally to the young children and teens as well as to the children within adults who also use the playroom.

There is a sandtray area that currently holds a growing menagerie of human, animal, and fantasy figures; a selection of miniature fences and buildings; and a variety of items from nature. In a dry or wet sandtray (20 in. × 30 in. × 4 in.) or a smaller deeper sand tub (12 in. × 15 in.) filled with white sand, children play out the metaphors of their internal and external worlds as Lowenfeld (1979) documented.

There is a dollhouse center that holds two houses for playing out the repeated separation or divorce situations COAs endure. There are miniature dolls, furniture, household items, food, rugs, lamps, "booze" bottles, and toys where COAs play out the external and internal traumas of their households and their lives (Kuhli, 1983).

There are tubs reminiscent of infant-toddler environments to elicit sensory-motor play for the infant-toddler within the child client—foam balls, colored serpentine, fabric and yarn scraps, water, and cornstarch. There are real baby bottles and pacifiers to complete the unfinished infant experience.

There is a construction area that holds such items as wooden blocks, Legos™, Tinkertoys™, and Lincoln Logs™. It is there that the children gain control over an unpredictable world. Though it seems things in their real world of addiction never quite fit right, here, they can easily fit things together.

A covered porch allows for woodworking and for water play with very wet, messy tubs. There is a yard where therapists are attacked with squirt guns and hoses and where children can expand their boundaries and their power.

The play environment becomes the safe home that children of alcoholics and addicts have not experienced. The materials are kept in their places, identified by picture and word labels. This provides predictability unknown in addictive homes. The stability, emotional support, and encouragement provided by the play therapist in turn provide the children with perhaps their first consistent positive relationship.

Individual and Group Play Therapy

The child enters treatment in individual therapy in which several observation sessions coupled with parent and family sessions allow the therapist to assess the child's issues. The therapist determines the best diagnoses and the appropriateness of individual, sibling, and/ or group treatment. Individual therapy allows children to open and reinforce the trusting part of themselves due to the relationship with the therapist and the predictability of the play setting. In individual therapy, children affected by parental addiction gradually let go of the old coping mechanisms they needed for survival and reorganize their internal worlds—their cognitive structures and their psyches.

COAs whose trauma and abandonment occurred in infancy and the first few years of life will particularly benefit from longer term individual therapy. It is in the silence of the world of play inhabited only by child and therapist that the child will begin to touch the unconscious worlds of his or her preverbal life.

Individual, longer term therapy is equally important for aggressive or acting-out children. These troubled children need the unconditional, positive regard of the play therapist as they show him or her their own inner torment as well as the acts of torment committed by the intimidator or martyr parent in the alcoholic family (Hammond-Newman, 1993). COA groups should be spared the projected hostility of these scapegoated children until they are more manageable and appropriately self-directed.

However, individual therapy alone for the child or teen from an addictive family keeps the veil of secrecy and the cloak of denial, insidious with addiction, ever-present. Group therapy, when the child or teen client is ready, allows the child from the addictive family to feel less alone. Until the group experience, the child has felt isolated with confusion and fear, depression and anxiety, and has felt guilty for intermittently hating one or both parents. The group allows the child to break the isolation and to break through additional denial. They learn in group that most alcoholics and addicts in other families behave with similar intimidation and predictability (Davis-Susser, 1991).

The group experience allows the children and teens to reorganize the external world through cooperative play and to learn about a world established by the therapist where children's needs and rights are more important than rigid rules. Group becomes the model for a healthy family where maladaptations—roles and rigid rules—to the unhealthy family system are transformed. Addictive families are either enmeshed or estranged. When the family is enmeshed, the children do not learn to establish boundaries effectively; when the family is estranged, the children do not know how to reach out to others. Many COAs find themselves ill-equipped to build friendships and lack adequate social skills with their peers.

Groups are multiaged with the age breakdown within groups of 4- to 7-year-olds, 7- to 11-year-olds, 11- to 14-year-olds, and 14- to 18-year-olds. Younger children require a therapist-child ratio of 1:4, and teens require 1:6. The groups are also conducted from the developmental play approach. Each child is free to choose his or her own activity or to engage other children in their activities. Teen groups will often plan projects in which all participate.

Family and Sibling Therapy

Treating members from addictive families in sibling or family sessions is generally not recommended in initial therapy. The family denial system—roles and rules—are so well intact that the therapist will have little else to address (Wegsheider-Cruse, 1981). The roles and masks that children wear to cope with the addictive family are discussed in the context of play therapy later in this chapter. The rules that chemically dependent families as well as other dysfunctional, unconscious families follow are "Don't talk, Don't trust, Don't feel" (Black, 1981). The play environment allows COAs to shed their masks and to begin to talk and to express feelings and gradually build trust through the metaphors of toy figures and toy structures.

When COAs live with their parents, the parents are sometimes in therapy or treatment simultaneously. Often, however, the recovering parent denies the effects of their alcohol and drug use on their children until they are 6 months to 2 years into recovery. The children then come to play therapy. Parents are educated about addictive family dynamics and the effects on children. They are given handouts and ongoing information to support the recovery process for their children.

Foster parents often need more education to understand the darker sides of the addictive world of the COA who is living in their home. They are encouraged to participate in the therapy process and are guided to support their COA's recovery.

Children who live in actively addictive homes need the protection of the play therapy environment as a safe haven. It is important to build a relationship with parents and to gently confront the active codependency or substance addiction. They should be encouraged to see their child's strengths and to take action on major problems. The still-diseased parent cannot be as fully included in the child's therapy process as parents who are pursuing recovery. The active addict exaggerates the children's problems to avoid their own or denies the children's problems to avoid facing their own pain.

Once there are cracks in this system of denial, family treatment is effective and often necessary. Younger children are often the first to allow denial to slip away. Sibling play therapy is an excellent opportunity to offer COAs new ways of relating as they approach the materials and games of the playroom together. COAs grow up without adequate supervision. Care for the children is dictated on any given day not by their developmental needs but by the amount of alcohol or drugs ingested by one or both parents. In the beginning of sibling therapy, the children are alternately threatened and relieved to have an intervener in their relationships. COAs either constantly trip over one another's boundaries or blame one another for their immaturity and inability to work things out. Then they withdraw from one another. Because addiction makes emotional closeness with parents sporadic or nonexistent, sibling therapy may be their only chance to achieve family closeness.

CASE ILLUSTRATION—SIBLING GROUP

The family entered therapy after the mother, aged 30, had been clean and sober for 2 years. Mom had also been in ongoing individual therapy and occasional group therapy since her release from a 4-month in-patient program 2 years previously. Dad had minimal alcohol use and, although codependent, had been more emotionally available to the children. However, as a farmer, he often worked long hours. Sherry (8), David (7), Randy (6), and Gary (4) all had symptoms resulting from living with their mother's drug use and resulting neglect and anger. Sherry was anxious, worried, and controlling. David also was anxious and was pseudomature. Randy had outbursts of anger directed at younger siblings, including 9-month-old Tommy, and at mother. Gary was extremely anxious and appeared to be hyperactive with attention-deficit hyperactivity disorder (ADHD). The children were each in individual therapy for 6 months. About once a month, one of them would request that their sister Sherry or brother David come with them.

Randy's energy was channeled into creativity as he attended to blocks, building logs, sandtray work, and drawings in play therapy. Gary improved dramatically through individual therapy, using sand, water, and paints to release his anxiety and to increase his attention span from 5 minutes to 30 minutes on any one project.

This change in ability to focus and attend was a typical example of a COA who initially exceeded the criteria for mild ADHD in the *Diagnostic and Statistical Manual of Mental Disorders*, Third Edition, Revised (DSM-III-R) (American Psychiatric Association, 1987), but who, after play therapy and intervention with parents, was discovered to have symptoms that were nonorganic in origin. Rather, they were a manifestation of the anxiety produced by the neglect and intermittent availability of the parents.

As the individual issues began to heal and individual symptoms began to subside, the children requested more and more sibling sessions. Mother also reported that most of their problems seemed to be in their sibling interactions. Each was functioning well in school and had by this time functional relationships with each parent. As they worked in the playroom as a sibling group, still directing their own play, each would walk up to one of the other's play and begin drawing on the same paper, moving the other's blocks or sand or dollhouse figures without asking permission. This naturally set up frustration in the other sibling who got verbally angry, pushed the other away or waited awhile to get passive revenge by, in turn, disturbing the other's play. Slowly, as their trust built, the therapist began to suggest that they ask one another if they wanted to play alone or if they would share their play. Observing the struggle of this boundaryless sibling group with immature social skills who were otherwise bright and creative children, this therapist was reminded of a session 3 years earlier when their father had come to talk with this therapist about a potential intervention for their mother who had relapsed after previous drug treatment. With furrowed brow and wringing hands, he described his fear as their mother had driven regularly 60 miles to obtain her prescription drugs. He then tearfully described coming home from work many evenings to find his wife loaded with drugs and Gary (1), Randy (3), David (4), and Sherry (5) alone upstairs with strewn toys, food spilled, and things in general disarray. In their formative relationships, there was no one to intervene and assist them in learning boundaries and sharing toys and activities. It was time. Sandtrays were a favorite for all of them. At least two trays were available during their sessions so that sharing was an option but not a requirement.

In a typical session, 4-year-old Gary intently created a town resembling the natural order of the farming community where he lived and the new order he had found within himself through individual therapy. Sherry used the dollhouse to play out her need for control externally and internally. She constantly reorganized the house's contents to get it "just right." Randy's aggression at home was nearly always in reaction to not getting what he wanted immediately. In the playroom, he played themes of control and containment of these emotions. He built containers and drew boxes and other enclosed figures. He spent 30 to 45 minutes precariously balancing things that would not stay put and attempted to control their positions. David participated more in sibling than individual therapy, improving in his ability to let go of controlling his younger brothers and respecting their boundaries. He was often the overseer, focusing only for a while on his own projects, then wanting to play with his siblings or to control his sibling's activity. When Gary moved from blocks to the sandtray, David approached Gary's sandtray and began to reach in without permission. Gary said boldly, "This is my work; you play in the other sandtray!" David, shocked by his younger brother's assertiveness, backed off immediately and pursued play in the other sandtray.

The Therapist's Role with Children of Alcoholics and Addicts

"When *is* my Mary time?!" 9-year-old Sam exclaimed to his mother after he had missed 2 weeks of therapy with this therapist, Mary. His mother reported with surprise how important the play therapy sessions were to Sam. Dad had been gone drinking for several months and only called home when he was drunk. Sam had grown to depend on his time in the play therapy room to work through his anger and loss.

In play therapy, the therapist offers Sam and other COAs compassion regarding the disease of addiction and compassion for the fear and tension from growing up in a disturbed home. The therapist also offers intuition, curiosity, love, and imagination in the relationship with the children. Information regarding the disease of addiction, which helps them to sort out their feelings and to let go of feeling at fault in this family maze, is also shared. The therapist is respectful when their worlds are disrespectful, predictable when their lives are chaotic, genuine and authentic when their world is manipulative and dishonest, responsible in their otherwise irresponsible world. The fields of human development and psychology offer the framework that holds the therapist-child relationship in play therapy.

The play therapy session for COAs is guided by their innate sense of what they need in order to break through their denial, to give up survival roles, and to release anger, sadness, fear, and shame. Sometimes children immediately engage the therapist as characters in their dramas or as receivers of their tension through balls or squirt guns. Some will build relationships with the therapist by asking him or her to fetch toys, water, or whatever they need to effectively play out their scenes even though they are surprised by the therapist's willingness to do so. Others will build, create, or dramatize on their own and simply want the therapist to observe. The therapist follows their lead. The therapist's respect for their dignity, their space, and their needs delights children affected by addicted parents too sick to offer such respect.

The play therapist's role with COAs will vary in complexity depending upon the level of functioning of the children's parents. COAs who are in environments where addiction is still active or who are in foster care are at highest risk for the severe symptoms and issues discussed in this chapter. The therapist often takes on a caseworker role with the child client, building support with schools, social service agencies, and extended families. COAs who have at least one parent in recovery need the therapist's support to deal not only with the continued immaturity and unpredictability of clean and sober parents but also with the loss of the parent to recovery programs. To save their lives, the addicted parents are often away from home in hospital treatment programs, therapy groups, and 12-step groups more often or for longer periods than they were away drinking or using. This is especially true for addicted mothers who often used the shelter of the home to hide their drinking or using. The therapist provides important stability for the child during this critical initial phase of family recovery.

The therapist's role in individual therapy is to build a relationship with the child that will allow the child to trust the environment and to use the playroom for optimum exploration and healing (Landreth, 1991; Moustakas, 1992). Group and sibling therapy is a dance whereby the therapist assists the children in building effective relationships and also focuses on the children's individual projects and needs.

Therapists observe, take notes, watch, and listen. Therapists comment on the content and quality of their play. The therapist wonders, ponders, asks questions, and asks projective questions. The therapist plays with the child or with play characters or roles assigned by the child. They approach the therapist tentatively or hostilely, or they try to figure out what will please. The therapist approaches them with unconditional, positive regard. The therapist delights in their courage to play their way to healing. They finally figure out that what pleases the therapist is for them to explore all aspects of themselves— to be themselves.

Treatment Stages

Family Roles in the Playroom: Initial Phase of Therapy

Much has been written about the roles that members play in chemically dependent families (Black, 1981; Wegscheider-Cruse, 1981). In Transforming Your Childhood, Transforming Your Life (Hammond-Newman, 1993), this author has identified the parents' roles as the Intimidator and the Martyr and the children's roles as Super-responsible, Troubled, Victim, Loner, and Clown—roles that apply not only to chemically dependent families but to all families with problems.

The oldest child in chemically dependent families will often play the role of the Super-responsible, achieving child whose job it is to make the family look good and to caretake the younger siblings. The second or middle child will often play the role of the Troubled, scapegoated child. This child becomes the object of projections of the sick parents. The parents delude themselves to believe that this child, rather than the addiction, is the source of their problems. The Loner child is more often one of the younger children in the family. This child is born into a family system with no place to fit. This child cowers from the behavior of the Troubled child and withdraws into a world of fantasy, books, and animals. The Victim child is observed more often in the abusive, addictive family. This is the child that is thoroughly disempowered by physical or sexual abuse from one or both parents or from victimization by siblings or persons outside the family due to parental unavailability and neglect. The youngest child plays the Clown role from a very young age; he or she pleases, jokes, and cajoles or projects hyperactivity to distract and disrupt the family tension.

Children approach the playroom as they approach life. Super-responsible children enter the playroom smiling but sometimes with concern because they are missing an "important" after-school activity. These children spend the first few sessions trying to find out what will please the therapist, often asking, "Is this all right?" or "Can I really do that?" They play out dramas with the toys where the protagonist is "in charge." It will be a while before they reveal the fear that lies beneath their bravado.

Troubled children often do not want to come to play therapy and may act-out for the parents before the session. Whether they want to be there or not, their play is aggressive, even sometimes destructive. The aggression is often directed at the therapist. Trusting the therapist to see the pain beneath their acting-out will come later in therapy.

Loner children enter play therapy timidly, engaging the therapist very little. They will usually choose safe, structured, nonmessy activities hoping not to reveal too much. The therapist joins them in parallel play and their worlds of loneliness and fantasy begin to open up. Victim children enter the room defeated. The blocks fall over and the Legos™

will not fit. The doll clothes will not go on right, and they are not good at drawing. It will be months before the pain and fury and shame that lies beneath this lethargy and negativity are tapped.

Clown children enter the room exhibiting anxiety through silliness, hyperactivity, and flitting from activity to activity. They are eager to please and enthusiastic about play. As the therapist follows their lead through the initial weeks of therapy, they begin to build trust and to settle in and settle down to reveal the turmoil within.

Exhibiting the denial typical to addictive families in their first few sessions, the children play out their roles and try not to reveal much about their true feelings. They also follow their family's rules. They rarely talk directly or play or draw directly about the addiction in initial therapy. They ignore the presence in the room of the beer cans and paraphernalia. When feelings come through in play, their faces often still exhibit flat affect. At first, they will play away from their feelings instead of into them.

Throughout this initial phase of therapy, the therapist follows, watches, and listens. Addicted parents are almost never able to sit for an hour and watch their child play or to play with their child. The therapist's presence and attention are an unusual experience for them. As the therapist honors and engages their family role, trust builds, and they begin to shed the role and reveal more of their true selves through play.

Play therapy literature already addresses with some depth the work with Troubled (acting-out, aggressive) and Loner (withdrawn) children (Schaefer, 1976; Schaefer & O'Connor, 1983). Also, the COA literature indicates greater likelihood of emotional and cognitive problems than behavioral (Bennett, Wolin, & Reiss, 1988). Therefore, the example that follows is of an oldest, Super-responsible child in the early phase of treatment. The Super-responsible child's well-developed "look good" image, even though they may be only 4 or 5 years old, leads their parents to believe they do not need help. It takes education and a gentle but firm approach to convince parents and other service systems that looking good all the time is not normal.

CASE ILLUSTRATION

When Shelley (5), the oldest of two children (her brother is 3), entered play therapy, she was described by her divorced codependent mother as "always smiling, and always very good." After her mother read some about COAs, she feared the potential effects of the progressive alcoholism in Shelley's father, who had visitation with her every other weekend. In the first session, Shelley set up a female child figure in the lower, left-hand room of the dollhouse, surrounded by dark rocks, twigs, and yarn . . .

THERAPIST: Tell me about this.

SHELLEY: This is a very happy girl.

THERAPIST: The girl is very happy.

SHELLEY: Yes.

THERAPIST: I wonder about all the dark stuff around her.

SHELLEY: Oh, she's very happy, so it doesn't bother her.

Therapist: She's very happy, so she doesn't notice the dark stuff.

The Issues for Children of Alcoholics

COAs have numerous complex issues as a result of the stressors of parental addiction (Roosa, Beals, Sandler, & Pullow, 1990). They may have incomplete bonding due to parental alcohol and drug use or to the chaos that accompanies change (such as the birth of a sibling) in the addictive family. This incomplete bonding may result in varying degrees of attachment disorder, which is played out in the playroom as they keep their distance from the therapist and choose materials that are the least animate and the most contained.

COAs develop low self-esteem (Hall, 1988) and shame regarding the parents' substance use and resulting behaviors (Naditch, 1987). This is played out in the playroom as fictional figures are assaulted verbally and physically. COAs are nearly always fearful about what has just happened or what might happen next, which gets played out in the playroom by tentative approaches to the materials and by treating dolls and toys with either hypervigilant attention or neglect.

Depression or anxiety, common COA symptoms (Roosa, Sandler, Gehry, Beals, & Cappo, 1988), are often covered with anger or acting-out. Depression and suicidal ideation are often revealed in play through death scenes with fantasy figures. Some COAs are organically hyperactive, some seem hyperactive. They often seem confused. Confusion for the children is easier to cope with than the stark reality of their lives, and it is a manifestation of the addict's or codependent's constant state of confusion. They play this out in the playroom by being undecided about what to do, by mixing paints or play dough, or by sifting sand.

The addiction literature has substantiated for years that COAs also are genetically predisposed and are at higher risk to develop alcohol and other drug addiction (Goodwin, 1971; Vaillant, 1988). More recent research substantiates a neuropsychological and neurophysiological basis for the propensity for addiction in COAs (Tarter, Laird, & Moss, 1990). Play about their own drinking or drug use is revealed (initially with silliness) by having a toy, doll, therapist, or themselves play the drunk. Hyperactivity in both the nonorganic symptom form and the organic form is more often present in COAs than in control groups (Goodwin & Schlesinger, 1975). Significant biological links have been established between hyperactivity and addiction in later life (Morrison & Stewart, 1973).

Addicted parents are never emotionally available enough to the child. In the play session, this "never enough" theme gets played out by the children collecting or "shopping" for numerous items, especially pretend food, by filling containers to overflow, toddler-style. They adapt their parents' coping mechanisms for this deficit and become perfectionistic, controlling, and guilt-ridden (Fleury, 1989). They play this out by arranging the dollhouse, fixing the cars, having to get it "right," compulsively cleaning, or building very careful structures with Lincoln Logs™ or Legos™.

By teen years, full-blown codependency patterns have developed. In the session, pleasing or defiant behaviors are exhibited with the therapist, and, in the play with the dollhouse or sandtray, many symbols of caretakers and victims, controllers and rescuers are displayed.

COAs' problems may have begun in the womb due to maternal alcohol and other drug use including nicotine and caffeine. They may suffer from fetal alcohol syndrome (FAS) or from severe effects of maternal drug use (FDE), remarkable by physical deformities and mental retardation (Giunta, 1988). More common, though, is fetal alcohol effect (FAE) and less severe fetal drug effects (FDE), that result in hyperactivity, attention deficit, behavioral problems, learning disabilities, motor problems, and hypersensitivity to light and sounds (Doberczak & Shanzu, 1988; Schneider & Chasnoff, 1988; Smith & Coles, 1991). FAE and FDE children may exhibit more tantrums, more acting-out, or more withdrawn behavior than the average COA. They are, however, reacting as much to their maladapted central nervous systems as to their disturbed family. Specialized play environments, which meet the varying degrees of developmental delays and inability to adequately process sensory stimulation, are necessary to effectively treat severe FAE and all FAS children. FAE children who are appropriately treated for accompanying hyperactivity do well in developmental play therapy.

As the issues begin to emerge and therapy progresses, parents, schools, or social service agencies may report an escalation in aggressive or acting-out behavior. This is common when children are working through the trauma of an addictive family, as others have reported in their work with other traumatized children (Norton & Norton, 1992). Some children from addictive families may perpetuate the family denial by withdrawing from play regarding critical issues and by avoiding play that easily reveals the family secrets. Other COAs will go to great lengths to determine what pleases the therapist, and deeper therapeutic work will be blocked for several sessions. This pleasing behavior is especially typical of female COAs (Berger, 1991).

CASE ILLUSTRATION

Shelley (5) entered the playroom on her third session reporting that she had had a very bad day with her teacher. She was smiling and yet expressing anger. This was a partial breakthrough for the "always very good" COA. This therapist encouraged her to use a pillow as her "very bad day" and kick it around the room for awhile.

SHELLEY: (Kicking pillow, speaking loudly and deliberately) I had an awful day. I hate my teacher. She is not fair.
THERAPIST: Shelley's kicking her very bad day!
SHELLEY: I'm kicking my teacher!
THERAPIST: The pillow is getting kicked!
SHELLEY: Yeah! (Continued repeating for 10 minutes)

This therapist purposefully avoided in this initial phase of therapy stating, "Shelley's mad. Shelley's kicking her teacher." The family rule was that Shelley did not get mad, and direct verbalization could cause her to suppress her anger once more.

The Play Deepens: Middle Phase of Treatment

Depression, which is indicated as a risk factor for COAs (Rolf, Johnson, Israel, Baldwin, & Chandra, 1988), sadness, fear, grief, and loss finally come flooding forth. As the trust bond with the therapist strengthens, the roles are dropped in the playroom, and the play deepens.

CASE ILLUSTRATION

Sam's alcoholic Dad had been gone for 4 months on a drinking binge that was a repeat of many throughout Sam's life.

Sam (9) approached the dollhouse and played out a theme he has been working through and elaborating for several sessions. He gathered numerous dollhouse-sized male figures that "take over" the dollhouse.

SAM: They need weapons. (Finds everything in room that could be small weapons and struggles to get them in place)

THERAPIST: It's hard to figure out how everything will fit and how it will work.

SAM: Ah! There's the man with the hook upstairs.

THERAPIST: The man with the hook looks mean.

SAM: Yeah, these are all the bad guys. The good guys are over here, and they're trying to escape!

THERAPIST: The good guys are trying to get away from the bad guys.

SAM: The Indians will help the good guys. (Sam is American Indian.)

THERAPIST: Oh good, the Indians come to the rescue.

SAM: Here's the sheriff, too. The sheriff and the Indian are defending the house.

THERAPIST: The two of them can defend it all on their own.

SAM: Yes! They got the guy with the red cloak. (Sam carefully removes red cloak from figure.) He lost his protection.

THERAPIST: Something could happen to him.

SAM: He falls and dies. Oh, he almost hit the kid! The kid almost died!

From careful observation over several sessions, Sam's metaphors became clear. Sam was playing out his fear and vulnerability through the attack of the "bad guys" (his father's alcoholism and internal pain). The "Indians" were the strength of his powerful mother who is a tireless political and social activist in Indian affairs. The sheriff was the super-responsible part of Sam who, with his Indian mother, can go it alone without his adopted FAE sister, a chronic runaway, or alcoholic Dad. The kid who almost got hit and nearly died (really hurt) was the vulnerable part of Sam. The male figure who lost his cloak was the alcoholic father—stripped, vulnerable, and hurtful.

Most children of alcoholics and addicts ingest drugs from early childhood. Some COAs report being fed liquor in a baby bottle. All COAs have told this author that they have had at least a sip of alcohol or have been inappropriately medicated or drugged by age 6 or 7. Many young COAs are given adult prescription or street drugs by their parents from a very young age to help them sleep or to perk them up. In addition, COAs are extremely affected by their parents' drinking, using, and resultant behaviors. Surprisingly, parental alcohol/drug use is not the foremost issue on children's minds. Their own emotional and physical safety is primary. When these issues manifest in the playroom in the middle phase of therapy, they give the baby doll pills and drinks when it is "sick" or tired, or they reveal to the therapist what the fantasy figure or character feels like when it is drunk. More common still the child will ask the therapist to engage in dramatic play where the child directs the therapist to be the "drunk," as 7-year-old Barney did in his fifth session.

CASE ILLUSTRATION

BARNEY: Have a beer!

THERAPIST: Oh, I don't know, I might get drunk.

BARNEY: Just one beer! (Hands therapist a beer can.)

THERAPIST: Oh, okay. (Therapist pretends to gulp.)

BARNEY: Here have another.

THERAPIST: Yeah, I really need another one! (Therapist pretends to gulp another.)

BARNEY: Here's another.

THERAPIST: (Again therapist "gulps" beer down, slurs, and staggers.) I like shtat beeer.

BARNEY: (Giggles) You look stupid like my dad.

THERAPIST: (Still slurring) Yeah, alcoholics sure look stupid!

BARNEY: (Giggling) My dad talks like that. (His eyes lower, his voice gets serious.) But my dad gets mean!

THERAPIST: (Normal voice) Alcoholics get mean when they drink.

BARNEY: (Throws beer can, tears in his eyes) I hate it.

THERAPIST: (Normal voice) You hate your dad's drinking and meanness.

His vulnerability was the cue to return to a normal voice. He had reached the depth of his pain, and he needed his therapist to be there with him, to support him emotionally as his alcoholic/addict dad's disease did not allow.

Children of parents who use illegal drugs face the same fears and threats that children of alcoholics face but additionally collude with the family's secrecy resulting from the fear that their parents will go to jail for their actions.

CASE ILLUSTRATION

Five-year-old Alice played out her feelings regarding her father's imprisonment for his involvement in burglary and drug dealing.

ALICE: (Handcuffing therapist) You're the bad guy.

THERAPIST: I'm the bad guy.

ALICE: Bad guys have to go to jail.

THERAPIST: Oh, I'm going to have to go to jail.

ALICE: Yes. (Finishes handcuffing therapist, and escorts her to far corner of room.) You have to stay here for a long time, and you can't have birthday parties or see your kids or anything.

THERAPIST: I'll really miss my kids and birthday parties.

ALICE: Tough! You shouldn't have given those drugs to those people.

THERAPIST: If I wouldn't have given the drugs to those people, I could be with my kids and have birthday parties.

ALICE: That's right! Okay now . . . (Leads therapist out of jail and removes handcuffs.) You put the handcuffs on me and put me in jail.

They then replayed the scenario with roles reversed. Since this therapist had understood that Alie's core issue was the separation from her father and not her father's illegal activity, Alice could then trust going a step further in exposing her own vulnerability (allowing the therapist to handcuff her) and putting herself in her father's place.

The COA literature also indicates that addictive families are at great risk for physical and sexual abuse (Christozov & Toleva, 1989; Reich, Earls, & Powell, 1988). Posttraumatic Stress Disorder is evident in these children (Bean-Bayog, 1987). The abuse issues for COAs are acted-out in the playroom as toy soldiers are wounded, Legos™ are torn apart, dolls are hidden in corners of the room, and child figures and perpetrators are buried in the sand.

Children of addiction often wish their unpredictable parent(s) dead, or they contemplate suicide themselves. This is played out in the playroom in bloody battles where no one survives and in toy ambulances that acquire numerous miles with emergency rescue trips across the playroom. As the disease progresses in the family, they also fear the alcoholic parent's death from the increasingly obvious danger in which alcoholism places their mother or father. Sometimes children will fear that their parent, in a drunken rage or careless stupor, will kill them.

CASE ILLUSTRATION

In a COA group one evening, Janie (10), her sister Sami (8), Janis (7), and Tony (7) were working with play dough at a table together. Sensory materials such as play dough can have a relaxing effect on children and slide them into their feelings.

JANIE: My Dad got drunk in town the other night and got in an accident and everyone (in the small, rural town) knows about it. I hate him!

THERAPIST: (Therapist moves close and responds to the pained, fearful look on Janie's face that the "hate him" statement does not adequately cover.) You hate what your Dad did, and you're scared for him.

JANIE: (Digs into play dough, tears well in her eyes.) I'm scared he's going to die. (Other three children watch wide-eyed, kneading the colored dough.)

THERAPIST: You are afraid your Dad might die from drinking too much or in a car accident. (Turning to others) Have any of you ever worried about Mom or Dad dying?

SAMI: (Begins furiously mixing play dough, gets tense, red in the face, tears well.) I think my Dad's gonna die.

THERAPIST: It hurts so much and it's confusing (replying to play dough mixing) to think about Dad dying.

SAMI: (Starts crying hard; therapist holds her.)

TONY: My Mom almost died from drugs before she came here (inpatient treatment program). I hope she stops; it's scary. (He "hides" one color of play dough inside another as he talks.)

THERAPIST: It's hard to even look at or think about Mom dying.

TONY: (Tears well.) I want it to go away. (Smashes play dough)

JANIS: My Dad says if he drinks one more he'll die.

THERAPIST: That is really scary!

JANIS: (Kneads play dough intensely to release tension and fear.) Mary (therapist), what if he drinks another beer?

Termination

As the children move out of the intensity of feelings of the middle phase of therapy, their play will change in quality. The issues become integrated, and there is evidence of resolution. The play becomes more creative and elaborate. The child becomes lighter and more hopeful and functions better in life outside the playroom.

Effective termination involves three to six sessions, depending upon the duration of therapy. The child will indicate readiness for termination by playing more independently of the therapist. The child may even direct the therapist to sit away from the child and to do something else. The child will play out themes of separation where all do well, or at least survive.

CASE ILLUSTRATION

For a year, Tammy (8), had been in therapy that was initiated by her maternal grandparents with whom she lived. Her mother was a drug addict and had been divorced for 7 years from Tammy's father, who lived out of state. Tammy had a 13-year-old half-brother, Tom, of whom she was very fond, but rarely saw because he lived out of town with his father. Her Mom's disease had progressed to the point that Mom could not maintain a home and was often on the streets. Having long been concerned for Tammy's welfare, her well-to-do grandparents gladly provided a safe home.

Initially in play therapy, Tammy spent many sessions playing out her need for control through building careful structures with blocks or Legos™. She later played themes of caring and mending hurts with the dolls, reflecting her newfound safety with her grandparents.

As her play deepened in the middle phase of treatment, the dolls were left alone, abandoned. The doll characters reflected Tammy's loneliness and fear. Tammy reported directly as a result of this play that Mom had left her many times to go and get drugs. Also, Tammy revealed many scenes of violence between her mother and her mother's boyfriend that left her cowering in the corner. She was sometimes rescued by a caring neighbor.

Tammy's core issue, however, was fear regarding potential kidnapping by her mother or one of her mother's "druggie" cohorts. Many scenes were played in the dollhouse where the child or children were kidnapped. This progressed to scenes of being kidnapped and rescued.

Toward the end of the year of therapy, Tammy's grandparents and father agreed that he was ready to take custody of Tammy and provide a stable home for her. This dollhouse scene integrated her months of work on her fears.

TAMMY: (spends 15 minutes setting up the dollhouse silently; the therapist sits close by and observes.) Ok, here are the kids—the sister and brother.

(A subtheme of therapy has been her wish for more closeness with her brother.)

They are playing together. The Dad is over here in the other room watching TV.

THERAPIST: So the kids are enjoying playing, and Dad is relaxing watching TV.

TAMMY: Right. The kids ask Dad, "Can we go outside and play?" (Dad doll replies through Tammy.) Yeah, but you kids be careful and stay close to the house. Tom, you take care of your sister. (Tom doll replies.) Ok, I will.

(Tammy moves dolls to play yard outside of dollhouse.)

TAMMY: (Picks up toy airplane and flies toward house.) The bad guys are coming.

THERAPIST: Uh, oh, it's the bad guys again.

TAMMY: Yeah, this guy's going to parachute down and try and steal the girl.

THERAPIST: Oh, no! He might steal her.

TAMMY: But the Dad hears the plane and runs to the door and yells, "Get in here right now!" (Tammy quickly maneuvers the dolls into the dollhouse.)

THERAPIST: Phew! They made it.

TAMMY: And the Dad locks the door and she's ok.

THERAPIST: The Dad can keep the girl safe.

TAMMY: Ok, let's play it again!

(Tammy enthusiastically replayed the scene with a new ending.)

TAMMY: So the kids are playing together (outside) and having fun. The bad guys are gone!

THERAPIST: So, the girl is safe!

TAMMY: (Beaming) Yes! (Hugs therapist.)

The last few sessions were spent on some exploration regarding Tammy's high risk for drug use and on drawing pictures of grandma's house, Mom, Dad's house, and the airplane that she would fly on to Dad's house. In her last session, she made good-bye cards and presents for the friends, family, and therapist she was leaving. This therapist made a card with pictures and messages about the year together and sent her off with some of the instant photos taken of her play.

CONCLUSIONS

The field of addiction has made progress in research regarding COA symptomatology, school prevention programs, genetic predisposition for addiction, and FAS and FDE. There is still very little documentation to date regarding COAs in play therapy. This writing and a book in progress by this author, *Spirits in the Playroom*, begin to rectify that. Much more research by and dialogue between play therapists who work with COAs are encouraged.

The developmental play therapy model has proven effective with COAs. Its empowering effect allows the children's true strengths to emerge in spite of the unconsciousness that denies the children's emotional health in the addictive family system.

Developmental play therapy allows children to work through their own compulsivity, perfectionism, control, denial, and guilt. In play therapy, anger and acting-out can be safely expressed and contained. Depression, anxiety, loss, and confusion emerge from the child for exposure and healing. Core shame and fear can be played out in the world of metaphors from the child's psyche (Allan, 1991). Budding codependency can be thwarted as the child bonds with the therapist in the safety of the playroom.

The initial phase of therapy exposes the masks that COAs wear to survive the addictive family system. As the masks begin to slip, the more vulnerable issues and feelings are revealed. Healing occurs through individual, sibling, and group play therapy.

As the play deepens, the child needs much support from the therapist to shed the guilt that accompanies exposing the family's secrets. The child further depends on the therapist, the safe-room environment, and the materials to release and yet contain the enormousness of the pain, fear, and shame that lie at the core of the wounded COA.

In the termination phase of therapy, COAs naturally integrate and resolve most of their issues according to their developmental abilities. They reach acceptance of those issues

over which they are powerless or that are irresolvable. They do not need to focus their energy as much on playing to heal and can now focus their energy on playing to create and playing to enhance growth.

When children develop wholeness of the spirit through play with the therapist, materials, and peers, the generational chain of addiction is more likely to be broken.

REFERENCES

Al-Anon Family Groups. (1973). *Alateen: Hope for children of alcoholics.* New York: Author.

Al-Anon Family Groups. (1986). *Al-Anon family groups.* New York: Author.

Alcoholics Anonymous World Services. (1957). *Alcoholics Anonymous comes of age: A brief history of Alcoholics Anonymous.* New York: Author.

Alcoholics Anonymous World Services. (1976). *Alcoholics Anonymous* (3rd ed.). New York: Author.

Allan, J. (1991). *Inscapes of the child's world.* Dallas, TX: Spring Publications.

American Psychiatric Association. (1987). *Diagnostic and statistical manual of mental disorders* (3rd ed., rev.). Washington, DC: Author.

Axline, V. (1969). *Play therapy.* New York: Ballantine. (Original work published 1947)

Bean-Bayog, M. (1987). Children of alcoholics. *Advances in alcohol and substance abuse, 6*(4), 1–3.

Bennett, L. A., Wolin, S. J., & Reiss, R. (1988). Cognitive, behavioral and emotional problems among school-aged children of alcoholic parents. *American Journal of Psychiatry, 145*(2), 185–190.

Berger, J. (1991). Comparative analysis of locus-of-control in children of alcoholic mothers and children of alcoholic fathers. (Doctoral dissertation, Adelphi University, 1991). *Dissertation Abstracts International, 51*(9), 3219–A, 0419–4209.

Black, C. (1981). *It will never happen to me.* Denver, CO: M.A.C. Publishers.

Blaine, H. T. (1988). Prevention issues with children of alcoholics. *British Journal of Addiction, 83,* 793–798.

Brown, K. A., & Sunshine, J. (1982). Group treatment for children from alcoholic families. In M. Altman & R. Crocker (Eds.), *Social groupwork and alcoholism* (pp. 65–72). New York: Haworth Press.

Brown, S. (1985). *Treating the alcoholic: A developmental model for recovery.* New York: Wiley.

Brown, S. (1988). *Treating adult children of alcoholics.* New York: Wiley.

Christozov, C., & Toleva, S. (1989). Abuse and neglect of children brought up in families with an alcoholic father in Bulgaria. *Child Abuse and Neglect, 13,* 153–155.

Cork, M. (1969). *The forgotten children: A study of children with alcoholic parents.* Toronto, Ontario, Canada: Addiction Research Foundation.

Davis-Susser, S. A. (1991). Group therapy for latency age children of alcoholics: A treatment outcome study. (Doctoral dissertation, Pace University, 1991.) *Dissertation Abstracts International, 51,* 5024–502B.

Doberczak, T. M., & Shanzu, S. (1988). Neonatal and electroencephalographic effects of intrauterine cocaine exposure. *Journal of Pediatrics, Neurology, and Community Medicine, 113,* 354–358.

Fleury, T. M. (1989). Child-rearing practices of alcoholic mothers and their children's behavior. (Doctoral dissertation, California School of Professional Psychology, Berkeley). *Dissertation Abstracts International, 49,* 3436–343B.

Gardano, A. C. (1988). Kinetic family drawings and its application to the evaluation of family structure with an emphasis on children from alcoholic families. (Doctoral dissertation, George Washington University). *Dissertation Abstracts International, 49,* 1385–138B.

Giunta, C. T. (1988). Patients with fetal alcohol syndrome and their caretakers. *Social Casework, 69,* 453–459.

Goodlad, J. (1984). *A place called school: Prospects for the future.* New York: McGraw-Hill.

Goodwin, D. W. (1971). Is alcoholism hereditary? *Archives of General Psychiatry, 25,* 545–549.

Goodwin, D. W., & Schlesinger, F. (1975). Alcoholism and hyperactive child syndrome. *Journal of Nervous and Mental Disease, 160,* 349–353.

Hall, J. C. L. (1988). Exploration of self-esteem in COAs. (Doctoral dissertation, California School of Professional Psychology, Fresno). *Dissertation Abstracts International, 48,* 3679B.

Hammond, M. (1985). *Children of alcoholics in play therapy.* Deerfield Beach, FL: Health Communications.

Hammond-Newman, M. (1993). *Transforming your childhood, transforming your life.* Unpublished manuscript.

Hoffman, S. (1986). *Alcohol use, misuse and addiction* (3rd. ed.). Salem, OR: State of Oregon, Office of Alcohol and Drug Abuse Programs.

Johnson, J. L., & Rolf, J. E. (1990). When children change: Research perspectives on children of alcoholics. In R. L. Collins, K. E. Leonard, & J. S. Searless (Eds.), *Alcohol and the family: Research and clinical perspectives.* New York: Guilford Press.

Johnson, V. E. (1980). *I'll quit tomorrow.* San Francisco: Harper & Row.

Kuhli, L. (1983). The use of two houses in play therapy. In C. E. Schaefer & K. J. O'Connor (Eds.), *Handbook of play therapy* (pp. 274–279). New York: Wiley.

Landreth, G. (1991). *Play therapy, the art of the relationship.* Muncie, IN: Accelerated Development.

Landreth, G, Homemyer, L., & Bratton, S. (1993). *The world of play therapy literature.* Denton, TX: The Center for Play Therapy, U. of North Texas.

Lerner, R., & Naditch, B. (1984). *Children Are People support group training manual.* St. Paul, MN: CAP, Inc.

Lowenfeld, M. (1979). The World technique. London: George Allen & Unwin.

Milam, J. (1981). *Under the influence.* Seattle, WA: Madrona.

Morrison, J. R., & Stewart, M. A. (1973). The psychiatric status of legal families of adopted hyperactive children. *Archives of General Psychiatry, 3,* 888–891.

Moustakas, C. (1992). *Psychotherapy with children: The living relationship.* Greeley, CO: Carron Publishers. (Original work published 1959)

Naditch, B. (1987). Rekindled spirit of a child: Interventions for shame with elementary age COAs. *Alcoholism Treatment Quarterly, 4*(2), 57–69.

Narcotics Anonymous World Services. (1986). *Narcotics Anonymous.* Van Nuys, CA: Author.

Norton, B., & Norton, C. (1992, June). *Reaching children through play therapy.* Symposium presented by Family Psychological Consultants. Portland: OR.

O'Connor, K. (1991). *The play therapy primer.* New York: Wiley.

Oaklander, V. (1978). *Windows to our children.* Moab, UT: Real People Press.

Oliver-Diaz, P. (1988). How to help recovering families struggle to get well. *Focus, 11*(2), 20–21, 49–50.

Pearce, J. (1980). *The magical child.* New York: Bantam.

Reich, W., Earls, F., & Powell, J. (1988). Comparison of the home and social environments of COAs and non-alcoholic parents. *British Journal of Addiction, 83,* 831–839.

Rogers, C. (1961). *On becoming a person, a therapist's view of psychotherapy*. Boston: Houghton Mifflin.

Rolf, J. E., Johnson, J. L., Israel, E., Baldwin, J., & Chandra, S. (1988). Depressive affect in school-aged children of alcoholics. *British Journal of Addiction, 83*, 841–848.

Roosa, M. W., Beals, J., Sandler, I. H., & Pullow, D. R. (1990). Role of risk and protective factors in predicting symptomatology in adolescent self-identified children of alcoholic parents. *American Journal of Community Psychology, 18*, 725–741.

Roosa, M. W., Sandler, I. N., Gehry, M., Beals, J., & Cappo, L. (1988). Children of alcoholics life-events schedule: A stress scale for children of alcohol-abusing parents. *Journal of Studies on Alcohol, 49*, 422–459.

Schaefer, C. (1976). *The therapeutic use of child's play*. New York: Jason Aronson.

Schaefer, C., & O'Connor, K. (1983). *Handbook of play therapy*. New York: Wiley.

Schneider, J. W., & Chasnoff, I. (1988). Motor assessment of cocaine-exposed infants. *Physical Therapy, 68*, 838.

Schweinhart, L. J., & Weikert, D. (1980). *Young children grow up: The effects of the Perry Preschool Project*. Ypsilanti, MI: High Scope Press.

Smith, A. (1988). *Grandchildren of alcoholics*. Deerfield Beach, FL: Health Communications.

Smith, I. E., & Coles, C. D. (1991). Multi-level interventions for prevention of fetal alcohol syndrome and effects of prenatal alcohol exposure. In M. Galanter (Ed.), *Recent developments in alcoholism: Vol. 9. Children of alcoholics* (pp. 165–182). New York: Plenum Press.

Tarter, R. F., Laird, S. B., & Moss, H. B. (1990). Neuropsychological and neurophysiological characteristics of children of alcoholics. In J. S. Searless & M. Windle (Eds.), *Children of alcoholics: Critical perspectives* (pp. 73–98). New York: Guilford Press.

Vaillant, G. E. (1988). Predicting alcoholism and personality disorder in a 33-year longitudinal study of children of alcoholics. *British Journal of Addiction, 83*, 831–839.

Wadsworth, B. (1971). *Piaget's theory of cognitive development*. New York: David McKay.

Wegscheider-Cruse, S. (1981). *Another chance: Hope and help for the alcoholic family*. Palo Alto, CA: Science and Behavior Books.

White, G., & Hammond, M. (1985). *Report on the children of alcoholics project*. Salem, OR: State of Oregon Alcohol and Drug Programs Office.

Woodside, M. (1988a). COAs: Helping a vulnerable group. *Public Health Reports, 103*, 643–648.

Woodside, M. (1988b). Research on children of alcoholics: Past, present, and future. *British Journal of Addictions, 83*, 785–792.

CHAPTER 18

A Structured Activities Group for Sexually Abused Children

SCOTT J. VAN DE PUTTE

INTRODUCTION

The literature documenting the experience of sexually abused children has focused on the child's experience of anxiety. These descriptions focused primarily on the psychological and physical manifestations of anxiety in children. The most familiar diagnosis of this anxiety by adults who do clinical work with children is that of Posttraumatic Stress Disorder (PTSD), in the *Diagnostic and Statistical Manual of Mental Disorders*, Third Edition, Revised (DSM-III-R), of the American Psychiatric Association (1987). The list of symptoms includes the following:

A. The person has experienced an event that is outside the range of usual human experience and that would be markedly distressing to almost anyone.

B. The traumatic event is persistently re-experienced in at least one of the following ways: 1) repetitive play in which themes or aspects of the trauma are expressed; 2) recurrent distressing dreams of the event; 3) suddenly acting or feeling as if the traumatic event were recurring; 4) intense psychological distress at exposure to events that symbolize or resemble an aspect of the traumatic event.

C. Persistent avoidance of stimuli associated with the trauma or numbing of general responsiveness as indicated by at least three of the following: 1) efforts to avoid thoughts or feelings associated with the trauma; 2) efforts to avoid activities or situations that arouse recollections of the trauma; 3) inability to recall an important aspect of the trauma; 4) loss of recently acquired developmental skills; 5) feelings of detachment or estrangement from others; 6) restricted range of affect; 7) sense of a foreshortened future.

D. Persistent symptoms of increased arousal as indicated by at least two of the following: 1) difficulty falling or staying asleep; 2) irritability or outbursts of anger; 3) difficulty concentrating; 4) hypervigilance; 5) exaggerated startle response; 6) physiological reactivity upon exposure to events that symbolize or resemble an aspect of the traumatic event. (p. 149)

Other diagnoses that are typically given to sexually abused children include over-anxious disorder and generalized anxiety disorder. Theoretical notions associated specifically with the experience of sexual assault, such as "identification with the aggressor" (Burgess, Hartmean, McCausland, & Powers, 1984) and "dissociation" (Spiegel, 1984), are perceived as adaptive efforts to defend against the experience of overwhelming anxiety. Even many of the more severe diagnoses given to adults abused as children, such as multiple personality disorder, are perceived as resulting from a "splitting off" of various aspects of the psyche. This "splitting off" is often perceived as the result of an experience of overwhelming anxiety that cannot be integrated by the immature psyche of the child (Putnam, 1989).

The sexual abuse of children has been perceived by the author to represent a failure in the perpetrating adult to empathize with the developmental needs of the child. Because of his or her sexual preoccupation with the child, the perpetrating adult does not engage the child in the types of activities that typically form the experiential foundation that allows the child to develop the ability to mediate his or her own experiences of anxiety. From this perspective the activities group described herein was structured to provide the sexually abused child with the types of experiences that support the child in mediating his or her anxiety. Utilizing the self theory of Kohut (1971) and the Theraplay concepts of structuring, intruding, nurturing, and challenging (Jernberg, 1979), a group approach to the treatment of sexually abused children was developed.

The preadolescent stage of development was perceived by the author as an ideal stage to intervene with child survivors. The child has not yet developed secondary sexual characteristics, and sexual concerns are not a primary issue at this time. The child is still motivated by his or her primary narcissistic needs but is also beginning to utilize language skills acquired in the preschool years to form more enduring relationships with members of his or her peer group. In addition, developmental research indicates that the preadolescent child's ability to integrate and process information about his or her environment shifts dramatically. The child begins to develop the ability to verbally process abstract concepts. In the opinion of the author, this combination of characteristics makes the preadolescent child particularly receptive to a structured group intervention designed to support the child in integrating his or her sexual abuse experiences into a cohesive sense of self-identity.

The activities group was perceived by the author as a supplement to individual therapy. Individual play therapy was perceived primarily as a means of allowing the child to reenact anxiety regarding the abuse in play. It is the belief of the author that the majority of sexually abused children must first develop the type of relationship with an adult in which they feel safe enough to confront the source of their anxieties through play. Once the experience of anxiety has been confronted and acted out, the child can begin the process of assigning that experience some sort of meaning through verbal interactions with others. The activities group was perceived as a means of allowing sexually abused children to develop the ability to verbalize their experiences by modeling the behavior of same-aged peers.

THEORETICAL FOUNDATIONS

Kohut (1982) perceived the self to be the core of an individual's psychological universe. The self was perceived to be an abstract mental structure defined and detected only through its manifestations. It consisted of the motivations, skills, and goals of an individual and of all of the tensions that existed between them. The infant develops a mature self through a developmental process of interacting with the environment. The parent is the primary mediator between the needs of the infant and the demands of the environment. According to Kohut (1971), the infant is born with two primary, innate, psychological needs: He refers to these primary narcissistic needs as the need for exhibitionism and the need for grandiosity. In addition, the child is born with the need to idealize his or her parent(s) as all-powerful, perfect, and loving. The infant self was perceived as diffuse, with no boundaries. Kohut (1987) perceived that it was the role of the parent to respond in an empathic manner to the innate psychological needs of their children. If the parents were able to respond with reasonable accuracy and timing, then the infant would come to experience a type of control over the environment comparable to what is experienced by adults over their bodies and their minds. Thus, the parent becomes for the child what Kohut referred to as "mirroring self object." A self object was defined by Kohut (1982) as simply any object perceived as a part of oneself.

If the parents reacted to the child's need for exhibitionism with responses that indicated the child is special, meaningful, and unique, the child learns to relish admiration and to be the center of someone else's gaze and preoccupation; the child develops the capacity to be assertive and to accept affection and attention. If the parents react to the child's need for grandiosity with responses that indicate the child is safe and well-provided for and that his or her world is predictable, they give the child a sense of impact on his or her environment; they make the child feel powerful, as if she or he is the center of the universe; and they counter fears of vulnerability and helplessness. The child comes to idealize the parent as a paragon of his or her future development, merges with the parent, and develops a sense of inner cohesion and integration.

The child begins to develop a more realistic understanding of his or her world, beyond the idealized image of the parent, and gradually to separate himself or herself from the parent through a process Kohut (1971) referred to as "transmuting internationalizations." The parent gradually begins to provide developmentally appropriate frustration of the child's primary narcissistic needs. This creates anxiety in the child. If the parent's ability to empathize with the child's developmental needs is well-developed, then this frustration will not be experienced by the child as overwhelming. In this way, the child develops the ability to tolerate anxious and ambivalent feelings, to be "self-refuting and self-soothing," and to rely on others (Golden, 1985).

At the most basic level, what sexual abuse represents is a denial of the child's developmental needs by the perpetrating adult in favor of the adult's ungratified sexual impulses. It is quite probable that the adult is expressing a variety of unmet needs from his or her own childhood by initiating sexual activity with a child. However, from the perspective of the abused child, the sexual activity makes little, if any, developmental "sense" to the child's immature body and demonstrates to the child that his or her body, as well as his or her being is a vehicle for the gratification of the perpetrating adult's needs. Rather than the adult utilizing his or her body and being to reflect the needs of the child, the child is forced to reflect the unmet narcissistic needs of the adult.

A Model for Group Structure

Jernberg (1979) described four different types of parent-initiated activities that form the foundation for positive emotional development in the child. The types of activities initiated by Theraplay therapists were categorized into four groups: structuring, challenging, intruding, and nurturing. The therapy model she developed consisted of engaging children in activities that, regardless of the client's age, replicated the essential parent-infant interaction that should ideally take place with a 6-month-old infant. The Theraplay therapist attempted to provide the child with the experiences of having an adult directly attend to his or her narcissistic needs and, at the same time, provided the frustration necessary to allow the child to begin to internalize a more realistic perception of his or her world.

Structuring activities focus the child on his or her own special physical characteristics and remind the child of reality limitations. They include such activities as outlining hands, feet, or body on paper; giving and clarifying directions; promoting respect for rules and order; and directing the child to move faster, slower, or in a different direction.

Challenging activities invite the child to compete against a goal stated by the therapist. They are intended to develop in the child a tolerance for anxiety and frustration and to teach that the positive and negative affect associated with competition could be channeled in a playful and nondestructive manner. Challenging activities include arm wrestling, pillow fighting, and hide-and-seek.

Intruding activities are activities in which the therapist unexpectedly invades the bodily space of the child and then, just as unexpectedly, withdraws. These activities are intended to be surprising and delightful and to catch the child off guard while emphasizing the child's separate physical existence from that of the therapist. Intruding activities encourage the child to develop tolerance for anxiety. The child learns to tolerate a developmentally appropriate amount of discomfort that resulted from being in a relationship in which she or he is depending on another. Intruding activities encourage the child to develop boundaries that separate him or her from caretaking adults. The adult caretaker intrudes into the physical space in close proximity to the child's body. The child learns to take delight in inviting others in but also to set limits in keeping others out, according to their own levels of comfort. Intruding activities include tickling, giving rides, counting freckles, playing variations of peek-a-boo, and teaching the child how Eskimos say hello (rubbing noses).

Nurturing activities directly address the developmental needs of the child. The therapist continually communicates to the child that she or he is safe and lovable, that it is all right to have certain needs, and that the therapist will take good care of him or her. These activities communicate that the therapist and other adults are engaged, consistent, and available and that they provide care on a noncontingent basis.

Theraplay activities such as those just described in the interventions were seldom used in the sexual abuse group. However, the structure of the activities group was based on the four categories of interaction described by Jernberg (1979). The activities of the group were tailored to address the developmental needs of preadolescent boys and girls.

PROCEDURE

Therapist Variables

The Structured Activities Group can be used by any mental health professional with experience and training in providing therapy services for sexually abused children. A working knowledge of support-group and activities-group models for providing group therapy to sexually abused children would provide useful background information for utilizing this model. A general knowledge of the treatment issues involved in working with sexually abused children would also be helpful.

The author has conducted groups with and without coleaders. In the opinion of the author, there are advantages and disadvantages to both situations. A major advantage in having two adult leaders is that, in a large group, two adults are able to provide more structure and stability. In addition, the adults are able to communicate differing perspectives and approaches, making the group a more diverse environment. The major disadvantage to having two group leaders is that possibilities for miscommunication between the group leaders and among group members and group leaders are increased dramatically with the addition of a second adult leader. This fact requires that the adult coleaders set aside extra time, in addition to the time spent together in group, to process each session and to plan interventions for the next group. The major advantage to having a single leader is that the group members have a single stable adult figure with whom to negotiate during the group session. This tends to make the group a more predictable environment for many group members. The major disadvantage to having a single leader is that if the leader finds it necessary to focus his or her attention on a particular member, other members may take advantage of this by acting-out.

Child Variables

Referrals for the group can be taken from a variety of children's health service organizations. Typical sources of referral are Child Protective Services and Juvenile Probation. For the preadolescent group, the age requirements that the author finds most useful are ages 8 to 11 years. Exceptions are made for younger children who are particularly verbal and who have been in individual therapy for an extended period of time. Exceptions are also made for 12- or 13-year-olds who appear to prefer a group in which they are able to play rather than simply talk.

The author has two primary requirements for group membership: (a) the child must have been in individual therapy for at least 2 to 3 months, long enough to have established a stable relationship with his or her individual therapist; and (b) the child must have demonstrated the ability and the willingness to verbalize some aspect of his or her molestation experiences. The group therapist and the individual therapist consult about the question of whether the child is ready to begin talking about his or her experiences of sexual abuse in group. Placing a child in a group who is not ready to begin verbalizing the experience of abuse can be counterproductive to progress in therapy. Premature entrance into group therapy can undermine the healing power of the therapeutic relationship, and it might give the child the message that his or her individual therapist has misunderstood his or her needs for safety, and has failed to respect the trust the child has invested in the therapist by disclosing the abuse.

The group can be run with either boys and girls, or with children of only one gender. One advantage of having a group with boys and girls in it is that the group members learn that sexual abuse is common among children of both genders and have the opportunity to listen to children of both genders tell their stories. The primary disadvantage the author has discovered is that even very young preadolescent boys and girls have more difficulty discussing sexual abuse issues in the presence of members of the opposite sex than they do in front of peers of the same sex. Over time, however, this inhibition tends to break down and, as members become comfortable with one another, they tend to talk more openly about their experiences. The author does not put a single child of one gender into a group of children of the opposite gender. In the author's experience, this tends to encourage the children of the same gender to pick on and victimize the lone member of the opposite gender.

The author is most comfortable with a maximum number of six children in a group with a single adult leader. With two adult coleaders, the author usually conducts a group of eight or nine members.

Technique

The group session is designed to be 90 minutes. The first 35-minute period is designed to be utilized as "check-in" time. During this time, each member is given an opportunity to introduce himself or herself to the other members and to talk about his or her experience of sexual abuse. The second 35-minute period is designed to be utilized as time for an activity. The final 20 minutes are designed as snack time and time for the therapist and group members to give feedback to one another about how their behavior affected other group members.

Group norms are perceived as very important by the author. From the very beginning, the therapist must emphasize to each member that group norms about sexuality are much different from expectations in the larger society and from the abusive family system. Before a member enters group, the therapist meets with each child. At this meeting, the rules of group are reviewed. The therapist also reviews with each prospective member expectations for his or her behavior in group. The member is told that the reason every member of the group is there is because some adult has done something sexual to them. The member is told that when he or she is in school, playing with his or her peers, or talking with nonperpetrating adults, sexual things are probably not talked about much. But that group is different. Group is a place where sexual things are talked about but not acted on. The member is told that sexual behavior in group is not allowed and that any members who are sexual with other members in group will no longer be able to attend. The prospective member is told that the group rules are as follows:

1. Keep yourself safe. Don't put yourself in a situation where you could get hurt.
2. Keep others safe. Don't purposefully hurt the feelings or body of other members. Don't threaten others.
3. Take care of the room. Don't destroy or break things in the room.
4. Talk about being sexually abused.

Any questions the prospective member has about the group are then answered by the therapist.

The role of the therapist in the sexual abuse group is to mediate the amount of anxiety experienced by each member as he or she attempts to begin the task of verbally processing their abuse experiences. The therapist does this by providing structuring, nurturing, intruding, and challenging activities that are tailored to the developmental needs of the children in the group.

The structuring aspect of group consists of the expectation that the members conform to the rules if they are to remain in the group. The group rules are designed to provide for the safety needs of all the members. During the final 20 minutes of group, while the members are eating a snack, the therapist again addresses each group member. At this time, the member is given feedback by the therapist and other members about how they have followed the rules. The therapist also tells each member what they have contributed to this group session. This gives the therapist an opportunity to emphasize what is special and unique about each child. It also gives the therapist an opportunity to interpret or reframe problematic behaviors.

Feedback can be given in a variety of ways. In the group as it currently functions, the members are given points for following the rules. At the end of 2-month's time, they trade in their points for small toys. If any member receives zero points on any particular rule (with the exception of the last rule), it is assumed they are not doing their part to keep group safe. The other members then vote on whether they feel this member should be allowed to attend the next group. In these votes, majority rules and the therapist does not vote, unless it is to break a tie. If any of the members get zero points for not following any of the rules for three consecutive sessions, they are not allowed to attend the next session. If this happens repeatedly, then it is believed this demonstrates that the child is not motivated to attend group and a different form of therapeutic intervention is found.

The check-in portion of the group is also structured. This is done primarily to help the members contain the intense anxiety they experience when they initially enter group. During check-in, the members are asked to introduce themselves to the group. They are asked to give their name, how old they are, what school they go to, who they live with, a good thing that happened to them the past week, and a bad thing that happened to them the past week. The members are then asked to say who molested them and how that person was related to them and to talk about one thing that person did to them when they molested them. The benefit of this structure is that each member knows the minimum that will be expected of them each group. In this way, they are able to anticipate and prepare for how much anxiety they will have to tolerate each session. Initially, the therapist or a more experienced walks the new member through check-in, asking the new member each question. Eventually the members internalize this structure and respond spontaneously. Once they are more comfortable with the anxiety they experience during check-in, they begin to offer more information. When the therapist feels the group member has internalized the structure of check-in and developed some tolerance for the anxiety inherent in that process, she or he modifies the structure of check-in and asks questions that are individually tailored to the needs of each member.

The intruding aspect of the group experience occurs naturally within the check-in portion of the group. It is not appropriate in a sexual abuse group for the therapist to physically intrude upon a child as suggested by a strict interpretation of Theraplay technique. The type of intrusion that occurs in the sexual abuse group is developmentally tailored to the needs of the preadolescent members of the group. The importance of the intrusive moments exist in facing what is most anxiety provoking and maintaining a sense of self.

New members of group are initially surprised by the often graphic and explicit descriptions of sexual abuse given by the more experienced members. For many new members, this surprise is initially quite unpleasant. However, over time, the members appear to enjoy the freedom the norms of group provide them and take great pride in their ability to talk about "gross" aspects of their experiences that would never be discussed with others outside of group.

The group members often develop what one member of the author's group referred to as a "gross meter," or a hierarchy of embarrassing and humiliating sexual acts. The children begin by talking about the least embarrassing aspects of their experiences and progress to talking about those experiences that are more embarrassing. Oftentimes, the members will remember new experiences that they had disassociated. These events are initially reported as individual occurrences. The children then begin to piece these individual experiences together, to sequence them, and to attempt to make sense of the events and assign them some sort of meaning. At some point in treatment, it often becomes quite important for a member to challenge himself or herself by processing the most embarrassing and humiliating aspects of the abuse in a single group session.

In group, the children compare their experiences. They learn that some aspects of their experiences of molestation were similar to those of other members. They learn that in some ways what they experienced was unique. They learn that they are not alone in feeling ashamed and damaged by their experiences and that, as bad as their experiences may have been, other group members have often experienced something worse. The children internalize a new understanding of their experiences based on an understanding of the experience of other members. Based on this understanding of their own experiences and the experiences of others, they are often quite willing to confront other members about particular aspects of their experiences that they may be denying or attempting to cover up. In this way, the intrusive aspect of group becomes self-perpetuating.

The nurturing aspect of the group session is structured to occur primarily during snack. Snack is provided to every member no matter what their behavior has been like during the rest of the group. The reasoning behind doing this is to give a message that, no matter how inappropriate a child's behavior is, the group acknowledges that the child still has needs that deserve to be addressed. This issue is one that is quite often tested by children who feel particularly worthless or damaged by their experiences.

The children compete in a variety of ways within the structure of the group. The stated purpose of the group is to talk about, and not act-out, past sexual abuse. The children compete for the attention of the therapist by choosing to adhere to this goal—or by choosing not to adhere to it. This "challenge" is built in to the process of group and is a major dynamic factor that contributes to the many directions in which group process may move. The therapist can either choose to introduce more anxiety by choosing an activity that challenges the members to further address the meaning of sexual abuse in their lives, or the therapist can choose an activity that is less challenging and allows each child to move at his or her own speed.

In the group the author runs, it is common practice not to introduce challenging activities after a particularly stressful check-in period. The message the therapist attempts to give with this type of intervention is that, even though the group members have been humiliated and hurt and feel damaged, they are still able to experience fun through participating in the same types of play activities in which their peers participate. Often, a game of baseball or tag or simply climbing on the playground equipment is sufficient to give this type of message. In addition, when a new member enters the group, the author usually allows the members to engage in free play for their activity so that the children can get to know the new member in the way that children come to know their peers best, through unstructured play. The introduction of a new member usually evokes a good deal of anxiety in the other members. The new member is a threat to their established places among the other members. The sight of the frightened newcomer the first time she or he faces talking about the sexual abuse in a group brings back memories about a time when they were more fragile and vulnerable. Free play allows the new members to express their anxieties in whatever way is most comfortable for them and to begin to develop a feeling of being connected to the new member through shared play. Free play also allows the new member to begin thinking of the group as a place where he or she comes to have fun, and not just a place where he or she has to talk about being sexually abused. Activities that can be adapted to the requirements of group are available in the work of James (1989) and Mandel and Damon (1989). A list of activities that the author has utilized in his therapy group is provided in the next section.

In addition to the therapeutic activities that are built in to the structure of the group, the therapist has a variety of other activities at his or her disposal to facilitate group process. These activities include the following types: (a) limit setting; (b) interpretation; and (c) modeling.

In addition to the limit setting implicit in the structure of group, the therapist will find it necessary to remind group members of the rules during group. The therapist also has an obligation to keep the group safe for all members. The group members tend to assume roles in the group based on either adhering to the rules of group or breaking the rules; and they compete with one another for the therapist's attention by assuming one role or another. It is important for the therapist to process with each member how they have decided to seek attention from adults during each session. If the member is willing, the next step in processing this information is to hypothesize why a particular member consistently seeks attention in a particular way and to generalize this behavior to the child's experiences in the lager world.

The second method through which the therapist can affect a change in perspective in group members is interpretation. An interpretation can provide structure, nurturing, challenge, or intrusion. The opportunity to interpret exists throughout the group process. The therapist must make decisions regarding timing and frequency. The therapist must decide whether to focus on group process or individual issues. She or he must also consider how group process and individual issues interact to produce behaviors in certain children. The structure of group presents a unique opportunity to help the members verbally process the needs and anxieties expressed in the play activity portion of the group through interpretation.

The final method through which the therapist can affect a change in the perspective of group members is modeling. The more experienced members model talking about their abuse experiences for the less experienced members. This dynamic is a major factor contributing to the less experienced members developing the belief that they are able to talk about their abuse experiences in group. The therapist can also model behaviors for the group members. In a group with male members, the author makes a point of modeling expressing feelings other than anger and aggression and talking matter of factly about sexual matters. He also models providing nurturing and emotional support for the younger members.

Games and Activities That Challenge Members to Deal with Sexual Abuse

The author has found the following activities to be useful in helping group members deal with issues pertaining to their sexual abuse during the activities portion of group:

ALIKE AND DIFFERENT.   This is a good game for introducing new members and helping the members get to know one another through play. The facilitator simply calls out a character trait, personal preference, or abuse event and asks everyone who has experienced this to go to one side of the room. Usually, the author begins with benign items such as "Everyone who likes chocolate ice cream go to this side of the room." He or she then proceeds to move into characteristics of the molest, such as "Everyone who was molested by a man go to this side of the room." The author usually begins "talking" about the molest by saying "Everyone who has been molested go to this side of the room" as an indirect way of showing members that everyone in the room shares this experience.

SINGING WITH MOVEMENT.   "My Body" by Peter Alsop (1983) and "Safe and Strong and Free" (Fjell, 1984) are the standards for sexual abuse groups. However, older latency members usually consider these songs somewhat immature. The author has found rap music a useful medium for older latency aged children to express feelings about sexual abuse. The children can create the music and beat with their bodies; commercial rap is often angry and talks about harsh realities, which encourages children to talk about the harsh realities of their own experiences; and rap has a reputation for saying the unsayable words (many of them sexualized) that are often censored by this society. All of this is not lost on children. Group members have created some intelligent and relevant rap songs with titles such as "Don't Sex Me In" and "Power to Children" complete with musical accompaniment, all on their own.

Status, Blobs, and Animals. This is a way of getting children to put into body language what they are feeling at the moment: "If you were an animal right now, show me what animal you would be."

Molester, May I? This "game" was invented by two group members and allows members to deal directly with their anger about having to listen to and obey the adult who was molesting them, as if he or she deserved their respect in order to maintain the appearance of conventionality. The members draw or construct a molester out of clay, paper and crayons, or cardboard materials. Each "molester" is then set up at the front of the room. Each child asks the molester "Molester, may I . . .?" The group then votes on whether the molester will say yes or no. Each member is then allowed to create his or her own response to the molester.

Role-Plays and Rehearsals. Group is an opportunity for children to role-play and rehearse difficult events in their lives that are related to their molestation experiences. Going to court, talking with police detectives, and confronting their molesters are the events members most typically want to rehearse.

Color-Your-Sexual-Abuse. The instructions are the same as for "Color-Your-Life" (O'Connor, 1983), but the child is asked to color his experience of sexual abuse, rather than his or her life.

Letters to . . . Letters to the molester and the "nonoffending parent" are the most common group activities. But the author has had children write letters to the lawyer who defended their perpetrator; to former therapists; and to dead parents, animals, and relatives who were somehow related to their molest experiences. The possibilities are endless. Usually these letters are written outside of group. The group is a place where, if the child is willing, she or he can read these letters out loud or pick out a member to whom she or he would like to read the letter. The purpose of reading the letter is to bring feelings long repressed and denied into the "real" world.

Ongoing Group Journals. Collectively creating a generic story and then writing it down or recording the story as it is created is a fun and interesting activity. It encourages the members to think of themselves as part of the group, as a collective entity and emphasizes everyone adding a piece to the collective unit. It also creates a sense of the collective consciousness of the group at that particular moment and creates an opportunity to interpret changes in the group stories over time. Usually, one child will throw something about their own molestation into the story; it is interesting to see what other members do with it.

Handouts. These usually consist of a series of sentence-completion activities that focus on a particular aspect of being molested, that is, keeping the secret, feelings, or ways of defending oneself from thinking about the molest. The author finds handouts most useful when, after each child has completed the "assignment," there is an activity in which the members can act-out and expand upon the words they have written on the paper.

Games That Challenge Just for Fun

The author has found the following activities to be useful in facilitating interaction, cooperation, and nonthreatening competition during the activities portion of the group:

SNAKE-IN-THE GRASS.   This is a game found in *The New Games Book*. One member is "the Snake." She or he lies on his or her stomach on the ground. All the other players place a hand on some part of the snake's body. The snake shouts "go," and begins crawling around on the floor attempting to tag other players who are standing. When tagged, the other players must get down on their stomachs and attempt to help the original snake tag other players until all of the players are snakes. It is best to play this in a fairly enclosed space or mark off a boundary (Flugleman, 1976, p. 93).

GROUP SAND PLAY.   This is a good activity for a small group or a large sandbox.

MUD PIES.   Messy, but lots of fun, the author uses this when he feels that the group is getting too abstract and needs some grounding. It is best to dress in something you do not mind throwing out and to get permission from all of the parents of the children to be involved. A garden hose and towels for cleaning are also recommended. Getting dirty and getting clean is often a theme in the play of sexually abused children, and this activity appears to have latent symbolic content. Given the symbolic possibilities, the author does not force children who are hesitant to participate in getting dirty. However, he does insist that those who get dirty make some attempt at cleaning up before leaving group.

"WAR".   This is somewhat controversial but nonetheless much in demand by groups with both male and female members. The author has no toy guns in his office, so blocks, fingers, and Lego™ creations are used for "weapons." The therapist typically joins this activity and can attempt to initiate peace talks and negotiate a cease-fire or a truce if so inclined. A miniature war against an imagined army of molesters is a typical theme of sandbox play. Capture-the-flag and pillow fights are variations of aggression-releasing activities that accomplish the same goal.

FIELD TRIPS.   At times, the author has allowed group members to earn trips to a local swimming pool or to a cultural or sporting activity.

Arts and Crafts Activities

The author has found the following arts and crafts activities to be useful during the activities portion of group in helping group members deal with issues pertaining to their sexual abuse:

CLAY.   Clay can be pounded, pulled, punched, and molded into almost anything. The activity is good for expressing feelings.

FINGER PAINTING.   This is another variation of mess-and-clean, with the added benefit of the child getting to keep what he or she has created and to have it admired by others.

DRAWING.   There are all sorts of drawing variations. The therapist should consult a good art therapy book such as *Windows to Our Children* by Violet Oaklander (1978).

Activities Utilizing the Camcorder and VCR

Activities utilizing the camcorder and VCR are useful in a variety of different ways. Most latency aged children like to see themselves on television and find these activities fun.

Reviewing videotapes gives the therapist the opportunity to give each member feedback about his or her performance and creates two opportunities for interpretation; once during the taping, and once during the review of the videotape. Videotape has the effect of making what goes on in group more concrete and accessible to the members. The tapes can be viewed as many times as the group members are willing to tolerate, and the children have difficulty denying what they have said or done on tape.

SEND A VIDEOTAPED MESSAGE TO THE MOLESTER.   The obvious advantage to this variation of the Letter to the Molester is that everyone—child, therapist, and molester (if it is decided the message is to be sent)—can actually see how the child is feeling while delivering the message.

ROLE-PLAYS.   Saved on tape, a series of role-plays collected over an extended period of time can be a powerful reminder of the progress a child has made in group. Often, the therapist will review these tapes with a child when he or she graduates.

MAKE A MOVIE ABOUT SEXUAL ABUSE.   This is a long-term project that often gets sidetracked before completion. However, it provides the opportunity for the members to create and take control of the outcome of a molest experience. The opportunity for role-plays, rehearsals, stage directions, scripting, and improvisation make this a project full of therapeutic possibilities. The major problem is how to depict sexual abuse in film without depicting sex. Films such as *Radio Flyer* do a good job of depicting the effects of physical abuse on children without actually showing the abuse itself. Films such as this can be shown to the group as a model of how they might approach this problem in making their own films.

CASE MATERIAL

Behavior Patterns

The types of behavior that can result from a denial of the child's developmental needs by a perpetrating adult careprovider in favor of the adult's ungratified sexual impulses are best described in three short cases:

CASE ILLUSTRATION 1

Jim was a 9-year-old Caucasian male living with his maternal aunt and her spouse. Jim reported being sexually abused by his mother's boyfriend, his mother, and several male and female friends of the family from the ages of 3 to 5 years. The abuse consisted of oral, anal, and vaginal intercourse. He was tied to furniture and videotaped in sexual acts with adults. He was defecated and urinated on and forced to defecate and urinate on adults. When Jim entered therapy as a 5-year-old, his behavior was quite sexualized. He climbed on top of other children and simulated anal intercourse; he masturbated publicly; and he attempted to remove his clothes in the therapy room. He was fearful of the dark, of water, and of sleeping alone. He was encopretic and enuretic. He had long temper tantrums and lashed out aggressively at any adult who attempted to provide comfort. Two years after beginning individual therapy and playing out the contents of his repeated molestations, he was placed in a therapy group at age 7. Although much younger than the majority of members, he soon began to verbalize the events surrounding his molestation.

CASE ILLUSTRATION 2

Mark was an 11-year-old Caucasian male living with his biological mother. Mark was sexually abused by a male friend of the family between the ages of 3 and 5 years during a time in his life when his parents were abusing drugs. The perpetrator recruited several children from the neighborhood and initiated sexual games within the group. He forced Mark and the other children to have oral and anal intercourse with him. He played a game he called "house" with Mark and made him have intercourse with a teen-aged female. Mark entered therapy at age 10 when he was referred by his mother who walked in on him and his sister engaging in intercourse. At the time of his referral, Mark was extremely irritable and defiant, had angry outbursts, argued with adults, and demanded that they treat him as if he were their equal. At various points in treatment, he became despondent and threatened suicide. A year after beginning treatment, Mark entered a therapy group for sexually abused boys.

CASE ILLUSTRATION 3

Jared was an 8-year-old Caucasian male living in foster care. His mother abandoned him and his sibling to live in another state when Jared was 3 years old. Jared reported being molested between the ages of 3 and 7 years by his biological father. He stated his father often snuck into his room and performed anal intercourse at night while he pretended he was asleep. Jared was referred for therapy at age 8 after being removed from his father's custody by Child Protective Services when his sister disclosed that the father had molested her. Jared was often tearful, acted immature, babyish, isolated himself from others, and "spaced out." His affect was extremely labile and at times inappropriate; he often appeared confused and disoriented, was easily distracted, had nightmares, wet his bed, and was frequently discovered having oral sex and/or intercourse with his older sister. Two to three months after beginning therapy, he disclosed that his father had also molested him, and he was placed in a therapy group for sexually abused boys.

These three cases were chosen because they illustrate a variety of behavior patterns that can develop when children are sexually abused as toddlers, and the abuse is not disclosed until preadolescence. Each of these male children was molested between the ages of 3 and 5 years. Each of these children displayed the symptoms of posttraumatic stress disorder. Despite these similarities, the anxiety they experienced was made manifest through a variety of different behavior patterns. The behaviors each child exhibited appeared to have more to do with the family dynamics that existed at the time the child was being abused than with the type of abuse suffered by each child.

Jim lived in a chaotic family where there was a great deal of drug use. Adult caretakers disappeared without explanation for days, months, or years at a time, only to return unexpectedly and reclaim their role as his primary careproviders. In the first 2 years of his life, he was cared for by his mother, his grandmother, and two of his maternal aunts for periods varying from several months to a year. In addition, the behavior of adults fluctuated markedly according to their level of intoxication. This child displayed an anxiety-driven hypervigilance that mimicked hyperactivity when he first entered therapy. He had no experiential basis for predicting how adults would treat him, and he reacted to the slightest perceived threat with hostility and anger. His mood fluctuations and radical changes in behavior reflected the chaos that existed in his nuclear family.

Mark was molested during a time when his needs were being neglected by his parents due to their involvement in drug use. Mark did not feel he could rely on his parents or other adults to provide for his protection or safety. He learned early in life to provide for his own needs. He became quite angry with adults when they made demands on him. He expressed the attitude that he made great efforts to be self-reliant and not make demands on adults; he felt, because of this, that he should be allowed to live his life as he pleased. When he did allow himself to become dependent on an adult, he was quite easily disappointed by the smallest frustration.

Jared was given consistent care and supervision by his father from the time of his birth. He reported pleasant memories of his father. When his father was jailed for molesting him and his sister, Jared experienced profound guilt due to the testimony he provided that helped to convict his father. Jared's regression and withdrawn behavior appeared to be a reflection of his relationship with his father. Much of the abuse was focused on Jared's bed- and pants-wetting. The father both humiliated and rewarded Jared for this behavior. In addition, Jared learned to compete with his older sister sexually for his father's attention. Jared developed a series of behaviors designed to make his father laugh, to distract him from the sexualized relationship with his older sister, and to draw attention to himself. When the attention he received began to be sexualized and aggressive, he withdrew into himself. When in therapy with his sister, these behaviors became most noticeable. Jared began focusing on his body functions, talking about genitals, falling down, crashing into walls, and in general acting in the role of a clown. The more he was ignored by adults, the more intensely incompetent and ridiculous his behaviors became. If the adults were at all punitive or rejecting in response to these behaviors, Jared typically curled up on the floor and began crying.

The treatment goals for Jim, Mark, and Jared differed dramatically. For Jim, the treatment goals focused on stabilizing his moods, decreasing his hypervigilance, and connecting him to a stable primary parent figure who could provide consistent structure. For Mark, the treatment goals focused primarily on freeing him to behave like a child instead of a small adult. For Jared, the treatment goals focused primarily on eliminating his tendency to withdraw into fantasy and to act-out his role as the sexualized clown in his family.

The single behavior pattern common to each of these children was the sexual acting-out with peers. Each of the children had transferred the sexualized mirroring of their needs by adult caretakers to their relationship with their preadolescent peers.

Therapeutic Interventions

In the pages that follow, examples of group interventions emphasizing the structuring, intruding, challenging, and nurturing aspects of group will be provided for at least one of the three children, Jim, Mark, or Jared. In addition, examples of interventions utilizing limit setting, interpretation, and modeling will also be given.

The following vignette illustrates a therapeutic intervention emphasizing the *structuring* aspect of group.

CASE ILLUSTRATION

Mark spent a good portion of an entire group threatening smaller group members with physical harm, resulting in several members asking that he be excluded from the next group session. After much discussion and arguing, a vote was taken, and Mark barely escaped being expelled from the group session after intensely lobbying his fellow 11-year-olds to allow him to remain. The therapist was able to utilize this sequence of events to point out that Mark appeared very motivated to stay in group and that the reason for this must be that he has some issues he needed to address. The therapist suggested that perhaps his problems following group rules had something to do with his upcoming court appearance, which he had failed to mention during group.

The following vignette illustrates a therapeutic intervention emphasizing the *intruding* aspect of group and how this process progressed over a period of time for one particular member.

CASE ILLUSTRATION

Jim had a distressing repetitive dream about his molester masturbating him with a baseball bat, the same baseball bat with which he physically abused Jim. During group check-in, he began by verbally processing this event. He proceeded to also process being defecated and urinated on by the same perpetrator. Although he had reported being urinated and defecated on as separate, individual events in previous sessions, by grouping these events together, he began the process of assigning new meaning to each event. His comment to the group was, "Those were the worst, the ones I never want to think about again." By forcing himself to talk about in group what he could not think about in the privacy of his own stream of consciousness, he sought, with the help and support of the other members, to take control of the painful and distressing dream that tormented him at night.

This process of coming to face to face with "the worst" of their molest experiences and maintaining a sense of wholeness despite intense anxiety and shame is an integral part of the group experience for all group members.

The next vignette illustrates a therapeutic intervention emphasizing the *challenging* aspect of group and how the structure of the group lends itself toward helping members verbalize the anxiety they express in their play during the activity portion of the group.

CASE ILLUSTRATION

During one group activity, members were attempting to make a movie about child sexual abuse. The members were suggesting scenes to be included in the movie. Jim suggested that a good scene would involve a father tying his son to his bed and inserting a variety of objects into the boy's "butt." The therapist told him it was good idea and asked him to draw a picture to give the group an idea of how it would look on camera. (The group later agreed by vote that this type of scene could not be filmed because no actor would agree to subject themselves to such treatment.) Up until this point, Jim had never mentioned being tied up during his abuse. During the next session, the therapist asked if Jim had been treated like the boy in the movie scene he had created. He then proceeded to verbally process a whole series of abusive experiences about which he had never talked before.

This vignette illustrates a therapeutic intervention emphasizing the *nurturing* aspect of group.

CASE ILLUSTRATION

Early in his group experience, Jim often annoyed older group members by poking at them, intruding on their physical space, or making inappropriate sexual gestures in their presence. As a result, he was often the recipient of threats and anger from older members. At one time, his behavior escalated to the point where he exposed himself to another group member. The therapist then led him to the waiting room and asked the receptionist to supervise him until group ended. When snack time came, the therapist went to retrieve Jim from the waiting room. Jim was told that if he could manage to demonstrate that he could keep himself safe for the next 15 minutes, he was welcome to come and eat snack with group. The first thing Jim did upon entering the room was to hit an older member as he took his seat. The therapist told Jim he would not be allowed to eat snack with group because his behavior had demonstrated he was not willing to follow the rules. This was a major disappointment to him, and he began crying, demonstrating his genuine pain at being excluded from a portion of group from which he had never witnessed another member being expelled. The therapist saved his snack. When group ended, the therapist brought Jim back to the group room, fed him his snack, and processed the events leading up to his expulsion from group.

The following vignettes illustrate therapeutic interventions utilizing *limit-setting* and *interpretation*.

CASE ILLUSTRATION

After being moved from one foster home to another, Jared began displaying his sexualized clowning behaviors in group, crashing into walls and falling down on the ground and then rolling around the floor. These behaviors had made an appearance early in his group experience but had quickly disappeared when he settled into the relatively stable environment of his first foster family. With the sudden change, Jared was once again faced with uncertainty in regard to expectations of his behavior. Initially, the therapist reminded Jared of the group rule stating that he should not hurt himself and that he was not earning points while rolling around on the floor. While giving out points, the therapist simply pointed out to Jared that he was "clowning around" like he did when he first entered group and that the therapist felt this indicated that in his new foster family he must be feeling a lot like he did when he lived with his dad. The therapist reassured him that he did not need to be a clown to get attention in his new family or in group.

The interpretation just explained was an attempt to lend structure to Jared's understanding of his own behavior. A more intrusive interpretation might have linked his clowning behaviors to his sexual acting-out with his sister and might have suggested that Jared was behaving in group as if he were still living in his father's family, although his living situation, despite the recent change, had improved dramatically. A more nurturing interpretation might simply have acknowledged his clowning behavior as a result of his feelings of anxiety and might have provided Jared with the message that he had good reasons to be anxious, given past experiences. A challenging intervention might consist of specific training in how to behave differently.

CASE ILLUSTRATION

In Mark's family, he often felt he was constantly competing for his mother's attention with two younger female siblings. Mark was, for a long time, coincidentally the oldest member in group and the member whom many of the children regarded as the group leader. This created a situation in which the younger members looked to him to provide for their needs. Mark enjoyed the power this gave him, but he resented his position because he felt it took away from his ability to be taken care of by the therapist. He often sought attention from the therapist and abused his power over the younger members by threatening them with physical harm, anticipating that the therapist would intervene on behalf of the younger member. When this occurred, Mark felt rejected and envious of the attention given to other members. At one point, Mark threatened Jim with a "beating" after group and told the therapist he could do nothing about what happened after group.

After several weeks of attempting to set limits and be the mediator in this ongoing conflict between the two members during group, the therapist decided to approach the problem in a different way. He affirmed Mark's perception that the therapist's control was limited to the boundaries of group but reminded him that the group rules stated he should not threaten other members and that he was not earning points when he was threatening Jim. The next group session, Mark, Jim, and the other members came back and processed the confrontation that occurred between Mark and Jim after group. The members reported that, after the previous week's group, Mark had put Jim in a head lock and told him not to tease him anymore. During the time the group processed this event, Mark told Jim he really liked him and did not want to hurt him, but Jim needed to stop annoying him by calling him names. Jim acknowledged that he liked Mark also and just wanted to play with him and to be treated like he was Jim's friend. The therapist told Jim and Mark that he felt they were both old enough to work out their own problems and did not always need his help. He told Mark he did not need to threaten the smaller children in order to get the therapist's attention and demonstrated he could get attention by spending time processing the event with him. The therapist told Jim he did not need to be annoying to get Mark's attention and asked Mark to tell Jim how he could get his attention in ways that would not provoke further threats.

The next vignette illustrates a therapeutic intervention utilizing *modeling*.

CASE ILLUSTRATION

Jared initially "spaced out," disassociated, or simply hid his head and wept during particularly anxiety-provoking moments in group. The therapist, upon noticing this, often sat him on his lap and assured him verbally that everything would be all right; this was an attempt to ground him in the present and provide comfort. Mark, upon witnessing the therapist provide comfort to Jared, immediately announced to the group that, if he ever cried in group, no one was to touch him and the therapist was not to sit him in his lap. This provided the therapist with an opportunity to process with Mark why the thought of others providing comfort to him in this way made him feel so uncomfortable.

The following vignette illustrates the type of progress each of the three cases made in group therapy.

CASE ILLUSTRATION

Jim initially entered the group and behaved as if it were the unpredictable, unreliable, and sexualized caretaker he had been exposed to since earliest childhood. Two years later, he expressed the desire to stay in group until he turned 11 so he could show younger members "how to talk about the stuff you never want to say." When Mark entered group, he immediately took charge of the situation, divided the members into those he liked and those he hated, and set about the task of scaring those whom he perceived as threats into giving in to his demands. One year later, he began to struggle with whether the members liked him because he was likeable or because they were scared of him. To his surprise, many members had managed to see through his bravado and to recognize that he, like many of the members, was only trying to protect a part of himself that had been brutalized and betrayed. When Jared entered group, he sank into a corner and drew into himself. A year and a half later, he faced leaving group due to a second change in foster homes. He pranced around the room crashing into walls and disintegrating into squeals of laughter as he attempted to avoid dealing with his feelings about leaving. During snack, he gave in to his feelings and cried while hugging Mark good-bye.

CONCLUSION

Children are, in fact, born with needs, as Kohut (1987) implied. However, it is only through interacting with empathic parental caretakers that children develop the narcissistic qualities that Kohut described as the need for exhibitionism and the need for grandiosity. Although the word *narcissism* implies solitude, singularity, and ego-centrism, the behavioral manifestations of those needs would not exist without the empathic responses of the parent. Although the word *empathy* suggests an understanding of and a willingness to consider the needs of others before the needs of self, the ability to empathize is grounded in the experience of narcissism. Narcissism does not exist in the vacuum of the child psyche, and empathy does not simply exist or not exist in the cavernous depths of the adult subconscious. Narcissism and empathy coexist in the relationship between child and parent. The meaning implied by the words *narcissism* and *empathy* is uniquely human and emerges only in the context of a human relationship.

It is because narcissism and empathy coexist in the parent-child relationship that the group is potentially such a powerful intervention in working with sexually abused children. Through a structured group intervention, the members can be provided with the types of empathic responses that were negated or overwhelmed by adult sexuality. The group has the potential to appropriately mirror the needs of the members. Thus, the child's relationship with the group becomes a metaphor for his or her relationship with parental caregivers, past and present.

Since the beginning of sexual abuse treatment, the therapy group has been considered an effective means of intervening on behalf of childhood sexual abuse survivors. The author has attempted to outline a perspective on group treatment of preadolescent survivors of child sexual abuse based on the Object Relations Theory (Kohut, 1971) and Theraplay technique (Jernberg, 1979). In the opinion of the author, the therapy group represents a unique opportunity to provide an environment that is conducive to helping children at this particular developmental stage to begin to integrate the experience of sexual abuse into a cohesive sense of self.

REFERENCES

Alsop, P. (1983). "My body." Moose Stool Music (BMI). Box 960, Topanga, CA.

American Psychiatric Association. (1987). *Diagnostic and statistical manual of mental disorders* (3rd ed., rev.). Washington, DC: Author.

Burgess, A. W., Hartmean, C. R., McCausland, M. P., & Powers, P. (1984). Response patterns in children and adolescents exploited through sex rings and pornography. *American Journal of Orthopsychiatry, 144*(5), 656–662.

Fjell, J. (1984). "Safe and strong and free." Honey Pie Music (BMI). Box 1064, Davis, CA.

Flugleman, A., & Turnbeck, S. (1976). *The new games book.* New York: Doubleday.

Golden, B. R. (1985). How theraplay facilitates healthy narcissism. *The Journal of Child and Adolescent Psychotherapy, 2*(2), 99–104.

James, B. (1989). *Treating traumatized children: New insights and creative interventions.* Toronto, Ontario, Canada: Lexington Books.

Jernberg, A. (1979). *Theraplay: A new treatment approach for children and their families.* San Francisco: Josey Bass.

Kohut, H. (1971). *The analysis of the self.* New York: International Press.

Kohut, H. (1982). Introspection, empathy and the semi-circle of mental health. *International Journal of Psychoanalysis, 59,* 413–425.

Kohut, H. (1987). *The Kohut Semina.* (M. Elivon, Ed.). New York: Norton.

Mandel, J. G., and Damon, L. (1989). *Group treatment for sexually abused children.* New York: Guilford Press.

O'Connor, K. J. (1983). The Color-Your-Life technique. In C. E. Schaefer & K. J. O'Connor (Eds.), *The handbook of play therapy.* New York: Wiley.

Oaklander, V. (1978). *Windows to our children.* Moab, UT: Real People Press.

Putnam, F. W. (1989). *Multiple personality disorder.* New York: Guilford Press.

Spiegel, D. (1984). Multiple personality as a post-traumatic stress disorder. *Psychiatric Clinics of North America, 7,* 101–110.

Author Index

Subject Index